Who's Who
in the
Liberal
Democrats?

Fifth edition

Published by PCA Books
on behalf of the
Liberal Democrats Parliamentary Candidates Association

Editor LINDA FORBES

Copyright © 2006 Liberal Democrats Parliamentary Candidates Association
Printed by Bell & Bain Ltd, Glasgow

British Library Cataloguing-in-Publication Data

A catalogue reference for this book
is available from the British Library
ISBN 1 85187 762 2

The Liberal Democrats exist to build and safeguard
a fair, free and open society in which we seek to
balance the fundamental values of liberty, equality
and community and in which no one will be enslaved
by poverty, ignorance or conformity

Preamble to Federal Constitution

Liberal Democrat Parliamentary Candidates Association

The PCA exists to support all Liberal Democrat parliamentary candidates
and aspiring candidates for Westminster,
the European and Scottish Parliaments, and
the Welsh and Greater London Assemblies.

It provides regular training, political briefings and
campaign support to its members,
and publishes *The Parliamentary Campaigner*,
The Candidate and *Who's Who in the Liberal Democrats*.

For further information, contact PCA Chair Gary Lawson
on 07941 553859
or by e-mail: gary@lawsononline.org

To join, contact PCA Membership Secretary Elliot Shubert
on 07764 611401
or by e-mail: membership@libdempca.org.uk

Membership is open to all candidates and aspiring candidates,
and costs £30 if paid by cheque,
or £25 if paid by direct debit.

Index

Subscribe to *Liberal Democrat News* for just £30 a year

Liberal Democrat News gives you the whole picture, covering news about the party that you will not find in the national media. Thousands of Liberal Democrats are already reading it to keep abreast of news and policy and also to join in party debates and gossip.

Liberal Democrat News brings you reports about the work of our Parliamentarians in Westminster, Brussels, Edinburgh and Cardiff. It keeps you in touch with local election campaigns and policy forums. The letters, features and columnists provide lively discussion on issues facing the party and the country.

Take out a subscription to **Liberal Democrat News** now and keep yourself informed of every aspect of the party's work and campaigning.

Subscribe online at:
www.libdems.org.uk/support/newssubscribe.html

020 7227 1327 ldnsubs@libdems.org.uk

Building on our successes

Rt Hon Sir Menzies Campbell MP QC CBE
Leader of the Liberal Democrats

As Leader of the Liberal Democrats, I'm delighted to be able to contribute this foreword to a book which has become essential reading within the party and for those outside that wish to know whom to contact and where.

We must continue to build on our General Election successes of 2001 and 2005. With 63 MPs in Westminster we now have the largest parliamentary team since 1929. We have consolidated our position in Scotland and Wales and have made advances in the Greater London Assembly and in Brussels.

We can be proud of our recent by-election success in Dunfermline and West Fife, where we beat Labour from third place in the Chancellor's own back yard!

In all these elections, we have benefited from our principled approach to multilateral solutions for international problems such as Iraq and Darfur, our commitment to a fairer society built by government we can trust, our defence of individual freedoms against their erosion by this authoritarian government and our belief that environmental action is essential at home and abroad to create a sustainable future for the generations to come.

Elected Liberal Democrat parliamentarians and assembly members know that we have the most committed activists in the country. They, like me, are grateful to all those Liberal Democrats who work not only at by-elections but all year round. And that work in each and every constituency is essential for us to build on our recent successes and to achieve the further progress that I know we can.

This fifth edition of *Who's Who in the Liberal Democrats?* underlines the depth of talent which we have in our ever-growing ranks and gives me enormous optimism and confidence in the party's future.

I commend it to you and wish the PCA every success.

Menzies Campbell

LIBERAL DEMOCRAT HISTORY GROUP

The Liberal Democrat History Group promotes the discussion and research of historical topics, particularly those relating to the histories of the Liberal Democrats, Liberal Party, the SDP and of liberalism.

Our activities appeal to anyone with an interest in the history of British Liberalism, whether academics, party activists or spare-time students of political history. We:

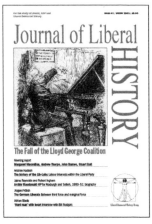

- Publish the quarterly *Journal of Liberal History*, containing articles, book reviews, biographies, and meeting reports.

- Publish books, including the *Dictionary of Liberal Biography, the Dictionary of Liberal Quotations* and *Great Liberal Speeches.*

- Organise evening discussion meetings, witness seminars and fringe meetings at Liberal Democrat Conferences.

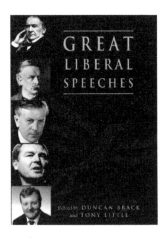

- Make resources available to students of Liberal history, including news of research in progress and guides to archive sources.

- Provide a concise history of the Liberal Democrats along with a more extensive *Liberal History Online* project.

Membership/subscription, including four issues of the ***Journal of Liberal History***, costs only £20.00 (£12.50 unwaged); from: Liberal Democrat History Group, 6 Palfrey Place, London SW8 1PA. Web: **www.liberalhistory.org.uk.**

The only organisation for the study of Liberal, SDP and Liberal Democrat history

The Federal Party Executive 2006

The Federal Executive is responsible for directing, co-ordinating and implementing the work of the Federal Party, including overall strategy, campaigning, organisation and staffing. The Federal Finance and Administration Committee and the Campaigns and Communications Committee both report to the FE. The FE has 29 voting members: the Party President (who chairs it) and three Vice Presidents; the Leader and two other MPs; one peer; one MEP; two councillors; three state party reps; and fifteen members directly elected by conference reps.

Leader **Rt Hon Sir Menzies Campbell MP**
Leader's Aide** **Carrie Henderson**
President & Chair **Simon Hughes MP**
Vice-presidents **Stan Collins** England
Judy Hayman Scotland **Lembit Öpik MP** Wales
Treasurer** **Tim Clement-Jones**
MPs' Representatives **Norman Lamb MP, John Thurso MP**
Chief Whip** **Paul Burstow MP**
MEPs' Representatives **Chris Davies MEP**
Peers' Representative **Lord Razzall**
Councillors' Representatives **Meral Ece, Chris White**
State Representatives **Paul Farthing** England
Roy Thomson Scotland **Peter Black AM** Wales
Chief Executive **Lord Rennard**
Chief Executive Scotland** **Derek Barrie**
Chief Executive Wales** **Stephen Smith**
Director of Fundraising & Membership** **David Loxton**
HQ Director** **Ben Stoneham**
Staff Rep **Kate Heywood**
Chair, Gender Balance Task Force** **Sandra Gidley MP**
Chair FFAC ** **David Griffiths**
Elected members **Qassim Afzal, Ramesh Dewan, Jock Gallagher, Tim Garden, James Gurling, Elizabeth Johnson, Stephen Lloyd, Tessa Munt, Candy Piercy, David Rendel, Mike Simpson, Robin Teverson, Gerald Vernon-Jackson, David Williams, Simon Wright**
** non-voting

Federal Conference Committee 2006

Chair **Duncan Brack**
Vice-Chairs **Ruth Polling, Andrew Wiseman**
Jon Ball, Catherine Bearder, Sarah Boad,
Sal Brinton, Dee Doocey, Gareth Epps, Sue Garden, Chris Maines,
Justine McGuiness, Jane Smithard
FE Representatives **Jock Gallagher, James Gurling**
FPC Representatives **Robert Adamson, Jeremy Hargreaves**
Staff Representative **Gordon Seekings**
English Representative **Andrew Wiseman**
Scottish Representative **Debra Storr**
Welsh Representative **David Bourne**
Chief Steward **Chris Jennings** (co-opted)
** non-voting

Federal Policy Committee 2006

The Federal Policy Committee is responsible for researching and developing policy and overseeing the Federal Party's policy-making process. This includes producing policy papers for debate at conference, and drawing up (in consultation with the relevant parliamentary party) the Federal election manifestos for Westminster and European elections. The FPC has 29 voting members: the Party Leader and four other MPs; the Party President; one peer; one MEP; three councillors; three state party reps; and fifteen members directly elected by conference reps. It must be chaired by one of the five MP members.

Leader **Rt Hon Sir Menzies Campbell MP**
President **Simon Hughes MP**
Elected Representatives **Robert Adamson, Charles Anglin,**
Phil Bennion, David Boyle, Sal Brinton, Theo Butt Philip,
Gareth Epps, Tony Greaves, Jeremy Hargreaves, Jo Hayes, Judith
Jolly, Susan Juned, Jonathan Marks, Julie Smith, Neil Stockley
MP Representatives **Alistair Carmichael MP,**
Ed Davey MP, Steve Webb MP, Roger Williams MP
English representative **Geoff Payne**
Scottish representative **Hugh O'Donnell**
Welsh representative **Peter Price**
MEPs' representative **Baroness Ludford**
Peers' representative **Lord Maclennan**

Councillor Representatives **Adam Carew,**
Stan Collins, Andrew Duffield
Non-voting co-optees **Duncan Brack** (FCC representative), **Robert**
Brown MSP, Jenny Randerson AM

Campaigns & Communications Committee

Chair **Ed Davey MP**
Staff contact **Sarah Morris** s.morris@libdems.org.uk

Constitutional Amendment FC1 to Article 8.2 submitted by English Liberal
Democrats at Federal Conference, Brighton 2006 proposes changes to the
Committee structure.

Federal Finance and Administration Committee 2006

The Federal Finance and Administration Committee is responsible for
planning and administering the budget and finances of the Federal Party,
directing its administration and ensuring its compliance with the
provisions of the Political Parties, Elections and Referendums Act 2000. It is
responsible to the FE, but normally also reports directly to the Federal
Conference. The FFAC has 14 voting members: the Chair , Party Treasurer
and five other members (all elected by the FE); the Party President; three
state party reps; and the Chief Executive and two other members of Federal
(HQ and Parliamentary) staff.

Chair **David Griffiths**
President **Simon Hughes**
Treasurer **Tim Clement-Jones**
Chief Executive **Lord Rennard**
FE Representatives **Jean Crossland, Paul Farthing, Edward Lord,**
David Rendel, Mike Simpson
FCC Representative **Andrew Wiseman**
English Representative **Stan Collins**
Scottish Representative **Douglas Herbison**
Welsh Representative **Aled Morris Jones**
Staff Representatives **Nigel Bliss, Douglas Janke**

Federal Appeals Panel

Chair **to be elected September 2006**
Elected by Federal Conference: **Viv Bingham, Celia Goodhart,
Philip Goldenberg, Stan Hardy, Susan Fenwick,
Rev Mark Soady, Paul Carter, David Ive, Baroness Falkner**
English Represntatives **Perter Lee, Valerie Silbiger, Chris Willmore**
Scottish Representatives **David Harcus, Elizabeth Dick,
Mike Rumbles MSP**
Welsh Representatives **Alan Masters, Cecilia Barton, Cllr Keith Davies**

The Panel should be contacted via **David Allworthy**,
Head of Compliance and Constitutional Support
d.allworthy@libdems.org.uk

International Relations Committee 2006

Chair **Robert Woodthorpe Browne**
Elected Representatives **Jonathan Fryer, Tony Greaves,
Linda Jack, Marie-Louise Rossi**
FE Representatives **Theo Butt-Phillip, Rabi Martins, Chris White**
State Party representatives
Susanne Lamido (England), **Karen Freel** (Scotland)
Liberal International **Lord Alderdice, David Griffiths**
Youth and Student Representative **vacant**
Parliamentary Representative **Baroness Ludford, Michael Moore MP**
Committee of Regions Representative **Lord Tope**
Staff member **Karla Hatrick**

ELDR Council Delegation

Elected members **David Bellotti, Ruth Coleman, Jonathan Fryer,
Jo Hayes, Justine McGuiness, Peter Price, Colin Ross,
Robert Woodthorpe Browne**
FE Representative **David Griffiths**
FPC Representative **Phil Bennion**
LDEG Representatives **Ahmed Mallick, Chris Foote-Wood**

G8 2006

Chair **Peter Lee** tel 01223 460665
English Party representatives **Ian Cuthbertson, Susanne Lamido, Balan Sisupalan** Scottish Party representative **Iain Smith**
Administration **Tim Pickstone** tim.pickstone@aldc.org
Eleanor Ritchie eleanor.ritchie@aldc.org

Gender Balance Task Force

Chair **Sandra Gidley MP** gidleys@parliament.uk
Vice chairs **Candy Piercey** candypiercy@cix.co.uk
Jo Swinson jo_swinson@yahoo.co.uk
Administrator Vacant
4, Cowley Street, London SW1P 3NB
020 7222 7999 gbtf@libdems.org.uk

Federal Party Staff

HQ 4 Cowley Street
London SW1P 3NB
tel 020 7222 7999
fax 020 7799 2170
e-mail info@libdems.org.uk **web** www.libdems.org.uk

Chief Executive **Lord Rennard of Wavertree MBE**
chris.rennard@libdems.org.uk
Political Assistant **Sarah Morris** ldcam@cix.co.uk
Office Manager & Committee Administrator **Kate Heywood**
kate.heywood@libdems.org.uk

ADMINISTRATION

HQ Director **Ben Stoneham** ben.stoneham@libdems.org.uk
Head of Compliance & Constitutional Support
David Allworthydavidallworthy@cix.co.uk
IT Support Consultant **Colin Rosenstiel** colin.rosenstiel@libdems.org.uk
Training Administrator **Lorna Spenceley** lspenceley@cix.co.uk
English Party Administrator **Paul Rustad** englishlibdems@cix.co.uk
Receptionist **Robert Hempenstall** robert.hempenstall@libdems.org.uk

Part-Time Receptionist & Information Coordinator
Emma Price emma.price@libdems.org.uk
London Region Administrator **Flick Rea** londonlibdems@cix.co.uk

CAMPAIGNS AND ELECTIONS

Director of Campaigns **Paul Rainger** prainger@cix.co.uk
National Campaigns Officer **Duncan Borrowman** borrowman@cix.uk
Internet & Communications Officer **Mark Pack** markpack@cix.co.uk

CONFERENCE & EVENTS

Conference Organiser **Stuart Marrit**
Assistant Organisers **Jane Stainer** j.stainer@libdems.org.uk
Emma Harris e.harris@libdems.org.uk
Sales Executive **Carol Caruna** c.caruna@libdems.org.uk

FINANCE

Director of Finance **Nigel Bliss** nbliss@cix.co.uk
Finance Officers **John Walsh** j.walsh@libdems.org.uk
Beau Wilson beau.wilson@libdems.org.uk

INTERNATIONAL OFFICE

Head of Office **Karla Hatrick** k.hatrick@libdems.org.uk
Programme Manager **Ellen Kelly** e.kelly@libdems.og.uk

POLICY & COMMUNICATIONS

Director of Policy & Communications
David Norman d.norman@libdems.co.uk
Head of Press Office **Mark Littlewood** mark.littlewood@libdems.org.uk
Senior Press & Broadcasting Officers
Andrea Kinnear a.kinnear@libdems.org.uk
Lena Pietsch lena.peitsch@libdems.org.uk
Mike Zorbas, Luke Croydon, Ben Wiseman

Policy & Research

Head of Policy & Research **Greg Simpson** simpsong@parliament.uk
Deputy Head of Policy & Research **Christian Moon**

Jonathan Wallace, Helen Banks, Chris Saunders
Polly MacKenzie, Marianne Sladowsky
Will de Peyer, Steve Toole, Matt Waldman

MARKETING, FUNDRAISING and MEMBERS' SERVICES

Director **David Loxton** davidloxton@cix.co.uk
Membership Services Manager **Ernest Baidoo-Mitchell**
e.mitchell@libdems.org.uk
Fundraising Manager **vacant**
Membership Development Officer **Dave Hodgson** dhodgson@cix.co.uk
Membership Officer **Matthew Wherry** m.wherry@libdems.org.uk
Customer Services Officer **Gordon Seekings**
membership@libdems.org.uk
Membership Assistant **Gemma Roulston** g.roulston@libdems.org.uk

LIBERAL DEMOCRAT NEWS

Editor **Deirdre Razzall** ldn@libdems.org.uk
News Assistants **Monica Howes** ldn@libdems.org.uk
Production Assistant **Jayne Martin-Kaye** jayne.martin-kaye@libdems.org.uk

LIBERTY NETWORK, BUSINESS FORUM

Liberty Network **Helen Jardine-Brown**
helen.jardine-brown@libdems.org.uk

LDYS

Administrator **Paul Pettinger**
tel 020 7227 1387

LIBDEMS CALLING

Supervisors **Steve Riley, Mark Turner**

WOMEN LIBERAL DEMOCRATS

Admin Support Officer **Debbie Enever** women@libdems.org.uk

THE PARTY AT WESTMINSTER

House of Commons

Leader **Rt Hon Sir Menzies Campbell MP QC CBE**
Deputy Leader **Dr Vince Cable MP**
Chief Whip **Paul Burstow MP**

Members of Parliament (63)
(for contact details, see under names in Who's Who? **Section)**

Danny Alexander (Inverness, Nairn, Badenoch and Strathspey), **Norman Baker** (Lewes), **John Barrett** (Edinburgh West), **Alan Beith** (Berwick-upon-Tweed), **Tom Brake** (Charshalton and Wallington), **Colin Breed** (S E Cornwall), **Annette Brooke** (Dorset Mid and Poole North), **Jeremy Browne** (Taunton), **Malcolm Bruce** (Gordon), **Paul Burstow** (Sutton and Cheam), **Lorely Burt** (Solihull), **Vince Cable** (Twickenham), **Menzies Campbell** (Fife North East), **Alistair Carmichael** (Orkney and Shetland), **Nick Clegg** (Sheffield Hallam), **Ed Davey** (Kingston and Surbiton), **Tim Farron** (West Moreland and Lonsdale), **Lynne Featherstone** (Hornsey and Wood Green), **Don Foster** (Bath), **Andrew George** (St Ives), **Sandra Gidley** (Romsey), **Julia Goldsworthy** (Falmouth and Cambourne), **Mike Hancock** (Portsmouth South), **Evan Harris** (Oxford West and Abingdon), **Nick Harvey** (North Devon), **David Heath** (Somerton and Frome), **John Hemming** (Birmingham Yardley), **Paul Holmes** (Chesterfield), **Martin Horwood** (Cheltenham), **David Howarth** (Cambridge), **Simon Hughes** (Southwark North and Bermondsey), **Chris Huhne** (Eastleigh), **Mark Hunter** (Cheadle), **Paul Keetch** (Hereford), **Charles Kennedy** (Ross, Skye and Lochaber), **Susan Kramer** (Richmond Park), **Norman Lamb** (Norfolk North), **David Laws** (Yeovil), **John Leech** (Manchester Withington), **Michael Moore** (Berwickshire, Roxburgh and Selkirk), **Greg Mulholland** (Leeds North West), **Mark Oaten** (Winchester), **Lembit Opik** (Montgomeryshire), **John Pugh** (Southport), **Alan Reid** (Argyll and Bute), **Willie Rennie** (Dunfermline and West Fife), **Dan Rogerson** (North Cornwall), **Paul Rowen** (Rochdale), **Bob Russell** (Colchester), **Adrian Sanders** (Torbay), **Robert Smith** (Aberdeenshire West and Kincardine), **Andrew Stunell** (Hazelgrove), **Jo Swinson** (Dunbartonshire East), **Matthew Taylor** (Truro), **Sarah Teather** (Brent East), **John Thurso**

(Caithness, Sutherland and Easter Ross), **Steve Webb** (Northavon), **Mark Williams** (Ceredigion), **Roger Williams** (Brecon and Radnorshire), **Stephen Williams** (Bristol West), **Phil Willis** (Harrogate), **Jenny Willott** (Cardiff Central), **Richard Younger-Ross** (Teignbridge)

Lib Dem-held constituencies

Aberdeenshire West and Kincardine (Robert Smith), **Argyll and Bute** (Alan Reid), **Bath** (Don Foster), **Berwickshire, Roxburgh and Selkirk** (Michael Moore), **Berwick-upon-Tweed** (Alan Beith), **Birmingham Yardley** (John Hemming), **Brecon and Radnorshire** (Roger Williams), **Brent East** (Sarah Teather), **Bristol West** (Stephen Williams), **Caithness, Sutherland and Easter Ross** (John Thurso), **Cambridge** (David Howarth), **Cardiff Central** (Jenny Willott), **Ceredigion** (Mark Williams), **Charshalton and Wallington** (Tom Brake), **Cheadle** (Mark Hunter), **Cheltenham** (Martin Horwood), **Chesterfield** (Paul Holmes), **Colchester** (Bob Russell), **Dorset Mid and Poole North** (Annette Brooke), **Dunbartonshire East** (Jo Swinson), **Dunfermline and West Fife** (Willie Rennie), **Eastleigh** (Chris Huhne), **Edinburgh West** (John Barrett), **Falmouth and Cambourne** (Julia Goldsworthy), **Fife North East** (Menzies Campbell), **Gordon** (Malcolm Bruce), **Harrogate** (Phil Willis), **Hazelgrove** (Andrew Stunell), **Hereford** (Paul Keetch), **Hornsey and Wood Green** (Lynne Featherstone), **Inverness, Nairn, Badenoch and Strathspay** (Danny Alexander), **Kingston and Surbiton** (Ed Davey), **Leeds North West** (Greg Mulholland), **Lewes** (Norman Baker), **Manchester Withington** (John Leech), **Montgomeryshire** (Lembit Opik), **Norfolk North** (Norman Lamb), **North Cornwall** (Dan Rogerson), **North Devon** (Nick Harvey), **Northavon** (Steve Webb), **Orkney and Shetland** (Alistair Carmichael), **Oxford West and Abingdon** (Evan Harris), **Portsmouth South** (Mike Hancock), **Richmond Park** (Susan Kramer), **Rochdale** (Paul Rowen), **Romsey** (Sandra Gidley), **Ross, Skye and Lochaber** (Charles Kennedy), **S E Cornwall** (Colin Breed), **Sheffield Hallam** (Nick Clegg), **Solihull** (Lorely Burt), **Somerton and Frome** (David Heath), **Southport** (John Pugh), **Southwark North and Bermondsey** (Simon Hughes), **St Ives** (Andrew George), **Sutton and Cheam** (Paul Burstow), **Taunton** (Jeremy Browne), **Teignbridge** (Richard Younger-Ross), **Torbay** (Adrian Sanders), **Truro** (Matthew Taylor), **Twickenham** (Vince Cable), **West Moreland and Lonsdale** (Tim Farron), **Winchester** (Mark Oaten), **Yeovil** (David Laws)

Shadow Cabinet and Parliamentary spokespersons

*members of Shadow Cabinet

Leader **Sir Menzies Campbell MP**
Deputy Leader **Dr Vince Cable MP**

Shadow Leader of the House and
Shadow Cabinet Office Minister **David Heath MP**

Party President and Shadow Attorney General and
Department of Constitutional Affairs **Simon Hughes MP**

Foreign & Commonwealth Office
Michael Moore MP
Jeremy Browne MP

Treasury **Dr Vince Cable MP**
Julia Goldsworthy MP, Colin Breed MP

Home Affairs **Nick Clegg MP**
Lynne Featherstone MP, Mark Hunter MP

Health **Steve Webb MP**
Sandra Gidley MP, John Pugh MP

Education **Sarah Teather MP**
Stephen Williams MP (HE/FE spokesperson)
Greg Mulholland MP (schools spokesperson)

Dept for Work & Pensions
David Laws MP
Danny Alexander MP

Dept for International Development **Susan Kramer MP**

ODPM **Andrew Stunell MP**
Dan Rogerson MP

DTI **Edward Davey MP**
Lorely Burt MP (Small Business spokesperson)
David Howarth MP (Energy spokesperson)

DEFRA **Chris Huhne MP**
Martin Horwood MP (Environment spokesperson)
Roger Williams MP (Rural Affairs spokesperson)

Transport **Alistair Carmichael MP**
Paul Rowen MP, John Leech MP

Defence **Nick Harvey MP**
Bob Russell MP, Willie Rennie MP

Culture, Media and Sport **Don Foster MP**

Scotland **Jo Swinson MP**
John Barrett MP

Northern Ireland **Lembit Opik MP**
Alan Reid MP

Wales **Lembit Opik MP**
Mark Williams MP

Chief Whip **Paul Burstow MP**
Deputy Whips **Adrian Sanders MP**
Jenny Willott MP
Science **Dr Evan Harris MP**
London **Lynne Featherstone MP**

The President of the Liberal Democrats and Ed Davey MP, Chair of the Campaigns and Communications Committee, also attend Shadow Cabinet meetings by virtue of party office.

Members of House of Commons Select Committees

CHAIRMEN

Constitutional Affairs: Rt Hon.Alan Beith MP
International Development: Malcolm Bruce MP
Science and Technology: Phil Willis MP

MEMBERS

Community & Local Government: John Pugh MP, Martin Horwood MP
Constitutional Affairs: Alan Beith MP (Chair), David Howarth MP

DCMS: Adrian Sanders MP
Defence: Willie Rennie MP, Mike Hancock MP
DEFRA: Dan Rogerson MP, Roger Williams MP
Dept for Work & Pensions: Greg Mulholland MP, Jenny Willott MP
DTI: Mark Hunter MP

Education: Paul Holmes MP, Stephen Williams MP
Environmental Audit: Tim Farron MP, David Howarth MP
European Scrutiny: Richard Younger-Ross MP

Finance & Services: Paul Burstow MP
Foreign Affairs: Paul Keetch MP, Richard Younger-Ross MP

Health: Sandra Gidley MP
Home Office: Jeremy Browne MP, Bob Russell MP
House Administration: John Thurso MP
Human Rights: Dr Evan Harris MP

International Development: John Barrett MP, Malcolm Bruce MP

Modernisation: Paul Burstow MP, Adrian Sanders MP

Northern Ireland Grand Committee: Lembit Opik MP, Greg Mulholland MP, Alan Reid MP

Procedure: Sir Robert Smith MP, John Hemming MP
Public Accounts: Annette Brooke MP, John Pugh MP
Public Administration: Paul Rowen MP, Jenny Willott MP

Regulatory Reform: Lorely Burt MP, John Hemming MP

Science and Technology: Dr Evan Harris MP, Phil Willis MP (Chair)
Scottish Affairs: Danny Alexander MP
Standards and Privileges: Nick Harvey MP

Transport: John Leech MP
Treasury: Colin Breed MP, John Thurso MP

Wales: Mark Williams MP

Europe
- how much do you really know?

Meet MEPs, Commission staff
and fellow Lib Dems in Brussels

Receive regular Newsletters
explaining
policy and institutions

Source campaign support and
information

**See www.ldeg.org for more details
on how to join us**

Prospective Parliamentary Candidates

The first points of call for anyone thinking about becoming a parliamentary candidate are the states' candidates offices in Cowley Street, London (for England: 020 7222 1204 **e-mail** candidates.office@ libdems.org.uk); Clifton Terrace, Edinburgh (for Scotland: 0131 337 2314 **e-mail** scotlibdems@cix.co.uk) and Bayview House, Cardiff (for Wales: 029 2031 3400 **e-mail** ldwales@cix.co.uk).

1 Ask for an application pack, which contains full information on the assessment process.

Asking for the pack does not commit you to anything. Please note all applicants for assessment must have been fully paid up members of the party for at least 12 months.

2 Fill in the application form.

Successful candidates come from all sorts of backgrounds; the form is a chance to let the assessors who you are, what you've done and why you think you'll be a good PPC or PEPC. We recommend that you take time to fill out and revise the form and really do yourself justice. Help and advice is available from the Candidates' Office and your Regional Candidates' Chair.

3 Attend an assessment day.

When there are sufficient applicants in your region, your RCC will invite you to attend an assessment day. You will be assessed for the qualities that make an effective PPC or PEPC. Sessions will include party knowledge, presentation skills, media, leading a team, campaigning and policy.

4 Apply to be selected as a PPC or PEPC.

All constituency and regional vacancies are advertised in **LibDem News** *and on the PCA website at* **www.libdempca.org.uk**

State and regional candidates committees

English Candidates Committee

Chair **Dawn Davidson**
ECE Representatives (directly elected):
**Glynis Dumper, Brian Orrell, Geoff Payne,
Jenny Shorten, Mark Valladares**

English Candidates Officer **Tamsin Hewett**
English Candidates Officer's Assistant **Eliane Patton**
4 Cowley Street, London SW1P 3NB
tel 020 7227 1204 **e-mail** candidates.office@libdems.org.uk

English Regional Candidates chairs

Devon and Cornwall **Glynis Dumper** tim.dumper@which.net
22 Woodville Road, Exmouth, Devon EX8 1SF **tel** 01395 276635

East Midlands **Penny Wilkins** penny@thecomputergeek.co.uk
16 Fowey Close, Wellingborough, Northants NN8 5WW
tel 01933 674 086

East of England **Sal Jarvis** sal@sjarvis.cix.co.uk
26 High Street, Graveley, Hitchin, Herts SG4 7LA **tel** 01438 727122

London **Brian Orrell** londonlibdems@cix.co.uk
24 Bina Gardens London SW5 0LA **tel** 0207 244 9039

North West **Bruce Hubbard** ia28@rapid.co.uk
91 Deyes Lane, Maghull, Merseyside L31 6DF **tel** 0151 526 4932

Northern **Doreen Hudart** doreen.huddart@newcastle.gov.uk
144 Biddlestone Road, Heaton, Newcastle upon Tyne NE6 5SP
tel 0191 240 1084

South Central **Liz Warner** lizwarner2000@hotmail.com
Staddles, Wildhern, Hatherden Rd, Andover, Hants SP11 0JE
tel 01264 735 303

South East **Margaret Ticehurst** ticehurstpark@aol.com
17 Park Lodge, Blackwater Rd, Eastbourne, Sussex BN21 4JE
tel 01323 731 767

West Midlands **Roger Gray**
8B Gibbons Grove, Wolverhampton WV6 0JF **tel** 01902 755 105

Western Counties **Gill Pardy** gillpardy@tiscali.co.uk
21 Fortescue Road, Bournemouth BH3 7JT **tel** 01202 552 009

Yorkshire and Humber **Stephen Fenton** stephenfenton1@aol.com
104 Askham Lane, York YO24 3HP **tel** 07751 963 215; 01904 337 757

Scottish Campaigns and Candidates Committee

Convener **Caron Lindsay**
tel 01506 414010 **e-mail** caron@cbahowden.icuklive.co.uk
Committee **Neil Wallace** (vice-convenor), **Helen Watt,
Norman Fraser, Iain Dale, Elspeth Attwooll MEP,
Jo Swinson MP, Iain Smith MSP, Andrew Arbuckle MSP,
Judy Hayman, Jamie Paterson, Rae Grant, Eileen McCartin,
Isabel Nelson, Simon Hutton, Fraser MacPherson**

Welsh Campaigns and Candidates Committee

Chair **Jenny Randerson AM** jenny.randerson@wales.gov.uk
**Mel ab Owain, Dominic Hagan, Barry Long, David Rees,
Nick Tregoning, Michael Woods**

House of Lords

Leader **Rt Hon Lord McNally of Blackpool**
Deputy Leaders **Lord Dholakia of Waltham Brooks** and **Lord Wallace of Saltaire**
Chief Whip **Lord Shutt of Greetland**

Peers

(for contact details, see under names in Who's Who? **Section)**

Lord Addington, Lord Alderdice of Knock, Lord Alliance, Lord Ashdown of Norton-sub-Hamdon, Lord Avebury, Baroness Barker, Baroness Bonham Carter, Lord Bradshaw, Lord Carlile of Berriew, Lord Chidgey, Lord Clement-Jones, Lord Dholakia, Lord Dykes, Lord Ezra, Viscount Falkland, Baroness Falkner of Margravine, Lord Fearn, Lord Garden of Hampstead, The Earl of Glasgow, Lord Goodhart, Lord Greaves, Baroness Hamwee, Baroness Harris of Richmond, Lord Holme of Cheltenham, Lord Hooson, Lord Hutchinson of Lullington, Lord Jacobs, Lord Jones of Cheltenham, Lord Kirkwood of Kirkhope, Lord Lester of Herne Hill, Baroness Linklater of Butterstone, Lord Livsey of Talgarth, Baroness Ludford, Lord Mackie of Benshie, Lord Maclennan of Rogart, Lord McNally, Baroness Maddock, The Earl of Mar and Kellie, Lord Methuen, Baroness Michie of Gallanach, Baroness Miller of Chilthorne Domer, Baroness Neuberger, Lord Newby, Baroness Nicholson of Winterbourne, Baroness Northover, Lord Oakeshott of Seagrove Bay, Lord Razzall, Lord Redesdale, Lord Rennard, Lord Roberts of Llandudno, Lord Rodgers of Quarry Bank, Lord Roper, Lord Russell-Johnston, Lord Sandberg, Baroness Scott of Needham Market, Lord Sharman of Red Lynch, Baroness Sharp of Guildford, Lord Shutt of Greetland, Lord Smith of Clifton, Lord Steel of Aikwood, Lord Taverne, Lord Thomas of Gresford, Baroness Thomas of Walliswood, Lord Thomson of Monifieth, Baroness Tonge, Lord Tope, Lord Tordoff, Lord Tyler, Lord Vallance of Rummel, Lord Wallace of Saltaire, Baroness Walmsley of West Derby, Lord Watson of Richmond

To see the full text of parliamentary
debates online, visit
www.parliament.uk

Liberal Democrat Responsibilities in the Lords

Leader **Lord McNally**

Deputy Leaders **Lord Dholakia** and **Lord Wallace of Saltaire**

Chief Whip **Lord Shutt of Greetland**

Deputy Whip **Lord Addington**

Whips **Baroness Harris of Richmond**
The Earl of Mar & Kellie
Lord Roberts of Llandudno

Home Office **Lord Dholakia**
Baroness Linklater of Butterstone (Penal Reform).
Baroness Harris of Richmond (Police)
Lord Avebury (Civil Liberties)
Earl of Mar and Kellie (Scottish Home Affairs)

Shadow Attorney General **Lord Thomas of Gresford**

Department of Constitutional Affairs (DCA) and Shadow
Lord Chancellor **Lord Goodhart**

Cabinet Office Lord Maclennan of Rogart
(with special responsibility for Civil Service Reform)

Foreign & Commonwealth Affairs **Lord Wallace of Saltaire**
Lord Avebury (with special responsibility for Africa)

Europe **Lord Dykes**

Defence **Lord Garden**

International Development **Baroness Northover, Lord Roberts of**
Llandudno

Culture, Media & Sport **Lord Clement-Jones, Baroness Bonham-Carter,**
Lord Addington (Sport)

Education and Children **Baroness Walmsley**

Further Education, Higher Education and Skills
Baroness Sharp of Guildford

Health **Baroness Barker, Baroness Neuberger**

Environment, Food & Rural Affairs **Baroness Miller of Chilthorne Domer**
Lord Livsey of Talgarth (Agriculture)
Lord Greaves
Lord Redesdale (Energy)

Office of the Deputy Prime Minister, Regional and Local Government
Baroness Scott of Needham Market, Baroness Hamwee
Communities and Local Government **Baroness Falkner of Margravine**

Northern Ireland **Lord Smith of Clifton, Baroness Harris of Richmond**

Scotland **Lord Maclennan of Rogart**

Trade and Industry **Lord Razzall**
Lord Vallance of Tummel
Lord Redesdale (Energy)
Lord Sharman

Transport **Lord Bradshaw**
Earl of Mar and Kellie, Earl of Glasgow

Treasury **Lord Newby**
Lord Oakeshott of Seagrove Bay

Wales **Lord Livsey of Talgarth, Lord Roberts of Llandudno**

Women's Issues **Baroness Thomas of Walliswood**

Department of Work & Pensions **Lord Oakeshott of Seagrove Bay**
Lord Addington (Disability)

Advisory team on legal matters:
Lord Goodhart, Lord Lester of Herne Hill, and **Lord Thomas of Gresford.**

Parliamentary Staff

Leader's Office

tel 020 7219 1433 **fax** 020 7219 0054
Chief of Staff **Norman Lamb** lambn@parliament.uk
Political Counsellor **Archy Kirkwood** kirkwooda@parliament.uk
Head of Office **Alison Suttie** suttiea@parliament.uk
Principal Aide to Sir Menzies Campbell MP **Carrie Henderson**
hendersonc@parliament.uk
Press Secretary **Puja Darbari** darbarip@parliament.uk
Speechwriter/ Policy Adviser **Euan Roddin** roddine@parliament.uk
Correspondence Manager **Anne-Marie Bunting**
buntinga@parliament.uk
Correspondence Assistant **Vicki Adamson** adamsonv@parliament.uk
Party Liaison/ Office Manager **Ian Sherwood** sherwoodi@parliament.uk

Chief Whip's Office

House of Commons
tel 020 7219 5654 **fax** 020 7219 5894
Secretary to Parliamentary Party **Ben Williams**
tel 020 7219 5654 williamsbp@parliament.co.uk
Deputy Secretary **Eleanor Pinfield**
tel 020 7219 1415 pinfielde@parliament.uk

Chief Whip's Office - House of Lords

Head of Office **Carolyn Rampton**
tel 020 7219 6548 ramptonc@parliament.uk
Parliamentary Assistant **Anne-Marie Christoffersen-Deb**
tel 020 7219 3114 christoffersendeba@parliament.uk
Senior Researcher **Elizabeth Hanna**
tel 020 7219 3178 hannae@parliament.uk
Senior Researcher **Tom Kiehl**
tel 020 7219 1229 kiehlt@parliament.uk
Senior Researcher **Neil Balmer**
tel 020 7219 5272 balmern@parliament.uk
fax 020 7219 2377

The Party in Europe

Leader of the UK Liberal Democrats **Diana Wallis MEP**
European Parliament, Rue Wertz, 1047 Brussels, Belgium

MEPs

(For contact details, see under names in Who's Who? **Section)**

Elspeth Attwooll Scotland, **Chris Davies** North West `
Andrew Duff Eastern, **Fiona Hall** North East
Chris Huhne South East, **Saj Karim** North West
Baroness Ludford London, **Liz Lynne** West Midlands
Bill Newton Dunn East Midlands, **Baroness Nicholson** South East
Diana Wallis Yorkshire, **Graham Watson** South West

ALDE Group

Leader **Graham Watson MEP**
e-mail **euro_office@cix.co.uk**

Austria 1 Independent
Belgium 6 (3 VLD, 3 MR)
Cyprus 1 Diko
Denmark 4 (3 V, 1 RV)
Estonia 2 (1 K, 1 ER)
Finland 5 (4 KESK, 1 SFP)
France 11 UDF-Europe
Germany 7 FDP
Hungary 2 SZDSZ
Ireland 1 Independent
Italy 12 (7 Margarita, 2 IDV, 1 MRE, 2 Radicals)
Latvia 1 LW
Lithuania 7 (2 LCS, 5 LLP)
Luxembourg 1 DP
Netherlands 5 (4 VVD, 1 D66)
Poland 4 UW
Slovenia 2 LDS
Spain 2 (1 CiU, 1 PNV)
Sweden 3 (2 FP, 1 C)
UK 12 (Liberal Democrats)

The Party in Local Government

Across Britain the Liberal Democrats have 4,746 Councillors and control or influence over 150 councils. Number of Councillors by Party as at 21st June 2006 was: Lib Dem 4,746, Labour 6,164, Conservative 8,482, SNP 189, Plaid Cymru 182, Others 2,257.

In the early 70s the arrival of "Community Politics" promoted by ALDC's predecessor, the Association of Liberal Councillors, produced great successes for the party in Local Government, most famously in the party's growth in Liverpool led by Sir Trevor Jones (Jones the Vote).

The problems of the late 70s caused by the Lib/Lab pact and the Jeremy Thorpe affair led to significant losses in local government most notably in the 1977 County Council elections when the party won just 90 seats nationwide.

The Thatcher 80s saw a period of sustained growth for the party in Local Government and success at a local level was often reproduced in Parliamentary success. Menzies Campbell and Paddy Ashdown both won their seats after several years of campaigning and building up their base through local Government. South Somerset District Council is still controlled by the Liberal Democrats and North East Fife was Lib Dem controlled until abolished by the Tories in May 1995.

During the 80s the advances in Local Government by the Alliance parties threw many councils into a balanced or hung situation. ALDC quickly became the experts in advising councillors on how to deal with the challenges and opportunities that this threw up.

The advance in local Government continued after the SDP and Liberals merged to form the Liberal Democrats - the low poll ratings that the party recorded nationally were never replicated in local elections and even in 1990 when on 6% in national opinion polls the party scored a significant double advance in the local elections of 1990 taking overall control of Tower Hamlets and Sutton London boroughs.

The 1990s saw the party making further advances in Local Government for the first time taking majority control of a significant number of councils. The

County Council elections of 1993 saw the Lib Dems take control of three county councils (Dorset, Somerset, Cornwall and the Isle of Wight) - compared to just one for the Tories. The unpopularity of the Major years saw the party win more councils in 1995 with a high point of 54 councils under Lib Dem control. With the election of a Labour Government and the return to opposition of the Tories many commentators predicted a rapid decline of Lib Dem local Government strength. However the years since the '97 election have shown that the Liberal Democrats local Government strength is surprisingly durable with the party holding on to many of its councils in the South and South East. In the 1999 Council elections the Tories made national gains of over 1400 - but mostly at Labour's expense. The Lib Dems had net losses of just 118.

Recent years have seen Liberal Democrat progress in the big cities and urban areas that were formerly Labour heartlands. Liverpool fell to Liberal Democrat control in 1998 and has been followed by Stockport, and, in 2004, Newcastle. In London, we took control of Islington at a by-election at the end of 1998; after holding control in 2002 we lost seats in 2006, but still run the council on the Mayor's casting vote. The general pattern of recent local elections has been mixed with gains and losses from both other parties in different areas.

Liberal Democrats made big gains in Cardiff and in Swansea, both of which Labour lost to NOC. And in Scotland in 2003, Liberal Democrats made a strong showing, winning eight seats in Aberdeen City. With 28 councillors, we are the biggest party in Aberdeenshire, sharing control with the Independents. We took four additional seats in Inverclyde, where the Tories disappeared and we have overall control. We won four seats in East Dunbartonshire and also won seats in Edinburgh, Glasgow, Dundee and Perth.

Today the party has outright control of 34 councils, stretching from Carrick in Cornwall to Inverclyde in Scotland, with minority control and influence over a substantial number of other councils.

Lib Dem Majority Councils

as at 21st June 2006

Metropolitan Districts (3)
Liverpool, Stockport, Newcastle-Upon-Tyne

Shire Counties (3)
Cornwall, Devon, Somerset

English Districts (20)
Cambridge, Carrick, Chesterfield, Durham City, Eastleigh,
Lewes, North Devon, North Norfolk, Oadby & Wigston,
Pendle, St Albans, South Lakeland, South Norfolk,
South Somerset, Three Rivers, Uttlesford,
Vale of White Horse,
Watford, West Lindsay, Woking

English Unitaries (4)
Bournemouth, Torbay,
Windsor & Maidenhead, York

London Boroughs (3)
Kingston-upon-Thames,
Richmond Upon Thames, Sutton

Scottish Councils (1)
Inverclyde

Elected Mayor (1)
Watford

Lib Dem Minority Controlled Councils

English Districts (2)
Harborough, Waverley

English Unitaries (5)
Bristol, Luton, Milton Keynes, Southampton, Portsmouth

Scottish Councils (1)
East Dunbartonshire

Welsh Councils (1)
Cardiff

LD Mayors with casting vote (1)
St Albans

Liberal Democrat Group
Local Government Association

Local Government House, Smith Square, London SW1P 3HZ
tel 020 7664 3235 **fax** 020 7664 3240 **e-mail** libdem@lga.gov.uk

Political Advisers **Oscar Plummer** oscar.plummer@lga.gov.uk
Rob Banks rob.banks@lga.gov.uk
Administration Officer **Anat Toffell** anat.toffell@lga.gov.uk

The Group office provides support to councillors active within the LGA
and offers an information service to the wider body of Liberal Democrat
councillors in the form of briefings, newsletters and conferences. In
addition, it advises Liberal Democrat MPs on issues relating to local
democracy and helps them keep in touch with their colleagues in local
government.

Group Executive

Leader **Richard Kemp** richard.kemp@liverpool.gov.uk
Deputy Leader **Gerald Vernon-Jackson**
wendy.burton@portsmouthcc.gov.uk;
Chair **David Williams** cllr.dwilliams@richmond.gov.uk
Secretary **John Commons** cllr.j.commons@notes.manchester.gov.uk
Ordinary Members **Pat Aston** aston@clara.net
Gordon Beever gordon.beever@kirklees.gov.uk **Carol Woods**
cllrcarolwoods@hotmail.co.uk
Derek Osborne derekosbourne@cix.co.uk
ALDC Representative **Laura Willoughby**
laura.willoughby@islington.gov.uk

Cabinet

includes elected members of Group Executive (see above) plus
Community Well-being Board Chair **David Rogers**
cllr.david.rogers@eastsussex.gov.uk; david.rogers@lewes.gov.uk
Improvement Board Vice Chair **David Williams**
cllr.dwilliams@richmond.gov.uk
Children & Young People Vice Chair **James Kempton**
james.kempton@islington.gov.uk; judith.tudhope@islington.gov.uk
Safer Communities Board Deputy Chair **Caroline Seymour**
cllr.c.seymour@northyorks.gov.uk
Environment Board Chair **Paula Baker**
cllr.paula.baker@basingstoke.gov.uk
Regeneration Board Chair **Chris White** chris.white@hertscc.gov.uk
Scrutiny Panel Vice Chair **Trevor Jones** d.t.jones@dorset-cc.gov.uk
Human Resources Panel Vice Chair **Dermot Roaf**
dermot.roaf@oxfordshire.gov.uk
Resources Panel Deputy Chair **Keith Whitmore**
cllr.k.whitmore@notes.manchester.gov.uk
European & Intl Panel Chair **Ruth Coleman** rcoleman@northwilts.gov.uk

CHILDREN & YOUNG PEOPLE BOARD

Vice Chair **James Kempton** james.kempton@islington.gov.uk;
judith.tudhope@islington.gov.uk
Member **Diane Packham** diane@derekpackham.plus.com;
diane.packham@newcastle.gov.uk
Member **Pauline Clarke** pclarke-cc@somerset.gov.uk
Sub **Martin Candler** martin.candler@stockport.gov.uk

COMMUNITY WELL-BEING

Chair **David Rogers** cllr.david.rogers@eastsussex.gov.uk;
david.rogers@lewes.gov.uk
Member **Maureen Robinson** maureen.robinson@nfdc.gov.uk
Rabi Martins Rabi_laay@hotmail.com; rabi@southallpartnership.co.uk
Sub **Laura Murphy** cllr.laura.murphy@wealden.gov.uk

ENVIRONMENT BOARD

Chair **Paula Baker** cllr.paula.baker@basingstoke.gov.uk
Member **Roger Symonds** mail@rogersymonds.org.uk
Member **Richard Knowles** cllr.r.d.knowles@oldham.gov.uk
Member **Humphrey Temperley** humphrytemperley@hotmail.com
Sub **Adam Carew** adamcarew@tiscali.co.uk

IMPROVEMENT BOARD

Vice Chair **David Williams** cllr.dwilliams@richmond.gov.uk

Member **John Commons** cllr.j.commons@notes.manchester.gov.uk

Member (4Ps) **Edward Lord** ce.lord@virgin.net

Sub **Lorna Spenceley** lspenceley@cix.co.uk

REGENERATION BOARD

Chair **Chris White** chris.white@hertscc.gov.uk

Member **Liz Lee** elizabeth.lee@lewes.gov.uk

Member **Alan Hockridge** alan.hockridge@lineone.net

Sub **Brian Golby** brian.golby@midbeds.gov.uk

SAFER COMMUNITIES BOARD

Deputy Chair **Caroline Seymour** cllr.c.seymour@northyorks.gov.uk

Member **Audrey Jones** cllr.a.jones@notes.manchester.gov.uk

Member **Paul Porgess** pporgess@cix.co.uk

Safer Communities – Fire **Christina Jebb**
Christina.Jebb@staffordshire.gov.uk

Sub **Barbara Todd** barbara.todd1@ntlworld.com

Sub (FIRE ONLY) **Gordon Beever** gordon.beever@kirklees.gov.uk

EUROPEAN & INTL PANEL

Chair **Ruth Coleman** rcoleman@northwilts.gov.uk

Member **Graham Tope** graham.tope@london.gov.uk

HUMAN RESOURCES PANEL

Vice Chair **Dermot Roaf** dermot.roaf@oxfordshire.gov.uk

Member **Simon Shaw** simon.shawsouthport@supanet.com

RESOURCES PANEL

Chair **Keith Whitmore** cllr.k.whitmore@notes.manchester.gov.uk

Member **Carol Woods** cllrcarolwoods@hotmail.co.uk

SCRUTINY PANEL

Vice Chair **Trevor Jones** d.t.jones@dorset-cc.gov.uk; j.rook@dorsetcc.gov.uk

Member **Lorna Spenceley** lspenceley@cix.co.uk

Greater London Assembly

Liberal Democrat Group Members and portfolios

Dee Doocey Chair of Economic Development, Culture,
Sport & Tourism Cttee dee.doocey@london.gov.uk
Baroness Hamwee Chair of Assembly; Chair of Budget Cttee
Sally.Hamwee@london.gov.uk
Geoff Pope Transport geoff.pope@london.gov.uk
Lord Tope Police, governance, human rights
Graham.Tope@london.gov.uk
Mike Tuffrey Environment mike.tuffrey@london.gov.uk

Member Liaison Manager **Nick Carthew**
Tel 020 7983 4962 nick.carthew@london.gov.uk
website www.gla.libdems.org.uk.

Association of London Government (ALG) Liberal Democrat Group

59½ Southwark Street, London SE1 0AL
tel 020 7934 9503 fax 020 7934 9624
Political Adviser **Stephen Knight**
Stephen.Knight@alg.gov.uk

Group Leader **Cllr Sean Brennan** – leader, LB Sutton
sean.brennan@sutton.gov.uk
Deputy Leader **Cllr Derek Osbourne** – leader, RB Kingston upon Thames
derekosbourne@cix.co.uk
Exec Mbr Children & Young People **Cllr James Kempton**
– leader, LB Islington james.kempton@islington.gov.uk
Committee Member **Cllr Paul Lorber** – leader, LB Brent
Committee Member **Cllr Serge Lourie** – leader, LB Richmond upon Thames
Committee Member **Cllr Keith Moffit** – leader, LB Camden
Committee Member **Cllr Nick Stanton** – leader, LB Southwark

Group spokespersons

Transport and Environment **Cllr Colin Hall** – LB Sutton
e-mail colin.hall@sutton.gov.uk
ALG Grants **Cllr Tracey Ismail** – LB Islington
e-mail tracey.ismail@islington.gov.uk
Greater London Employers Forum **Cllr Lorraine Zuleta** – LB Southwark
e-mail lorraine.zuleta@southwark.gov.uk

London Fire and Emergency Planning Authority (LFEPA)
Group Leader **Mike Tuffrey** – London Assembly Member
LB appointee **Cllr Ed Butcher** – LB Haringey
e-mail ed_butcher@blueyonder.co.uk

The Party in England

4 Cowley Street, London SW1P 3NB
Administrator **Paul Rustad** englishlibdems@cix.co.uk
tel 020 7227 1325 **fax** 020 7222 7904
Membership Development **Dave Hodgson** dhodgsona@cix.co.uk
tel 01234 330346, 07976 205116
Chair **Stan Collins** stanstheman@cix.co.uk
Treasurer **Jonathan Davies** jonathandavies@cix.co.uk
Chair English Candidates Committee **Dawn Davidson**
Dawn.Davidson@Brighton-Hove.gov.uk
FE representative **Paul Farthing** pfarthing@targetdirect.co.uk
Chair FFAC **David Griffiths** davidgriffiths@griffithshicks.co.uk
Chair Federal Appeals Panel **Susan Fenwick**
s.fenwick@btopenworld.com
Broker **Gordon Taylor** tel 07768 607015 gordontaylor@beeb.net

English Council Executive 2006

Chair **Stan Collins** stanstheman@cix.co.uk
Vice-Chair **Philip Goldenberg** goldenberg@cix.co.uk
Candidates Committee Chair **Dawn Davidson**
Dawn.Davidson@Brighton-Hove.gov.uk
English Party Staff Representative **Paul Rustad**
englishlibdems@cix.co.uk

Regional representatives

Devon & Cornwall **Keith Baldry** keithjbaldrey@lineone.net
East of England **Steve Jarvis** steve@sjarvis.cix.co.uk
East Midlands **Richard Church** rchurch1@btconnect.com
London **Sean Hooker** cllr.s.hooker@barnet.gov.uk
Northern **Eileen Blakey** emblakey51@yahoo.co.uk
North West **Gill Gardiner** gillgardiner@wirral.gov.uk
South Central **Chris Jennings** chrisjennings@btinternet.com
South East **Mike Simpson** mikeg.simpson@virgin.net
West Midlands **Tracey O'Brien** tjob1@tiscali.co.uk
Western Counties **Neil Halsall** neil.halsall@southglos.gov.uk
Yorkshire & the Humber **John Smithson** john.smithson@kirklees.gov.uk
LDYS **Mark Gettleson**

Directly elected by English Council

Ian Cuthbertson icuthbertson@cix.co.uk
Jonathan Davies jonathandavies@cix.co.uk
Philip Goldenberg goldenberg@cix.co.uk
Shirley Holloway shirley.holloway@blueyonder.co.uk
Brian Orrell londonlibdems@cix.co.uk
Geoff Payne geoff@geoffpayne.org.uk
Mike Simpson mikeg.simpson@virgin.net
Jenny Shorten, Dave Smithson, Steve Sollitt
Liz Warner, Penny Wilkins
Co-options
Jean Crossland ALDC

English Finance and Administration Committee

Chair **Jonathan Davies** (Treasurer ECE) – ex-officio
Stan Collins (Chair ECE) – ex-officio
Dawn Davidson (Chair ECC) – ex-officio
Members **Ian Cuthbertson, Shirley Holloway,**
Brian Orrell, Mike Simpson (elected by and from ECE)

English Appeals Panel

Chair **Peter Lee** tel 01223 460665

English Council representatives on other bodies

Federal Executive **Paul Farthing**
Federal Policy Committee **Geoff Payne**
Federal Conference Committee **Andrew Wiseman**
Joint States Membership Committee **2 vacancies**
G8 **Ian Cuthbertson, Susanne Lamido**
cilia2000@slamido.freeserve.co.uk
Balan Sisupalan balansisuplan@aol.com

English Candidates Committee

Dawn Davidson (chair), **Glynis Dumper, Brian Orrell, Geoff Payne,**
Jenny Shorten, Mark Valladares

The Party in Scotland

Our opportunity has never been greater

Nicol Stephen MSP
Leader of the Scottish Liberal Democrats

It has been a very good year for the Liberal Democrats in Scotland. Our results in last year's UK General Election were our strongest for more than half a century. Our share of the vote went up from 16% to more than 22%. We came second in share of the vote and number of seats. We won two new constituencies in Inverness, Nairn, Badenoch and Strathspey, and in East Dunbartonshire, where our new MP Jo Swinson is now the youngest member of the House of Commons. Perhaps most remarkable of all, the Liberal Democrat share of the vote in Scotland's four-party system was for the first time higher than our share across the whole of the UK.

Following these successes came the stunning Liberal Democrat victory in the Dunfermline and West Fife Westminster by-election. We achieved a swing of more than 16% to win the seat from Labour. The gain was all the more remarkable as it was not expected - or predicted by the nation's political pundits or media. It emphasised that it is the Liberal Democrats who are the only party with growing momentum in Scotland. In similar circumstances the SNP failed to win in the Cathcart and Livingston by-elections.

In Dunfermline Willie Rennie was an excellent candidate and is now establishing himself as a very effective Member of Parliament. To understand his success you need to analyse some of the new trends in Scottish politics. Increasingly the Liberal Democrats are winning votes among young people and in new parts of Scotland. Time and again the Liberal Democrats are winning mock elections and other political contests in our schools, colleges and universities. And in large parts of Scotland, historic loyalties are shifting. People are no longer willing to vote the same way. Traditional class-based or family-based voting patterns are breaking down. Increasingly when offered the opportunity people are switching to the Liberal Democrats.

The scale of the progress we are making has been emphasised not only in Dunfermline but also in the recent Moray by-election and in local government results. In Moray, in circumstances where our vote would traditionally have been significantly squeezed we saw our vote increase from 12% to 20%. In local government we sensationally won the King's Park by-election in Glasgow from fourth place last time, and in the last few weeks we won the Lochardil by-election in Inverness, notably in a Scottish Parliament seat currently held by the SNP.

The reason for all these successes is that the Liberal Democrats in Scotland are increasingly seen as a party of the future. We are determined to reject the bitter battles and name-calling of the other major parties. We are determined to fight a positive campaign.

Clearly major UK and international issues, such as the fight against terrorism, the war in Iraq and the handling of the Middle East crisis will continue to be at the forefront of the political agenda in Scotland. However, in the next few months what will be influencing voters the most will be the key issues that will dominate next year's Scottish Parliament elections.

The Liberal Democrats will be focusing on three major themes. The first relates to energy and the environment. Scotland can become the green energy powerhouse of Europe. The Liberal Democrats are determined to support this vital investment - and reject new nuclear power in Scotland. The second is our positive approach to young people. We will promote positive policies to encourage and support young people, investing not only in our schools but also in excellent sports and community facilities. The third will be our commitment to a pro-enterprise environment. As Scotland's Enterprise Minister I have already delivered a cut in business rates and the Liberal Democrats want to see further action to give Scottish businesses a greater competitive advantage.

Our opportunity has never been greater. Our experience in government in Scotland since 1999 has significantly increased our strength and credibility. All the evidence of recent elections and current opinion polls points to Liberal Democrats making major gains in the forthcoming election. We are now well placed to be Scotland's largest party after next year's General Election. The challenge now is to deliver.

Scottish Liberal Democrats

4 Clifton Terrace, Edinburgh EH12 5DR
tel 0131 337 2314 **fax** 0131 337 3566
e-mail administration@scotlibdems.org.uk
Leader **Nicol Stephen MSP**
Deputy Leader **Michael Moore MP**
President **Malcolm Bruce MP**
Convener **Judy Hayman**
President **Malcolm Bruce MP**
Convener **Judy Hayman**
Vice Convener (Campaigns & Candidates) **Caron Lindsay**
Vice Convener (Conference) **Helen Watt**
Vice Convener (Policy) **Robert Brown** MSP
Treasurer **Douglas Herbiso**n
Elected to Federal Executive **Roy Thomson**

Parliamentary Representatives

European Parliament **Elspeth Attwooll** MEP
UK Parliament **John Barrett** MP
Scottish Parliament **Margaret Smith** MSP

Regional Representatives

Central Scotland **Nicol McLaughlan, Rev Ian Murdoch**
Greater Glasgow **Norman Fraser, Isabel Nelson**
Highlands & Islands **John Melling, Jamie Paterson**
Lothian **Craig Harrow, Marilyne MacLaren**
Mid Scotland & Fife **Anthony Garrett, Avril Simpson**
North East Scotland **Dr Liz Dick, Paul Johnston**
South of Scotland **Brian Logan, Ron Waddell**
West of Scotland **Eileen McCartin, Helen Watt**
Non-voting representatives from Associated Organisations
ASLDC **Kate Dean** SGLD **Richard Burnett-Hall**
SWLD **Jacquie Bell** SYLD **Iain Kennedy**

BUSINESS COMMITTEE

Convener **Douglas Herbiso**n
Executive **Anthony Garrett Tony Hutso**n

Campaigns & Candidates **Jamie Paterson**
Conference **Helen Watt** Co-opted **Brian Logan**

CAMPAIGNS & CANDIDATES COMMITTEE

Convener **Caron Lindsay**
tel 01506 414010 **e-mail** caron@cbahowden.icuklive.co.uk
Committee **Neil Wallace** (vice-convenor), **Helen Watt,**
Norman Fraser, Iain Dale, Elspeth Attwooll MEP,
Jo Swinson MP, Iain Smith MSP, Andrew Arbuckle MSP,
Judy Hayman, Jamie Paterson, Rae Grant, Eileen McCartin,
Isabel Nelson, Simon Hutton, Fraser MacPherson

CONFERENCE COMMITTEE

Convener **Karen Freel**
Vice Conveners **Debra Storr, Helen Watt**
Executive **Fred Mackintosh, Ian Yuill**
Directly elected **Dr Liz Dick, Caron Lindsay, Stuart Smith**
Debra Storr, Helen Watt
Policy **Robert Brown MSP** Co-opted **Ron Waddell, Mike**
Falchikov Ex-Officio **Tavish Scott MSP**
MPs **John Barrett** ASLDC **Paul Johnston**
SGLD **Alison MacLachlan** SYLD **Helen Herd**

POLICY COMMITTEE

Convener **Robert Brown MSP**
Executive **Marilyne MacLaren Rev Iain Murdoch**
Directly elected **Gordon MacDonald, Hugh O'Donnell, Ben Strachan**
Co-opted **Alan Costello, Jane-Claire Judson, Antonia Swinson**
Federal Representatives **Dr Gurudeo Saluja**
House of Lords **Jamie Mar & Kellie** MEP **Elspeth Attwooll**
MPs **Alistair Carmichael** ASLDC **Paul Edie**
SGLD **Prof Denis Mollison**

APPEALS TRIBUNAL

Convener **Malcolm Bruce MP**

Representatives on Federal Committees

Federal Executive **Derek Young**
Campaigns & Candidates Committee **Dr Derek Barrie**
Conference Committee **Karen Freel* Debra Storr**
Policy Committee **Keith Raffan**
Equal Opportunities **Dr Gurudeo Saluja**
Finance & Administration Committee **Douglas Herbison**
G8 **Iain Smith** Joint States Candidates **Dr Derek Barrie**

What's going on in Scotland?

Find out from

Clifton Terrace Focus

the official gazette of

Scottish Liberal Democrats

4 Clifton Terrace, Edinburgh EH2 5DR

PARTY HQ STAFF

Chief Executive **Martin Hayman**
Director of Campaigns & Elections **Derek Barrie**
derekbarrie@cix.co.uk
HQ Manager **Suzette Macgregor**
administration@scotlibdems.org.uk
Membership & Development Officer **James Spence**
membership@scotlibdems.org.uk
Campaigns Officer **Charles Dundas**
Constituency Development Officer **Jon Fox**

Members of the Scottish Parliament

Constituencies

George Lyon Argyll & Bute
John Farquhar Munro Ross, Skye & Inverness West
Mike Pringle Edinburgh South
Jeremy Purvis Tweeddale, Ettrick & Lauderdale
Nora Radcliffe Gordon
Euan Robson (Roxburgh & Berwick)
Mike Rumbles West Aberdeenshire & Kincardine
Tavish Scott Shetland
Iain Smith North East Fife
Margaret Smith Edinburgh West
Jamie Stone Caithness, Sutherland & Easter Ross
Jim Wallace Orkney

Regions

Andrew Arbuckle Mid-Scotland & Fife
Robert Brown City of Glasgow
Ross Finnie West of Scotland
Donald Gorrie Central Scotland

Liberal Democrats in Government

Nicol Stephen Deputy First Minister and
Minister for Enterprise & Lifelong Learning
Ross Finnie Minister for Environment & Rural Development
Tavish Scott Minister for Transport
Robert Brown Deputy Minister for Education & Young People
George Lyon Deputy Minister for Finance and Public Service Reform
Margaret Smith Whip

Scottish spokespersons

Danny Alexander MP – House of Commons: Work & Pensions
Cllr Andrew Arbuckle MSP – Finance; and Transport & Local Govt
Elspeth Attwooll MEP - Europe
John Barrett MP – House of Commons: Scotland
Malcolm Bruce MP – Chair, International Development Select Committee

Sir Menzies Campbell MP - Leader, Liberal Democrats
Alistair Carmichael MP – Shadow Secy of State for Transport
Donald Gorrie MSP – Culture, Sport & Older People
Baroness Linklater of Butterstone – House of Lords: Home Office
The Lord Maclennan of Rogart - House of Lords: European Constitution;
and Scotland; The Earl of Mar & Kellie - House of Lords: Whip
House of Lords: Scottish Home Affairs; and Transport
Michael Moore MP - Shadow Secy of State for Foreign & Commonwealth
Affairs; Deputy Leader, Scottish Liberal Democrats
John Farquhar Munro MSP - Gaelic Language
Mike Pringle MSP – Deputy, Justice; Jeremy Purvis MSP – Justice
Nora Radcliffe MSP - Environment & Rural Development; Equal
Opportunities; Alan Reid MP – House of Commons: Northern Ireland
Willie Rennie MP – House of Commons: Defence
Euan Robson MSP – Health and Communities
Iain Smith MSP – Education; Margaret Smith MSP – Chief Whip
Jamie Stone MSP - Enterprise, Lifelong Learning (including Tourism)
Jo Swinson MP – House of Commons: Shadow Secy of State for Scotland

Scottish members of the House of Lords

The Earl of Glasgow, Lord Kirkwood of Kirkhope, Baroness Linklater of
Butterstone, Lord Mackie of Benshie, Lord Maclennan of Rogart, The
Earl of Mar & Kellie, Baroness Michie of Gallanach, Lord Russell-
Johnston, Lord Steel of Aikwood, Lord Thomson of Monifieth

The Party in Wales

We're the Official Opposition now

by Lembit Opik MP
Leader of the Welsh Liberal Democrats

Back in 2004 I predicted further successes would be secured by the Welsh Lib Dems, following a record breaking performance in the Local Elections that year. Well, it happened, and we doubled our MPs in the 2005 General Election. This was in fact the best result for the Lib Dems in any nation in the UK.

So, just as Wales contributed almost half of the entire Council seat-gain achieved by the Lib Dems across Britain in '04, so also we contributed a 100% increase in the number of Parliamentarians in '05.

This was the consequences of persistent investment by the Lib Dem Assembly Members, MPs and existing local councillors and activists. We were assiduous in our targeting methods. We also followed the Parliamentary selection process faithfully.

Hence our spectacular gain over Labour in Cardiff Central by Jenny Willot MP. In addition, we won back the West Wales seat of Ceredigion from the Welsh Nationalists. In fact, Mark Williams MP's victory was the first time in history Lib Dems have gained a seat from Plaid Cymru. Our four Parliamentary seats make the Welsh Lib Dems the Official Opposition Welsh Party in Westminster.

Looking ahead, we'll focus on consolidating what we've got and driving towards more Assembly Members and council seats in forthcoming elections. Watch out for further gains in Ceredigion and Swansea, as well as other promising developments in Wrexham. There's no magic in success. We just do it by the book, and make sure to try and inspire the public with clear principles and well thought out Liberal and Democratic policies. But it is working, and I feel the Welsh Lib Dems have proved a seven-year journey from the First Division to the Premier Political League has neared its destination.

Welsh Liberal Democrats
Democratiaid Rhyddfrydol Cymru

Bayview House, 102 Bute Street, Cardiff CF10 5AD
Telephone 029 2031 3400 Fax 029 2031 3401
e-mail enquiries@welshlibdems.org.uk
web demrhydcymru.org.uk
President **Rob Humphreys**
Vice President **Nick Bennett**
Leader **Lembit Opik MP**
Assembly Leader **Mike German AM**

National Executive

Chair **Rob Humphreys** e-mail r.humphreys@swansea.ac.uk
Vice Chair **Alison Goldsworthy** alison@cardiffwestlibdems.org.uk
Treasurer **Alastair Baker** alistair@creativerealisation.com
Secretary **Jon Burree** nburree@aol.com

Committee Members

Nick Bennett e-mail darpar@cambrensis.uk.com
David Bourne davidabourne@hotmail.com
Jon Burree nburree@aol.com
Mike German AM mike.german@wales.gov.uk
Aled Morris Jones
Tudor Jones tudor@tgbabell.freeserve.co.uk (Chair, Conference Cttee)
Jim Kelleher, Ben Lloyd
Veronica Watkins veronica.watkins@newport.gov.uk
Kirsty Williams AM kirsty.williams@wales.gov.uk

Party Staff

Chief Executive **Stephen Smith** 029 2031 3400
stephen.smith@welshlibdems.org.uk
Party Manager **Ian Walton** 029 2031 3400 fax 029 2031 3401
ian.walton@welshlibdems.org.uk
Administrator **Karen Roberts** 029 2089 8741
Karen.roberts@welshlibdems.org.uk
Campaigns Officer **Jon Aylwin** 02920 313400
jon.aylwin@welshlibdems.org.uk
Head of Media **Gareth Price** 029 2089 8426
gareth.price@welshlibdems.org.uk
Policy Officer **Dewi Knight** 029 2031 3400
policy.office@welshlibdems.org.uk

Brecon and Radnor **Deanna Leboff** 99 The Struet, Brecon LD3 7LS
01874 625739 brecrad@cix.co.uk
Cardiff Central **Jon Aylwin** 133 City Road, Roath, Cardiff
02920 471167 office@cardiffcentral.org.uk
Montgomeryshire **Rhiain Selby** 3 Park Street, Newtown, Powys SY16 1EE
01686 625527 montgomeryldp@cix.co.uk
South East Wales **Phillip Melish** 101a The Highway, New Inn, Pontypool,
Torfaen NP4 0PN
01495 740358 phillip.mellish@wales.gov.uk
South Wales West **Nick Tregoning** 70 Mansel St, Swansea SA1
01792 536353 ldwaleswest@cix.co.uk
North Wales **Wendy Davies**
Kenmar, Chester Rd, Rossett LL12 0DL
01244 571918 wendy.davies@wales.gov.uk

Members of the Welsh Assembly

Leader **Mike German AM** (South Wales East) 02920 898352
Mick Bates AM (Montgomeryshire) 02920 898340
Peter Black AM (South Wales West) 02920 898361
Eleanor Burnham AM (Wales North) 02920 898343
Jenny Randerson AM (Cardiff Central) 02920 898355
Kirsty Williams AM (Brecon & Radnorshire) 02920 898358

Portfolios

Mike German Leader, Local Government, Europe
Mick Bates Environment, Planning and Countryside
Peter Black Social Justice, Education
Eleanor Burnham Culture, Sport and Welsh Language
Jenny Randerson Finance, Economic Development and Transport
Kirsty Williams Health

Welsh members of the House of Commons

Lembit Opik MP (Montgomeryshire), **Mark Williams MP** (Ceredigion),
Roger Williams MP (Brecon & Radnorshire),
Jenny Willott MP (Cardiff Central)

Welsh members of the House of Lords

**Lord Carlile, Lord Hooson, Lord Livesey, Lord Thomas, Lord Roberts,
Baroness Walmsley**

The Alliance Party of Northern Ireland

88 University Street, Belfast BT7 1HE
tel 028 9032 4274 **fax** 028 9033 3147
e-mail alliance@allianceparty.org

The Alliance Party – the Liberal Democrats' sister party in Northern Ireland - was formed in April 1970 to give political expression to those who felt that Nationalist and Unionist political parties did not reflect their political views. It is the only political party to receive significant support and membership from both Catholics and Protestants. The Alliance is a member of the European Liberal Democratic and Reform group (ELDR) and of Liberal International. Former leader and the first Speaker of the Northern Ireland Assembly, John Alderdice, sits on the Lib Dem benches in the House of Lords. The leader of the party (since October 2001) is David Ford who was formerly an active Liberal Democrat in Orpington.

Vision of shared future

With six Members of the Legislative Assembly (MLAs), in the Northern Ireland Assembly, the Alliance is the only party with a cross-community vision for a shared future in the next Assembly. We will fight our corner on issues that others ignore, and ask the awkward questions that they dodge. We now have the first female Assembly member from East Belfast and the best gender balance of any party. We are now the only party that can provide constructive opposition to a future Executive, and are the only centre party in the Assembly. I am immensely proud of the team that I lead.

David Ford MLA

Leader **David Ford** MLA david.ford@allianceparty.org
Deputy Leader **Eileen Bell MLA** eileen.bell@allianceparty.org
President **Tom Ekin** tom.ekin@allianceparty.org
Chair **Trevor Lunn** trevor.lunn@allianceparty.org
Hon Treasurers **Mervyn Jones** mervyn.jones@allianceparty.org
and **Stewart Dickson** stewart.dickson@allianceparty.org
General Secretary **Stephen Farry** stephen.farry@allianceparty.org

Members of the Legislative Assembly (MLA)

Leader **David Ford MLA** South Antrim
Deputy Leader **Eileen Bell MLA** North Down
Chief Whip **Kieran McCarthy MLA** Strangford
Seamus Close MLA Lagan Valley
Naomi Long MLA East Belfast
Sean Neeson MLA East Antrim

Alliance Party Staff

General Secretary **Stephen Farry** stephen.farry@allianceparty.org
Administration **Debbie Spence**alliance@allianceparty.org
PA to Party Leader **Marjorie Hawkins**
marjorie.hawkins@allianceparty.org
Press Officer **Steven Alexander** steven.alexander@allianceparty.org
Policy & Development Officer **Allan Leonard**
allan.leonard@allianceparty.org

Party Spokespersons

Europe **Colm Cavanagh** colm.cavanagh@allianceparty.org
Enterprise, Trade & Investment **David Alderdice**
david.alderdice@allianceparty.org
Social Development **Eileen Bell MLA** eileen.bell@allianceparty.org
Agriculture and Rural Development **Frank McQuaid**
frank.mcquaid@allianceparty.org
Health, Social Services & Personal Safety **Geraldine Rice**
geraldine.rice@allianceparty.org
Regional Development **John Mathews** john.mathews@allianceparty.org
Equality & Community Relations **Margaret Marshall**
margaret.marshall@allianceparty.org
Children **Marjorie Hawkins** marjorie.hawkins@allianceparty.org
Education **Naomi Long MLA** naomi.long@allianceparty.org
Environment **Seamus Close MLA**seamus.close@allianceparty.org
Justice & Human Rights **Stephen Farry** stephen.farry@allianceparty.org
Local Government **Stewart Dickson** stewart.dickson@allianceparty.org
Finance & Personnel **Tom Ekin** tom.ekin@allianceparty.org
Councillors Association **Trevor Lunn** trevor.lunn@allianceparty.org
Culture, Arts & Leisure **Yvonne Boyle** yvone.boyle@allianceparty.org

The Party and Funding

Under the spotlight

Party political fundraising is increasingly under the spotlight in spite of the passing of the Political Parties Elections and Referendums Act back in 2000; and a number of Select Committees and the Electoral Commission itself will undoubtedly be making further recommendations for reform later in the year.

Even if the current scandal of loans for peerages leads to state funding however, we will undoubtedly still need to raise our own funds, not least from the efforts of our members.

Any fundraising strategy must be based on transparency, accountability and a clear understanding of the purposes for which money is being raised.

A successful strategy depends on our ability to arouse political enthusiasm and, above all, demonstrate a link between financial support and results at elections. Encouraging potential donors to invest in campaigning success is therefore crucial.

This means that more than ever before, our fundraising efforts must be interlinked with the Party's campaigning strategy and activity, especially in target seats. To contest the general election effectively and win more than our current number of seats, we need to give adequate support to candidates, upgrade our internet presence, improve our databases and the quality and quality of our opinion research.

Introducing new donors and encouraging existing donors to give more is crucial and one of our key instruments in this is Liberty Network - our Liberal Democrat supporters club. Please do join, and encourage others known to you locally as donors or potential donors to do so. There will almost certainly be a direct benefit to our hard-working candidates!

Lord Tim Clement-Jones
Federal Treasurer

The Party in Print

Liberal Democrat News

4 Cowley Street London SW1P 3NB
Tel 020 7222 7999 Fax 020 7222 7904
e-mail ldn@cix.co.uk
Editor **Deirdre Razzall**

Liberal Democrat Image

Retailer of policy information and other party material
Craig Card, Lib Dem Image
11 High Street, Aldershot, Hampshire GU11 1BH
Tel/Fax 01252 408282 libdemimage@ldimage.demon.co.uk

Liberator

Liberator Publications
Flat 1, 24 Alexandra Grove, London N4 2LF
e-mail collective@liberator.org.uk

Grassroots Campaigner

Free to gold and silver members of ALDC, £7 to others
ALDC, The Birchcliffe Centre, Hebden Bridge,
West Yorkshire HX7 8DG
Editor **Mark Alcock** mark.alcock@aldc.org

Challenge

Quarterly magazine of the Green Liberal Democrats
Editor **Paul Burall** paulburall@prburall.demon.co.uk

Clifton Terrace Focus

The official gazette of Scottish Liberal Democrats
4 Clifton Terrace, Edinburgh EH2 5DR
e-mail scotlibdems@cix.co.uk

Journal of Liberal Democrat History

published by Liberal Democrat History Group
Editor **Duncan Brack**
e-mail journal@liberalhistory.org.uk

The Legal Democrat

Journal of the Liberal Democrat Lawyers Association
2 Green's Yard, North Hill, Colchester CO1 1QP
Editor **Jo Hayes**
e-mail johayes@greenyard.demon.co.uk

Interlib

Quarterly newsletter of Liberal International British Group
1 Whitehall Place, London SW1A 2HD
Tel 020 7839 5905 Fax 020 7925 2685

The Party Online

The party's main website is
www.libdems.org.uk
and includes links to a host of related groups
LDO (Liberal Democrats Online) developed the party's e-mail service
and has established a discussion list for LDO members. It's safe and
secure with no annoying adverts. The main aim of
LDOMEMBERSTALK is to allow members to freely discuss e-
campaigning; for example to ask questions and get answers from other
LDO members. Or perhaps you might have some news or ideas about
using e-mail or the web for party campaigning. Visit
http://lists.libdems.org.uk/wws to find out more about the lists you can
join or control your membership of the list.
To join LDO see listing under SAO section.

Specified Associated Organisations (SAOs)

Association of Liberal Democrat Councillors (ALDC)

Birchcliffe Centre, Birchcliffe Road, Hebden Bridge, West Yorkshire
HX7 8DG Tel 01422 843785 Fax 01422 843036
e-mail mail@aldc.org **web** www.aldc.org

Officers

President **Andrew Stunell MP**
Chair **Cllr Sarah Boad**
Treasurer **Jean Crossland**
Vice chairs **Cllr John Commons, Mike Ward**
Secretary **Cllr Willie Wilson**

Staff

Chief Executive **Cllr Tim Pickstone**
tim.pickstone@aldc.org
In overall charge of the Association's direction and strategy. He has specific responsibility for managing the Party's G8 process and plays an active role in delivering front-line advice, council support and training to Lib Dem councillors and the wider party.

Political Officer **Cllr Mark Alcock**
mark.alcock@aldc.org
Gives front-line telephone support on a range of issues. Also edits the member's magazines Grassroots Campaigner and Goldmine and maintains the ALDC website.

Political Officer **Cllr John Bridges**
john.bridges@aldc.org
Writes the comment each week on the By-Election results in ALDC column in Lib Dem News, edits Election Briefing, organises ALDC conference fringe gives front-line telephone support and is responsible for ALDC publications.

Scottish Officer ***Dr Derek Barrie**
derek.barrie@aldc.org
Is in charge of all ALDC's operations in Scotland.

Training and Council Support Officer (Northern) ***vacant**
Responsible for providing training and support to council groups.

Training and Council Support Officer (Southern)
*Cllr Roger Symonds roger.symonds@aldc.org
Responsible for providing training and support to council groups.

Executive support officer
*Eleanor Ritchie eleanor.ritchie@aldc.org
Responsible for administration of G8, awards grants to local parties facing elections to help improve their campaign.

Office Manager **Val Pilling** val.pilling@aldc.org
Oversees the day-to-day running of the organisation, deals with the accounts and oversees the Support Staff.

Membership and Database Officer **Emma Hall** emma.hall@aldc.org
Responsible for membership and maintaining database, runs Direct Debit system, promotes membership and helps with the By-Election service.

Membership and Database Assistant ***Dina Ball** dina.ball@aldc.org
General support, assists with direct debits and members' payment enquiries and helps with the By-Election service.

Elections and IT Support Assistant ***David Ball** david.ball@aldc.org
General support, dispatches publication orders, membership queries, updates computer software and server backup and administers the By-Election service.
* Part time

Association of Scottish Liberal Democrat Councillors and Campaigners (ASLDC)

Convener **Willie Wilson**
Vice-Convener **John Morrison**
Secretary **Paul Edie**
Treasurer **Paul Johnston**
Committee **Margaret Kennedy, Alec Nicol, Fraser Macpherson, Ian Yuill, Marilyne MacLaren, Caron Lindsay**
ALDC Scottish Officer **Dr Derek Barrie**
e-mail derekbarrie@cix.co.uk

Agents & Organisers Association

Chair **Victoria Marsom**
4 Cowley Street, London SW1P 3NB
Tel 020 7227 1214
e-mail agents@libdems.org.uk or ldagents@cix.co.uk
Web www.ldagents.org.uk
Helps facilitate the exchange of ideas among agents and organisers
and to represent the views of agents within the party. The association
also arranges training events, are the publishers of a number of key
party publications and offer help-lines and one-to-one assistance for
agents and others throughout campaigns.

*Association of Liberal Democrat Trade Unionists (ALDTU)

The Association is the party's organisation of trade unionists. It exists to
support Liberal Democrat members in the trade union movement and to
input into party policy. Membership is open to trade unionists and
associate membership is open to those who support union aims.
Contact **Andrew Hudson**
30 Leigh Road London E10 6JH
020 8529 2993 (work)
Membership Secretary **Angela Whitelegge** 020 7730 2311

*Association of Liberal Democrats in Engineering and Science (ALDES)

ALDES exists to provide a resource of engineering and scientific
know-how to support the party. It also enables engineers and
scientists within the party to discuss common concerns.
Secretary **Richard Balmer**
79 Links Drive, Solihull, B91 2DJ
0121 603 0661 Fax 0121 608 7057
e-mail richard_balmer@cix.co.uk
Website www.aldes.org.uk

Business Motion FB5 at Federal Conference, Brighton 2006 refers.

*DELGA

(Liberal Democrats for lesbian, gay,
bi-sexual and transgender equality)
President **Dr Evan Harris MP**
Chair **Alison Wheeler** chair@delga.org.uk
c/o 4 Cowley Street, London SW1P 3NB
Tel 020 7227 1321 **e-mail** info@delga.org.uk
Web http://www.delga.org.uk

Ethnic Minority Liberal Democrats

Chair **Fiyaz Mughal** fiyaz@fiyaz.freeserve.co.uk
Vice chairs **Peter Perren** pete@pjperren.com
Vice Chair **Claudia Wilmot** claudia.wilmot@morganstanley.com
Vice Chair **Hew Jaff** hjkurd@hotmail.com
Campaigns Director **Norsheen Bhatti** kiki_bhatti@hotmail.com
Secretary **Jay Sharma** jaysharma_uk@yahoo.co.uk
Treasurer **Dorrie Valerie** dorrievalery@btinternet.com
Membership Secretary **Anne Diamond** annediamond1@aol.com
Events Co-ordinator **Miriam Hussain Chowdhury** mhc919@hotmail.com
Media Officer **Dave Raval** dave.raval@ttp.com
Executive members
Cllr Meral Ece meral.ece@islington.gov.uk
Patrick Murray patrick_malcom_murray@hotmail.com

Liberal Democrat Youth and Students

4 Cowley Street, London SW1P 3NB
tel 020 7227 1387
e-mail ldys@cix.co.uk **web** www.ldys.org.uk

Chair **Mark Gettleson**
Vice-chairs
David Bourne (Finance),
Steve Harper (Communications) **e-mail** steven.harper@gmail.com
Adam Edwards (Membership)
Campaigns **Adi Smith**
Executive **Amanda Crane, Nasim Bazari, Matt Fensome, Paul Hardling,
Simon Drage, Martin Jopp, Andy Higson, Paul Seery**
English Convenor **Chris Gurney**
Wales Chair **Adi Smith**

Scottish Young Liberal Democrats

4 Clifton Terrace, Edinburgh EH12 5DR
tel 0131 337 2314 **fax** 0131-337 3566 **e-mail**
administration@scotlibdems.org.uk
web www.ldys.org.uk
Convener **Tom Clement** t.m.a.clement@sms.ed.ac.uk

Parliamentary Candidates Association

President **Rt Hon Sir Menzies Campbell MP**
Patron **Lord Rennard of Wavertree**

Vice Presidents
**Paul Holmes MP, Baroness Northover, Jane Smithard,
Jenny Willott MP** and **Robert Woodthorpe Browne**

Executive
Chair **Gary Lawson** gary@lawsononline.org
Deputy Chair **Tessa Munt** tessa@tessa4wells.com
Vice-Chairs **John Stevens** sue@sbaldwin1.freeserve.co.uk
Martin Turner martin.turner@unforgettable.com
Secretary **Jo Christie-Smith** johanna.christiesmith@ntlworld.com
Membership Secretary **Elliot Shubert** e.shubert@ntlworld.com
Treasurer **Mike Dixon** mike@mikedixon.org
Marketing Officer **Liz Leffman** lizleffman@clothesource.net
Recruiting Officer **James Quinlan** james.quinlan@ntlworld.com
Conference Organiser **Ben Abbotts** benjamin@llm.co.uk
Training Officer **Jill Hope** spes@cix.co.uk
Parliamentary Campaigner **Jane Smithard** and **Robert Woodthorpe Browne**
Communications / *The Candidate* **Antony Hook**
antony@doverlibdems.org.uk
Who's Who **Linda Forbes** linda@lindaforbes.co.uk
Focus on Government **Jock Gallagher** jyg@cix.co.uk
Policy Officer **Justine McGuiness** jezmcguinness@aol.com
European Officer **John Ryan** JRyan2002@aol.com
Peers List **Dr Julie Smith**
Business Liaison Officer **Elliot Shubert** e.shubert@ntlworld.com
Fund-raising Officer **Karen Gillard** karengillard@yahoo.com

The PCA represents and supports the party's front-line candidates

Women Liberal Democrats

**The WLD constitution pledges to eliminate all inequality
based on gender**

Scottish Women Liberal Democrats

President **Elspeth Attwooll MEP**
Chair **Jacquie Bell** sbell@easynet.co.uk
Vice Chair **Eileen McCartin**
Treasurer **Nikki Thomson**
Secretary **Joanna Toomey**
Committee **Ruth Currie, Katy Gordon, Caron Lindsay**,
Amy Roger, **Antonia Swinson, Jo Swinson MP, Helen Watt**

Associated Organisations (AOs)

The groups listed below have certain rights of consultation over policy papers, as defined within the Federal Party's constitution.

DAGGER

(Democrat Action Group for Gaining Electoral Reform)

Chair **Joan Davies**
Russell Lodge, Parkend, Lydney, Gloucestershire GL15 4HS
01594 562 617 **e-mail** johan.parkend@uk.co.uk

DAGGER works for the introduction of Proportional Representation by the Single Transferable Vote - the only system acceptable to genuine democrats. STV maximises the power of the voter and also ensures that most people will be represented in parliament by an MP that they have chosen.

Green Liberal Democrats

e-mail info@greenlibdems.org.uk **web** www.green.libdems.org.uk
Chair Adam Carew
Weald House, Forest Road, Whitehill GU35 9BA
CHALLENGE Editor **Paul Burall** paulburall@prburall.demon.co.uk

Executive Members
Catherine Bearder cbearder@cix.co.uk
James Blanchard jamesblanchard@yahoo.com
Jonathan Coles jwaco@btopenworld.com
Jane Mactaggart jane.mactaggart@hmc-oxford.com
Graham Neale graham@bigvan.com
Dave Rickard daverickard@waitrose.com
Steven Toole tooles@parliament.uk
Martha Vickers martha@mmvickers.freeserve.co.uk

Green Liberal Democrats campaign within the party to put the green perspective at the heart of all of our policies. They produce a quarterly political journal Challenge and maintain a high profile within the party, especially at federal conferences. They also maintain links with and work with a number of green campaign groups outside the party in order to influence the wider debate on green politics.

Scottish Green Liberal Democrats

President **Nora Radcliffe MSP**
Convener **Prof Denis Mollison** denis@ma.hw.ac.uk
The Laigh House, Inveresk, Musselburgh EH21 7TD
Vice-Convener **Dr Liz Dick** edickl@aol.com
Secretary **Richard Burnett-Hall** r.burnetthall@btopenworld.com
Treasurer (and Membership) **Robin Hill** r.l.hill@ed.ac.uk
82 Constitution Street, Dundee DD3 6JG 01382-204410
Committee
Alison McLachlan talisker.1@virgin.net; **Fraser Macpherson**
fraser.macpherson@irrv.org.uk; **Dr Gurudeo Saluja**
gsaluja@aberdeenshire.gov.uk, **John Stuart** johnstuart@talktalk.net

Liberal Democrat Christian Forum

Chair **Martin Turner**
President **Alan Beith MP**
Organiser **Debbie Enever, Vicki Adamson**
4, Cowley Street, London, SW1P 3NB
Tel: 020 7227 1224
e-mail office@christianforum.libdems.org
web www.christianforum.libdems.org

The LDCF is a voice of Christian faith in the Liberal Democrats and the voice of Liberal Democracy amongst Christians. Our practical focus is to develop a positive Christian input into the Party's activities at national, regional and local levels. LDCF seeks to support members through prayer and fellowship. LDCF welcomes Christians from all backgrounds who are members and supporters of the Liberal Democrats and associated Parties.

Liberal Democrat Disability Association

Chair **Gemma Roulston**
98 Colesmead Road, Redhill, Surrey RH1 2EQ
Tel 01737 277607 gemma.roulston@btopenworld.com
Vice-chair **Susan Carson**
32 Croft Street, Lower Broughton, Salford, Manchester M7 1LR
Tel 0161 792 2010 susancecilia.Carson@ntlworld.com
Secretary **Hannah Saul**
57 Badgers Road, Buckingham MK18 7EU hannah_saul@hotmail.com
Treasurer **Chris Holman**

141a Bilton Road, Rugby CV22 7AS **Tel** 01788 565037
chrisholman@cix.co.uk
PCA Rep **Robert Adamson**
Askgard, Sessay, Thirsk, North Yorkshire YO7 3BE
Tel 01845 501058 robert@adamson.freeserve.co.uk
EMLD Rep **Anne Diamond**
9 Honister Gardens, Stanmore, Middlesex HA7 2EH
annediamond1@aol.com 020 8907 8457

Liberal Democrat European Group

web: **www.ldeg.org**
President **Chris Davies MEP**
Chair **Ed Featherstone** ed.featherstone@btinternet.com
Vice Chairs **Catherine Bearder, Phil Bennion**
Treasurer **Derek Honeygold,** Secretary **Karen Freel**
Committee **S Arnold** (Yorks & Humber), **P Bennion** (East Midlands), **P Billenness, R Bryant, S Currie, G Dunk** (Wales), **J Fryer** (London), **S Hobden** (South West), **J Pindar** (North West), **D Millar** (Scotland), **S Quigley** (South East), **R Sutton** (West Midlands), **A Witherick** (East of England), **C Foote-Wood** (North East)
Co-optees **L Forbes** (Newsletter), **A Mallik, K Sharp, C Weaver** (website)

LDEG is the forum for those committed to closer integration and expansion of the EU. The group provides campaigning support and material to activists, organises seminars and fringe meetings at conference. It also arranges regular visits to the European institutions.

Liberal Democrat Humanist & Secularist Group

web: **www.scotlibdems.org.uk/humanists**
Chair & Membership Secretary **Simon Jones** sqing@btinternet.com
Vice Chair **Mike Quinton** patmikequinton@supanet.com
Secretary and Publicity **John White** John.White@concore.co.uk
Treasurer **Roger O'Brien** roger@obrien3.demon.co.uk
Elected Members **Vera Head** vera@co10hp.fsnet.co.uk **Mike Pictor** m.pictor@uk.co.uk **Luke Croydon** Luke@Brillsongs.com

The Group's principal purpose is to promote humanist / secularist ideas in Liberal Democrat thinking as an alternative to those stemming from religious beliefs and attitudes.

Liberal Democrats Online

If you are interested in Internet-related policy issues, or in the use of the Internet for campaigning, try the website for Liberal Democrats Online (LDO) at www.online.libdems.org

Chair **Becky Harvey** beckyharvey@cix.co.uk Vice-chair **Rob Fenwick** libdems@rfen.co.uk Treasurer **David Martin** davidrossmartin@btinternet.com Secretary **Pete Dollimore** pete.dollimore@tiscali.co.uk Membership Secretary **Susanne Lamido** cilia2000@slamido.freeserve.co.uk

Executive

Jon Ball jonball@cix.co.uk **Simon Hanson** ldo@orac.demon.co.uk **Alison Wheeler** libdems@alisonwheeler.com **Alan Window** awindow@cix.co.uk

Liberal Democrats for Peace & Security

Chair **Gareth Epps**

1 The Green, Charlbury, Oxford OX7 3QA

tel 07950 035 836 **e-mail** garethepps@cix.co.uk

Secretary **Margaret Godden**

97b Divinity Road, Oxford OX4 1LN

tel 01865 721530 **e-mail** margaret.godden@rmplc.co.uk

Formerly the Liberal Democrat Peace Group, LDPS works to co-ordinate, inform and develop constructive initiatives across a broad range of issues related to the promotion of peace, security, armament controls and disarmament. Mailings include information, contacts, campaign news and updates. Membership £10 (£5 unwaged): cheques payable to 'Liberal Democrat Peace Group'.

Liberal International

Secretary General **Jan Weijer**s

1 Whitehall Place, London SW1A 2HD

Tel 020 78395905 Fax 020 7295 2685

e-mail all@liberal-international.org

web www.liberal-international.org

British Group

Publicises the work of Liberal International, arranges overseas visits, provides hospitality for visiting liberals and keeps Liberal Democrats informed of liberal activities world-wide. It also arranges meetings and

LIBERAL
International british group

Founded in 1947, Liberal International is the pre-eminent network for liberal parties and for the strengthening of liberal democracy around the world. The British Group publicises the work of Liberal International, provides hospitality for visiting liberals and keeps Liberal Democrats informed of liberal activities world-wide. It also arranges meetings and seminars and produces regular newsletters.

WWW.LIBG.ORG.UK

The LIBG website contains details of forthcoming events, information on how to join LIBG, extracts from *"Interlib"*, the quarterly newsletter of Liberal International British Group and contact details.

LIBG'S CALENDAR OF EVENTS INCLUDES

THE LIBG ANNUAL DIPLOMATS RECEPTION
- A Major Event of the London diplomatic calendar attended by many MPs & Peers.

LIBG FORUMS: *Variety of topics and high profile speakers including in the past year Ambassadors, High Commissioners and a former UN Assistant Secretary General*

LIBG ORGANISED OVERSEAS VISITS

LIBG DELEGATES ATTEND LI CONGRESSES AROUND THE WORLD
- 2005 was in Sofia, Bulgaria and 2006 will be this November in Marrakech, Morocco

For further information please contact: info@libg.org.uk or call David Griffiths on 07768 682409.

seminars, produces regular newsletters and raises funds for Liberal International's work. The British Group is represented at Congresses and Executive meetings of LI.

President **Lord Garden KCB**
Vice-presidents **Lord Alderdice, Peter Billenness, Sharon Bowles,**
David Griffiths, Rt Hon Charles Kennedy MP, John Melling,
Richard Moore, Graham Watson MEP
Chair **Sharon Bowles**
Vice-chair **Gary Lawson**
Secretaries **Gary Lawson, Ahmad Mallick**
Treasurers **Dai Liyanage, David Rebak**
Executive Committee
Lord Dykes, Tom Dale, Nilmini de Silva, Derek Partridge,
Frances Peacock, Bruce Ritchie, James Sandbach, Baldev
Sharma, Monika Skowronska, Anneliese Waugh, Robert
Woodthorpe Browne

54 St Botolphs Road, Sevenoaks, Kent TN13 3AG
Tel: 01732 779476 or 07941 553859 Fax 0870 1210659 e-mail info@libg.org.uk
web www.libg.org.uk

Other groups

ALTER (Action for Land Value Taxation and Economic Reform)

Chair **Tony Vickers**
62 Craven Road, Newbury, Berks RG14 5NJ
tel 01635 230046
e-mail info@libdemsalter.org.uk
web www.libdemsalter.org.uk

CentreForum

The liberal think tank
6th Floor, 27 Queen Anne's Gate, London, SW1H 9BU
tel 020 7340 1160 **fax** 020 7222 3316

E-mail info@centreforum.org **web** www.centreforum.org

CENTREFORUM

CentreForum is the UK's leading liberal public policy think tank.

It is an independent forum for new and progressive debate.

Subscribers receive a copy of all CentreForum publications and invitations to seminars and meetings.

For more information call 020 7340 1160 or email info@centreforum.org

CentreForum also runs FreeThink, a discussion website open to all.

It's the place to debate domestic and international issues.

Visit it at www.freethink.org and join the debate.

www.CentreForum.org
6th Floor, 27 Queen Anne's Gate,
London SW1H 9BU

The Chard Group

Chair **Frances Mackenzie**
204 Orchard Avenue, Bridport, Dorset DT6 5RL
Tel 01308 425068

Chinese Liberal Democrats

Objective: To provide a bridge between the Liberal Democrat party and
the Chinese community in the United Kingdom
Chair: **Linda Chung** lindachung@talktalk.net
Other committee members include: **Paul Bensilum,**
Hong-Ling Dyer and **Merlene Toh Emerson**
web www.chineselibdems.org.uk

EARS (Election Agents Record System)

EARS is run for the Liberal Democrats by Datatrans Ltd.
Tel 020 8407 0155 **e-mail** info@datatrans.co.uk
Web www.datatrans.co.uk/ears.

Liberal Democrats Business Forum

4 Cowley Street, London SW1P 3NB
Tel 020 7227 4914 **fax** 020 7799 2170
e-mail businessforum@libdems.org.uk
web www.libdemsinbusiness.org.uk
Works with businesses nationwide to keep them in touch with the policies
and activities of the Liberal Democrats.

Liberal Democrat Education Group

Chair **Denys Robinson** denys.robinson@london.gov.uk
Vice-chair **Katherine Egan**
Secretary **Robert Jones**
rshjones@btinternet.com
Treasurer **Anthony Bowen** bowen@jesus.cam.ac.uk
Membership Secretary **Julian Wates** j.wates@ntlworld.com
web www.libdems.org.uk or www.lga.gov.uk/libdemgroup

Liberal Democrat History Group

Chair **Tony Little**
Editor, Journal of Liberal History **Duncan Brack**
journal@liberalhistory.org.uk
Membership Secretary **Patrick Mitchell** subs@liberalhistory.org.uk
6 Palfrey Place, London SW8 1PA
For assistance with historical queries, email
Secretary **Graham Lippiatt** enquiries@liberalhistory.org.uk

Liberal Democrat Image

Publishers of party promotional material and suppliers of campaign
items from rosettes to posters; recruitment pads to canvass cards
Proprietor **Craig Card**
11 High Street, Aldershot GU11 1BH **tel/fax** 01252 408282
e-mail libdemimage@ldimage.demon.co.uk

Liberal Democrat Lawyers Association

LDLA has more than 200 members. The recommended subscription is £50
(with a minimum of £30) with students, pupils and trainees £10. It publishes
The Legal Democrat and currently has working parties looking at

Constitutional Change; Access to Justice; briefing parliamentary party and local councillors; appointed CPD provider by ILEx It also holds an annual residential conference; the 80 Club lecture; fringe meetings at the federal conferences; and produces a regular newsletter. There is an annual dinner and other opportunities for networking.

President **Lord Lester of Herne Hill QC**
Deputy President **Joyce Arra**m
Chair **Jonathan Marks QC**
e-mail jmarks@4pumpcourt.com
Vice Chairs **David Ive David Owen-Jone**s;
Treasurer **Lynne Ravenscrof**t
Secretary **Mrs Jo Jackson** Tel 023 92 513853 **e-mail** joldlaadsec@aol.com
Editor Legal Democrat **Jo Haye**s
web www.libdemlawyers.org.uk
Webmaster **John Lambert**

Liberal Democrat Muslims Forum

Objectives To provide Muslim members with a forum to help formulate and influence Liberal Democrat and government policies
Chair **Prof. Karrar Khan** karrar.k@ntlworld.com
Contact **Nasser Butt** nasserbutt@blueyonder.co.uk

Liberal Democrats in Public Relations

Chair: **Chris Fox** chris.fox@tateandlyle.com
Treasurer **Clive Parry**
committee includes **Alan Leaman, David Thompson,**
Elizabeth Jackman, Charlotte Parry

Liberty Network

4 Cowley Street, London SW1P 3NB
tel 020 7227 4914 **fax** 020 7799 2170
e-mail info@libertynetwork.org.uk
www.libertynetwork.org.uk
Director **Helen Jardine-Brown**
The Network enables senior professionals and high-profile supporters to come together at a series of quality political and social events, to engage with one another and with the Front Bench team to help the crucial fund-raising challenge.

National Liberal Club

1 Whitehall Place, London SW1A 2HE
Tel 020 7930 9871 Fax 020 7839 4768
Membership Secretary **Rosemary Tweddle**
e-mail membership@nlc.org.uk **web** www.nlc.org.uk

Peel Group

The Peel Group was formed by Liberal Democrats who believe that attracting new members and voters, who might have once thought of themselves as moderate Conservatives (but have since not voted or voted Labour), is vital to the electoral interests of the party.

Chair **Marie-Louise Rossi**
Administrator **Sue Baldwin**
National Committee
Baroness Nicholson MEP, Chris Huhne MP, Lord Rennard, John Stevens, Lord Dykes, Lord Lee of Trafford, Graham Bishop, Dr Harold Elletson
e-mail info@peelgroup.org.uk / mlrossi@cix.co.uk
website www.peelgroup.org.uk
tel/fax 020 8529 7339

The Gladstone inheritance

A brief party history prepared by the Liberal Democrat History Group

The Liberal Democrats are the successors to two important reformist traditions in British politics – those of liberalism and of social democracy, which became separated from each other in the early part of the twentieth century, but are now reunited, in the shape of the Liberal Democrats. This section provides a concise history of the Liberal Party, SDP and Liberal Democrats, for a longer version, see the website of the Liberal Democrat History Group, at www.liberalhistory.org.uk.

ORIGINS
Whilst the history of the Liberal Democrats stretches back 150 years to the formation of the Liberal Party in 1859, Liberal political thought can be traced back a further 200 years to the ferment of the English Civil War, and the reaction that set in with the restoration of the monarchy in 1660. Despite various currents of radical thought around the powers of the state and the monarchy, there was no organisation that could reasonably be regarded as a political party in the modern sense, liberal or otherwise, at this time.

The eighteenth century saw the gradual establishment of relatively formal parliamentary groupings, the Whigs and the Tories. Broadly speaking, the Tories were defenders of the Crown and the established Anglican Church, while the Whigs drew their inspiration from the Glorious Revolution of 1688, which established the supremacy of parliament over the monarchy.

In the 1770s the revolt of the American Colonies and the French Revolution opened up a renewed debate about the ideological basis of government. Under Charles James Fox, the Whigs resisted Pitt's authoritarian measures during the Napoleonic Wars and a prolonged period in opposition also encouraged the Whigs to embrace a more popular agenda, in the form of religious toleration and electoral reform. A Whig government under Lord Grey passed the Great Reform Act of 1832, which began the process of extending the franchise and, thereby, the need for politicians to engage both with ordinary electors and with radical elements outside Parliament. Out of this process grew the political parties that we recognise today.

The Conservative Party came into existence in 1835 but it took longer for a cohesive liberal party to emerge. Uneasy alliances between the aristocratic Whigs and the middle-class liberals, elected after 1832 to represent the newly enfranchised industrial regions, could not be relied upon. There was also the problem of how to accommodate radical opinion, barely represented in the Commons, but which looked to Parliament for a reforming lead. The glue to bind the various factions together was provided by the Peelites, a small but influential band of free-trade Conservatives, who broke with their party in 1846 over the abolition of the Corn Laws (duties on imports of grain). Free trade, which appealed both to the radicals and the working classes (because it kept food cheap) and the industrial manufacturers (because it made it easier for them to export) became a pre-eminent Liberal cause well into the twentieth century.

74

THE LIBERAL ASCENDANCY

The Liberal Party finally coalesced on 6 June 1859, when Whigs, Peelites and Radicals met at Willis' Rooms in St James Street, London, to agree to overthrow a minority Conservative government. The Liberals governed Britain for most of the following thirty years, benefiting from further extensions of the franchise in 1867 and 1885.

Liberal leader and four-times Prime Minister William Gladstone dominated British politics. In the 1850s he established his reputation for prudent financial innovation by replacing taxes on goods and customs duties with a progressive income tax, a modest step towards the redistribution of income, and by establishing parliamentary accountability for government spending. Gladstone won strong support from nonconformists for his attitude to religious questions, which at that time deeply affected basic liberties and education. After victory in the 1868 general election, Gladstone's government disestablished the Church of Ireland and, in 1870, passed the first Education Act. In 1872, the Liberals established the secret ballot, but Liberal differences over Irish university education allowed the Conservatives to win in 1874.

Gladstone returned to power in 1880, partly because of the renown he had won for defending the rights of oppressed minorities in the Balkans. The Liberal government became increasingly concerned with bringing peace to Ireland, where sectarian differences and economic problems were intermingled. This was reflected in the growth of a Home Rule party which, following the 1885 election, held the balance of power in the Commons. Gladstone made an unsuccessful attempt to navigate a devolution bill on to the statute book, and in the process split the Liberal Party, losing the 1886 election and keeping the party out of power for the next twenty years, apart from a minority administration in 1892–95.

Ireland was not the only source of dissension. There was no obvious successor to Gladstone and when he eventually retired, in 1894, his replacement, Lord Rosebery, proved to be weak and indecisive. The party was split between those who thought the government should stick to the traditional Liberal approach of small government and political and constitutional reform and those – the 'New Liberals' – who argued for intervention to help the poorer sections of society. The 1892 Newcastle Programme was the first step in the Liberals' embrace of a more interventionist economic and social policy.

THE NEW LIBERALISM

The Liberal Party was still in the doldrums in 1900, when the Conservatives won a comfortable election victory on the back of Boer War-inspired patriotism. The next few years, however, were to see a startling comeback, culminating in the 1906 Liberal landslide, on a par with Labour's 1997 victory, as the Liberals exploited Conservative splits over protective tariffs and education. A further factor, secret at the time, was an electoral pact which ensured that the new Labour Party and the Liberals did not oppose each other, thereby maximising the progressive vote.

The Liberal government of 1906–15 was one of the greatest reforming administrations of the twentieth century. Led by towering figures such as Asquith, Lloyd George and Churchill, it broke the power of the House of Lords and laid the foundations of the modern welfare state. Labour exchanges were introduced, old-age pensions were paid by the state for the first time, and the national insurance system was created. This was the realisation of the New Liberal programme – removing the shackles of poverty, unemployment and ill health so as to allow people to be free to exercise choice and realise opportunity.

From the outset the Liberals had difficulty passing legislation through the Tory-dominated House of Lords. The crunch came when the Lords rejected Lloyd George's 1909 'People's Budget', which introduced a supertax on high earners to raise revenue for social expenditure and naval rearmament. Two elections were fought in 1910 on the issue of 'the peers versus the people'. In both, the Liberals triumphed, though lost their majority, remaining in power with the support of Labour and Irish Nationalist MPs. In 1911, with the King primed to create hundreds of new Liberal peers if necessary, the Lords capitulated and the primacy of the House of Commons was definitively established.

DECLINE
The strains of fighting the First World War, however, brought the Liberal ascendancy to an end. The disastrous split in 1916 over the direction of the war, which saw Lloyd George supplant Asquith as Prime Minister, left the Liberal Party divided and demoralised. In the 1918 and 1922 elections, factions led by the two former colleagues fought each other rather than the Conservative and Labour Parties. The party's grassroots organisation fell apart, allowing the Labour Party to capture the votes of the new working-class and women voters enfranchised in 1918.

The Liberals reunited around the old cause of free trade to fight the 1923 election, which left them holding the balance of power in the Commons. Asquith's decision to support a minority Labour government, however, placed the party in an awkward position and effectively polarised the political choice between Conservatives and Labour; the disastrous 1924 election relegated the party to a distant third place as the electorate increasingly opted for a straight choice between the other two parties.

Despite a renewed burst of energy under Lloyd George, which saw the party fight the 1929 general election on a radical platform of Keynesian economics, the Liberals were by then too firmly established as the third party to achieve any direct influence on government. They split again in the 1930s and continued to decline until the mid-1950s. By 1957 there were only five Liberal MPs, and just 110 constituencies had been contested by the party at the previous general election. Despite the political irrelevance of the party itself, however, the huge impact of the Liberal thinkers Keynes and Beveridge, who underpinned government social and economic policy for much of the post-war period, showed that Liberalism as an intellectual force was still alive and well.

REVIVAL
Revival came with the election of Jo Grimond as party leader in 1956. His vision and youthful appeal were well suited to the burgeoning television coverage of politics, and he was able to capitalise on growing dissatisfaction with the Conservatives, in power since 1951. In 1958, the Liberal Party won its first by-election for thirty years, at Torrington in Devon, and in 1962, Eric Lubbock (later Lord Avebury) won the sensational by-election victory of Orpington. Many commentators speculated that the Liberals would make a substantial breakthrough at the next general election.

Unfortunately, the party was hampered by organisational difficulties and progress was slow, with a loss of votes and seats under Wilson's Labour governments of 1964–70. Revival came once more in the 1970s with Jeremy Thorpe as leader, peaking in the two general elections of 1974, with 19 and 18 per cent of the vote (though only 14 and 13 seats, respectively, in Parliament).

One reason for the revival in Liberal fortunes was the development of community politics, in which Liberal activists campaigned intensively to empower local communities and win council seats. This strategy was formally adopted by the party in 1970 and was most successful in Liverpool. Although Liberals found it difficult to translate success in local government into Parliamentary seats, David Alton's by-election victory in Liverpool Edge Hill in 1979 showed that it could be done.

Following Labour's defeat in the 1979 election, the internecine strife and growing success of the left within the party alienated many MPs and members. Moderate Labour leaders such as Shirley Williams had worked with the Liberal Party during the referendum on membership of the European Community, and during the Lib-Lab Pact which kept Labour in power in 1977–78. On 26 March 1981 a number of them broke away from Labour to found the Social Democratic Party (SDP). The new party attracted members of both the Labour and Conservative Parties and also brought many people into politics for the first time. The Liberal Party and SDP formed an Alliance later the same year, agreeing to fight elections on a common platform with joint candidates.

The Alliance's political impact was immediate, wining a string of by-election victories and topping the opinion polls for months. Fighting on a platform of opposition to the extremism of Thatcher's Conservatives and Foot's Labour Party, the two parties won 26 per cent of the vote in the 1983 general election, the best third-party performance since 1929. Labour won 28 per cent of the vote, but gained 209 MPs, compared to 23 for the Alliance.

The Alliance gained further by-election victories in the 1983-87 Parliament, and made significant progress in local government, but tension between the leaderships of the two parties also became apparent. David Owen, the SDP's leader from 1983, was personally less sympathetic towards the Liberals than had been his predecessor Roy Jenkins, and was also more determined to maintain a separate (and in practice more right-wing) identity for his party, despite its numerical disadvantage in the House of Commons. Differences emerged on economic questions and, principally, on defence, with the SDP much more strongly in favour of a British nuclear deterrent than the Liberals. The 1986 Liberal Assembly was the scene of a particularly damaging disagreement over nuclear weapons, and the 1987 election campaign was not lacking in tension. The Alliance's share of the vote dropped to 23 per cent in the 1987 general election.

A NEW PARTY
In the days following the 1987 election, the Liberal leader, David Steel, immediately proposed a merger of the two parties. There then followed a lengthy period of negotiations between the two parties, the new party's constitution and even its name being subjects of intense controversy. Merger was eventually approved by a majority

of both parties and the new party was born on 3 March 1988, with Paddy Ashdown elected as its first leader in July. David Owen led a significant faction of Social Democrats who would not be swayed from their opposition to merger, but after a couple of encouraging by-election results, the 'continuing SDP' declined into irrelevance and wound itself up in 1990.

After a difficult birth, the new party suffered a troubled infancy. Initially known as the Social & Liberal Democrats, it took some time before the name 'Liberal Democrats' took hold, and the membership of the new party fell to a much lower level than that of its two predecessors combined. Recapturing the enthusiasm of former supporters seemed a daunting task, even before Conservatives and Labour could be tackled. The nadir was reached in the 1989 European elections, when the party secured just 6.2 per cent of the vote, being beaten decisively into fourth place by the Green Party.

Under Ashdown's tireless and inspiring leadership, however, slowly but surely morale, finances and membership recovered. In 1990 the Liberal Democrats re-established themselves on the political scene by winning the Eastbourne by-election, overturning a substantial Tory majority. In the 1992 general election the party won 17.8 per cent of the vote and 20 seats. Paddy Ashdown was consistently described in opinion polls as the most popular party leader and the party's policies, especially its pledge to raise income tax to invest extra resources in education, were widely praised.

Five years of weak and unpopular Conservative rule after 1992 paved the way for further advances. In 1995, the Liberal Democrats became the second party of local government, beating the Conservatives, and in many urban areas became the main opposition to Labour. The party won its first-ever seats in the European Parliament in 1994, and by-election successes continued, even after Tony Blair's election as Labour leader, which had seen many political commentators predicting that 'moderate' New Labour would destroy the Liberal Democrats.
In 1997, the Liberal Democrats won 46 seats, the highest number won by a third party since 1929. Whilst the party's overall share of the vote fell slightly, to 16.8 per cent, ruthless targeting of resources on winnable constituencies showed how the detrimental effects of the first-past-the-post electoral system could be countered.

Early in the 1992 Parliament, in a speech at Chard, Ashdown had signalled the end of the Liberal Democrat policy of 'equidistance' between the two largest parties, and instead indicated that he would be prepared to work with Labour to defeat the Conservatives. Ashdown and Blair had even discussed a formal coalition between their parties once the Conservatives were ousted, but the scale of Labour's triumph made such an arrangement impossible. Instead, in July 1997, five Liberal Democrats were appointed to a joint cabinet committee on constitutional reform. It is difficult to identify what, it anything, the committee achieved, and Blair reneged on his original promise to hold a referendum on electoral reform. The relationship between the two parties did not long outlast Ashdown's resignation as party leader in 1999.

A NEW LEADER AND A NEW APPROACH

Ashdown led the Liberal Democrats through a series of elections in 1999 before standing down. The introduction of proportional representation helped the party increase its representation in the European Parliament from two to ten MEPs, the largest national contingent in the European Liberal group. The elections to the new Scottish Parliament proved even more successful, resulting in a Labour – Liberal Democrat coalition government. In the elections to the Welsh Assembly, the party won six seats; a coalition with Labour, which had also failed to gain an overall majority, was established in 2000.

On 9 August 1999, Charles Kennedy was comfortably elected leader of the Liberal Democrats, after a contest between five MPs; Simon Hughes was his nearest challenger. From the outset he was less inclined to work with Labour, focusing instead on replacing the Conservatives as the principal party of opposition.

Although the party gained Romsey from the Conservatives in a by-election in 2000, and made significant gains from Labour in local government elections, commentators generally felt that it would be difficult for the Liberal Democrats to hold on to all their parliamentary seats at the following election. The party defied such expectations in 2001, however, winning 52 seats and increasing its overall share of the vote (for the first time since 1983), to 18.3 per cent. A new feature was a significant increase in the share of the vote in Labour strongholds.

The events of 11th September 2001, and the Labour government's decision to join the US invasion of Iraq in 2003, transformed the political situation. The Liberal Democrats became the only one of the three main parties to oppose the war, and also the steady infringements of civil liberties perpetuated by New Labour in the name of the war on terror. The party's critique of over-centralised and micro-managed public services, its proposals for a fairer tax system (a local income tax to replace the Council Tax, and a new 50 per cent rate of income tax for earnings above £100,000), its consistent support for strong environmental policies, and its opposition to Labour's introduction of tuition and top-up fees for university students, all also provided it with a popular and distinctive policy platform.

Combined with the growing public distrust of Tony Blair and the continuing disarray of the Conservatives, this led to electoral dividends in the 2001–05 Parliament. Two by-election gains (Brent East in 2003 and Leicester South in 2004), continued advances in local government elections (including beating Labour into third place in 2004), two more gains in the European elections in 2004, and continued success in Scotland and Wales (with a continuation of the Labour – Lib Dem coalition in Scotland, though not in Wales, where Labour fared slightly better in 2003 than in 1999) all led the party to enter the 2005 general election in an optimistic mood.

And the results indeed provided grounds for celebration. The Liberal Democrats emerged from the contest with 62 seats, the highest number of Liberal MPs since 1923, and 22.7 per cent of the vote, a 4 per cent increase from 2001. The party fared particularly well against Labour, gaining 12 seats from the party of government and overturning large majorities in Labour strongholds such as Hornsey & Wood Green, Cambridge and Manchester Withington, as well as winning from third place in Falmouth & Camborne and Bristol West. The party did particularly well amongst students and Muslim voters, and beat the nationalists and the Tories to take second place in Scotland. Above all, the conventional wisdom that Liberals always lose support under periods of Labour government was well and truly undermined.

The election results were not all good news, however, with a net loss of two seats to the Conservatives, and the failure to win a whole string of Conservative-held seats with narrow majorities. This contributed to an unhappy party conference, which saw two defeats for the leadership position, partly reflecting left-right tensions within the party (though these were never as deep as journalists liked to pretend) and clearly expressed dissatisfaction with Kennedy's somewhat lackadaisical leadership style.

Kennedy seemed to dispel some of the disquiet, however, with an effective end-of conference speech, but throughout the autumn his parliamentary colleagues became increasingly exasperated with the party's drift and lack of direction. Events suddenly accelerated in early January 2006, with Kennedy's announcement (forestalling an ITN news story) that he had been receiving treatment for alcoholism. His fondness for drink had been an open secret in the party for years, but allegations of drunkenness, although they had often been aired in the media, had always been vigorously denied. In an attempt to reassert his authority, Kennedy announced that he was calling a leadership election in which he would be a candidate.

Over the following thirty-six hours, however, the bulk of the parliamentary party decided that they had had enough, and queued up to call on Kennedy to stand down – citing not just his alcoholism but also his lack of effective leadership and drift over policy positions. In the face of this, Kennedy took the decision to resign as leader, which he announced on 7 January.

The ensuing leadership contest, although marred by two personal scandals revealed in the media, enjoyed a far higher level of media coverage than either of the two previous leadership elections. In February an impressive by-election win in Dunfermline & West Fife – the seat next to that of the man expected to be the next Labour leader, Gordon Brown – demonstrated that the party remained an electoral force despite two months of almost universally negative press coverage, and was still able to take seats from Labour.

The leadership result was announced on 2 March. Simon Hughes' campaign never really recovered from his media problems of late January, and he ended up third with 12,081 votes to Chris Huhne's 16,691 and Sir Menzies Campbell's 23,264. Although Huhne had fought an energetic campaign, it was not enough to overcome his relative lack of profile – he had only been elected to the Commons the year before, although he had previously been an MEP for six years – and on the redistribution of Hughes's second preferences, the final outcome was Campbell 29,697 and Huhne 21,628. The party thus opted for its former Deputy Leader, who had taken over as Acting Leader after Kennedy's resignation.

The recovery of the Liberal Party, and its successors, from the period after the Second World War, when it nearly disappeared altogether, is one of the most remarkable stories in British politics. The Liberal Democrats' next challenge is to cast off their third-party status and make a genuine bid for government.

Who's Who
in the
Liberal
Democrats?

Abbreviations

BC, CC, DC, PC, TC
   Borough, County, District, Parish or Town Council

Cttee	Committee
Exec	Executive
Gp	Group
LP	Local Party
Mbr	Member
PPC	Prospective Parliamentary Candidate (Westminster)
PEPC	Prospective Parliamentary Candidate (Europe)
PSPC	Prospective Parliamentary Candidate (Scottish Parliament)
Secy	Secretary

A

AALDERS-DUNTHORNE, Andrew Paul *b* Nov 3, 1969 *m* Donna 2 *s* Kielen, Marc *education* Bowthorpe High School, Norwich; City College, Norwich (degree, environmental biology); Univ of East Anglia (PGCE) *career* army officer; staff cytogenetist, contract research laboratory; currently science teacher Norwich Middle School *party* joined young SDP, founder mbr Liberal Democrats; mbr (Eaton ward) Norwich City Council 1996, Heigham ward 2000; Wensum Ward (after boundary review) 2004- ; opposition spokesman for Environment, Leisure & Community Services; now former exec mbr Personnel and Best Value and exec Exec Mbr for the Community; PPC Norwich South 1997, 2001, 2005 reducing Home Secretary Charles Clarke's majority; former vice chair Norwich South LP; chair Norwich area campaigns Cttee *special interests* education, science, armed forces *other mbrships* Association of Teachers and Lectures; Association for Science Education; Institute of Supervision and Management *recreations* family life, mbr of local Anglican Church, swimming, cycling, hill-walking, environment (runs after-school ecology club) *address* The Old Forge, New Street, Fressingfield IP21 5PG *tel* 07946 658329 *e-mail* andrew.aaldersdunthorne@talk21.com

ABBOTT, Chris *b* Jul 10, 1950 *m* Glynis 2 *s* 1 *d education* Starbeck School, Harrogate *career* self-employed electrical contractor *party* joined Liberal Party 1968; founder mbr Lib Dems; mbr Redcar & Cleveland Borough Council 1987- (leader, Liberal Democrat Gp 1999-), cabinet mbr, Housing and Neighbourhood Renewal May 2003- ; mbr Cleveland County Council 1985-96; mbr Whitby Town Council 1978-84 *special interests* campaigner for recognition of traditional counties; activist, community politics since 1974 *other mbrships* exec mbr Association of British Counties; exec mbr Yorkshire Ridings Society *recreations* freshwater fishing, reading, e-mails and history *address* 39 Essex Close, Redcar, Yorkshire TS10 4BY *tel* 01642 487557 *e-mail* chrisabbott@cix.co.uk

ABBOTTS, Benjamin Peter *b* Sept 22, 1975 *m* Zara (neé Pollock) Oct 24, 2003 *education* Geoffrey Chaucer School, Canterbury, Univ of Bristol (BSc Politics) *career* Public Affairs Consultant, Shandwick 1998-2001; Account Director Edelman Worldwide 2001-03; Divisional Director, The Communication Gp 2003-04; Senior Vice President, LLM Communications 2004- ; *party* PPC Sevenoaks 2005, Bromley and Chiselhurst 2006 (by-election) where Tory majority was reduced to 633 from 13,342; mbr English Council, PCA Exec; South East England Region Exec, Sevenoaks LP Exec *special interests* Europe, penal affairs, former Soviet states, constitutional and parliamentary reform *recreations* house restoration, football, travel, walking *address* 16 Oakhill Road, Beckenham, Kent BR3 6NQ *tel* 0208 658 5562 *mobile* 07973 353421 *fax* 0207 269 9367 *e-mail* benjamin@llm.co.uk

AB-OWAIN, Melvyn *b* Nov 5, 1958 *education* Ysgol Aberconwy, Conwy; St David's Univ College, Lampeter *career* freelance organiser (mainly for Liberal Party 1984-86); tax inspector Inland Revenue 1986-88; manager Rhyl Citizens Advice

Bureau 1988-92; senior administrator, Gwynedd Magistrates Courts Cttee 1992-94; Target Seats Officer Wales, West Midlands, Campaigns Dept, Liberal Democrats 1994-2001; grants project manager, Wales Council for Voluntary Action 2001- *party* joined Liberals 1978; chair Lampeter student Liberals 1981-83; agent Conwy Constituency 1991-2.; vice chair of Clwyd North West Lib Dems 1992-93; PPC Caernarfon 2001 *special interests* environmental issues (especially to do with birds and mammals), history (especially Welsh and maritime history); foreign affairs *other mbrships* British Trust for Ornithology, RSPB, Wildfowl and Wetlands Trust, Mammal Society, Liberal International *recreations* bird-watching, painting, travel, war games *address* 31 Coed Bedw, Abergele, Conwy LL22 7EH *tel* 01745 826528 home 07887 931567 business *e-mail* melabowain@cix.co.uk

ADAMSON, Robert Moray *b* Aug 8, 1949 Doncaster *engaged* Eileen 2 *d* (Claire & Cheryl) *education* St Luke's College, Exeter; Univ of Lancaster, Dip Org Psychology *career* civil servant, producing training material for Fire Service Officers; management training; running small TV studio and creating training videos about emergency planning and preparedness *party* having left Civil Service in 1996 became politically active and have served as Regional Chair and on the English Council in addition to being Deputy Party President 2006; PPC Darlington 2001, 2005; mbr Federal Policy Cttee; Yorkshire and The Humber European election candidate 1999, 2004, local candidacies include North Yorkshire County Council 2001, 2005; Hambleton District Council 1999, 2003; current chair Vale of York LP; exec mbr PCA; mbr LDDA; Deputy Party President 2006- ; *special interests* disability issues *recreations* reading, Internet, games, my family, films (particularly comedies & "tear jerkers"), Suduko, taking time to enjoy simply being alive *address* Asgard, Sessay, Thirsk, North Yorkshire YO7 3BE *tel* 01845 501058, 07801551337 mobile *e-mail* Robert@Robertadamson.info *web* www.Robertadamson.info

ADAMSON, Vicki: Organiser; Liberal Democrat Christian Forum, and Women Liberal Democrats *qv address* 4 Cowley Street, London SW1P 3NB *tel* 020 7227 1224 *e-mail* office@christianforum.libdems.org *web* www.christianforum.libdems.org

ADDINGTON, 6th Baron (UK 1887) Dominic Bryce Hubbard: Deputy Chief Whip *b* Aug 24, 1963 *s* of 5th Baron Addington (d 1982) and Alexandra Patricia, nee Millar *education* Hewett; Norwich City College; Univ of Aberdeen (MA) heir brother, Hon Michael Hubbard *career* fund-raiser, counsellor Apex Trust; events management Milton Broadway *party* entered House of Lords at 22 as youngest serving peer; Lords spokesperson Culture, Media and Sport (Sport) 1993- ; disability spokesperson 1994- *other mbrships* vice-president British Dyslexia Association; vice-president UK Sports Association *recreations* rugby (plays for local XV, old boys XV), football (captain Commons and Lords football and rugby team: played in Parliamentary World Cup 1994, 1999) *clubs* NLC *address* House of Lords, London SW1A 0PW

AFZAL, Qassim Chair Liberal Democrat Friends of Kashmir *b* Feb 8, 1960 Manchester *m* Zahra 1 *d* Hamza 2 *s* Zaynab, Hussain *education* MA/BA in Middle-Eastern studies, MA international business; certificate in languages; currently researching (part-time) PhD in political equality within diversity, Univ of Salford *career* TV presenter, *The Week Today*, issues, current affairs (social, political, economic, cultural: local to international) *party* chair and mbrship secy of Manchester Blackley LP; elected cllr Manchester Cheetham ward 1998, 2003; PPC Manchester Gorton 2005 (10.98% swing, 33.2% share of vote, selected 6 weeks before campaign), Birmingham Small Heath and Sparkbrook 2001; Euro candidate NW Region 2004; chairman Liberal Democrats Friends of Pakistan (LDFP), chair, Lib Dem delegation (with Party President Simon Hughes MP) to Kashmir leadership and Pakistan President Musharraf, Prime Minister Shoukat Aziz, and Foreign Minister, and opposition Parties, Brussels HQ, NATO delegate re WMD 2005; Chair Fringe Conference: Assistant Secretary General to NATO & Michel Moore MP foreign affairs team; chaired working Cttee re faith schools for the Lib Dem education Shadow Secretary Phil Willis MP; spokesperson for FE on ELDR Congress & LI Congress, FE, IRC, FCC (exec mbr), elected to interim peer panel; PCA Media and Communcations spokes 1999; mbr ALDC *special interests* mover, seconder, author of motions, conference speaker re assisted dying, Iraq, anti war campaigner, Peace re India Pakistan over Kashmir, civil liberties, trains, faith schools *other mbrships* LGA Equalities Exec, portfolios: race equality, faith issues, human rights; NW regional Lib Dem equality think-tank, Manchester LD Multi-cultural Working Gp, Consultation Probation Board, NHS Race and Health Board, JJ Housing Association Management Board; Customs & Excise Consultation; Secretary General to Community Advisory Service, a charitable organisation *publications* currently writing about political equality delivering research papers: Status of Diverse Business Community, Middle-Eastern Studies faith gps, Women and the Veil, theological text authenticity, International Marketing, the global textile industry, business networking etc *recreations* time with wife and kids, poetry, photography, gym, flying, dance, music, travelling, politicking, News Night and Star Trek *style* Cllr Qassim Afzal MA *address* ABI House, 339 Cheetham Hill Rd, Manchester M8 0SN *tel* 0161 205 2885 mobile 07956 873046 *e-mail* qassim.afzal@ntlworld.com *web* www.qassim-afzal.com

AHMED, Farid *m* Kalpana 1s 2 *d education* International Business School, Univ of Hull, MBA; Kings College, Univ of London BSc Chemistry *party* joined Walthamstow Liberals1984; chair of Young Liberals; school governor *special interests* foreign affairs, international trade, ethnic issues *other mbrships* Exec mbr Campaign for Racial Equality; Association of Corporate Treasurers *recreations* cricket (ECB level 1 Coach); flying light aircraft, golf *address* 67A Grove Hill, South Woodford, London E18 2JA *tel* 0208 989 5603 mobile 07802 94 2781 *e-mail* ahmedfirani@yahoo.co.uk

AINSLIE, John Bernard *b* Aug 2, 1921 *m* Shelagh 1 *s* 3 *d education* Harrow School; Trinity College, Oxford *career* Army: acting captain 1942-46; farmer, Church Farm Mildenhall, Marlborough 1951-90 *party* joined Liberal Party 1949; chairman, Devizes Constituency Liberal Democrats; mbr Wiltshire County Council (chairman 1985-89); PPC Devizes; Euro candidate *special interests* agriculture, environment, community politics *other mbrships* Action for the River Kennet (ARK) *recreations* music, theatre, reading *address* Pennings, Mildenhall, Marlborough, Wilts SN8 2LT *tel* 01672 513477 home 01672 512385 business *fax* 01672 515765

ALDERDICE of NOCK, Lord John Thomas: Life Peer cr 1996: Deputy President Liberal International *b* Mar 28, 1955 *m* Joan 2 *s* Stephen, Peter 1 *d*

Anna *education* Strandtown Primary School 1960-63, Ballymena Academy 1964-73, The Queen's Univ of Belfast (MB BCh BAO) 1978; Royal College of Psychiatrists MRCPsych 1982, FRCPsych 1997, Hon FRCPsych 2001 *career* consultant psychiatrist 1988- ; lecturer, senior lecturer in psychiatry 1990-99; Exec medical director, South & East Belfast Health & Social Services Trust 1993-97 *party* joined Alliance Party of Northern Ireland 1978; vice-chair 1987, party leader 1987-98); mbr Belfast City Council 1989-97; vice-president Liberal International 1992-2000, deputy president 2000- , president British Gp 2001-04; elected Northern Ireland Forum 1994-96; treasurer European Liberal Democrat and Reform Party 1995-99; appointed to House of Lords (Liberal Democrat) 1996; elected Northern Ireland Assembly 1998-2003, Speaker of the Northern Ireland Assembly 1998-2004; vice-president ELDR 1999-2003; Federal Policy Cttee 2001-03 *special interests* Northern Ireland, foreign affairs, mental health, conflict and its resolution, psychology of terrorism *other mbrships* Independent Monitoring Commission 2003- ; *recreations* reading, gardening, music, gastronomy *publications* numerous political, psychoanalytic articles *address* House of Lords, London SW1A 0PW *tel* 020 7219 5050 home 028 9079 3097 business 028 9073 7539 *e-mail* alderdicej@parliament.uk

ALEXANDER, Daniel Grian MP (Inverness, Nairn, Badenoch & Strathspey maj 4,148) *b* May 15, 1972 Edinburgh *m* Rebecca 2005, no children (yet) *education* Lochaber High School, Fort William; St Anne's College, Oxford, BA (Hons) PPE *career* press officer Scottish Liberal Democrats 1993-95; Director of Communications, European Movement 1996-99; Head of Communications, Britain in Europe 1999-2004; Head of Communications, Cairngorms National Park 2004- ; *party* MP spkspn Work and Pensions; mbr Scottish Affairs Select Cttee *special interests* Highlands and Islands issues, Europe, welfare reform, housing *recreations* fishing, hill-walking, cricket, reading, pensions *address* Constituency Office, 1a Montague Row,Inverness, IV3 5DX *tel* 01479 811540 home 01463 711280 business *e-mail* danny@highlandlibdems.org.uk *website* www.dannyalexander.org.uk

ALLAN, Richard *b* Feb 11, 1966 education Oundle School, Northants; Pembroke College, Cambridge Univ (BA Archaeology and Anthropology); Bristol Poly (MSc Information Technology) *career* field archaeologist, Britain, France, The Netherlands 1984-85, Ecuador 1988-89; IT systems (to support primary care) NHS 1991-97; MP 1997- *party* mbr Avon County Council 1993-96; PPC Sheffield Hallam 1997 (elected), 2001 (re-elected with increased majority); chair, Information Select Cttee 1998-2001, parliamentary spokesman on Information Technology 2001- ; mbr Home Affairs Select Cttee from 1997-98; Employment Select Cttee from 2000-01; Liaison Select Cttee; co-chair (with Ed Davey), party's Wired Working Gp 2002- *special interests*- development of e-democracy, e-Govt *other mbrships* board mbr Parliamentary Office of Science and Technology; trustee of the Industry and Parliamentary Trust; director Sheffield City Trust, charitable company that runs major Sheffield sporting and entertainment venues; Amnesty International, World Development Movement, Hallamshire Historic Buildings Society, Friends of Porter Valley

ALLIANCE, Lord Sir David Alliance: Life Peer cr 2004, CBE *b* Jun 15, 1932 *m* (dis) 2 *s* 1 *d education* Etehad School, Iran *career* chairman Coats Viyella Plc (retired 1999); chairman N Brown Gp Plc *party* (mbr for several years) *special interests* foreign affairs *other interests* mbr Prince's Youth Business Trust, Council for Industry and Higher Education, Univ of Manchester Foundation, Weizmann Institute; Fellow Royal Society for the Encouragement of Arts, Manufacturers and Commerce; Fellow City and Guilds of London Institute; Hon Fellow Shenkar College of Textile Technology and Fashion *honours* LLD Manchester; LLD Liverpool; DSc Heriot-Watt; Hon Fellow UMIST; Hon Fellow Shenkar, FRSA, CI Mgt, CompTI, Hon. FCG *recreations* art, reading, *objets d'art* *address* Mermaid House, 43A Acacia Road, London NW8 6AP *tel* 0207 493 7735 business *fax* 020 7493 7739 *e-mail* alliancedav@yahoo.co.uk

ALLIE, James LLB MA PGCE *b* Sept 12, 1969 *education* St James' Catholic HS, Grahame Park, Barnet; Univ of Leicester; Univ of Keele, Univ of Huddersfield; Univ of Westminster *career* various casual jobs 1988-1998; lecturer in law Calderdale College 1999-2000; social welfare lawyer Hoxton Trust Legal Advice Service 2000-05; housing lawyer in private practice *party* joined 2000; Cllr LB Brent 2002- , housing spokesperson; chair campaigns Cttee Brent LP, exec mbr; PPC Brent South 2005 *special interests* housing policy, social welfare law, refugee, asylum issues, policing and crime, race, criminal justice *recreations* golf, motor-biking, opera *clubs* NLC, 606 Lots Rd Jazz club, Finchley Golf Club *style* Cllr James Allie *address* 91 Clifford Gardens, Kensal Rise, London NW10 5JG *tel* 020 8969 6419 *e-mail* borborallie2003@yahoo.co.uk

AMBACHE, Jeremy Noel *b* Dec 16, 1946 Chislehurst *m* Ann 1973 *2d education* Bedales School; Sussex University, BA Social Psychology; York University M. Phil, Social Work and Social Administration; Kingston University MA Management and Public Sector Strategy *career* Social Worker, Birmingham Social Services 1971-73; Team Manager, Hammersmith Social Services 1974-80; Coordinator for Community Homes, Brent Social Services 1981-84; Area Manager, Croydon Social Services 1984-90; Divisional Director, Berkshire Social Service 1990-91: Assistant Director, Bedfordshire Social Services 1991-93; Director of Social Services, Knowsley 1993-2000; Director of Social Services and Housing, Bromley 2001-2002; Management Consultant 2002- ; (including Senior Researcher for Susan Kramer, MP) *party* London Region Cttee 2006- ; helped draft White Paper - Promoting Independence, Protecting Individuals 2003; conference representative for Putney; target ward candidate, Graveney,Tooting; PPC Tooting 1987, Putney 2005; mbr PCA *other mbrships* Putney Lawn Tennis Club *special interests* NHS, local government, Police, criminal justice, race relations and social care *publications* various articles in Social Care and Health journals *recreations* tennis, yoga, travel, walking, France, and campaigning *address* 17 Hazlewell Road, Putney SW15 6LT *tel* 020 8785 9650 *e-mail* ambachej@aol.com

AMOS, Gideon *b* Jan 16, 1965 Liverpool *m* Caroline Ellis 1995 3 *s* 1 *d education* Wells Cathedral School; Oxford Polytechnic/Brookes Univ: BA Architecture, DipArch (postgraduate diploma architecture), DipUD (postgraduate diploma in urban design), MA (urban design), mbr Royal Institute of British Architects 1993, Royal Town Planning Institute 2004 *career* architectural assistant various practices 1990-93; development designer WS Atkins 1993-97; director, Planning Aid for London 1997-2000; Director, Town & Country Planning Association (TCPA) 2000- *party* joined Wells Liberal Association 1982; secy, other offices Oxford Polytechnic Alliance Society 1084-92; 85-88 Secy Oxford East LP 1985-88; deputy president Oxford Polytechnic Student Union, governor Polytechnic 1988-89; local election candidate 1989, 1990, 1991; mbr (Oxford Central) Oxford City Council 1992-96, gp leader, leader of opposition 1995-96; approved Westminster candidate 1995- ; mbr and conference representative Hackney LP 1997-2000 *special interests* sustainable development, community participation, housing, planning, development, architecture, urban design, regeneration, conservation, local Govt, disability *other mbrships* RIBA, RTPI, FRSA, NLC, Urban Design Gp, TCPA, National Trust, Hackney Society, PCA *recreations* running, bringing up children *publications* various articles, pamphlets *address* 33 Sharon Gardens, South Hackney, London E9 7RX *tel/fax* 020 8525 8124 home 020 7930 8903 business *e-mail* gideon.amos@btopenworld.com

ARBUCKLE, Andrew David MSP *b* Apr 12, 1944 *2d education* Bell Baxter High School, Cupar; Elmwood College, Cupar – National Diploma in Agriculture *career* farmer, East Fife; former President Fife NFU; Agricultural Editor, Dundee Courier & Advertiser 1986-2005 *party* North East and Central Fife; convenor Mid Scotland and Fife Regional party; list candidate Mid Scotland and Fife 1999, 2003; Fife Regional Cllr 1986-1995; Fife Cllr 1995- ; convenor North East Fife LD Association 1999-2002; MSP Mid Scotland and Fife 2005- ; Finance, Local Govt and Transport, Spokesperson, Scottish Parliamentary Gp 2005- ; *other mbrships* former mbr St Andrews Univ Court, Tay Road Bridge Board, former chair Fife Athletic Club *recreations* former Scottish pole vault champion, sport, music, reading *address* The Scottish Parliament, Edinburgh EH99 1SP *tel* 0131 348 5800 or 0770 352 8378 *email* andrew.arbuckle.msp@scottish.parliament.uk

ARMITAGE, Alan Edmund *b* Dec 13, 1950 *m* Jane 1 *s* 2 *d education* Fettes College, Edinburgh; St James School, Maryland, USA; Univ of York *career* ICL Computers 1972-84 (account manager Ministry of Defence, European Institutions, British Telecommunications); ITL 1984-89 (branch manager, Aerospace ICL Secure Systems) 1989-96; sales manager Platinum Technology, Computer Associates 1997-2000 ; European security products manager AppGate Ltd (small Swedish software company) 2000-01, European partner manager *party* joined Jan 2002; mbr Oxford City Council (Summertown) May 2002; organiser Oxford West & Abingdon and Wantage constituencies Jan 2003- ; previously Conservative Cllr on Aylesbury Vale District Council 1989-93, deputy leader of the council 1990-93; European PPC for Pro Euro Conservative Party 1999, South East Region special *interests* immigration, civil liberties, education, leisure services, environment *other mbrships* lay mbr Immigration Appeal Tribunal; European Movement *recreations* music, history *address* 92 Southmoor Road Oxford OX2 6RB *tel* 01865516115 home 01865249813 business *e-mail* oxford92@aol.com

ARRAM, Joyce Muriel F.Inst L.Ex., FRSA *b* Mar 24, 1935 *education* Camden School for Girls (Frances Mary Buss Foundation); Central London Polytechnic; North London Polytechnic *career* Legal Exec (45+ years in legal profession): Alexander JLO Solicitors 1997- ; mbr Council of Institute of Legal Execs (ILEx) 1976-2004 (longest serving Council mbr), elected Honorary VP 2004; certified Licensed Conveyancer 1987; mbr Council for Licensed Conveyancers 1988-1989; Treasurer Central London Branch of ILEx; associate mbr City of Westminster and Holborn Law Society *party* joined Liberals pre 1956; candidate GLC 1964, LBCs Camden, Haringey and Barnet, PPC (Liberal Party) 1966, 1968 and 1974 (twice) S.E. Essex and Ruislip/Northwood; active in Summer Stock and Civil Rights campaigns USA particularly in Florida 1962-3; Secy Liberal Democrat Lawyers Association 1992-2001, Deputy President 2001-; mbr exec cttee Lib Dem Friends of Israel; mbr Liberal International, WLD *special interests* Governor Kingsway College of Further Education 1986-1998; Trustee National Benevolent Fund for the Aged 1988- ; Trustee Institute of Legal Execs Benevolent Fund 1999- ; convenor of local Neighbourhood Watch; Woman Freemason (past Master of Lodge); mbr Capital Women's Forum (formerly Network) (organisation for women at the top of their professions); Fellow Royal Society of Arts (1990); involved in RSA Coffee House Challenge 2004/5 and mbr RSA London Region Cttee *clubs* National Liberal Club; RSA *recreations* the arts, gardening, entertaining, owned by cat *style* Joyce M Arram, F.InstL.Ex., FRSA *address* 1 Summerlee Gardens, East Finchley, London N2 9QN *tel* 020 8444 8578

ASGHAR, Ali *b* Aug 12, 1951 *m* 3 *s* 2 *d education* Mirpur HS, Azad, Kashmir; Trent Bridge School 1965; People's College, Nottingham (GCSE English); Nottingham Trent Univ (Higher English Language, Communications Studies) 1996-97 *party* joined Feb 2003; mbr Nottingham City Council, chair Older Persons Services; Social Services; chair Elderly Voices Conference; advocate, Older Persons Services; Sheriff of Nottingham *special interests* environment; community politics; human rights; welfare rights *recreations* Tai Chi, reading *address* 1 Dovedale Road, Bakersfield, Nottingham NG3 7GS *tel* 01159116195 home 0115 9423364 business *e-mail* ali_asgharameer@yahoo.co.uk

ASHDOWN of Norton-sub-Hampton, Rt Hon Lord: **Sir Jeremy John Durham (Paddy) PC (1989) KBE (2000) Life Peer cr 2001 GCMG, Leader of the Liberal Democrats 1988-99** *b* New Delhi Feb 27, 1941 *m* 1961 Jane Courtenay 1 *s* Simon 1 *d* Kate *education* Bedford; Language School, Hong Kong (qualified first-class Chinese interpreter) *career* Royal Marine 1959-72, served in Borneo, Persian Gulf and Belfast; commander Special Boat Section (SBS) in Far East; Foreign Office 1971-76, First Secy British Mission, UN Geneva; Westland Helicopters 1976-78; senior manager Morlands Ltd 1978-81; unemployed for four months in 1981; youth officer Dorset County Council 1981-83; parliamentarian 1983- ; non-Exec director Time Gp 1999-2002; non-Exec director Independent News Group 2000-2002; High Representative in Bosnia Herzigovina.2002-2006 *party* PPC Yeovil 1976; elected MP for Yeovil 1983, re-elected 1987, 1992, 1997 (with 21.1% maj) stood down 2001; Leader of the Liberal Democrats 1988-99; sometime parliamentary spokesman on Trade and Industry, Education and Science, Northern Ireland *publications* *Beyond Westminster* (1994); Citizens' Britain (1989); *The Ashdown Diaries Vol 1* (1999) *Vol 2* (2001) *recreations* walking, gardening, wine-making *address* House of Lords, London SW1 0PW

ATTWOOLL, Elspeth MEP (Scotland) *b* Feb 1, 1943 *m education* Tiffin Girls, Kingston upon Thames; St Andrew's Univ (Queen's College, Dundee), LL.B, MA politics & philosophy; speaks fluent French, some German, Dutch, modern Greek *career* Univ senior lecturer in jurisprudence and comparative law, Univ of Glasgow 1966-98; MEP Scotland 1999- *party* president Scottish Women Liberal Democrats 1998- ; mbr Scottish Party Exec; candidate at local, Westminster, Euro, Glasgow; Scottish party spokesman on Europe; elected European Parliament 1999, re-elected 2004; mbr Cttee on Employment and Social Affairs. Cttee on Regional Policy, Transport and Tourism; mbr Cttee on Fisheries; substitute mbr, Agriculture & Rural

Development Cttee; mbr delegation for relations with Canada; substitute mbr Cttee on Environment, Public Health and Consumer Policy; substitute mbr delegation for relations with Japan; mbr Liberal International, Centre Forum *other mbrships* Scottish Human Rights Centre; IVL (International Association for Social and Legal Philosophy), AUT *recreations* reading (particularly legal theory, detective fiction) *address* Suite 1, Floor 2, Olympic House, 142 Queen Street, Glasgow G1 3BU *tel* 0141 243 2421 *fax* 0141 243 2451 *e-mail* info@elspethattwoollmep.org.uk *web* www.elspethattwoollmep.org.uk

AUSTEN, John Maurice *b* May 31, 1931 *m* 1 *d education* Dartford GS; Erith GS *career* RAF and banking *party* joined Liberals 1953; former secy and auditor of local parties; mbr Lib Dem History Gp, ALTER, LDEG, John Stuart Mill Institute, Liberal International, Liberal Political Studies Gp, Lib Dem Humanist and Secularist Gp; formerly school governor, mbr Rates Valuation Tribunal *special interests* electoral reform, direct democracy, land value taxation, republicanism *other mbrships* Electoral Reform Society, Swiss Railways Society, various Sherlock Holmes societies *address* 104 Lion Road, Bexleyheath, Kent DA6 8PQ *tel* 020 8303 2639 *e-mail* jmausten104@hotmail.com

AVEBURY, 4th Baron (UK 1900) Eric Reginald Lubbock Mbr Lords Foreign Affairs team *b* Sept 29, 1928 *education* Upper Canada College; Harrow; Balliol College, Oxford (BA) *m* 2 1985 Lindsay Stewart 1 *s* (2 *s* 1 *d* from previous marriage) *career* Rolls-Royce (aero-engine div) 1951-53; Production Engineering Ltd (management consultant) 1955-60; Charterhouse Gp 1960-62; director C.L. Projects Ltd *party* joined Liberals 1960 in Orpington; won Downe Ward in UDC election 1961; PPC Orpington 1962 (by-election): elected, served as MP until 1970; succeeded to title, went to House of Lords 1971; chair Liberal Party Housing Cttee 1962-63; sole Liberal on 1965 Speaker's Conference on Electoral Law 1965; Chief Whip 1963-70; chair Liberal Party Race Relations and Immigration Cttee; mbr Lords Foreign Affairs team speaking frequently on conflict resolution, asylum policy and human rights. *publications* numerous including *One Vote One Value* on PR *special interests* president Fluoridation Society 1972-84; president Conservation Society 1973-81; mbr Royal Commission on Standards of Conduct in Public Life 1975-76; chair Parliamentary Human Rights Gp 1976- ; president London Bach Society, Steinitz Bach Players 1984 *other mbrships* Buddhist, active patron of Angulimala, the Buddhist Prison Chaplaincy *address* 26 Flodden Road, London SE5 9LH *e-mail* ericavebury@hotmail.com

B

BAKER, Norman John MP (Lewes maj 8,474**)** *b* Jul 26, 1957 Aberdeen *m* 1 *d education* Royal Liberty School, Romford; Royal Holloway Univ, London *career* prior to election as MP in 1997, held variety of jobs including regional Exec director Our Price, clerk Hornsey Railway Station, manager wine shop, teacher English as a Foreign Language *party* elected Lewes District Council, Beddingham Parish Council 1987; led Lib Dems to victory Lewes DC elections, leader of council 1991; elected

MP for Lewes 1997; environment spokesman 1997-99; broadcasting and consumer affairs spokesman 1999-2001; Home Affairs spokesman 2001-02; Shadow Environment and Rural Affairs Secy 2002-06; voted *Channel 4 Opposition MP of the Year* 2002 *special interests* environment, animal welfare, civil and human rights *recreations* music, collecting records and occasionally singing in a 60's rock band *address* 204 High Street, Lewes BN7 2NS *tel* 01273 480281 *fax* 01273 480287 *e-mail* via *web* at www.normanbaker.org.uk

BAKER, Paula *b* Oct 9, 1948 *m* Martin 2 *d* Jane, Heather *education* St Mary's Grammar, Northwood; Univ of Essex (BA Telecomms Eng) *career* telecommunications engineering (Post Office Telephones, London); lecturer in electronics, Basingstoke College of Technology); now full-time Cllr *party* founder mbr SDP, Liberal Democrats; regional secy SDP; elected Basingstoke & Deane Borough Council 1987, Leader of Council 1995-98; Mayor 2005-6; deputy chair LGA Environment Board; mbr of UK Delegation to EU Cttee of the Regions, serving on the Sustainable Development Commission; mbr Green Liberal Democrats, WLD, ALDC *special interests* waste management, planning, telecomms *other mbrships* National Trust, Hampshire Wild Life Trust, Overton Community Association, Overton Parish Council, HDRA *recreations* gym, early Flemish art, gardening, *The Archers* *address* 59 Winchester Street, Overton, Basingstoke, Hants RG25 3HT *tel* 01256 771219 *e-mail* paulabaker7@aol.com

BAKHAI, Nigel *b* Jul 2, 1971 *education* Brighton College 1984-89; Univ of Bradford 1989-92 (BSc Hons Politics/History); Univ of Nottingham 1992-94 (MA International Relations; Diploma in Logistics) 1999 *career* mbr Institute of Logistics and Transport; management trainee Tie Rack 1994-95; replenishment assistant Mothercare 1995-97; distribution co-ordinator House of Fraser 1997-99; inventory controller, key accounts manager, Electrolux Home Products 1999- *party* joined 1987; Exec mbr Ealing Southall, campaign manager 2001 GE; mbr London Region Exec 2001- , campaigns, policy sub-Cttee; mbr English Council; treasurer Ealing Borough co-ordinating Cttee 2001- ; London regional co-ordinator, EMLD (Ethnic Minority Lib Dems) *address* 51 Azalea Close, Azalea Court, Hanwell, London, W7 3QA *tel* 0208 579 8299 mobile 0786 798 3932 *e-mail* nbakhai@aol.com

BALMER, Richard BSc (Eng), CEng, MICE, FCIWEM **Secy ALDES** *b* Feb 16, 1938 Status *m* Sue 2 *s education* Portsmouth Grammar School 1946-56, Kings College, London Univ. 1956-59 *career* chartered civil engineer, mainly in water business, with 5 years in Uganda, 4 years in Plymouth, 15 years with Severn Trent as an engineer/economist; consultancy work in the Middle East and India *party* joined 1981; Solihull MBC Cllr 1988 96; agent 1992 General Election; Hon Sec ALDES 1996- ; chair Nuneaton and North Warwickshire 2004- ; mbr several party policy working *special interests* ensuring party has properly informed and balanced view of science-related matters in the political domain (eg energy, GM technology) *other mbrships* mbr, Institution of Civil Engineers, fellow, Chartered Institute of Water and Environmental Management, mbr Solihull Methodist Church, National Trust *recreations* travel, history *publications* professional papers, ALDES briefing notes *address* 79, Links Drive, Solihull, B91 2DJ *tel* 0121 603 0661 *fax* 0121 608 7057 *e-mail* richard_balmer@cix.co.uk

BARING, Sue *b* Jun 5, 1930 Esher *m* twice, 4 *ch* 13 *gch education* Heathfield School *career* magistrate 1965-88, mbr Parole Board for England and Wales 1971-74 and 1979-83; chair Inner London Probation Cttee 1999- 2000; trustee Howard League for Penal Reform 1978- ; trustee Liberty 2004- ; board mbr Almeida Theatre 1993-2003; chair British Inst of Human Rights 1989-2004, 1981 and 1995 Governor of Kings College, London and of the Delegacy of Kings College Medical School-Vice Chair for 1989-95; chair Board of Advisors - Centre for Medical Law and Ethics at King's College, London 1989-95 *party* mbr Westminster LP; joined SDP 1981 then Liberal Democrat party; PPC Reading East 1987, East Hampshire 1992; local election candidate, Bayswater, 2004, 2006; mbr Lib Dem Lawyers Assoc; taken part in various policy working parties *special interests* criminal justice, penal reform, education and the arts *recreations* walking, gardening, theatre, grandchildren; *style* Hon Mrs Susan Mary Baring OBE JP *address* 18 Cleveland Square, London W2 6DG *tel* 020 77061806 *fax* 020 7706 1805 *e-mail* suebaring@aol.com

BARKER, Baroness Liz: Life Peer cr 1999: Lords Spokesperson on Health *b* Jan 31, 1961*education* Dalziel High School, Motherwell; Broadway School, Oldham; Southampton Univ *career* field officer Age Concern *party* joined Liberal Party in 1979, mbr Union of Liberal Students, chair 1982-83; mbr Liberal Party National Exec 1982; mbr Liberator Collective (publisher of *The Liberator*) 1983-86;. Federal Policy Cttee 1997, former chair Liberal Democrat Federal Conference Cttee (to 2003); mbr various party policy working gps, including Future of Social Services, Liberal Democracy, Freedom and Fairness for Women and An Age of Opportunity; created Life Peer 1999; Lords spokesperson health, social care, pensions *special interests* health, social services, problems of ageing, poverty, civil liberties *other mbrships* ACCTS trade union; trustee Andy Lawson Memorial Fund *address* House of Lords, London SW1A 0PW *e-mail* barkere@parliament.uk

BARKER, Michael John *b* Feb 16, 1954 widower 2 *s* 1 *d education* Forest Grammar School, Wokingham 1965-72; Univ College, Swansea 1973-76 (BA Hons Political Theory and Govt); Univ of York 1976-77 (postgraduate diploma in social administration) *career* Sheffield City Polytechnic, 1977-79; research assistant Dept of Public Administration Albermarle Market Research, London 1979-83; market research Exec Argyll Foods plc, London, 1983-84; market research manager Hintons plc, Stockton-on-Tees 1984-85; marketing manager The Health Warehouse Ltd, Darlington (proprietor of health food shop, wholefood bakery, delicatessen, vegetarian restaurant)1985- *party* founder mbr SDP; candidate London Borough of Merton; agent for Bruce Douglas-Mann, Mitcham & Morden 1983; Liberal Democrats, Darlington, 1984; mbrship lapsed during 1990s due to time devoted to being single-parent family and running own business; rejoined Lib Dems 2002; constituency chair, 2004; local Govt candidate *recreations* bringing up children, Reading Football Club, gardening, chess, avoiding DIY chores *address* 19, Stanhope Rd, Darlington, Co Durham DL3 7AP *tel* 01325 283081 *e-mail* mjbarker2@hotmail.com

BARLOW, Roger John *b* Apr 14, 1951 *m* Ann 1 *s* Edward 1 *d* Eleanor *education* Oxford (BA) 1972; Cambridge (PhD) 1977; Open Univ (MA Education) 1998 *career* research in particle physics Oxford, Hamburg, Geneva, Stanford; currently Professor of Particle Physics, Manchester Univ *party* joined the Liberals 1980;

branch secy Warrington South; chair Knutsford; non-candidate Tatton (stood down for Martin Bell) 1997; PPC Warrington South 2001, Halton 2005 *other mbrships* British Association, Institute of Physics, Fulbright Alumni Association *address* 23 Trouthall Lane, Knutsford, Cheshire WA16 0UN *tel* 01565 722989 home 0161 275 4178 business *fax* 0161 273 5867 *e-mail* Roger.Barlow@man.ac.uk

BARNARD, Kay BSc PhD *b* May 11, 1948 nee Burns *m* Jim 1 *s* William 1 *d* Jenny *education* Colstons Girls School, Bristol; Leeds Univ (BSc biochemistry); Kings College, London (PhD biochemistry) *career* research associate MIT, Mass, USA 1973-75; medical research Bristol Univ 1976-83; senior scientific officer Food Research Institute, Bristol 1983-89; National Kidney Fund Research Fellowship, Bristol Univ 1989-91; director, food processing company, farming company 1992-2000, 1976-2004 *party* various offices over years, from branch to constituency chair; English Council mbr since 1986; county Cllr (won Tory seat with 30% swing) 1993-97; handed over to another winning Lib Dem; number three on SW Euro list 2004; PPC Bristol South 2005 (increasing LD vote by 55% and moving to second place behind Labour) *special interests* health, science (particularly the environment), agriculture, education *other mbrships* Univ of Bristol Council 1993-2002; NRA, Regional Rivers Advisory Cttee 1993-97; Environment Agency Regional Environment Protection Cttee 1996-97; Primary Care Trust non-exec director 2000-03 *recreations* violin (at low level), wood carving, walking *publications* many scientific publications *address* Keward Farm, Pawlett, Bridgwater, Somerset TA6 4SE *tel* 01278-683066 *fax* 01278-684664 *e-mail* jbarnard@globalnet.co.uk

BARNARD, Mark Anthony *b* Dec 28, 1967 Shoreham *m education* Blatchington Mill School, Hove *career* sales director 1987-90; MD 1990-96; MD and owner 1999- ; *party* mbr South East Region; former City Councillor 1999-2003; spokesperson on the Environment and on Housing; PPC Thanet North 2005 *recreations* current affairs, reading, property market *address* Copwood House, 24 Bolsover Road, Hove, Sussex BN3 5HP *tel* 01273 245428 home 07881814506 mobile *fax* 01273 245428 *e-mail* mark.barnard8@btinternet.com

BARNARD-LANGSTON, Jennifer Mary (known as Jenny) *b* Jan 29, 1950 *m* fostered 30 teenagers *education* Maud Allen Secondary School, Littlehampton; Ringmer College; Lewes Tertiary College; Sussex Univ *career* nurse; foster parent; owner, manager Agape Trust (home providing supported living for young homeless); psychotherapist, working from GP surgery *party* joined January 2002 (defected from Tories); chair, Brighton & Hove LP 2002- ; magistrate 2006- ; *special interests* health, education, community politics *other mbrships* vice chair, community health trust; lay ember, Brighton & Hove PCT; Sussex Univ Council; governor, Lewes Tertiary College Corp 1990-2000, chair 1996-2000 (appointed new principal); governor comprehensive school, formerly chair, successfully managed application for Performing Arts Status, oversaw two OFSTED inspections (appointed new headteacher) 1990- ; chair. junior school (oversaw successful application for Beacon School Status, two OFSTED inspections, appointed new headteacher) 1990- *recreations* reading *publications* jointly wrote *Strategy for Prevention of Suicide in Brighton & Hove address* 3 Mile Oak Gardens, Portslade, East Sussex BN41 2PH *tel* 01273 245428 home 07881 814506 mobile *fax* 01273 245428 *e-mail* jenny.barnardlangston@ntlworld.com

BARON, Christina Murray *b* Oct 1, 1950 *m* Alan Butt Philip *qv* 1 *d* Frances 2 *s* David, Theodore *qv* **education** St Leonard's School, St Andrews: City Univ, London **career** lecturer, SOAS, Univ of London (British studies) 1986-99; lecturer, Univ of Bath, 1998-date (British history/British studies); chair, Somerset Partnership NHS and Social Care Trust 1997-2004 **party** joined Liberals, Rochdale 1965; Lib Dems at foundation; sub-agent, Isle of Ely by-election 1973; PPC Hemel Hempstead, Feb, Oct 1974; Bridgwater, 1979; president (last), Women's Liberal Federation, 1986-88; agent, Somerset, North Dorset 1984 Euro election; Wells City Cllr 1976-99, Mayor 1980-81 **special interests** increasing representation of women at every level; mental health legislation, provision **other mbrships** founder trustee, Nancy Seear Trust; active Anglican (PCC, St. Thomas, Wells); first woman full mbr, National Liberal Club; mbr Avon and Somerset Probation Board 2004- **recreations** Lundy Island, visiting old churches, opera, arguing with Conservatives **address** The Old Vicarage, St Thomas Street, Wells, Somerset BA5 2UZ **tel/fax** 01749 675071 **e-mail** christina.baron@fsmail.net

BARRETT, John MP (Edinburgh West maj. 13,600) *b* Feb 11, 1954 *education* Forrester High School; Telford College; Napier Polytechnic *m* 1 *d career* company director *party* convener Lothian Region; vice president Scottish Liberal Club; mbr Edinburgh City Council 1995-2001, gp spokesperson Transport & Economic Development; parliamentary agent for Donald Gorrie MP 1997; mbr, Scottish Party Exec 2001- ; chair, Edinburgh West local development Cttee 2000-01; PPC Edinburgh West 2001 (elected); mbr, International Development Select Cttee; secy, All Party Microfinance, Microcredit Gp; All Party Gp on Zimbabwe; Shadow Minister of State for Scotland *other interests* former board mbr Edinburgh & Lothians Screen Industries and Edinburgh Filmhouse *other mbrships* Amnesty International *recreations* cinema, music, travel, meeting people *address* House of Commons, London SW1A 0AA; 1a Drumbrae Avenue, Edinburgh EH12 8TE *tel* 0131339 0339 *fax* 0131 476 7101 3 *e-mail* barrettj@parliament.uk *website* www.johnbarrettmp.com

BARRIE, Derek Andrew MA (Hons), PhD Chief of Staff Scottish Liberal Democrats *b* Aug 3, 1942 *m education* Bell-Baxter HS, Cupar; Univ of St Andrews (MA Hons, modern & mediaeval history 1964; PhD 1992) *career* history teacher 1968-88; full-time Lib Dems 1989- *party* joined Scottish Liberal Party 1961; PPC East Fife 1966; agent East Fife then North East Fife 1970, Feb and Oct 1974, 1979, 1983; campaign manager 1987; mbr North East Fife DC 1977-88, council chair 1984-88; part-time ALDC Scottish Officer 1989-90; target seats officer, Scotland 1991-92; campaigns officer, Scotland 1992-99; director Campaigns & Elections, Scotland 2000-2003, Chief of Staff 2003- ; campaign manager, Edinburgh West 1992, West Aberdeenshire & Kincardine 1997, Aberdeen South 2001 *special interests* mbr COSLA 1980-84; Univ Court, Univ of St Andrews 1980-1984 *recreations* former RU referee, golf, gardening, reading, theatre *publications* various campaigning publications for ALDC, Scottish Liberal Democrats; editor *Clifton Terrace FOCUS address* 13, Lindsay Gardens, St Andrews, Fife, KY16 8XB *tel* 01334 475502 *fax* 01334 475502 *e-mail* derekbarrie@cix.co.uk

BATCHELOR, Anthony John OBE, MA, BSc (Econ) *b* Apr 6, 1941 *education* Northampton Town and County School; King Charles 1 School, Kidderminster; Univ College London; Birmingham Polytechnic BSc (Econ) Hons; Keele Univ MA in US History and Politics *career* researcher, campaigner, Liberal Party Organisation 1962-64 (mainly preparations for by-elections in Central Norfolk, Colne Valley, Stratford-upon-Avon, Belfast South and Leeds South); Kidderminster College 1965-2000: head, business and social studies, deputy principal, principal and chief Exec; Open Univ social and political sciences tutor, counsellor 1971-99; AEB chief examiner GCE O-level Govt and Politics 1980-85, A-level Govt and Politics 1986-2000; Edexcel: principal examiner GCE 'A' General Studies 2000- , GCSE Citizenship Studies 2003- ; educational consultant Schools Curriculum and Assessment Authority 1993-97, Qualifications and Curriculum Authority 1998- , Marches Consortium (PGCE programmes) since 2000; researcher Host Policy Research, 2003-04 *party* joined Liberal Party 1957; founder mbr, secy Kidderminster Liberal Association 1958-60; mbr Party Council, National Exec, Candidates Cttee, Standing Cttee 1974-83; president, West Midlands Liberal Federation 1974-77, chair 1977-80; parly candidate, South Worcs 1964, Kidderminster February and October 1974, Wyre Forest 1983, 1987; Euro candidate, South Birmingham, 1979; mbr Kidderminster BC 1967-74, Wyre Forest DC 1973-87, gp leader 1979-85; ldr council 1979-83, 1984-85; v chair 1985-86; chair 1986-87; mbr Leominster Liberal Democrats since 1987 *special interests* economic policy and citizenship issues *other mbrships* mbr Court, Univ of Birmingham 1979-83, 1984-86 *publications* regular contributor to *Politics Review, Citizenship File, Liberal Democrat News* columnist on constituency boundary matters since before 1997 General Election; (with Trevor Green) *Revise for GCSE Citizenship Studies-Edexcel* Heinemann 2004; (with Edward Little and Gareth Davies) *Revision Express for A Level General Studies* Pearson pub 2004 *address* Tudor Cottage, Collington, Bromyard, Herefordshire HR7 4NE *tel* 01885 410241 *e-mail* aj.batchelor@virgin.net

BATES, Michael (Mick) AM Welsh Spokesperson on Environment, Planning and Countryside *b* Sept 24, 1947 *m* Buddug Thomas 1 *s* Daniel 1 *d* Ruth *education* Loughborough College School; Worcester College of Education; Open Univ *career* teacher 1970-77; farmer 1977- ; AM 1999- ; *party* joined Welsh Liberal Democrats 1980; party spokesperson for Agriculture and Rural Development 1999- ; European Affairs 1999-2001; Environment, Planning and Transport 2000-01; Education and Lifelong learning 2001-03; Environment, Planning and Countryside 2003- ; *special interests* planning; Community Politics; Community Regeneration; Heritage; Rural Affairs; environment; education; transport; formation of co-operative companies *other mbrships* trustee Institute of Health; trustee Llanfyllin Union; Workhouse Restoration project; director Primestop Producers Limited *recreations* painting, poetry, farming, Bob Dylan *address* National Assembly for Wales, Cardiff Bay, Cardiff CF99 1NA *tel* 02920 898340 *fax* 02920 898341 *e-mail* mick.bates@wales.gov.uk

BATSTONE, Dinti Wakefield *b* Dec 6, 1971 *m* Matthew Sept 2004 1 *s* William James 2005 *education* Benenden School, Kent 1984-88; Rugby School 1988-90; Pembroke College, Cambridge Univ 1991-94; College of Law, London 1994-96; INSEAD, Fontainebleau, France 2001 *career* Linklaters (law firm) London, Hong Kong 1997-99; Pearson Television/ RTL Gp 1999-2000; freelance consultant, translator and interpreter 2002- ; *party* joined 1999; mbr LB Lambeth 2002-06, gp chair 2002-03; European parliament candidate (Number 4 on London List) 2004 *special interests* European, international affairs *recreations* languages (UK Young Linguist of the Year 1990), travel *e-mail* dintiwakefield@yahoo.com

BEANSE, John Derek *b* Jan 5, 1947 *education* Yardley Primary School, Chingford, London, E4; Sir George Monoux Grammar School, Walthamstow, London, E17; Sidney Sussex College, Cambridge (Hons Mod Languages - French & German); Goldsmiths' College, London (PGTC); as student worked two summers for Deutsche Bundespost in Frankfurt, Ludwigshafen; attended courses in Paris, Lyon & Univ of Lausanne (Switzerland) *career* teacher in comprehensive schools:at different times Head of House; Head of Sixth Form; Head of Modern Languages; now languages examiner, tutor and also give travel talks to various gps *party* joined Liberal Party in 1974; PPC Chingford and Woodford Green in 2001, 2005 (against Iain Duncan Smith); five times local election candidate in LB of Waltham Forest; currently chairman and press officer of Chingford and Woodford Green Liberal Democrats, also former chair (thrice times 3 years); *Focus* editor for over 20 years.; wrote and moved two motions, both passed overwhelmingly: 1) (at Edinburgh) response to Jenkins Commission report; and 2) Emergency motion on Community Health Councils (Bournemouth, 2000); have spoken frequently at conference (part of speech on Euro debate, at Bournemouth 2001, broadcast live on BBC TV *special interests* community and current affairs; mbr and accredited speaker Electoral Reform Society; former chair Waltham Forest Community Health Council; spoke on Carlton TV's *Your Shout* on abolition plans for Community Health Councils *other mbrships* ALDC; LD Christian Forum; Alzheimers Society; CPRE; Movement for Christian Democracy *recreations* travel; photography; music (classical, folk, musicals) *address* 47 Mansfield Hill, Chingford, London, E4 7SS *tel* 020-8529-0741 *e-mail* johnbeanse@yahoo.co.uk

BEARDER, Catherine Zena *b* Jan 14, 1949 *m* Professor Simon Kenneth Bearder (married within week of meeting, spent following few years in huts in game reserves studying hyenas and bush babies in Transvaal) 3 *s* Timothy, Ian, Peter *education* Reed JM&I School, Hertfordshire (failed 11+); Hawthorns School, Frinton on Sea, Essex (a school for young ladies that failed in this case) St Christopher School, Letchworth Herts (left at 15) *career* family farm in Hertfordshire, organising strawberry pickers and farm shop (*Miss Hertfordshire* 1966, *Dairymaid of Royston* 1967, *Dairymaid of Hertord* 1968); Beckwith and Son, antique dealers, Hertford; research assistant to husband, South African game reserves; time out to raise children; fund-raising for local Wildlife Trust; manager Bicester Citizens Advice Bureau; national development officer Nat Fed Women's Institutes; constituency organiser Oxford West and Abingdon Liberal Democrats; development officer Victim Support, Oxfordshire (Magistrates Court Witness Service) *party* joined 1995; PPC Banbury 1997, Henley 2001; Euro candidate, South East 1999, 2004; chair Banbury LP 1998; regional Exec mbr 2000-2; English Region rep 2001; chair, regional conference Cttee 2003-4; mbr Wendlebury Parish Council 1986-92, Cherwell District Council 1995-97, Oxfordshire County Council 2003- ; mbr Green Liberal Democrats Exec, PCA, Women Lib Dems, Ethnic Minority Liberal Democrats, LDEG Exec *special interests* fighting social exclusion, protecting the environment *other mbrships* trustee, director Oxfordshire Rural Community Council; mbr Oxfordshire Racial Equality Council; Friends of the Earth; Charter 88; Women Environmental Network; Institute of Advanced Motorists; United Nations Association *recreations* driving (winner, West of England Woman Car Driver of Year 1992), gardening; believed to be party's only expert on hyenas, painting *address* Sun House, 2A Stanley Road, Oxford OX4 1QZ *tel* 01865 792960 home 07786 170949 mobile *e-mail* cbearder@cix.co.uk

BECKERLEGGE, Philip Treglown *b* Dec 20, 1942 *m* Sarah 2 *s career* solicitor, partner London City firm specialising in private client residential property *party* joined 1960; regional chair (3 years); regional president (3 years); constituency chair, president; mbr National Exec, Party Council of Liberal Party; chair regional candidates Cttee; mbr national candidates Cttee ; PPC Cirencester & Tewkesbury 1979, 1983, 1987; PPC Cotswold constituency; mbr Cotswold District Council1979-87 Cirencester Town Cllr 1999-2003 *special interests* local issues: trustee housing charity for young people, trustee Opportunity Play gp' chair governors Cirencester Deer Park School (mixed, all ability 11-16 comprehensive) *other mbrships* Reform Club *address* 12 Park Street, Cirencester, Glos GL7 2BW *tel* 01285 640252 home 020 7427 6496 business *e-mail* philip.beckerlegge@yahoo.co.uk

BECKET, David William *b* Mar 19, 1936 *m* Anne 2 *d education* Midhurst Grammar School; Southampton Technical College; Southampton Univ *career* ICL (and predecessors) 1962-1991 *party* joined 1991; Berkshire County Cllr 1993-98; chair Newbury Area Highways & IT; West Berkshire UA Cllr 1997-2000, chair Transportation; mbr Newcastle under Lyme LP (West Midlands Region) and chair 2001-03; Newcastle under Lyme Borough Cllr 2002- , cabinet mbr 2002-03; mbr ALDC *other mbrships* CAMRA *special interests* transports *recreations* bell-ringing, walking, cooking, travel in Eastern Europe *address* 25 Ladygates, Betley, Crewe CW3 9AN *tel* 0845 4581950 *e-mail* david.becket@newcastlelibdems.org.uk

BEGG, Margaret Ann *b* Nov 7, 1942 Cambridge *m* 2 *s education* Perse School for Girls, Cambridge; Univ of Nottingham BA Hons French with Spanish; Coventry Butts College ESOL certificate *career* Adult lecturer in French, Spanish, ESOL in Leicestershire, Lancashire, Warwickshire and Coventry 1964-2000 *party* exec mbr Warwick & Leamington LP (West Midlands Region); elected Warwick DC 1984, currently Environment Portfolio holder and Exec mbr *other mbrships* ALDC, United Nations Association, European Movement, Charter 88, Friends of the Earth *special interests* environmental and energy issues, electoral and parliamentary reform, planning and development *recreations* badminton, swimming, walking, music, art and architecture *LD quirk* in favour of nuclear power as part of the solution, alongside renewables and energy efficiency, to our future energy needs *style* Cllr *address* Garden House, Clarendon Crescent, Leamington Spa CV32 5NR *tel* 01926 423822 *e-mail* mbegg@cbegg.com

BEITH, Rt Hon Allan James PC (1992) MP (Berwick on Tweed maj: 8,632) *b* Apr 20, 1943 *m 1* Barbara (died 1998) 1 *s* (died 2000) 1 *d m 2* Baroness (Diana) Maddock *qv* 2001 *education* King's, Macclesfield; Balliol, Nuffield Colleges, Oxford; Hon DCL, Univ of Newcastle-upon-Tyne *career* Univ lecturer in politics, Univ of Newcastle-upon-Tyne; MP 1973- ; *party* joined Liberal Party 1958; mbr Tynedale District Council; elected MP Berwick-upon-Tweed 1973 by-election (majority 57) successfully defended seat in the two 1974 GEs (three elections in less than a year); and subsequent GEs to 2005; Chief Whip (Liberal) 1976-85; Deputy Leader Liberal Party (to David Steel) 1985-88; spokesman on Parliamentary and Constitutional Affairs 1983-87, Foreign Affairs 1985-87; Alliance spokesman on Foreign Affairs 1987; mbr of Treasury Select Cttee 1987-94; Liberal Democrat spokesman on Treasury Affairs 1987-94, Home Affairs 1994-99; mbr of House of Commons Commission 1979-97; Deputy Leader Liberal Democrats 1992-2003; vice-chair All-Party Arts and Heritage Gp; exec mbr All-Party Parly Gp on Nonprofit Making Mbrs' Clubs; mbr of the Intelligence and Security Cttee of the Speaker's Cttee on the Electoral Commission; chairman of Select Cttee on Constitutional Affairs *other mbrships* vice-president, National Association of Local Councils; chairman of trustees, Historic Chapels Trust *recreations* historic buildings, boats, music, walking *other interests* Methodist preacher *address* House of Commons, London SW1A 0AA *tel* 020 7219 3540 *fax* 020 7219 5890 *e-mail* cheesemang@parliament.uk *web* www.alanbeith.org.uk

BELL, Jacqueline Dianne *b* May 21, 1958 *m* Simon 1980 1 *s* Huw Matthew Apr 15, 1981 *education* City School , Sheffield; Univ College of North Wales, Bangor (BA Honours Social Theory and Institutions (Social Administration); Univ of Edinburgh (CQSW, Diploma in Social Work) *career* instructor to mentally ill, Middlewood Hospital, Sheffield 1979-80; CAB Volunteer, Middlewood Hospital Sheffield 1979-80; shoe sales assistant, Hughes and John, Aberystwyth 1980-81; Children's Column, *Cambrian News,* Aberystwyth (Yes, she was Dewi Dragon!!) 1980-91; volunteer, Penicuik CAB, 1981-83, 1986-87; clerical, administrative assistant Lothian Victims Support Scheme 1983-84; social worker Lothian Regional Council 1987-96, Midlothian Council 1996-2003, Edinburgh Council 2003- *party* joined 1989; mbr Dunbar Branch Cttee 1991- , vice convenor 1993-96, convenor 1996- ; mbr East Lothian LP Exec 1993- , vice convenor 1997-99, 2001-04, convenor 2000-1; Cttee mbr Scottish Women Liberal Democrats 2000- , convenor 2004- ; mbr Women Liberal Democrats, Scottish Women Liberal Democrats, PCA, Liberal Democrat European Gp, Liberal Democrat Christian Forum, Liberal Democrat Disability Association; candidate East Lothian Council: Dunbar 1992, Tyninghame 1995, North Berwick 1999; Scottish Parliament, South of Scotland List 1999; Lothian List and Midlothian 2003; PPC Midlothian 2001, Richmond (Yorkshire) 2005; mbr Dunbar Community Council 2000- ; successfully presented motions, amendments to Scottish Conference 1998- , Federal Conference 2000- *special interests* community care, disability, agriculture other mbrships BASW, The National Trust, Belhaven Parish Church Congregational Board, Dunbar John Muir Association, Dunbar Community Woodland Association, Scottish Downs Syndrome Association *recreations* horse riding, tapestry, Latvia (house available to rent), travel, amateur drama *address* Braeside, 2 High Street, Belhaven, Dunbar, East Lothian, EH42 1NP *tel* 01368 863110 home 0131 536 7900 work 07721 585474 mobile *fax* 0131 536 7898 *e-mail* sbell@easynet.co.uk

BELL, Mike *b* Nov 21, 1973 Weston-super-Mare *single* no children *education* Worle School, Broadoak Sixth Form *career* Deputy Editor, Property News 2003- ; Project Co-Ordinator, Young Enterprise 2002-2003; Campaigns Officer, Liberal Democrats 2001- ; Constituency Agent, Brian Cotter MP 1995-2001; Campaigns Assistant, Graham Watson MEP 1993-1995 *party* mbr Weston-super-Mare LP, Western Counties Region; councillor, North Somerset UA; Exec Mbr for Finance & Performance; councillor, Weston-super-Mare Town Council; mbrship secy, Weston-super-Mare LP; PPC Woodspring 2005, Weston super Mare 2006- ; mbr ALDC *special interests* finance and procurement, pensions *style* Cllr *address* Mansfield Three, 203 Longridge Way, Weston-super-Mare BS24 7HR *tel* 01934 522248 home, 01934 622000 work, 07765 902348 mobile *e-mail* mike@michaelbell.org *website* www.mikebell.org.uk

BENNION, (Roger) Phillip *b* Oct 7, 1954 *m* Penny (nee Foord) *education* QEGS Tamworth; Univ of Aberdeen (BSc Agriculture 2.1); Univ of Birmingham (BA 1st History/Economic and Social History); Univ of Newcastle upon Tyne (PhD Agronomy and Plant Breeding, Oilseed Rape) *career* lecturer in crop production, Shuttleworth College 1983-84; farmer, Haunton Manor Farm, near Tamworth 1985- *party* joined 1987; PPC, Lichfield 1997, 2001; European PPC, West Midlands, 1999, 2004 (No 3 on list); mbr Lichfield District Council 1999- ; mbr, Staffordshire County Council, 2002- , gp spokesperson Education and Social Services; vice-chair, West Midlands Region 2000-02; Rural Affairs and Agriculture, Mbr of Spokesman's Advisory Panel 1997- ; agricultural advisor to Liz Lynne MEP; mbr Federal Policy Cttee 2003-04 *special interests* agriculture, rural affairs, CAP reform, renewable energy, alternative crops, rural regeneration, trade policy, WTO, transport *other mbrships* National Farmers' Union (Staffordshire county chairman 1996), mbr of NFU West Midlands Combinable Crops Board with special responsibility for oilseeds, alternative crops and biotechnology; National Oilseeds, Proteins and Alternative Crops Cttee 1998 until abolition 2003; Home Grown Cereals Authority R&D Cttee 2000-03; vice-chair Staffordshire Rural Economic Forum *recreations* theatre, opera, art, art history, political economy, history, independent travel, cricket (played Derbyshire County League cricket for many years, now a umpire on the league list) *address* Haunton Manor Farm, Haunton, Tamworth, Staffs, B79 9HN *tel* 01827 373274 home 07831 136512 mobile *e-mail* phil.bennion@btconnect.com

BERENT, Anna *b* Oct 7, 1926 *widowed* 2 *s education* Dartington Hall School; Portsmouth Municipal College; London Polytechnic (now Univ of Westminster) *career* journalist on variety of publications - trade, children's and *The Australia and New Zealand Weekly*; career interrupted by marriage, children, move to Milan (for seven years); completed degree in 1966, worked as research technician in Health Service *party* foundation mbr SDP, foundation mbr Lib Dems; mbr Islington SDP Exec; mbr of the Islington LP Exec; elected to Islington Council, Mildmay ward, May 2002; Deputy Mayor 2005-6 *special interests* campaigned against major policies affecting Islington, proposed trunk roads through London, surface Channel Tunnel Rail Link through Islington (instead of in the deep tunnel eventually conceded); organiser local events, festivals; campaigned successfully for retrieval of local park that had come to be thought of as merely a traffic roundabout.; the environment *other mbrships* Green Liberal Democrats, Amnesty, Mildmay Community Partnership, Newington Green Action Gp, Groundwork, school *recreations* reading, travel, ballet, theatre *address* Islington Town Hall, Upper Street, London N1 2UD *tel* 020 7359 7087 *e-mail* anna.berent@islington.gov.uk

BERMAN, Dr Rodney *b* Apr 20, 1969 *ptnr* Nick Speed *education* Woodfarm High School, Thornliebank, Glasgow, 1980-86; Univ of Glasgow (BSc Hons in Pharmacology 1990); Univ of Glasgow (PhD in Pharmacology 1994) *career* research fellow, Univ of Wales College of Medicine Cardiff 1994-99; senior researcher, Welsh Liberal Democrat gp, National Assembly for Wales 1999-2004; Leader, Cardiff County Council 2004- ; leader, Welsh Liberal Democrat gp, Welsh Local Govt Association 2004- ; President, Conference of Atlantic Arc Cities 2005-07 *party* joined Scottish Liberal Party 1986, founder mbr Liberal Democrats 1988; previously secy, chair Cardiff Central LP; chair South Wales Central Assembly Electoral Regional Cttee; PPC Rhondda 1997, Cardiff South and Penarth 2001; elected (Plasnewydd ward) Cardiff County Council 1999; gp ldr Liberal Democrat

2000- ; leader of opposition 2000-04; Welsh representative, ALDC Standing Cttee 2000-04; Assembly candidate Cardiff South and Penarth 2003 *special interests* local Govt, environment, transport, equalities, science *other mbrships* Friends of the Earth Cymru *recreations* travel, music, cooking, science fiction *publications* various scientific research papers *address* 11 Roath Court Road, Roath, Cardiff, CF24 3SB *tel* 029 2031 0554, 07788 745 195 mobile *fax* 029 2048 2897 *e-mail* rberman@cix.co.uk

BERRIDGE, Janet Mary *b* May 2, 1952 Birmingham *m* Michael Berridge *qv* *education* Harrison Barrow Girls GS; Birmingham Polytechnic (diploma in Modern Foreign Languages for Business) *career* Cologne Trade Fair Co 1973-77; PA to MD and supervising stand construction UNIPLAN exhibition stands 1977-82; PA to MD EMI Music, Central Europe 1982-92; freelance translator to music industry 1992-95; freelance translator (German, French, Spanish, Dutch, Russian, into English) 1995- ; *party* mbr Canterbury and Whitstable LP 2000- ; secy 2000-04, treasurer 2004- ; *special interests* the arts, justice system; voluntary work; music *other mbrships* NLC, Liberty, Liberty Network, Amnesty International, Musicians' Benevolent Fund, Howard League for Penal Reform, National Association of Official Prison Visitors *recreations* theatre, ballet, concerts, cooking, walking, swimming, cycling, reading, music *publications* numerous articles in CD booklets for German record labels *LD Quirk* enjoy assisting in catering for lunches, dinners, etc *address* 3 Shaftesbury Road, Canterbury CT2 7LE *tel* 01227 470027 *fax* 01277 470028 *e-mail* mhnu80@dsl.pipex.com

BERRIDGE, Michael John *b* Jun 1, 1942 *m* Janet *qv* (nee Hickinbotham) 1993 *education* St Paul's School 1956-61; Corpus Christi, Cambridge 1961-65 MA Classics; Wuppertal Univ 1980-89 MA Modern Languages *career* various office jobs 1965-78 (GLC, Province of Ontario, Simpsons, Toronto) freelance translator since 1980 (German, six other languages into English) *party* Cambridge Univ Liberal Club 1961-65 (recruited by Michael Steed); Wembley North Young Liberals 1965-70; mbr Canterbury & Whitstable Lib Dems since 2000; Canterbury city Cllr 2003- ; mbr Liberty Network 2004 *special interests* organic/local food, transport, music (Grade VII piano 2000) *other mbrships* life mbr Festiniog Railway Society, Dignity in Dying Society, National Trust *recreations* swimming, bridge, music-making *publications* English translations in numerous classical CD booklets (notably Berlin Classics) *address* 3 Shaftesbury Road Canterbury CT2 7LE *tel* 01227 470027 *fax* 01227 470028 *e-mail* Michael.Berridge@canterbury.gov.uk

BIRCH, Eileen L *b* May 1 *m* Michael 1 *s* Adam *education* Univ of Wolverhampton 1995-98 LLB (Hons); Bilston High School for Girls (left 1964 *party* secy, Wolverhampton LP; candidate, Ettingshall ward Wolverhampton City Council *special interests* crime and crime prevention, local community *other mbrships* various local gps, including Parkfields Tenants and Residents Association, Parkfields Ettingshall Neighbourhood Safety Cttee, Wolverhampton South Neighbourhood Watch Association, Heart of Bilston *recreations* family, local interests, writing, internet *publications* short stories, poems published in *Serendipity*, an online magazine *address* 56 Whittaker St Wolverhampton WV2 2EB *e-mail* ettingshallfocus@lycos.co.uk *web* gps.msn.com/LiberalDemocratAlternative

BLACK, Peter AM *b* Jan 30, 1960 Clatterbridge, Wirral *m* Angela (nee Jones) Jul 20, 2000 *education* Wirral Grammar School for Boys; Univ College of Swansea, BA Hons English & History *career* Land Registry for Wales 1983-99; Welsh Liberal Democrat Assembly mbr for South Wales West 1999- ; mbr City and County of Swansea Council 1984- ; *party* mbr Welsh National Exec; mbr Federal Exec; chair Welsh Assembly Education Cttee; Welsh Lib Dems Assembly Candidate for Swansea East 1999 and 2003; number 1 on Regional Assembly List South Wales West 1999 and 2003; mbr Swansea and Gower LP; mbr ALDC *special interests* housing *recreations* film, poetry *style* Cllr Peter Black AM *address* 115 Cecil Street, Manselton, Swansea SA5 8QL *tel* 01792 473743 home 029 20 898744 office 07774 256123 *fax* 029 20 898362 *e-mail* peter.black@wales.gov.uk *web* www.peter-black.net

BLACKBURN, Christopher Gary Andrew *b* Jun 9, 1982 Blackpool *partner* Lyn-Su Floodgate *qv education* Lostock Hall High School 1993-98; Runshaw College 1998-2000; Univ of Manchester 2000-03 (2:1 BA Hons Politics and Modern History) *career* Recruitment Consultant, Strive (Supply Chain & Logistics) Exec Management Recruitment *party* joined April 1, 2000; Stockport local election candidate 2006 *special interests* student issues, housing, top-up fees, regional government *other mbrships* Chorley FC Independent Supporters Trust; Friends of Real Lancashire; Official England Rugby Supporters Club; Campaign for Real Ale, Sale Sharks Supporters Club *recreations* rugby union (Sale Sharks RUFC), football (Chorley FC), cricket (Chorley CC, Lancashire CCC) *address* 69 Mounsey Road, Bamber Bridge, Preston, Lancashire, PR5 6LU *tel* 01772 465309 home 07941 700676 work 0161 4777 555 business *e-mail* lankylancastrian@yahoo.com

BLACKIE, Robert (Rob) *b* Jul 29, 1973 *education* Oxford (BA History, Economics 1995); LSE (MSc Development Studies Environment) *career* environmental economist Namibian Ministry of Environment & Tourism 1996-98; freelance consultant economics, environment 1998-89; researcher Institute of Development Studies Univ of Sussex 1999; Liberal Democrat Treasury Advisor 1999-2004; Liberal Democrat Director of Research 2003-05; consultant Blue Rubicon 2006- ; *party* chair Vauxhall Lib Dems 2002-04; agent Vauxhall Lib Dems 2006; mbr International Development Working Gp 2003-04, Macroeconomics Working Gp 2002-03 *special interests* development issues, inequality issues, environment, human rights, African politics, economic policy *recreations* Mugendo kickboxing, Wu Shu, music *address* basement, 356 Coldharbour Lane, London SW9 8PL *e-mail* rob.blackie@bluerubicon.com

BLACKMORE, Roger *b* 1941 Woodcote *m* 3 *ch education* Abingdon School, Berkshire; Shebden College, Devon; Leicester Univ, BA Social Sciences *career* college lecturer *party* leader of Leicester City Council; former chair and President, East Midlands Region; PPC Gainsborough 1970, 1974, 1979, North Devon 1983, Wansdyke 1987; mbr ALDC, Green Liberal Democrats *other mbrships* English Heritage, Woodland Trust *special interests* environmental issues *publications* Uses of Referendums New Outlook 1974 *recreations* photography, walking, local history *style* Cllr *address* 15 Mellor Road, Western Park, Leicester *tel* 0116 285 6394 home 0116 252 6048 work

BLANCHARD, James Christopher *b* Mar 23, 1977 Leicester *ptnr* Helen SEM Greaves *education* Newcroft Primary School; Shepshed High School; Hind Leys Community College; Univ of Leeds *career* LDYS Head of Office 2004-05; Charter 88, Campaigns and Media Officer 2005- ; *party* joined Leeds North West 2000; Islington LP 2001; Cllr, LB Islington 2002-06; recruitment secy 2003, social secy 2004; PPC Hackney North and Stoke 2005, Huddersfield 2006- ; accredited party trainer; LDYS general exec mbr 2003-04, vice-chair mbrship development 2006; Green LD exec mbr 2002- ; *special interests* the environment and ecological economics, education, youth politics, political engagement, electoral and constitutional reform *other mbrships* Charter 88, NLC, CAMRA *recreations* often neglected but music, reading, films, comics, board-games, scuba diving, refereeing association football *tel* 07753958214 *e-mail* jamesblanchard@yahoo.com

BLOOM, Louise Anne *b* 7, 1964 *partner* Keith House *qv* 2 *d education* Rodway High School, Bristol 75-82; Kingston Polytechnic (BA Hons Applied Social Science specialising in European Politics and Economics) 1982-85 *career* account handler various advertising agencies1985-90; research, admin asst Lib Dem Gp, Royal Borough of Kingston 1991-93; freelance conference organiser, press, PR manager 1994-97; Independent Living Scheme asst co-ordinator, Kingston Association of Disabled People 1997-98; information officer, Richmond Advice and Information on Disability 1998-2000; Greater London Assembly Mbr May 2000-Feb 2002; advocacy project manager MIND, Southampton & New Forest Feb 2002- *party* joined Liberal Party 1982; chair Kingston Poly Liberal Club 1983-85; Exec mbr NLYL. 1984-86; vice chair, Green Lib Dems 1995-2001; just about every job Kingston LP (except treasurer!) 1984-2000; sub-agent Richmond Park 1997; failed to get elected Kingston Council in 1986 (missed by three votes), 1994, 1998; Exec mbr London Region 1996-2000; LEA School Governor 1986-2000; mbr London Assembly, London Fire & Emergency Planning Authority, vice chair Environment Scrutiny Cttee May 2000-Feb 2002 mbr Eastleigh Borough Council, Exec mbr Environment May 2002- ; Exec mbr South East England Regional Assembly Jul 2002- ; mbr Hedge End town council May 2003- ; mbr LGA Environment & Regeneration Exec Jul 2003- ; *special interests* environment, disability, equalities issues, social policy *other mbrships* Greenpeace, Amnesty International, Howard League for Penal Reform recreations travelling, theatre, music, reading *address* 52 Woodstock Close, Hedge End, Southampton SO30 0NG *tel* 01489 787336 mobile 07932 032045 *fax* 01489 787336 *e-mail* louisebloom@cix.co.uk

BOAD, Sarah Elizabeth Chair ALDC *b* Feb 22, 1958 *m* Alan 1987 1 *d* Claire 1999 1 *s* Simon 2003 *education* Monmouth School for Girls 1966-76; Univ College of Swansea 1976-79 (BSc Metallurgy): CEng MIMMM 1986 CSci 2005 *career* Morganite Electrical Carbon Ltd, Swansea 1980-86; Dunlop Aviation, Coventry 1986-91; national co-ordinator, mbrship development exec (responsible for local branches, increasing mbrship) Institute of Materials, Institute of Materials Minerals and Mining 1991- *party* joined SDP 1982; founder mbr Liberal Democrats 1988; mbr LLiw Valley BC 1986-87; mbr Warwick DC 1987-99, gp leader 1989-99; mbr Warwickshire CC 1994- , deputy gp leader; mbr Royal Leamington Spa Town Council 2002- ; PPC Warwick and Leamington 1992; mbr FCC 1992- ; mbr ALDC Standing Cttee 1988- , chair 1996-2001, 2004- ; mbr WLD, LDO, ALDES, LDEA *special interests* local govt, early years education (mbr policy paper working gps); maternity services, equal opportunities, especially for women *recreations* spending time with her children *publications* You Can do It (ALDC) *address* 33 Parklands Avenue, Royal Leamington Spa, Warwickshire CV32 7BH *tel* 01926 339822 *fax* 01926 423683 *e-mail* sarah@boad.me.uk

BODDY, Nigel *b* Feb 17, 1959 Darlington *education* Northumbria Univ 1992 (law degree, postgraduate in legal practice); Northumbria Univ 1997 (solicitors exams) *career* company director 1983-87; Civil Servant 1987-95; solicitor admitted 1999, currently working on defending criminal cases and other high street solicitor services in Middlesbrough; one of a large family of north country solicitors *party* PPC Hartlepool 2001 (sought, unsuccessfully, re-selection for 2004 by-election); European PPC Northern Regional list 2004; currently preparing Sedgefield constituency in case of by-election should Tony Blair decide to resign; former branch chair Darlington; parliamentary researcher, Edinburgh (for two MSPs, MP) after opening of new Scottish Parliament (his warnings about cost over-runs on Scottish Parliament Building went unheeded) *special interests* education (Save Hurworth School Campaign, Save Queen Elizabeth College Campaign, Save Darlington College Campaign), environment (Ghost Ships Campaign), law, crime, economics, social security and benefits (Save the Neville Parade Post Office Campaign), NHS (Save Hartlepool Hospital Campaign); family has long tradition of public service: maternal aunt Wendy Monro-Crichton worked for 'The Control Commission Austria 1945 to 1948' and knew Stalin Kruschev and Gromyko, went on to teach journalists at Napier Univ; maternal grandfather, Tommy Harrison (as a lad of 17) took part in famous World War 1 military engagement in Hartlepool when German ships shelled the town; Nigel's mother Jennifer Boddy aided the introduction of comprehensive education in home town of Darlington; his cousin, Sam Watson, was president Durham Miners Union , member Labour Party, and who persuaded Aneurin Bevan to make a speech to 1957 Labour conference when Bevan made now-famous "naked into the conference chamber" line; another Watson cousin was a Labour MP in Scotland; second-cousin Gertrude Bell worked for Foreign Office in the 1920s and drew the map of Iraq out of old Ottoman Empire; her father, Nigel's cousin, Sir Hugh Bell, founded the steel industry on Teesside and built North Yorkshire County Hall *recreations* swimming *address* 14 Fife Road, Darlington *tel* 01325 465043 home 07730 511659 mobile *e-mail* nigel_boddy@hotmail.com

BONE, Emma Jane *b* Feb 25, 1972 Rossendale, Lancs *single education* BA (Hons) Philosophy *career* constituency organiser/ researcher Lembit Opik MP, Mick Bates AM, and Montgomeryshire Liberal Democrats 2005- ; computer programmer in Direct Mail industry, experience in IT, both programming and helpdesk support, customer services, administration, project coordination and business analysis *party* current PPC Filton and Bradley Stoke (Western Counties); PPC Huddersfield 2005 *special interests* environment, education, small businesses *recreations* reading, sewing, gardening, and delivering!! *Style* Miss *address* 14 Savages Wood Road, Bradley Stoke BS32 *tel* 07977016509 *e-mail* info@fabslibdems.org.uk *web* www.fabslibdems.org.uk

BONES, Christopher John *b* Jun 12, 1958 *m* Gail 1s 1d *education* Dulwich College, London; Aberdeen Univ; Manchester Business School *career* Shell Petroleum Company, 1982-87, Diageo plc, 1987-99 including spells of working in USA, Hong Kong: various roles most notably, HR director UDV Europe, gp compensation and benefits director; gp organisation effectiveness and development director (reporting to main board responsible for organisation development and design, change management, culture, Exec education and learning and development) Cadbury Schweppes plc 1999- *party* joined SDP 1981; founding president SDP Students 1981-82; chair West Cheshire SDP 1985-86; fought various local election campaigns; joined Liberal Democrats in 1993; Exec mbr Oxford East Liberal Democrats 2000; speechwriter for David Owen 1987 General Election, Paddy Ashdown 1997 General Election; mbr Liberty Network 2004 *special interests* industry, education, training *other mbrships* Fellow, Royal Society of Arts; Fellow, Chartered Institute of Personnel and Development; regular lecturer in HR strategy and leadership, Henley Management College *recreations* theatre, gardening *publications* The Self-Reliant Manager (Routledge 1994); monthly columnist *HR Magazine address* The Thatched Cottage, 2, Mill Lane, Iffley, Oxford OX1 4EJ *tel* 01865 711453 home 02078305063 business *fax* 01865 711481 *e-mail* chris.bones@csplc.com

BONHAM CARTER, Baroness (Jane) *b* Oct 20, 1957 *education* St Paul's Girls' School; Univ College London *career* television producer Ten Alps/ Brooke Lapping Productions; Director of Communications Liberal Democrats 1996-98; editor Channel 4's *A Week in Politics* for 1993-96; producer BBC's *Panorama, Newsnight party* mbr Campaigns and Communications Cttee; Advisory Board Centre Forum *other interests* Rehabilitation for Addicted Prisoners Trust; council mbr Britain in Europe *address* House of Lords, London SW1A 0PW

BONKERS, 38th Lord cr 1067 (Rutland); Grand Cross of Rutland (with oak leaves) OM, PC, MC, *s* of 37th Lord, Ambassador of Rutland to the Court of St James, Lib Dem spokesman on outer space in the House of Lords *b* St Pancras Day 18__ *education* Uppingham; Univ of Rutland at Belvoir; hon. degrees Oxford, Cambridge, Samarkand, Harvard, St Petersburg, Sorbonne *m.* First Lady Bonkers (Harlequins and England) 1905 *heir* Viscount Barking *career* statesman, soldier, diplomat, philosopher, traveller, industrialist, author, philanthropist, all-round Good Egg *party* chair Rutland Young Liberals 1892-1905; MP Rutland South-West 1906-10, Cllr (Bonkers Hall Ward) 1910-, Liberal and Lib Dem spokesman on numerous subjects1910-, unsuccessful candidate for leadership in the Lords 1997 *publications* 102 volumes of *Memoirs* from 1902, *Thoughts on Free Trade* (1906), *The Glory of the British Constitution* (1910), *The Case for Electoral Reform* (1911), *An End to War* (1914), *The Coming Prosperity* (1929), *Edward the Great, Our New King* (1936), *An End to War,* second edition (1939), *The Death of Socialism* (1944), *The Death of Conservatism* (1950), *Jo Grimond: Our Next Prime Minister* (1963), *Jeremy Thorpe: Our Next Prime Minister* (1969), *David Steel* (1982), *Paddy Ashplant: Our Next Prime Minister* (1996), *Charles Kennedy: Our Next Prime Minister* (2001), *The Party Above Scandal* (2005), *Ming Campbell: Our Next Prime Minister* (2006) *special interests* **Editor's note:** *ENTRIES SUBMITTED UNDER THIS HEADING DELETED ON LEGAL ADVICE recreations* cricket, reading *Liberator*, firing ink pellets at Lord Steel of Aikwood *clubs* MCC, NLC, Reform, Rutland County Cricket, Harpo's, Mashie-Niblick *style* The 38th Lord Bonkers *address* Bonkers Hall, Rutland *tel* Rutland 7 *website* www.lordbonkers.com

BOWLES, Sharon Margaret MEP *b* Jun 12, 1953 *m* Andrew Horton 2 *s education* Our Lady's Convent, Abingdon; Reading Univ; Oxford Univ *career* European patent and trade mark attorney *party* joined 1986; mbr Federal Exec; PPC

Aylesbury 1992, 1997; PEPC Buckinghamshire and Oxford East 1994, third on SE Region European List 2000, 2005; became MEP for SE Region May 2005; co-chair International Relations Cttee; vice president ELDR Party (Bureau); vice chair British Gp, Liberal International; vice chair (science) and co-founder ALDES *special interests* European, international affairs, science and technology, small businesses *other mbrships* Anti-Slavery International; National Liberal Club *recreations* music, sport *address* Broadway House, Bourne End, Hemel Hempstead, Hertfordshire HP1 2RU *tel* 01442 876561 *e-mail* bowles@powernet.co.uk

BOYLE, David Courtney *b* May 20, 1958 *m* Sarah Burns 1 *s* Robin born Jul 15, 2004 *education* Clifton College, Bristol; Trinity College, Oxford (philosophy and theology); Harlow Technical College (NCTJ journalism) *career* reporter *Oxford Star* newspaper 1981-5; editor *Town & Country Planning* magazine 1985-8; head of development Rapide Productions (making TV documentaries) 1988-91; roving freelance writing getting what work possible, including: rewriting signs on Sainsbury's petrol pumps 1992, associate producer Channel 4 schools series *Time Capsule* 1993, editing Shandwick's European newsletter 1994, representing New Economics Foundation at G7 summit in Nova Scotia 1995, training in business writing, Das Island in Persian Gulf 1996, writing Comic Relief's annual report 1997, Uzbekistan editor for *CIS Today* magazine 1998, co-founder *Ethical Performance* 1999, mbr of Downing Street review of volunteering policy 2000, co-founder of Time Banks UK 2001, co-founder of London Time Bank 2002; senior associate New Economics Foundation 1999- , and author; editor *New Economics* 1988-98, *Radical Economics* 1999- , *New Democrat* 1989-91, *Liberal Democrat News* 1992-8; occasional contributor to *New Statesman,* and other rags *party* signed up by Dermot Roaf in Oxford during 1979 general election; local election agent Oxford 1982-5, Oxford W and Abingdon Liberal exec 1982-5; secy Alliance 'shadow city council' 1983-5; wrote Oxfordshire county election manifesto 1985; co-founder joint Liberal Ecology Gp/SDP Greens magazine *Challenge*; Liberal Assembly press office team 1986-7, Federal Policy Cttee (1998-), PPC Regents Park & Kensington N 2001; mbr Meeting the Challenge review gp 2005- ; *other mbrships* Green Lib Dems, Folklore Society, Royal Society of Arts, TCPA *publications* *Building Futures* (1989), *What is New Economics?* (1993), *World War II: A Photographic History* (1998), *Funny Money: In Search of Alternative Cash* (1999), *Why London Needs its Own Currency* (2000), *Virtual Currencies* (FT report 2001), *The Tyranny of Numbers* (2001), *The Money Changers* (2002), *Authenticity: Brands, Fakes, Spin and the Lust for Real Life* (2003), *The Little Money Book* (2003), *Blondel's Song: The capture and imprisonment of Richard the Lionheart* (2005) *special interests* time banks and co-production, future of money, currently writing book about John Cabot; award-winner Observer/Arvon poetry competition; Winston Churchill Fellow (both 1996) *recreations* piano, walking, talking in restaurants *address* 56 Dale Park Road, Crystal Palace, London SE19 3TY *tel* 020 8653 3845 *email* dcboyle@gmail.com *web* www.david-boyle.co.uk

BRACK, Duncan MSc **Chair, Federal Conference Cttee** *b* Jan 24 1960 *education* George Watson's College, Edinburgh; Hertford College; Oxford Univ (BA, pol & econ); Birkbeck College, Univ of London (MSc politics & administration) *career* research assistant LPO 1984, David Alton MP 1985, Archy Kirkwood MP 1985-87; parliamentary officer, RCN 1987-88; director of policy, Liberal Democrats 1988-94; senior research fellow, Chatham House (Royal Institute of International Affairs)

1995-98, Head Sustainable Development Programme, Chatham House, 1998-2003, Associate Fellow, Chatham House, 2003- ; freelance researcher, writer and editor 2003- ; *party* v chair ULS 1983-84; v chair Liberal Information Network (LINk) 1984-88; chair Lib Dem History Gp 1993-99; Editor, *Journal of Liberal History* 1993- ; Federal Conference Cttee 1995- , v-chair 1997-2003, chair 2003- ; v-chair 'Meeting the Challenge' policy review working gp 2005-06; mbr various working gps on environment, energy and trade policy *publications* include *Why I am a Liberal Democrat* (ed Lib Dem Publications 1996), 'Liberal Democrat Policy' in *The Liberal Democrats* (Don MacIver, ed Harvester Wheatsheaf 1997); *Dictionary of Liberal Biography* (ed Politico's Publishing 1998); *Dictionary of Liberal Quotations* (ed Politico's Publishing 1999); *Great Liberal Speeches* (ed Politico's Publishing 2001); *Trading for the Future: Reforming the WTO* (with Nick Clegg MEP, Centre Forum 2001); *International Trade and the Montreal Protocol* (Chatham House 1996); *Trade and Environment: Conflict or Compatibility?* (ed Chatham House 1998); *International Trade and Climate Change Policies* (Chatham House 1999); *Trade, Investment and Environment* (with Halina Ward ed Chatham House 1999), *Prime Minister Portillo...and Other Things that Never Happened* (ed with Iain Dale Politico's Publishing, 2003), *Multilateral Environmental Agreements and the WTO* (Chatham House, with Kevin Gray, 2003), *Controlling Imports of Illegal Timber: Options for Europe* (Chatham House and FERN, with Chantal Marijnissen and Saskia Ozinga, 2002); many papers and book chapters on trade and environment issues, and international environmental crime *recreations* theatre, music, cinema, bridge, ice-skating, swimming *address* 38 Salford Road, London SW2 4BQ *tel* 020 8674 0612 *e-mail* duncan@dbrack.org.uk

BRADSHAW, Lord Professor William (Bill) BA MA: Life Peer cr 1999: Lords Spokesperson on Transport *b* Sept 9, 1936 *education* Slough GS; Univ of Reading *career* BR management trainee 1959, various appointments London, West divisions; divisional manager Liverpool 1973; chief operating manager LMR 1976; deputy GM 1977; Chief Ops Manager BR HQ 1978; director Policy Unit 1980; GM Western Region BR 1983-85; senior Visiting Research Fellow, Centre for Socio-Legal Studies, Fellow, Wolfson College, Oxford 1985-2002; Honorary Fellow Wolfson College, Oxford 2004- ; Professor of Transport Management,, Univ of Salford 1986-92; chairman Ulster Bus and Citybus Ltd 1987-93; non-Exec director Lothian Regional Transport 1997-2000; special adviser HoC Select Cttee 1992-97; chairman Bus Appeals Cttee 1998-2000; mbr board British Railways 1999-2001; mbr Commission for Integrated Transport 1999-2001 *party* chair Transport panel 1994; mbr Oxfordshire County Council 1993- ; v chair Thames Valley Police Authority 1997- ; chair Oxfordshire GTE (promoting guided bus system in county) *recreations* growing hardy perennials, playing mbr brass band *address* House of Lords, London SW1A 0PW

BRAKE, Thomas Anthony MP (Carshalton and Wallington maj: 1,068) **Shadow Secy for International Development** *b* Melton Mowbray, Leicestershire May 6, 1962 *m* Candida Goulden 1 *s* 1 *d education* Lycee International, Paris; Imperial College, London; speaks fluent French, conversational Portuguese, Russian *career* senior consultant IT, Cap Gemini; MP for Carshalton and Wallington 1997- *party* joined 1983 to help William Goodhart, then Alliance candidate North Kensington; Cllr LB of Hackney 1988-90; Cllr LB of Sutton 1994-98; mbr environment policy working gp that produced *Costing the Earth;* PPC Carshalton and Wallington 1992 (reduced Tory majority by nearly 4,500), 1997 (elected and overturned 10,000 majority), 2001 (re-elected with increased majority); mbr parliamentary environment team, special responsibility for transport in London, water, land-use and planning and aviation 1997-2001; shadow transport minister 2001-03; shadow secy of state international development 2003-05; shadow secy of state transport 2005-06; shadow minister local govt 2006- ; environment select Cttee 1997-2001; accommodation and works Cttee 2001- ; mbr Transport Select Cttee 2001-03; president Air Safety Gp; mbr Franco-British Parliamentary Relations Gp; mbr All-party Parliamentary Gp on Human Rights *special interests* foreign affairs, transport, environment *other mbrships* Amnesty International, Greenpeace, Oxfam *recreations* running *address* House of Commons, London SW1A 0AA *tel* 020 8647 9329 home 020 8255 8155 business *fax* 020 8395 4453 *e-mail* info@tombrake.co.uk

BREED, Colin MP (Cornwall South East maj: 6,507**) Shadow Treasury Spokesperson** *b* May 4, 1947 London *education* Torquay GS *m* Barbara Jane 3 *s* Matthew, Nicholas, Jonathan 1 *d* Deborah *career* manager, Midland Bank 17 years working throughout Devon, Cornwall (youngest manager, area office Plymouth); post in venture capital, then merchant banking; proprietor small distribution business (which enabled him to nurse constituency) 1992-97; MP 1997- *party* town, district Cllr 1982-92; Mayor of Saltash 1989 and 1995; PPC SE Cornwall 1997 (elected), 2001 (re-elected; mbr of Trade and Industry parliamentary team 1997-2001; Shadow Minister of Agriculture and Rural Affairs 2001-03; mbr European Scrutiny Select Cttee 2006- ; Radioactive Waste sub Cttee; treasurer All-party Cricket Gp *other interests* mbr General Medical Council; co-chair of CAABU, Council for Arab British Understanding; local Methodist preacher *publications* *Roots to Recovery* (on future of rural Britain) 2000; *Checking out the Supermarkets* (on profitability) 2001 *recreations* golf, watching sport *address* House of Commons, London SW1A 0AA; Barras Street, Liskeard, Cornwall PL14 6AD *tel* 01579 344 577 *fax* 01579 347 019 *e-mail* breedc@parliament.uk *web:* www.colinbreed.org.uk

BRETTLE, Rob *b* Sept 18, 1963 Manchester *party* joined Liberal Democrats 1998; previously mbr Liberal Party; mbr Manchester Gorton LP, North West Region; vice-chair Manchester City Party 2004-05; mbr Manchester City Party Candidates Cttee 2003- ; secy Manchester Gorton LP 2005-; secy Manchester Blackley LP 2001-04; secy North Warwickshire Liberal Assoc 1981-1989; mbr Regional Candidates Cttee 2002- ; accredited Returning Officer; mbr Liberal Party National Exec 1988-1989; candidate North Warwickshire BC, Atherstone South, 1983; Manchester City Council, Moston, 2002; Manchester City Council, Harpurhey, 2003; Manchester City Council, Fallowfield, 2004 (30 votes short); mbr ALDC, DELGA; Liberal International British Gp, Green Liberal Democrats, Agents & Organisers Association, Atherstone Liberal Club, Liberal Democrat Friends of Somaliland *other mbrships* Manchester Friends of the Earth, Friends of Platt Fields (Manchester), Secy Christian Mission Historical Association, Shareholder in Friends of the Earth (Birmingham) Ltd, Vice-Chair National Federation of Bus Users 1986-1988; Laird of Camster *special interests* buses & bus services, electoral reform/STV, church history, Somaliland, Commonwealth Games, amateur vexillologist *recreations* travelling, steam trains, collecting Commonwealth Games ephemera, choral singing *address* 56 Kingsbridge Court, Kingbridge Road, Manchester, M9 5SW *tel* 0161 202 4622 *e-mail* rob@fallowfield-libdems.org.uk

BRIGHT, Ruth Kathleen *b* Jan 28, 1967 *m* Diccon Bright.1 *d* Orla *education* Alton College, Hants; London School of Economics (BSc Econ Govt) *career* Age Concern 1992-2001; project manger, Advice Service for Carers of people with Alzheimer's *party* joined Liberal Party at LSE 1985; Southwark Cllr 1994-2002, deputy gp leader 1999-2002; PPC Eat Hants 2002- *special interests* health, social services, Russia , Central and Eastern Europe *other mbrships* Parkinson's Disease Society; Alzheimer's Society; Gp b Strep Support (national charity tp raise awareness of Gp b Strep, infection that can kill or disable newborn babies) *recreations* playing with the baby! *address* 6 Greenfields Avenue, Alton, Hants, GU34 2ED *tel/fax* 01420 590317 *e-mail* ruthkbright@hotmail.com

BRINTON, Sarah Virginia (Sal) *b* Jan 4, 1955 *m* Tim Whittaker 2 *s* 1 *d* 2 *wards education* Churchill College, Cambridge (BA, MA Cantab) 1981-84; Anglia Polytechnic Univ (PhD Hon) 2003 *career* floor manager BBC Radio, TV 1974-81; Venture Capitalist 1984-1992; bursar Selwyn, Lucy Cavendish Colleges, Cambridge 1992-2002; board mbr East of England Development Agency 1998-2004, deputy chair 2001-04; chair Cambridgeshire Learning and Skills Council 1999-06; IDeA senior peer Clearing House; training consultant; Exec Director Association of Universities of the East of England 2006- ; East Anglian Businesswoman of the Year 1997; finalist in Mid Anglia Businesswoman of the Year 1995,1996, 2000; National Training Awards judge 2002- ; non-exec Director, Univ for Learning (Learndirect), St Johns Innovation Centre Ltd, Christian Blind Mission UK *party* joined 1974; PPC SE Cambridgeshire 1997, 2001, Watford 2005 (re-selected 2006); Cambridgeshire County Cllr 1993-2004; education spokesperson 1993-97, gp leader/leader of the opposition 1997-2004; mbr FPC and FCC 2006- ; mbr education and higher education working party 1994-97; party trainer; mbr PCA (past vice chair), WLD, ALDC, LDCF *special interests* education and skills, HE, economic development, local Govt *other mbrships* Institute of Directors *address* 9 Fairlawns, Langley Road, Watford, WD17 4UH *tel* 01023 238552 home 07768 821187 mobile *e-mail* salbrinton@cix.co.uk

BROMLEY, Nicholas John (Nick) *b* Mar 11, 1957 *m* Helen (nee Derry) 1 *s* Hugo *education* Wellington College, Berkshire 1970-75; MA (hons) English Language and Literature, Oxford University 1978; Diploma in Law, Polytechnic of Central London 1980; called to the Bar 1981; qualified mediator, Centre for Effective Dispute Resolution 2003 *career* practised briefly at the Bar, took civil service exams 1983; worked for Department of Social Security, Department of Health and HM Treasury until 1996; Private Secretary to Minister for Social Security and the Disabled 1998; director of health research for the Centre for Reform 2000-2005; *party* joined 1998; candidate in district and county elections; branch chair, mbr LP exec; mbr Health Working Group 1999-2000, Public Services Working Group (Huhne Commission) 2001-02; PPC Waveney 2005 election *special interests* health reform, social security reform, European Union, public spending control, civil liberties, dispute resolution *other mbrships* trustee Charles Dickens Museum, London, trustee of the Beccles Regeneration Partnership, chairman of parish council *recreations* riding (horses and bikes), walking, fencing, collecting books and prints *publications Funding Federalism* 1999; *Universal Access – Individual Choice: International Lessons for the NHS* 2001, *What Makes Hospitals Successful?* 2004, *Online Pharmacy Patient Choice or Peril?*, published by Centre for Reform (now

CentreForum) www.centreforum.org *address* Shadingfield Hall, Shadingfield, near Beccles, Suffolk, NR34 8DE *tel* 01502 575660 *e-mail* bromleian@aol.com

BROOKE, Annette MP (Mid Dorset & North Poole maj: 5,482**) Shadow Spokesperson, Children, Young People and Families** *b* Jun 7, 1947 *m* Mike 2 *d education* Romford Technical School; London School of Economics (BSc Hons Economics); Hughes Hall, Cambridge (Certificate of Education) *career* partner with geologist husband in consultancy trading in minerals and gemstones; teacher; lecturer (economics) Open Univ *party* mbr Poole BC 1986- , chair Planning Cttee 1991-96, chair Education Cttee 1996-2000; Mayor of Poole 1997-98; lead mbr for Education, board mbr Dorset Careers, vice chair Poole Town Centre Management Board; PPC Mid Dorset and Poole 2001 (elected), 2005 (re-elected); spokesperson for Children, Young People and Families 2006- ; Education spokesperson 2005-06; spokesperson for Children 2004-05; Deputy Whip 2001-04; spokesperson, Home Affairs Team 2001-04 *specialist interests* discrimination, committed to fighting for equality of opportunity; campaigns for equal treatment on concessionary bus fares for senior citizens, people with disabilities; passionate about improving opportunities for children, adults with special needs *other mbrships* RSPB, Wessex-Newfoundland Society, Poole Local Agenda 21 *recreations* gym, reading and shopping with daughters *address* House of Commons, London SW1A 0AA constituency Broadstone Liberal Hall, 14 York Road, Broadstone, Dorset BH18 8ET *tel* 01202 693 555 *e-mail* brookea@parliament.uk *web* www.annettebrookemp.org

BROOKE, Eric William *b* Mar 23, 1971 *education* St Giles College (Sep 2001) TESOL, Univ of Hertfordshire 1992-96 (computer science, information systems); Exeter College 1991-92 (A levels) *career* Cornwall County Councillor (Newquay North) and Cabinet Mbr (Community Services) May 2005- ; Dan Rogerson's Organiser Nov 2004-Jul 2005; Campaign officer Hartlepool Sep 04-Nov 04; campaign team leader Consumers' Association-*Which?* 2002-03; creative consultant Make Stuff Happen June 2002-Aug 02; head of campaigns National Canine Defence League Oct 2001-Feb 02; campaign adviser Strategy Public Relations Aug 2001-Sep 01; communications consultant Action for Blind People Jun 2001-Aug 01; General Election manager (Wales) Liberal Democrats Mar 2001-Jun 01; campaigns adviser NSPCC Nov 99-Mar 01; National Exec mbr NUS 1998-99; president Univ of Hertfordshire Students' Union 1996-98; governor Univ of Hertfordshire 1996-98; information system consultant, Pure Imagination Ltd 1994-95; accredited national trainer NUS 1992-98 *party* joined March 1999; communications co-ordinator Welsh Assembly1999; GE manager Wales 2001; PPC 2001; *Final Flourish* co-coordinator, Leader's Tour office 2001; party trainer *special interests* creativity, Spanish, education, environment, economy, Europe, IT, young people *other mbrships* Friends of Earth, Amnesty International, PADI, Project AWARE, British Mountaineering Council, YHA *recreations* diving, hiking, climbing, cooking *e-mail* ericbrooke@mac.com

BROPHY, Jane Elisabeth *b* Aug 27, 1963 *m* 2 *s* 1 *d education* Chorlton High School, Manchester 1972-79; Alsager Comprehensive, Cheshire 1979-81; Univ of Leeds (Biochemistry BSc Hons) 1984; Leeds Metropolitan Univ (Nutrition and Dietetics, post-grad diploma) 1987 *career* allied NHS health professional (dietician) 1987-88; campaigner, researcher *Save the Ozone Layer* United Nations Association 1988-89; parliamentary press assistant Lib Dems1989-90; nutritionist, research &

information manager The Vegetarian Society UK 1990-94; expert witness on nutrition "McLibel Case" 1996; health promotion advisor (CHD) NHS Salford & Trafford Health Authority 1994-98, special educational needs programme co-ordinator 1998-2002; chief officer South Manchester NHS CHC May 2002-Sept 2003; five a day co-ordinator, Oldham Primary Care Trust Sept 2003- *party* joined Liberals 1985; last chair Young Liberals, co-chair new SLD youth organisation 1987-88; vice-chair Green (Liberal) Democrats 1988-91; chair Liberal Democrat Animal Protection Gp 1991-94; mbr Federal Policy Cttee 1989-90; mbr Federal Conference Cttee 1990-91; mbr environment, sustainable development, health, animal protection, genetic engineering federal policy gps 1980s, 1990s; wrote, moved Federal Conference motions, policy papers on animal protection, genetic engineering 1990-91; vice-chair Altrincham and Sale West LP 2003; mbr (Village Ward) Trafford MBC 1994-98, 2003- , deputy gp leader *special interests* food policy, nutrition, science, public health, health care, NHS, education (special needs interventions for autism, Aspergers, ADHD); local Govt; voluntary, statutory sectors partnership; environment, recycling, global warming, transport other *mbrships* PEACH (Parents for the Early Intervention of Autism in Children); ALDC; National Childbirth Trust; WLD; LGA; Green Liberal Democrats *recreations* family, social activities, music, walking in countryside; reading, cinema, internet *publications* nutrition consultant *Baby & Child Vegetarian Recipes* (Ebury Press), and *The World in Your Kitchen* (New Internationalist) *address*.22 Meadow Bank, Timperley, Altrincham, Cheshire WA15 6QP *tel* 0161 962 7107 home 07968 566572 mobile *e-mail* jane.brophy@bigfoot.com or jane@brophys.com or jane.brophy@trafford.gov.uk

BROWN, Keith John Esquire, JP FBDO AMIOP SMC *b* Jun 21, 1949 *education* Forest Hill School; City and East London College; Univ of London *career* ocularist, Moorfields Eye Hospital 1970, Kent Co-Ophthalmic and Aural Hospital, Maidstone 1973, Kent and Sussex Hospital, Tunbridge Wells 1975; private practice: Brown Poole & Partners, Tunbridge Wells 1972, Brown and GiMpel Southborough 1979; Hawkhurst, Southborough, Maidstone, W Malling 1981; consultant ocularist, Keelers Cromwell Hospital 1984; Trotters, Edinburgh 1986; Dolland and Aitchinson Gp 1987; Chaucer Hospital Canterbury 1988; BUPA Hospital, Hastings 1998 *party* chair Cranbrook and District, PPC Tonbridge and Malling 1997, Tunbridge Wells 2001; mbr Tunbridge Wells BC 1994-98; chair, Hawkhurst Parish Council 1992-98, mbr DELGA *special interests* Stonewall; Freeman City of London; fdr fellow British Association of Dispensing Opticians 1986 *recreations* cooking, walking, vintage public transport vehicles *clubs* NLC, Town House *address* Linnet House, Cranbrook Road, Hawkhurst Kent TN18 4AX *tel* 01580 754253 home 01580 753668 business *fax* 01580 754254 *e-mail* mail@keithbrown.info

BROWN, Philip James: Chair, Perth Liberal Democrats *b* Dec 14, 1966 *m* Gwynneth (née Edwards) Sept 3, 1993 2 *d education* Highdown Comprehensive, Reading; Leicester Univ (BA, Geography), *career* systems administrator, Wellcome Trust 1998-2003; Regional Organiser, Mid-Scotland and Fife Liberal Democrats 2003-04; Regional Administrator, Capability Scotland 2004- ; *party* mbr LDO, ASLDC, Convener, Perth Liberal Democrats 2005- ; Mid-Scotland & Fife Region Exec; Perth & Kinross Council candidate, May 2007 *special interests* information technology *recreations* football, ska *address* 34 Woodside Crescent, Craigie, Perth

PH2 0EW *tel* 01738 783656 home 07812 839396 mobile *e-mail* philip007brown@clara.co.uk

BROWN, Robert MSP Glasgow Regional list *b* Dec 25, 1947 *m* Gwen 1 *s* 1*d* *education* The Gordon Schools, Huntly 1959-65; Aberdeen Univ (LLB 1st Class Hons) 1969 *career* solicitor, senior civil partner Ross Harper & Murphy; Glasgow councillor 1977-92; mbr of Scottish Parliament 1999- *party* treasurer, secretary, chair Aberdeen Univ Liberal Society 1966-89; secy, Aberdeen Liberals 1969-71; PPC Glasgow Rutherglen 1974, 1979, 1983, 1987, 1997, 1999, 2003; councillor, Glasgow District 1977-92; leader, Liberal Democrat Gp 1977-92; member, Scottish party exec; vice-chair, Scottish party policy cttee 1995- ; campaign organiser, Greater Glasgow Liberal Democrats 1997- ; responsible for Scottish manifesto 1997, 1999, 2001, 2003; elected Scottish Parliament, Glasgow Regional list 1999; communities, housing spokesperson 1999-2003; Convener, Scottish Party policy cttee 2003- ; mbr Scottish Lib Dem negotiating team May 2003; education, young people spokesperson 2003-05; convenor Scottish Parliament cttee for education and young people 2003-05; Deputy Minister for Education and Young People 2005- ; *special interests* human rights, housing *other mbrships* Law Society of Scotland; chairman Rutherglen and Cambuslang CAB 1993-99; president Overtoun Park Bowling Club 1977- ; *recreations* history; science fiction *address* The Scottish Parliament, Edinburgh, EH99 1SP *tel* 0141 243 2421 *fax* 0141 243 2451 *e-mail* robert.brown.msp@scottish.parliament.uk *web* www.robertbrownmsp.org.uk

BROWNE, Jeremy MP (Taunton maj: 573**)** *b* May 17, 1970 *m* Charlotte *education* Nottingham Univ (Politics); elected President of Students' Union *career* financial consultancy with Dewe Rogerson, Edelman Communications Worldwide and ReputationInc, specialising in corporate reputation management *party* personal assistant to Alan Beith MP 1993; PPC Enfield Southgate 1997, Taunton 2005 (elected); Director of Press and Broadcasting working with Paddy Ashdown and Charles Kennedy; spokesman on Foreign Affairs 2005- ; *special interests* education (Governor at Ladymead Community School) *other mbrships* Advisory Board of Reform think-tank *recreations* travel; sports: football (Queens Park Rangers), rugby and cricket; restaurants; walking

BRUCE, Malcolm MP (Gordon maj:11,026**)** *b* Nov 17, 1944 *education* Wrekin College, Shropshire; St Andrew's Univ (Hons Graduate, Economics and Politics); Strathclyde Univ (MSc Marketing); barrister (Gray's Inn) *m* 2 May 23, 1998 Rosemary Vetterlein 2 *d* 1 *s*, and 1 *s* 1 *d* (from previous marriage) *career* journalism (*Liverpool Daily Echo*); commerce (Boots, the Chemist); local Govt (NE Scotland Development Authority), 1981-84 established, with partner, Aberdeen Petroleum Publishing (producing weekly newsletter, *Aberdeen Petroleum Report*, reference book on North Sea, *Scottish Petroleum Annual*) *party* joined Liberals 1962; president Univ Liberal Club, St Andrew's Univ; founder mbr Social and Liberal Democrats 1988; PPC North Angus 1974, West Aberdeenshire 1979, Gordon 1983 (elected); re-elected 1987, 1992, 1997, 2001; 1983-85 parliamentary spksn Scottish Affairs; 1985-87; Energy 1987; 1987-88 Trade and Industry; 1988-90 Natural Resources (Energy and Conservation); 1988-92 leader Scottish Liberal Democrats; 1990-92 Scottish Affairs; 1992-94 Trade and Industry; 1994-99 Front Bench spksn The Treasury; candidate for party leadership 1999; chair Parliamentary Party 1999-2001; Shadow Secy of State, Department of Food, Rural Affairs and Agriculture (DEFRA)

2001-02; Shadow Secy of State, Trade and Industry 2003-05; mbr Parliamentary Assembly, Council of Europe 1999- ; president, Scottish Liberal Democrats 2000- *other interests* Rector of Dundee Univ 1986-89; national vice-president National Deaf Children's Society, president Grampian branch *recreations* theatre, music, walking *address* House of Commons, London, SW1A 0AA *tel* 020 7219 6233 and 01467 623413 (constituency) *fax* 020 7219 2334 and 01467 624 944 **(constituency)** *e-mail* brucem@parliament.uk *web* www.malcolmbruce.libdems.org.uk

BRUCE, Rosemary *b* Jan 19, 1972 *education* Newstead Wood School for Girls; Univ of Dundee *m* Malcolm Bruce MP *qv* 1998 1 *d* Catriona *b* Sept 15 1 *s* Alasdair *b* Mar 14 2002 *career* asst mngr Toby restaurant, Beckenham; PA to director of marketing *Financial I* 1996-98; PA to managing director, DC Gardner 1998-99, both part of Euromoney Publications plc; office manager, diary secy to Malcolm Bruce MP 1999- *party* chair Scottish YLDs 1993-95; former Exec mbr London region; Exec mbr PCA 1997-98; PPC Beckenham 1997 (twice GE, by-election); campaign officer Gordon 2004-*special interests* provision of education, training; getting more women, young people involved in politics *recreations* listening, playing music, theatre, reading, swimming, walking *address* Grove Cottage, 7 Grove Terrace, Torphins, Banchory, Kincardineshire AB31 4HJ *tel* 013398 89120 *fax* 013398 82656 *e-mail* brucer@parliament.uk

BUCKLEY CARPENTER, Diana Fay *b* Nov 1, 1949 *d* of naval WW2 hero *m* 1 racing driver 1 *d* Amy 1 *s* William *m* 2 chiropractor 2 *d* Misty, Suki *education* Farlington, Sussex, excelled in acting, poetry, sport and all things that evaded prep; Central School of Speech and Drama, winning Rodney Millington Award for best actress, from *Spotlight* (casting directory) *career* acting in theatre, film, television; "resting" in London's famous and fashionable watering holes, attending on the rich and famous; former proprietor interior horticultural firm, servicing London's premier businesses; employment consultant (set up City's first industrial agency); account director, training information and IT learning management systems; instructional officer teaching drama in young offenders institution *party* elected Earley Town Council 1987; Wokingham DC 1994 various chairs; council chair 1996, vice-Chair 1995; various police consultative gps; Learning and Skills Partnership; unitary cabinet mbr, community safety & social Inclusion 2001/02; school gov; Community Health Council, mbr, Crime and Policing working gp 1995-96 and advisor 2001; Chiltern Region policy gp 1996-97; LP chair 2000/2; vice-chair 2002/4; secy PCA 2003-04 *special interests* young people, crime prevention, drugs *other mbrships* British Actors Equity, Public & Commercial Services Union *recreations* writing, art, film, upholstery and soft furnishings *publications* in the making (beware!) *address* 8 Stanton Close, Earley, nr Reading, Berks *tel* 0118 926 7302 mobile 07887 502646 *e-mail* Diana49@tiscali.co.uk or bestmoomy@hotmail.com

BUCKLITSCH, Peter James *b* Jan 30, 1949 *m* Rosalyn 1 *s* Charles 1 *d* Karensa *education* King's College School, Wimbledon; Fellow, Institute of Financial Accountants; Mbr British Computer Society *career* started as articled clerk, moved into computers 1985; ran own law stationery company alongside Plan Computers 'until the wretched John Major destroyed the economy and my business' 1990; started again with document imaging company, Open Systems & Imaging Ltd, selling mainly to MoD; moved company into record management systems, currently UK distributors for Worklift Record Management software *party* joined 1990; Cllr

Mayfield ward 1995-99; vice chair (personnel) 1995-97, chair IT Panel 1995-99; Exec mbr Wealden LP 1994-2003, vice chair 1998-2003; lost local election (Jarvis Brook ward) on lottery draw after tie 2003; short-listed for Northeast Region Euro list 2003; short-listed for Christchurch, Blaydon 2003; PPC Dartford 2005 *special interests* IT in govt, transport, defence *other mbrships* Nightingale Gun Club *recreations* golf, clay shooting *address* Bellsmead, Station Road, Rotherfield, East Sussex TN6 3HR *tel* 01892 853256 home 01892 600911 business *fax* 01892 600919 *e-mail* peter.bucklitsch@os-and-i.com

BULLAMORE, Tim *b* February 22, 1966 *div* 1 *d* born 2000 *education* Univ of Bath (MBA, 2004); Abbey Grange CE High School, Leeds 1979-84 *career* Barclays Bank 1984-87; Youth Hostels Association 1987-88; Ibbs & Tillett (classical music management) 1988-1990; Really Useful Gp 1990-92; *The Bath Chronicle* (journalist) 1993-1999; *The Times* 1999- specialising in obituary writing – shortlisted for Specialist Writer of the Year, British Press Awards, March 2002; co-ordinator of London Lives, tributes to the victims of the July 7 bombings, *The Times, July 2005*; freelance journalism/sub-editing; work has appeared in *The Daily Telegraph, Independent, Guardian, BBC Music Magazine, Cosmopolitan, Press Gazette, Woman magazine, Press Association, British Medical Journal* and *Liberal Democrat News*; served RAOC (TA) 1983-89 (best young soldier award, 1988) *party* chair Bath LP January 2004 – January 2006; architect of successful GE campaign in Bath, 2005; PPC Gloucester 2001 (40% increase in share of vote); cllr Bath (Weston ward) May 1999- ; gp press officer 1999-2001; Business Services spokes 2001-03; I&DEA leadership academy, Spring 2004; I&DEA accredited peer since Oct 2003; moved motion on passive smoking at federal conference March 2004; summated motion on Post Offices at federal conference March 2005; organiser of Bath (Weston ward) Golden Jubilee Celebrations, June 2002; co-organiser of Three Tenors Concert in Bath, Aug 2003; chair of governors, Weston All Saints Pri Schl, Bath, 2001- ; *special interests* media, the arts and the rejuvenation of Bath Spa *other mbrships* National Union of Journalists; International Association of Obituary Writers; Lib Dem History Society *recreations* dining out, bringing up my daughter, enjoying beautiful city of Bath, classical music, opera *publications* *Fifty Festivals,* the History of the Bath International Music Festival, 1999; *British Towns* (contrib), 1999; *Chin Up Girls!* Womens' obituaries from the Daily Telegraph (contrib), 2006; recent papers to Fifth Great Obituary Writers' Conference (New Mexico, June 2003), Sixth Great Obituary Writers' Conference (New Mexico, June 2004), Seventh Great Obituary Writers' Conference (Bath, June 2005), Death, Dying and Disposal Conference (Bath, September 2005), *address* 13 Belmont, Lansdown Road Bath BA1 5DZ *tel* 01225 330037 or 07836 617030 *e-mail* tim@bullamore.co.uk

BULLION, Alan *b* Pembury, Kent *single education* PhD, Univ of Southampton; BA (Hons) First Class, Open University *career* journalist on agriculture and biofuels, also worked in book and magazine publishing *party* joined 1983; local cllr in 1980s; mbr and chair Tunbridge Wells LP; PPC Hammersmith and Fulham 2005; mbr ALDC, DELGA, ELDR, ALDTU *other mbrships* UNA, European Movement *special interests* defence, Europe, rural affairs *publications* published widely on Sri Lanka, India, biofuels *recreations* music, film, travel, reading, writing, walking *style* Dr *address* Flat 7, Oak House, Oak Road, Tunbridge Wells, Kent TN2 3AN *tel* 01892 549871/01892 533812, 07840 854328 mobile *e-mail* alan.bullion@informa.com

BURNETT, John *b* Sept 19, 1945 *education* Ampleforth College; Britannia RN College, Dartmouth; College of Law, London *m* Billie 2 *s* Robert, George 2 *d* Alice, Laura. *career* Royal Marine Commando, active service in Borneo, Middle East (retired as Lt 1971); solicitor, practised in London until 1976, then senior partner of his Devon law firm; mbr Law Society's National Revenue Cttee 1985-97; farmer breeding Devon cattle *party* Liberal/SDP Alliance candidate West Devon and Torridge 1987 (halved then Tory MP Emma Nicholson's maj to 6,468); 1997 (elected), re-elected 2001; mbr of parliamentary Home Affairs and Legal Team, spksn on legal affairs 1997- ; Shadow Ministerial Spokesman, Home Office; Shadow Law Officer (Solicitor General); mbr Finance Bill Cttee 1997- , Procedure Select Cttee; Speaker's Fine Art Cttee; trustee Parliamentary Contributory Pension Fund; House of Commons Mbrs Fund; mbr Joint Cttee (of both Houses) on Consolidation Bills *other mbrships* NFU; council Devon Cattle Breeders Association; Royal Marines Association; Royal British Legion *other interests* active mbr Torrington RC church; campaigning for capital expenditure on local village primary s, retention of local community hospitals which he considers crucial to the rural community *recreation*s walking, swimming, tennis and travel *address* 21-25 St James Street, Okehampton, Devon EX20 1DJ *tel* 01837 55881

BURNHAM, Eleanor AM (North Wales) **Welsh Assembly Spokesperson on Culture, Sport and Language** *b* 1955 *m* 1 *s* 1 *d* *education* business graduate, Welsh-speaking *career* lecturer, complementary therapist *party* Welsh Assembly candidate Delyn 1999, elected for North Wales 2004 *recreations* solo singing, gardening, arts, cooking, reading *address* Orchard House, Burton Road, Rossett, Wrexham, LL12 0MY *tel* 01244 570694 *fax* 01244 570694 *e-mail* eleanor.burnham@wales.gov.uk

BURSTOW, Paul MP (Sutton and Cheam maj: 2,846**) Chief Whip** *b* May 13, 1962 Carshalton *education* Glastonbury HS for Boys 1981-85; South Bank Polytechnic (BA Hons Business Studies) *m* Mary 1 *s* 2 *d* *career* buying dept Allied Shoe Repairs, Carshalton before working for printing company, Cheswick *party* 1986-96: organising secy Association of Social Democrat Cllrs, ALDC from 1988; political secy 1996-97; elected Sutton LB Council (Rosehill ward), with 28 other Liberal/SDP Alliance Cllrs, giving party control for first time 1986; re-elected twice (with increased majorities); chair Highways and Transportation Sub-Cttee, Environmental Services Cttee, deputy leader Council 1991-97; chair Disability Forum 1991-97; PPC Sutton and Cheam 1992 (biggest swing to Lib Dems in Greater London); elected 1997, re-elected 2001, 2005; parliamentary spksn on Disabled People, mbr Local Govt Team with special responsibility for Social Services and Community Care 1997-2001; Shadow Minister for Older People 2001-03; Shadow Health Secy 2003-05; Shadow Minister for London 2005-2006; Chief Whip 2006- ; chair All-Party Gp on backcare, co-chair All-Party Gp on Ageing and Older People, and Primary Care and Public Health; vice-chair All-Party Gps on Disability, Local Govt, Social Care and MS, and secy All-Party Gps on Carers and Skin *other mbrships* parliamentary ambassador for NSPCC; patron of Relatives and Residents Association *recreations* cooking, reading, walking, gym *address* House of Commons, London SW1A 0AA constituency Epsom House, 312-314 High Street, Sutton, Surrey SM1 1PR *tel* 020 8288 6555; constituency Epsom House, 312-314 High Street, Sutton, Surrey SM1 1PR tel 020 8288 6555 *fax* 020 8288 6550 *e-mail* info@paulburstow.org.uk *web* www.paulburstow.libdems.org.uk

BURT, Lorely Jane MP (Solihull maj:279**)** *b* Sept 10, 1954 *m* Richard Burt, Lib Dem Gp Leader, Dudley MBC 1 *d* 1 step *s education* High Arcal Grammar School, Dudley Technical College, Univ College of Swansea, Open Univ (MBA, BSc (econ) Hons, FInstSMM *career* assistant governor, HM Prison Service; personnel research officer, Beecham; personnel and training manager, Forte, UK; personnel and training manager, Europcar; HR consultant, Mercers; MD Kudos Leisure Limited; MD Ace Communications Ltd; Director Mansion House Gp; currently consultant for Cintica Ltd, Longden Training Ltd. Umabica Ltd. *party* joined 1995; elected Cllr Dudley MBC, Kingswinford South (quadrupling the previous vote to win seat for first time for party 1998; Federal Policy Cttee 1999; PPC Dudley South 2001 (increasing Lib Dem vote from 11% to 15%); elected Cllr St James' Ward, 2002 (winning second seat for first time for party); resigned as a Cllr 2003 to concentrate on fighting the parliamentary seat of Solihull; chair Dudley South LP 2001-03;mbr West Midlands Regional Exec 2001- ; Euro Candidates' WM List 2004; elected MP for Solihull 2005; appointed Small Business Spokesperson 2006- ; *special interests* finance and tax, business and anything which makes constituents unhappy *recreations* rugby (watching), theatre, cinema, good friends, good food *address constituency* 41 Warwick Rd, Olton, Solihull B92 7HS *tel* 07957 812805 *fax* 01384 86154 *e-mail* contact@solihull-libdems.org.uk

BURT, Richard *b* May 22, 1954 Farnborough, Hampshire *m* Lorely Burt MP 1 *s* James 1 *sd* Emma *education* Farnborough Grammar School; BEd (Birmingham Univ); BA (Open Univ) *career* journalism, teaching, community arts and Fire Service before running sportswear manufacturing and supply company for ten years; councillor since 1996 *party* mbr West Worcestershire, selected as PPC 2006; vice chair and media co-ordinator West Midlands Region; Gp Leader, Dudley MBC 1998-2004; PPC Dudley South 1997, Dudley North 2001, Shrewsbury & Atcham 2005; campaign manager Ludlow constituency, 2001 GE *other mbrships* trustee: Association for Shared Parenting, keeping children in contact with parents after separation or divorce special interests social justice and peace *recreations* fell running, walking, watching rugby, reading, music *tel* 07970 713 032 *e-mail* richard@richardburt.org *web* www.richardburt.org

BUTT, Nasser *b* May 22, *1958 m* Rukhsana 2 *s* Tahir, Humza 2 *d* Sophia, Zanoobia *education* early education in Lahore, Bradford; Bradford College; graduated in finance, accountancy (ACCA) London *career* finance graduate, accountant with 20-year successful corporate career IBM, Dunn & Bradstreet, Yorkshire Water, Bradford & Bingley, ASDA, Level 3 Communications; head of finance 1998- ; strategic development, building four businesses since 1996 *party* joined 1991, Crawley; PPC Mole Valley; targeted, won (from Tory) council seat Sutton 2002; served on local, regional, national Cttees since 1992; chair national Multi-Faith Forum, Ethnic Minority Liberal Democrats 1993-2003; founder chair Liberal Democrats Muslims Forum Jun 2004; spokesperson, advisor on Ethnic Minority political, diverse cultures and religious issues *special interests* international Muslim organisation (expertise in Islamic theology); belief in Islam as moderate, tolerant and peace-creating faith that has no room for extremism; experienced community leader; trustee *Amicus Vision*, SE charity combating social exclusion, enabling people to take control of their own lives; three other charities *address* 60 Benhill Avenue, Sutton, Surrey SM1 4DW *tel* 07710 389336 *e-mail* nasserbutt@blueyonder.co.uk *web* www.butt.libdems.org

BUTT PHILIP, Alan *b* Aug 15, 1945 *m* Christina Baron *qv* 2 *s* David, Theodore *qv* 1 *d* Frances *education* Eton College (King's Scholar); St John's College, Oxford 1964-68 (1st Class Hons, Politics, Philosophy, Economics); Nuffield College, Oxford 1968-70; DPhil (Oxon) 1971 *career* financial controller, ICFC Ltd 1970-75; Research Fellow, Univ of Bath 1975-78; lecturer 1978-88, senior lecturer 1988-92, Reader in European Integration 1992- ; Jean Monnet 'chair' in European business 1990- ; visiting professor, Univ of Virginia 1994, ESCP-EAP, Paris 2002; winner Charles Douglas Home Memorial Award 1989 *party* joined Liberal Party 1957; president, Oxford Univ Liberal Club 1965-66; chair, Central Islington Liberal Association 1971-75; president Central Islington Liberal Association 1975-77; mbr Finance & Admin Board, National Exec, Liberal Party 1974-76; editor *New Outlook* 1975-78; PPC Wells Feb, Oct 1974, 1979, 1983, 1987; Euro candidate Somerset 1979, South West England list 1999; chair, Wells LP 1998-2001, President, Wells LP 2005- ; *special interests* European Union institutions, policies (especially single European market, regional policy, environment, enlargement); civil liberties; constitutional, electoral reform; exchange of students, staff in higher education *other mbrships* convenor, trustee, John Stuart Mill Institute; president Bath & Wansdyke branch, European Movement; treasurer St Thomas, Wells with Horrington Parochial Church Council; mbr Liberty, Electoral Reform Society, Green Liberal Democrats; mbr Royal Institute of International Affairs, European Union Studies Association (USA); Friend of the Red Squirrel (Cumbria) *recreations* music (playing piano, violin, harpsichord; singing); travel; reading; cathedrals, old churches *publications* *The Welsh Question* (1975); articles, monographs and book chapters on aspects of EU lobbying, policies, policy implementation, European Liberalism *address* The Old Vicarage, St Thomas Street, Wells, Somerset BA5 2UZ *tel* 01749 675071 home, 01225 383013 business *fax* 01749 675071 *e-mail* alan@buttphilip.freeserve. co.uk

BUTT PHILIP, Theodore John Apr 4, 1983 *s* of Dr Alan Butt Philip *qv* and Christina Baron *qv education* Stoberry Park Infants, Primary Schools, Wells; Walker Upper Elementary School, Charlottesville, Virginia; The Blue School, Wells; Lancaster Univ, 2002 (BA Hons Politics and International Relations); Univ of the West of England 2005- (studying for PGDL) *career* student *party* joined Wells 1994; chair, Wells City Branch, 2001-2; Wells City & Rural Branch 2005- ; Somerset rep, Western Counties Regional Exec 2006; mbr, English Council, 2002- ; mbr, Federal Policy Cttee, 2002-4 and 2005- ; County Council candidate for Wells 2005; mbr LDYS; mbr Liberal Democrat Peace and Security Gp *other mbrships* Liberty (National Council for Civil Liberties); Electoral Reform Society; governor, Soberry Park School *special interests* local Govt; Somerset history; electoral reform; civil liberties *club* National Liberal Club *recreations* reading; walking; travel; drinking (real ale, good wine); thinking *address* The Old Vicarage, St Thomas Street, Wells, Somerset BA5 2UZ *tel* 01749 675 071 home 07811871274 mobile *fax* 01749 675 071 *e-mail* theo@buttphilip.com

BYRON, Josephine (Jo) *b* Jul 1, 1953 *m* David 1 *s* 1 *d education* St Mary's RC School Grimsby; Manor House, Brigg (Scholarship); Luton Univ *career* Aerospace industry: financial analyst, finance manager, procurement, project manage *party* founder mbr Emersons Green Residents Association 1997; joined Lib Dems 1998; mbr oldest parish council in England; South Gloucestershire Unitary Authority 1999- (took seat from Labour giving first Lib Dem majority), vice chair of council, contracts and competitive tendering leader 2000; English Council mbr 1999- ;

community services leader 2000-03; PPC Solihull 2001 (increased winnability from 64th to 40th in five months); Exec mbr WLD 2002, vice chair 2003; policy adviser Bristol North West Exec; Lib Dem mbr Strategy Cttee, Standards Board for England 2004; invited speaker on bullying 2004 Standards Conference; approved candidate special circumstances: able to move to any winnable seat, does not work, has no caring responsibilities, husband works from home *special interests* new communities, environment, planning, standards in local Govt; speed reading (more than 2,500 words per minute) *other mbrships* Bristol Univ Court 2004- *recreations* singing, doorstep canvassing *address* 8 Home Field Close, Emersons Green, Bristol. BS16 7BH *tel/fax* 01454 864074 mobile 0787 030 2967 *e-mail* jo.byron@southglos.gov.uk

C

CABLE, Vincent MP (Twickenham maj: 9,965**) Shadow Chancellor** *b* May 9, 1943 York m Rachel (Wenban Smith) 2004; Olympia (Rebolo) 1968, died 2001 3 *ch* Paul, Aida and Hugo *education* Poppleton Road Primary, Nunthorpe Grammar, York; Fitzwilliam College, Cambridge (BA Hons, Natural Science and Economics); Glasgow Univ (PhD); currently Visiting Fellow, Nuffield College Oxford *career* Finance Officer, Kenya Treasury 1966-68; lecturer in Economics, Glasgow Univ 1968-74; Diplomatic Service, 1st Secretary, Latin American Dept 1974-76; Overseas Development Institute, Deputy Director 1976-83 (Special Advisor to Rt Hon John Smith 1978-79); Special Advisor, Economic Affairs, to Commonwealth Secretary General 1983-89 (seconded to work with Mrs Brundtland re UN Commission on Sustainable Development 1986-87); Shell International, Group Planning 1989-93; Head of Economics, Royal Institute of International Affairs 1993-95; Chief Economist, Shell International 1995-97; elected MP for Twickenham 1997- ; *party* Labour Cllr in Glasgow and PPC Hillhead 1970; SDP/Liberal Alliance PPC York 1983, 1987; Liberal Democrat PPC Twickenham 1992, elected 1997, re-elected 2001, 2005; Shadow Chancellor *recreations* dancing (Ballroom and Latin) *publications Public Services: Reform with a Purpose* Centre for Reform (2005), *Multiple Identities* Demos (2005), *Regulating Modern Capitalism* Centre for Reform (2002), *Globalisation and Global Governance* Chatham House/Pinter (1999), *China and India: Economic Reform and Global Integration* Royal Institute of International Affairs (1995), *Global Super Highways* Royal Institute of International Affairs (1995), *Trade Blocs* (with David Henderson) Royal Institute of International Affairs (1994), *The World's New Fissures* Demos (1994), *Developing with Foreign Investment* (with B Persaud) Croom Helms (1987), *The Commerce of Culture* (with L C Jain and A Weston) Lancer (1985), *Protectionism and Industrial Decline* Hodder & Stoughton (1983), Editor of *Development Police Review* to 1983, *British Interests and Overseas Developments* ODI (1979); contributor to many books including: *The Orange Book: Reclaiming Liberalism* (Ed: Paul Marshall and David Laws) (2004), Daedalus: *The Future for the State* (1995), *The Red Paper for Scotland* (Ed: Gordon Brown) (1975); major contributor to: *Our Common Future* The World Commission on Environment and Development (1987), Report of the Commission on Global Governance (1989), Commonwealth Export Group Report on Debt (Lord Lever) (1985), Commonwealth Export Group Report on Climate Change and Sea Level Rise (Sir Martin Holgate) 1988 *style* Dr *address* 2a Lion Road, Twickenham TW1 4JQ tel 020 8892 0215 fax 020 8892 0218 *e-mail* cablev@parliament.uk web www.vincentcable.libdems.org.uk

CALDER, Jonathan Peter *b* Mar 25, 1960 *education* Robert Smyth School, Market Harborough; Univ of York (BA Philosophy); Univ of Leicester (MA Victorian Studies) *career* communications officer, British Psychological Society (Division of Clinical Psychology); formerly employed by Golden Wonder Ltd (mbr Pot Noodle tasting panel) *party* Liberal Party 1978; secy York Liberal Students 1978-80; mbr *Liberator* Collective 1983- ; mbr Harborough DC (Market Harborough North) 1986-91; Lord Bonkers' literary secy 1990- ; mbr Federal Policy Cttee 2000-04; weekly columnist *Liberal Democrat News* 1999- ; sometime contributor to leaders' speeches *recreations* reading, walking, Shropshire; played chess for Leicestershire 1984-99 *publications* contributed chapters to *Professional Psychology Handbook* (BPS Books, 1995), *Making and Breaking Children's Lives* (PCCS Books, 2005), 'Defending Families' (*Liberator* 'Passport to Liberty' 5), (with David Boyle) 'Cohesive Communities' (*Liberator* 'Passport to Liberty' 5); articles, reviews for *Liberator* and *Liberal Democrat News*; articles for *The Guardian, Guardian* website, *Open Mind, Shropshire Magazine, Computer & Video Games*; gave Richard Jefferies Society Birthday Lecture, Aldbourne, Wiltshire 1997, writes Liberal England blog http://liberalengland.blogspot.com *address* 26 Scotland Road, Market Harborough, Leicestershire LE16 8AX *e-mail* calder@postmaster.co.uk

CAMPBELL, Gordon *b* Nov 16, 1963 Dunfermline *m* 2 *ch* Lewis and Amy *education* Queen Anne High School, Dunfermline
career Department of Employment 1981-86; Dunfermline Building Society 1986- , currently Head of Social Housing *party* mbr Dunfermline1981-88, Inverness, Nairn & Lochaber 1991-93, Perth 1993-2000, Dunfermline 2001-03, Perth 2003- ; secy and press officer Perth LP; PSPC Perth 2003 (increased vote share by 2%); PPC Perth & North Pertshire 2005 (increased vote share by 7%) *address* 59 Garvock Hill, Dunfermline KY12 7UR *tel* 01383 736073 *e-mail* gordongcampbell59@yahoo.co.uk

CAMPBELL, Rt Hon Sir Menzies CBE QC MP (North East Fife maj: 12,571**)
Leader, Liberal Democrats** *b* May 22, 1941 *m* Elspeth Mary Urquhart 1970 *education* Hillhead High School, Glasgow; Glasgow Univ (MA Arts 1962, LLB Law 1965); Stanford Univ, California, USA (post-graduate International Law 1966-67) *career* called to Bar (Scotland) 1968; Advocate Depute, Crown Office 1977-80; Queen's Counsel (Scotland) 1982 *honours* CBE 1987; Privy Cllr 1999; knighted 2004 New Year Honours *party* chair, Scottish Liberals 1975-77; PPC NE Fife 1974-83 elected 1987; chief Foreign Affairs & Defence Spokesperson 1992-97, Shadow Foreign Secy 1997-2003; Deputy Leader, Liberal Democrats Feb 2003-06, becoming Leader in 2006; Shadow Secy of State for Foreign & Commonwealth Affairs Oct 2003-06; mbr Select Cttees: Mbrs' Interests 1988-90; Trade & Industry 1990-92; Defence 1992-97, 1997-99; Joint Cabinet Cttee 1997-2001 *other mbrships* president Glasgow Univ Union 1964-65; Scottish Sports Council 1971-81; chair Royal Lyceum Theatre Company, Edinburgh 1984-87; Broadcasting Council for Scotland 1984-87; Clayson Cttee on Liquor Licensing Reform in Scotland; trustee Scottish International Education Trust; part-time chair, Medical Appeal Tribunal; part-time Chair VAT Tribunal (Scotland); board, British Council; UK Delegation to the North

Atlantic Assembly 1989- ;UK Delegation to the Parliamentary Assembly of CSCE 1992 *recreations* competed in 1964 Olympic, 1966 Commonwealth Games, captain, UK athletics team 1965-66; holder UK 100 metres record 1967-74 *address* House of Commons, London, SW1A 0AA *tel* 020 7219 0559; North East Fife Liberal Democrats, 16 Millgate, Cupar, Fife KY15 5EG *tel* 01334 656361 *e-mail* nefifelibdem@cix.co.uk (constituency) gradys@parliament.uk (London)

CANNON, David John *b* Aug 23 1950 Tiverton *education* Bideford Grammar School; Univ of Birmingham (BSc Mathematics(1971 *career* British Rail Computing Division 1971; privatisation refugee, took voluntary redundancy 1995 *party* joined Liberal Party 1973; various local party offices; elected Crewe & Nantwich Borough Council 1994; elected mbr Cheshire County Council 2004-05; **PPC** for Crewe & Nantwich 1997, 2001; editor *Christian Focus* (newsletter of LD Christian Forum) 2000-05 *recreations* walking *address* 43 Lunt Avenue, Crewe, Cheshire CW2 7LZ *tel/fax* 01270 668135 *e-mail* dcannon@cix.compulink.co.uk

CARD, Craig William *b* May 21, 1960 *m* Leola 1989 *education* Bay House Secondary *career* retail management Burton Gp plc 1976-88; proprietor O & R Printing 1988; partner, party's Liberal Democrat Image 2000- *party* joined 1984; mbrship secy Aldershot LP 1985-92, chair 1994-96, candidate Aldershot BC 1986, 1987, 1988, 1990; mbr Rushmoor Council (Mayfield) 1991- , chair Development Management Cttee 1986-88, gp leader 1999- *address* 24 Cheyne Way, Farnborough, Hampshire, GU14 8RX *tel* 01252 656033 home 01252 510005 business *e-mail* libdemimage@ldimage.demon.co.uk

CAREW, Adam *b* Mar 20, 1969 Greenwich *education* St Matthew's School, Bohunt; South Downs College; Universities Southampton and Worcester; Merrist Wood and Duchy Colleges; degree in Social, Economic and Political History specialising in English Radicalism; qualifications in Ecology, Environmental Science, Art and Sculpture, Business, Management Studies *career* almost full-time in local Govt, previously Arts Management, Ecological Consultant, FE lecturer *party* joined Liberals aged 14, lapsed and rejoined in 90s; chair Green Liberal Democrats; PPC NE Hants 2005; gp ldr and County Cllr – Whitehill, Bordon and Lindford; District and Town Cllr – Whitehill Walldown; mbr Federal Policy Cttee 2006- ; reserve mbr LGA Environment Board; mbr PCA Exec; mbr NE Hants LP Exec; former mbr English Council; Regional Policy Cttee; South Central Regional Exec; successful constituency Press Officer NE Hants 2002-05; events and fundraising officer Woolmer Forest branch 2002-04; Vice Chair of National Younger Cllrs Forum *special interests* wildlife conservation, green issues, history, post modernist theory, archaeology, landscape, heritage, walking, outdoor pursuits, english folk customs and traditions, the arts, public speaking, Fairtrade *address* Weald House, Forest Road, Whitehill, Hants GU35 9BA *tel/fax* 01420) 47 2743 *e-mail* adam.carew@hants.gov.uk or adam_carew@easthants.gov.uk

CARLILE, Lord Alexander Charles: QC, LLB, AKC, Life Peer cr 1999 *b* Feb 12,1948 *m* Frances 3 *d education* Epsom College; King's College London; College of Law *career* called to the Bar, Grays Inn, 1970; QC 1984; MP Montgomery 1983-97; Recorder of the Crown Court 1986; deputy High Court judge, honorary Recorder Hereford 1996; Independent Reviewer of terrorism legislation 2001; non-Exec Director of Wynnstay Gp plc *party* Leader of Welsh Lib Dems; 1988-97;

parliamentary Home Affairs spokesperson; chair Welsh party1992-97, president 1997-99 *special interests* Central Europe, Wales, visual arts, law recreations art, music, Italy *other mbrships* lay mbr General Medical Council 1989-99; Fellow, Institute of Advanced Legal Studies, NACRO, White Ensign *clubs* Athenaeum *style* Lord Carlile of Berriew *address* House of Lords, London SW1A 0PW *tel* 020 7400 1800 *fax* 020 7404 1405 *e-mail* carlileqc@aol.com

CARMICHAEL, Alistair MP (Orkney & Shetland maj:6,627) **Shadow Secy of State Transport** *b* Jul 15, 1965 *m* 2 *s education* Port Ellen Primary School; Islay High School; Aberdeen Univ (LLB, Dip LP) *career* solicitor, procurator fiscal, hotel manager, MP 2001- *party* chair Scottish Liberal Students 1984-85; PPC Paisley South 1987; secy Orkney LP 1989; General Election agent Banff & Buchan 1992; convener, Gordon LP 1998-2000; Scottish election agent, Gordon 1999; elected to Parliament for Orkney & Shetland 2001; Northern Ireland Spokesperson 2001-05; shadow Home Affairs team 2005-06; Scottish Party spokesperson Energy Review Oct 2001- ; Select Cttees: International Development 2001-02; Scotland 2001- ; mbr, All-Party Fishing Gp 2001- , All-Party Offshore Oil & Gas Industry Gp 2001- , Scottish Affairs 2003- *other mbrships* Director, Aberdeenshire Women's Aid; Church of Scotland Elder *recreations* music, amateur dramatics *address* House of Commons, London, SW1A 0AA *tel* 0207 219 8307; Orkney Liberal Democrats, 31 Broad Street, Kirkwall, Orkney, KW15 1DH *tel* 01856 876541 *fax* 01856-876162; Shetland Liberal Democrats, 171 Commercial Street, Lerwick, Shetland, ZE1 0HX tel 01595 690044 *fax* 01595 690055 *e-mail* carmichaela@parliament.uk

CARR, Hubert *b* Mar 22, 1942 *m* Bridget Lewis 2 *d education* Monkton Combe School, Bath; Univ of Durham; Open Univ *professional qualifications:* Chartered Engineer; mbr Institution of Civil Engineers; mbr Institution of Structural Engineers; mbr Institution of Highways and Transportation *career* design office, Howard Humphreys & Sons 1960-1962; site engineer Blackwall Tunnel, Mott Hay & Anderson 1962-63; site engineer Swanley by-pass 1963-64; design team leader M5 motorway, Somerset, Freeman Fox & Partners 1965-71; design of New Covent Garden, external roadworks, chief engineer Losinger Systems Ltd (pre-stressing sub contractors) 1971-73; design team leader A10 Norfolk, Husband & Co 1974; structural engineer Ahmed Hamdi Tunnel, Egypt: Halcrow &Co 1975-76; project engineer Jebel Ali Airport, Halcrow 1976-77; self-employed consulting engineer 1978- ; consultant planning inspector DoE 1981-90 *party* joined 1991; DC candidate 1992, 98; mbr Surrey County Council 1993- 97; chair LP 1994 –96; mbr Mole Valley District Council 1999-06, gp secy, deputy gp leader 2002-06; PPC Horsham 2001; mbr ALDC; mbr ALDES, currently Vice Chair - Engineering *special interests* planning policy; the built environment, buildings, roads; sustainable issues *other mbrships* deputy, then chairman Halcrow Staff Association (independent TU) 1976-78; council mbr, Institution of Civil Engineers 1978-81; various professional Cttees *recreations* model railways; designed (nearly finished building) own car *address* 87 Copthorne Road, Leatherhead, Surrey KT22 7EE *tel* 01372 817 504 home 0845 644 1101 business *fax* 0208 773 0442 *e-mail* hubertcarr@googlemail.com

CARR, Jane *b* Jun 9, 1963 *m* Andy 2 *d* Samantha, Jasmine 1 *gd* Tara-Jane *education* Walton Girls High School, Grantham; De Montfort Univ, Leicester *career* sales, marketing 1981-85; childcare provider 1985-89; social work, Lincolnshire Social Services, specialising in child protection, domestic violence, family support

1989-2002; social care provider, managing own company, Ward Andrews Associates 2002- ; *Working Women of the Year* 1995 *party* joined from Liberals; constituency chair Grantham and Stamford 1989-2003; regional conference secy 2001-03; elected to SKDC 1985-89, vice chair Recreation; PPC, Grantham and Stamford 2001; shortlisted European candidate 2003; secy WLD 2002; currently PPC North East Milton Keynes *special interests* employment rights, women's issues, children's rights, small business *other mbrships* Business and Professional Women UK (past regional president); mbr national council, Britain in Europe; UNISON; BASW; school governor *recreations* reading, gardening, films, good company, shopping, food *address* 31 Kilpin Green North Crawley, Newport Pagnell MK16 9LZ *tel* 01234 391487 home 01234 391031 business 07860 860 870 mobile 01234 391 031 *fax e-mail* jane.carr@mklibdems.co.uk

CARTHEW, Nick *b* Mar 20, 1962 *m* Andree *career* various jobs in music and advertising industries 1979-92; director Tridias toyshops 1992- ; Head of Office for Dr Jenny Tonge MP 1997-2001; Head of Office London Assembly Liberal Democrat Gp 2001- ; *party* joined Liberal Party 1976; chair Richmond and Barnes Liberal Democrats 1985; agent for council elections 1980- ; mbr (Town Ward) LB Richmond upon Thames 1988-2000, chair Leisure Services, senior vice chair Education *special interests* regional govt, international development *recreations* Brentford Football Club; watching all sports *address* 26 Townshend Terrace, Richmond, Surrey TW9 IXL *tel* 020 8948 4586 home 020 7983 4962 business 07773 782639 mobile *e-mail* nick.carthew@london.gov.uk

CHAPMAN, Mark *b* Mar 3, 1973 Hitchin *ptnr* no *ch education* to A-level *career* sales, marketing and, most recently, in technical roles *party* mbr and v-chair Mid Bedfordshire LP (Eastern Region); Mid Beds cllr 2003- ; Recruitment Officer, Eastern Region; PPC Mid Beds 2005; mbr Green Lib Dems *other mbrships* benefactor to WWF *special interests* environment, Govt use of IT, opportunity and social mobility *recreations* cricket, football, golf, reading, music *address* 15 Ivel Road, Shefford, Beds SG17 5LB *tel* 01462 629480, 07915 063255 mobile *e-mail* m_r_chapman@hotmail.com *web* www.mark-chapman.co.uk

CHAPMAN, Peter Jeffrey *b* Feb 8, 1945 *m* Pat 1972 1 *s* 1 *d education* Univ of Exeter 1963-66 BA German and French *career* 17 years in manufacturing industry 1966-1983; 19 years in travel industry 1983-2002 *party* joined 1999; vice-chair, agent Beaconsfield Liberal Democrats; PPC Beaconsfield 2005 *special interests* small business sector, the euro, the EU *other mbrships* Electoral Reform Society *recreations* hill-walking, cross-country skiing *address* 86 Fulmer Drive, Gerrards Cross SL9 7HE *tel* 01753 883573 *e-mail* peter.pjchapman@btopenworld.com

CHAPPELL, David *b* Feb 10, 1953 Hartlepool *liberated* 1 *ch education* Hartlepool Technical Day School; Bell College; Napier College; ONC Construction (with distinction); HNC Building *career* five years banking; 28 yeas construction industry as quantity surveyor, including work in Saudi Arabia, Zimbabwe *party* GE agent 1974 and 2001; re-founded and chaired Suffolk County co-ordinating Cttee; mbr Eastern England and LP exec; PPC Bury St Edmunds 2005 (vote up 48%); mbr PCA, ALDC, Green LDs, Association of Liberal Democrat Engineers and Scientists *special interests* foreign affairs, debt relief, helping people *other mbrships* Liberty Network, John Mills Institute *recreations* walking, travelling, countryside *LD quirk* prefers campaigning to 'politicking' *address* Lodge Barn Cottage, The Green, Fornham All Saints, Bury St Edmunds IP28 6JX *tel* 01284 764891 home 01638 661062 work 07803 956373 mobile *e-mail* david@thewizardstower.demon.co.uk

CHATFIELD, Jonathan Peter *b* May 3, 1970 *m* Dot (2000) *education* Weymouth Grammar School 1981-86; Weymouth College 1986-88; Univ of Bradford 1988-91; currently studying for MBA, Warwick Business School *career* president, Students' Union, Univ of Bradford 1991-92; graduate training scheme, British Railways Board 1992-93; station manager, Enfield 1993-94, Cambridge 1994-96, sales, marketing manager, Stansted Express 1996-2000, business manager, Network Rail 2000- *party* joined Liberal Democrats 1988; vice chair, SE Cambridgeshire 2001-04; mbr Histon Parish Council 2001-05; South Cambridgeshire District Council 2002- ; PPC SE Cambridgeshire 2005 *special interests* transport, education *other mbrships* Histon Parish Church; Univ of Bradford Graduates' Association; tutor, The Leadership Trust *recreations* cycling, hill-walking *address* 2 Parr Close, Impington CB4 9YH *tel/fax* 01223 520 132 *e-mail* j.chatfield@ntlworld.com

CHIDGEY of Hamble-le-Rice, Lord David: cr Life Peer 2005 *b* Jul 9, 1942 *m* 3 *ch education* Admiralty College, Portsmouth; Portsmouth Polytechnic (graduated mechanical engineer Portsmouth Naval Base before reading Civil Engineering, Portsmouth Polytechnic); Fellow, Institution of Civil Engineers; Fellow, Institute of Highways and Transportation; mbr Institute of Transport; Fellow Institute of Engineers of Ireland; Companion, Institute of Mechanical Engineers; Companion, Royal Aeronautical Society *career* chartered engineer: associate director Eastleigh-based international consulting engineers, senior advisor to Govt departments *party* mbr Alresford TC and Winchester City Council mid-1970s to early-1990s; chair, Hants and Wight Region 1992 -94; Euro candidate Hampshire Central 1988; Hampshire Central 1989 (by-election); PPC Eastleigh 1992, 1994 (by-election) elected MP; re-elected 1997, 2001; spokesman Employment & Training; previously spokesman Transport, Trade & Industry; mbr Foreign Affairs Cttee; mbr Chairmen's Panel *recreations* golf, county cricket, good company *address* House of Lords, London SW1A 0PW *tel* 020 7219 6944 *fax* 020 7219 5436

CHRISTIE-SMITH, Johanna Alison Elizabeth (Jo) *b* Jul 5, 1971 Redhill *divorced education* Hazelwick Comprehensive School, Crawley, Reigate VIth Form College, BSc(Econ) Hons International Relations, Univ of Wales, Aberystwyth *career* independent outsourcing & offshoring consultant & contractor, Strategy & Project Manager Barclays Bank plc 1995-2005 *party* Beckenham, London Region; Secy PPCs Association (PCA); mbr of English Council; PPC 2005 Mitcham & Morden; council candidate 2006, Clockhouse Ward, LB of Bromley *special interests* civil liberties, crime & rehabilitation of offenders, social justice and mobility, international affairs, London policy *other mbrships* CentreForum, Liberty, Amnesty International, National Liberal Club, Chair of Crystal Palace Safer Neighbourhoods Police Panel, governor Churchfields Primary School, volunteer with Friends United Network, an organisation working with underprivileged children in Islington & Camden *recreations* travel (esp. Middle East & India), gym, cooking & eating food and occasionally gardening *address* The Garden Flat, 110 Crystal Palace Park Rd, London SE26 6UP *tel/fax* 020 8249 7265, 07957 769341 mobile *e-mail* johanna.christiesmith@ntlworld.com

CHUNG, Linda: Chair, Chinese Liberal Democrats *education* Tapton School, Sheffield; Univ of Westminster (LLB Hons) *career* business and management consultancy; director of ISIS Offshore, international executive recruitment; employment tribunal member; non-executive director of health trust *party* candidate in Hampstead Town (LB Camden) 2006 local elections; vice-chair Camden Chinese Community Centre *other mbrships* founder mbr and vice-chair to Lord Chan, Chinese in Britain Forum 1996-2004; Director, Mind in Camden 1998-2001; Chinese National Healthy Living Centre vice-chair 1992-2001; founder mbr and chair, Council of Employment Tribunal Members' Associations 1998-2001 *special interests* health and environment, employment, business and economic development, community engagement *recreations* running, ballet and contemporary dance, travel *address* 15 Langland Gardens, London NW3 6QE *tel* 020 7794 2592 *e-mail* lindachung@talktalk.net

CHURCH, Clare Alison (nee Hamblen) *b* Glasgow Jan 7, 1974 *m* Sebastian 1 *s education* Glasgow Caledonian Univ 1992-95 BA (Hons) Nursing; City Univ London 2000-02, BSc (Hons) Midwifery *career* Registered General Nurse (surgical, high dependency) 1995-2000, Glasgow hospitals; Registered Midwife, St Thomas' Hospital, London 2000- *party* joined Liberal Democrats 1991; secy Scottish Young Lib Dems 1991-94; mbr Scottish Exec 1994-2000; Scottish Campaigns and Candidates Cttee 1996-2000; Scottish Conference Cttee 1995-99; Cllr East Dunbartonshire Unitary Authority 1995-99; PPC Ayr 1997, West Renfrewshire 2001; Scottish PPC Glasgow Maryhill 1999, Dumfries 2003; treasurer Women Liberal Democrats 2002- ; mbr Federal Health Policy Working Gp 2003 - *special interests* health, education *other mbrships* mbr Royal College of Midwives *recreations* swimming, film, travel *address* 6 Rothery Terrace, Foxley Road, London, SW9 6EY *tel* 020 7582 4511 home 07973 736024 mobile *fax* 020 7793 9355 *e-mail* clarehamblen@hotmail.com

CHURCH, Richard *b* Apr 11, 1958 Northampton *single education* Oakham School; Reading Univ BA (Hons) Politics 1981 *career* former director, Church's China; full time Cllr *party* mbr Northampton LP (former chair); gp ldr Northamptonshire County Council; mbr Northampton Borough Council (former gp ldr); former Mayor of Northampton; chair East Midlands Region; PPC Northampton North 1992, 2001, Wellingborough 2005; Euro candidate Northampton & South Leicestershire 1989 and East Midlands 2004; mbr LD Humanist & Secular Gp (mbrship secy); mbr ALDC *other mbrships* British Humanist Society *special interests* local govt, environment, international affairs *recreations* gardening, local history *style* Cllr *address* 3 Kinglsey Gardens, Northampton NN2 7BW *tel* 01604 719097 *e-mail* rchurch1@btconnect.com

CLARK, Duncan *b* Jan 30, 1972 Lewisham *m* 1 *ch education* Collingwood College, Camberley; Univ of Huddersfield (BA Hons History and Politics); Sheffield Hallam Univ (PG Diploma Housing Administration) *career* Sabbatical Welfare Officer, Univ of Huddersfield Students Union 1993-95; Area Housing Manager, Pavilion Housing 1997-2001; Housing Officer, The Guiness Trust 2001-03; Senior Property Manager, Servite Houses 2003- ; *party* mbr Surrey Heath, selected as PPC 2006, chair Frimley Green, Mytchett and Deepcut branch; councillor, Surrey Heath BC and Windlesham PC 1999- ; International Officer Student Liberal Democrats England & Wales 1991-93; mbr ALDC *style* Cllr *address* 163 Frimley Green Road,

Frimley Green, Camberley, Surrey GU16 6JX *tel* 01932 722296 work, 0773 965 7277 mobile, 01252 835224 home *e-mail* duncan@surreyheathlibdems.org.uk *web* www.surreyheathlibdems.org.uk

CLARK, Reginald Blythe *b* Sedgefield, Co Durham Mar 15, 1958 *m* Judith Anne 1 *s* Tom 1 *d* Laura *education* Brinkburn Comprehensive, Hartlepool; Christ Church, Oxford (MA); rugby Blue 1978 & 79; President Vincents Club *career* City career with Yamaichi Securities, Swiss Bank Corporation, JP Morgan; ten years European finance director, Kobe Steel, Japan; currently chief Exec, Global Human Capital Management Gp plc, managing director, Loxko Venture Managers Ltd, Fellow of Institute of Management Consultants; mbr of Securities Institute *party* Federal Treasurer 2000-05; PPC Hartlepool 1997; former treasurer Richmond & Barnes LP; chair Kew Ward; secy City Liberal Democrats *special interests* commercial, fiscal policy *other mbrships* National Liberal Club, Garrick Club *recreations* cycling, jogging, rugby *address* 5 Maze Road, Kew, Richmond, Surrey TW9 3DA *e-mail* rclark@globalhcmgp.com

CLARKE (nee Jones), Helen Ceri *b* Oct 12, 1974 *m* Jonathan Clarke May 29, 2005 *education* Redhill School, Stourbridge, West Midlands; Halesowen College, West Midlands; Welsh College of Music and Drama at Neath College, South Wales *career* five years as traffic warden, South Wales Police; administrator Welsh Liberal Democrats.; educational support officer Swansea College; currently working for Peter Black AM as PA/caseworker *party* joined 2001; minute secy Swansea and Gower LP 2001-03, vice chair 2002- ; secy Welsh Policy Cttee 2003; mbr Welsh National Exec 2004; local candidate, Morriston 2003, 2004; candidate Neath, National Assembly for Wales 2003 *special interests* trade union issues, public services, policing and crime, education *other mbrships* UNISON representative for South Wales Police, Swansea College *recreations* tennis, cats, socialising *address* 28 Vicarage Road, Morriston, Swansea SA6 6DH *tel* 01792 541982 *e-mail* h.jones14@ntlworld.com

CLEGG, Nicholas William Peter MP (Sheffield Hallam maj: 8,682) **Shadow Home Secy** *b* Jan 7, 1967 *m* 2 *s education* Westminster School; Cambridge Univ; Univ of Minnesota USA; College of Europe, Belgium *career* journalist, consultant 1990-94; EU development assistance projects in Former Soviet Union 1994-96; senior adviser to Vice President of the European Commission 1996-99; MEP, East Midlands 1999-2004; part-time lecturer at Sheffield University 2004-05; chair of economics working gp for European Policy Centre, a think tank 2004-05 *party* joined 1993; elected MEP 1999; mbr Campaign and Communications Cttee; chair, Third Age Campaign Team; mbr, working gp on Liberal Democrat philosophy, principles; elected MP Sheffield Hallam 2005 *special interests* globalisation, Europe, foreign affairs; education, constitutional reform *other mbrships* commissioner, Independent Commission on Proportional Representation (Univ College London) 2003-04; elected board mbr European Movement 2004; advisory board Centre Forum; Britain in Europe; Amnesty International *recreations* outdoors (skiing, mountaineering), theatre *publications* political columnist Guardian Unlimited; regular contributions to Financial Times, The Independent, several local, regional newspapers; pamphlets: Doing Less To Do More (CER);.Reforming the WTO (CentreForum); Learning from Europe: Lessons in Education (CER, co author); Reforming the European Parliament (Foreign Policy Centre, co author) *address* 85

Nethergreen Road, Sheffield S11 7EH *tel* 0114 230 9393 *fax* 0114 230 9614 *e-mail* cleggn@parliament.uk

CLEMENT-JONES of Clapham, Baron Timothy Francis: CBE 1988, cr Life Peer 1998: Lords spokesperson on Culture, Media and Sport *b* Oct 26, 1949 *education* Hailebury; Trinity College, Cambridge MA *m* 1 Dr Veronica Yip 1974 (d 1987) *m* 2 Jean Roberta Whiteside 1s *career* solicitor: articled clerk Howard Chance 1972-74, assoc Joynson-Hicks & Co 1974-76, corporate lawyer Letraset International Ltd 1976-80, asst head (later head) legal services LWT Ltd 1980-83, legal director retailing div Grand Met plc 1984-86; gp company secy, legal advisor Kingfisher plc (formerly Woolworth Holdings plc) 1986-95; director Political Context Ltd 1996- ; co-founder, partner Independent Corporate Mentoring (ICM) 1996-99; v-president Eurocommerce (Euro Retail Federation) 1992-95; chairman DLA Upstream (public affairs practice of DLA Piper Rudnick Gray Cary international law firm) 1999- ; *party* chair LD Lawyers Association; chair Liberal Party 1986-88; chair FFAC 1991-98; director Euro Election Campaign 1992-94; v-chair GE Gp 1994-97; chair London Assembly, Mayoral Campaign 2000, 2004; Federal Party Treasurer 2005- ; Lords spokesman on health 1998-2004; Lords spokesman on Culture, Media and Sport 2005- ; v-chairman All Party Autism Gp 2001- ; v-chairman All Party China Gp 2005- *other mbrships* trustee Cancer BACUP; chair Crime Concern 1981-95; chair The Context Gp; chair of trustees Treehouse School for autistic children 2001- ; governor Hailebury School; Law Society, FRSA, FCIPR, board mbr CentreForum *recreations* walking, travelling, reading, diving, eating, talking *address* House of Lords, London SW1A *e-mail* timcj@atlas.co.uk

CLIFFORD-JACKSON, Vivienne Helen divorced 1 *d* Isabella Jackson *education* County Girls' School, East Sheen; London Univ; Royal College of Nursing, Garnett College Roehampton; Brunel Univ *career* qualified Registered Nurse 1971; midwife 1976; clinical teacher 1982; Diploma in Nursing 1984; Registered Nurse Tutor 1986; Masters Degree 1991; staff nurse, night sister, ward sister, nurse teacher, researcher, lecturer and latterly recruitment manager; worked The Netherlands, exchange United States; *Best Recruitment Consultant for Norfolk* 2002; in Top Ten Women in Norfolk 2003; wrote *Toolkit* for DoH, advised on recruitment strategies at national level; currently one day per week local Cheshire home; sessional lecturer at local FE college; and occasional consultancy *party* founder mbr SDP 1981; met husband canvassing, had first Alliance baby; chair Richmond and Twickenham, negotiated local Alliance; mbr LB Richmond and Twickenham 1982, chair Community Health Council, school governor; moved to Norfolk 1990; PPC Mid Norfolk 2001 and 2005, increased vote by 9%; mbr South Norfolk District Council 2004; cabinet 2004; Leader 2005; exec mbr South Norfolk LP; first-school governor *special interests* health care, housing, complementary therapies, environment; raising aspirations *other mbrships* British Horse Society; Nurse and Midwives Council; Royal Norfolk Agricultural Association (vice-president Royal Norfolk Show) *recreations* committed Christian active in church; horse riding; gym; yoga *publications* various *address* Clifford House, 8 Badger Close, Mulbarton, Norfolk NR14 8NT *tel/fax* 01508 571346, 07717 296 202 mobile *e-mail* vivienne@cliffordconsulting.org.uk vcjackson@s-norfolk.gov.uk

CLUCAS, Flo: OBE (2005) *b* Sept 5, 1947 *m* John 2 *s education* Bellerive Convent, FCJ Liverpool; St Mary's College, Bangor; Liverpool Institute of Higher Education; Liverpool Univ *career* dental nurse; GPO telephonist, journalist, civil servant local Govt officer, teacher, HE tutor *party* joined 1981; secy, chair Liverpool Garston; mbr NW Regional Exec, chair; mbr Federal Exec; conference representative 1981-2004; PPC Halton 1987, Crosby 1992, Garston 1997, Wirral South by-election 1997; Euro candidate 1989, 1994, 1999, 2004; elected mbr Liverpool City Council 1986-2004: variously education, policy and resources spokesperson; deputy gp leader, deputy leader of council 1998-99, chair Policy and Resources 1998-99, Exec mbr Environment 1999-2002, Exec mbr Housing, Neighbourhood Services and Community Safety 2002-2004, European Affairs 1998-2004, Eurocities Representative 1998-2004; leader Lib Dem Gp NW Regional Assembly; Exec mbr Economic Development and Europe 2006- ; First Vice-President ALDE Gp Cttee of the Regions, full mbr CoR 2006-2010 *special interests* Europe, local Govt, education, regional affairs; regeneration *other mbrships* chair Liverpool Institute for Performing Arts (HE institution) 2001-04; Cttee of the Regions 2002-04; North Mersey Comunity Health Trust Board 2000-02; Atlantic Area PMC 2000-02; NW Europe Interreg 3B PMC 2002-04; Merseyside Objective 1 PMC 1998-2004; chair NW Regional Assembly European and International Affairs KPG 2001-04; Exec, policy Cttee mbr NWRA; Citysafe Partnership; Newheartlands HMRI Pathfinder Board; NW Regional Housing Forum; Urbact PMC; Cohesion Forum 2002/2004 *recreations* travel in France, Old Dudes and Dudettes, Merseycats, old films *publications* joint-author *A Vision for the City's Parks* (Liverpool City Council) *address* 209 Hunts Cross Ave Liverpool L25 9NB *tel* 0151 428 6957 home 0151 225 2601 business *e-mail* flo.clucas@liverpool.gov.uk

COLE, Sally *b* Apr 13, 1978 St Leonards-on-Sea *education* Winton House School; Claverham Community College; Bexhill Sixth Form College; Goldsmiths College, Univ of London (BA Communications) *career* Press and Campaigns Officer to Graham Watson MEP 1999-2000; Parliamentary Researcher to Tom Brake MP 2000-2002; POLD Education Advisor 2002; Account Administrator, Make Stuff Happen Ltd 2002-03; Administrator, Greenwich Council 2004; Research Officer to Islington Council Lib Dem Group 2004- ; *party* mbr (and secy) Richmond and Twickenham LP, London Region; candidate for Tooting Graveney Ward, Wandsworth, 2002; mbr ALDC *special interests* environment, transport, education *recreations* reading, writing, film, LRP *address* 124 Clifden Court, Clifden Road, Twickenham TW1 4LR *e-mail* sally_cole@yahoo.com

COLE-HAMILTON, Alex *b* Jul 22, 1972 *m* Gill *education* Madras College, St Andrews, Univ of Aberdeen *career* president, Aberdeen Univ SRC 1999-2000; organiser, West Edinburgh Liberal Democrats 2000-2001; Scottish Liberal Democrats Communications Officer (Scottish Parliament) 2001-03; policy, communications officer Fairbridge, Scotland 2003- ; *party* joined 2000; worked professionally for party for three years; PSPC Kirkcaldy, Mid-Scotland, Fife list 2003; ward organiser, Crail; conference delegate; mbr Mid-Scotland, Fife Exec; PPC Kirkcaldy and Cowdenbeath 2005 *special interests* foreign affairs (Middle East), international development, social justice and inclusion *other mbrships* Amnesty International *recreations* learning Arabic; scuba diving; indoor rock climbing *address* 19/2 Dalgety Road, Edinburgh *tel* 07786 554 661 home 0131 661 5880 business *e-mail* alexcolehamilton@gmail.com

COLEMAN, Cllr Christopher Francis *b* Nov 18, 1978 Cheltenham *education* St Edward's School Cheltenham; Univ College Northampton (graduated LLB Hons June 2000); Staffordshire Univ (Legal Practice Course 2001) *career* solicitor with local firm of solicitors (Criminal Law) *party* activist age 12, joined 14, College Ward Liberal Democrats, Cheltenham; organised Univ branch; Youth and Students representative Northampton LP exec; ward election agent Northampton BC elections 1999; LDYS candidate National Union of Students exec elections 2000 (while at Staffordshire Univ); co-opted exec Stoke-on-Trent LP; PPC Stoke-on-Trent South 2001 (increased share of vote); mbr executive Cheltenham LP 2002- ; mbr Cheltenham Borough Council (St Paul's Ward) 2002- ; PPC Forest of Dean 2005 (increased share of vote) *special interests* prison reform, youth work, human rights *recreations* youth leader, Church Lads' and Church Girls' Brigade St Paul's Company, Cheltenham; leader St Paul's Breakfast Club for children and young people; keen supporter Cheltenham Town FC and Sheffield United FC *style* Cllr Chris Coleman *e-mail* chriscoleman@email.com

COLEMAN, Ruth 1 *d* Rachel 3 *s* Daniel, Jonathan and Matthew *education* Manchester High School for Girls; Univ of York; Univ of Manchester *career* mathematics teacher (secondary school, FE college) to 1990; councillor since 1991; senior mbr, Peer Clearing House, Improvement and Development Agency May 2003-2006; IdeA Peer, Rural Excellence Programme April 2006- ; *party* joined Liberal Party as teenager; founder mbr Liberal Democrats; mbr UK delegation to ELDR Council; chair, LGA Local Govt International Bureau 2005- ; full mbr ELDR Group, EU Cttee of the Regions 1998- ; formerly vice-chair Federal Policy Cttee; deputy leader, LGA Liberal Democrat Gp; leader, North Wiltshire District Council 1994-99, 2003-5; PPC Toxteth, Macclesfield, Woodspring, Leeds Central; PEPC SW England; chair Young Liberals, Liberal Students, PCA *special interests* EU, international development, local democracy, equality *recreations* travel, jazz, yoga *address* 2 Maple Terrace, Yeadon, Leeds, LS19 7HL *tel* 0113 229 0266 *email* ruth.coleman2@ntlworld.com

COLLETT, Adrian Paul *b* Mar 30, 1958 *m* Pam 2 *adult stepchildren* 2 *step-grandaughters education* Salesian College, Farnborough *career* retail management: MacFisheries, Mac Market Supermarkets, International Supermarkets; switched to full-time local Govt, political work 1980s *party* joined Liberals 1976; agent Aldershot 1979, 1983, 1987; PPC 1992, 1997, 2001 (reducing Conservative majority from 19,188 to 5,334), 2005; mbr Hart DC 1980-92, gp ldr Liberal/Alliance/Lib Dem nine years, council leader 1986-88; mbr Hampshire CC 1983- , v chair Planning & Transportation 1993-97, gp leader 1997- ; mbr Yateley TC *special interests* environment, civil liberties, equalities, health *recreations* hill-walking, rambling, gardening, reading, music (classical to punk but particular fondness for David Bowie's seminal works of 1970s) *address* 47 Globe Farm Lane, Darby Green, Blackwater, Hampshire GU17 0DY *tel/fax* 01252 873786 mobile 07718 146606 *e-mail* acollett@cix.co.uk

COLLINS, Scott Jon *b* Oct 9, 1970 Northampton *separated* 2 *ch* 1 *d* 1 *s education* Sponne School,Towcester, Northants; studying for degree Social Science with Politics (OU) *career* security supervisor for national company, Hygiene Services Transport Manager *party* East Mids Regional Exec mbr/secy 2004- ; Northampton LP Exec mbr/secy 2004- ; County Council candidate in St James Division 2005

(3rd); Brook Ward, Towcester 2003 (elected) Towcester Town Council; PCA mbr and approved for parliamentary elections *special interests* environment, education, European reform, electoral reform, further devolution to regions and countries within UK *recreations* rugby, reading, music, good food, debating, real ale, collecting cufflinks and ties *address* 34 Boughton Green Road, Kingsthorpe, Northampton NN2 7SP tel 01604 474778 home 07883 751620 mobile *e-mail* scott_collins@hotmail.com

COLLINS, Stan (Stanley Bernard) Chair, English Liberal Democrats *b*1948 *education* Roundhay School, Leeds; UMIST (BSc Chemistry) *career* IT from 1970 until retirement in 2001; consultant on handling US environmental claims, London Insurance Market *party* joined Liberals 1974; mbr Liberal National Exec 1983; chair Westmorland and Lonsdale 1983-86, founding chair W&L Liberal Democrats 1988-89; campaign organiser numerous local elections; PPC 1987, 1992, 1997 (reduced Tory majority from 17,000 to 4,000); many media appearances including half-hour debate with Peter Mandelson on eve of Littleborough and Saddleworth by-election (Mr M lost his temper when asked what Labour stood for!); mbr FPC 2000- ; mbr FE 2001- ; chair English party, federal vice-president (England) and mbr FFAC 2004- ; Euro candidate North West England 2004; mbr South Lakeland DC 1979- (gained seat as 'paper' candidate); chair finance cttee 1990-99; mbr Cumbria CC 2005-; mbr Lake District National Park authority 2005- ; leader various campaigns including successful Staveley by-pass campaign 1981-89, Westmorland General Hospital 1985-6; Save Abbey Home 1996; campaign to stop further damage to Lakeland communities by second homes and to remove their 50% Council Tax discount *special interests* rural affairs, foreign affairs, economics, science and technology and impact on society and environment; inventing phrases like *Tory Free Zone* (Kendal 1990), *Genteel ethnic cleansing* (second homes 1998), and some best edited out *recreations* cooking; eating; fell-walking; travel; reading (especially science, history, biography); gardening when in mood or grass gets too long; occasional inventor including fearsome diesel-powered pogo stick; likes lying in hammock with book and long cold drink on hot summer days *publications* newspaper, magazine articles on second homes, rural housing, broadband, IT for rural areas, numerous other subjects, 'England 2020'; ambition is for Liberal Democrats to be contenders for office, power in all parts of country, at every level of government by 2020 *address* 8 Gowan Close, Staveley, Kendal, Cumbria LA8 9NW *tel* 01539 821086 *e-mail* stanstheman@cix.co.uk

COMMONS, John Patrick Bryans *b* Jan 3, 1956 *education* St. Bede's College Manchester; Manchester Polytechnic *career* president Manchester Polytechnic Student's Union; manager community projects, Methodist Church; parliamentary agent Liberal Party, Liberal Democrats Sheffield Hillsborough 1983, 1987, Knowsley South bye-election 1990; Congleton 1992; Berwick-upon-Tweed (Rt. Hon Alan Beith MP) 1997; political consultant *party* PPC (Liberal) Manchester Moss Side1979, Sheffield Hillsborough 2001; mbr (Levenshulme Ward) Manchester City Council 1985- ; ALDC trainer; former *Liberal Democrat News* columnist, consultant/provider of ALDC election results service; Secy-General Young Liberal Movement (England); vice-president LYMEC (European Community Liberal Youth Movements); mbr regional, national Exec, finance Cttee Liberal Party; chair Manchester City Liberal Democrats, currently chair candidates Cttee; served in every ward, constituency officer role; representative at every conference from 1975; panel of Federal Conference chairs; vice-chair ALDC Management Cttee, secy of Lib Dem Gp Exec at LGA and mbr of LGA Improvement Board; mbr arts policy working gp *special interests* community politics, European, North American issues, libraries, museums, sport *other mbrships* local Govt peer mbr, Audit Commission Comprehensive Performance Assessment Teams; non-Exec director Central Manchester Primary Care Trust and chair of CMPCT Audit Cttee; former deputy chair LGA Cultural Services Exec; vice-chair Manchester Mayo Association; National Library of Ireland, Dublin; Museums Association Council *recreations* museums, bridge, travel, cinema, theatre, Manchester United *address* 37 Cromwell Grove Levenshulme, Manchester M19 3QD *tel* 0161 224 9366 home 0161 234 3002 office *e-mail* johncommons@levenshulme.com; cllr.j.commons@manchester.gov.uk

COOKE, Stephen (Steve) *b* Oct 2, 1974 Kilembe (Uganda) *m* 2 *ch education* Irish Intermediate and Leaving Certificates, DipHE Combined Studies (Wolverhampton Univ), DipHE Politics and Government (Open Univ), BA (Hons) First-class (Open Univ) *career* various IT/Web related jobs; currently web developer for Manchester Metropolitan Univ *party* mbr Salford LP (chair 2004, 2005) in NW region; councillor; candidate for Gosport council – Rowner Holbrook ward – 2002, Salford council – Langworthy ward – 2003, Salford council – Claremont Ward – 2004; PPC Ellesmere Port and Neston 2005 *other mbrships* Amnesty International, New Politics Network, Peace Pledge Union, River Valley Credit Union (board of directors), Unison (branch officer at Manchester Metropolitan Univ) *special interests* environment, children and young people, lifelong learning, human & animal rights, constitutional affairs, international development *recreations* reading, camping, fencing *address* 49 Rydal Crescent, Swinton, Lancashire M27 5WS *tel* 0161 7941289, 07790 668191 *e-mail* steve@stevecooke.org *website* http://www.salfordlibdems.f2s.com/wordpress/

COOKSEY, Stephen John *b* Jan 11, 1944 *m* Margaret 2 *s* Leighton James, Ross Edward *education* Middlesbrough High School for Boys; Univ of Leeds *career* political research assistant Univ of Bristol 1965-66; political research office Univ of Leeds 1966-69; research, welfare officer Univ of Bradford Students Union 1969-72; administrator Univ of Bradford 1972-81; assistant registrar Univ of Salford 1981-89; registrar Roehampton Institute 1989-93, academic secy 1993-98; registrar Univ of Buckingham 1998-2001; deputy director Open Univ validation services 2001- *party* joined 1962; chair Leeds ULS 1964-65; agent Cleveland constituency 1964; PPC Leeds South 1970; Pudsey Feb 1974, Oct 1974; 1979; Skipton & Ripon 1987; Mole Valley 1997; European candidate Leeds 1984; vice chair Yorkshire Liberal Federation 1976-87; president Yorkshire Liberal Federation 1987-89; chair Yorkshire Candidates Association 1971-81; mbr South-East Liberal Democrats Exec 1992-96; mbr Liberal Party Council 1971-88; mbr Liberal Party National Exec 1976-88; mbr Horsforth Urban District Council 1971-74, chair Housing Cttee 1973-74; mbr West Yorkshire County Council 1974-82, gp secy 1974-80; mbr Leeds City Council 1980-89, gp leader 1982-89; mbr Mole Valley District Council 1999- , chair Planning Cttee 1996-98; gp leader 2000-05; elected to Surrey County Council 2005 *special interests* local Govt; Europe; environment *other mbrships* ALDC; National Trust; English Heritage; CAMRA; Dorking & District Preservation Society; Ramblers Association *recreations* travel; theatre; music; walking; political history *address* Parklands, 43 Deepdene Avenue, Dorking, Surrey RH5 4AA *tel* 01306 881663 mobile 07971686108 home 020 7447 2514 business *fax* 01306 881663 *e-*

mail stephen.cooksey1@btinternet.com (home); s.j.cooksey@open.ac.uk (office); cllr.cooksey@mole-valley.gov.uk and stephen.cooksey@surreycc.gov.uk (council)

COOPER, Mark Geoffrey BA Hons *b* Apr 16, 1948 *m* Sue Tippett GP 5 *s education* Taunton's School, Southampton 1964-67; Univ of Leeds 1967-70 (BA Hons social science) 1970; PGCE 1973; union secy 1968-69 *career* Auckland Regional Authority, NZ, 1970-71; Joseph Lucas (Sales & Service) Birmingham 1971-72; St. Mary's College, Southampton, 1973-04 (head, geography, economics) *party* joined Liberals 1979; *Focus* editor 1985-95; mbr Romsey TC (mayor 1991-92); Test Valley BC 1986- , gp leader 1991-2001, council leader 1995-1998; PPC Romsey 1997 (11.8% swing from Con), put family first at by-election 2000; PPC Southampton Itchen 2001; Hampshire County Councillor 2005- ; *special interests* planning, design, conservation *style* Cllr Mark Cooper *address* 22 The Thicket, Romsey SO51 5SZ. Hampshire *tel* 01794 516028 *fax* 01794 513590 *e-mail* cooper22tt@aol.com

COPE, Trevor Andrew *b* Mar 12,1953 *m* Shirley Erica 2 *s* David, Erian 1*d* Treley Emma *education* M(Ed), B(Ed), Dip (IE) Exeter Univ; A (mus) LCM-London College of Music *career* teacher *party* joined 1968; chair various dates Brixham, East Devon, Honiton, Exmouth; mbr East Devon District Council 1992- ; mbr Exmouth Town Council 1995- ; Mayor of Exmouth 2004 *special interests* education, armed forces *recreations* bus enthusiast, model bus collector, stamp collector, marathon runner *address* 67 Winston Road, Brixington, Exmouth EX8 *tel* 01395 270128 *e-mail* trevor.cope@talk21.com

CORDWELL, Dr John Edward *b* Jun 29, 1944 *m* Jun (nee Ashworth) 1 *s* James 1 *d* Emma *education* Univ of Liverpool BSc maths and physics; BSc Honours metallurgy; PhD in metallurgy 1971 *career* research officer, electricity supply industry until early retirement 1994; lay school inspector; copy-editor and proof-reader specialising in educational and strategic planning texts 1994 *party* joined Liberals early 1970s (attracted by environmental policies); mbr Gloucestershire County Council 1981- , and chair County Council 2000-01; for many years chairman of Planning and Transportation, and subsequently Cabinet portfolio holder, Strategic Planning and Transport 2001-05, currently shadow portfolio holder; mbr SW Regional Assembly, vice-chair of its Regional Spatial Strategy Steering Gp; mbr SW LGA; mbr SW Regional Development Agency's Infrastructure Board Advisory Gp (representing SW Regional Assembly); county Euro spokesperson until 2005 (when Tory council withdrew mbrship), representing the county on the EU Conference of Peripheral Maritime Regions (CPMR) and Atlantic Arc Commission; but continuing mbr transport gp of AAC; former vice-chair SW UK Brussels Office Joint Cttee; Euro candidate, West Midlands 1999 *special interests* environment; planning and transport from local to Europe-wide; Malta *other mbrships* Wotton-under-Edge Town Council 1979- , four times mayor (longest serving mbr); mbr Society for Editors and Proofreaders; Life Mbr CPRE; school and language college governor, former chair, vice-president, Wotton-under-Edge Civic Society *recreations* genealogy and local history; growing cacti, vines and other Mediterranean plants, indoor water gardening, book collecting, pub quizzes *address* Greenlea, Haw Street, Wotton-under-Edge, Gloucestershire GL12 7AG *tel* 01453 842439 *fax* 01453 521705 *e-mail* cordwell@clara.net or john.cordwell@gloucestershire.gov.uk *web*: www.cordwell.clara.net

CORLETT, Neil *b* Jun 10, 1966 *m education* Calday Grammar School, West Kirby 1977-84; Reading Univ 1984-89; College of Europe, Bruges 1990-91 *career* European Commission two years; European Parliament eleven years, currently Head of press service, ALDE gp in European Parliament *party* joined 1998; mbr Brussels/Europe branch; PEPC, North West England 2004 *special interests* European Community affairs *recreations* painting, photography, running, travelling *tel* 00 32 2 284 2077 *e-mail* ncorlett@europarl.eu.int or ncorlett@f2s.com

COTTER, Lord Brian: cr Life Peer 2006 *b* Aug 24, 1938 m Eyleen 2 *s* 1 *d education* St Benedicts; Downside, Somerset (4.5-minute-miler at age 16); North London Polytechnic *career* largely·self-employed, manufacturing and services until winning Weston-super-Mare 1997; now Commons spokesman on trade and industry and small business *party* joined Liberals in 1983 (Margaret Thatcher was effectively his recruiting sergeant); active at many levels of local party, mbr Woking DC 1986-90, chair Youth sub-cttee; PPC Weston-super-Mare 1997 (elected), re-elected 2001; vice chair All Party Parliamentary Small Business Gp, vice chair All Party Retail Gp, vice chair All Party China Gp, joint-chair All Party Manufacturing Gp, treasurer Autism Gp; former vice president PCA *special interests* development of fair legal and tax framework designed to promote and encourage small businesses, fair trade and international development issues (patron of SURF, a national charity for Rwandan widows) *other mbrships* NLC *recreations* reading, films, music *publications* Creating an Entrepreneurial Culture - Unleashing the Potential of Britain's Small Businesses (Centre for Reform 2001) *address* Brian Cotter, House of Lords, London SW1A 0PW *e-mail* brian@briancotter.org

COWAN, John Lessels *b* Jan 9, 1975 *seeking heiress education* Univ College, Suffolk *career* advertising sales Exec Puma Publishing 1997-99; marketing Exec McGuffie Brunton 2000-01; chief Exec Marlingford Sports Marketing 2001- *party* joined 1990; vice president Young Lib Dems 1992-93; vice chair Mid-Norfolk 1993-94; mbr Federal Sustainable Economy Policy Gp 1993-94; Eastern Region rep English Council 1994- ; leader Lib Dem Gp Barnham Broom PC 1996- ; mbr Charles Kennedy's leadership campaign team 1999; mbr English Council Exec 1999-2000 *special interests* Europe *other mbrships* European Movement, EMLD, LDEG *recreations* motor-sports, contemporary arts *address*.3 Chapel Close, Barnham Broom, Norwich *tel* 01603 759425 *e-mail* cowan@totalise.co.uk

COX, Michael Francis *b* May 14,1958 1 *s* 1 *d education* Salesian College, Shrigley, Bollington, Cheshire 1969-75; Thornleigh College, Bolton, Lancashire 1975-77; Brunel Univ 1977-81 *career* trainee Chartered Accountant Cooper Basden & Adamson 1981-85; qualified CA Cooper Lancaster 1985-87; Deloitte Haskins & Sells 1987-88; partner Cooper Lancaster 1988-97; founding partner Cox Costello & Horne 1997- *party* joined Liberals 1986; treasurer Hayes & Harlington Liberals 1987-90; secy City Liberal Democrats 1990-97; chair Ruislip Northwood LP 1985-98; vice chair Hillingdon LP 1999-2001, chair 2001-2004; GLA candidate Ealing & Hillingdon 2000, 2004; PPC Ruislip Northwood 2001, 2005; elected Cllr Ruislip Manor 2002; deputy gps leader 2002- ; chair Hillingdon Council Environment Overview & Scrutiny 2002- *special interests* chair Yugoslav Lifeline Humanitarian Organisation 1999-2000; treasurer Hillingdon Homestart 2002-05; governor Whiteheath Infant, Junior Schools 1998- ; company secy London Youth Games 1997-2004 *recreations* golf (badly), football (spectator) *address* 23 Breakspear

Road, Ruislip, Middlesex HA4 7QZ *tel* 01895-472965 home 01923-771977 business 01923-771988 *fax e-mail* michaelfcox@blueyonder.co.uk

CRAWFORD, Andrew *b* Jan 17, 1958 *ptnr* Jane Hanna 1 *s education* Neath Grammar School 1969-72, Gravesend Grammar School 1972-73, Isleworth Grammar School 1973-76; Manchester College, Oxford 1993-96 (2.1 in Philosophy, Politics and Economics); president JCR 1994-95; Associate of the Chartered Institute of Bankers *career* on three years unpaid leave to fight next General Election; finance administrator (part time) Epilepsy Bereaved 1999- ; risk manager Abbey National Treasury Services 1997-2003; risk manager Lehman Brothers, London 1996-97; head of internal audit; Crown Financial Management 1990-93; assistant vice president Chemical Bank 1981-89; management trainee; Lloyds Bank International Limited 1976-81 *party* joined 1989 in Winchester; rapid promotion from humble deliverer of *Focus* to constituency treasurer 1990-92; helped LP take control Winchester City Council; after Univ helped run campaign office, Henley 1997 General Election; Cllr (Greendown Ward) Vale of White Horse District Council 1999- (held 2003), elected (Marcham Division) Oxfordshire County Council 2001; completed hat trick Jan 2004 taking Wantage TC; deputy mayor of Wantage May 2004; PPC Wantage 2005 *special interests* environment, international relations, transport (especially rail), winning elections, public and consumer finance *other mbrships* trustee Wilts and Berks Canal Trust; trustee Courthill Trust, Wantage Youth Hostel on the Ridgeway; Sustrans, River Thames Alliance *recreations* walking, watching organic vegetables grow *publications* more *Focus* than you can shake the proverbial stick at. 1991- *address* 4 Charlton Road, Wantage, Oxfordshire OX12 8ER *tel* 01235 772782 home 01235 772851 *fax/*business *e-mail* andycrawford@dial.pipex.com

CROZIER, George Alex, senior political adviser to Lib Dem parliamentary party *b* May 22, 1972 *education* Croeswylan School, Oswestry 1983-88; North Shropshire College 1988-90; Univ of Southampton 1990-93 (BSc Politics/International Studies) *career* researcher, press officer Diana Maddock MP, 1993-97; researcher Liberal Democrat Leader's Office (then Paddy Ashdown MP) 1997-98; head of research, senior speechwriter, Leader's Office, 1998-99; senior political adviser Parliamentary Party; head Communications Unit, 1999- ; deputy director Lib Dem Parliamentary Resource Centre, 2003-05 *party* joined 1989; party activist 1990- ; exec mbr (co-opted) Student Lib Dems 1992; exec mbr Southampton Lib Dems 1992-93; casework officer Christchurch, Eastleigh, Littleborough and Saddleworth by-elections 1993-95; mbr (staff) housing policy working group 1995-96; absent votes officer, researcher Winchester by-election 1997; editorial board mbr (staff), 1998 Policy Review; mbr HQ results analysis team, local elections 1998-99, 2002-03, general election 2001; mbr editorial board *Parliamentary Campaigner* (PCA newsletter) 1999- ; helped set up Lib Dem extranet 2000-01; head General Election communications team, 2001, 2005; accredited senior party trainer 2002- ; local election candidate Tower Hamlets LBC 2002 *special interests* the internet/IT and politics, international affairs, polling, electoral analysis *other mbrships* Friends of the Earth; exec cttee, Lib Dems in PR (LDiPR); exec cttee Government Affairs Group, Chartered Institute of Public Relations (CIPR GAG); Westminster gym *recreations* eating out, music, quizzes *publications* co-editor *Research Resources Handbook* for parliamentary staff; editor *Signposts for the Next Ten Years*, a pamphlet of speeches by Paddy Ashdown 1999; lead draftsman, party strategy consultative paper 1999; editor *Liberal Democrat End of Year Report* 2003; numerous party briefings, reports *address* 23 Aberavon Road, Bow, London, E3 5AR telephone 020 7219 3374 office 07740 477374 mobile *fax* 020 7219 5713 *e-mail* crozierg@parliament.uk (work), crozierg@yahoo.co.uk (personal)

CUTHBERTSON, Ian Michael *b* Oct 24, 1945 Bradford *partner* Carol Runciman *qv* 1 *s* 2 *ss* 2 *sd education* Bradford GS; West Cheshire Central College of FE; Univ of Bradford *career* local govt officer 1964-67 (Bradford CBC); civil servant 1967-75 (Min of Power, Min of Defence); programmer/analyst, technical specialist, development team leader, company director 1975-87; consultant 1987- (specializing in HCI/usability, corporate systems and database development, systems migration, data collection/exchange and embedded systems applications, team-building and project management; information systems manager 2003- ; p/t teacher, lecturer 1993- ; *party* joined 1994; Treasurer Vale of York LP 2003-6, secy 2001-02; Treasurer Yorks & Humber Region 1998-99, chair 2000-01 and 2003-04; vice chair English Council Exec 2001; treasurer English Party 2002-05; PPC Dewsbury 2001 and Selby 2005; candidate Heworth ward, City of York 1999; elected as Cllr for Strensall ward, City of York 2003; Returning Officer; Assessor and Facilitator; Agent; accredited Party Trainer mbr of ALDC, PCA, Friends of LDYS *special interests* education, finance, party and candidate development *other mbrships* Centre Forum *recreations* music (singing, performing, listening), theatre, walking, cycling, sailing *publications* author, contributor to and editor of various technical papers *style* Cllr Ian Cuthbertson *address* Spurr House, Plainville Lane, Wigginton, York YO32 2RG *tel* 01904 764356, 07944 259074 *e-mail* icuthbertson@cix.co.uk

D

DAHRENDORF, Lord Ralf: Life Peer cr 1993 *b* Hamburg 1929 *education* Hamburg Univ (DPhil); London and sociology (PhD sociology) *career* professor of sociology, taught at various European and American universities; Mbr German Bundestag; Commissioner EEC; Director London School of Economics 1974-84; Warden St. Anthony's College, Pro-Vice-Chancellor Univ of Oxford.1987-97 *party* joined German Free Liberal Party 1967; elected to the Bundestag 1969, Foreign Office minister in Willy Brandt's Govt; mbr of Commission of European Economic Communities (responsible for Foreign Trade and External Relations) 1970-71, reappointed (responsible for Research, Science and Education) 1973-74; adopted British citizenship 1988, created Liberal Democrat life peer 1993; mbr Lords European Union Cttee, sub-Cttees on trade and economic affairs, and delegated powers and deregulation *publications* numerous books include *Class and Class Conflict* 1959; *Society and Democracy in Germany* 1966; *The Modern Social Conflict* 1988; *Reflections on the Revolution in Europe* 1990 *address* House of Lords, London SW1A 0PW

DAKERS, Andrew Stuart *b* Apr 30, 1979 *education* Open Univ (MSc Development Management) 2000-02; Huddersfield Univ 1998-99; Hampton, Surrey 1992-97; Colet Court, London 1989-1992 *career* London & South East Campaigns

Officer, WWF-UK 2005-; Communications & Business Change Advisor, GlaxoSmithKline, London 2003-04; United Nations, New York 2002; *AY UP!* radio, magazine (Univ of Huddersfield Students' Union) 1998-1999; Kiira College Butiki, Jinja, Uganda 1998; Computing Associates, London 1994-98 *party* joined 2000; vice chair of Hounslow Borough Liberal Democrats 2003; approved PPC Apr 2004 *special interests* international development, community politics, environment, corporate social responsibility *other mbrships* Brentford Recycling Action Gp; Centre Forum; Institute of Public Relations, Government Affairs Group; Open Univ Development & Environment Society; Chatham House; United Nations Association *recreations* travel, scuba diving, hiking, music, theatre, fine art *address* The Cedars, 2 Upper Butts, Brentford, Middx TW8 8DA *tel* 07788 116159 or 020 8568 2209 *e-mail* hi@andrewdakers.com *web* www.andrewdakers.com

DALE, Thomas Edward (Tom) DL 1996 *b* Clacton-on-Sea Mar 14,1931 *education* Colchester Royal Grammar School; Gosfield School, Halstead; LSE; London Univ Institute of Education (hons degree in economics, PCGE) *career* National Service Royal Artillery; teacher 1951-55; Warden, Cambridge International Centre 1960-65; PR consultant to various political and semi-political orgs 1966-85; director T.E.A.M. Promotions Ltd 1986- (now part-time); secy, The Hampden (Educational) Trust 1967- ; overseas fund-raising manager Fight-for-Sight appeal of Inst of Ophthalmology and Moorfields Eye Hosp; dctr Mercialodge Ltd 1987- ; corporate fund-raising mngr YMCA Foyer, Colchester 1999-2000 *party* org secy British Gp Liberal International 1965-96, v president 1997- ; assistant to Rt Hon Jeremy Thorpe 1967-76; research assistant Lord Russell Johnston 1986-87; secy Lib Pty International, Euro Affairs Co-ord Cttee 1980-86; Liberal Party international officer 1976-85; mbr exec ELDR 1977-85; Liberal Party Council until 1986; NEC 1976-81; secy, vice-chair, chair Eastern Region 1962-80; secy, Halstead Lib Association 1952-54; held every office in Harwich Division Lib Association; PPC Harwich (four times), Central Suffolk; president Harwich LP; president, Essex North LP; secy Liberal Summer School 1967-74; Lib Euro Action Gp 1971-75, 1976-82 *local Govt:* mbr (for Brightlingsea) Essex CC 1965-66, 1972-77, 1981-97 (Lib Dem Gp leader 1989-93, council chair 1995-96); Tendring DC 1979-95, chair Finance Cttee, mbr 2000-02, chair Regulatory Cttee 2001- 02; St Osyth PC 1979-87; Brightlingsea TC 1991- (mayor, 1996, 1997, 1999); chair Consumer Affairs Cttee ACC 1986-89; Cttee mbr Essex Association of Local Councils 2000- *other interests* pres, Univ of London SU 1957; governor LSE 1981-86; chair governors Gosfield School 1976-83, now foundation governor; governor NE Essex Tech College 1982-88 ; mbr EA Tourist Boarrd 1981-97; Kent and Essex Sea Fisheries Cttee 1981-97; Essex Flood Def Cttee 1993-97; East of England Region Flood Def Cttee 1995-99; mbr Court, Essex Univ 1997- ; Freeman of Brightlingsea 1994- *clubs* NLC (mbr General Cttee) *address* 38 High Street, Brightlingsea, Essex CO7 0AQ

DASH, Brian David *b* Jun 24 1939 *m* 2 *s* 2 *d education* Gosport Central School; Portsmouth College of Technology; Southampton Technical College; Portsmouth Polytechnic; IEE Part III; HNC Electrical Engineering; HND Mechanical Engineering; Chartered Engineer; MIMech E, MIEE Dip Mgt Studies (Dist) *career* student apprentice, technical staff trainee CEGB; operations engineer Marchwood, Fawley power stations, reliability and efficiency engineer Fawley power station *party* founder mbr SDP 1981; vice chair Hants & Wight Region 1989-93; New Forest district Cllr 1983-87, 1993-03; Hants County Cllr 1989- ; Hythe & Dibden parish Cllr 1983-2003; agent New Forest East 1997, PPC 2001; PPC New Forest East 1995 *special interests* education, economics *other mbrships* Hants Wildlife Trust, governor Langdown Junior School, Noadswood Comprehensive, Totton 6th Form College; co-chair Hythe Skate & Ride; Waterside Neighbourhood Family project; Hythe Town Centre Development Gp; never a mbr of Young Conservatives! *recreations* nine grandchildren, golf, travel, reading (politics) *publications* co-author of IMechE technical papers *address* 38 Jones Lane Hythe Southampton Hants SO45 6AX *tel* 02380 846019 home 07850 543261 mobile *fax* 02380 840422 *e-mail* dashes@globalnet.co.uk; brian.dash@hants.gov.uk

DATE, Geoffrey *b* Mar 11, 1943 *s* of Andrew and Margaret Date (nee Watson) *m* Tricia (nee Fowler) 1 *s* Stephen 1 *d* Sarah *education* qualified 1971: Chartered Institute of Public Finance and Accountancy *career* director South Devon Accountancy Ltd *party* mbr Devon CC 2001- ; South Hams DC 1995 - ; Totnes TC 1991- ; chair Totnes LP 1994-98; mbr English Council *recreations* wine, reading, pub quizzes *address* 4 Brooklands, Totnes, Devon TQ9 5AR *tel* 01803 865183 *fax* 01803 865622 *e-mail* geoff.date@devon.gov.uk

DAVEY, Edward MP (Kingston & Surbiton maj:8,966) **Shadow Secy of State for Trade and Industry** *b* Mansfield, Notts Christmas Day, 1965 *m* Emily Gasson *qv* July 2005 *education* Nottingham HS; Jesus College, Oxford (PPE 1st class: president JCR 1985-1988); Birkbeck College, London Univ (MSc Economics) *career* during gap year worked in pork pie factory, Boots plc, hitch-hiked round Spain, holiday courier in France; senior economics advisor, Lib Dem MPs (mainly Alan Beith and Paddy Ashdown); closely involved in developing policies such as penny-on-income-tax for education, making the Bank of England independent; costed 1992 election manifesto); Omega Partners (management consultants) specialised in postal services, worked on projects for post offices in 28 countries including Belgium, South Africa, Sweden and Taiwan 1993-97 *party* Shadow Secy of State for Trade and Industry 2006- ; Shadow Office of the Deputy Prime Minister 2002-05; previously spokesman for London LibDems on the economy, employment and tourism; mbr Federal Policy Cttee, various other policy gps; PPC Kingston and Surbiton 1997 (elected after three recounts: maj 56), re-elected 2001, 2005; economic affairs spokesman in Malcolm Bruce's Treasury team; promoted by Charles Kennedy to deputy Matthew Taylor's Treasury team (with responsibility for public spending and taxation policy); spokesman on London (worked with Susan Kramer's mayoral campaign); mbr Procedure Select Cttee 1997-99, Treasury Select Cttee 1999- ; mbr Standing Cttees, including Finance Bills, the Bank of England, Govt Resources and Accounts Bills, Govt for London Bill *special awards* from Royal Humane Society, Chief Constable British Transport Police 1994 *publications Random Facts* (regular local newspaper column); *Making MPs Work for Our Money* (Centre Forum, 2000) available at *web* www.edwarddavey.co.uk *recreations* walking, cinema, music, squash, swimming, football (Notts County, Kingstonian FC) *address* House of Commons, London SW1A 0AA *constituency* 21 Berrylands Road, Surbiton, Surrey KT5 8QX *tel* 020 8288 0161 *fax* 020 8288 1090 *e-mail* daveye@parliament.uk *web* www.edwarddavey.co.uk

DAVIES, Chris MEP for NW England *b* Jul 7, 1954 *m* Carol 1 *d* Kate *education* Cheadle Hulme School, Stockport; Cambridge Univ, Gonville & Caius College *career* marketing and communications consultant *party* joined 1974; Liverpool City

Cllr 1980-84, chair Housing Estate Management sub-Cttee 1980-1; deputy chair Housing & Building Cttee 1982-3; chair Housing & Building Cttee 1982-3; mbr Oldham Borough Council 1994-98; PPC Littleborough & Saddleworth 1987, 1992, 1995 by-election: elected; PPC Oldham East 1997; MP for Littleborough & Saddleworth 1995-97; MEP (North West of England) 1999, re-elected 2004; leader of the UK gp of Liberal Democrats in European Parliament 2004-06; Lib Dem environment spokesman, European Parliament; mbr and ELDR spokesman on the Environment, Public Health and Food Safety Cttee; mbr Budgetary Control Cttee; Delegation mbr to the EU-Cyprus Joint Parliamentary Cttee *recreations* fell running *address* 4 Higher Kinders, Greenfield, Saddleworth, Oldham OL3 7BH *tel* 01457 870236 home 0161 477 7070 business *fax* 0161 477 7007 *e-mail* chrisdaviesmep@cix.co.uk

DAVIES, Jonathan *b* Jan 29, 1962 *education* Gravesend School for Boys; Christ Church, Oxford; The College of Law; qualified as solicitor 1986 *career* Reynolds Porter Chamberlain, partner 1989- (specialising in financial services, insurance) *party* founder mbr SDP 1980, and organised Alliance's first successful election campaign in Oxford – Central Ward 1982; local party officer in Haringey, Hendon South, Hendon, and Finchley and Golders Green (treasurer 2006-); London Regional Officer, chair 1993-5 and 2002-4, secy 1990-93, treasurer 1995-2000; treasurer, English Party 2006- ; mbr Federal Finance and Administration Cttee 2001-03; one of the Party's constitutional experts - member of the Constitutional Review working group, 1992-3; councillor: Childs Hill Ward, LB of Barnet 1994-98; PPC Finchley & Golders Green 1997, Hertsmere 2005; GLA candidate (Barnet & Camden) 2000; parliamentary and local govt election agent, including 1992 and 2001 General Elections *address* 6 Carlton Close, London NW3 7UA *tel* 020 8455 5956 *e-mail* jonathandavies@cix.co.uk

DAVIES, Nicola Sian *b* Aug 21, 1973 *education* Univ of Wales Swansea (BA Hons, MA) *career* local govt affairs manager for telecommunications industry; former parliamentary researcher Lord Livsey, Lembit Opik MP; A-level politics, philosophy teacher *party* joined 1992; PPC Birmingham Hodge Hill 2005 and in 2004 by-election; West Midlands Euro list candidate 2004; PPC Birmingham Edgbaston 2001; exec mbr PCA 2003-05; former mbr West Midlands Exec, Liberal International *special interests* environment and planning *recreations* travel, sport (swimming, mountain biking), cinema *address* 1 Manor Farmhouse, Lime Avenue, Leamington Spa CV32 7DB *tel* 01926 315 013 *e-mail* nicola_s_davies@yahoo.co.uk

DAWE, Jennifer Ann (Jenny) *b* Edinburgh, Apr 27, 1945 *divorced* (nee Beveridge) *4 s* Robert, Gavin, Kenneth, Craig *4 gs 1 gd education* Trinity Academy, Edinburgh; Aberdeen Univ; Edinburgh Univ MA, PhD (Thesis: A History of Cotton-growing in East and Central Africa) *career* librarian, Tanzania and Malawi 1966-80; part-time Tutor, American & Commonwealth History department, Edinburgh Univ 1985-87; Admin & Information Officer, Lothian Community Relations Council, 1988-90; Welfare Rights Officer, Lothian Regional Council, 1990-96; Senior Welfare Rights Officer, Welfare Rights Team, East Lothian Council 1996- ; *party* mbr Edinburgh West, local council candidate 1992 & 1995; PPC Edinburgh Pentlands, 1997; elected as Edinburgh City Councillor, October 1997; leader of LibDem Gp, City of Edinburgh Council 1999- ; joined party in 1961, while still at school; held various offices within Local Parties, including Treasurer, Mbrship Secy, Convener; past mbr of Scottish Policy Cttee and Scottish Conference Cttee; editor of '*Clifton Terrace Focus*' from Edition 1 in Oct 1993 to Nov 1997 *other mbrships* Amnesty International; World Development Movement; Refugee Council supporter special interests human rights; social justice; electoral reform; fair international development recreations travel, reading, gardening *style* Cllr Dr *address* City Chambers, High Street, Edinburgh; *tel* 0131 529 4987 *e-mail* jenny.dawe@edinburgh.gov.uk; jenny.dawe@tiscali.co.uk

DEARDEN, Stephanie *b* Feb 3, 1956 Blackburn *div* 3 *ch* in wedlock *education* Intack County Primary, Ballakermeen High School, Everton 2nd Modern *career* Engineer, manager at 21, worked for PO as technician; worked for many years in transport as a logistics manager, IT engineer and then director before commiting to raising her family *party* exec mbr Battersea & Tooting LP; Tooting branch mbr, secy, Press & Publicity Officer, conference delegate; PPC Tooting 2005; candidate Graveney (target ward) Focus Team; cllr; mbr DELGA, GBTF, WLD, LDCF, LDO *other mbrships* Environmental Forum, Education Overview & Scrutiny, Schools Admissions Forum, Wandsworth Community Empowerment Fund Network, Churches Together Tooting *special interests* eating out, railways and transportation *recreations* travelling, Command & Conquer, RA2 *LD quirk* won 1st prize for best Focus in London region in 2005 *style* Rev Sister *address*14 Effort Street, Tooting London SW17 0QR *tel* 07985 649807 *fax* 020 7771 2551 *e-mail* stephanie@stephaniedearden.org *web* http://www.stephaniedearden.org/

DEAVIN, Christopher Edward *b* Aug 6, 1967 *m* Helen *education* Churcher's College, Petersfield; Plymouth Univ (Politics/Law); Imperial College (MBA) *career* Euromoney Publications PLC; *Financial Times*; Datamonitor PLC; Standard and Poor's Jan 2002- ; *party* Advisory Board, Liberal Democrat Business Forum; mbr Liberty Network; mbr Twickenham Riverside mbrship development secy) and St Margaret's Ward branch; supporter CentreForum; created long-term business plan for Federal Party (2002) working with the Chief Exec, Treasurer and others as part of a wider initiative to increase professionalism and fundraising at a national level *special interests* funding, effectiveness of the Federal party, constitutional reform in UK *other mbrships* The Pimlico Strollers Cricket Club, Esher CC, The Friends of The Lord's Taverners; The Scotch Malt Whisky Society *recreations* Playing cricket, watching Portsmouth Football Club, reading - especially *Private Eye,* travelling *address* 16 Alexandra Road, East Twickenham, Middlesex, TW1 2HE *tel* 0208 892 7181 mobile 07879 408467 *e-mail* Christopher_Deavin@StandardandPoors.com

DEEDMAN, Derek *b* Mar 25, 1947 Bournemouth *m* 4 *s* 1 *sd education* Stourfield/Beaufort Secondary School -1964, qualified as Public Finance Accountant 1969 *career* local govt officer (public finance accountant) Bournemouth CBC 1964, Brighton CBC 1970, East Sussex CC 1974, took early retirement 1997 *party* mbr and chair Arundel & South Downs LP in SE Region, cllr Adur DC 1976-84 and 1986-90 (council chair 1981-83, deputy ldr 1986-90), cllr West Sussex CC Bramber Castle division, PPC Gravesend 1992, Arundel & South Downs 2001 and 2005; mbr ALDC, LD Agents & Organisers Assoc *other mbrships* Make Votes Count *special interests* public transport, highways, finance *publications* Focus for many years *recreations* family, canaries, reading *style* Cllr *address* 13 Canons Way, Steyning, West Sussex BN44 3SS *tel* 01903 814314 home, 01903 879917 (cllr business only) *e-mail* derek.deedman@tiscali.co.uk or derek.deedman@westsussex.gov.uk

DERING, Stephen Matthew *b* Frimley, Surrey May 21, 1977 *education* post-graduate Exec diploma in management, Barking College; Univ of Wales, Swansea 1996-98; Mary Hare Grammar School, Newbury 1989-96 *career* regional director, deafPLUS 2003- ; public affairs officer Shelter 2001-03; campaigns manager South Wales West Liberal Democrats 1999-2001; manager West Norfolk Deaf Association 1998-99 *party* joined 1991 (age13); mbr (Thornton ward) LB Lambeth 2002 (youngest Cllr in Lambeth, first profoundly deaf mbr in borough's history) *special interests* disability, housing *other mbrships* Chartered Institute of Managers, Institute of Public Relations *recreations* gym, water sports, travel *address*15 Quayview Apartments, Arden Crescent, London E14 9WA *tel/fax* 020 7790 6147 *e-mail* dering@cix.co.uk

DEWAN, Ramesh *b* May 2, 1947 *m* 1 *d education* St Xavier, Jaipur; NCRT, Northern Poly *party* mbr Federal Exec for ten of last twelve years and Federal Policy Cttee for three years; director Liberty Network; founder chair of Asian Liberal Democrats; chaired Ethnic Minorities Working Gp; mbr WLD *other mbrships* advisory board mbr CentreForum; Fawcett Society *special interests* equal opportunities, greater autonomy for English regions *address* 31 West Drive, Harrow Weald, Middlesex HA3 6TX *tel* 020 8861 0500 *fax* 020 8861 2129

DHOLAKIA of Waltham Brooks, Baron Navnit: Life Peer cr 1997, OBE, DL: Deputy Leader of Liberal Democrats in House of Lords: Lords Spokesperson on Home Office and Legal Affairs President of the Liberal Democrats 2000-04; *Asian of the Year* (2000); Pravasi Bharatiyan Sanman Award (2003) *b* Apr 3, 1937 *m* Ann 2 *d* Anjali (lawyer), Alene (doctor) *education* India, UK *career* appointments with Commission for Racial Equality, Police Complaints Authority, Ethnic Minority Advisory Cttee of Judicial Studies Board, Lord Carlile's Cttee Parole Systems Review; magistrate; mbr Board of Visitors HM Prison Lewes *party* joined Liberals in Brighton, 1950s; House of Lords front bench spokesman, Home Affairs; mbr House of Lords Appointments Commission; mbr advisory board Centre Forum; president of the party 200-04; patron The Liberty Network; trustee Parliamentary Appeal for Romanian Children *other interests* Deputy Lieutenant, County of West Sussex (Jun 1999); chair, National Association for the Care and Resettlement of Offenders (NACRO), chair Race Issues Advisory Cttee; council mbr Save the Children Fund; Howard League for Penal Reform, mbr ed board Howard Journal; trustee Mental Health Foundation; gov Commonwealth Institute; mbr Management Board, Policy Research Institute on Ageing & Ethnicity; trustee The Ghandi Trust, Dr J *m* Singhvi Foundation, Pallant House Gallery, Chichester, British Empire & Commonwealth Museum, Bristol; mbr LSE's Mannheim Centre for Criminology and Criminal Justice; mbr Home Secy's Race Forum; v pres Tower Hamlets Race Equality Council; v pres The Family Welfare Association; patron Friends of ASRA, Greater London Housing Association; AHISMA, for Quality of Life; FOCUS; Gatwick Detainees Welfare Gp; Hope for Children; Indo-Caribbean Sanatan Cultural Society; International School for Information & Technology, Hyderabad, India; JANUSZ, The World Trust; Mid. Sussex Mediation; Memorial Gates Trust; Debate of the Age; NRI Club International (Birmingham); Naz Foundation; Oxford Centre for Hindu Studies; Pan Project; PRESET; SIA, The National Development Agency for the Black Voluntary Sector; FEMAH Foundation for Ethnic Minorities Action for Health; Spitalfields Life; Student Partnership World Wide; Thare machi - Starfish Initiative; UNA, International Year for the Culture of Peace (2000); Royal Holloway Campaign for Resource; 4 SIGHT (West Sussex Association for the Blind); Wise Thoughts; Prisoners Abroad; India International Foundation; Purley Park Trust; Punjabie Theatre Academy; council mbr Indian Jewish Association UK; Commission on the Future of Multi-Ethnic Britain; Caine Prize for African Writing; *recreations* cooking, photography, gardening *address* House of Lords, London SW1 0PW *tel* 020 7219 5203 *fax* 020 7219 2082

DHONAU, Mary *b* May 30, 1958 Reading *m* 5 *ch* 3 of whom are adult and one who suffers from severe autism *education* Headington County School Oxford; Royal College of Music (singing and operatic studies) *career* coordinator of the National Flood Forum (a grassroots organisation set up to help people at risk of flooding *party* mbr and vice-chair Worcester LP in West Midlands; PPC Worcester 2005; mbr PCA, ALDC *special interests* flooding *recreations* singing when I've got the time *address* 1 Waverley Street, Worcester WR5 3DH *tel* 01905 353104 home 01905 351933 work 07754592534 mobile *e-mail* mary@dhonau.eclipse.co.uk *website* www. marydhonau.com

DIXON, Michael David (Mike) Treasurer PCA *b* Aug 14, 1957 *m* Pam 1979 1 *s* Andy 1 *d* Vicky *education* Rushcliffe Comprehensive; experimental 2-year art foundation course, Nottingham *career* K Shoes, London, Nottingham and Birmingham 1975-83; sales and marketing, Dasco Shoe Care Ltd 1983-88; training advisor Chamber of Commerce 1988-90; proprietor catering company 1990-97; boat builder 1997-2003; Liz Lynne MEP 2003-05; Stratford-upon Avon Lib Dems 2003-05; organiser City of Birmingham 2005- ; *party* joined 1998; chair Wyre Forest LP 1999; mbr Exec English Council 2000- ; exec PCA 2000- , treasurer, mbrship secy 2002- ; mbr Crime and Policing Working Party 2000, W Mids Regional Exec 2001; agent county by-election 1999; candidate district elections 1999-2000; PPC Wolverhampton SW 2001, Edgbaston 2005; canvass and campaign manager West Worcs 2001; PEPC West Midlands 2004; core-team mbr Hodge Hill By-election (ran in-house printing, managed back of house) Jul 2004; ran the re-run fraud elections Aston and Bordesley 2005; accredited trainer: Campaigns, Agents and Mbrship *special interests* law and order; policing; defence *recreations* spending as much time as possible with my new grandson, cooking, walking, blues and baroque music *address* 22 Warbler Place, Kidderminster, Worcs DY10 4DZ *tel/fax* 01562 742146 *e-mail* mike@mikedixon.org

DONALDSON, Iain Colin *b* Jun 13, 1964 *education* Wright Robinson High School; Openshaw Technical College *career* sales, marketing and administration life and, pensions industry 1984-93; finance administration Univ of Manchester 1993-2003; Research Secy, Univ of Manchester 2003- *party* joined Liberal Democrats at foundation 1988; currently chair of Candidates Cttee for City of Manchester Liberal Democrats; mbr North West Regional Exec; mbr English Council; mbr Manchester City Council 1992- , mbr Community Regeneration *special interests* markets, community development, enablement, community regeneration, licensing and legal affairs, environment and environmental planning *other mbrships* Green Liberal Democrats, DELGA, Agents Association, PCA, ALDC *recreations* reading, writing, cycling, karaoke *address* 2 Abbeywood Avenue, Debdale, Manchester M18 7JZ *tel* 0161 231 6869 *e-mail* donaldsonic@btopenworld.com

DOOCEY, Dee OBE: London-wide Mbr, Greater London Authority *m* Jim 1 *s* Mark *career* management consultant, former MD international fashion company *party* elected Greater London Assembly Jun 2004; chair Economic Development, Culture, Sport and Tourism Cttee (the Assembly's lead cttee on the Olympics, and which also develops and analyses policies on housing, economic development, culture, sport and tourism for London); mbr of the Metropolitan Police Authority, and sits on its Planning Performance and Review Cttee; campaign mngr/agent Twickenham 1992, 1997; finance director Liberals, Liberal Democrats for ten years; financial advisor to parliamentary party 1979-89; fmr mbr Richmond LBC (8 yrs), fmr chair Housing; fmr chair WLD; mbr FCC *special interests* housing, homelessness, regeneration of communities *recreations* theatre, skiing *clubs* NLC *address* 21 Percy Road, Hampron, Middlesex, TW12 2HW *tel* 020 7983 4797 *e-mail* dee.doocey@london.gov.uk

DOUGHTY, Sue *b* Apr 13, 1948 *m* David Vyvyan Orchard 2 *s* 2 *sd education* Mill Mount GSI, York; Northumberland College of Education (CertEd); Hon Fellow Chartered Institute of Waste Management *career* teaching East Riding of Yorkshire 1970-71; work-study analyst Northern Gas 1971-75; CEGB 1975-76; O&M analyst Wilkinson Match 1976-77; career break (maternity; charity activity) 1978-82; industrial consultant 1982-88; IT Project Manager Thames Water 1989-98; management consultant 1999-2001; MP for Guildford 2001-05; re-selected as PPC Guildford 2006; parliamentary consultant *party* joined Liberal Party in Newbury; former exec mbr Chilterns region; constituency chair, Reading East; currently President – Women Liberal Democrats; deputy president Federal Party with responsibility for Women *special interests* environment, mental health, equality *other mbrships* Green Liberal Democrats; County Club, Guildford; Institute of Directors *recreations* walking, gardening, theatre, delivering *Focus* *address* The Hall, Woking Road, Guildford, GU1 1QD *tel* 01483 306000 *fax* 01483 306031 *e-mail* orcharddoughty@cix.co.uk

DUFF, Andrew Nicholas OBE MEP Eastern Region *b* Christmas Day, 1950 Birkenhead *education* Sherborne School, Dorset; St John's College, Cambridge (BA Hons, MA Cantab, MLitt); L'Institut d'Etudes Europeennes, L'Universite Libre de Brussels *career* research officer, Hansard Society; consultant EC affairs; research fellow Joseph Rowntree Trust; director Federal Trust, London; board mbr, Trans-European Policy Studies Association, Brussels *party* joined Liberals 1974; mbr Cambridge City Council (Castle ward) 1982-90 (gp leader 1988-90); v-president Liberal Democrats; chair English Council; mbr Federal Exec, Federal Finance and Admin Cttee 1994-97; PPC Huntingdon 1992; Euro candidate Cambridgeshire 1984, 1989, 1994, Eastern Region 1999 (elected MEP); co-ordinator Constitutional Affairs Cttee; mbr Charter Convention 1999-2000; mbr European Convention 2002-03 & chair Liberal caucus; first v-president, delegation, EU-Turkey; substitute mbr Cttee on Foreign Affairs, Human Rights, Common Security and Defence policy *publications* inc *Understanding the Euro* (Federal Trust, Kogan Page 1998), *The Treaty of Amsterdam* (Federal Trust, Sweet & Maxwell 1997) *address* Orwell House, Cowley Road, Cambridge CB4 0PP *tel* 01223 566700 *fax* 01223 566 698 *e-mail* mep@andrewduffmep.org www.andrewduffmep.org

DUFFIELD, Andrew John Richard *b* Jan 12, 1963 *m* Helen 1 *s* Jay 1 *d* Maia *education* Plymouth College; Durham Univ (St Chad's); officer training

Britannia, Royal Naval College, Dartmouth *career* currently senior manager Newcastle Univ Students Union; previously A&E,T&O manager NHS; retail area manager Bass; seaman officer Royal Navy *party* joined 1990; PPC Tynemouth 1997, Sedgefield 2001, Hexham 2005; Euro candidate Northern Region list 1999; mbr Northumberland County Council (Morpeth Kirkhill) 2001-2005; mbr Alnwick District Council (Rothbury South Rural Ward) 2003- ; *special interests* All libertarian pursuits: free, fair and sustainable global economics; in particular, fiscal reform through phased removal of taxes on income, enterprise and value added, replaced by charges on use of natural and community-created resources (esp. Land Value Taxation) and re-cycling wealth to fund a universal, non-means tested citizen's income. *other mbrships* Exec ALTER (Action for Land Taxation & Economic Reform) *recreations* walking in Northumberland with family and 2 English Springers. *publications* still working on blockbuster; several unpublished board games *address* Riversview, Physic Lane, Thropton, Northumberland NE65 7HU *tel* 01669 620 450 home; 07762 329367 mobile *e-mail* duffieldX@aol.com

DUNDAS, Charles Christopher *b* Jul 19, 1978 Bellshill, North Lanarkshire *m* Siobhan Mathers Dec 11, 2004 *education* Whitburn Academy, West Lothian; Univ of Glasgow (MA, History) *career* finance assistant, National Australia Banking Gp 2001-2002: assistant to Iain Smith MSP 2002- ; North East Fife constituency organiser 2003- ; *party* president, Glasgow Univ LibDems (GULD) 1998-99; PPC Glasgow Baillieston 2001; PSPC Glasgow Springburn Ward 2003; PPC Livingston May 2005; agent to Sir Menzies Campbell MP 2005; by-election candidate Livingston Sept 2005; mbr Edinburgh North & Leith *special interests* constitutional reform, civil liberties, international affairs, progressive taxation, the arts *other mbrships* Fellow, Society of Antiquaries of Scotland; life mbr, Glasgow Univ Union *recreations* history, cinema, literature *address* 63 Madeira Street, Leith, Edinburgh, EH6 4AX *tel* .0131 553 5462 home, 07966 119741 mobile *e-mail* mail@charlesdundas.org.uk *website* www.charlesdundas.org.uk

DUNK, George *b* Jan 13, 1951 eldest son of Gordon (dcsd) and Helen – St Ives, Cornwall and Westerham, Kent *m* Sandra Mason (dcsd) of Cape Town, Mar 31, 1990 *education* South Bromley College; Bromley College of Technology; City of London Poly (including studies at CIFE Bruges) *career* former marine insurance broker at Lloyd's; co-founder and Chair of the GST Group, Athens; Director Delta Publishing Ltd; independent arbitrator and mbr Valuation Tribunal Service; freelance travel writer and political adviser *party* joined Liberals 1967; former Chair SE England YLF; International Vice-Chair NLYL; LYMEC; EFLRY; PPC Kent 1974, Woking 1979; former Chair, Agents Association; successful Party agent electing 39 candidates to public office; former deputy leader of the twenty-seven strong Opposition Gp on LB Southwark and Vice-Chair London Region; former mbr policy working gp on aviation, airports and air travel; currently organising research and liaison visits for party members to European institutions for and on behalf of LDEG; mbr LDEG Exec *special interests* founder Sahara Action Committee 1977; development and maintenance of fair democratic processes in South Africa, Kenya and Sierra Leone and how the NHS treat our elderly *recreations* sailing; watching cricket and rugby; exploring; motoring; flying and photography *clubs* London Cornish (life member); South Africa Society; The Newlands Club (rugby); Univ of Cape Town Yacht Club; Surrey County Cricket Club; Great Western Society and the Cape Hope Flying Club *publications* "The Forgotten War" 1980 *address* 2 Dean

Close, London SE16 5PH *tel* 020 7252 1920 home 07944 908389 mobile e-***mail*** george.dunk@btinternet.com

DUNN, Jody *b* Jul 27, 1969 *m* 2 Martin, 2000 2 *s* Charlie, Cameron 2 *d* Saskia, Lucy *education* City of London School for Girls, Barbican; Woodhouse Sixth Form School; St Andrew's Univ (BA Hons Spanish, International Relations); City Univ (post-graduate diploma in Law (CPE) with commendation 1996-97); Inns of Court School of Law (graded outstanding, top 15 in country; finalist World Debating Championships in Cork 1996; winner European Debating Championships in London 1997 (received trophy from Cherie Blair); multi-lingual English, Finnish, Spanish, conversational Swedish, French, basic German and Dutch *career* left school at 17; DJ London stores; DJ, radio presenter Finland (three years); travelled (for two years) DJ-ing in Malta, Sweden, Bermuda, Cyprus; BBC CWR (Coventry and Warwickshire Radio); Barrister criminal law, now family law specialist Amicus Chambers Jul 2003- ; law specialist, columnist *Middlesbrough Gazette party* PPC Hartlepool by-election 2003 (committed to being an MP who lives, works in town) *publications Control Your Divorce* (Jun 2003); *How to Help the Children Survive the Divorce* (Jul 2004) *recreations* judo (brown belt); languages, poetry, travel *address* 33 Spalding Road, Hartlepool TS25 2JS *e-mail* info@hartlepool-libdems.org.uk *web* www.hartlepool-libdems.org.uk

DUNPHY, Peter Gerard *b* Jun 24, 1966 Consett *m education* St Bedes, Lanchester, Durham; Univ of Liverpool 1985-88 BA (Hons) Politics *career* financial services recruitment 1989- ; founder, now Group CEO, Darwin Rhodes (financial recruitment) 1996- ; *party* joined SDP in 1982; worked for Ian Wrigglesworth MP 1985-86; National Secretary (1985-86) and National Chair (1986-87) of Young Social Democrats; mbr of 'Yes to Unity' campaign 1987; founder mbr Liberal Democrats; PPCs Association Exec 1998- , chair 2000-2002; director, Liberty Network; mbr Westminster LP; PPC Hornsey & Wood Green 1992, Dagenham (by-election) 1994, Walthamstow 2001; local election agent 1990, 94, 98, 2004, 05. 06; cllr London Borough of Waltham Forest 2002-2006; mbr PCA, LD Humanists and Secularists, Liberty Network *special interests* financial services, taxation, international affairs, pensions *other mbrships* National Liberal Club, National Secular Society, CAMRA life mbr *recreations* football (Newcastle United season ticket), travel, psephology, music, occasional Cossack dancing *address* 13 Queensborough Mews, London W2 3SG *tel* 07966 531863 *e-mail* petergdunphy@hotmail.com

DYER, Hong Ling *b* Sept 19 1977 China 1 *s education* Holton-Arms School, Bethesda, MD USA 1989-95; MA from Univ of Aberdeen 1998-2001; postgraduate certificate from Institut International des Droits de l'Homme 2004 *career* researcher at Liberty National Council for Civil Liberties 2001-02; researcher to Tom Brake MP 2002-06; Project Officer with Islington Strategic Partnership 2006- ; *party* mbr Twickenham & Richmond (London), Fundraising Secy of Mortlake and Barnes ward *other mbrships* Chinese Liberal Democrats, Liberty, YHA *special interests* urban regeneration, enterprise, overseas development *recreations* cycling *quirk* Liberal Lunching (LLC) *style* Ms *address* 27 Rosemary Gardens, London SW14 7HD *tel* 07950487683 *e-mail* hl20037@hotmail.com

DYKES, Lord Hugh John Maxwell MA (Cantab) MSI: Life Peer cr 2004: Lords Spokesperson on Europe *b* May 17, 1939 *education* Weston Super Mare

Grammar School; Pembroke College, Cambridge Univ (MA Econ), MSI *m* 3 *s* (one dec) *career* one-time stockbroker, investment analyst; Euro consultancy dealing with single currency and Euro Union; director Dixons plc (Far Eastern Division) 1985- *party* Conservative MP Harrow East 1970-97; special advisor, PPS Edward Heath's Cabinet Office but felt increasingly at odds with Thatcherite Toryism; former chair, Conservative Gp for Europe, Anglo-French, German and Spanish Parliamentary Gps, Euro Movement; MEP 1974-77; spoken on behalf of candidates in French, German elections (also speaks Spanish, Italian and Russian) awarded Federal Order of Merit (Germany), Chevalier de l'Ordre National de Merite (France), Medaille pour l'Europe, Luxemburg; joined Lib Dems, Sept 15 1997; won top male place on London Euro list 1999; advisor to Paddy Ashdown on Euro policy; mbr of the party's defence, foreign and European affairs team; mbr working gp on the EU Convention in 2001 *other mbrships* vice president British-German Association, chaired its annual conference 2002 *publications* once regular contributor to financial pages of City magazines, more recently a number of articles on foreign affairs, economics and finance special interests co-founder *Conservatives for Fundamental Change* following visit to South Africa in 1985 *recreations* music, theatre, gymnastics, walking and reading *clubs* Beefsteak, Garrick, Carlton NLC *address* Second Floor, 49 Berkeley Square, London W1X 5DB *tel* 020 7495 4379 *fax* 020 7629 5677; House of Lords, London SW1A 0PW

E

EAGLING, Russell: MSc *b* Jun 9, 1977 *education* The Minster School 1985-95; Staffordshire Univ 1995-98; Alfred Univ New York 1997; Westminster Univ 2004-05 *career* correspondence administrator Rt. Hon Paddy Ashdown MP; campaign manager East Midlands European election 1999; Head of UK Office Nick Clegg MEP 1999-2001; press, events organiser David Laws MP 2001-02; teacher Hubei Univ, Wuhan PR China 2003-04; New Media manager, CentreForum 2005- ; *party* joined 1995; treasurer Staffordshire Univ Liberal Democrats 1997-98; treasurer LDYS 1998; campaigns officer East Midlands 1999-2002; PPC South Derbyshire 2001; artworker Romsey 2001 General Election; approved party trainer specialising in artwork, candidate LB Camden election 2006 (Fortune Green ward) *special interests* China, America, UK constitution, penal reform *recreations* travel, languages (especially Spanish, Mandarin) *address* 31a Christchurch Hill, London NW3 1LA *tel* 020 7435 0799 *e-mail* russell@russelleagling.com *web* www.russelleagling.com

EARNSHAW, Charles Anthony (Tony) *b* Jun 13, 1953 *m* Estelle 2 *s* 1 *d education* Bingley Grammar School; Kingston Polytechnic BA (Hons) 1975; FPMI *career* Friends Provident Life Office 1975-78; Stewart Wrightson Benefit Consultants/Willis Consulting 1978-88; Kingsgate Consultancy (founder) 1988-92; SBJ Benefit Consultants 1992-98 (amalgamation of Kingsgate and SBJ Associates); MD, Northern Trust Global Advisors Ltd 1998-; founder chairman Association for Multi Manager Investing (AIMMI) *party* joined Liberal Party 1968, chairman Baildon Young Liberals, served on various constituency Cttees Shipley,

Yorks)1969-72; mbrship lapsed; joined Liberal Democrats 1996 *special interests* race relations; religious tolerance; peace; fair trade; development issues; pensions, investment *other mbrships* Dorking Tennis and Squash Club; Mole Valley Poets; Institute of Directors (MinstD); Pensions Management Institute; St Paul's Church, Dorking *recreations* music, especially jazz; playing sax, piano, guitar; theatre; poetry; books; plus a little tennis, golf *publications* *From Cradle to Grave* (collection of poetry) 1996; *Bull Run* (collection of poetry) 2001; *Kenyan Journey* (poetry); various articles in professional publications *address* Fonthill Cottage, Coldharbour Lane, Dorking, Surrey RH4 3BN *tel* 01306 880053 home 0207 982 3340 business *e-mail* tonyearnshaw@dsl.pipex.com

ELDRIDGE, Colin William *b* Apr 3, 1977 **ptnr** Christine Doyle *education* St. Bartholomew's School, Newbury (A-levels Politics, Economics and History); Univ of the West of England, Bristol (BA Hons Politics) *career* campaign organiser, Graham Watson MEP 1999 Euro elections; sales manager, United Marketing Ltd 1999-2001; business development exec, Esmerk Ltd. 2001-02; head, Exec Mbrs Office, Liverpool City Council 2002-03; Sales and Marketing consultant 2003- ; Director, Wash and Press Centre Ltd. 2005- ; *party* joined Newbury Liberal Democrats 1993 (during by-election); elected Bristol City Council (Cotham Ward) May 1998 as Britain's youngest Cllr; re-elected 1999 (after boundary changes); deputy whip Liberal Democrat Gp 1998-retired 2001 at the age of 24; PPC Woodspring 2001; elected Liverpool City Council (Church Ward) 2004; PPC Liverpool Wavertree 2005 (achieved 12% swing) *special interests* Electoral Reform *other mbrships* Friends of the Earth. *recreations* eating out; cooking; watching, playing sport *address* 50 Rathbone Road, Wavertree, Liverpool, L15 4HQ *tel* 0151 734215 home 07717 495301 mobile *e-mail* colin@wavertreelibdems.co.uk

ELENGORN, Martin David *b* Sept 17, 1944 *party* joined 1976; at various times chair Teddington ward association, secy Twickenham constituency association; Cllr Teddington ward LBRT from 1982, successively chair Highways, General Purposes, Planning and Transport and Standards Cttees between 1983 and 2002; deputy leader 1992-94; opposition spokesman on Transport and Environment 2002- ; vice-chair Standards 2002- ; 1986-2002 variously vice-chair London Ecology, London Boroughs Transport, London Planning Advisory, ALG Environment Cttees *special interests* environment, transport, nature conservation *address* 10 Albert Road, Teddington, Middx TW11 0BD *tel* 0208 977 1187 home 0207 898 1741 business *e-mail* cllr.melengorn@richmond.gov.uk

ELGOOD, Paul *b* Nov 10, 1971 Brighton *education* Blatchington Mill School, Hove; St John's College, York *career* senior manager for national charity; parliamentary researcher 1989-90 *party* mbr Brighton and Hove LP in SE Region; parliamentary researcher 1989-90; South East Region Management Cttee 1997; Cllr Brunswick & Adelaide ward 1999- ; gp leader Brighton and Hove City Council 1999-2005; chair, Brighton and Hove City Council's Equalities Forum 2003- ; PPC East Worthing and Shoreham 2001, Hove 2005; mbr ALDC *special interests* equalities, community safety and local govt finance *other mbrships* trustee Brighton Racecourse, Sherlock Holmes Society of London *recreations* travel, US presidential history *address* 7 Palmeira Court, 32 Palmeira Square, Hove BN3 2JP *tel* 07796 614333 *e-mail* paul.elgood@brighton-hove.gov.uk *web* brighton-hovelibdems.org.uk

ELLIS, Jonathan *b* May 21, 1968 *m* Joanne (nee Cannon) 1997 *education* Danum Comprehensive, Doncaster; St Edmund's, Canterbury; Durham Univ (BA History); diploma Health Services Management; Loughborough Univ (MBA); Leicester Univ (PGCE) *career* currently chief Exec Empty Homes Agency; adviser on international development to Diocese of St Albans; trustee of Asylum Aid and Broadway (homeless charity in London); associate trainer Centre for Strategy and Communications; formerly Oxfam campaign manager (leading campaign against asylum vouchers) and senior manager in NHS *party* joined Liberals 1985; chair Durham ULS 1987-8; exec mbr North Bedfordshire LP 1992; chair Leicester East 1994-05; Leicester South vice chair 1997-98; PPC Bosworth 1997 and 2001; chair East Midlands Region 1999-2001 *special interests* asylum-seekers, refugees, homelessness, poverty; *other mbrships:* Amnesty International, Oxfam, Church Action on Poverty, Action for Southern Africa, Free Tibet campaign *address* 64 Stephenson Wharf, Apsley, Herts HP3 9WY *e-mail* jjellis@fish.co.uk

ENEVER, Debbie *b* Jul 27, 1981 *m* Perry Enever *education* Kings College Cambridge (BA, History) 1999-2002; City Univ, London (post graduate diploma in Law) 2002-4 *career* worked as Head of Ofice, Women Liberal Democrats since graduation; continuing to study part-time *party* joined 1997, after standing as Lib Dem - and winning - mock election at school; active in student branch at Univ, secy for two years; Exec mbr Chatham and Aylesford LP 2002, constituency chair 2004; candidate in local elections 2003 *special interests* human rights, equal opportunities *address* 53 Upper Luton Road, Chatham, Kent ME5 7BH *tel* 01634 830950 *e-mail* debbie.enever@cantab.net

EPPS, Gareth Daniel Chair, Liberal Democrats for Peace & Security *b* Apr 28, 2972 *education* Magdalen College School, Oxford; Univ of Manchester *career* currently senior account manager, Green Issues Communications, Reading 2002- ; variety of roles for Liberal Democrats including assistant Campaigns Officer, South East; LDYS communications officer (twice); parliamentary researcher 1996-2002 *party* joined 1992; mbr FCC 1997- ; former mbr FE, FPC, English Council Exec, CCC; district Cllr West Oxfordshire DC (Freeland & Hanborough ward) 2000- ; PPC Witney 2001; mbr, *Liberator* Collective, Liberal Revue Team; chair Liberal Democrats for Peace & Security *other mbrships* United Nations Association; CAMRA; New Economics Foundation; Friends of the Earth *recreations* Krautrock, cricket, Manchester City Football Club *publications* regular contributions, *Liberator* *address* 1 The Green, Charlbury, Oxford OX7 3QA *tel/fax* 01608 810573 mobile 07950 035836 *e-mail* garethepps@cix.co.uk

EXLEY-MOORE, Tania Chantelle *b* May 30, 1969 Scarborough *div* 1 *s* Harry Horatio aged 5 *education* self-educated from 11-16 whilst living in Borneo; Scarborough VI Form College; Teesside Univ, BA (Hons) Humanities; Nottingham Univ, MA Victorian Literature; Huddersfield Univ PGCE; York Univ doctoral research ("Visions of Masculinity in the novel of the 1850s"!) *career* P/T Adult Ed Lecturer Yorkshire Coast College, Scarborough 1993-1996; FE Lecturer in English & ESOL Bury College 1996-1998; lived in Sweden 1998-1999; Head of English and RE, Symbister House JHS, Shetland 1999-2000; teacher: A level English/History/Media Studies, Scarborough VI Form College 2003- ; AQA Examiner 2003- ; *party* PPC Scarborough and Whitby 2005 (doubling our share of the vote), re-selected 2006; chair of Scarborough Young Liberals 1985-1988;

Shetland Lib Dem Policy Cttee 1999-2001; mbr PCA; mbr Yorkshire and Humber Regional Policy Cttee and Regional Conference Cttee *special interests* education, electoral reform, environment, civil liberties, the arts *other mbrships* International Arthurian Society *recreations* opera, theatre, classical music, film, reading, summers in Shetland *address* 38 Chantry Drive, East Ayton, Scarborough, North Yorkshire, YO13 9EY *tel* 01723 865312, 07761 279194 mobile *e-mail* exley-moore@lineone.net

EZRA of Horsham in the Co of West Sussex, Baron Derek: Life Peer 1982, Kt 1974, MBE 1945 *b* Feb 23, 1919 *s* of late David and Lillie Ezra *education* Monmouth School; Magdalene College, Cambridge (MA) *m* 1950 Julia Elizabeth, *d* of Thomas Wilkins, of Portsmouth, Hants *career* army 1939-47; mbr UK Delegation to Euro Coal and Steel Community 1952-56; National Coal Board: joined 1947, regional sales mangr 1958-60, director general marketing 1960-65, mbr Board 1965-67, deputy chair 1967-71, chair 1971-82; chair British Iron and Steel Consumers' Council 1983-87; director, Redland plc 1982-89, Solvay SA 1979-89; chair: Associated Heat Services plc 1966-, British Institute of Management 1976-78, Energy and Technical Services Gp plc 1990-; industrial adviser to Morgan Grenfell 1982-87; president Coal Industry Society 1981-86, Institute of Trading Standards Adminstration 1987-92; hon Fellow, Magdelene College Cambridge; Liveryman Worshipful Co of Haberdashers *party* joined Liberal Party 1936 as active mbr Cambridge Univ Liberal Club (alongside Richard Wainwright former Liberal MP Colne Valley); headed 1938 delegation, organised by Liberal Club, to Paris to meet leading French politicians including M. Paul Reynard, later wartime Prime Minister; while in army and at NCB, unable to take an active part in politics; in 1983 cr life peer on recommendation of David Steel (to introduce industrial experience to Liberal benches in House of Lords; initiated 1984 debate which led to creation of a Select Cttee to look into UK's weakening trade position; with Lord Falkland, represented party; chair sub-Cttee 'F' of European Select Cttee; worked closely with Nancy Seear, then leader in Lords; under Lord Jenkins became spokesman on economic affairs; energy spokesman under Lord Rodgers; now concentrates on impact of energy on environment *style* The Rt Hon Lord Ezra, MBE *address* House of Lords, London SW1A 0PW

F

FALCHIKOV, Michael G (Mike) *b* May 26, 1937 London *divorced* 1 s 1 d 3 *gdch* *education* Welwyn Garden City GS, Oriel Coll. Oxford (BA Mod Langs) *career* lecturer, then Senior Lecturer in Russian, Univ of Edinburgh - retired 1999 *party* joined Liberal Party 1959, Lib Dems 1988, currently mbr of South Edinburgh LP, held various offices in local party over a period of 35 years, Regional Party Chair (Lothian) 2000-2005, mbr Exec Scottish Liberal Party 1977-83 approx - on local negotiating team at start of Alliance, currently mbr Scot Lib Dems Conference Cttee and Mbrship Development Cttee, PPC Linlithgow 1992, many times council candidate/agent in Edinburgh council elections 1971-2003, helped in many by-elections and every parliamentary election since 1970 (first canvass experience in North Devon 1959) *publications* translations from Russian and articles in professional journals *recreations* football (season ticket Hibernian FC), listening to music (esp jazz), travel, films *address* 1 Strathearn Road, Edinburgh EH9 2AH *tel* 0131 447 1296 *e-mail* M.Falchikov@ed.ac.uk

FALKLAND, 15 Viscount of (1620): Premier Viscount of Scotland; Lucius Edward William Plantagenet Cary; also 15 Lord Cary (1620) House of Lords Spokesman on Culture, Media and Sport *b* London May 8, 1935 *s* of 14 Viscount (d 1984) and his 2 w Constance Mary, nee Berry (d 1995) *education* Wellington College *m* 1 1962 (dis 1990) Caroline Anne 1 *s* (Lucius, Master of Flakland) 2 *d* (Hon Samantha, Hon Lucinda (and 1 *d* decd) *m* 2 Nicole 1 *s* Hon Charles *b* 1992) Heir *s*, Master of Falkland *career* 2Lt 8 King's Royal Irish Hussars; journalist; theatrical agent; former chief exec C T Bowring Trading (Hldgs) Ltd *party* joined SDP 1984; mbr House of Lords Select Cttee on Overseas Trade 1984-85; dep chief whip 1988-2001 , spksn on Culture, Media and Sport 1995- ; elected hereditary peer under Lords Reform Act 1999; deputy president All Party Arts and Heritage Gp, deputy chair London Arts Gp, deputy chair All Party Gp on Alcohol Abuse; secy All Party Motorcycle Gp *recreations* golf, motorcycling, cinema, racing, reading *clubs* Brooks, Sunningdale GC *style* The Rt Hon the Viscount of Falkland *address* House of Lords, London SW1A 0PW

FALKNER, Baroness Kishwer Khan: Life Peer cr 2004 *b* Mar 9, 1955 *m* 1 *child education* St Joseph's Convent School Karachi, Pakistan; London School of Economics; Univ of Kent *career* Chief Exec Student Partnerships Worldwide, charity supporting young people in Africa, Asia; Chief Programme Officer, Political Affairs Division Commonwealth Secretariat 1999-03, Director International Affairs, Liberal Democrats 1993-99 *party* PPC Kensington and Chelsea 2001 *address* House of Lords, London SW1A 0PW

STEBBING **FARRANT, Susan Rietta (Sue)** *b* Plymouth *single* 1 *s* Ben 1 *d* Bryony, both born 1982 *education* Plymouth High School for Girls; Univ of London, Wye College, BSc, PhD from Department of Environmental Studies and Countryside Planning *career* self-employed management consultant (communications and business process development) 1989- ; previously worked in voluntary sector (joint planning); four years as officer in Women's Royal Army Corps *party* mbr Newbury LP (South Central Region); cllr West Berkshire Council; mbr South Central Region Policy Cttee; accredited GBTF trainer; PPC South Swindon 2005; local election candidate West Berkshire Council 2003, Newbury Town Council 1997, 2000 *special interests* housing, human rights, criminal justice policy, disability issues, environment, arts and culture *other mbrships* Amnesty International; Prison Reform Trust; Charter 88; Berks, Bucks, Oxon Wildlife Trust *recreations* hill walking, sailing (badly), music (jazz and classical), eating out with friends *publications* various books and articles on social housing *style* Dr *address* 18 Croft Lane, Newbury, Berkshire RG14 1RR *tel* 01635 37067 home 07946 874002 mobile *e-mail* s.farrant@btclick.com

FARRINGTON, Jade Lynne *b* Mar 16, 1986 *education* Thomas Alleyne's High School, Uttoxeter; Burton College; Goldsmiths College, Univ of London *party* joined 2001; Youth & Student rep Burton LP 2001-04, mbrship secy 2003-04; Exec

Lib Dem Disability Association 2002-03; mbrship secy Lib Dem Peace Gp 2003-04; Exec LDYS 2002-054, mbr policy Cttee 2003-05; convenor West Midlands LDYS 2002-03; Youth and Student Rep, West Midlands Region Exec 2002-03; organiser Norwich South 2004-05; GE agent and organiser Watford 2005 *special interests* education, civil liberties *other mbrships* CAMRA, Agents & Organisers Association *recreations* music and gigs (especially rock), photography, Spurs, St Helens RLFC *address* 42a Gautrey Road, London SE15 2JQ *e-mail* jade.farrington@gmail.com

FARRON, Timothy James (Tim) MP (Westmorland and Lonsdale maj: 267**)** *b* May 27, 1970 son of Christopher, Susan Farron 2 *d* 2 *s education* Lostock Hall HS; Runshaw College, Leyland; Univ of Newcastle upon Tyne *m* Rosie (nee Cantley) 2 *d* 2 *s career* Univ administrator: Head of Faculty Administration, St Martins College, Lancaster 2002- ; Univ administrator Lancaster Univ 1992-2002 (in adult education 1992-95, students with disabilities 1995-97, central administration 1997-02) *party* joined Liberal Party 1986, merged Liberal Democrats 1988; president Newcastle Univ Union 1991-92; mbr NUS National Exec 1989-90,1991-92; mbr Lancashire CC 1993-2000, deputy gp leader 1997-2000; mbr South Ribble BC1995-99; PPC Westmorland and Lonsdale (target seat) 2001 (achieved highest Lib Dem/Liberal vote and smallest Tory majority since pre-WWI), elected 2005; spokesperson for Youth Affairs 2005-06; mbr Education Select Cttee 2005- ; PPS to Ming Campbell 2006- ; *special interests* health, transport, education, agriculture *recreations* football (Sunday league goalkeeper, Blackburn Rovers fanatic); music, pop culture; walking; cosmology, historic-car rallying; reading *other mbrships* Lakes Line User Gp; Cumbria Wildlife Trust; mbr AUT, St Thomas Church Milnthorpe, Liberal Democrat Christian Forum *address* 8 Dallam Chase, Milnthorpe, Cumbria LA7 7DW *tel/fax* 015395 64665 *e-mail* tim@timfarron.co.uk

FARTHING Paul *b* Aug 29, 1966 *education* Eggars School, Alton College, Manchester Univ, Warwick Univ *career* Charter 88 1989-93, Young Minds 1993-94, Burnett Associates 1995-98, Head of Marketing, English Churches Housing Gp 1998-99, Target Direct 1999- , currently MD *party* joined 1984; chair student wing 1988-89; Cllr LB Richmond 1990-96 chair Housing 1993-96; chair London Region 1996-98; chair English Party 1997-2000; mbr Federal Exec 1997- *special interests* constitutional reform, democratic participation (chair Charter 88 Council) other mbrships Royal Commonwealth Club; Fellow, Institute of Direct Marketing; mbr, Institute of Fundraising recreations wine tasting, reading, travel, films *address* 1 Victoria Terrace, Cheltenham GL52 6BN *tel* 01242 574434 home 01242 258700 business *e-mail* pfarthing@targetdirect.co.uk

FEARN, Lord Ronnie: Life Peer cr 2001, OBE 1985 *b* Feb 2, 1931 *m* Joyce 2 *ch education* King George V Grammar School, Southport *career* banking, apart from two years Royal Navy; MP 1987-2001; House of Lords 2001- *party* mbr Southport Borough Council 1963, gp leader; Merseyside County Council, gp leader; Sefton Borough Council, gp leader; mbr Federal Policy, Conference Cttees; mbr North West Regional Exec; PPC Southport 1987 elected; re-elected 1992, 1997; retired from Commons 2001; variously spokesman for England, transport, health, tourism, Local Govt and Housing. Stood down in 2001; created life peer 2001 *other interests* voluntary youth leader in Southport for 21 year *other mbrships* Fellow of the Chartered Institute of Bankers, mbr North West Tourist Board; governor King George V Grammar School, Southport *recreations* amateur dramatics, sport, people, politics *address* House of Lords, London SW1A 0PW; Shakespeare Street, Southport PR8 5AB *tel* 01704 533 555 *fax* 01704 533 535 *e-mail* southportldp@cix.co.uk

FEATHERSTONE, Ed *b* Apr 20, 1948 *m* Lesley 2s James, Timothy *education* City of Leicester Boys Grammar School; Britannia Royal Naval College, Dartmouth; Royal Naval College, Greenwich; Joint Service Defence College; Open Univ *career* awarded scholarship to Royal Naval College 1964; served as a Seaman Officer on General List of Royal Navy 1965-91, taking early retirement as Commander; career highlights include attendance at coronation of the King of Tonga, specialisation as aircrew with 3000 flying hours in fixed and rotary-wing aircraft with RN and RAF, Lynx helicopter Flight Commander, front-line service in Amphibious Headquarters ship in Falklands conflict; MoD Staff Officer in Operational Requirements, Operational Requirements Officer for NATO Frigate Project; Joint HQ Staff Officer in first Gulf War; since 1991, partner in small bookbinding business in Islington *party* joined 1996 after taking a degree in politics with the Open Univ; elected mbr London Borough of Islington 1998 and appointed opposition chief whip; organised delivery programme in historic Hillrise by-election which gave control of Islington to Lib Dems; appointed chair Performance Review; PPC South West Herts 2001, 2005; in 2002 successfully defended ward with increased majority; appointed chair, Overview and Scrutiny; former mbr Globalisation Policy Working Gp, Defence Policy Working Gp *special interests* foreign affairs, defence, performance management, the European Project, Inland Waterways of Great Britain *other mbrships* Sea Cadet Association (former chair, vice president Clapton and Hackney Sea Cadets), Fleet Air Arm Officers Association (former chair, Defence Sub Cttee); Liberal Democrat European Gp, former secy, chair 2006- ; Wendover Arm Trust; ALDC *recreations* walking, but now rarely without a leaflet *address* 6 North Road, Berkhamsted HP4 3DU *tel* 07889 953974 *e-mail* ed.featherstone@btinternet.com

FEATHERSTONE, Lynne MP (Hornsey and Wood Green maj:2,395**)** *b* Dec 20, 1951 *single* 2 *ch education* South Hampstead HS; Oxford Brookes Univ *career* own design company; strategic design consultant for UK's largest transport consultancy; worked at Univ College Hospital; director of electrical business with ten branches across London *party* Haringey Council: elected 1998, leader Opposition Gp 1998-2003; mbr Greater London Assembly 2000-05, chair Assembly Cttee on Transport 2003-05; elected MP 2005, appointed spokesperson for Police, Crime and Disorder 2005; Environmental Select Cttee 2005; London spokesperson 2006; mbr ALDC, PCA *special interests* transport, policing and equality issues *publications* textbook on marketing architecture *address* House of Commons, London SW1A 1AA *tel* 020 8340 5459 *fax* 020 8347 8214 *e-mail* lynne@lynnefeatherstone.org *web* www.lynnefeatherstone.org/blog.htm

FIERAN-REED, Emily Bella BA (Hons, Dunelm), FRSA *b* Sept 18, 1978 Ormskirk *education* Brook Lodge 1983-1990; Rainford High School 1990-97; St. Helens College 1997-98; Univ of Durham 1998-2001; City Univ, London 2002-3; Thames Valley Univ 2003-4; Goldsmiths College, Univ of London 2003-4 *career* Sears Gp plc 1995-97; Aintree NHS Trust 1997-98; Fazakerley Adult Support Services 1997-98; PUSH Guide to Which Univ 1998-99; North Press 1999-2001; Durham Students' Union president 2001-2002; Merton Borough Council 2003 *party* joined 1997; elected mbr LDYS Women's Cttee 1998; served at every level including secy, treasurer and president, Durham Univ branch 1998-2002; National

Council rep Durham City 2001-2; mbr, LDYS student NUS Cttee 2001-3; NUS Exec mbr 2002, 2003; mbr, Liberal Democrat Lawyers Association 1999-2004 *special interests* crime and justice, human rights, higher education, mental health *other mbrships* Fellow, Royal Society of Arts; Inner Temple; British Psychological Society; Britain in Europe; Christian Lawyers' Fellowship; Human Rights Lawyers Association; Amnesty International; Greenpeace; hon life mbr Durham Students' Union *recreations* music, walking, travel, reading, watching films, history, art, theatre, cooking *publications Inter Alia* (Law Journal) (2001-4); contributions to *PUSH Guide to Which Univ* (1998-1999); various local and national newspaper articles *address* Apartment A, Stanmore Street Mews, Stanmore Street, London N1 0LQ tel.07740 102215 home;.0207 7130743 business *e-mail* emilyfieranreed@dunelm.org.uk

FINNIE, Ross CA, MSP Minister for Environment and Rural Development *b* Greenock Feb 11, 1947 *m* Phyllis (nee Sinclair) 1971 1d Jill *b* 1974 1 *s* Graham *b* 1976 *education* Greenock Academy; admitted mbr Institute of Chartered Accountants of Scotland 1970 *career* new business development division Arthur Andersen & Co 1970-73; manager corporate finance British Bank of Commerce 1973-74; manager corporate finance 1974-78 director 1978-86 James Finlay Bank; local director corporate finance Singer & Friedlander 1986-91;self employed Ross Finnie & Co Chartered Accountants, Corporate Finance Advisers 1991-99 *party* joined Greenock Young Liberals 1965; mbr Greenock LP exec 1977- , 1989-91; mbr Inverclyde District Council 1977-96 then Inverclyde Council 1995-99, convener Planning & Development Cttee 1977-80; gp leader 1988-99; PPC Renfrewshire West 1979, Stirling 1983 mbr Scottish Liberal Party Exec 1979-86; chair Scottish Liberal Party 1982-86; chair Scottish General Election Cttee 1995-97; chair Scottish Candidate Vetting Panel 1998-99; Scottish PPC Greenock & Inverclyde 1999; elected to Scottish Parliament as regional list mbr for West of Scotland 1999, re-elected 2003; appointed Minister for Rural Affairs in Scottish Exec 1999; portfolio extended to Minister for Environment and Rural Development 2001- *other mbrships* Exec Cttee The Scottish Council Development and Industry 1976-88; Cttee Church and Nation, Church of Scotland 1993-98 *recreations* voracious reader, ardent rugby supporter (president Greenock Wanderers RFC 1990-92) *address* 91 Octavia Terrace, Greenock PA16 7PY *tel* 01475-631495 home 0131-3485783 business *fax* 0131-3485966 *e-mail* Ross.Finnie.msp@scottish.parliament.uk

FLOODGATE, Lyn-Su *b* London May 27, 1983 *ptnr* Christopher Blackburn *education* Coombe Girls' School 1994-99, New Malden, Surrey; Coombe Sixth Form 1999-2001 *career* orders administrator, JPM Resources, Chorley, Lancashire 2003- *party* joined Liberal Democrat Youth & Students, Dec 1999 in Kingston-Upon-Thames; helped set up South West London LDYS; LDYS vice chair (mbrship development) 2001-02, vice chair (communications) 2002; currently chair North West LDYS; mbrship secy Chorley LP; speaker various federal, regional conferences and appeared BBC's *Despatch Box, Westminster Live*; approved PPC; PEPC North West, 2004 European Elections (youngest candidate in UK) *special interests* youth Issues, sport, regional devolution, transport, ethnic minorities especially Chinese community *other mbrships* Fulham FC Supporters Club *recreations* watching football, cricket, Formula 1 racing, reading, listening to music, good food *address* 8B Back Fazakerley Street, Chorley, Lancashire PR7 1BQ *tel* 01257 232 097 home 07906 645 894 mobile *e-mail* mail@lynsufloodgate.org.uk

FORBES, Linda Craig: Publications Officer, PCA *b* Oct 9, 1957 Inverness *education* Lanark Grammar School; Glasgow College of Nautical Studies; School of Maritime Studies, Plymouth Univ; studying MSc Architecture (Advanced Environmental and Energy Systems) at UEL/CAT *career* publishing: editorial, production and management roles at Argus Business Publications Ltd, Scholastic Ltd, Pearson Education 1981- ; navigator Merchant Navy 1974-81 *party* first delivered leaflets 1980s, PPC Warwick & Leamington 2001, 2005; chair Warwick & Leamington LP 2002; candidate Warwick DC and Leamington TC elections 2003 (doubled vote); mbr PCA Exec 2004- ; ALDC Management Cttee 2005- ; exec mbr LDEG 2006- ; mbr LDEA; non-councillor mbr FE Councillors Working Gp 2006; mbr Green LibDems *special interests* education, dementia care, transport, environment, eco-building and alternative energy *other mbrships* Amnesty, Association for Environment Conscious Building, CentreForum, Centre for Alternative Technology, Chartered Institute of Purchasing and Supply, Cloud Appreciation Society, Institute of Environmental Management and Assessment *publications* Who's Who in the Liberal Democrats 2006; LDEG Newsletter; plus many others *recreations* learning Spanish, wine, arts generally, satisfying curiosity *LD quirk* aiming to set record for the number of constituencies lived in within a year *tel* 07740 091779 *e-mail* linda@lindaforbes.co.uk *skype* linda_forbes

FORD, David MLA: Leader of the Alliance Party of Northern Ireland *b* Feb 24, 1951 *education* Warren Road PS, Orpington; Dulwich College; Queens Univ, Belfast (BSc Economics); Northern Ireland Polytechnic (Certificate in Social Work) *m* Anne 3 *d* Janet, Ruth, Helen 1 *s* Martin *career* staff volunteer Corrymeela 1972; social worker, Northern Health and Social Services Board 1973; community services officer, Carrickfergus Borough Council 1978; senior social worker, NHSSB 1980; General Secretary, Alliance Party 1990-98; Assembly Mbr, South Antrim 1998- *party* former mbr, Orpington Liberal Party; joined Alliance on foundation; General Secy 1990-98; won council seat Antrim 1993, re-elected 1997, 2005; candidate Northern Ireland Forum South Antrim 1996; elected Northern Ireland Assembly South Antrim 1998, re-elected 2003; Chief Whip, 1998-2001; Leader 2001; former spokesman, agriculture, rural development, the environment; secy All-Party Group on International Development; PPC South Antrim 1997, 2000, 2001, 2005 *special interests* rural issues, environment, public transport, electoral reform, community relations *address home* Feamore, Barnish, Kells, Co Antrim BT42 3PR, tel/fax 028 2589 8170 *address work* Parliament Buildings, Stormont, Belfast, BT4 3XX, tel 028 9052 1314, fax 028 9052 1313 *e-mail* david.ford@allianceparty.org

FORDHAM, Edward Thornton (Ed) *b* Mar 13, 1971 Kingston-on-Thames *education* Spalding GS; Univ of Nottingham (BA Hons ancient history) 1990-93; president Univ of Nottingham Union *career* academic registry, Staffordshire Univ; academic warden Thompson House hall of residence; Lib Dems Campaigns and Elections Department; head of mayor's office Watford; interim Head of Office Lib Dem Gp, LGA 2006 *party* joined 1988; chair Spalding LP 1988-89; secy, chair Nottingham Univ 1991-94; mbr East Midlands regional Exec 1990-93; LDYS student development officer 1992-94; chair Stoke-on-Trent LP 1995-98; mbrship co-ordinator West Midlands Region 1996-97, chair 1997-99; accredited party trainer; PPC Stoke-on-Trent Central, 1997; mbr (Stoke West) Stoke-on-Trent City Council 1998-2002, deputy gp leader; constituency organiser Yeovil 1999; campaigns co-ordinator Western Counties 1999-2002 *special interests* homelessness, higher education (especially student unions) broadcasting, arts and culture, Ireland *other mbrships* Robert Bloomfield Society, Landmark Trust, Society for Roman Studies *recreations* chess (former player Lincolnshire county team); ancient numismatics; satire (from 1959) *publications History of Roman Catholic Church, Spalding address* 147A High Street, Watford, Hertfordshire WD17 2ER *tel* 01923 222 152 home 01923 278060 business *e-mail* edfordham@cix.co.uk

FOSTER, Don MP (Bath maj: 4,638) **Shadow Secy of State for Culture, Media and Sport** *b* Preston, Mar 31, 1947 *m* Victoria 1 *s* 1 *d education* Lancaster Royal Grammar School, Keele Univ, Bath Univ *career* teacher, curriculum developer, Univ lecturer, public sector consultant, Mbr of Parliament *party* Liberal Cllr Avon County Council 1981-89; gp leader, chair education Cttee; Exec mbr Association of County Councils. 1985-89; Alliance PPC, Bristol East 1987; MP for Bath 1992- ; .former party spokesman for Education (mbr Education and Employment Select Cttee 1996-99), Environment, Transport and the Regions, Transport now Shadow Secy of State for Culture, Media and Sport *special interests* local Govt, education, third world issues, culture, media, sport (not least Bath Rugby) *other mbrships* Honorary Fellow , Bath College of Higher Education; Institute of Physics, Amnesty International *recreations* watching Bath Rugby, gardening, travelling, music, reading *publications* numerous, most recent *From the Three Rs to the Three Cs* 2003 *address* House of Commons, London SW1A 0AA *tel* 020 7821 8905 home 020 7219 4805 business *fax* 020 7219 2695 *e-mail* fosterd@parliament.uk

FOULGER, Jef *b* Sept 6, 1955 *m* Julia 1 *s* 2 *d education* Colfe's GS; Langley Park Boys School; associate, Chartered Insurance Institute; FE lecturer *career* senior consultant BDO Stoy Hayward 1999- ; consultant Bradstock Financial Services 1991-99; pensions consultant Noble Lowndes 1987-91 *party* joined 2002; local candidate, ward organiser Bromley 2002; mbr Pensions Policy WG 2003-04; mbr and vice-chair LD Christian Forum; PPC Beckenham 2005 *special interests* pensions, education (chair of governors Unicorn Primary School), faith in society *other mbrships* St Johns (CoE) Church; Society of Financial Advisers; Park Langley Tennis Club *address* 97 South Eden Park Road, Beckenham, Kent BR3 3AX *tel* 020 8658 6243 home 020 8315 8751 business *e-mail* jef.foulger@ntlworld.com

FOX, Bridget Caroline *b* Jul 14, 1964 *education* Dr Challoner's High School for Girls, Little Chalfont 1977-82; Balliol College, Oxford (BA History & Modern Languages: French) Balliol 1983-86; diploma library and information studies, Polytechnic of North London 1988 *career* information officer, Sports Council 1988-97; senior customer services consultant SIRSI Ltd 1997- ; Exec Cllr, LB Islington 2002- *party* joined Liberal Party Oxford, 1984; education officer, Oxford Univ Student Union 1984-85; national vice chair, Student Democrats 1988; Cllr (Sele ward) Hertford TC 1987-1992; mbr Chilterns regional Exec;, Council for Regions of England; chair, LINk 1993-95; mbr *Reformer* editorial board; chair Islington LP 1996; vice chair London Region 1996-97; PPC Hampstead & Highgate 1997, East Ham 2001, PPC Islington South & Finsbury 2005, coming within 500 votes of taking this Labour seat; Cllr (Barnsbury Ward) LB Islington 1998-2006, lead mbr Environment 1998-2000, joint deputy leader 1999-2006; chair Partnership Cttee 2000-2002, Exec mbr for Sustainability 2002-06 *special interests* environment, urban policy, international aid and development, human rights *other mbrships* ALDC, Amnesty International *recreations* music, cinema, relaxing with friends

151

address 20 Morton Road, Islington, N1 3BA ***tel*** 07966 255821 home 020 7527 3043 business ***e-mail*** bridgetfox@cix.co.uk

FOX, Paul ***b*** Jun 2, 1964 ***m*** Cyd Lee Fox ***family*** parents deceased, 1 brother ***education*** The Cathedral School, Llandaff, Cardiff; All Saints School, Bloxham, Banbury; Balliol College, Oxford (BA Modern History & Economics) ***career*** local Govt officer 1986-1997, including Assistant Director of Education (Resources), Hertfordshire County Council 1993-97; advisor to Local Authority Associations on Education Finance 1995-97; senior director, international public finance, at City firm Fitch IBCA Ltd. 1997-99; director of finance, Lewisham College 1999-2001; director PF Public Finance Ltd 2003- ; ***party*** joined Liberal Party 1983; organiser Cirencester & Tewkesbury 1983; mbr Liberal Party Council 1983-88; NUS Officer in Lib/SDP Alliance-controlled Oxford Univ Students Union 1984-95; national treasurer ULS 1987-88, Student Democrats 1988-99; mbr, Manifesto Costings Gp 1996-97; Cllr (Hillrise Ward) LB Islington 16 Dec 1999 (by-election victory that gave Liberal Democrats control), lead mbr for Finance, Jan 2000-May 2003 (during which council tax cut from highest in London, while improving front-line services); GLA candidate London North East 2000; mbr London Region Exec 2000-01, chair London Region 2001-02; PPC West Ham 2001, North Wiltshire 2005; mbr Wiltshire County Council (after by-election in Chippenham Sheldon division) 2004-05; vice chair Chippenham LP 2006 ***special interests*** public finance, public services, history, party strategy ***recreations*** family, friends, steam railways ***address*** 18 Chapel Mews, Chippenham Wilts SN15 3AU ***tel/fax*** 01249 462975 ***e-mail*** paul@pjfox.freeserve.co.uk

FREEL, Karen ***b*** Jul 18, 1969 ***m*** Ian Yuill ***qv*** 1 ***d education*** St Mirin's & St Margaret's High School, Paisley; Clydebank College; Glasgow Caledonian Univ (BA Hons politics & sociology) ***career*** currently having career reak; liaison officer to Elspeth Attwooll MEP 2000-04; MD BEL Consultants 1998-2000; client administration manager, ICM Career Ltd 1997-98;.various administration positions, including national newspaper 1994-97 ***party*** joined SDP 1987 then Liberal Democrats; mbr Scottish Conference Cttee 1990- , convenor 2000- ; mbr Scottish Party Exec 1994-96, 2000; vice chair, Women Liberal Democrats 1999-2001; Scottish Officer, PPCs Association 2000- ; mbr Federal Conference Cttee 1999- ; Westminster PPC 1997; Scottish Parliament 1999, 2004; mbr Aberdeen City Council 2000- ***special interests*** foreign affairs, fisheries, women in public life ***other mbrships*** Friend of the Tate; Friend of Aberdeen Art Gallery; Friend of Aberdeen International Youth Festival ***recreations*** listening to music, reading, cinema, eating out ***address*** 57 Countesswells Crescent, Aberdeen AB15 8LN ***tel*** 01224 310746 home 01224 522186 business ***fax*** 01224 310746 ***e-mail*** kfreel@aberdeencity.gov.uk

FRYER, Jonathan ***b*** Manchester 5 Jun 1950 ***education*** Manchester GS; Univ Poitiers (Institut Tourain); St Edmund Hall, Oxford Univ; South Bank Univ, MA (Oxon) Oriental Studies, MSc Environment and Developmental education (completing) ***career*** journalist Reuters 1973-74; freelance based Brussels, Geneva, London (reported from nearly 130 countries since debut covering Vietnam war); visiting lecturer Univ of Nairobi, London School of Journalism; regular broadcaster; president Association of Foreign Affairs Journalists 1997- ***party*** secy NW YLs 1968-69; Oxford Univ Liberal Club; Euro candidate, London SE 1979, 1984, 1994, London Region List 1999, 2004; PPC Chelsea 1983, Orpington 1987, Leyton 1992;

mbr Bromley LBC 1986-90; former chair overseas development policy panel; former chair Liberal International British Gp; elected mbr ELDR council; Federal Policy Cttee; Exec Lib Dem Euro Gp; mbr Broadcasting Policy WG 2001 *publications* various include *The Great Wall of China*, Isherwood (reissued as *Eye of the Camera*), *George Fox and the Children of the Light, Soho in the Fifties and Sixties special interests* Quaker *clubs* NLC *address* 35 Forest Drive West, London E11 1JZ *tel* 020 8556 6032; 7 Av. de la Sauvagine (bte 95), B-1170 Brussels *tel* 32-2-672.1168 *e-mail* jfl0@soas.ac.uk

G

GALLAGHER, Jock FICS, MCJI, mbr Federal Executive *b* Mar 31, 1938 Greenock *m* Sheenagh Glenn Jones 1970 *education* Greenock HS; Stowe College, Glasgow; Wulfrun College, Wolverhampton *career* NS Royal Artillery 1956-58; journalist various newspapers 1958-66; BBC producer 1966-70, BBC programme head 1970-90; Director BBC Radio Show, Earls Court 1988; member Central Agricultural Advisory Council, Asian Programmes Committee; rep to European Broadcast Union, Commonwealth Broadcasting Association; chairman, MD BroadVision (production, communications) 1990-2003; Executive Director Association of British Editors 1990-99; editor *British Editor* 1991-99; chair Euro Editions Ltd, publisher *The Europe Quarterly, Who's Who in the Media?* 1997-2000; chair Health Independent Limited 2001-05; associate director The Young Programme 2004- *party* joined Greenock Young Liberals 1952; mbr Sutton Coldfield BC 1966-69; served at every level from ward treasurer through regional chair to NEC; founder mbr Lib Dems; v chair West Midland Region 1994-97; regional media co-ordinator 1994-96; Euro candidate Herefordshire and Shropshire 1994 (polled 44,000 votes); PPC Birmingham Edgbaston 1997 (didn't poll 44,000 votes!); mbr PCA Exec 1993- , chair 2003-05, chair *Focus on Government* group 2005- ; WM Region campaign director 1997 GE; mbr Federal Exec 2002, 2004, 2005 ; mbr Campaigns and Communications Cttee 2002; mbr Federal Conference Cttee 2004; PCA rep English Candidates Cttee 2002-05; media trainer for PPCs; founder, editor *Who's Who in the Liberal Democrats?* 1998-2005; author PCA's *Rough Guide to Campaigning special interests* media politics (moderator Free Media Conference, Warsaw 1993; media specialist OCSE 1994-98; Foreign Office Free Expression panel 2003- ; UK UNESCO Communications Cttee 2004- , chair Freedom of Expression Cttee 2005-); further education (former vice-chair FE college, regional mbr Further Education Funding Council); NHS (provided consultancy services, various NHS groups) *other mbrships* Founding Fellow (deputy chair 2005-), Institute of Contemporary Scotland; mbr Chartered Institute of Journalists; Association of European Journalists; chair Press Freedom Network 2001- ; hon mbr Society of Editors; juror, associate director, trustee Young UK programme 2003- ; *recreations* reading (voraciously), writing (lazily), golf (badly) *publications A Many-coated Man* (tribute to Laurie Lee), *Portrait of a Lady* (biog Lady Isobel Barnett), *Life and Death of Doris Archer* (biog Gwen Berryman), *The Archers Omnibus* (40 years of the serial), *The Archers Saga* (trilogy of novels that gave the soap family a past), various specialist media reports *address* Home Barn,

Ribbesford, Bewdley, Worcs DY12 2TQ *tel* 01299 403110 home 07956 807163 mobile *e-mail* jyg@cix.com.uk

GALLOP, Anne BA (Hons) *b* Sept 20, 1941 Coulsdon, Surrey *div* 3 *ch* 3 *gch education* Beckenham GS; Bedford College, London Univ (social vice president ULU) *career* banking, secretarial, PA , bringing up family in UK and France *party* joined Liberals 1979; founder mbr Liberal Democrats; activist in France, Hastings and Sutton; Hastings rep on SE Region Exec 1987-90; Cllr LB Sutton (elected 1995); appt LFCDA, gp leader 1998-2000; appt by mayor to LFEPA; gp leader, deputy chair 2002- ; v-chair LD Christian Forum 2001-04; LGA Fire Exec 2001-05; LGIU Mgt Assembly, Exec 2000- ; mbr LGA Fire Forum 1998- ; candidate Sutton/Croydon GLA 2000; PPC Croydon South 2001 *special interests* emergency planning; Fire Service inc resilience; special education; citizen advocacy (advocate working with people with profound learning difficulties; *other mbrships* NLC, Charter 88, Howard League for Penal Reform, Greenpeace *recreations* reading, music, opera, cross-country skiing, walking *address* 61 Redruth House, Grange Road, Sutton, SM2 6RU *tel* 0777 999 1197 *e-mail* ag003f0267@blueyonder.co.uk

GARDEN, Sue FRSA *b* Feb 22, 1944 *m* Lord Garden *qv* 2 *d education* Westonbirt School; St Hilda's College, Oxford *career* teacher UK, Germany; various posts City and Guilds of London Institute 1988-2000, including Head of External Relations; consultant, adviser to City & Guilds 2000- ; voluntary work including CAB adviser, SSAFA Forces Help caseworker; Vice-President Institute of Export *party* joined 2001; candidate LB Camden elections 2002; exec mbr Hampstead Town; fought Finchley and Golders Green 2005; elected FCC 2004, 2005 *special interests* education, especially vocational, FE, HE; welfare, social issues, international affairs, equal opportunities *other mbrships* World Traders' Livery Company (Liveryman, Court Assistant, Junior Warden 2006); Vice-Chairman Oxford Univ Society, president London branch *address* 14 Alvanley Court, 250 Finchley Road, London NW3 *tel* 020 7435 2796 home 07778 282790 mobile *fax* 020 7209 0859 *e-mail* sue.garden@blueyonder.co.uk

GARDEN of Hampstead in London Borough of Camden, Baron Tim: KCB MA MPhil FRAeS FRUSI FCGI: Life Peer 2004: Lords Spokesperson on Defence *b* Apr 23, 1944 *m* Sue *qv* 2 *d education* King's, Worcester; St Catherine's, Oxford (MA Physics, Honorary Fellow); Magdalene, Cambridge (MPhil International Relations); Royal College of Defence Studies *career* RAF 1963-96 as pilot (command posts included V-bomber squadron, helicopter station), RAF Director of Defence Studies 1982-85, Assistant Chief of the Air Staff 1991 (responsible for forward planning for all three services as Assistant Chief of the Defence Staff (Programmes) at MOD, Air Marshal Commandant Royal College of Defence Studies; Director Royal Institute of International Affairs 1996-98; visiting professor Centre for Defence Studies, King's College London 2000- ; broadcaster and journalist 1996- *party* joined 1999; mbr LDEG Exec 2002-4; FPC 2003-5 ; FE 2004-; foreign and security policy advisor 1999-04 ; mbr Liberty Network 2003-; deputy chairman National Liberal Club 2003-04. President Trading Standards Institute 2005- ; defence spokesman in Lords 2005- ; mbr of Select Cttee on Delegated Powers and Regulatory Reform 2004- ; President Liberal International British Group 2004- ; *special interests* European defence, international affairs, arms control, counter terrorism, Israel-Palestine, proliferation, arms sales and corruption *other mbrships* Fellow of Royal Aeronautical Society;

Fellow of Royal United Services Institute; Fellow City & Guilds of London Institute; CB 1992; KCB 1994; Légion d'Honneur 2003; Wells Professor Indiana University 2004; president London & South East Region Air Training Corps, chairman RAF Oxford & Cambridge Society, president Adastral Burns Club *recreations* photography, typography, writing, bridge, wine, pontificating *publications* Can Deterrence Last?; The Technology Trap; and hundreds of articles *address* 14 Alvanley Court, 250 Finchley Road, London NW3 6DL *tel* 02074352796 home 07770 470819 business 02072192747; *fax* 0207 209 0859 *e-mail* gardent@parliament.uk *web* www.tgarden.demon.co.uk

GARNETT, Martin Charles *b* May 10 1956 *m* Lesley (nee Brooks) 1 *s education* Bentley Grammar School, Calne 1968-74; read biochemistry Univ College Swansea, 2i, 1977; PhD *Biochemistry of Oxygen Toxicity* Univ College London 1981 *career* post-doctoral research assistant, Cancer Research Campaign Laboratories, Univ of Nottingham 1981-1991; lecturer, Drug Delivery, School of Pharmacy, Univ of Nottingham 1991-2004, senior lecturer 2004- ; nano-technology research work at Nottingham has focused on improving administration of drugs, including targeting drugs with monoclonal antibodies, incorporation of drugs into nano-particles and developing non-viral methods for DNA delivery (gene therapy) *party* joined 1992; Erewash LP exec 1993, various exec officer posts 1994- (including terms as chair, sec y vice chair); candidate parish, borough, county council elections; mbr Draycott PC 1995-1999; PPC Erewash 1997, 2001, 2005 *special interests* education (parent governor Friesland foundation school), higher education, science policy, transport *other memberships* Biochemical Society, British Association for Cancer Research, European Association for Cancer Research, Controlled Release Society *recreations* renovating early-Victorian family home; woodwork; other practical work; old British motorcycles (owns 750cc Triumph Bonneville with sidecar); keeps fit by commuting to work by bicycle; archery (longbow) *publications* sixty four refereed publications in scientific journals, 4 patent applications *address* 10 Derby Road, Draycott, Derbyshire DE72 3NJ *tel* 01332 872889 home 0115 9515045 business 0779 2684120 mobile *e-mail* martin.garnett@ghcom.net

GARRATT, Andrew Charles William *b* Nov 4, 1966 *education* Sandown High School, Isle of Wight; Kings College, Univ of London; Queen Mary College, Univ of London; Univ of Southampton *career* freelance PR consultant 2004- ; PR Manager, Univ of Portsmouth 2001-04; Campaigns Officer, Liberal Democrats 1999-2001; head party liaison for Paddy Ashdown 1997-99; constituency agent for Diana Maddock 1993-97 *party* joined merged party 1988; Cllr, Southampton City Council 1991-98 (deputy leader of opposition 1993-98); Cllr, Bournemouth Borough Council 1999- (cabinet mbr since Lib Dems took majority control 2003); PPC Bournemouth East 2001, 2005 *special interests* science policy; higher education; disability rights, particularly those of deaf people *other mbrships* Royal National Institute for Deaf People; Friends of the Earth; National Cued Speech Association; National Trust *recreations* playing piano; amateur astronomy; photography; travel (especially Australia and New Zealand); occasional skydiving and bungy jumping *e-mail* andrewgarratt@cix.co.uk

GASH, Julia Mary *b* Jun 22, 1963 *education* Redhill Comprehensive School; Brighton Polytechnic, BA Hons Visual Communication; Central St Martins, Post Graduate Diploma in Printmaking; Middlesex Univ, PGCE Art and Design *career*

established award-winning contemporary-lifestyle brand *Gash*, 1990, which operates as a female-friendly web portal and growing number of shops selling designer lingerie, erotic accessories; won NatWest Export Award for Small Businesses 1997; invited to Buckingham Palace to celebrate the achievements of young people of Britain 1999; cover girl for *The Observer Magazine* feature on women pioneering changes in sex industry Jul 2003; advisory panel mbr Durex *party* joined in Sheffield Hallam 2002; approved PPC; mbr Censorship Policy Working Gp 2003; PEPC second on list Yorkshire and Humber 2004 *special interests* European politics (key national spokesperson on euro, contributing to many flagship media productions on issue); established UK's first permanent Eurozone in Devonshire Quarter, Sheffield; sexual politics (delivered keynote speech, Conference 2002 in pornography debate; seen as one of influential figures in promoting changes in attitudes towards sexuality in Britain) *other mbrships* European Movement, Britain in Europe *recreations* yoga, travelling *publications* published comments etc. can be read on the www.gash.co.uk press gallery *address* 19 Westfield Terrace, Sheffield S1 4GH *tel* 07973 1999 69 home 0114 276 3733 business *fax* 0114 278 7604 *e-mail* julia@gash.co.uk or julia@juliagash.org *web* www.juliagash.org

GASSON, Emily Jane *b* Jun 23, 1970 *m* Ed Davey MP *qv education* Frensham Heights School , Farnham, Surrey; Durham, Oxford Universities *career* own business specialising in tackling anti-social behaviour 2005- ; Head of Legal Services, South Somerset Homes Limited 2000- ; legal aid solicitor in rural high street practices 1995-2000 *party* joined 1989; PPC Regents Park and Kensington North 1997, Dorset North 2001; currently PPC Dorset North 2001- ; various offices in local parties; mbr Housing Policy Forum 2003-044, advising on legal aid and court reforms; mbr Liberal Democrat Lawyers Association *special interests* housing policy, access to justice *recreations* swimming, painting, bell-ringing, travel *address* 78 St James St, Shaftesbury, Dorset SP7 8HF *tel/fax* 01747 858668 home 01935 404529 business *e-mail* emily@egasson.fsnet.co.uk

GEE, Stephen Mark *b* Jun 16, 1960 *m* Anne (nee Pollard) 1 *s* Christopher 1 *d* Sophie *education* Raynes Park High School; Reading Univ (BSc Hons), MRICS (Mbr of the Royal Institution of Chartered Surveyors) *career* quantity surveyor Cyril Sweett and Partners 1981-85; founding, managing partner John Rowan and Partners (developing business to one of top 50 surveyors in country) 1985- *party* joined 2001; policy coordinator Epsom and Ewell LP; mbr Sports Policy Working Gp; candidate for Tattenham Ward 2003, Nork Ward 2004, Reigate and Banstead Council; candidate Banstead West ward Surrey County Council 2003; PPC Wimbledon 2005 *special interests* sport, economics, business, foreign affairs *other mbrships* mbr Royal Institution of Chartered Surveyors *recreations* football, cricket, golf, skiing *address* 98 Nork Way, Banstead, Surrey SM7 1HP *tel* 1737 362810 home 020 8567 6995 business *fax* 020 8566 1181 *e-mail* sgee@jrp.co.uk

GEE-TURNER, Adrian John *b* Nov 9, 1965 *m* Leonie 2004 1 *s education* Stowe School; FE Cambridge Marketing College (Dip Marketing); Fellow Chartered Institute of Marketing career Exec Mbr Medical Marketing Gp - Institute of Marketing, Medical Devices Aerosol Drug Delivery System since 1986- ; *party* joined 1996, cllr on LBC Hackney 1998-2002, positions held included Chair of Council Gp, Chair of Scrutiny and Overview, lead on Agency Direct, Finance and Pensions; Mbrship Secy Hackney Liberal Democrats 2002-2003; PPC Dagenham

2001, Croydon North 2005; exec mbr ALDTU (Assoc Lib Dem Trade Unionists) *other mbrships* East London Britain in Europe (chair) *address* Flat B 205 Stoke Newington Church Street, Stoke Newington, Hackney, London N16 9ES *tel* 0789 999 0443 *e-mail* adrian.geeturner@btinternet.com

GEORGE, Andrew Henry MP (St Ives maj: 11,609) **Shadow Secy for International Development** *b* Dec 2, 1958 *m* Jill 1 *s* Davy 1 *d* Morvah *education* Mullion, Cury, Helston Comprehensive School; Sussex Univ (BA); Oxford Univ (MSc Agricultural Economics) *career* deputy director, community development charity, development worker, research consultant *party* MP for St.Ives 1997- ; Shadow Fisheries Minister 1997-2001; Agriculture Select Cttee 1997-2000; Shadow Disabilities Minister 1999-2001; Regional Affairs Cttee 2001- ; PPS to Charles Kennedy 2001-02; Shadow Secy for Rural Affairs 2002-05; Shadow Secy for International Development 2005- ; vice-chair All-Party Asthma Gp 2004- , chair 2001-4; secy All-Party Local Hospitals Gp 2002- ; vice-chair All-Party Rugby Union Gp Gp 2002- ; Roma Affairs Gp; vice-chair All-Party Fisheries Gp 2003- *other mbrships* president Council for Racial Equality in Cornwall *special interests* Third World, Cornwall, economic development, housing, fishing industry, agriculture, social exclusion, devolution, small nations, racism, domestic violence, immigration, environment, minority gps *recreations* sports including: football (various Commons football teams), cricket (mbr Leedstown Cricket Club), rugby (mbr Lords & Commons Rugby Team), tennis (mbr Hayle Tennis Club), swimming, cycling *publications* The Natives Are Revolting Down In The Cornwall Theme Park* (1986); *Cornwall At The Crossroads* (1989); *A Vision Of Cornwall* (1993); *A View from the Bottom Left-hand Corner* (2002) *address* House of Commons, London, SW1A 0AA *tel* constituency office 01736 360020 *fax* 01736 332866 *e-mail* georgea@parliament.uk or Andrew@andrewgeorge.org.uk

GERMAN, Michael James OBE AM Leader of Lib Dems in National Assembly of Wales *b* May 8, 1945 *education* St Mary's College, London, The Open Univ, Univ of the West of England *m* Veronica Watkins 2 *d* *career* teacher, head of music, various schools in Cardiff; Director, European Unit; Welsh Joint Education Cttee *party* PPC Cardiff Central 1974, 1979, 1983, 1987; mbr Federal Exec, Federal Policy Cttee; chair, Welsh Lib Dems, Campaigns & Election Cttee 1990-97; campaign director, Welsh Lib Dems 1991-97; mbr (Cathays Ward) City of Cardiff Council 1993-96, joint leader of council 1987-91; Leader, Welsh Lib Dems, National Assembly for Wales, 1999- ; mbr, National Assembly for Wales, South Wales East 1999- ; Deputy First Minister 2000-03, Minister for Economic Development 2000-01, Minister for Rural Development and Wales Abroad 2002-03 *special interests* economic development, education *recreations* music, travel *address* National Assembly for Wales, Cardiff CF99 1NA *tel* 02920 898741 *fax* 02920 898354 *e-mail* michael.german@wales.gov.uk

GIDLEY, Sandra Julia MP (Romsey maj: 125) **Shadow Health spokesperson** *b* Mar 26, 1957 *m* Bill Gidley 1 *d* 1 *s* *education* six different primary schools; Alton Eggars Grammar School, AFCENT International School; Windsor Girls School, Hamm, Germany; Bath Univ (BPharm 2:1) 1975-78 *career* pharmacist 1979-2000 community pharmacy manager mainly in supermarket sector 1979-81, 1991-2000, locum pharmacist 1982-91; antenatal teacher National Childbirth Trust 1990-94), MP for Romsey 2000-, *party* joined 1994; town, borough Cllr 1995-2003; vice chair

Region 1999-2000; elected MP for Romsey by-election 2000, re-elected 2001; LibDem Health spokesperson 2000-2002, spokesperson for women's issues 2001-03, then Minister 2003-05; spokesperson for older people 2005-06; mbr Health Select Cttee 2001-03 chair Gender Balance Task Force 2002-2004 *special interests* health, education, environment. Reproductive rights, HIV AIDS development work *other mbrships* mbr Royal Pharmaceutical Society *recreations* reading, cookery, theatre, badminton *address* 3a Victoria Place, Love Lane, Romsey, Hants SO51 5SB *tel* 01794 517652 home, 01794 511900 constituency, 020 7219 5986 HoC office *fax* 01794 512538 constituency, 020 7219 2324 office *e-mail* gidleys@parliament.uk

GIFFORD, William Lyell *b* Aug 22, 1950 *m* Carolyn (nee Mortimore) 1 *s* 1 *d* *education* Bedales School; Univ of Birmingham BA in Medieval & Modern History *career* bookshop manager 1972-80; computer & IT sales 1980-2005; marketing consultant 2005- *party* founder mbr Liberal Democrats, joined Liberal Party 1980; chair Warwick & Leamington Liberal Democrats (twice); Cllr (Milverton Ward, Leamington Spa) Warwick District Council 1995- , mbr of Exec 2003- ; Cllr since formation of Leamington Spa town council in 2002; mayor, Royal Leamington Spa 2001-02; governor Brookhurst Primary School, Leamington Spa 1994- *special interests* local, national and international politics *other mbrships* Amnesty International *recreations* walking, reading *address* 22 Augusta Place, Leamington Spa, Warwickshire CV32 5EL *tel* 01926-338776 home 024-7667 1912 business *e-mail* bill.gifford@warwickdc.gov.uk

GILBERT, Terence Anthony (Terry) *b* Jul 20, 1964 *m* Marie Osborn, Jul 2001 **1** s born 2005 *education* County High School, Clacton-on-Sea; BA Economics/SPS, Churchill College, Cambridge 1984-7; MA Social Work, Univ of Kent 1992-4 *career* Probation Service, 1989-2002; Political Advisor 2002-03; writer, househusband 2003- ; *party* joined Liberal Party 1983; founder mbr Lib Dems, 1988; various constituency Execs; Ipswich Borough Cllr, 2000-2002; PPC Ipswich, Jun 2001; mbr Social Care Policy Working Gp, 2002-3; political advisor, LB Tower Hamlets 2002-3; political organiser Norwich 2004; secy Norwich South LP 2005- ; *special interests* criminal justice, environment, Iraq war, satire *other mbrships* Amnesty International, Friends of the Earth *recreations* travel, cycling, hoping Liverpool FC will win the Premiership *address* 81 Rosary Road, Norwich NR1 1TG *tel* Norwich 219495 *e-mail* tagilbert@msn.com

GILL, Parmjit Singh *b* Leicester 1967 *career* information management, security consultant for local council dealing mainly with data protection, security issues; MP 2004- *party* joined 1994; PPC Leicester South 2001, 2004 by-election (elected in sensational by-election with 22% swing from Labour: party's first ethnic minority MP); mbr (for Stoneygate Ward) Leicester City Council 2003- (increasing Lib Dem vote by 400 per cent); cabinet link Social Services; under his stewardship Social Services Department increased Audit Commission rating from *fair* to *good other mbrships* Amnesty International; Anti-Slavery International; mbr national Exec Anti-Racist Alliance (ARA).*special interests* crime prevention, taxi licensing, racism *address* House of Commons, London SW1A 0AA *tel* 020 7219 3000 *constituency* 92 London Road, Leicester LE2 0QR *e-mail* gillps@parliament.uk *web* www.leicester-libdems.org.uk

GILL, Rosalind Mary *b* Jul 30, 1971 *education* St Albans High School 1978-89; Cambridge Univ (BA Joint Hons French and German) 1989-93, Brunel Univ (MA Britain and the European Union) 1993-94 *career* Exec officer Property Holdings, Department of the Environment 1995; organiser Watford Liberal Democrats 1996; assistant West Worcestershire LP GE 1997; assistant Liberal Democrat gp Berkshire County Council 1997-98; organiser Oxford West and Abingdon Liberal Democrats 1998-99; assistant Liberal Democrat Gp, Suffolk County Council 1999-2001; head of office, Norman Lamb MP 2001-03; English tutor 2003-2004; political assistant Liberal Democrat gp, East of England Regional Assembly 2003- ; support officer Liberal Democrat Gp, Luton Borough Council 2004-05; outreach assistant, Univ of East Anglia 2006- ; *party* joined 1994; European PPC, East of England list 1999, 2004; LDYS International Officer 1997; vice chair Liberal Democrat European Gp 2004-06; former mbr various local party execs *special interests* Europe *other mbrships* Amnesty International, European Movement, Friends of the Earth *recreations* swimming, jogging, socialising, cinema, spending time with my partner *e-mail* rosalindgill@btinternet.com

GILLARD, Karen *b* Mar 3, 1974 *education* Inns of Court School of Law 2001-2003; College of Law Guildford 1999-2000; Univ of Plymouth 1996-99 Devonport High School for Girls *career* advertising rep 1992-93; Civil Servant 1994-97; working toward career at Bar 2000- ; chair Board Directors South West Employment Centre *party* joined party Sept 2001 having defected from Conservative Party (previous career in Tories interesting but not enough space here!); on defection, only Lib Dem Cllr Plymouth City Council; lead election campaign that saw three returned 2003; vice chair Plymouth Lib Dems 2001- ; PPC Plymouth Sutton since Jul 2003 *special interests* defence, foreign affairs, Local Govt reform *other mbrships* mbr Honorary Society Middle Temple 1999- *recreations* listening to audio books, good food and drink, evenings out without talk of the Lib Dems generally *address* 6 Rutland Road, Mannamead, Plymouth Pl4 7BG *tel* 01752 517391 home 07974 756729 business *e-mail* karen.gillard@plymouth.gov.uk

GLASGOW, The Earl of; Patrick Robin Archibald Boyle; DL *b* Jul 30, 1939 *m* 1 *s* 1 *d education* Eton College; Sorbonne Univ *career* Sub-Lt Royal Naval Reserve 1960; assistant director in films and television documentary producer; founder, Kelburn Country Centre 1977 *party* transport spokesperson in House of Lords 2005- ; *other mbrships* ACTT *recreations* theatre, cinema, skiing *style* 10th Earl of Glasgow, Lord Boyle, Viscount of Kelburn, 10th Lord Boyle, 4th Baron Fairlie; succeeded to titles 1984; hereditary mbr House of Lords 1984-99; elected hereditary member of House of Lords 2005- ; *address* House of Lords, London SW1a 0PW

GLOVER, Gary *b* Jul 7, 1966 *m* Julie 1 *s* 2 *d education* Surrey Square, Walworth Secondary School *career* local Govt officer (housing) *party* joined 1992 North Southwark & Bermondsey LP; LP chair, vice chair various years; general election campaign chair 1997; agent to Simon Hughes 2001; agent to all candidates Southwark Local election (63 cllrs) 2002 *special interests* community politics, mbr implementation gp on Southwark community councils; director National Tenants & Residents of England; mbr ODPM ministers Sounding Board; various national tenants think tanks *other mbrships* national parks and open spaces organisations *recreations* watching Millwall Football Club; watching Harry Glover (aged 8) in local football league games *address* 18 Moreton House, Slipper Place, Bermondsey,

London SE16 *tel* 07949130439 home .business/*fax* 020 7525 1782 *e-mail* gary@bermondsey2000.freeserve.co.uk

GODDARD, Stephen Howard (Steve) MA, DPhil (Oxon) *b* May 19, 1969 *education* Queen's College, Taunton 1980-87; St John's College, Oxford 1987-98 *m* 1 *d* 1 *s career* lecturer in French, various Oxford colleges 1993- ; occasional political organiser, agent in local elections *party* joined 1990; almost immediately sent off leafleting by Evan Harris (later MP for Oxford West); campaigned Oxford local elections, various parliamentary, local Govt by-elections, most recently Dunfermline West; recruited wife to party 1993, followed by more than 150 new mbrs; candidate Central ward, Oxford City Council 1995 (second to resurgent Labour); Cllr Wolvercote ward 1996 2002 (stood down); gp secy 1998-99, deputy leader 1999-2000 (acting leader late 1999); PPC Oxford East 2001 (8% swing against Cabinet Minister Andrew Smith, pushing Tories into third place), 2005 (12% swing reducing Labour's majority to 963), re-selected April 2006 *special interests* environment; Europe, foreign affairs; constitutional reform *recreations* bird-watching; reading (especially historical novels, science-fiction, French); telefantasy (Dr Who, Buffy the Vampire Slayer etc); ineffectual gardening *style* Dr Steve Goddard *address* 60 Rosamund Road, Oxford, OX2 8NX *tel* 07790 360275 *e-mail* stevegoddard26@yahoo.com

GOLDENBERG, Philip MA (Oxon), FRSA, FSALS *b* Apr 26, 1946 London *m* Lynda Anne (formerly Silver, née Benjamin) 3 *s* 1 *d education* St Paul's School London; Pembroke College Oxford; 2nd class honours, Classical Moderations, FHS *Literae Humaniores career* City solicitor specialising particularly in corporate governance and employee share ownership; partner in S J Berwin 1983-2004; consultant to Michael Conn Goldsobel 2004- ; responsible for conception and enactment of Liberal proposals for employee profit-sharing in 1978 Finance Act; legal adviser to Liberal Party on merger with SDP 1987-88; joint author original constitution Liberal Democrats; legal adviser, RSA's *Tomorrow's Company* Inquiry 1995; advised DTI on Company Law Review 1998-99; advised on formation of Labour-Liberal Democrat Joint Cabinet Cttee 1997, procedural provisions of Scottish Coalition Agreement 1999; mbr National Council 1992-2004, Finance and General Purposes Cttee 1994-2004, Confederation of British Industry; secy The Liberal Democrats (Trustees) Ltd 1990; writer, lecturer on legal topics, media training and experience *party* mbr Woking Borough Council 1984-92 and 2003- (deputy gp ldr 2005-); PPC (Liberal) Eton & Slough 1974 (twice), 1979 (Liberal/SDP Alliance); Woking 1983, 1987, 1997; European PPC, Dorset & East Devon 1994; mbr Federal Policy Cttee 1988-9, 1990-92; mbr Federal Conference Cttee and SE Region Exec 1997- ; Treasurer 1999-2001; chair 2001-04; mbr, English Liberal Democrats Exec 2001- (vice-chair 2005-); English Liberal Democrats Finance & Administration Cttee, 2003- ; elected Interim Peers panel 1999; mbr, Federal Appeals Panel 2000-; Council, Make Votes Count 1999- ; Council mbr, The City in Europe 2001- ; Federal Trust Working Party on Corporate Social Responsibility 2001-2; secy, Oxford Univ Liberal Club 1966; mbr, Standing Cttee, Oxford Union 1967-68; chairman, St Marylebone YLs, secy, St Marylebone LA, 1968-69; press officer, Westminster LA, 1969-72, president, Watford LA, 1980-1; vice-chairman 1976-78, 1980-81, secy 1978-79; Home Counties Regional Liberal Party; mbr, Liberal Party Council 1975-88; NEC 1977/84; successor National Exec 1984-5, 1986-87; council agenda Cttee 1976-80; candidates Cttee 1976-85;

Assembly Cttee 1985-87; involved in national negotiations with former SDP on candidate selection for 1984 Euro-elections, 1987 General Election; mbr Liberal policy panels on reform of Govt, taxation and social society; industrial relations, employment *other mbrships* Electoral Reform Society; Wider Share Ownership Council; London Regional Council, CBI; chair of governors, Annie Lawson School, Ravenswood Village 1997- ; trustee, Tuberous Sclerosis Association 2000- ; trustee, RSA 2004- (joint treasurer 2005-); NLC; Society for Advanced Legal Studies *special interests* corporate finance, Govt, constitutional law, special educational needs, liberal economics *publications* Fair Welfare 1968; joint editor New Outlook 1974-77; part author with Sir David Steel Sharing Profits 1986; consultant editor Guide to Company Law CCH 1990-2001; mbr editorial advisory board Business Law Review 1994-04; author The Business Guide to Directors' Responsibilities S J Berwin, 2001, numerous articles *address* Toad Hall, White Rose Lane, Woking, Surrey GU22 7LB *tel* 01483 765377 *e-mail* goldenberg@cix.co.uk

GOLDSWORTHY, Alison Rachel (Ali) *b* Jan 17, 1983 *ptnr* Cllr James Blanchard *qv education* Newent Community School; Haberdashers' Monmouth School for Girls; Univ of Bath; Charles Univ, Prague *career* student and odd jobs students do! *party* LDYS Exec 1999-20000, 2001-03, chair 2002-03; Euro Candidate 2204 Welsh Liberal Democrats; mbr Welsh Finance and Admin Cttee 2003-04 *special interests* youth affairs, education *other mbrships* NUS, LDEG *recreations* riding, travel, smiling, laughing *address* c/o 4 Parc Close, Llangybi, Usk, Gwent, NP15 1PN *tel* 07974 353021 *e-mail* mail@voteali.org.uk

GOLDSWORTHY, Julia MP (Falmouth & Camborne maj:1,886) **Shadow Chief Secy to the Treasury** *b* Sept 10, 1978 *education* Truro School, Cambridge Univ (BA Hons History), Daiichi Univ of Economics (Japan), Birkbeck College London (PgC Economics) *career* with Carrick District Council, focusing on regeneration issues, building and developing links with local businesses in the area *party* Shadow Chief Secretary to the Treasury 2006- ; Shadow spokesperson on Health 2005-06; mbr Public Administration Select Cttee 2005- ; senior political adviser to Parliamentary Party (economy and education) 2003-04 *special interests* education, economic policy, housing *publications* co-authored In from the Cold: A Report on Cornwall's Affordable Housing Crisis and Cornish Students: 3 Years More Hard Labour? *recreations* art, music, theatre, rowing *address* 75 Trelowarren Street, Camborne, Cornwall TR14 8AL *tel/fax* 01209 716110 *e-mail* info@juliagoldsworthy.org *web* www.juliagoldsworthy.org

GOODHART, Lady; Celia McClare *b* Jul 25, 1939 *m* 1966 William Howard, Lord Goodhart QC *qv* 1 *s* 2 *d* 5 *gch education* St. Michael's Limpsfield, Surrey 1946-56; St Hilda's College, Oxford 1957-60 (MA; Hon. Fellow 1989); *career* HM Civil Service, MAFF 1960-66; Private Secy to Permanent Secy 1964-66; Principal 1966; Principal, Queen's College, London 1991-99 *party* founder mbr SDP 1981; PPC SDP/Liberal Alliance for Kettering 1983, 1987; European candidate Northamptonshire 1984; chair SDP Environment Policy Cttee 1985-87; Women for Social Democracy 1986-88; Women Liberal Democrats 1988; president East Midlands Liberal Democrats 1989-91; mbr SDP National Cttee, Policy Cttee; Liberal Democrats Federal Exec 1988-90 *special interests* environment, education, organisation *other mbrships* Hon Fellow City & Guilds Institute 2002; Chair Board of Trustees, Oxford Univ Society 1996-2004; Family Planning Association 1999-

2005; First Forum 2002-04; London Region of Girls' Schools Association 1996-99; Youth Clubs UK 1988-91; North Thames Gas Consumer Council 1979-82; president, Schoolmistresses and Governesses Benevolent Institution 1991- ; London Marriage Guidance Council 1990-95; Board of Trustees of Childline 1999- ; RCOG Ethics Cttee 1999-2002; St. Bartholomew's Hospital Ethical Cttee 1979-86; The Prince's Youth Business Trust Advisory Council 1988-91; All Saints Cttee (chairmen of major charities) 1988-91; Women's National Commission 1986-89; National Gas Consumers Council 1979-82; Data Protection Cttee 1976-78; Elizabeth Nuffield Education Fund 1972-82; Trustee, Council for Protection of Rural England 1987-91; Governor, Goldsmiths College London Univ 2003- ; Isaac Newton Comprehensive School 1977-81 *address* 11 Clarence Terrace, Regent's Park, London NW1 4RD and Youlbury House, Boars Hill, Oxford OX1 5HH *tel* 020 7262 1319 and 01865 735477 *fax* 020 7723 5851 *e-mail* 11clarence@freeuk.com

GOODHART, Baron Sir William Howard Goodhart: Life Peer cr 1997, Kt 1989, QC: Shadow Lord Chancellor *b* Jan 18, 1933 *m* Celia McClare Goodhart *qv* 1 *s* 2 *d education* Eton; Trinity College, Cambridge (MA); Harvard Law School (LLM) *career* barrister 1960-2003 (QC 1979) *party* joined SDP 1981; PPC Kensington 1983, 1987, 1988 (by-election), Oxford West & Abingdon 1992; chair SDP Council Arrangements Cttee 1982-88; Lib Dem Conference Cttee 1988-91; mbr Federal Policy Cttee 1988-97, vice-chair 1995-97; chair Lib Dem Lawyers Association 1991-94; co-draftsman SDP constitution 1981 and Lib Dems 1987; created life peer 1997; Shadow Lord Chancellor *special interests* Human Rights; legal system; constitution *other mbrships* vice-president International Commission of Jurists; Justice (vice-chair of Council), Cttee on Standards in Public Life 1997-2003; trustee, Fair Trials Abroad *recreations* walking *publications* Specific Performance (with Professor Gareth Jones) *address* House of Lords, London, SW1A 0PW *tel* 020 7219 5449 *fax* 020 7723 5851 *e-mail* goodhartw@parliament.uk

GORDON, Katy *b* Jan 23, 1966 *education* MA (Hons) French Studies IIi (Univ of Aberdeen); PgDip Careers Guidance (Napier Univ and Glasgow Careers Service); CIPD in HR (4 modules); A1 Assessor qualification *career* research assistant, ACER Freeman Fox 1990; trainee accountant, Ernst & Young 1990-91; various roles with Careers Service, Glasgow 1993- ; *party* chair Glasgow South LP, previously secy; jointly set-up local policy forum in Glasgow South branch; candidate Knightswood Park council by-election 2005; PPC Glasgow South West 2005 (doubling share of vote); exec mbr PCA, Scottish Conference Cttee, Scottish WLD, Gtr Glasgow LDs, Glasgow Area Campaigns Cttee *other mbrships* Chartered Institute of Careers Guidance, CIPD *special interests* Europe, civil liberties, electoral reform recreations gourmet cookery, hill walking, travel, current affairs *address* Flat 3/1, 26 Battlefield Avenue, Glasgow G42 9RJ *tel* 0141 636 0214 home 07799 060921 mobile *e-mail* katy.gordon@careers-scotland.org.uk

GORDON, Tim *b* Aug 26, 1971 London *m* no *ch education* William Ellis Comprehensive; Queens' College, Cambridge; College of Europe, Bruges; INSEAD, France *career* European Commission 1993-94; research assistant to Lord David Steel in House of Commons 1994; Financial Times 1995-99; The Boston Consulting Group BCG 2001- ; party mbr Westminster, Islington LPs; PPC Rotherham 2005; council candidate Islington 2006; mbr policy working gps on Commerce, and Employment and Trade Unions *special interests* international affairs incl. defence,

European affairs, business policy, govt reform, education, environment *publications* various articles in Financial Times on business and education recreations travel, reading, running, theatre *address* 3 Purley Place, London N1 1QA *tel* 0789 065 8870 *e-mail* timgordon21@hotmail.com

GORRIE, Donald MSP (Central Scotland Region) **Scottish Parliament Spokesperson on Communities, Standards Cttees** *b* India 1933 *m* 2 *s* 6 *gch education* Stirling, Oundle; Corpus Christi College, Oxford (2nd Class Honours Classics, Modern History) 1953-57; broke Scottish Native record 880 yards 1955; Oxford Blue 1955-57; president Oxford Univ Athletic Club 1957; won Silver Medal, World Student Games and won championships in US, Canada, international races Norway, Czechoslovakia; qualified athletics coach *career* second lieutenant (National Service) Royal Artillery, including service Germany 1951-53; teacher Gordonstoun 1957-60; PE department Marlborough College 1960-66; research, adult education lecturing, secondary school, college 1966-69; director of research, director of administration Scottish Liberal Party 1969-75; small-business start-ups including Edinburgh Translations; full-time Cllr Edinburgh Corstorphine to 1997; MP 1997-2001; MSP 1999- *party* PPC West Edinburgh 1970, February 1974, October 1974, 1992; MP West Edinburgh 1997-2001 (only non-Labour MP in 51 constituencies across central Scotland); parliamentary spokesperson Scottish education, local govt, youth, housing; elected Scottish Parliament 1999, re-elected 2003; spokesperson Culture, Sport and Older People's Issues, Convener of Procedures Cttee, Standards Cttee; former mbr Communities, Justice 1 Cttees, local govt, transport, environment, finance cttees; mbr Edinburgh Town, then District, then City Council 1971-97, gp leader 1980-96; mbr Lothian Regional Council as sole Liberal 1974-82, leader Alliance, then Liberal Democrat gp 1982-96 *other mbrships* president City of Edinburgh Athletic Club, Corstorphine Amateur Athletic Club; past chairman Edinburgh Youth Orchestra; board mbr Queen's Hall, Edinburgh; former board, Cttee mbr Edinburgh International Festival; founder, first convenor Edinburgh City Youth Café, Diverse Attractions (award-winning community drama venue in the Edinburgh Festival Fringe); Lothian Association of Youth Clubs, Royal Lyceum Theatre, Castle Rock Housing Association, Scottish Chamber Orchestra, Edinburgh College of Art, Telford and Stevenson Colleges, Edinburgh Zoo *recreations* reading, music, history, theatre, youth activities, visiting ruins *address* Scottish Parliament, Edinburgh EH99 1SP *tel* 0131 348 5796 *e-mail* donald.gorrie.msp@scottishparliament.uk

GRAHAM, James Peter David BA (Hons) *b* Oct 25, 1974 Beckenham *education* Pickhurst School; St Olave's GS; Univ of Manchester (BA Hons Theology, Religious Studies: dissertation *Why are Richard Dawkins' views on evolution and culture controversial?*) *career* campaigns, press officer New Politics Network 2004- ; press officer Liz Lynne MEP 2002-04; campaigns, development organiser Leeds Liberal Democrats 2000-02; communications officer (sabbatical) LDYS 1998-2000 *party* joined 1995; candidate (Church End) Barnet LBC 2006; literature officer and candidate's aide, East Dunbartonshire 2005; member Federal Exec 2003-5; vice chair Green Liberal Democrats 2002-05; candidate (Leamington Clarendon ward) Warwick DC 2003; organiser *A Radical Agenda for a Radical Liberal Century - second New Radicalism Conference* 2002; secy Leeds City and District exec 2002; agent Leeds North West 2001; vice president LDYS 2000-02; party rep *Young Political Leaders Programme*, Boston College Irish Institute (Oxford, Boston,

163

Washington) 1999; mbr LDYS Constitution Working Group 1999; candidate (Hulme ward) Manchester City Council 1997 by-election, 1998; chair Manchester Univ Liberal Democrats 1996-97; candidate (Fallowfield) Manchester City Council 1996 *special interests* civil liberties, constitutional reform, e-campaigning, economic reform, environment, science and technology *other mbrships* life mbr Manchester Univ Film Society; life mbr Manchester Students Union; New Economics Foundation; Y-Bilderberg *recreations* blogging, board games, comic-books (especially UK), film, forteana, SMS, miscellaneous geekery *address* 19 Village Road, Finchley, London N3 1TL *e-mail* semajmaharg@gmail.com *web* http://liberati.net/quaequamblog

GRANT, Richard F *b* Feb 11, 1953 2 *s education* Burley Primary School, New Forest; Twynham Secondary, Christchurch *career* estate agent 1969- *party* joined 1990; former chair, vice chair Ringwood, Bransgrove and Burley LP; Exec mbr of former New Forest LP; past president Liberal Democrat Small Business Association; attended PPC assessment *special interests* rural, country life; pop music, scooters/mods, environment; conservation; business affairs, letter writing to the media and TV *other mbrships* Associate, Chartered Management Institute; Hon Fellow, Property Consultants Society and holder of a PCV licence *publications* local newspapers, *Estates Gazette, Mortgage Introducer;* professional related magazines *address* Grantlands, Burley (New Forest National Park), Ringwood, Hampshire BH24 4AZ *tel* 01425 402499 *e-mail* rfg@grantlands.fslife.co.uk

GRAYSON, Richard Sean BA (Hons), DPhil: *b* 18 Apr 1969, Hemel Hempstead *s* of Donald, Jannat Grayson *m* Lucy Harland 1995 1 *s* Edward *education* Hemel Hempstead Comp School 1980-87; Univ of East Anglia (BA 1st Class Hons English and America History) 1987-91, General Secy, Students' Union; The Queen's College, Oxford (DPhil Modern History) *career* tutor in history, politics at colleges of Oxford Univ 1994-97; associate lecturer Open Univ 1997-98; Director, Centre for Reform (now CentreForum) 1998-99; Lib Dem Director of Policy 1999-2004; lecturer in British politics, Goldsmith College, Univ of London 2004- *party* joined 1988; Political Officer Student National Exec 1990-91; National Youth & Student Officer 1991-92; mbr English Policy Cttee 1992-93; mbr HE Funding Gp 1993-94; mbr Tertiary Education Working Gp 1994-96; mbr Globalisation Working Gp 1999-2000; Director of Policy 1999-2004; mbr Green Lib Dems 2000-; mbr Liberal Summer School Cttee 2000- ; PPC Hemel Hempstead 2005; mbr Meeting the Challenge Working Gp 2005-06 *recreations* QPR FC; genealogy; films; 1978 MG BGT owner, driver *publications* joint editor *The Reformer* 1997-99; *Austen Chamberlain and the Commitment to Europe: British Foreign Policy 1924-29* 1997; *Liberals International Relations and Appeasement: The Liberal Party, 1919-39* 2001; several articles on 20th century UK politics and international policy in academic journals *style* Dr Richard Grayson *address* Department of Politics, Goldsmiths College, New Cross, London, SE14 6NW *tel* 07974 920627 *fax* 01442 235385 *e-mail* rsgrayson@talk21.com

GREAVES of Pendle, Lord Tony: BA, Life Peer cr 2000 *b* Bradford (he says he has forgotten date) *m* 2 *d education* Oxford Univ (BA Hons in Geography) *career* sometime teacher; various Lib Dem party jobs; second-hand bookseller, Liber Books, specialising in Liberal, political and election themes *party* joined the Liberals 1960 (at Oxford and in Wakefield); chair Union of Liberal Students; national chair

Young Liberals mbr Lancashire CC 1971-98 (including spell as gp leader); mbr Colne BC, Pendle BC (including leader of council) for 30 years; moved keystone amendment at 1970 Assembly which committed party to community politics, crucial to its survival during 1970s; in mid-Seventies set up and worked as organising secy Association of Liberal Cllrs (ALC) at Hebden Bridge (the organisation grew from desk-and-phone in Sunday Schoolroom to successful national network and resource centre promoting and supporting massive growth in local Liberal campaigning and numbers of Cllrs from 700 to 2,600 during his time); managed Liberal Publications for five years; former *Liberal Democrat News* columnist; created life peer 2000; Lords Spokesman on Environment, Food and Rural Affairs 2002-03, 2005- ; *publications Merger* (with Rachel Pitchford), many pamphlets *recreations* climbing, hill-walking, cycling *address* House of Lords, London SW1AA 0PW; Hartington Street, Winewall, Colne, Lancs BB8 8BD *tel* 01282 864346

GREEN, Matthew Roger *b* Apr 1970 *m* Sarah 1 *d* Abigail *education* Priory School, Shrewsbury; Shrewsbury, Sixth Form College Univ of Birmingham *career* sales, marketing manager, Plaskit Ltd 1991-96; self-employed in PR, timber products, hotels 1996-2003; MP 2001-05 *party* joined 1993; mbr South Shropshire DC 1994-95; mbr West Midlands Regional Exec 1995-2000; Regional Media Co-ordinator 1996-97; Exec mbr PCA (various positions, now vice-president) 1995- ; PPC Wolverhampton South West 1997, elected MP for Ludlow 2001, re-selected 2005; chair Joint States Candidates Cttee 2001-05; mbr Federal Exec 2004- ; Shadow Minister, Youth Affairs 2001-05; Shadow Local Govt Minister 2002-05 *special interests* youth affairs, housing, planning, local Govt finance, agriculture, defence *other mbrships* National Liberal Club *recreations* mountaineering, playing cricket, cooking (and eating!) *publications* publisher Who's Who in the Liberal Democrats? (first edition 1998) *address* 33-34 High Street, Bridgnorth WV16 4DB *tel* 01746 766 465 *e-mail* mghome@btinternet.com

GREEN, Michael Andrew *b* Jan 10, 1967 *m* Irina Kaneva 2000 1*d education* MBA, INSEAD, Fontainebleau, France 1998-99; BA (Hons) Russian Studies, Univ of Leeds 1985-90; Chatham House Grammar School, Ramsgate, Kent 1978-85 *career* NatWest Markets, London 1990-95; NatWest Markets, Moscow 1995-98; Internet start-ups, London 2000-01; Mizuho Corporate Bank, Ltd, London 2001- ; *party* joined in Thanet South the Saturday before the 1983 General Election; Sabbatical Leeds Univ Union Officer 1988-89, ULS National Exec mbr 1987-90; PPC St Albans 2005 *special interests* foreign affairs esp. Russia and the CIS, immigration policy, macroeconomics *other mbrships* Amnesty International, CAMRA, European Movement, Friends of St Albans Abbey, Friends of the Earth, St Albans Civic Society, St Albans Liberal Club, Tottenham Hotspur Supporters Trust *recreations* popular music, reading and travel, season ticket-holder at Tottenham Hotspur FC *address* 31 Hart Road, St Albans, Herts AL1 1NF *tel* 01727 863821 home 07866 493094 mobile *e-mail* michael.a.green@ntlworld.com

GREEN, Simon *b* 1957 *m* Mary Akerman dentist 1 *s* 1 *d education* scholarship Royal Grammar School; studied analytical biochemistry at NESCOT; applied biology, Portsmouth; agriculture, farm management WSCAH *career* agronomist, lecturer in agriculture, crop husbandry, rural affairs plus working sheep farmer; formerly scientific research officer, veterinary biochemist MAFF *party* press officer, LP chair (three terms); Euro candidate, South West 1999; candidate district, county;

PPC key seat West Dorset 2001 (made it fifth most-winnable seat); defeated Shadow Home Secy, Oliver Letwin, in mock Roman election (conducted in authentic Roman togas made famous by televised intervention of centurion Tacticus alias Billy Bragg!) in run up to GE *special interests* UK and European agriculture, rural affairs; widely-acknowledged as expert on farming, rural life; active environmental campaigner; Europe; education; transport; human rights; electoral reform; involved in promoting Fair Trade initiatives and improving links with new central and eastern European EU countries *publications The Future of Rural Education, The Impact of Urban Economic Migration on Rural Areas and Strategies for Minimising Housing Impact in Rural Areas*; recreations photography (Licentiate of the British Institute of Professional Photographers 1990), sailing, cricket *e-mail* maill@stubcroft.com

GREENFIELD, Christopher John *b* Dec 28, 1948 *m* Gillian 1 *s* 1 *d education* Kingswood Grammar, Glos; Univ of Leeds, Michigan State Univ, Univ of Bristol, Cambridge Univ (Corpus) BA (Hons), MA (Ed) MEd EdD *career* researcher, field officer Rowntree Social Services Trust 1971-74; organiser, Pudsey Liberal Association 1974-75; parliamentary assistant Richard Wainwright MP 1975-77; PGCE 1977-78; comprehensive school teacher Huddersfield 1978-80; teacher International School, Bahrain 1980-82; Quaker (UK) Middle East Secy 1982-86; head-teacher Sidcot School, North Somerset 1986-97; principal International College, Sherborne 1997- *party* joined Young Liberals having heard Jo Grimond in Bristol, 1963; first Liberal Assembly (Central Hall Westminster) 1964; formed YL branch (Warmley, South Glos, 250 mbrs by 1968, chairman, then president; chairman Leeds Univ Liberal Society 1969-70; mbr ULS Exec; delegate Party Council, Party Exec; elected Leeds City Council 1973-76; West Yorkshire County Council 1976 by-election, re-elected 1977-80; PPC Leeds NE Feb 1974, Oct 1974, Leeds West 1979 (won 25% of vote), Kingswood (Bristol) 2001 *special interests* foreign affairs (especially Middle East), Islam, education, local Govt, constitution *other mbrships* elder Society of Friends (Quakers); directors Rowntree Reform Trust; Secondary Heads Association; National Liberal Club; past chairman, British Association of International Study Centres; advisory board, Institute for Citizenship *recreations* history, writing, lecturing, walking, reading *publications The White Robed Queen* (history of Sidcot School).1994; *By Our Deeds* (based on experiences as headteacher) 1997; *The Bridge* (history of International College, Sherborne) 2000; *World Class* (global role of British boarding schools: with P A Hardaker); numerous articles, chapters in books, journals *address* Sedgemoor, Martock Road, Long Sutton, Somerset TA10 *tel* 01935 814743 *fax* 01458 241191 *e-mail* cjgreen@jrrt.org.uk

GREENFIELD Mark *b* Nov 8, 1951 Maidstone *m* Myroon (nee Rahim) May 1974 1 *s* Edward James 1 *d* Laura Margaret *education* Oldborough Manor School, Maidstone; Maidstone & Medway College of Technology; Newcastle-Upon-Tyne Polytechnic BSc (Hons) Nursing Science *career* Nurse Tutor Sunderland School of Nursing/Bede College of Health Studies, Sunderland Health Authority 1983-1995; senior lecturer, Division of Adult Chronic Care, Univ of Northumbria 1995- ; *party* Chair Maidstone Young Liberals 1971-73; candidate Maidstone Borough Council North Ward 1973; chair Sunderland Liberal Association 1981-82; Sunderland City Councillor Bishopwearmouth / Thornholme Ward 1980-2004; Liberal Democrat Gp Leader 1986-1992, 2000-2004 Sunderland City Council; PPC Sunderland South 2001, Houghton & Washington East 2005 *special interests* the health & social care economy, strategic change & modernisation of primary health care, welfare of older people, elimination of ageism in health and social care, implementation of the National Service Framework for Older People, an older people's champion; founder mbr and trustee City of Sunderland Millennium Orchestral Society; mbr of The Woodland Trust, Durham Wildlife Trust, and working to enhance & protect our woodlands *recreations* attending live jazz sessions/festivals, collecting & listening to jazz recordings, woodland walking, & investing time with my two young grandchildren.

GREENLAND Duncan Taylor Deputy Treasurer Liberty Network *b* Jan 2, 1948 *m* Barbara 1982 1 *d* Anne Marie 1 *s* Jonathan *education* Lewes County Grammar School; Brasenose College, Oxford (PPE) 1966-69; City Univ Business School *career* international education, training (based USA and Paris); co-founder Study Gp International 1990-99; vineyard and property investments France *party* organising secy Oxford Univ Liberal Club; involvement lapsed while living abroad; joined Liberal Democrats West Sussex 1995, became actively involved with West Hampstead/Camden branch 2000- ; founder mbr, deputy treasurer -Liberty Network 2003-; mbr FFAC 2004-; FFAC representative Federal Conference Cttee *other mbrships* trustee, chair Centre Forum Exec *address* 15 Greville Place, London NW6 5JE *tel* 0207 328 5271 *e-mail* dtguk@aol.com

GRIFFIN, John Howard *b* Jan 29, 1953 *m* Amanda 3 *s* *education* Truro School; Fitzwilliam College, Cambridge (natural sciences); Birmingham Univ (MSc mineral chemistry); Plymouth Polytechnic (MPhil environmental geochemistry) *career* applied chemistry research; scientific editing, publication, communications Centre for Ecology and Hydrology 1988- *party* mbr Cambridge Univ Liberal Club; joined Liberal Democrats 1989; currently vice-chair of Henley LP; contested council elections unsuccessfully 1989, 1991, 1993; mbr South Oxfordshire DC 1995-2003, chairman of council 2002-03, chair planning, Lib Dem gp chair 1999-2003; mbr ALDC *special interests* environment, sustainable development, fair trade, international justice, planning, countryside issues *other mbrships* Chilterns shadow conservation board; Oxfordshire countryside access forum; World Development Movement; YHA; Cyclists touring club *recreations* cycling, walking *address* 29 Thames Mead, Crowmarsh Gifford, Wallingford OX10 8EX *tel* 01491 838523 *e-mail* johngriff9@aol.com

GRIFFITHS, David Brandon Chair, Federal Finance and Administration Cttee *b* Nov 8, 1940 *m (dis)* 1 *s* 1 *d* 1 *gs education* The City of London School; Hendon Preparatory School; articled Chartered Accountant to HD Solomon FCA, qualified Chartered Accountant (ACA) 1965, admitted as Fellow (FCA) i1970 *career gp* chief accountant, Ladbroke Gp Limited 1972-77; financial, acquisitions director Ladbroke Racing Limited, Ladbroke and Co Limited 1977-80; joint MD Caterers Buying Association Limited, Petersbug Press Limited 1980-85; senior partner Griffiths Hicks 1985- *party* joined Liberal Party 1960, founder mbr of Liberal Democrats; currently, chair Federal Finance and Administration Cttee, registered party treasure for PPERA compliance; treasurer Liberal International (World Liberal Union); former PPC Clwyd South, Paddington North; Euro candidate Hertfordshire and Thames Valley; chair, later organising secy Liberal International British Gp; former UK Delegation leader, Oxford and Canada LI Congresses; former Cllr, gp leader Watford Borough Council; former chair English Council of the Regions, Chilterns

Region, Aylesbury, Watford, Paddington North LPs ;former agent:- Aylesbury (captured council; close second in GE), South West Herts (Three Rivers: control retained, good second in GE), Watford, Paddington North; former chair, Paddington North Young Liberals, treasurer London League of Young Liberals *special interests* foreign affairs; human rights; taxation, finance *other mbrships* British Numismatic Society, Queens Park Rangers Supporters *recreations* QPR season ticket holder, numismatics *publications* several pamphlets on numismatic token related subjects *address* The White House, Lower Kings Road, Berkhamsted HP4 2AA *tel* 01442 833861 home 01442 864800 business *fax* 01442 870992 *e-mail* David.Griffiths@Griffithshicks.co.uk

GURLING, James *b* Jul 26, 1966 parents Jill & Peter, sister Sarah *education* Macaulay C of E Primary School, Clapham, London; Archbishop Tennison's Grammar School, Kennington Oval, London; Furzedown Secondary School, Streatham, London; Univ of Hull (BA Jt Hons History & Politics) *career* vice president (finance & administration), Hull Univ Students Union 1988-89; Sales Exec, Cooperative Press 1989-91; Parliamentary Agent, Dr Jenny Tonge, Richmond & Barnes and Campaign Exec Lib Dem HQ 1991-93; Account Manager, Thomson Regional Newspapers Ltd 1993-94; Account Director, Hill & Knowlton UK Ltd 1994-98; Head of Parliamentary Affairs, British Retail Consortium 1998; Board Director, GPC (Government Policy Consultants) 1998-2000; Head of Public Policy & Government Affairs, Hutchison 3G UK Ltd 2001-05; Partner, Media Strategy Ltd 2005- *party* joined SDP 1985; Regional Convenor Yorkshire & Humberside students & national Cttee mbr 1986-87; Candidate (St Andrews Ward) Hull City Council by-election 1987, 1988; National Treasurer LD Students 1988-89; candidate (Avenue Ward) Humberside County Council 1989, Organiser Lib Dem Students 1993; candidate (Springfield Ward) LB Wandsworth and Agent all council candidates, Battersea constituency 1994; mbr London Region Exec 1993-95; Exec mbr, secy Agents Association 1997; Press Aide to Rt Hon Paddy Ashdown MP General Election Tour 1997; elected (Newington Ward) LB Southwark 1998, opposition spokesperson press, culture, Re-elected 2002, Exec mbr Service Delivery/Communications & Performance Improvement 2002-5, vice chair Overview & Scrutiny & Chair of Planning 2005-6, re-elected 2006, chair of Gp; Leadership campaign agent and adviser to Rt Hon Charles Kennedy MP 1999- ; mbr of Federal Exec, Conference Cttee, Campaigns & Communications Cttee 2004-; General Election Media Intelligence Unit manager 2005; former editor The Reformer and mbr exec cttee Centre for Reform *special interests* energy, media, communications & broadcasting policy, retail *other mbrshps* Commonwealth Club, Reform Club, Guildable Manor of Southwark; Friends of Tate, Shakespeare's Globe, Royal Academy of Art; Institute of Contemporary Art; Kennington Park *e-mail* jgurling@btinternet.com

GURNEY, Chris *b* Dec 28, 1981 Tye Green, Hertfordshire *partner* Ruth Polling *qv* *education* Royal Grammar School, High Wycombe; Univ of Exeter (BA Hons History and Politics); currently completing dissertation (on Judith Butler, William Connolly and the political) for MA in Critical Global Studies *career* self-employed *party* joined April 2000; mbr Federal Policy Cttee 2002-3; mbr International Relations Cttee 2002-3; chair LDYS policy cttee 2002-4, mbr LDYS conference cttee 2001-4; mbr LDYS Federal Exec 2001-3; mbr English Council 2001-; mbr Exeter LP exec 2001-3; mbr Islington LP exec (recruitment officer) 2006-; mbr macro-economics working gp *special interests* international politics, feminist and post-identity politics, contemporary continental philosophy, activating young mbrs *other mbrships* Amnesty International, Friends of the Earth, CND *recreations* films, reading, football, cricket, clubbing, delivery *address* 26 Rahere House, Central Street, Islington EC1V 8DE *email* herculinebarbin@hotmail.co.uk

H

HALL, Brian C.Eng, MIMechE *b* May 19, 1948 *m* Anne 2 *s* Peter, Stephen 1 *d* Zoe *education* Univ of Sussex (BSc Hons Mechanical Engineering); London Business School (MSc Business Administration) *career* Shell UK exploration, production 1974-77; project engineer responsible for Brent A (North Sea oil production platform), Esso Europe, Esso exploration, production 1979-86; senior project engineer evaluating oil production economics 1986- ; owner, MD Airstream Communications Ltd (trade magazines) *party* rejoined 1993; elected West Sussex County Council 1993, 1997, 2001; elected Mid-Sussex District Council May 2003, gp leader 2003-04; elected mbr Federal Exec 2001, 2003; elected mbr Federal Policy Cttee 2001, 2003, 2004; represents Lib Dems on South East England Region's planning Exec, LGA Economic Regeneration Exec *special interests* economic regeneration, business strategy *other mbrships* elder Religious Society of Friends (Quakers) *recreations* photography, travel, theatre, cinema *publications* publisher two trade titles *Brushwork* and *Tool* Business+*Hire address* Wiston, Coppice Way, Haywards Heath, West Sussex RH16 4NN *tel* 01444 450347 home 01444 440188 business *fax* 01444 414813 *e-mail* brianhallz@aol.com *web* www.Lib-Dem.com

HALL, Colin Christopher *b* Jan 17, 1961 *ptnr* Cate Ison 2 *s* Tom, David 1 *d* Emma *education* Dayncourt School, Nottinghamshire; Huddersfield Polytechnic (BA Hons Literature) *career* senior manager, gp networking, communications J. Sainsbury plc 1982-98; IT consultant 1998-2003; constituency organiser, agent to Tom Brake MP 1998-2004, business co-ordinator 2004; lead Cllr for environment LB Sutton 2001-05; Deputy Leader LB Sutton from May 2006 *party* joined 1994; various ward, borough party posts; agent for parliamentary elections 1997, 2001; borough elections 2002 *special interests* environment, sustainability, municipal waste strategy, economic development, regeneration *other mbrships* Friends of the Earth; mbr Chartered Institute of Waste Management; technical adviser to IEEE *recreations* tennis, athletics, travel *address* 30 Clifton Road, Wallington, Surrey SM6 8AN *tel* 020 8647 5963 home 020 8669 2225 business *fax* 020 8647 5963 *e-mail* colin.hall@sutton.gov.uk or hallc@parliament.uk

HALL, Fiona Jane MEP North East England *b* Jul 15, 1955 *education* Worsley Wardles GS; Eccles College; St Hugh's College, Oxford (BA Hons upper II, modern languages) 1976; Oxford Polytechnic, Postgraduate Certificate in Education 1977 *career* mbr of the European Parliament North East of England, Jun 2004- ; international polling station supervisor, Kosovo (per OSCE) Nov 2001; senior researcher Lib Dem Deputy Leader, Rt Hon Alan Beith MP, Oct 2001; election agent Alan Beith, 16 county council candidates 2001; constituency organiser Berwick-upon-Tweed 1999-2001; Regional Media Co-ordinator North East May-Dec 2000; press, political officer Lembit Öpik MP, Richard Livsey MP 1997-99; assistant to Newcastle City Cllrs in South Gosforth (elections, campaigning, casework) 1994-97; vice chair, chair Druridge Bay Campaign, biggest environmental campaign in the North East; blocked nuclear power and halted sand-extraction on Northumberland coast 1989-96; lobbying for Oxfam, World Development Movement on international development issues; part-time, supply teacher Northumberland County Council, Workers Educational Association 1986-95; parent governor, Whittingham First School 1984-89; part-time playgp leader 1983-86; teacher self-help school, Naledi, Gaborone, Botswana 1977-79 *party* joined Jan 1, 1993 (New Year resolution!); European candidate North East list (top woman on zipped list) 1999; elected to the European Parliament 2004 (North East's first Liberal Democrat) *special interests* environment, international development *recreations* exploring new places, learning new languages, walking, writing (published poet), time with family *address* 55A Old Elvet, Durham DH1 3HN *tel* 0191 383 0119 *fax* 0191 375 7519 *e-mail* fiona@fionahallmep.co.uk

HALL, Katie *b* Dec 29, 1966 *m* 1 *s education* Leeds Univ (BSc Hons) *career* current: organiser, Wells constituency; public affairs, communications consultant, Somerset 2002-03; London, Amsterdam, Brussels 1992-99; political adviser Lib Dem gp LB Islington 2001-02; political adviser Nick Clegg MEP, Brussels 1999-2001; press, policy officer Paddy Ashdown MP 1990-92, communications aide Matthew Taylor MP 1989-90 *party* joined 1985 Leeds; vice chair Western Counties; Euro candidate 2004; candidate Sedgemoor DC 2003; Exec mbr Lib Dem History Gp 1998- ; treasurer Brux & Lux Lib Dems 1998-2001; adviser Paddy Ashdown 1992-96; mbr steering gp Campaign for Women; Exec WLD; Exec Islington LP; London Region policy Cttee, mbr Federal policy working gps; candidate Barnsbury ward 199; international vice-chair British Youth Council 1988-90; Exec Young Liberals 1986-88; Exec Leeds NW 1986-89, chair student branch Leeds NW 1987-89; mbr ALDC, Green Liberal Democrats; party trainer *special interests* environment, equalities, Europe. *other mbrships* Shark Trust, La Leche League *publications* co-author *Winning From Control* (ALDC 2002); co-author *Dictionary of Liberal Quotations* (1999) *Dictionary of Liberal Biography* (Politico's 1998) *recreations* admiring baby, by-elections, cooking *address* 47 Chilton Road, Bath, BA1 6DR *tel* 01225 471 024 *fax* 01225 471 287 *e-mail* katiehall@cix.co.uk

HALL, Richard *b* Aug 19, 1964 Oxford *education* Keele Univ BA History/Politics 1987; Microsoft Certified Systems Engineer 2000; currently studying MA in Modern History, Reading Univ *career* 14 years research work in rtrade union movement for various unions; 6 years in IT industry, public and private sectors *party* joined in 1998 following 15 years active mbrship of Labour Party; mbr Greater Reading LP, South Central region (secy Central Branch); conference delegate (twice); key campaigner Park Ward, Reading East; Labour PPC Newbury 1992; Reading borough candidate 1999, 2001, 2004, mbr PCA (approved candidate) *other mbrships* Motorcycle Action Group *special interests* world and domestic economy; Middle East; Latin America; US foreign policy; public sector IT policy; beating Labour; the Reading Labour Party especially Martin Salter MP *publications* Park Ward Focus, Reading Focus *recreations* dinghy sailing *LD quirks* proficient organiser; extremely good at practical tasks from making stakeboards to putting IT to party use on a limited budget *address* 17 Burnham Rise, Emmer Green, Reading RG4 8XJ *tel*

01189474280 home 07708412718 mobile *e-mail* richard@richardhall.org.uk *web* www.richardhall.org.uk

HALL-MATTHEWS, Dr David *b* Mar 19, 1967 Horsham *education* Christ's Hospital; Lincoln College Oxford (BA); School of Oriental and African Studies, London (MA); St Antony's College, Oxford (DPhil) *career* lecturer in International Development, School of Politics and International Studies, Univ of Leeds *party* mbr Camden LP in London Region; PPC Leeds North West 2001, Hemsworth 2005; mbr policy working groups on International Development and International Trade *special interests* governance, development and food security in South Asia and Southern Africa; higher education *publications* Peasants, Famine and the State in Colonial Western India Palgrave Macmillan 2005 *address* 42 Radcliff Buildings, Bourne Estate, Portpool Lane, London EC1N 7SN *tel* 020 7681 7375 home 077 9291 0493 mobile *e-mail* dnjhm@hotmail.com

HALSALL, Neil *b* Sept 21, 1944 Leigh, Lancashire *m* Joyce (nee Widdows) Apr 1, 1967 1 *d* 1 *s education* Moseley Hall Grammar School; Manchester College of Commerce *career* trainee accountant at BWA Ltd; accountant at ICI Pharmaceuticals Division and Commercial Manager at Zeneca Pharmaceuticals; retired from paid employment February 1996; mbr Chartered Institute of Management Accountants and Chartered Institute of Secretaries and Administrators until retirement *party* joined Liberal Party in early 1970s but lapsed and rejoined in mid 1980s; mbr Northavon LP, Western Counties region; past secy and chair LP, past Treasurer of regional party and currently chairman of regional party; Returning Officer for PPC selections; mbr Northavon District Council 1991 till disbanded 1996; mbr South Gloucestershire Council (unitary) 1995- including six years as Leader 1999-2005; mbr Thornbury Town Council 1988- including one year as Mayor; mbr ALDC, WLD, DELGA *other mbrships* chairman Two Bridges Drug and Alcohol Trust; chairman Thornbury Sea Cadet Unit; Treasurer Thornbury FM community radio; mbr South Gloucestershire Leisure Trust and many small charities and trusts *recreations* hill walking, militaria and my community; now looking for (some) time to myself too! *address* 3 Nightingale Close, Thornbury, Bristol, BS35 1TG *tel* 01454 414311 home 07776 236145 mobile *e-mail* neil.halsall@southglos.gov.uk

HAMES, Duncan John *b* Jun 16, 1977 *education* Watford Boys; New College, Oxford (Student Union Exec; Union Standing Cttee; mbr British Universities debating tour of California) *career* management consultant Deloitte 1998 - ; board mbr, South West of England Regional Development Agency 2003- ; previously NHS hospital trust recruitment, GP practice clerk *party* joined 1995; LDYS student development officer 1997; Lib Dems Online Exec 2002; honorary vice-president LDYS 2001-02; FFAC 2002; GBTF trainer, candidate coach; PPC Westbury 2005, Chippenham (selected 2006); district Cllr, Holt, West Wiltshire *special interests* digital divide in rural communities *other mbrships* central board mbr, Wiltshire Young Enterprise; governor, Westwood with Iford School *recreations* good food and good company *publications* LDO Guide to E-mail Campaigning 2001 *address* 126 The Midlands, Holt, Trowbridge, Wiltshire BA14 6RG *tel* 01225 782964 home 07711 526879 *fax* 08707 622665 *e-mail* Duncan@hames.org *web* www.hames.org

HAMWEE, Baroness Sally Rachel: Life Peer cr 1991: Lords spokesperson on ODPM matters *b* Jan 12, 1947 *education* Manchester High School for Girls; Girton

College, Cambridge *career* admitted solicitor 1972; former partner Clintons Solicitors now consultant specialising in media and entertainment *party* joined1976; mbr LB Richmond upon Thames Council 1978-98; chair Planning Cttee1987-91; v chair Policy & Resources Cttee1987; chair London Planning Advisory Cttee1986-94; past standing-Cttee v chair and pres ALDC; mbr NEC Liberal Party 1978-88; Fed Exec Lib Dems 1989-91; appointed to House of Lords 1991 as only second Lib Dem working peer in ten years; mbr General Election teams 1992, 1997; mbr House of Lords Select Cttee on relations between central and local govt 1995-96; House of Lords spksn, Local Govt 1991, Housing and Planning 1993; leader Environment, Transport and Regions team, leader Transport, Local Govt and Regions team 1997-2005; elected London-wide mbr London Assembly (GLA) 2000, re-elected 2004; deputy chair 2000-01, 2002-03, 2004-05; chair 2001-02, 2003-04, 2005-06; chair Budget Cttee 2000- ; deputy chair Business Management and Appointments Cttee, the 7 July Review (London Resilience) Cttee, the Audit and Inspection Cttee, mbr of Economic Development, Culture, Sport and Tourism Cttee, and the Planning and Spatial Development Cttee *other mbrships* past mbr (past chair) Council of Refuge 1991-2005, Parents for Children 1977-86; legal advisor Simon Community 1980; vice-president (past president) Town and Country Planning Association; mbr Joseph Rowntree Foundation Inquiry 1991 *address* House of Lords, London SW1 0PW

HANCOCK, Mike CBE (1992) MP (Portsmouth South maj: 3,362): **mbr House of Commons Chairman's panel** *b* Apr 9, 1946 Portsmouth *m* 2 ch *education* Portsmouth schools *career* director BBC Daytime, district officer MENCAP 1987-97; MP 1984-87, 1997- *party* joined SDP (from Labour) 1981, fdr mbr Liberal Democrats; mbr (Labour) Portsmouth City Council (Nelson, then Fratton ward) 1971- chair Planning 1991-97; Hampshire CC 1973- , leader Labour Opposition 1981, (SDP 1981), council leader (Lab/Lib Dem joint administration) 1993-97; PPC Portsmouth South 1983, 1984 (by-election: elected), 1987 (lost seat by 205), 1992 (lost by 242), re-elected 1997, 2001, 2005; mbr Defence Select Cttee; mbr HoC chairman's panel; bureau mbr Assembly of European Regions, Atlantic Arc, Council of Europe, Western European Union Parliamentary Delegation, NATO Parliamentary assembly *special interests* animal rights (supporting ban on hunting with dogs; co-sponsor parliamentary bill to ban live export of animals) *awards* CBE, 1992; honorary alderman of Hampshire *address* Albert Road, Southsea, Portsmouth PO5 2SE *tel* 02392 861 055 *fax* 02392 830 530 *e-mail* portsmouthldp@cix.co.uk *web* www.mikehancock.co.uk

HANSON. Anders Paul *b* Nov 25, 1975 Gothenburg, Sweden *education* Tapton School, Sheffield; Staffordshire University (BA Hons Geography) *career* Midland Mainline 1998-2002; Liberal Democrats 2002-05; WHSmith 2005- ; *party* joined 1995; activist in Stoke-on-Trent, Hereford, Sheffield 1995-98; mbr English Council 1997-2002 and 2004-5; vice-chair LDYS 1998-99; mbr English Council exec 1999-2002 and 2004; Derby city councillor Kingsway 2000-02, Mickleover 2002-03; PPC Derby South 2001; Welsh Assembly election agent Mid and West Wales 2003; local and general election agent Eastleigh 2004-5 *special interests* transport, community regeneration, urban design, education, Europe *other mbrships* The Civic Trust, The National Trust *recreations* meeting friends, walking, comedy, musicals, family history, music, reading, architecture, history *address* 25 Lydgate Hall Crescent, Crosspool, Sheffield, S10 5NE *tel* 07909 917 195.*e-mail* ahanson@clara.co.uk

HANSON, Simon BSc *b* May 18, 1971 *education* BSc computer communications *career* MD Orac Communications (IT consultancy), clients include British Airways, British Telecom, UnumProvident *party* chair Stourbridge LP, local and federal conference rep; exec mbr Libdems Online (LDO); mbr ALDC; mbr West Midlands Conference Cttee *special interests* school governance (local primary school governor); fair-voting STV, increasing number of local Cllrs, web *recreations* digital photography, salsa dancing, live music *address* 53 Chawn Hill, Pedmore, Stourbridge, West Midlands DY9 7JA *tel* 01384 373688 *fax* 0870 1641741 *e-mail* libdem@orac.demon.co.uk

HARDING-PRICE, David *b* Sept 7, 1956 St Albans *m* Sharon (nee Hillier) Aug 21, 1982 2 *d education* Lincoln Grammar School; Workshop College, Fulbourn School of Nursing (Cambridge) *career* Staff Nurse, Cambridge 1980-82; Community Psychiatric Nurse, Richmond Surrey & Grimsby 1982-89; Clinical Nurse Specialist, Grimsby 1989-95; Nurse Counsellor, Falkland Islands 1995-97; GP Liaison Nurse, Paddington 1998-2005; Team Clinical Co-ordinator, Skegness 2005- ; *party* past chair LP in East Midlands; PPC Lincoln 1992, Newark 2001, Sleaford and North Hykeham 2005; past mbr PCA *party record* "Not had a number one hit yet!" ☺ *other mbrships* Royal College of Nursing *special interests* health, social affairs, education and public transport *publications* various articles in health journals, co-author of *Drug Misuse* and *Caring for Children*, chapters in textbooks *special interests* co-founder of MATTDOTCOM, only United Kingdom based community charity for teenagers with cancer and other long term illnesses *recreations* season ticket holder for Lincoln City FC, music, radio & amdram, swimming *address* Lincoln *fax* 01522 540938 *e-mail* study@mattdotcom.org.uk

HARDY, Stephen Philip MBE (1999) *b* Jan 10, 1948 *m* Susan 1 *s* 1 *d education* Nottingham High School; Jesus College; Cambridge; Institute of European Studies, Brussels Univ *career* qualified as a solicitor 1974, various posts private practice, industry; currently company secy Ibstock Gp Ltd. (country's leading brick makers); director , company secy various not-for-profit regeneration companies Merseyside, East Midlands, South East (awarded MBE for pioneering Ibstock Community Enterprises Ltd) *party* joined Liberal Party 1966; founder mbr SDP, Liberal Democrats; vice chair South Notts area SDP 1983-84; PPC North East Derbyshire 1983, 1987, 1997, Bexhill and Battle 2001; cllr Rother DC 1999-2003, leader 2001- 03 *special interests* environment; transport; regeneration; arts; Europe *other mbrships* Greenpeace, National Trust, CPRE, Friends of the Earth *recreations* tending allotment; classical music *publications* *EEC Law* (Sweet and Maxwell) 1974 *address* White Horse Cottage High Street Robertsbridge, East Sussex TN32 5AN *tel* 01580 881309 home 020 7563 3000 business *e-mail* stephen@stephenhardy.org.uk

HARGREAVES, Jeremy MA (Oxon) **Vice Chair, Federal Policy Cttee** *b* Jan 2, 1974 *education* Whitgift School, Croydon; Christ Church, Oxford (MA *Literaae Humaniores*), Academical Clerk (Choral Scholar); president Oxford Reform Club; secy Student Union; mbr Hebdomadal Council *career* Head of Office, Islington Lib Dems; European affairs manager GJW Govt Relations; mbr, management board European Movement 1996-2001 and 2004- ; chair national development Cttee 1997- 99, 2000-01, president, Young European Movement 1996-7 *party* joined 1990; mbr Federal Policy Cttee 2001- , vice chair 2004- ; convenor, Conference Access Gp; chair LDEG 2004-06; mbr several policy working gps including *Meeting the*

Challenge; PPC Croydon Central 2005, Rushcliffe 2001; Westminster Press Office 1996, 1997 GE *special interests* Europe, foreign affairs, education, local Govt, business *recreations* music, travelling *publications Wasted Rainforests* (about party policy-making), *It's About the Public, Stupid*; *Private Sector Working*; *Campaigning on Europe*; regular articles in party publications, especially about Europe, public services *address* 21a Huntingdon Street, Barnsbury, London N1 1BS *tel* 07974 241 304 *e-mail* jeremy@jeremyhargreaves.org *web* www.jeremyhargreaves.org

HARPER, Rosalyn Jane *b* Sept 7, 1973 *education* Nottingham Law School (Postgraduate Diploma in legal practice) 1996-97; Nottingham Trent Univ: LLB (Sandwich Law Degree) 1992-96; Sixth Form College, Colchester 1990-92 Hockerill County Boarding School 1985-90 *career* solicitor, currently a consultant at JPMorgan, previously with international law firm, investment bank *party* PPC Surrey Heath 2002, elected Federal Exec 2003, 2004; vice chair LDYS 2002-03; Exec mbr Camden Borough LP *special interests* crime, home security, education, health, women *recreations* five-a-side football, films, theatre, catching up with friends *address* 48 Glassonby Walk, Camberley, Surrey GU15 1SQ *tel* 07980 757 388 *e-mail* rosharper2@netscape.net

HARRIS of RICHMOND DL, Baroness (Life cr 1999), Cllr Angela Felicity Harris: House of Lords Whip *b* Jan 4, 1944 Lancashire *m* 1 (dis 1974) 1 *s* Mark *m* 2 John *education* Canon Slade GS, Bolton; Ealing College of Hotel & Catering *career* air stewardess (Channel Airways) 1963-65; employment asst Oxfordshire County Council 1971-76 *party* joined Liberals 1974; asst agent, Henley-on-Thames; formed first Liberal branch in Richmond, Yorkshire 1976; agent, candidate's press officer; Euro candidate 1999; former Chief Steward, Federal Conference; mbr Richmond TC 1976-80, 1993- (Mayor 1993); Richmondshire DC 1978-89 (chair 1987-88); North Yorkshire CC 1981-2001 (first woman chair 1991-92); appoint to Lords 1999: former chair European Union Select sub-Cttee F, former mbr European Union Select Cttee, Whip; president of City of York Liberal Democrats *other mbrships* magistrate 1982-98; Northallerton Health Trust; DL of the County of North Yorkshire 1994; Court, Univ of York 1996- ; chair North Yorkshire Police Authority 1994-2001; deputy chair National Association of Police Authorities 1997-2001; patron Lister House British Legion, Trauma International; Hospice Homecare Support Gp; President of National Association of Chaplains to the Police *recreations* music, reading political biographies, watching sport on TV *address* House of Lords, London SW1A 0PW *tel* 020 7219 6709

HARRIS, Dr Evan MP BA (Hons), BM, BS **(Oxford West and Abingdon** maj: 7,683) *b* Oct 21, 1965 *education* Blue Coat School (state selective) Liverpool 1977-84; Harvard High School, Los Angeles 1985; Wadham College, Oxford 1985-88; Oxford Univ Clinical Medical School 1988-91 *career* qualified in medicine 1991; junior hospital doctor 1991-94; honorary registrar public health medicine 1994-*party* joined SDP 1985; elected MP Oxford West and Abingdon 1997, re-elected 2001, 2005; junior health spokesman 1997-99; spokesman higher education, science and women's issues 1999-2001; Shadow Health Secy 2001-03; spokesperson for Science 2005- ; *special interests* science (mbr, Science and Technology Select Cttee 2005-); medical ethics; race, immigration; equality, discrimination; HIV/AIDS; secularism *recreations* football, bridge, chess *address* 27 Park End Street, Oxford,

OX1 1HU *tel* 01865 245584 and 0207 219 5128 office *fax* 01865 245589 *e-mail* harrise@parliament.uk

HARVEY, Nicholas Barton (Nick) MP (North Devon maj:4,972**) Shadow Defence Secy *b*** Aug 3, 1961 Chandler's Ford *m* Kate (nee Fox) 1 *d* 1 *s education* Sherbe House School, Chandler's Ford; Queen's College, Taunton; Middlesex Univ *career* communications, marketing City consultants Dewe Rogerson; freelance consultant *party* joined Liberals 1974; as president-elect of Middlesex Univ's Students Union 1981, took outgoing Trotskyist Exec to High Court to prevent illegal donation of Union funds; agent Finchley, 1983; candidate Barnet Council 1986; PPC Enfield Southgate 1987 (v Michael Portillo), North Devon 1992 (elected maj: 794), re-elected 1997, 2001, 2005; parliamentary transport spokesman 1992-94 (opposed rail privatisation, pressed for funds to be switched from road to public transport); trade and industry 1994-97; English Regions 1997-99; front-bench Health spokesman 1999-2001; Shadow Secy for Culture, Media and Sport 2001-03; chair Campaigns and Communications Cttee 1994-99, chair Joint States Candidates Cttee 1994-99; mbr Federal Exec 1994-99, 2004 *special interests* Europe *other mbrships* Greenpeace, Friends of the Earth, Amnesty International *recreations* football, music, walking *address* House of Commons, London SW1A 0AA *tel* 020 7219 6232 *constituency* 23 Castle Street, Barnstaple, Devon EX31 1DR *tel* 01271 328631 *fax* 01271 345664 *e-mail* harveyn@parliament.uk *web* www.nickharvey.org.uk

HASWELL, Susan Jane *b* Mar 3, 1964 *m* Martyn West (retained own name for business purposes) 1 *ch education* King Edwards Grammar School; Bournville School of Art (fashion & art) *career* media sales manager, CPS Data Systems; account manager, Rote PR/Osborns/Shandwick; set up own business, Haswell Public Relations Ltd in 1997, merging in 2002 to Haswell Holden Ltd (currently CEO) *party* mbrship secy Bromsgrove LP (West Midlands Region); PPC Bromsgrove 2005 *other mbrships* MCIPR (Chartered Institute of Public Relations) *special interests* corporate social responsibility *recreations* travel, swimming, good food, spending time with family *address* Cornerflag, 18 Victoria Road, Bromsgrove, Worcestershire B61 0DW *tel* 01527 873937 day, 07966 301698 eve *e-mail* s.haswell@btinternet.com *web* www.haswellholden.com

HAYES, Josephine *b* 1955 *education* Colchester County HS for Girls; Lady Margaret Hall, Oxford (BA, Greats Class I, 1978); City Univ (Diploma in Law, 1979); called to the Bar, 1980; Yale Law School (LLM 1981); *career* barrister in private practice in London 1982-; founder mbr and former chair Assoc of Women Barristers **party** founder mbr; elected mbr Federal Policy Cttee, ELDR council delegation, interim peers panel; mbr International Relations Cttee; Chair Westminster and City of London LP; mbr exec Lib Dem Lawyers Assoc; Editor Legal Democrat magazine; mbr Green Lib Dems. Women Lib Dems (former Chair), ALDC, Lib Dem History Group *special interests* law reform, equal opportunities, energy policy, fair trade, environment *memberships* CentreForum, Friends of the Earth, Woodland Trust, Reform Club *recreations* walking with dog, gardening, reading, music, films, visual arts *publications* Atkin on landlord & tenant; various articles on law, judiciary etc *address* 5 Cathedral Mansions, 262 Vauxhall Bridge Road, London SW1V 1BP *tel* 020 7828 4578 home 07813 800741 mobile *e-mail* josephine.hayes@goughsq.co.uk

HAYMAN, Judith Lynne (Judy) Convener, Scottish Liberal Democrats *b* Mar 28, 1944 *m* Dr Peter Hayman 2 *d* Kate *b* 1969 Rachel *b* 1972 (both married) 1 *s* Martin *b* 1971 4 *gd* Phoebe 2000, Elise 2003, David 2005 (Hayman), Sam 2006 (Byrne) *education* Withington Girls' School, Manchester; Univ of Nottingham (BA Hons English) 1965; Univ of London (PGCE) *career* senior English teacher, Heathfield Grammar School, Gateshead; Musselburgh Grammar School; part time FE, adult education *party* joined Liberals 1970s; long-time activist East Lothian LP, mbr Exec, various sub-Cttees, five years as convener; candidate East Lothian and South of Scotland List (number three, fourth place) Scottish PPC 1999, 2003, 2007; PPC East Lothian 2001 (third place, 7.5% increase in vote); party spokesperson Arts and Broadcasting 1999; mbr 10-strong negotiating team on partnership agreement for Govt between Lib Dems, Labour 2003; mbr Scottish Exec 1999- ; candidate assessment panel (Scotland); convener Scottish Party 2004- ; federal vice president 2004- ; mbr Green Liberal Democrats *special interests* education, environment, arts, international development, human rights *other mbrships* community Cllr 1996-2004; former trustee Theatre Alba; former associate mbr Scottish Association of Playwrights; director .Pageant Players Community Theatre; Amnesty International; Oxfam; Friends of the Earth; John Muir Trust; Shelter; Royal Shakespeare Company.(locally); East Lothian Housing Association; Rail Action Gp East Scotland; environmental pressure gps *recreations* theatre, tennis, gardening, walking, reading, travel *address* The Knoll, Longnewton, Haddington, East Lothian EH41 4JW *tel* 01620 810218 *e-mail* judy.hayman@which.net

HEALY, Denis *b* Feb 11, 1960 *m* Alison 1 *s* Sean 1 *d* Maria *education* All Hallows Comprehensive School, Macclesfield, Cheshire 1971-78; Univ of Lancaster, BA (Hons) English Literature 1978-81 *career* graduate Management Trainee, Cadbury Schweppes 1981-84; 14 years senior marketing management experience, food industry; currently senior manager, Business Link South Yorkshire (responsible for helping make Yorkshire & Humber region best UK place to start, grow a business); extensive experience of regional economic development, marketing *party* joined 2001; PPC Hull North 2005 (re-selected 2006); chair, Haltemprice & Howden LP *special interests* regional economic development, business support, inward investment, marketing *other mbrships* mbr, Chartered Institute of Marketing *recreations* soccer refereeing, amateur dramatics, driving 1962 Morris Minor *address* 12 The Poplars, Leconfield, Beverley HU17 7NB *tel* 01964 551113 home *07736 367544* business *e-mail* denis@denishealy.org.uk *web* www.denishealy.org.uk

HEATH, David CBE (1989) MA MP (Somerton and Frome maj: 812) **Shadow Leader of the House**, Shadow Cabinet Office Minister with roving brief on human rights and civil liberties *b* Mar 16, 1954 Westbury *m* 2 ch *education* Millfield; St John's College Cambridge (MA Physiological Sciences); City Univ, London *career* registered optician; consultant World Wide Fund for Nature 1990-91; mbr Audit Commission 1994-97 *party* mbr Somerset CC 1985-97; leader 1985-89; leader Opposition 1989-91; chair Avon and Somerset Police Authority 1993-96; chair Somerset CC Education Ctteee1996-97; vice-chair Association of County Councils 1994-97; mbr Audit Commission 1994-979; vice-president Local Govt Association; PPC Somerset and Frome 1992; 1997 (elected), re-elected 2001, 2005; front bench spksn on Europe; spokesman Work and Pensions 2001-02; Shadow Minister, Home Office; 2002-05; Shadow Leader of the House 2005 -; Shadow Cabinet Office

Minister 2005 -; mbr Modernisation Committee 2005 -; mbr Standards & Privileges Cttee 2001-05 , Select Cttee on Foreign Affairs 1997-2001; chair All Party Parliamentary Gp on Eye Health and Visual Impairment, mbr All-Party gps on Pharmacy, Diabetes, United Nations, Romania, Parliamentary Assembly OSCE *special interests* local govt, the environment, law and order *address* The House of Commons, London SW1A 0AA *tel* 020 7219 6245; 14 Catherine Hill, Frome, Somerset BA11 1BZ *tel* 01373 473 618 *fax* 01373 455 152 *e-mail* davidheath@davidheath.co.uk *web* www.davidheath.co.uk

HEMMING, John MP (Birmingham Yardley (maj:2,672) *b* Mar 16, 1960 *m* 4 *ch education* King Edward's School, Edgbaston; Magdalen College, Oxford *career* Director of JHC plc *party* elected Birmingham City Council 1990, gp leader 1998- ; PPC Birmingham Hall Green 1983, Birmingham Small Heath 1987, Birmingham Yardley 1992, 1997, 2001, 2005 (elected); appointed Regulatory Reform Select Cttee 2005 *other mbrships* Friends of the Earth, Greenpeace, Musicians Union *recreations* playing jazz music (piano, guitar); reading; spending time with the children *address* 1772 Coventry Road, Yardley, Birmingham B26 1PB *tel* 0121 722 3417 *e-mail* john.hemming@jhc.co.uk *web* www.yardley.libdems.org.uk

HERBISON, Douglas: Scottish Party Treasurer *b* Jun 25, 1951 *m* 2 *d education* Univ of London (BSc Hons Economics) *career* MD Europa Analytica *party* mbr Central Scotland LP; mbr Motherwell DC 1973-79; mbr EU Economic & Social Cttee 1981-84; Euro Advisory Gp 1995-2002; PPC Cumbernauld 1983, Cunninghame North 1987, 1992, Inverclyde 2005; European election candidate Strathclyde West 1984, 1989, 1994; Banff & Buchan 2001; Scottish list 2004; Scottish Election Candidate Glasgow Kelvin 2003, List Candidate City of Glasgow 2003; Scottish party treasurer 2003- *address* 20 Princes Gate, Bothwell, Glasgow G71 8SP *tel* 01698 813504 *e-mail* douglas.herbison@btopenworld.com

HEYWOOD, Kate *b* Aug 10, 1978 Leeds *single* no *ch education* Arden School, Knowle, Solihull 1989-94; Solihull Sixth Form College 1994-96; Univ of Kent, Canterbury 1996-2000 *career* education, welfare officer, Kent Union 2000-01, treasurer 2001- 2002; HE National Cttee, NUS 2001- 2002; ethical, environmental Cttee, retail trade Cttee NUS Services Limited 2001–02; parliamentary assistant Tom Brake MP 2002-03; office manager David Chidgey MP 2003- 2004; Exec secy Liberal Democrats May 2004- *party* Exec mbr Camberwell and Peckham LP 2005; mbr Lib Dem Christian Forum *other mbrships* All Saints Church, Peckham *special interests* education, foreign affairs *recreations* cycling, knitting, cinema, reading *style* Miss *address* 4 Cowley St, London SW1P 3NB *tel* 0207 340 4916 *fax* 020 7799 2170 *e-mail* kate.heywood@libdems.org.uk

HICKS, Nigel Stuart ARICS *b* Jun 11, 1955 Truro *m* Sheelagh 2 *d* Fiona, Michelle *education* Falmouth GS; Trent Polytechnic, Nottingham (HND quantity surveying) *career* chartered quantity surveyor: private practice Plymouth (major projects included Derriford Hospital, MOD establishments); Sellafield; Swindon (projects included West Swindon Leisure Centre, work at Harwell); Tarmac Construction (for construction of Swindon prison); Crown House Engineering (based Glasgow but worked from home on sites in Wales, England); ALSTOM (formerly Cegelec, formerly GEC), projects included Jubilee Line extension, fourteen months Korea *party* LibDem candidate Redditch BC 1992 then joined the party!; mbrship secy

177

(increased mbrship from less than 100 to more than 200 in 12 months: local party won regional award); PPC Warwick and Leamington 1997, Meriden 2001, Redditch 2005 (only party to increase share and number of votes); elected Redditch BC (Abbey ward, defeated Labour mayor) 1999 (moved to Winyates ward when boundaries changed in 2004), chair Planning Cttee *recreations* previously played Sunday rugby, now prefers to go for good meal with wife; to simply be a tourist; as a Cornishman, loves the beach *style* Cllr Nigel Hicks *address* 20, Jays Close, Winyates Green, Redditch. Worcs B98 0SF *tel* 01527 523036 *e-mail* nigel.hicks@converteam.com

HIRST, Peter John *b* Sept 9, 1950 *m* Catherine Gaynor 2 *d* Sophie, Georgina *education* Werneth School, Oldham 1955-60; Rydal School, Colwyn Bay 1960-67;Univ of Manchester, Manchester Medical School 1967-73 *career* locum consultant physician 1988-2003; presently training to be a Life Coach; *party* joined 1988; PPC Stroud 2004; North West Regional Exec 1995-98; Congleton LP Exec 1991- , vice chair 2004 ; Congleton borough Cllr 1999-2002; Middlewich town Cllr 1999- ; Federal Conference Rep 1993 ; Chair Dane Valley Branch of Congleton Lib Dems 2004- ; mbr Green Liberal Democrats, LDEA, LDEG, LD Online, ALDC, PCA, *special interests* environmental sustainability, foreign affairs, transport, effective campaigning, education, health, community relations *other mbrships* CentreForum; Liberal International; Greenpeace; Friends of the Earth; World Development Movement; ERS; Charter 88; Amnesty International; Soil Association; The Woodland Trust; CPRE; NPN *recreations* gardening, digital photography, walking *publications* Local Shops:article in *Challenge* Spring 2003 pp 15-16 *address* 33 Rushton Drive, Middlewich CW10 0NJ *tel* 01606 737108 home 07760 203439 mobile *fax* 01606 737108 *e-mail* peter@hirst51836.fsnet.co.uk

HOBAN. Wayne *b* May 23, 1952 *m* Christine 1 *s* Matthew *education* Hawick High School, Napier School of Science & Technology; Ipswich Civic College; diploma College of Radiographers *career* apprentice motor mechanic; NHS radiographer, currently superintendent radiographer Royal Free Hospital *party* joined 1992; treasurer, chair Hornsey & Wood Green branch 1992-97; chair, president Haringey LP 1997-2001; mbr London Region Exec; English Party representative; PPC Enfield Southgate 2001; mbr LB Haringey 2002- , deputy gp leader; GLA candidate Enfield Haringey 2004; mbr Liberal International *special interests* school governor; co-ordinator of radiographic services to UN ICTY mortuary in Bosnia 1997-2001; founder of Trauma Imaging Gp (professional organisation formed to promote trauma and forensic radiography); honorary lecturer City Univ, Middlesex Univ, Univ of Western England, Univ of Central England; governor Homerton Hospital Foundation Trust 2004- *recreations* family, walking, travel, socialising *clubs* National Liberal Club *style* Cllr Wayne Hoban *address* 46. Blake Road, Bounds Green, London, N11 2AH *tel* 020 8368 2659 *e-mail* wayne.hoban@btinternet.com

HOBSON, Phylip (Phil) Andrew David *b* Sept 21,1968 Christchurch, Gwent *education* St. Joseph's RC High School, Tredegar Park, Newport, Gwent; Instituto Cervantes, Manchester *career* newspaper, magazine publishing 1988-98; telecoms 1998-2002; The Liberal Democrats 2002-2004; The Office of Michael German OBE AM, Regional Manager 2004- *party* joined 1991; secy Monmouth LP 1993-94; vice chair 1994-95; vice chair Manchester Central LP 1998-99, secy 2000-01; secy, Monmouth LP 2003, vice chair 2004-, DNO for South Wales East 2002- ; mbr

National Exec, Welsh Liberal Democrats 2003; mbr Welsh Candidates Cttee 2003; elected treasurer Welsh Liberal Democrats 2004; agent numerous local by-elections 1993- ; *Elections*: Monmouthshire County Councillor 2004-, Liberal Democrat Gp Leader, Monmouthshire County Council 2004- ; PPC Kensington by-election 1988, Manchester Central, 2001; Monmouth-Mynwy, 2005; Welsh Assembly Election Newport West 2003; candidate, South Wales East Regional List 2003; Chepstow Town Councillor 1993-96, 2002- , Mayor of Chepstow 2004-2005 *special interests* European Union, transport, environment, economics, planning, language and cultural identity, arts *other mbrships* Republic, Chepstow Athletic Club, ALDC, Liberal Democrat European Group *recreations* walking, gardening, arboriculture, mountain biking, modern art, reading, writing, travel, language, architecture *address (English)* Yr Hen Archdy, 8 Church Road, Chepstow NP16 5HP *address (Cymreig)* Yr Hen Archdy, 8 Heol-yr-Eglwys, Cas-Gwent NP16 5HP *tel* 079 6634 3978 *e-mail*: phylip.hobson@wales.gov.uk; philhobson@monmouthshire.gov.uk

HOLBROOK, Simon Andrew *b* Jul 21, 1957 Huddersfield *separated* 3 *ch education* Mirfield High School; Loughborough Univ (BSc Chemical Engineering *career* 22 years at Unilever in Research and Development, Environmental Management and Health & Safety; currently working for Environment Agency, responsible for managing permit under Pollution Prevention and Control Regulations *party* joined SDP 1981; PPC 1987; break from politics in 1990s to concentrate on career and family, currently Wirral Councillor and former Chair of Planning Cttee; PPC 2001 and 2005; mbr Association of Lib Dem Engineers and Scientists *address* 20 Reedville, Birkenhead, Ch43 4UH *tel* 0151 513 5656 *e-mail* simon.holbrook@wirral-libdem.org.uk

HOLMAN, Christopher Robin (Chris) *b* Feb 12, 1942 Truro *m* Maggie 1970 1 *d* Judith 1 *s* Alastair *education* The Grammar School, Plympton 1953-60; Rugby College of Engineering Technology *career* 'industrial gypsy' constructing and commissioning steam turbine generators for power stations from Hampshire to Caithness and Suffolk to Belfast, various places in between, with postings in Egypt, Cyprus, South Africa and India 1965-89; project management, sales in Rugby 1989-92; full-time Cllr *party* joined the Young Liberals at 14 (parents activists in SW Devon); first election experience Tavistock 1955 (candidate Richard Moore); subsequently active in locality of the power stations he worked; cttee mbr, officer branch and constituency in Cheshire, Caithness and Northumberland; campaigned against Bob Maclennan, then Labour, in both 1974 elections; past chair Rugby & Kenilworth LP; regional, and federal conference rep; exec mbr Liberal Democrat Disability Association; mbr Rugby BC 1994-; chair Licensing and Safety Cttee; mbr Warwickshire CC 2001-05; *special interests* environment, local residents, chair Mayday Trust *recreations* bowls, cycling, walking, birdwatching *other mbrships* Rugby Bowling Club, Rugby Sport for the Disabled Association, plus various national organisations, incl. AIUK, RSPB, ERS, ITDG, Free Tibet, National Trust, Ramblers *style* Cllr *address* 141a Bilton Road, Rugby, Warwickshire *tel* 01788 565037 home 07979 552905 mobile *fax* 01788 571477 *e-mail* chrisholman@cix.co.uk

HOLME of Cheltenham, Rt Hon Lord Richard Holme: Life Peer cr 1990, PC 2000, CBE 1983 *b* Eggleton May 27, 1936 *education* St John's College Oxford (MA); Harvard Business School *m* 1958 Kay Mary 2 *s* Hon Richard Vincent, Hon

John Gordon 2 *d* Hon Nicola Ann, Hon Penelope Jane *career* officer Gurkha Regiment; chairman Constitutional Reform Centre 1984-94; Threadneedle Publishing Gp; director Penguin Books; Prima Europe Ltd 1991-99; director Rio Tinto plc (formerly RTZ Corporation plc) 1995-98 (currently adviser to chairman) *party* joined Liberals 1959; PPC East Grinstead 1964, 1965 by-election, Braintree 1974, Cheltenham 1983, 1987; secy Parliamentary Democracy Trust 1979-95; president Liberal Party 1980-81; adviser David Steel, Paddy Ashdown; created life peer 1990: Lords spokesman on N Ireland 1990-2000; chair 1997 General Election Campaign; mbr Joint Constitutional Cabinet Cttee with the Labour Govt 1997 *other interests* chair, co-founder English College in Prague 1991- ; Visiting Mbr Nuffield College Oxford, Visiting Professor of Business Middlesex Polytechnic, chair of governors Cheltenham Ladies' College; Chancellor Univ of Greenwich, Visiting Professor Thunderbird Business School in Arizona; former vice-chair Independent Television Commission; chair Broadcasting Standards Commission; chair Environment Commission, International Chamber of Commerce; co-chair World Business Council's Cttee on Corporate Social Responsibility; vice-chair global business coalition preparing for the Earth Summit in *publications* The Peoples Kingdom 1987 *recreations* reading, walking, opera *clubs* Reform, Brooks's *style* The Rt Hon Lord Holme of Cheltenham CBE *address* House of Lords, London SW1A 0PW

HOLMES, Paul MP (Chesterfield maj: 3,045) **Chairman of the Liberal Democrat Parliamentary Party** *b* Jan 16, 1957 *m* Rae 1 *s* 2 *d education* Prince Edward Primary School, Manor Top, Sheffield; Firth Park Secondary School; Univ of York (history degree); Univ of Sheffield (PGCE) *career* teacher Chesterfield Boys School 1979-84; teacher Buxton Community School 1984-2000 *party* mbr Chesterfield Borough Council 1987-95, and 1999-2003; elected MP for Chesterfield 2001, re-elected 2005; Shadow Minister for Arts and Culture 2006- ; Shadow Spokesman, Work and Pensions 2002-05; Spokesperson for People with Disabilities 2001-05; mbr Select Cttee for Education and Skills; Friend of UNICEF in the Commons *special interests* education, disability, human rights, international development *recreations* history, literature, walking *address* House of Commons, London SW1A 0AA *tel* 0207219 8158 *fax* 02072191754 *e-mail* chestefield@cix.co.uk

HOOK, Anthony James FRSA BA (Hons) PGDL PGDPLS *b* Apr 10, 1980 *education* Dover Grammar School for Boys; Univ College London; City Univ London; Inns of Court School of Law; The Inner Temple *career called to the Bar 2003;* Temple practice civil, criminal law; made court debut Apr 2, 2004 *party* joined Oct 1998; LDYS student development officer 1999-2000, vice-chair (finance) 2000-2001 including 2001 GE; PPC Dover 2001 (youngest Liberal candidate, one of youngest of any party for centuries); campaign director local elections Dover 2003 (when Lib Dems won balance of power); mbr Green Liberal Democrats, Peel Gp, EMLD, Liberal History Society; author *Growing Branches* (guide to building youth, student branches); mbr Federal defence policy working gp 2000 *special interests* foreign policy, crime and policing, freedom of information, human rights, youth policy *other mbrships* FRSA, RSA Young Leader of Year 2002 *recreations* walking, all outdoor pursuits, youth work, Scouts *publications Political Parties, Elections and Referendums Act* Autumn 2004 *tel* 07967 136099 *e-mail* antony@doverlibdems.org.uk

HOOPER, David William Giles *b* Jun 25, 1930 *education* King's School, Chester; Liverpool Univ; Churchill College, Cambridge; UMIST *m* 2 *ch* *career* hd of Science, Chester College of Higher Education 1963-82; researcher, dealer in nineteenth century photographs 1982- ; *party* chair Univ of Liverpool Liberal Socy 1955-56; mbr Chester RDC 1966-70; secy (sometime trsr and chair) Chester Liberal Assoc 1969-88; secy Cheshire Liberal Party 1975-76; president Chester LibDems 1996-97 *special interests* history of science; visiting France and art exhibitions *address* 36 Flag Lane North, Chester CH2 1LE *tel* 01244 380844 *e-mail* hooper@chesternet.co.uk

HOOSON, Baron Hugh Emlyn QC: Life Peer cr 1979 *b* Mar 26, 1925 *m* 2 *d* *education* Denbigh GS; Univ College of Wales, Aberystwyth (BA Law) *career* Royal Navy (Fleet Air Arm) 1943-46; called to the Bar, Gray's Inn 1949; QC 1960, Deputy Chairman Flintshire Quarter Sessions 1960-72; Merioneth Quarter Sessions 1960-67; Recorder Merthyr Tydfil and Swansea 1971, elected Leader Wales and Chester Circuit 1971-74, Recorder of Crown Courts, Deputy High Court Judge 1972-91; non-Exec director of Laura Ashley plc 1985. chair 1995; chairman Trustees of the Laura Ashley Foundation 1986-97; non-Exec chair Severn River Crossing plc 1991-2000 *party* PPC (at age 22in 1947) Caernarvon Boroughs (seat was abolished in boundary review before election); Conway 1950, 51; MP for Montgomeryshire 1962-79; chair All-party parliamentary gp for World Govt 1966-70; spksn for Defence, Foreign Affairs, Home Affairs, Legal Affairs, Agriculture and Welsh Affairs 1962-79; Leader Welsh Liberal Party 1967-79; raised to the peerage 1979; president Welsh Liberal Party 1983-86; Lib Dem spksn on Welsh Affairs 1996-2001 *special interests* law, constitution, agriculture, defence, Welsh affairs, Euro affairs, international affairs (rapporteur of working party chaired by Congressman John Lindsay (later Mayor of New York) which first suggested the West should seek détente with the Communist World, then greeted with incredulity by the Govt Establishments *other mbrships* president of the National Eisteddfod of Wales at Newtown 1966, honorary White Bard of the National Gorsedd of Bards 1967; president International Musical Eisteddfod, Llangollen 1987-93 *recreations* music, theatre, reading, walking *address* The Rt Hon Lord Hooson QC, Summerfield Park, Llanidloes, Powys *tel* 01686 412298; House of Lords, London SW1A 0PW

HOPE, Jill Susan *b* Jan 12, 1952, Birmingham *education* Headlands Grammar Sch, Swindon; Univ of Southampton, BA Hons English 1973; PGDip Business Studies, City of London Business School 1975 *m* 1976, Shaun (qv), 1 **s** (John 1983), 3 **d** (Susan 1981, Kate 1989, Rose 1991) *career* media and finance: IPC Magazines, London 1973-74, Barclaycard 1974-1978, area manager HSBC 1978-2001, business advisor, Business Support Northamptonshire 2005- ; *party* chair, Northampton LDs 1998-2000, Cllr West Hunsbury Ward, Northampton BC 1999-; training officer, PCA 2004- ; PPC Harborough 2001, 2005 *special interests* planning, education, NHS *recreations* swimming, literature, theatre, art, writing, campaigning, listening to Radio 4, writing seditious letters to local press *style* Cllr Jill Hope *address* 27 Rectory Lane, Milton Malsor, Northampton NN7 3AQ *tel* 01604 858395 home, 0116 257 1117 LD Constituency office, 07887 995653 mobile *e-mail* spes@cix.co.uk

HOPE, Shaun Horan *b* Feb 17, 1947, Padiham, Lancs *education* St John's RC, Padiham; Camden Cmmnty Sch (formerly Sir Wm Collins Sec) Somers Town, London; Royal Holloway London, BSc Sp Hons Chemistry 1968 *m* 1976 Jill Susan (qv) 1s, 3d *career* electronics, business, H Educ: Engineer, Plessey Semiconductors, 1968-72, Sales: Monsanto 1972-77, Director. Mason Corp. Hldgs 1977-98, Alumni Officer Cranfield Univ 2000- *party* Hampstead Labour Party, Young Socialists 1963; treasurer, Northampton Liberal Democrats 1999-2003, Harborough LP 2004- , South Northants DC candidate 1999, 2003 (twice), Northants CC candidate 2001, parish Cllr 2003- ; agent Northampton 2003 *special interests* planning, women's issues; international relations; maths & computer science *other mbrships* treasurer Northampton Rail Users' Association; Milton Malsor History Society *recreation* swimming, database design & programming, theatre, art, music, campaigning, writing provocative letters to local rags *style* Shaun Hope *address* 27 Rectory Lane, Milton Malsor, Northampton NN7 3AQ *tel* 01604 858395 *work* 01234 754992 *fax* 01604 858181 *mob* 07985 007696 *e-mail* spes@cix.co.uk and s.hope@cranfield.ac.uk

HORWOOD, Martin Charles MP (Cheltenham maj 2,305) *b* Oct 12, 1962 *m* Dr Shona Arora 1 *d* Maya 1 *s* Sam *education* Cheltenham College 1976-80; Queen's College Oxford (BA Hons, Modern History) 1981-84 *career* national chair Union of Liberal Students 1984-85; commercial, voluntary sector marketing posts 1985-90; , donor marketing manager Oxfam GB 1990-95, director communications and fundraising Oxfam India 1995-96; director of fundraising Alzheimer's Society 1996-2001; senior consultant, then head of consultancy, for range of national charity clients Target Direct Marketing 2001- *party* joined Cheltenham Young Liberals 1981; president Oxford Student Liberal Society 1983; national chair Union of Liberal Students 1985-86; chair Liberal Information Network (LINk) 1987-90; co-editor *New Democrat International*1989; mbr Vale of White Horse District Council 1991-95, deputy gp leader 1993-95; mbr North Hinksey Parish Council 1991-95; PPC Oxford East 1992, Cities of London & Westminster 2001, Cheltenham 2005; elected MP May 2005; mbr ODPM Select Cttee 2005- ; secy All Party Parliamentary Gp on Corporate Responsibility 2005- ; mbr Lib Dem Home Affairs team 2005-06; Shadow Environment spokesperson 2006- ; *special interests* world development, international affairs, charity, voluntary sector *other mbrships* Amicus (trade union), Ashridge Management College Alumni, Institute of Fundraising, Survival International, World Development Movement, Amnesty International, Alzheimer's Society, CPRE, Leckhampton Green Land Action Gp; Cheltenham Civic Society; Friends of National Star College; Gloucestershire Wildlife Trust; governor, Cheltenham Bournside School 2006- ; *recreations* travel, photography, astronomy *address* 16 Hewlett Road, Cheltenham, Glos GL52 6AA *tel* 01242 224889 constituency office, 020 7219 8256 House of Commons *e-mail* mhorwood@arorahorwood.net

HOUSE, Keith *b* Jun 2, 1965 Southampton *partner* Louise Bloom *qv* 2 *d* 2 *s* from early marriage *education* Wildern Secondary School, Barton Peveril College *career* full time Cllr; ldr Eastleigh Borough Council 1994- ; Head of Mbrship Services, Lib Dems 1990-99; LGA Planning Exec Chair 1999-2001; LGA 4ps Chair 2002-2005; Founding Chair, South East England Regional Assembly 1999-2000; Board Mbr, South East England Development Agency 2002- ; *party* joined Liberal Party in 1983; past chr, secy, agent, current mbr Eastleigh LP (South Central); Founding Chair, Hampshire & IOW Lib Dems 1988-92; candidate for Eastleigh Borough Council 1991- , Gp Leader 1992- ; Hampshire County Council 2001- ; Environment Spokesman, Hedge End Town Council 1988- , Chair 1991-92; Bursledon Parish

Council 1987-88, 2003+; Hamble-le-Rice Parish Council 2004- ; Hampshire Fire and Rescue Authority 2005- ; mbr ALDC, assorted others lapsed but there in spirit - Greenpeace, Amnesty International, Liberty *other mbrships* Royal Town Planning Institute, Royal Society for the Arts, Barton Peveril College *special interests* international election observer for OSCE, civil liberties, environment *recreations* travelling to unusual places, including rock/folk/county gigs around the world *style* Cllr *address* Pine Glen, Bridge Road, Bursledon, Southampton SO31 8AH *tel* 07768 357918 *fax* 023 8040 4225 *e-mail* keith.house@eastleigh.gov.uk *web* www.eastleigh.gov.uk/keithhouse

HOWARTH, David MP (Cambridge maj:4,339) *b* Nov 10, 1958 *m* 2 *ch education* Queen Mary's, Walsall; Clare College, Cambridge; Yale Law School *career* university lecturer in law and economics *party* elected Cambridge City Council 1987, leader of Opposition Gp 1990-2000, leader of Council 2000-03; PPC Cambridge 1992, Peterborough 1997, Cambridge 2001, 2005 (elected); Shadow DTI (Energy) spokesperson 2006- ; Shadow Community and Local Govt spokesperson 2005-06; Select Cttees from 2005: Environmental Audit; and Constitutional Affairs; mbr Federal Policy Cttee 1989 *other mbrships* Friends of the Earth, Amnesty International *recreations* squash, running *address* 1st floor, Eastern Court, 182-190 Newmarket Road, Cambridge CB5 8HE *tel* 01223 304421 *e-mail* david.howarth@cambridgelibdems.org.uk *web* www.davidhowarth.org.uk

HOWELLS, William Davyd (Will) *b* May 20,1979 *education* Skinner's School for Boys, Tunbridge Wells 1990-97; Univ of Leeds (MPhys in Physics with Astrophysics)1997-2001 *career* finance and commercial services officer Leeds Univ Union 2001-02; Leeds Univ Library 2002-04; Napier Univ Learning Information Services 2004- ; *party* joined 2002; ward election agent, Leeds May 2003; ward candidate, Leeds, May 2004; vice-chair (finance) LDYS 2003-05; secy LDYS Scotland 2005-06; mbr, spokesperson's gp on BBC Charter Review 2004 *special interests* higher education, constitutional reform, media *other mbrships* Society of Genealogists; Electoral Reform Society *recreations* music, cult TV and film, blogging (www.willhowells.org.uk/blog) *e-mail* will@willhowells.org.uk

HOWES, Monica BSc *b* Sept 12 (some time ago), London *m* Hugh 2 *ch education* Haberdashers' Aske's School; Johannesburg HS for Girls; mature student Polytechnic of Central London, now Univ of Westminster (BSc Hons Class I) 1976 *career* secretarial work in theatre; after postgraduate study twenty years in Open Univ as course manager, then Director External Relations, finally Director International Office *party* four times Westminster candidate, once Euro candidate; assistant to editor *Liberal Democrat News* *special interests* mbr Women's National Commission; health (former mbr several health authorities); greater opportunities for women *recreations* opera, theatre, travel *address* 34 Berks |Hill, Chorleywood, Herts WD3 5AH *tel* 01923 282323 *fax* 01923 286533 *e-mail* monica.howes@ntlworld.com

HOWSON, Professor John Orrell *b* May 16, 1947 Hackney *div* no children *education* Tottenham County, LSE, Oxford Universities *career* teacher, Univ lecturer and head of department, Govt adviser, company director *party* joined Liberals in 1996 and mbr of Liberal Democrats since foundation; adviser to parliamentary education team; President of LDEA; PPC Reading East 2005; many local candidacies over past 30 years; currently mbr Regional Exec (South Central) and local party exec; *special interests* education, the law (licensing law) *publications* many and varied; regular writer on education issues *recreations* walking *style* Prof *address* 70 Rewley Road Oxford OX1 2RQ *tel* 01865 203270 home 01865 242468 business 07958 702292 mobile *e-mail* johowson@tiscali.co.uk

HOYLE, Robert (Bob) MA, MSc, DPhil *b* Leeds Apr 12 1956 *s* of Prof P Chandra and Dr TB Hoyle *m* Sarah Margetts *education* Merchant Taylors' School, Liverpool; Christ's & Churchill Colleges Cambridge; Univ of Bristol; Wolfson College & Christ Church Oxford, Oxford; Brookes Univ; Inner Temple (Duke of Edinburgh Scholar); Open Univ *career* academic, lawyer *party* Oxford city Cllr 1992-2002; deputy Lord Mayor of Oxford 2001-02 (first civic officer from ethnic minority; first Liberal Democrat); PPC Luton North 1997; mbr Oxford East exec 2000-02; mbr Crime & Policing, Planning working gps; ethnic minority mbr EMLD; chair Assoc of Liberal Democrat Co-operators *special interests* UK constitution *recreations* mathematics, gp relations, socialising *clubs* Frewen Club, Oxford *style* Dr Bob Hoyle *address* 8 Tyndale Road Oxford OX4 1JL *tel* 01865 727929 *fax* 01865 727929 *e-mail* bob727929@ntlworld.com

HUDSON, Veena *b* Feb 3, 1979 *education* Spalding HS 1990-95; Queen Elizabeth Grammar School 1995-97; Univ of Reading (BA Hons German, French with Dutch, Spanish *career* parliamentary assistant to Nick Clegg MEP, Brussels 2001-02; head of office LDYS 2002-03; parliamentary assistant to Nick Clegg MEP, Brussels 2003-04 *party* mbr South Holland and The Deepings LP; LDYS; WLD; EMLD: Euro candidate No 3 East Midlands list (highest placed woman, youngest candidate) 2004 *special interests* international trade, development, environment, youth and gender equality *other mbrships* Greenpeace, Amnesty International *recreations* photography, acting, theatre-going *address* 125 London Road, Spalding, Lincs PE11 2TW *e-mail* veenahudson@hotmail.com

HUGHES, Simon Henry Ward MP (Southwark North and Bermondsey maj: **5,406): President of Liberal Democrat Party; Shadow Secy of State for Constitutional Affairs, and Shadow Attorney General** *b* May 17, 1951 Cheshire *education* Woodford Primary, Llandaff Cathedral, Cardiff; Christ College, Brecon; Selwyn College, Cambridge read Law; College of Europe, Bruges, certificate in Higher Euro Studies *career* called to Bar, Inner Temple 1974; trainee EEC, Brussels 1975-76; mbr Secretariat, Directorate and Cttee on Human Rights, Council of Europe 1976-77; barrister 1978- ; MP 1983- ; Hon Fellow South Bank Univ 1994 *party* joined Liberal Party 1971 (inspired by campaigns for international justice in South Africa, Palestine); founder mbr Lib Dems 1988; elected youngest opposition MP in sensational Bermondsey by-election Feb 1983 (with swing of 50.9 per cent), re-elected 1983, 1987,1992,1997 (seat expanded, renamed), 2001, 2005; runner up to Charles Kennedy in leadership election 1999; candidate in leadership election in 2006; variously front-bench spokesperson on Housing; Local Govt; Education, Science & Training; Environment, Natural Resources & Food; Urban Affairs & Community Relations; Health and Social Welfare 1995-2001; Shadow Home Secy 2001-03; London Mayoral candidate 2004; Parliamentary Spokesman (in Shadow Cabinet) for London; won *The Spectator*-Highland Park Mbr to Watch award 1985; National Motivation Week's Most Motivated MP award 1989; Green MP of the Year 1992; Epolitix Environment Champion 2005; mbr HoC Accommodation and Works

Cttee; Ecclesiastical Cttee of Parliament; introduced Parliamentary Bills on Empty Property, Access to Information, to set up Parish and Community Councils in London, Disestablishment of Church of England, Equal Rights for War Pensioners, to require Queen to pay income tax and to change sexist rules of succession to the throne; officer Parliamentary All-Party South Africa Gp; v chair All-Party Asthma Gp; mbr All-Party Bangladesh Gp, Anti-Racist Alliance, Liberal Democrats Against Apartheid, One World Democrats *other interests* patron, Missing People Helpline; chair Save Guy's Campaign (fighting to maintain services at Britain's flagship hospital which is situated in his constituency) 1994-99; former mbr C of E General Synod; joint chair Council of Education in the Commonwealth; past-president British Youth Council; president Southwark Chamber of Commerce, Redriff Club in Surrey Docks; trustee, director Rose Theatre Trust; chair governors St. James' Primary School, Bermondsey *publications* books on human rights, the law, defence, political realignment *recreations* music (church music to Eurovision), theatre, history, sport (Wales RFU, Glamorgan CCC, Millwall FC, Hereford FC), the countryside, travel, spending time with family, friends *address* House of Commons, London SW1A 0AA *tel* 020 7219 6256 *fax* 020 7219 6567 *e-mail* simon@simonhughesmp.org.uk *web* www.simonhughes.org.uk/

HUHNE, Chris MP (Eastleigh maj:568) **Shadow Environment Secy** *b* Jul 2, 1954 *m* 3 *ch education* Univ de Paris-Sorbonne; Magdalen College, Oxford (MA 1st class Hons PPE) *career Young Financial Journalist of the Year* 1981; *Financial Journalist of the Year* 1991; council mbr Royal Economic Society 1993-98; council mbr Consumers' Association, 2002-04; freelance journalist India 1975-76; *Liverpool Daily Post and Echo* reporter 1976-77; Brussels correspondent *The Economist* 1977-80; leader-writer *The Guardian* 1980-84; economics editor and columnist *The Guardian* 1984-90; assistant editor, columnist *The Independent on Sunday* 1990-91; business editor, head of department *The Independent* and *The Independent on Sunday* 1991-94; economics director, MD sovereign ratings IBCA Ltd 1994-97; gp MD Fitch IBCA Ltd 1997-99; elected MEP for South East England Jun 1999; economic spokesman of the European Liberal Democratic and Reformist gp (ELDR), European Parliament, 1999-2005; mbr, Economic and Monetary Affairs Cttee; substitute mbr Budgets Cttee; delegation mbr ASEAN; council mbr Britain in Europe, 1999- ; board director Policy Network 2001-04 ; mbr TransAtlantic Policy Network 2000-05 *party* fdr mbr SDP; council candidate Islington 1982, Alliance PPC, Reading E 1983; Oxford W & Abingdon 1987; chair Lib Dem press & broadcasting policy panel, 1994-95; economics advisor policy unit, GE 1997; mbr Economic Policy commission 1998; director Electoral Reform (Ballot Services) Ltd to 1995; mbr Advisory Board, Centre Forum; jt chair (with Lord Wallace) Global Security, Stability and Sustainable Policy panel, 1999-2000; board *Liberal Democrat News* 1999- ; president ALTER 2000- ; chair expert commission on Britain's adoption of Euro 2000; chair, public services policy gp 2001-2 ; deputy leader Liberal Democrat European parliamentary party (LDEPP) 2001-03; MEP South East England 1999-2005; MP Eastleigh 2005- ; contested party ldrship 2006 *publications Both Sides of the Coin: the arguments for the Euro and European Monetary Union* (with James Forder writing the arguments against) 1999, second edition 2001; *The Ecu report: the single European currency* (with Michael Emerson) 1991; *Real World Economics: essays on imperfect markets and fallible Govts* 1990; *Debt and Danger: the world financial crisis* (with Lord Harold Lever) 1985, second edition 1987; various articles in books, journals (see www.chrishuhne.org) *recreations* family, film *clubs* NLC *address* Liberal Democrat Office, 109a Leigh Road, Eastleigh, SO50 9DR; House of Commons, London SW1A 0AA *tel* 023 8062 0007 *e-mail* chris@chrishuhne.org.uk

HUMPHREYS, Robert Owen (Rob) BSc (Econ) President & Chair of National Exec Cttee, Welsh Liberal Democrats *b* Nov 4, 1957 *m* Catrin Evans 1 *d* Rosa Melangell *education* Welshpool High School, Montgomeryshire; Ruskin College, Oxford (mature student: diploma in labour studies); Univ of Wales, Cardiff (BSc Econ First Class *History of Ideas*) *career* factory worker Montgomeryshire seven years; mature student Oxford (trade union scholarship), Cardiff; Univ lecturer continuing education, cultural studies Univ of Wales Swansea 1992- (including co-ordination of *Community Univ of the Valleys* project 1993-98); Director for Wales, NIACE Dysgu Cymru *party* mbr Swansea & Gower Liberal Democrats; president Welsh Liberal Democrats 2002-04, re-elected unopposed 2004-06; deputy president 2000 02; mbr Welsh national Exec Cttee 1998- , chair 2002- ; mbr Welsh Policy Cttee 1998- ; campaigns and elections Cttee 2000- ; mbr Federal Exec 2001-03; candidate Bridgend and South Wales West regional list, National Assembly for Wales 1999, Cynon Valley and South Wales central regional list 2003; Welsh Exec representative on team which negotiated partnership Govt in National Assembly; appointed by Secy of State for Wales to Cttee of Welsh European Programme Exec1997; appointed by Welsh Minister of Education to independent investigation into student hardship and funding 2000, joint author subsequent report *Investing In Learners* (Rees Report); Exec mbr Wales Friends of Searchlight; chair *Right to Vote* Cttee, All-Wales Ethnic Minorities Association *special interests* post-16 education, lifelong learning; community development; citizenship; anti racist and anti-fascist work; culture, arts; professional research interests also include national identity, lectured Finland, Germany, USA; works with Univ of Joensuu (Finland) EU trans-national project; with BBC Wales in producing multi-media educational materials; adjudicator Welsh Schools Debating Championships 2000- ; adjudicator literary competitions, South Wales Miners' Eisteddfod 1994-99; chair literary events National Literature Centre for Wales; occasional commentator on historical, cultural affairs BBC Wales radio, television *other mbrships* chair National Institute for Adult Continuing Education in Wales (NIACE *Dysgu Cymru*) 2004-06; board NIACE (England and Wales); Fellow, Univ of Wales National Centre for Public Policy; advisory board Council for Education in World Citizenship Cymru; Exec Universities Association for Continuing Education Cymru; Amnesty International, Electoral Reform Society *publications* various on Welsh cultural history, lifelong learning; edited collections *Universities and Communities*; *Communities and their universities: the challenge of lifelong learning*; *Opening up the Keep* (about writer Gwyn Thomas); *Voyages* (about writer Alun Richards); various academic publications *recreations* mountain walking, football (Wales, Shrewsbury Town - a born optimist!); running (former county level senior athlete, club captain Pegasus Athletics Club, Cardiff); cycling; cinema; literary history; popular culture *clubs*: Shrewsbury Town Supporters Club *address* 35 Cathedral Road, Cardiff CF11 9HB *tel* 029 20 370900 office 07734 698063 410560 mobile *fax* 029 20 370909 *e-mail* rob.humphreys@niacedcorg.uk

HUNT, Jon *b* Apr 29, 1958 *m* Marcia 3 *s education* Monkton Combe School, Bath; St Aubyns School, Tiverton; East Anstey Primary School; diploma, health economics, Univ of Tromso, Norway; MA (Cantab) classics, economics St John's

College, Cambridge *career* established Englemed News, on-line medical news agency 1999; medical correspondent *Birmingham Post* 1988-99; *Express and Star*, Wolverhampton; *West Somerset Free Press party* PPC Birmingham Perry Barr 2001, 2005; Cllr (Perry Barr) Birmingham City Council 2003- ; chair, education and lifelong learning scrutiny cttee, 2005- , gp leader, West Midlands Passenger Transport Authority 2005- ; chaired education and training in regeneration task and finish cttee, 2004-05 *special interests* education, transport, local democracy, public accountability *other mbrships* chair of governors, Calshot Primary school; Beeches Evangelical Church, Great Barr; Royal Economic Society *address* 52 Perry Avenue, Perry Barr, Birmingham B42 2NS *tel* 0121 240 9689 home 07837 604161 mobile *e-mail* jon@perrybarr.com

HUNT, Jonathan Nigel *b* Jul 16, 1943 *m* Veronica 2 *s* Daniel, Oliver *education* primary, secondary in private sector, tertiary, public sector *career* trainee, assistant editor, editor *Baker & Confectioner, Master Builder*, London; *Daily Nation* gp Arusha, Tanzania; sub-editor, feature writer *TVTimes*, London; business sub-editor, writer, deputy business editor, *Pendennis* editor *The Observer*; editor, two management magazines; columnist, business editor, city editor *Today*. *Sunday Today*; freelance, contract publisher, adviser to TECs, edited *Agenda*; part-time editor special reports *Financial Times*; other freelance work *party* joined Liberals 1973; founding chair Peckham constituency association 1974; PPC Uxbridge 1979, Dulwich 1983; Gillingham 2001; various policy panels; Cllr LB Southwark 2002- ; president Camberwell & Peckham LP *special interests* embarrassing establishments of all kind; race relations; trade, employment, corporate issues; small business, regeneration; sport *recreations* watching football (Arsenal, Dulwich Hamlet); growing oranges and lemons (near Granada, Spain) *publications* work on starting, running small business; *Marketing for Young Businesses*; various industrial histories *address* 1a Anderton Close, Champion Hill, London SE5 8BU *tel* 020 7737 3793 *e-mail* jh@writeon.demon.co.uk or jonathan.hunt@southwark.gov.uk

HUNTER, Mark James MP (Cheadle maj:3,657) *b* Jul 26, 1957 *m* Lesley 1 *s* Robert 1 *d* Francesca *education* Audenshaw Grammar School *career* professional, newspaper advertising industry for over 20 years, lately business development manager Guardian Media Gp, local newspaper division; full-time Leader of Stockport MBC May 2002- ; *party* joined Liberal Party mid-70s; active Young Liberal; youngest ever mbr Tameside MBC 1980 (aged 22); represented Droylsden West ward for nine years, led opposition Liberal Gp; elected North Marple ward Cllr, Stockport MBC 1996, chair Education Cttee three years then Deputy Gp Leader; succeeded as Leader of the Council May 2002; PPC Ashton-under-Lyne 1987, Stockport 2001, 2005 (elected – by-election following death of Patsy Calton); Shadow Home Affairs spokesperson 2006- ; Shadow ODPM spokesperson 2005-06 *special interests* local Govt, community politics *other mbrships* ALDC; Amnesty International; National Trust; Marple Civic Society; Marple Band *recreations* watching beloved Manchester City Football Club; reading; theatre; travel; eating in good restaurants *address* home: 34 Cote Green Road, Marple Bridge, Stockport SK6 5EW; office: Town Hall, Stockport SK1 3XE *tel* 0161 427 8836 home 0161 474 3302 office *fax* 0161 474 3308 *e-mail* hunterm@parliament.uk and cllr.mark.hunter@stockport.gov.uk

HUPPERT, Julian Leon MRSC *b* Jul 21, 1978 California, USA *education* Trinity College, Cambridge – MA, MSc, PhD; The Perse School; Sydney Grammar School; Kings College Choir School *career* research Fellow, Trinity College 2004- ; CEO Cambridge Laboratory Innovations 2003-05; business analyst, Monis Software 2000-01; OECD team member, Bulgarian education review 2000 *party* joined 1996; mbr Cambridge LP Exec 2001- ; Cllr (East Chesterton), Cambridgeshire County Council, 2001- , gp deputy leader 2004- ; whip, EERA 2005- ; PPC Huntingdon 2005 (2nd place); mbr Regional Policy Cttee; mbr PCA, ALDC, ALDES, Green LDs *special interests* transport (esp. sustainable and cycling), international affairs, liberal policing *recreations* squash, percussion, St John Ambulance, travel *style* Cllr Dr – but only where necessary! *publications* various scientific papers; *OECD Review of Bulgarian Education Policy address* 5 Scarsdale Close, Cambridge CB4 1SL *tel* 01223 423561 home 07876 192717 mobile *e-mail* julian@julianhuppert.org.uk *web* www.julianhuppert.org.uk

HUTCHINSON of Lullington, Baron Jeremy Nicolas: Life Peer cr 1978, QC 1961 *b* Mar 28, 1915 *education* Stowe, Magdalen College Oxford (MA) *m* 1 1940 (m dis 1966) Dame Peggy Ashcroft DBE (d 1991) 1 *s* Hon Nicholas St John Hutchinson 1 *d* Hon Eliza *m* 2 1966 Jun formerly wife of Franz Osborn *career* mbr Cttee on Immigration Appeals, Cttee on Identification Procedures; Professor of Law, Royal Academy 1988 *party* created Labour life peer 1978; joined SDP 1981, now sits as LibDem in House of Lords *other interests* vice chairman Arts Council 1977-79; trustee Tate Gallery 1977-84 (chairman 1980-84), Chantrey Bequest 1977- *recreations* cricket, the arts *clubs* MCC *style* The Rt Hon Lord Hutchinson of Lullington, QC *address* House of Lords, London, SW1A 0PW

J

JACKSON, David *b* Apr 30, 1971 Glasgow *m* 2 *ch education* St Thomas Primary, Riddrie; St Mungo's Academy, Bridgeton; Univ of Glasgow MA (Hons) *party* Secy and President, Glasgow Univ Liberal Democrats 1989-93; Secy Glasgow Rutherglen Liberal Democrats 2000-2002; Grade A listed candidate, PPC for Glasgow Rutherglen 2001, Glasgow East 2005, and PSPC for Glasgow Baillieston 2003; convenor, Glasgow Rutherglen LP 2003- ; *other mbrships* European Movement *special interests* Europe, sport *recreations* competitive swimming, cycling (as a method of commuting – 50 miles per week, about 50 miles more than David Cameron?!?) *LD quirks* see recreations above – I am the most competitive liberal I know! *style* Mr is just fine *address* 16 Hilary Drive, Baillieston, Glasgow G6 6NP *tel* 0141 573 7128 home 07795 510300 mobile *e-mail* d.jackson2@ntlworld.com

JACKSON, Ian Andrew *b* Feb 7, 1949 *m* Jo 3 *d education* St Cuthbert's GS Newcastle on Tyne 1960-67; Newcastle Polytechnic 1967-70 *career* management accountant (Charted Institute of Management Accountants) in distribution sector *party* Tynemouth Liberals 1972-1976 (vice chair, district council candidate); founder mbr Fife Social Democrats 1981-87; treasurer, mbr Scottish Council, agent district, regional, parliamentary (Dunfermline West 1984), European (Central Scotland 1986) elections; community Cllr Dalgety Bay 1984-87; Lichfield Liberal Democrats 1990-; chair, regional, federal conference rep; English Council 2000-02; agent for all elections 1995- ; district, city Cllr Lichfield 2003- ; PPC Lichfield 2004 *special interests* transport; planning; environment *other mbrships* chair Leomansley Action Gp.1992-2000; vice chair Lichfield Rail Promotion Gp 1999- *recreations* hill-walking (Munro Bagger, 26 to go!); choral singing; Newcastle *address* 13 Walsall Road, Lichfield, WS13 8AD *tel* 01543-414732 home 07771818530 business *e-mail* ianjackson@lichfieldlibdems.org.uk

JACOBS, Lord Sir Anthony Jacobs: Life Peer cr 1997, kt 1988 *b* Nov 1931 *m* 2 *ch career* FCA; chairman three major companies: Nig Securities Gp 1957-72; Tricoville Gp 1961-90; British School of Motoring 1973-90; House of Lords 1997 *party* joined Liberals 1972; served on Housing, Economic Cttees; economics, taxation advisor to party 1973-78 (working closely with John Pardoe MP); PPC Watford Feb and Oct General Elections 1974 (increased share of the vote from 6% to 24%); joint-treasurer of the Party 1984-87; keen supporter of merger; chair of English Party; federal vice-president; created life peer 1997; speaks on range of subjects including disparity between prices paid by British, European and US consumers; banning use of hand-held mobile phones in cars; campaign for justice for condemned pilots of 1994 Chinook Helicopter crash *other mbrships* Tate Gallery Millennium fund-raising Cttee for the new Tate Bankside Gallery of Modern Art; mbr Crown Estate Paving Commissioners 1980- ; trustee Jacobs Charitable Trust; chairman board of governors Haifa Univ 1992-2001 *publications Help for the First Time Buyer recreations* art, golf, reading, theatre, opera, travel *address* House of Lords, London SW1A 0PW

JAMES, Simon *b* April 1, 1967 York *m* Montserrat Medina Fernandez 1 *ch* Kiron James Medina *education* Stamford School; South Bank Univ (BSc Physical Sciences with Computing) *career* assistant to London Region Media coordinator 1994; organiser, Paddy Ashdown's European election tour 1994; administration officer, Kingston Council Liberal Democrat Gp 1995-98; Communications Officer, Local Government International Bureau 1998-2002; web and publications manager, Medical Research Council 2002; Communications Manager, Nuclear Industry Association 2003-; *party* mbr Kingston LP (London); cllr (executive mbr for Economic Development and Regeneration; vice-chair ALG Economic Development, Regeneration and Europe Steering Group; alternate member of the Congress of the Council of Europe); PPC Spelthorne 2005, Tooting 2001, 1997; council candidate Kingston 2002, Wandsworth 1998, 1994; mbr PCA, LDEG *other mbrships* Nation Liberal Club, ERS, European Movement *special interests* Europe, environment and energy *publications* various scientific papers *recreations* running, cycling and watching cricket and American football *style* Cllr *address* 84 Mount Pleasant Road, New Malden KT3 3LB *tel* 020 8942 3541 *e-mail* simon.james@councillors.kingston.gov.uk

JARDINE-BROWN, Helen *b* Aug 6, 1972 *ptnr* Andy Mayer *education* Univ of Southampton (Winchester School of Art) BA Hons Textiles; Cranbrook School, Kent *career* acting Head of Treasurer's Unit, Liberal Democrat HQ and Exec Director, Liberal Democrat Business Forum 2005- ; J-B Consulting: freelance design consultancy 2003-04; Head of Creative Direction for jewellery manufacturers Gruppo Graziella srl, Arezzo, Italy 2002-03; Private Label Business Manager for

Menswear Division of Marzotto SpA, Arezzo, Italy 1998-02; designer for silk manufacturer Ratti SpA, Como, Italy 1998; designer for the necktie division of Mantero Seta SpA, Como, Italy 1997-98 *party* mbr North Southwark & Bermondsey LP; council candidate for South Bermondsey 2006; Liberal Democrat Foreign Press Liaison (GE campaign 2005) *other mbrships* National Secular Society *special interests* health, education, secularism recreations poker, painting, embroidery, cooking *address* 37 Tyers Estate, Bermondsey Street, London SE1 3JG or 4 Cowley St, London SW1P 3NB *tel* 020 7340 4914, 07745 758962 mobile *e-mail* helen.jardine-brown@libdems.org.uk

JARVIS, Sal *b* May 6, 1959 *m* Steve 2 *s* 1 *d education* Faringdon Girls Grammar School; Oxford College of FE; Hatfield Polytechnic; Homerton College, Cambridge (BA Hons Humanities) *career* Herts CC, National Children's Homes: supporting families in crisis; childminder, learning support assistant; WEA tutor; A-level tutor in political and moral philosophy; currently special-needs co-ordinator, class-room teacher mainstream primary school *party* founder mbr; former constituency chair, local election agent, last Chilterns Region chair, currently East of England Regional candidates' chair; district Cllr 1999 *special interests* education and training, inclusion issues, children's services *other mbrships* Amnesty International; Action Aid *recreations* horse-riding, bridge, old cars, family, poetry *publications* contributor to *Idea*, a Cllr's guide; some poems *address* 26, High Street, Graveley, Hitchin, Herts, SG4 7LA *tel* 01438 727122 *e-mail* sal@sjarvis.cix.co.uk

JARVIS, Steve *b* Jun 12, 1956 *m* Sal *qv* 1 *d* 2 *s education* Francis Bacon School, St.Albans; Hatfield Polytechnic *career* engineer 1978 – development manager, programme manager, product manager, business development director during a career with GEC, STC, ICL, STC and Nortel Networks; MD, Quinata Ltd 2001 *party* joined Liberal Party 1979; mbr North Herts DC 1992- , gp leader 1999- ; PPC NE Herts, 1997; chair NE Herts 1997-2000, agent 2001; chair Chilterns Regional policy Cttee 2000-02; chair East of England region policy Cttee, 2003; chair East of England Region 2004- ; PPC South Holland and The Deepings 2005 *special interests* political marketing *other mbrships* CPRE *recreations* bridge, golf, old cars *address* 26 High Street, Graveley, Hitchin, Herts *tel* 01438 727122 home 01438 361547 business *fax* 01438 362058 *e-mail* steve.jarvis@quinata.co.uk

JEBB, Christina Rita, FRSA *b* Jun 27, 1949 *m* Henry Jebb 2 *d* 1 *s* (plus twin grandsons) *education* Aston Park School, Birmingham; St Agnes Convent High School, Birmingham; Holte Grammar School, Birmingham; Open Univ; Keele Univ *career* teacher, lecturer (French, mathematics) 1970-86; nursing, then voluntary sector 1986-91; county, district, parish Cllr 1989- ; mbr Stoke-on-Trent and Staffordshire Fire Authority 1989-2005; Staffordshire Police Authority 1990-97, 2000- ; hypnotherapist, NLP practitioner, holistic therapy consultant 1997- ; local youth, community management Cttees 1989- , chair 1999- ; mbr North Staffordshire Health Authority 2000-2002; mbr North Stoke Primary Care Trust 2002-03; mbr LGA Fire Exec 2001-04, deputy chair; mbr LGA Safer Communities Board 2004- ; mbr West Midlands fire authorities Regional Management Board 2004- ; chair Staffordshire Moorlands DC 2003-04; mbr Fire Service NJC 2001- , chairman NJC Employers side 2004, deputy chair 2005- ; *party* founder mbr Liberal Democrats; LP elected federal conference representative; Health Association mbr, former chair; mbr WLD, ALTER, PCA; LP chair, secy, treasurer various occasions; PPC Staffordshire

Moorlands 1992, 1997 (increased vote share on both occasions) *special interests* fire, police issues; health & environmental improvement; taxation reform; community politics *other mbrships* Soroptimist International (Newcastle & District president 2001-02); Business Women's Club of Ivanovo, Russia; various campaigning, environmental, community and women's organisations *recreations* family, DIY, reading, meditation, travel *publications* co-author *Recognising the signs of sexual abuse in children* (Out of School Alliance); author *Usui Teate Shoden*; *Usui Teate Okuden*; *Usui Teate Shinpinden*; *Reiki Kara Teate*; *Hypnotherapy – An interactive workshop*; *Exploring Auras – An interactive workshop*; *Thermo-Auricular Therapy*; *address* Endon Bank, Church Lane, Endon, Stoke-on-Trent ST9 9HF *tel* 01782 503615 home 01782 503615 business *fax* 01782 503615 *e-mail* Christina.Jebb@staffordshire.gov.uk *web* www.christinajebb.co.uk

JENNINGS, Christopher Edward *b* Jul 15, 1965 *m* Mandy (nee Smith) Jul 1995 1 *d* Molly (May 1997) *education* Hadham Hall School, nr Ware, Hertfordshire 1976-82; Southgate Technical College 1982-86; Cambridge College of Arts and Technology 1986-88 *career* apprentice technician DER Ltd 1982-86; electronics engineer Ripul Ltd 1986-88; sales engineer Treston Ltd 1988-90; retail manager B&B HiFi 1990-92; home insurance advisor A-plan Insurance 1992-96; estate agent Chancellors 1996-2003; estate manager Peverel OM Ltd 2003- *party* joined Liberal Party 1987, Hertford and Stortford; Newbury constituency vice chair; Didcot Branch chair, secy; Wantage LP chair, vice chair, computer officer, secy; agent for Neil Fawcett, PPC Wantage 2001; Chilterns Region recruitment officer, European officer; South Central European Office; Chilterns Region conference Cttee, chief steward; South Central conference Cttee mbr and conference chief steward; federal conference stewards team 1988- (currently deputy chief steward); returning officer; mbr Agents Association, ALDC *special interests* European issues; governor St. Birinus School Didcot; chair All Saints School, Didcot School Association (ASSA); chair Didcot Arts and Community Association (DACA), Northbourne Community Centre management Cttee *recreations* computing, photography, ballooning *address* 59 Derwent Ave, Didcot, Oxfordshire OX11 7RF *tel* 01235 816080 *fax* 01235 519510 *e-mail* chrisjennings@btinternet.com

JOLLY, Judith *b* Apr 27, 1951 *m* Ian (cllr North Cornwall District Council) 2 *s* Andrew (constituency organiser, North Cornwall) Stephen (student, international politics) *education* King's High School for Girls, Warwick; Leeds Univ (BSc control engineering); Nottingham Univ (PGCE mathematics) *career* teacher/lecturer comprehensive schools, College of St Mark & St John (HE) 1974-94; British Council, Oman 1994-97; chair Cornwall European campaign for Robin Teverson 1994; agent for Paul Tyler 1997; head of political staff for Robin Teverson MEP 1997-99; regional campaigns, media coordinator 2000-01; non exec director Mental Health & Learning Disability Trust 1997-2000; vice chair NHS Primary Care Trust 1997 - 2002; chair NHS Primary Care Trust 2005- ; director: CAB, Credit Union, Launceston MCTi, Peninsula Arts, East Cornwall Bach Festival *party* joined Liberal Party 1984; treasurer SE Cornwall 1986-88; chair North Cornwall LP 1998-2001; mbr regional exec 1992-94, 2000- ; mbr PCA Exec 1998- 2005, FPC 2004 - ; PPC Plymouth Devonport 2005, gained 8,000 votes, 11.2% swing Lab to Lib Dem *special interests* disadvantaged communities, how they can help themselves; Middle East *recreations* reading modern novels, singing, gardening *address* Oakleigh House,

Congdons Shop, Launceston, Cornwall PL15 7PN *tel* 01566 782411 *e-mail* judithjolly@oakleigh.eclipse.co.uk

JONES, Lord Nigel: Life Peer cr June 2005: former MP for Cheltenham 1992-2005 *b* Mar 30, 1948 Cheltenham *m* 1 *s* Sam 2 *d* (twins) Amy, Lucy *education* Prince Henry's Grammar School, Evesham *career* consultant, project manager for many large development projects UK, overseas (Middle East, Scandinavia, Hong Kong and Jamaica) 1965-71; ICL 1971-92; MP 1992-2005 *party* joined Liberal party 1973; borough council candidate Cheltenham 1976; elected Gloucestershire County Council (Cheltenham) 1989 when Liberal Democrats in minority control; vice chair Public Protection Cttee; PPC (against Charles Irving) 1979; 1992 elected MP, re-elected 1997, 2001: mbr Select Cttee on Science & Technology 1993- ; Select Cttee on Standards and Privileges 1997-99, Select Cttee on International Development 1999-01; Public Accounts Select Cttee Jun 2002-05; House of Lords Information Cttee 2006- ; former Exec mbr Commonwealth Parliamentary Association, Inter-Parliamentary Union; former chair British-Ghana Gp; former chair British-Botswana Gp; chair Parliamentary Beer Club *other interests* mbr council of British Association for Central, Eastern Europe *other mbrships* United Nations Association *recreations* all sports, watching Cheltenham Town, Swindon Town, cricket, gardening *address* House of Lords, London SW1A 0PW *tel* 020 7219 4415 *e-mail* jonesn@parliament.uk

JONES, Paul Michael *b* Feb 22, 1952 *m* Diane 1 *s* Christopher 1 *d* Michelle *education* Wallasey Technical GS; Aston Polytechnic, Birmingham (HNC Business Studies) *career* Royal Engineers 1969-77; Steeplejack, Zambia 1977-79; various sales, marketing positions 1979-91 including marketing manager Simong Engineering, sales manager Bass Gp plc, sales director Metsec Gp PLC; proprietor own business 1991-99; currently house husband, director Dane Housing, councilor, school governor *party* joined 1999; councilor Congleton BC 1999- , portfolio holder, performance 2001-2, gp, constituency press officer *special interests* crime, policing particularly drugs legislation; mbr planning and legislation policy working gp *other mbrships* Chartered Institute of Marketing (MCIM); British Mensa *recreations* golf, bridge *The Times* crossword *address* Croft House, 1 Hillesden Rise, Congleton, Cheshire CW12 *tel* 01260 274426 home 07973 139003 business *e-mail* p.m.jones@tesco.net

JONES, Peter *b* 1956 Sutton Coldfield *m* Katy 1979 1 *d* Hazel 1 *s* Matthew *education* Malvern College; Univ of East Anglia *career* director, printing firm *party* mbr Chiltern LP (vice-chair 2006), South Central region; councillor Chiltern DC 1991- ; PPC Milton Keynes SW 1997, Aylesbury 2001, 2005; mbr ALDC *special interests* planning *recreations* watching Leeds United, Wycombe Wanderers or Chesham United, playing golf, refereeing local minor league football *LD quirk* frequent speaker at national and regional conferences *address* 20 The Warren, Chartridge, Chesham, Bucks HP5 2RY *tel* 01494 784681 home 07850 972507 mobile *fax* 01494 791638 *e-mail* peter.m.jones@btinternet.com

JONES, Terrye *b* Nov 5, 1952 *ptnr* Robin Teverson 3 *d* Victoria, Lucy, Zoe *education* Helston Grammar School *career* MD printing factory in Launceston, Cornwall; KCS Trade Print Ltd specialising in integral products, new anti-fraud pin number technology *party* joined 1990; chair Falmouth and Camborne constituency;

past vice-chair, PPCs Association; PPC 1992 and 1997 of Falmouth Camborne 1992, 1997; past chair, Cllr Kerrier District Council *special interests* housing issues (especially for social and first-time buyers), homeless issues; management, growth of small businesses *other mbrships* mbr, Primary Management Gp 1 in Cornwall; mbr Direct Marketing association *recreations* art, folk singing *address* 32 College way, Gloweth, Truro, TR1 3 RX *tel* 01872 279792 home 01566 773696 business *fax* 01872 278378 *e-mail* terrye@kcsprint.co.uk

JONES, Sir (Owen) Trevor kt 1981 known by most Liberal Democrats as Jones the Vote *b* 1927 *s* of Owen, Ada Jones of Syserth *party* President of the Liberals 1972-73; elected Liverpool City Council 1968, Liverpool Metropolitan Council 1973-91 (leader 1981-83); PPC Toxteth 1974 *style* Sir Trevor Jones *address* 221 Queens Drive, Liverpool L15 6YE

JONES, David Trevor (known as **Trevor**) *b* Jun 21, 1944 Oldham *m* Stella (nee Johnson) Aug 3, 1968 *2 s 2 d education* Counthill Grammar School, Oldham; London School of Economics (BSc Econ 1965) *career* Local Govt Officer 1965-1982; sub postmaster 1982-2002 *party* elected to West Dorset DC 1973, Dorchester Town Council 1976, Dorset County Council 1992; PPC Preston North 1970, West Dorset 1979, 1983, 1987; National Chairman Association of Liberal Councillors 1976-85; Chairman (subsequently MD) Liberal Democrat Publications to 1998; chair of Policy and Resources and subsequently Leader, Dorset County Council, 1993-2001; Mayor of Dorchester (Casterbridge) 1982, 1992, 2002; vice chair Scrutiny Panel, Local Govt Association; chair of Audit and Scrutiny Cttee, Dorset County Council; chair, Dorset Ambulance NHS Trust; Gp Leader Dorset Fire and Rescue Authority; mbr Peer Clearing House, IDeA; mbr Local Govt Pension Cttee *special interests* the Arts (Chair, Dorset Mobile Cinema Charity) *recreations* football, bowls and birdwatching *address* Syward Cottage, Syward Road, Dorchester, DT1 2AJ *tel* 01305264335, 07980 893717 mobile; *e-mail* trevor@sywardcottage.co.uk

JUBY, Geoffrey William *b* Feb 7, 1954 Norwich *m* Nemia 1 *s* Kenneth, 1 *d* Maria *education* CSEs plus C&G 706/1&2 Diploma in Management Catering *party* mbr Gillingham & Medway in SE Region; gp ldr on Medway Council; cllr Gillingham South ward; mbr Kent & Medway Fire & Rescue Authority; elected 1996 to Gillingham BC (stood 1994, 1995, 1996); elected Medway UA 1997, 2000, 2003; PPC Medway 2001, 2005 *special interests* regeneration, health, education *recreations* church activities, cricket, travel and racing *address* 16 Franklin Road, Gillingham, Kent ME7 4DF *tel* 01634 575544 or 07740 590098

JUNED, Susan Aysha *m* Shahid 2 *d* 1 *s education* PhD Biology; MSc Biodiversity; BSc Ecology *career* research: biodiversity, sustainable development; currently Govt Liaison Officer for NISP (helps business manage environmental impacts) *party* mbr Stratford on Avon District Council 1990- , leader of council: May 1997-2000; mbr Warwickshire County Council 1993-2005, education spokesman May 1994 - 2005; PPC Stratford on Avon 1997, 2001, 2005; Euro candidate West Midlands 1999; mbr Federal Policy Cttee; trustee, founder, chair, Warwickshire Energy Efficiency Advice Centre *special interests* environment, energy efficiency, sustainable development, education, agriculture *recreations* cycling, walking, reading, music *address* 15 Fenwick Close, Alcester, Warwickshire, B49 6JZ *tel/fax* 01789 762751 *e-mail* susanjuned@cix.co.uk

K

KARIM, Sajjad Haider MEP North West England *b* Jul 11, 1970 Blackburn, son of Conservative Cllr *m* Zahida 1 *s* 2 *d education* Walter Street County Primary, Brierfield; Mansfield High School, Brierfield; Nelson and Colne College; City College, London (law); College of Law, Chester *career* partner Marsdens, solicitors, Nelson; MEP 2004- *party* mbr Pendle Council 1994-2002; MEP North West of England 2004- ; mbr International Trade Cttee; *special interests* human rights, international trade, foreign affairs *other mbrships* Law Society *recreations* football *address* 8 Manchester Road, Nelson BB9 7EG *tel* 01282 613616 *fax* 01282 616177 *e-mail* info@sajjad.karim.org.uk

KAUSHIK, Murari *b* July 11, 1954 Bangalore, India *m* Gita (nee Iyengar) for 24 years 2 *d* Maya, Anita *education* Bearwood College, Berkshire; Manchester Business School, MBA *career* international banking and iInvestments 1979- ; currently European Bank for Reconstruction and Development (EBRD) *party* mbr Winchester LP, South Central Region; activist, recent local candidate and PPC New Forest West 2005 (came second) *other mbrships* Fairthorne Manor Golf Club (Hampshire), Bangalore Club, Bangalore Golf Club, Karnataka Golf Club, Karnataka State Cricket Association (Bangalore) *special interests* financial matters, election monitoring *recreations* rambling, golf (merely competent), chess (County/Club player when younger), visiting museums *address* 23 Cherry Gardens, Bishop's Waltham, Southampton, Hampshire SO32 1SD *tel* 01489 890413 *e-mail* murarikaushik@hotmail.com

KEATING, Chris *b* Dec 23, 1980 *education* Haberdashers' Aske's School, Elstree; St John's College, Cambridge (BA Economics) *career* constituency organiser, Eastbourne Liberal Democrats 2002-05; borough organiser, Islington Liberal Democrats 2005- ; *party* joined during 1997 General Election; chair Cambridge Student Liberal Democrats 2000-01; candidate Cambridge City Council 2002; LDYS Exec 2003-05, vice-chair campaigns 2004-05; accredited party trainer *special interests* political philosophy, youth and student politics *address* Flat 2, 81 Hartham Road, London N7 9JJ *tel* 07760 491413 mobile *e-mail* c.j.keating.99@cantab.net

KEAVENEY, Paula Clare *b* Dec 29,1959 Beckenham *ptnr* no *ch education* Sydenham High School, Edinburgh Univ (MA Philosophy and Politics); Univ of Central Lancashire (diploma in journalism) *career* specialist book orderer for Borders in Liverpool 2005- ; previously radio journalist BBC Radio Lancashire, BBC Radio Cleveland; marketing, press officer Refugee Council, Save the Children Fund; head of communications, Muscular Dystrophy Campaign; head of media and PR, NCH; fundraising and marketing manager, Autism Initiatives; deputy manager, Business in the Arts *party* joined 1981; mbr Liverpool Garston, NW Region; elected mbr Liverpool City Council; PPC Garston 2001, 2005, Battersea 1997 *publications* *Marketing for the Voluntary Sector* (Kogan Page 2001) *address* 75 Canterbury

Street, Garston, Liverpool, L19 8LQ *tel* 0151 494 0341 *e-mail* paula@garstonld.org.uk web garstonld.org.uk

KEETCH, Paul Stuart MP (Hereford maj:962) *b* May 21, 1961 *m* Claire Elizabeth Baker 1 *s* William *education* Hereford High School for Boys; Hereford Sixth Form College *career* self-employed business consultant 1979-95; non-Exec director London computer company 1996- ; MP for Hereford 1997- *party* joined Liberal Party 1975; former mbr Federal Exec; Cllr Hereford City Council 1983-1986; MP for Hereford since May 1997; spokesperson for Health 1997; Education and Employment 1997-99; Shadow Secy of State for Defence 2002-05 (spokesperson 1999-2002); mbr Foreign Affairs Select Cttee 2005- ; founder All Party Parliamentary Cider Gp; founder All Party Parliamentary British-Lithuania Gp; chair Liberal International British Gp 2005 *special interests* national heritage, defence, foreign affairs *recreations* watching cricket and cricket, especially with son; swimming; cycling; entertaining friends and family *address* 39 Widemarsh Street, Hereford HR4 9EA *tel* 01432 341483 *fax* 01432 378111 *e-mail* paulkeetch@cix.co.uk *web* www.paulkeetch.libdems.org.uk

KELLY, Jacqeline *b* Dec 20, 1979 *education* Univ of Stirling, Univ of Copenhagen (BA Hons English, Postcolonial Literature) *career* Commission for Racial Equality 2001-03; parliamentary account manager, NewsDirect 2003- ; volunteer Shelter Families Project 2003- *party* joined 1996; mbr Edinburgh Central LP; Scottish PPC, Falkirk West 2003; candidate Scottish council elections, Edinburgh Dalry 2003; campaign literature manager, sub-agent Edinburgh Central 2003 *special interests* equality, economic issues *other mbrships* Public and Commercial Services Union; founder, chair *Frock the Vote recreations* cinema; art of Lucian Freud, Tracey Emin; post-colonial literature; cities; lunch; drinking beer *publications* contributions to *Scottish Left Review, Morning Star address* 1/4 Dryden Gait, Edinburgh, EH7 *tel* 07765 803 152 *e-mail* jacquelineekelly@hotmail.com

KEMPTON, James *b* Sept 17, 1960 *ptnr* Tim Dean *education* Eltham College 1972-79; Univ of York 1980-83 (BA Hons History & Politics); PGCE Univ of London 1998-99 *career* teacher, Plashet School, East Ham 1999-2002; Chief Exec, Royal College of Paediatrics and Child Health 1996-98; senior manager Royal College of General Practitioners 1989-96; British Medical Association 1983-89 *party* mbr LB Islington council Holloway ward 1994-2002, St Mary's Ward 2002- ; joint deputy leader of council 2000- , lead mbr children and young people; formerly chair education, libraries Cttee; Exec mbr regeneration education 2000-04; formerly deputy leader, opposition; chief whip; children's services spokesperson for LD councillors in England; vice chair LGA Children & Young People Board, ALG Children Young People & Families Steering Group; mbr Children's Workforce Development Council; mbr ministerial board of stakeholders for Children, Young People & Families, ministerial advisory group, London Challenge, ministerial advisory group Schools' Capital Policy; governor City & Islington College, governor St Mary Magdalene School; PPC Dagenham, 2005, Erith & Thamesmead 2001, Islington North 1997 *other mbrships* FRSA *special interests* education and health *publications* *Private Sector Working* (ALDC) *address* 10 Halton Road, Islington, London N1 2EU *tel* 0207 359 0398 *fax* 0207 359 0398 *e-mail* james.kempton@islington.gov.uk

KENNEDY, Rt Hon Charles, MP (Ross, Skye & Lochaber maj: 14,249**) Leader of Liberal Democrats 1999-2006** appointed Privy Council, Oct 1999 *b* Inverness Nov 25, 1959 *m* Sarah Gurling 2002 1 *s* Donald James 2005 *education* Lochaber High School, Fort William, Univ of Glasgow (president of Union; won The Observer mace for Univ debating), graduated MA Jt Hons Politics and Philosophy *career* journalist, broadcaster BBC Highland; awarded Fulbright Scholarship to Indiana Univ, United States, where he taught public speaking and carried out graduate research in speech communication, political rhetoric and British politics while working towards a PhD at Indiana *party* in 1983, he sought SDP nomination for Ross, Cromarty & Skye, made flying weekend visit for hustings (won from a field of six), returned UK for the General Election and less than six weeks later was elected MP for largest constituency in Britain (defeating sitting Tory minister) and youngest MP; spksn on range of welfare state issues, first for SDP-Liberal Alliance, then Lib Dems; in mid-eighties served on All Party Select Cttee on Health and Social Services, mbr Commons Select Cttee which set up televising of Parliament; first SDP MP to back merger with Liberals after 1987 General Election, moved successful motion at party conference; *The Spectator's* Mbr to Watch 1989; party president 1990-94; parliamentary spksn European Affairs 1992-97; Agriculture, Food and Rural Affairs 1997-99; party leader 2002-06 *address* House of Commons, London SW1A 0AA **constituency office** 1A Montague Row, Inverness IV3 5DX *tel* 01463 714377 *fax* 01463 714380 *e-mail* charles@highlandlibdems.org.uk *web* www.charleskennedy.org.uk

KEY, Eleanor *education* RIBA, UCL (Dip Arch UCL, BA Hons Architecture) *career* architect in Zimbabwe; senior architect, design team-leader London architects practice (working on urban regeneration, affordable housing, public buildings); projects include social housing, Arsenal stadium redevelopment; Sadler's Wells Theatre 1999- ; *party* joined 1978 (started early delivering, addressing, stuffing envelopes, manning jewellery stall at fetes, jumble sales; at school, Univ helped with canvassing, collecting signatures for local elections, format and editing *Focus* and election literature; Manchester Univ Liberal Party 1984-86; North West Surrey Liberals 1977-92 mbr Camden borough party (formerly Holborn and St Pancras) 2000-, active in the constituency Jan 2001- ; PPC Holborn and St Pancras; mbrship secy H&SP 2002- , secy 2002-03; Exec mbr Camden Borough Party 2001- , secy 2002-04; established successful *Pub of the Month* (social which has activated mbrs); mbr London Region candidates Cttee 2004- ; mbr Camden Campaign Cttee (GLA, European, Parliamentary elections); mbr PCA, Green Liberal Democrats *other mbrships* Exec Wildlife Society Mashonaland branch (Zimbabwe) 1993-96 (PR, fund raising: organised wine tasting tours, two film premieres, theatre night, designed, printed advertisements, flyers; co-ordinated rebuilding of Wildlife Shop; mbr Wildlife Volunteer Service 1994-96 (annual surveys of game Mana Pools, Gonarezhou National Parks, protection and care of baby rhino, Chewore; LEA governor Holy Trinity and St. Silas School; Crown Residents' Association *recreations* mbr church choir, St. Mary Magdalene's, London; sketching, walking, gym, writing, reading, theatre, cinema, rowing (international standard. 1980-84); crew - Little Britain Challenge Cup 1997 *address* 14 Orchard Way, Congleton, Cheshire CW12 4PW *tel* 01260 281951 *e-mail* elkey02@yahoo.co.uk

KHALSA, Satnam Kaur *b* Panjab 1955 (moved to Hounslow when 13) *m* Harjinder Singh *qv* 3 *ch education* Cranford Comprehensive School; North East

London Univ (BSc Hons Biological Sciences); qualified as accountant 2001; ACCA *career* DSS; time out to raise children; DTI 1985; auditor LB of Hounslow; Royal Borough of Kingston upon Thames; private sector; NHS; auditing local authorities, mostly in the London area *party* mbr Ethnic Minorities Lib Dems 2002; exec mbr Hounslow Borough LP 2003- ; candidate Heston West by-election 2004 *other mbrships* founder British Sikh Women's Organisation; Truth & Justice campaign; Hounslow Environment Watch; CARE (Community Action for Recycling and the Environment) and Fairtrade in Hounslow *recreations* paints, kirtan, walking, gardening *address* 39 Ash Grove, Heston, Middlesex TW5 9DU *tel* 020 8577 3148

KHAN, Karrar A, JP *b* Jun 28,1943 *m* Asma Apr 7 1985 2 *s* 2 *d education* Punjab Univ, Lahore (BPharm; BA); London Univ (PGDip in Pharm Tech); Portsmouth Univ (PhD) MRPharmS *career* head of Pharmaceutical development at Boots Pharmaceuticals/ BASF Pharma 1982 -2001; director Pharmacy operations OSI Pharmaceuticals 2001- 2003; Pharmaceutical Consultant, Visiting Professor (DeMontfort Univ) *party* PPC Rushcliffe 2005 *other mbrships* President Lions Club 2005 *publications* over 40 in scientific journals *tel* 0115 914 6758 *e-mail* karrar.k@ntlworld.com

KIDD, Heather Mary *b* Jan 31, 1954 *m* Trevor Kidd 4 *d b* 1985,1987, 1989, 1994 *education* Kings Manor School, Shoreham-by-Sea, West Sussex; Queen Mary College, Univ of London (BSc Hons Biology); Chelsea College for Science Education, Univ of London (PGCE) *career* science teacher, Camden School for Girls 1976-82; Angmering School, Angmering, West Sussex 1982 –85; Community College, Bishop's Castle, Shropshire 1999- ; *party* joined 1996; elected (Chirbury Ward) South Shropshire District Council 1997, chair Health, Housing 1998, joint leader 2001, leader 2003- ; chair Ludlow LP 2001-04 (during which Matthew Green elected MP); elected LGA LD Gp Housing Exec 2003-05; Affordable Housing Portfolio Holder for Shropshire Partnership; lead LD Gp to LGA Lib Dem Green Council of the Year Award 2006 *special interests* rural housing especially local needs; community safety; youth issues, education *recreations* bell ringing, gardening (if time *address* Eastville, Chirbury, Montgomery, Powys SY15 6BH *tel* 01938 561651 home 07980 635518 business *fax* 01938 561479 *e-mail* heather.kidd@southshropshire.gov.uk

KILLEYA, Adam David Evan *b* Jul 13, 1981 *engaged* Merryn Pearce *education* Derby High School & Holy Cross College, Bury; Balliol College, Oxford BA Hons, PPE, 2002; Bristol University, PGCE in Citizenship, 2005 *career* Assistant Language Teacher, JET Programme, Ichihasama-cho, Japan 2002-2004; Teacher of Personal Development, Citizenship and Politics, Saltash.net Community School 2005- ; *party* South East Cornwall, Devon & Cornwall Region; previously Oxford West & Abingdon 1999-2002; Bury North 2002-04; Bristol West 2004-05; mbr Devon and Cornwall Regional Exec; mbr South East Cornwall Exec; English Council Representative 2006; PPC Bolton North East 2005; mbr LDYS, ex Vice-Chair; Hon V-Pres, Federal LDYS; Hon V-Pres, Devon and Cornwall LDYS *other mbrships* NASUWT *special interests* education; youth issues; constitutional reform *publications* co-editor of Young, Free and Liberal - A Young Person's Guide to Liberal Democracy *recreations* writing, reading, single malts *address* 164, St Stephen's Road, Saltash, Cornwall *tel* 07950 655 562 *e-mail* adam_killeya@yahoo.co.uk

KING, Iain *b* Jan 29, 1971 Bristol *m* Victoria King (nee Malzone) May 28, 2005 no *ch education* Fellow of International Administration of Post Conflict Societies, Wolfson College, Cambridge Univ 2004; Diploma in Journalism, City Univ, London 1994; MA in Politics, Philosophy and Economics, Pembroke College, Oxford 1992 *career* Director of Programmes, Westminster Foundation for Democracy 2005- ; Campaign Director, Europe First (the non-sectarian 'Gilliland' campaign), Belfast 2004; Head of Planning, UN interim administration mission in Kosovo 2003; Head of Political Affairs, EU Mission in Kosovo 2001-02; Regional Head of Reconstruction and Development, EU, northern Kosovo 2000; freelance political consultant, election monitor and journalist 1997-2000; Editor, Liberal Democrat PCA Candidates' Briefing 1995-2000; senior Northern Ireland researcher, Liberal Democrats 1995-1999; Lib Dem Policy Communications Officer 1995-97; researcher, BBC Radio Five Live 1995; Lib Dem Policy Unit and Northern Ireland researcher 1993-95; editor of national student newspaper UniVieW 1992-94 *party* joined June 1991; Federal Conference rep since 1996; elected to interim peers panel, 1999; PPC Old Bexley and Sidcup 1997, against Sir Edward Heath (winning 16% of the vote, the best Lib Dem result in London from third place in Labour's landslide year); mbr PCA, ALDC, Lib Dem Humanist and Secularist Group *special interests* international affairs; international administrations in post-conflict societies; Northern Ireland; ethics, meta-ethics and philosophy publications *Why the World Could Not Transform Kosovo* (Cornell Univ Press, due May 2006; contributed to and compiled several Liberal Democrat policy papers and policy summaries in the mid-1990s *recreations* running, reading, travelling, anything different *contact* via: 28B Lyndhurst Road, NW3 5PB *tel* 07788 454929 *e-mail* iainbking@yahoo.com

KING, Lionel A *b* Jul 2, 1936 West Ham, East London *m* Sally Lancaster 1964 1 *s* Daniel 1971 1 *d* Joanna 1970 *education* Leyton County High School; Birmingham Univ (BA Hons, Modern Langs); research scholar 1959-60 *career* former FE senior lecturer in TV Production/Media Training; retired 1993, latterly freelance journalist, writer/broadcaster *party* joined 1959; chair Univ Liberal Soc 1960; mbr West Midlands Liberal Federal Exec 1961-79, vice-chair 1961-63, chair 1963-64; mbr Liberal Party Council 1962-65; Party Exec 1963-64; English Council 1996-2001; various offices Handsworth/Perry Bar LP 1972-85; Solihull and Meriden LP 2005- ; candidate Birmingham MBC 1961, 1965-68, 1974-75; PPC Kidderminster 1964, Sutton Coldfield 1970, Walsall South 1987; mbr LCA/LDPCA 1960 - (thought to be longest serving member of approved list of PPCs); mbr LDEG, LD History Gp *other mbrships* CentreForum, ERS, New Politics Network, NUJ, The Cricket Society *special interests* mbr West Bromwich Trades Council 1975-75; Management Cttee, New Midland Housing Association 1981-96; Hon Nat Sec Ageusic Anomic (self-help gp for people deprived of sense of taste/smell) *recreations* listening to live/recorded jazz; travel; languages; cricket (still active club player); reading history, politics and biographies *publications* radio play, Tv drama, numerous newspaper/magazine articles, contributions to anthologies, county cricket histories including *Who's Who of Cricketers 1800-1992,* currently writing first novel *address* 18 Thistlewood Grove, Solihull B93 0DW *tel* 01564 784228 *e-mail* lionel@sheila64.wanadoo.co.uk

KINGSLEY, Jennifer *b* New York City *m* Stephen 2 *s education* BSc (Econ) Social Anthropology, London School of Economics; MA International Relations, Georgetown Univ; DELF (French Proficiency Diploma); p/t courses in counselling, training courses for Victim Support, CRUSE (bereavement) *career* journalist, editor, cllr LBC Kensington and Chelsea (until May 2006), volunteer worker, wife and mother! *party* PPC Kensington and Chelsea 2005; mbr Kensington and Chelsea LP; mbr PCA *other mbrships* numerous local community gps and heritage and arts organizations, St. George's Hanover Square, London, Parochial Church Council, school governors' board of St. George's Primary School *special interests* writing (the printed word!), youth justice, education, performing and visual arts *publications* varied articles in local, national and international press *recreations* attending visual, performing arts and political events, writing, reading, hiking, gym, gardening, meeting people and cementing friendships, savouring family life *address* 5 Thurloe Street, London SW7 2SS *tel* 020 7598 9793 07899 796525 mobile *e-mail* jennykingsley@btopenworld.com

KIRK Madeleine Anne (neé Lyden) *b* Feb 13, 1953 Manchester *m* David 1975 1 *d* 1 *s education* Loreto Grammar, Manchester; St John's College, Manchester; Leeds Metropolitan University *career* Bank Officer, Standard Chartered Bank 1971-83; Finance Officer, Amateur Swimming Association 1991-99; Finance Officer, Joseph Rowntree Foundation 2000- ; *party* mbr York Outer (Yorkshire & the Humber); Regional Treasurer, previously Regional Chair; PPC Leeds East 1997, Elmet 2001 and 2005, York Outer 2006; City of York Cllr 1995- ; Ryedale Cllr 1991–95; PEPC Yorkshire & the Humber 1999; mbr ALDC and WLD *special interests* education, supporting small retailers, electoral and parliamentary reform *recreations* walking, reading *style* Cllr *address* 9 Melcombe Avenue, Strensall, York YO32 5BA *tel* 01904 491464, 07851741458 mobile *e-mail* kirkyork@aol.com *web* www.madeleinekirk.org.uk

KIRKWOOD of Kirkhope, Lord Archy: cr Life Peer 2005, Kt 2003 *b* Apr 22, 1946 *education* Cranhill School, Glasgow; Heriott-Watt Univ (BSc in pharmacy) *m* Rosemary 1 *s* 1 *d career* solicitor, notary public later partner in Hawick *party* elected MP 1983-2005; parliamentary spksn on health, social services and social security 1985-87 and Alliance overseas development spksn 1987; Scottish whip 1987-88; spksn on social security and welfare 1989-94; Deputy Chief Whip, campaign co-ordinator, Chief Whip 1992-97; Shadow Cabinet Mbr without portfolio 1997-2003; Select Cttees: Finance & Services 1992-97, Selection 1992-97, Liaison 1992-97, 1997-05, Court of Referees 1997-05, chair Social Security 1997-2001, chair Work & Pensions 2001-05, mbr, former trustee, Low Pay Unit, House of Commons Commission; sponsored two Private Mbrs Bills: *Access to Personal Files* 1987; *Access to Medical Reports* 1988; treasurer All-party AIDS gp; mbr of parliamentary human rights gp; vice-chair, All Party Post Office Gp 2001-05; director Centre Forum *other interests* chair, Rowntree Reform Trust 1985- ; mbr board of governors Westminster Foundation for Democracy 1998- *recreations* riding, ski-ing, photography *address* House of Lords, London SW1A 00PW *e-mail* kirkwooda@parliament.uk

KISSELL, Roslyn Anne *education* BA; CQSW; Diploma Applied Social Studies, Institute of Personnel Management (Education and Training); post-grad cert, State Policy and Social Change; post-grad Diploma in Govt Studies career administration NHS, Marriage Guidance Council; personnel-management advisor local MIND cttee; probation officer 1975-96; helped set up and taught on Caring for Adolescents course, Univ of Hertfordshire *party* joined Liberals 1960s; mbr WLD 1999, vice chair 2001-02; PPC assessor 2002- ; elected cllr 1999, v chair, planning 1999, environment, leisure 2000; mbr Police Forum; county council candidate 2001; mbr parish council Jul 2003; Policy Officer for SE Region 2005- ; Returning Officer 2006- ; mbr SE Candidates Cttee; mentor for SE PPCs *other mbrships* WLD rep Women's Advisory Cttee, United Nations Association (WACUNA); formerly school governor; mentor Princes Trust, Sussex Probation Service; mentor dyslexic offenders in partnership with NACRO and Prison Service under a European Project; Soroptomist International, Howard League for Penal Reform, National Trust, Friends of the Tate *recreations* bridge, theatre (where now works), travel *e-mail* roslyn@kissell.fsnet.co.uk

KISSMANN, Edna *b* Dec 20, 1949 *education* BA (Suma cum Laude) Hebrew Univ of Jerusalem; Master of Science (cum Laude), Boston Univ *career* co-owner, partner Kissmann Langford Ltd (strategic communications consultancy, specialising in global healthcare industry, crisis and issues management); formerly (for 20 years) with Burson Marsteller: head of Healthcare Business (NYC), joint MD (London), CEO (Germany), Global Practice Chair for Healthcare (out of London office), Chief Knowledge Officer; manager, Press Response and Monitoring unit, office of late Israeli Prime Minister Yitzak Rabin *party* joined 2002; mbr Exec Islington LP; Liberty Network *special interests* health, foreign affairs *other mbrship:* First Forum; International Women's Forum, London; management Cttee Oxford Centre for Diabetes, Endocrinology and Metabolism; Reform Club, Home House *recreations* theatre, music, rambling, travel, people-watching *address* Flat 404, Waterloo Gardens 2, Milner Square, London, N1 1TY *tel* 207 607 1400 home 0207 292 3672.business *fax* 0207 292 3678 *e-mail* ednas@kissmannlangford.com

KNIGHT, Stephen John *b* May 15, 1970 *m* (dis) 1 *sd* Carmen *education* Teddington School 1981-86; Richmond upon Thames College 1986-88 Exeter College, Oxford 1988-89; Univ of Southampton 1989-92 (BSc Hons Physics) *career* public relations officer, Jubilee Sailing Trust, Southampton 1993-94; PR consultant, Argyll Consultancies PLC 1995-96; political adviser Liberal Democrat Gp, Association of London Govt 1996- *party* joined Social and Liberal Democrats 1988; treasurer Oxford Univ Social and Liberal Democrats 1989; mbr Federal Science Policy Working Gp 1991; president Southampton Univ Students Union 1992-93; candidate Southampton City Council elections 1992, 1993, 1994; elected LB Richmond upon Thames Council (Teddington Ward), 1998, 2002, Exec mbr education 2001-02, deputy opposition leader 2003- *special interests* London governance, education, youth issues *recreations* sailing, photography, cinema *publications* contributor to *It's About the Public, Stupid – Liberal Democrats' Experience of Managing PFI Contracts* (pub LGA Lib Dem Gp) *address* 73 Harrowdene Gardens, Teddington TW11 0DJ *tel* 020 8977 4541 home 020 7934 9503 office *fax* 020 7934 9603 *e-mail* cllr.sknight@richmond.gov.uk home; stephen.knight@alg.gov.uk office

KNOWLES, Moira *b* Jan 18, 1922 *education* Knocknagor Public Elementary School 1927-32; Princess Gardens School, Belfast 1932-35; Roedean School 1935-38; Magee Univ College, Trinity College Dublin 1938-42 *career* BBC 1943-52; British Red Cross (Malaysia) 1952-53; Education Dept, Federation of Malaysia 1953-57; Hong Kong Govt1957-77 *party* joined 1948 St Andrews; local rep Crail1979-2002; agent several council, parliamentary elections; Hon Vice Chair; mbr

Liberty Network *special interests* community politics (chair Crail Community); guided walks; conservation (vice-chair Crail Preservation Society); former museum curator *other mbrships* National Trust for Scotland (still a volunteer) *recreations* golf, bridge, travel *publications* leaflets on local walks *address* 3 Kirkmay House, Marketgate, Crail, Fife KY10 3TH *tel* 01333 450315

KRAMER, Susan Veronica MP (Richmond Park maj 3,731**) Shadow Secy of State for International Development** *b* Jul 21, 1950 *m* John Kramer 1 *s* Jonathan 1 *d* Abigail 2 *cats* Whittington, Nell *education* St Paul's Girls' School; St Hilda's College, Oxford (BA, MA PPE); Univ of Illinois (MBA) *career* partner Infrastructure Capital Partners (advising on financing infrastructure projects, central Europe, Italy); formerly vice-president Citibank, Chicago; former board mbr Transport for London; director Specialty Scanners plc; *party* joined 1994; London mayoral candidate 2000; Euro candidate, London 1999; PPC Dulwich & West Norwood 1997; currently MP Richmond Park (elected May 2005); former mbr Federal Exec, London Region Exec, chair Twickenham and Richmond Liberal Democrats *special interests* transport, community politics, environment, youth services *other mbrships* governor Paxton Primary School, Lambeth; NLC; HACAN, numerous local associations Richmond and Kingston; *recreations* sitting in sun; strolling in Richmond Park, Kew Gardens; theatre; eating chocolate; playing with surrogate grand-child (aged 3) *address* House of Commons, London SW1A 0AA *tel* 020 7219 6531 *e-mail* kramers@parliament.uk

L

LAITINEN, William James *b* Aug 15, 1981 Vermont USA *career* search Consultant 1998- ; MD/Owner of Exige International 2001- *party* mbr Solihull and Meriden, PPC Meriden 2005 *special interests* environmental sustainability and reform (local and international), economics as a tool in global conservation and educational reform *recreations* yoga, film, reading, food and wine *tel* 0121 711 2334 work 078121 63336 mobile; *e-mail* william@exigeinternational.com

LAKE, Matthew Eldon (Matt) *b* May, 1968 *m* Deborah Roberts 2 *s* Daniel, Nathan *education* Perdiswell Primary School, Worcester 1973-77; Powick C of E Primary School, Worcestershire 1977-79; Chase High School, Malvern 1979-86; Staffordshire Univ 1986-89 *career* Employment Service 1989-2001; Citylife 2001- *party* supporter Liberal Party, Liberal Democrats since age 13; rejoined party after leaving Employment Service 2001; chair, Ilford South LP 2002-04; GLA candidate Havering & Redbridge 2004; candidate (Barkingside Ward) LB Redbridge by-election Apr 2003, (Goodmayes Ward) increased vote share from 18% to 32% in 2002; PPC Ilford South 2005 – achieved best LD result since 1974 – 20.5% vote share (up from 11.3%), votes increased from 4,647 to 8,761 *other mbrships* elder Chadwell Heath Baptist Church 1999 *tel* 07904 311313 mobile *e-mail* matt_lake@btopenworld.com

LAMB, Norman Peter MP LL.B (North Norfolk maj:10,606) **Shadow Secy for DTI** *b* Sept 16, 1957 *m* Mary 2 *s education* Wymondham College; Univ of Leicester (Law); City of London Polytechnic *career* solicitor (specialist in employment law); Norwich City Council 1982-86; partner Steele and Company 1986-2001; MP 2001-*party* mbr Norwich City Council 1987-91 gp leader; PPC North Norfolk 1992, 1997 (missed by just two per cent), 2001 (elected), 2005 (re-elected); deputy spokesman International Development 2001-02, Treasury spokesman 2002-03, PPS to Charles Kennedy 2003-05; Chief of Staff in Leader's Office 2006- ; *other mbrships* Law Society, Employment Lawyers Association *special interests* Africa *publications* *Remedies in the Employment Tribunal* 1998 *clubs* NLC *recreations* football (Norwich City season ticket-holder), art, travel *address* House of Commons, London SW1A 0AA *tel* 020 7219 8480; 15 Market Place, North Walsham, Norfolk NR28 9BP *tel* 01692 403752 *fax* 01692 500818 *e-mail* info@normanlamb.org.uk *web* www.normanlamb.libdems.org.uk

LAMBERT, Matt *b* Aug 31, 1963 *m* Heidi (neé Rumble) Aug 1, 1992 2 *s* 1 *d education* Bryanston School, Univ of Essex (BA Government) *career* research assistant, Liberal and Liberal Democrats Whip's Office 1985-88; Senior Partner and Managing Director, European Public Policy Advisers, London and Brussels 1998-99; Managing Director, Grayling European Strategy, Brussels and Director, Westminster Strategy, London 1999; Director of Government Affairs, Microsoft Ltd 1999 -; *party* PPC Maldon and East Chelmsford 2005; Councillor, Chelmsford Borough Council, Rothmans Ward 1999-2003; previous mbr, Brussels and Luxembourg LD 1992-1997 *special interests* civil liberties; child protection on the Internet *other mbrships* Fellow RSA *address* 104 Vicarage Lane, Great Baddow, Chelmsford CM2 8JD *tel* 01245 471 418

LAST, Professor John William CBE *b* Jan 22, 1940 *m* Sue 3 *s* 4 *gson* 2 *gd education* Sutton Grammar School, Surrey, Trinity College ,Oxford : MA Oxford 1965 PPE; D.Litt City Univ 1995 *career* Littlewoods, Liverpool 1969-93, ultimately Head of Corporate Affairs; United Utilities director of public affairs 1993-98; non-Exec chairman: Dernier Property Gp 1996- ; chair, Bute Communications Ltd, Cardiff 2004- ; part-time professorship at City Univ, London 1998- ; *party* adopted as PPC Ilkeston 1963; mbr Vale of Clwyd LP; joined Peel Gp 2001; Hon Treasurer Welsh Liberal Democrats 2002; deputy Federal Treasurer 2003**;** chair Candidates Cttee, Welsh LDs 2004-06; *special interests* cultural matters, economic matters *recreations* music, hill-walking *publications* *A brief history of museums* (fourth edition 2003), *The Last Report on Local Authority Museums* (1991), *A future for the Arts* (1987) *address* Llannerch Hall, nr St Asaph, Denbighshire LL17 0BD *tel* 01745 730060 *fax* 01745 730545 *e-mail* last@llanerch.wanadoo.co.uk

LATHAM, Philip Ronald *b* Nov 12,1942 *m* Jean Aug 28, 1965 *education* Sedbergh School; Open Univ (BA Hons English) Univ of Sunderland MA (Cultural and Textual Studies) *career* teacher of English and Communication 1970-1993; teacher of English as an additional language 1994- ; **party** PPC Hexham 2001, North Durham 2005, elected Tynedale Council 1995, chair; Community, Health & Culture scrutiny; mbr of North East Regional Assembly *special interests* social and community enterprise; chair: Friends of Libraries in Tynedale, Craftwrite Ltd *recreations* beekeeping, running slowly, walking, gardening, reading *address* 22 Station Close, Riding Mill, Northumberland NE44 6HE *tel* 01434682494,

07753605036 mobile *e-mail* info@philiplatham.org.uk *website* www.philiplatham.org.uk

LAWMAN, Sandra Joy *b* Sept 22, 1958 *partner* Colin Kolb *education* Manchester High School for Girls; Durham Univ, Fellow Association of Accounting Technicians, qualifications in Business French, Business German, Japanese *career* taught English in Tokyo on leaving Univ, various accounting, admin jobs 1984-89; accounts supervisor All Nippon Airways,London 1989-97; director Dudley Miles Company Services 1997-99; corporate , trust manager, Campaign to Protect Rural England 1999-2004; Secy to Trustees managing South London and Maudsley NHS Trust Charitable Funds Jul 2004 ; *party* helped European election Manchester 1984; joined SDP Camden, Mar 1985; treasurer Camden SDP; candidate LB Camden 1986; founder mbr Liberal Democrats, Vauxhall LP Exec 1987- (including chair, treasurer); Cllr LB Lambeth 1990-94, 1995-2002, chair Children's Services, Social Services, chair Liberal Democrat Gp; PPC Norwood 1992, Croydon North 2001, Croydon South 2005; Euro candidate London list 2004; representative federal, London regional conferences; agent Streatham constituency in LB Lambeth elections 2006; mbr London Regional Exec 2006- ; *special interests* health, social services (mbr social care policy working party 2002-03, health working party 2003-04); Japanese mental health issues (lectured Tokyo 2002); study tour to Japan Feb 2006 *other mbrships* board mbr Liberal Democrat Business Forum; mbr Centre Forum, LDEG, WLD, History Gp, subscriber *Liberator*; chair Lambeth Twinning Association May 2004- ; lay board mbr South London and Maudsley Mental Health NHS Trust; board mbr Mosaic Clubhouse, Balham; president Manchester High School Old Girls Federation Jun 2004- ; *recreations* music (mbr Monteverdi Society, English Chamber Choir); theatre (especially Young Vic); food *address* 6 Kirkstall Road, Streatham Hill, London SW2 4HF *tel/fax* 0208 671 7214 home 0207 919 2460 mobile 07958 245 945 *e-mail* sandra@lawman-kolb.co.uk

LAWRENCE, Angela founder WITS (Women in Target Seats) Campaign *b* Jul 13, 1947 *m* Steve 2 *s* 1 *d education* North Kesteven Grammar School, Lincolnshire; Kesteven College of Education (teacher training) *career* primary school teacher on and off until 1997; Lib Dem Gp Support Officer, West Berks. 2002-03; currently SE Region Campaigns Assistant (to Neil Fawcett) *party* joined SDP 1987; founder mbr Lib Dems; mbr Oxford West and Abingdon LP; elected Vale of White Horse DC 1991, opposition spokesperson, housing 1995-2000, chair, housing 2000-2003, deputy leader 2000-02, chair policy, 2002-2003, chair environmental overview; stood down from Council May 2003 (but worked to ensure seat was held); mbr LGA Housing Exec; chair LGA Rural Housing Task Gp; PPC Witney 1997; Cotswold 2001; formerly mbr Federal Policy Cttee, Federal Conference Cttee; minutes secy PPCs Association; mbr two Housing Policy Working Parties; conference voting rep, and regular attendee since 1991; chair Abingdon Branch Lib Dems; founder WITS (Women in Target Seats) Campaign *special interests* housing (there's a surprise), environment, Agenda 21, social exclusion - access; equal opportunities *recreations* tennis, singing *address* 221 Radley Road, Abingdon, OX14 3SQ *tel/fax* 01235 525436 *e-mail* alawrenceb@cix.co.uk

LAWRIE, John OBE (1990) MA *b* Oct 3, 1942 youngest of 5 children of Thomas Lawrie CBE, Marjorie (nee Jennings) *education* Edinburgh University (MA 1964) *formerly* mbr Securities Institute *career* Commonwealth Statistics office, Melbourne,

Australia (1965), Scottish Provident, Edinburgh: investment mngr 1980, chief investment mngr, Scottish Provident (Ireland) 1991-98, exec chair, Aberdeen Asset Management (Ireland) 1998-2000; dctr IFG plc 2000-; *party* joined Scottish Liberals 1960; president, Edinburgh University Liberal Club 1963-64; secy Scottish Young Liberals 1963-65; cllr Edinburgh Corporation 1971-75; parly election agent Edinburgh Pentlands (1970-79), council election agent seven times, council candidate four times; treasurer Scottish Liberal Party 1975-83, exec mbr 1983-86, chair 1986-87; mbr Scottish negotiating team for Liberal/SDP merger 1987-88; interim trsr, Scottish Social and Liberal Democrats 1988; exec mbr 1988-92; Scottish rep Federal Exec 1988-91; hon president Edinburgh South Liberal Democrats; *formerly* mbr Scottish Appeals Tribunal and Scottish rep on Federal Appeals Panel; *other interests* board mbr Edinvar Housing Association 1973- (chair 1979-82); UK and Ireland chair, The Samaritans 1996-99 (v chair 1993-96), Scottish rep, exec mbr 1990-93); mbr Exec Cttee Telephone Helplines Association 1996- (chair 1999-2002; trsr 1996-99 and 2004-); board mbr Penumbra (2003-); board mbr Edinburgh Cyrenians (2003-); mbr Commission on Boundary Differences and Voting Systems (The Arbuthnott Commission), 2004-6; *recreations* hill-walking *address* 14 Greenhill Terrace, Edinburgh EH10 4BS *tel* 0131-447 3410; *e-mail* johnflawrie@yahoo.co.uk

LAWS, David Anthony MA MP (Yeovil maj: 8,562**) Shadow Secy of State for Work and Pensions** *b* Nov 30, 1965 *education* St George's College, Weybridge (winner *The Observer* Mace National Schools Debating Competition 1984); Kings College, Cambridge (scholarship: double first in economics) *career* vice-president JP Morgan 1987-94; MD Barclays deZoete Wedd 1992-94; economic adviser to LibDems 1994-97; dctr of policy and research 1997-99 *party* joined 1984; author 1994, 1995 Alternative Budgets; PPC Yeovil 2001 (elected MP in succession to Paddy Ashdown); Spokesman on Defence 2001-03; Shadow Chief Secy to the Treasury 2003-05; Shadow Secy of State for Work and Pensions 2005- ; *special interests* education, economics, social welfare, pensions *other mbrships* Institute of Fiscal Studies *recreations* rugby, history, running, athletics *address* House of Commons, London SW1A 0AA *tel* 020 7219 8413 **constituency** Spring Cottage, Lydmarsh, Chard, Somerset TA20 4AA *tel* 01935 423284 *fax* 01935 433652 *e-mail* enquiries@yeovil-libdems.org.uk *web* www.yeovil-libdems.org.uk/

LAWSON, Gary Adam: Chair, PCA *b* Oct 19, 1963 Frimley, Surrey *m* Tricia neé Newton Apr 7, 1990 2*d* 1*s education* Portsmouth Grammar School; SOAS, London Univ, BA Economics and Politics; Cranfield School of Management, Cranfield Univ, MBA; currently London Univ, LLB *career* corporate treasurer, Reed Elsevier 1991-95; treasurer, Morgan Stanley Global Securities 1995-98; Exec Director, J P Morgan 1998-2001; managing partner, Chandos Partners 2001-03; Chief Exec, Sector Treasury Services 2004- ; charity trustee and non-exec director, Hyde Housing Gp 2004- ; *party* PPC Portsmouth North 2005; PCA chair 2005- (exec mbr since 2003); International Relations Cttee 2004- ; English Council rep 2006; Liberal Democrat Lawyers Association exec 2005- ; LIBG vice-chair 2006- , secy 2004; exec mbr Sevenoaks LP 2001-04; mbr Brussels and Luxembourg LP (lived Luxembourg 1993-98); mbr Federal Policy Working Gps: Censorship 2003, International Development 2004, International Trade & Investment 2004; International Law 2006 *other mbrships* NLC, Royal Commonwealth Society, Hampshire CCC, Electoral Reform Society, Atlantic Council, LDEG, CentreForum *special interests* social enterprise, international trade, international legal system, global development, international relations, electoral and parliamentary reform *publications* various articles on WTO, GATS and armed forces procurement *recreations* cricket (represented Luxembourg internationally), fine wines, fishing *address* Chandos, 54 St Botolphs Road, Sevenoaks, Kent TN13 3AG *tel* 01732 779476 home 07941 553859 mobile *fax* 0870 121 0659 *e-mail* gary@lawsononline.org *website* www.lawsononline.org

LE BRETON, Christopher David Glossop *b* Aug 15, 1964 Kitale, Kenya *education* Bryanston School; Geography at School of African & Asian Studies, Univ of Sussex; Univ of Grenoble; MSc Agricultural Economics at Wye College, Univ of London; languages: French, German, Russian, Serbian, Sinhalese *career* campaigner London Cycling Campaign 1989-91; campaigner Friends of the Earth 1989-91; project manager, Braunschweig, Germany 1992-94; Environment task manager, European Commission Tacis 1994-97; Exec Director, Global Legislators Organisation for Balanced Environment 1997-99; OSCE monitor to Georgian Parliamentary Elections 2000; consultant to EU and US regarding New regional environmental centres Russia, Central Asia, Caucasus, Moldova 1999-2005; Co-ordinator CycleMark/ Strategic Rail Authority, 2001; environmental adviser, European Agency for Reconstruction, Ministry of Environment, Serbia *party* PPC Greenwich and Woolwich 2005; mbr Greenwich LP 1999- ; mbr exec 1999-2003; campaigns cttee 1999-2002; candidate Trafalgar ward by-election 1999; Eltham South council election 2002; Brussels party 1992-97, mbr Green Liberal Democrats exec 2002-06; mbr, Liberal International; DELGA special interests international affairs, sustainable urban living, travel
(visited 90 countries around world) other mbrships Chatham House, Greenwich Cyclists, Friends of Greenwich Park, Friends of National Maritime Museum, Supporter-Sustrans *recreations* cycling, sculling, surfing, hiking *publications Dead Easy And Not Even A Puncture; A Short Ride Across The Himalayas*; Mountain-biking UK 1989; *Letter from Serbia* Green Liberal Democrats Challenge 2004 *address* 39 Azof Street, Greenwich, London SE10 0EG *tel* 020 8853 3431 *e-mail* azof@hotmail.co.uk and www.chrislebreton.com

LE BRETON, William (Bill) *b* Dec 13, 1950 *m* Sheila 1 *s* Tim 1 *d* Sophie *education* Millfield, London School of Economics *career* founding partner Oct Communications, Liverpool *party* joined 1978, previously campaigned for Paul Tyler in Bodmin 1974; mbr Medina Borough Council 1979-88,leader of council 1981-86; Isle of Wight County Council 1985-88; chair ALDC 1991-96, president 1996-98; campaigner, activist Liverpool 1989- *special interests* pursuit of liberty, friendship and excitement *other mbrships* Liverpool Racquets Club, MCC, Mountain Bothies Association *recreations* cricket, climbing, tennis *publications* co-editor Passports to Liberty *address* Gondal House, Rimington, Lancashire BB7 4DX *tel* 01200 445012 home 0151 236 2323 business *e-mail* bill@octobercomms.co.uk

LEE, Anne BA PhD FIPD *b* Oct 14, 1953 *m* 1 *d* 1 *s education* Shenfield School; Open Univ (BA), Univ of Surrey (PhD), Graduate Mbr, British Psychological Society; Fellow, Chartered Institute of Personnel Development, associate mbr Secondary Heads Association *career* Unilever, Industrial Society and J P Morgan; Visiting Fellow Univ of Surrey; headmistress independent girls' senior school; acting principal independent primary school; education and business advisor; writer; director Next Chapter Ltd (company supporting those who work in education);

Development Officer, Univ of Surrey *party* joined Liberals late 1970s; mbr Public Services Working Gp 2001-02; PPC South Norfolk 2001, Woking 2005; led Simon Hughes MP's leadership campaign 1999; mbr Guildford BC 1999-2003 *special interests* education, health, financing and management of public services *recreations* family, walking, music, travel *style* Dr Anne Lee *address* The Post House, West Clandon, Woking, Surrey GU4 7ST *tel* 01483 222610 *fax* 01483 225495

LEE, Lord John Robert Louis, DL FCA *b* 1942 Manchester *m* Anne Monique (nee Bakirgian) 2 *d education* William Hulme's Grammar School, Manchester; qualified Chartered Accountant 1964 *career* co-founded investment banking gp; board mbr number of public, private companies; currently non-exec director Emerson Development (Holding) Ltd; chairman Association of Leading Visitor Attractions 1990- ; regular contributor on investment in smaller public companies to *Financial Times; civic, charitable: previously* - vice chairman North West Conciliation Cttee, Race Relations Board; Trustee, home for discharged prisoners; chairman National Youth Bureau; chaired review for Govt into Health Education Authority 1992-8; chairman Christie Hospital NHS Trust 1992-98; Museum of Science and Industry, Manchester 1992-99; mbr English Tourist Board 1992-99; High Sheriff of Greater Manchester 1998-99 *currently* chairman trustees, governor Withington Girl's School, Manchester; founded Lee & Bakirgian Family Trust *party* Stretford Young Conservatives, NW Bow Gp; PPC Manchester Moss Side, Oct 1974; MP Pendle (Nelson and Colne) 1979-92; PPS to Rt. Hon. Kenneth Baker MP (Lord Baker) and Rt. Hon. Cecil Parkinson (Lord Parkinson) 1981-83; Under Secy of State (Defence Procurement) Ministry of Defence 1983-86; Under Secy of State Department Employment 1986-89; Minister of Tourism 1987-89; mbr Defence Select Cttee 1990-92; 1922 Exec 1992; resigned from Conservative Party 1997; chaired North West Britain in Europe; joined Liberal Democrats 2001; chair Commission on Tourism Policy 2003; director Lib Dem Business Forum; deputy Treasurer Lib Dems; president Altrincham-Sale West Liberal Democrats 2004; appointed Life Peer in 2006 *recreations* golf, salmon fishing, art and antiques, cinema *address* Bowdon Old Hall, 49 Langham Road, Bowdon, Cheshire, WA14 3NS; 1 The Gateways, Sprimont Place, Chelsea, SW3 3HX *tel* 0161 928 0696 and 020 7589 6153 *fax* 0161 929 5096 *e-mail* johnleedl@aol.com

LEECH, John MP (Manchester Withington maj:667) *education* Manchester GS; Loreto College (Mosside); Brunel Univ (history and politics) *career* trainee manager at McDonalds; call centre insurance claims handler for RAC in Stockport *party* elected Manchester City Council 1998, deputy leader of opposition 1998- , deputy leader Liberal Democrat Gp 2003- ; elected MP 2005; mbr Transport Select Cttee 2005- ; Shadow Transport spokesperson 2006- ; founded All Party Parliamentary Gp on Light Rail; mbr Parliamentary Football Team *special interests* housing, planning, transport *recreations* football (Manchester City fan), amateur dramatics *address* 53b Manley Road, Whalley Range, Manchester M16 8HP *tel* 0161 226 6542 *e-mail* leechj@parliament.uk

LEES, Jonathan Campbell *b* May 30, 1969 *m* Melanie 2s Ethan Noah 1 *d* Izzy Mei *education* Ratton School; Open Univ *career* bank two years; one voluntary work Wood Green (community, social, young people); church youth, community work eight years; qualified youth work, ran project two years; community development manager, housing association five years, currently works as Programme Manager for national charity *party* joined 2001; Exec mbr LP; borough Cllr 2003, gp leader 2005-; PPC Epsom & Ewell 2005 *special interests* community development, regeneration, young people, affordable housing *recreations* football, golf, church, gym *address* 5 William Evans Road, Epsom, Surrey KT19 7DE *tel* 01372 749149 home 07801 432459 mobile *e-mail* jmeilees@yahoo.co.uk

LEFFMAN, Liz: Marketing Officer PCA *b* Mar 23, 1949 *partner* Mike Flanagan *education* Christ's Hospital School for Girls, Hertford; Univ of Leeds (BA Philosophy and History of Art); London Business School (London Exec Programme); Oxford Brookes Univ (MA in coaching and mentoring practice, graduating this year) *career* account director J Walter Thompson 1976-81, account director Saatchi and Saatchi 1981-82; marketing manager National Dairy Council 1982-85; marketing, business development director Courtaulds Textiles 1985-92; director, Clothesource Management Services, consultancy specialising in textile trade and, in particular, in Eastern Europe 1992- *party* joined SDP 1981; re-joined Lib Dems 2000; currently mbrship secy, Witney LP; marketing officer PCA 2004- ; PPC Witney 2005 *special interests* overseas trade, small business enterprise *other mbrships* director, The Kairos Foundation (international educational charity); mentor co-ordinator for the Oxfordshire Prince's Trust *recreations* singing with local choral society, walking, cooking, entertaining *address* 10 Park Street, Charlbury, Oxfordshire OX7 3PS *tel* 01608 810153 home 01608 810153 business *fax* 01608 813067 *e-mail* lizleffman@clothesource.net

LELLIOTT, Mark I.Eng MIEE *b* Haslemere, Nov 25, 1955.*m* Suzan (active Lib Dem, Cllr) 1979 *education* Woolmer Hill, Haslemere; Weybridge, Guildford Technical Colleges *career* defence industry then engineer, video tape editor BBC *party* joined Liberal Party; with wife, founder mbr Liberal Democrats; both elected Cllrs 1995, part of team which wrested Haslemere TC from Tories for first time in century, re-elected 2003, Mayor of Haslemere 1998, gp leader; PPC Surrey Heath 2001 (one of four SE seats that made gains against Tories and Labour) *special interests* environment, transport.*recreations* cycling, reading, theatre, keeping fit, skiing, riding (owns Russian motorcycle); holidays in Siena *address* Birch House, Cherry Tree Avenue. Haslemere. Surrey. GU27 1JP *tel* 01428 644499 *e-mail* mark_Lelliott@onetel.net.uk

LESTER of Herne Hill, Baron Anthony Paul Lester: Life Peer UK 1993, QC 1975 *b* Jul 3, 1936 *m* Katya 1 *s* Hon Gideon (associate artistic director American Repertory Theater, Cambridge, Massachusetts) 1 *d* Hon Maya (barrister) *education* City of London, Trinity College Cambridge (BA), Harvard Law (LL.M) *career* 2nd Lt Royal Artillery 1956; called to the Bar, Lincoln's Inn 1963 (bencher 1985), mbr Northern Ireland Bar, Irish Bar; former recorder South Eastern circuit 1987; special adviser to: Home Secy (Roy Jenkins)with special responsibility for developing policy on race relations, sex discrimination and human rights 1974-76, Standing Commission Human Rights in Northern Ireland 1975-77; former chair Board of Governors James Allen's Girls'; president Interights (International Centre for Legal Protection of Human Rights); mbr Board: Salzburg Seminar 1997, Euro Roma Rights Center; mbr Editorial Board *Public Law*, editor-in-chief *Butterworths Human Rights Cases*; hon visiting professor of law UCL; honorary degrees Open Univ, Universities of Durham, Ulster, the South Bank and Univ College London *party* former chair, treasurer Fabian Society; founder mbr SDP; president Lib Dem

Lawyers' Association; created Life Peer 1993; mbr Parliamentary Cttees on human rights, European Union Law *special interests* human rights (campaigned for thirty years to make the European Human Rights Convention directly enforceable in British courts; introduced two Private Mbrs' Bills which became models for Human Rights Act 1998); LIBERTY Human Rights Lawyer of the Year 1997 *publications* articles, books on human rights, constitutional law including *Justice in the American South* (1964), *Shawcross and Beaumont on Air Law* (ed jtly, 3 edn 1964), *Race and Law* (jtly 1972); consultant editor, contributor *Constitutional Law and Human Rights in Halsbury's Laws of England* (fourth edition, 1973, re-issued 1996); contributor to *British Nationality, Immigration and Race Relations in Halsbury's Laws of England* (fourth edition 1973, re-issued 1992), *The Changing Constitution* (ed Jowell and Oliver, 1985), co-editor *Human Rights Law & Practice* 2nd edition (Butterworths 2004) *recreations* walking, sailing, golf, water colours *style* The Lord Lester of Herne Hill, QC *address* House of Lords, London SW1A 0PW; Blackstone Chambers, Blackstone House, Temple, London, EC4Y 9BW *tel* 020 7353 4612 *e-mail* info@odysseustrust.org

LEUNIG, Tim *b* Feb 26, 1971 *education* Univ of Oxford (BA History and Economics, MPhil Economics, DPhil Economics) *career* Prize Research Fellow, Nuffield College, Oxford 1995-97; lecturer in economics, Royal Holloway College, Univ of London 1997-98; lecturer in economic history LSE 1998- ; director, Kingston Borough Liberal Democrat Property Company 2003- *party* joined 1989; held various offices including chair, Ealing Acton & Shepherds Bush LP 1997-2002; council candidate 1998; newsletter editor Kingston Borough LP 2002- ; economic advisor Lib Dem Treasury & Environment teams 1997- , economic advisor to Federal Policy Cttee 2002- ; mbr eight federal working gps 1997- , including chair Macroeconomics 2003, housing (twice), Liberal Democracy, local economics, public services, urban, transport), mbr, Women Liberal Democrats 2001- *special interests* economics, environmental policy, taxation, transport *other mbrships* American Economic Association, Amnesty International, Institute for Fiscal Studies, London cycling campaign, Roadpeace, Royal Economic Society *recreations* gardening, reading, walking *publications* number of academic publications (see *web*), articles in *The Reformer*, letters in *The Economist, Financial Times, Liberal Democrat News address* 52a Berrylands Road, Surbiton, Surrey, KT5 8PD *tel* 020 8241 0140 home 020 7955 7857 business *fax* 020 8241 0140 home 020 7955 7730 business *e-mail* tim@leunig.net *web* www.leunig.net

LINDON, Karl Anthoney DipPsych *b* Aug 19, 1980 *ptnr* since 1989 *career* Civil Service, Ministry of Defence 1999, assistant press office manager 2001-03, Exec officer, Defence Medical Services Department 2003- ; *party* joined 1997; chair LDYS Hemel Hempstead 1997-99; chair London DELGA 2000-02; mbr Newington Ward Exec 1999- ; approved PPC 2004- ; council candidate Faraday Ward, Southwark 2006; mbr PCA *special interests* experienced equality activist, knowledge of foreign affairs, local community action issues and psychology *other mbrships* director of own company Beyond Ego Ltd; student mbr British Psychological Society; on court mbr of Badminton Association of England *address* Flat 2, 91 Camberwell Road, London SE5 0EZ *tel* 07734 461 022 *e-mail* karl@lindon.org.uk *web* www.lindon.org.uk

LINDSAY, Caron *b* Jul 31, 1967 Inverness *m* 1 *d education* Wick High School *career* currently working for Willie Rennie MP; previous boring jobs only there to finance political involvement; after birth of daughter became volunteer breastfeeding counsellor which is not at all boring *party* mbr 1983-89, 91- ; various positions held in East Midlands; candidate in Carrick, Cumnock and Doon Valley 2003, Kirkton Ward, West Lothian Council 2003; Convener, Campaigns and Candidates Cttee, Scottish Liberal Democrats 2005- ; mbr STV Working Group for 2007 Local Govt Elections 2004- ; Scottish and Federal Conference rep, exec mbr, West Lothian Lib Dems 2000- ; ASLDC exec mbr 2004- ; facilitator and assessor of candidates 2002- ; accredited party trainer in campaigns and selection subjects 1998- ; Campaign Manager for Livingston by-election 2005; mbr ALDC, WLD *other mbrships* Baby Milk Action, Parent Mbr, School Board, St John Ogilvie Primary School, Livingston *special interests* child development, infant feeding issues, supporting new parents, early years education *recreations* reading, music, cookery, wine and chocolate, one day will learn to dance if I ever have any spare time *LD quirk* got detention in 1983 election campaign for skipping school to go canvassing for Bob Maclennan in Caithness *address* 139 Buchanan Crescent, Livingston,West Lothian EH54 7EF *tel* 01506 414010, 07821 882543 mobile; *e-mail* caron@cbahowden.icuklive.co.uk

LINKLATER of Butterstone, Baroness Veronica: Life Peer cr 1997 *b* Apr 15, 1943 Dunkeld *m* Magnus Duncan Linklater 2 *s* 1 *d education* Cranborne Chase School; Sorbonne; Univ of Sussex, Univ of London (Diploma, Social Administration); Honorary Doctorate Univ College 2001, Queen Margaret Univ College, Edinburgh *career* child care officer, LB Tower Hamlets 1967-68; visitors' centre (co-founder), Pentonville Prison 1971-77; governor, three Islington schools 1970-85; Winchester prison project, Prison Reform Trust 1981-82; founder, administrator, then consultant to The Butler Trust 1983-87, trustee 1987-2001, vice president 2001- ; JP Inner London 1985-88; moved to Scotland 1987; children's panel mbr Edinburgh South 1989-97; co-ordinator, trustee, vice chairman Pushkin Prizes (Scotland) 1989- ; president Society of Friends of Dunkeld Cathedral 1989-; cttee mbr Gulliver Award for the Performing Arts in Scotland 1990-96; founder, exec chairman The New School, Butterstone (for educationally fragile children) 1991-2004, president 2004- ; trustee Esmée Fairbairn Foundation 1991- ; chairman Rethinking Crime and Punishment 2001- ; patron The Sutherland Trust 1993-2003; trustee The Young Musicians Trust 1993-97; director The Maggie Keswick Jencks Cancer Caring Centres Trust 1997-2004; mbr Beattie Cttee (on post-school provision for young people with special needs) 1998-99; foundation patron Queen Margaret Univ College, Edinburgh 1998; patron, The Airborne Initiative 1998-2004; trustee Development Trust, Univ of the Highlands and Islands 1999-01; patron National Schizophrenia Fellowship Scotland 2000- ; Secy, The Scottish Peers Association 2000- ; mbr Scottish Cttee, Barnardo's 2001- ; chancellor's assessor Napier Univ Court 2001-04; advisory board mbr The Beacon Fellowship Charitable Trust 2003- ; patron The Autism Intervention Research Trust 2004- ; patron The Calyx, Scotland's Garden Trust 2004- ; adviser Koestler Award Trust 2004- ; patron The Probation Boards Association 2005- ; council mbr Winston Churchill Memorial Trust 2005- ; chairman All Party Parliamentary Gp on Offender Learning and Skills 2005- ; patron Action for Prisoners' Families 2005- ; *party* PPC Perth & Kinross 1995; Life Peer created 1997 *special interests* criminal justice (especially young people in trouble); education *especially special educational needs .recreations* family, music, theatre, reading *address* 5 Drummond Place, Edinburgh, EH3 6PH *tel* 0131 557 5705 *fax* 0131 557 9757 *e-mail* v.linklater@blueyonder.co.uk

LISHMAN, (Arthur) Gordon CBE; BA (Econ), FRSA *b* Nov 29, 1947 *s* of late Dr Arthur Birkett Lishman and Florence May Lishman; *m* Margaret Ann (née Long); 1*s* Chris b 1976 2*d* Philippa b 1978, Katie Brodie-Browne b 1982; expecting grandparenthood in 2006! *education* Colne Grammar School; Univ of Manchester; Honorary Fellow, Univ of Central Lancashire *career* director general, Age Concern 2000- ; Liberal Party Research Department 1968-70; Liberal Party Community Politics, Local Govt Officer 1970-72; organiser, North Yorkshire Liberals 1972-74; Age Concern England, 1974-; field officer 1974-77, head of fieldwork 1977-87, operations director 1987-2000; director, Age Concern Enterprises Ltd, 1995- ; mbr, Steering Gp for Commission on Equality & Human Rights; Secy General, Eurolink Age 2001- ; board mbr and secy, AGE – the European Older People's Platform 2001- ; International VP, International Federation on Ageing 2001- ; *party* joined Liberals Mar 1963; various offices – Burnley Young Liberals, Manchester Univ Liberal Club, Union of Liberal Students, National League of Young Liberals;. former editor *New Politics, Liberator, New Outlook*; wrote, summed-up community politics resolution Liberal Assembly 1970; founding mbr, secy, Cttee mbr; returning officer, president, chair, Association of Liberal Cllrs and ALDC; frequently mbr Liberal NEC and standing Cttee, Lib Dem Federal Exec, Federal Policy Cttee; chair International Relations Cttee 1992-2006; chair Westminster Foundation for Democracy Steering Cttee; delegation leader European Liberal & Democrat Party Council; mbr, Liberal International Exec .*special interests* ageing societies; equality and human rights, the political ideas of liberalism in 21st century *recreations* reading, family, eating & drinking, travelling *clubs* National Liberal *style* Mr. *address* Age Concern, Astral House, 1268 London Road, London SW16 4ER; 42 Halifax Road, Briercliffe, Burnley, BB10 3QN; 408 Keyes House, Dolphin Square, London, SW1V 3NA *tel* 020 8765 7701(w); 01282 422527, 0207 798 8936(h); 07778 271177(m) *fax* 0208 679 6997(w); 01282 452414(h) *e-mail* agl@ace.org.uk

LIVSEY OF TALGARTH, Lord Richard Arthur Lloyd Livsey: Life Peer created 2001, CBE 1992, DL: Lords Spokesperson on Wales *b* May 2, 1935 *m* Rene 2 *s* 1 *d education* Talgarth CP School; Bedales; Seale-Hayne Agricultural College; Reading Univ *career* National Service commission RASC; development officer, ICI Ltd (Agricultural Division); farm manager Blair Drummond Estate, Perthshire; senior lecturer in farm management, Welsh Agricultural College; Liberal, then Lib Dem MP Brecon and Radnorshire *party* joined Liberals 1961; MP for Brecon and Radnorshire 1983-1992 (lost by 300 votes), 1997 (regained seat with 5000 majority)-2001, leader of Welsh party in Commons 1988-92; mbr Welsh Affairs Select Cttee, Shadow Secy of State for Wales 1997; heavily involved in devolution settlement for Wales; created life peer after standing down as MP2001; Lords' spokesman agriculture, rural affairs *special interests* agriculture, rural affairs, animal health, environment, waterways, Welsh Assembly, Wales *other mbrships* EU Environment, Rural Affairs sub-Cttee D; president European Movement, Wales *recreations* music (mbr Talgarth Choir), fishing, cycling, watching rugby, cricket *address* House of Lords, London SW1A OPW *tel* 020 7219 6234 *fax* 020 7219 2377

LIYANAGE, Dayantha (Dai) Porambe MBE, FMS, MCMI *b* Colombo, Sri Lanka May 18 1944 *m* Mary (nee Quirke) 1972 2*d* Aoife b 1981, Claire b 1983 *education*

Royal College, Colombo; Brunel Univ *career* management consultancy, GLC, London Boroughs of Barnet, Ealing, Tower Hamlets & City of Westminster, British Shoe Corporation, Zambia Consolidated Copper Mines, National Criminal Intelligence Service, Urpol Policy Consultants *party* constituency chair, v chair Home Counties and SE region, mbr Kent CC (first Asian), Gillingham BC, Medway UA, Mayor of Medway; fact finding tour of South Africa, peace mission to Sri Lanka; served on David Steel's commission on reasons for lack of ethnic minority involvement in politics; Inner City Working Gp, mbr Federal Policy Cttee, ELDR Council, Treasurer LDEG & LIBG *special interests* served on OFWAT CSC, National Lottery Charities Board (SE region), Kent Police Authority, chair school governing body, chair Havengore Education & Leadership Mission, V Chair Kent Assn for the Blind, Chair Medway Family Support Service, Chair Medway Action against Racial Attacks, Trustee Medway REC; International Election Monitor, Sri Lanka *clubs* Round Table, 41 Club, Medway Rotary Club (President), officer Rotary District 1120 *address* 28 Woodpecker Glade, Wigmore, Gillingham, Medway ME8 0JR *tel* 01634 388979 (h) 07721 506603 (m) 01634 318453 (b) *e-mail* liyanage@blueyonder.co.uk *website* www.urpol.com

LLOYD, Stephen *b* Jun 15, 1957 Mombasa *education* Loreto, Mombasa, Barrow Hills nr Godalming, St Georges College, Weybridge *career* Head of Diversity Services, Grass Roots Gp (£110 million turnover performance-improvement company) 1998- ; fourteen years experience in this sometimes controversial but important area; recognised as one of leading diversity proponents in the country; he has worked with around 300 companies, Govt departments and public sector organisations on diversity issues 1990-98; various campaigning, development, press roles within the charity sector; former trustee RNID; patron BSHT; previously MD of own radio production company *party* mbr of SDP from formation, founder mbr Liberal Democrats; active since 1998; chair Maidenhead LP; recruitment officer Chilterns Region; mbr English Council; PPC Beaconsfield 2001; PPC Eastbourne (top ten target seat) 2005 (re-selected 2006) *special interests* managing diversity within the UK and Europe, corporate social responsibility, small business sector, welfare and benefits system, prevention of crime, prisons, accountability in Govt, EU *recreations* movies, old and new, classic cars, sailing, political history mbrships Institute of Directors, Charter 88, Woodland Trust, Amnesty International *address* 18 Bradford Street, Eastbourne, East Sussex BN21 1HZ *tel* 01323 747928 *e-mail* stephone.lloyd@grg.com *web* www.eastbournelibdems.org.uk

LLOYD-WILLIAMS, David *b* Mar 7, 1944 *m* Angela *education* Mount Grace School, College of Estate Management *career* building surveyor 1964-73; antiques dealer 1974- *party* joined Liberal Party 1980; mbr North Yorkshire County Council 1981- ; gp leader 1990-96; assistant agent Ryedale by election 1986; PPC Richmond (North Yorks) 1987l ACC gp secy 1989-96; LGA gp secy 1996- ; CCN gp leader 1996-2001; Ryedale LP fundraiser 1992-2002; substitute mbr CLRAE 2000- *special interests* community safety (mbr North Yorks Police Authority, local CDRP) *recreations* collecting nice things; old buildings; gardening; antique restoration *publications* paper on community safety, presented in Prague in 2003 CLRAE *address* Hawthorn House, Langton Road, Norton Malton YO17 9AD *tel* 01653 693016 *fax* 01653 696183 *e-mail* dlloydwilliams@btopenworld.com

LORD, C Edward *b* Jan 13, 1972 Littleborough, Lancashire *ptnr* Cllr Laura
Willoughby MBE *qv education* Bury Grammar School 1976-90; Univ of Essex BA
Public Policy and Public Management 1990-94 *career* national Exec mbr NUS
1994-96; freelance PR, fundraising and events organiser 1994-97; deputy director,
Friends of the Hebrew Univ of Jerusalem 1997-98; development director, Liverpool
John Moores Univ 1998-2000; development director, The City Univ 2000-02; chief
Exec, Crusaid 2002-03; public affairs and fundraising consultant 2003- ; interim
Chief Exec, Imperial College Union 2004-05; non-exec chairman 4ps – Public
Private Partnerships Programme 2005- ; *party* Deputy Federal Treasurer 2005- ; mbr,
FFAC 2006- ; observer at FE 2005- ; board mbr, Liberty Network and Liberal
Democrat Business Forum 2005- ; English Council 2006- ; LGA Liberal Democrat
Gp Cabinet 2005- ; London Region Exec 2006- ; London Region Campaigns Cttee
2006- ; Islington Local Party Exec 2004- ; mbr ALDC, DELGA, LIBG; cttee mbr
Liberal Democrat Friends of Israel *public service* mbr, LGA Strategy & Finance
PRG 2005- ; Mbr, LGA Improvement Board 2004- ; Trustee, Central Foundation
Schools of London 2004- ; Trustee, The Refugee Council 2003-04; Trustee, The
Honourable The Irish Society 2002-04; 2005- ; Justice of the Peace 2002- ; Cllr,
Corporation of London 2001- ; Trustee, City Parochial Foundation 2001-05;
Governor former Chair, Sir John Cass's Foundation School 2000-04; Lay Council
Mbr/Adviser, College of Optometrists 2000-03; Trustee, St Botolph's Homelessness
Project 2000-02; Trustee, Anglo-Israel Association 1997-2000; Board Mbr, The
Pride Trust 1996; Trustee, British Youth Council 1995-97 *special interests*
machinery of Govt; constitution; education; equalities; local/regional democracy;
culture, media and sport; home affairs *other mbrships* Freeman, City of London and
the Worshipful Companies of Leathersellers, Spectacle Makers and Fletchers also
liveryman *clubs* National Liberal (cttee mbr), Reform, Soho House and Lancashire
CCC; associate, Adam Smith Institute; associate mbr, Institute of Economic Affairs;
subscriber, Centre Forum; mbr Countryside Alliance, English Heritage, Lords'
Taverners, National Trust, The Tate; shareholder and former VP, West Ham United
Football Club; shareholder Rochdale Association Football Club *recreations* music,
theatre, cinema, art, heritage, watching live cricket and football, swimming, urban
and country walking, reading, good food, fine wines, travel *publications Liberating
Universities* 2000 *style* Cllr C Edward Lord, JP *address* 114d Blackstock Road,
London N4 2DR; Mbrs' Room, Guildhall, London EC2P 2EJ; Treasurer's Office, 4
Cowley Street, London SW1P 3NB *tel* 020 7354 5147 home, 020 7222 7999
business, 07974 431 484 mobile *fax* 020 7799 2170 *e-mail* ce.lord@virgin.net or
edward.lord@libdems.org.uk *website* www.edwardlord.com

LOTHERINGTON, John Charles *b* February 26, 1957 *education* Solihull School,
1968-75; Peterhouse, Cambridge 1976-80 *career* Haberdashers' Aske's School:
assistant master 1980-89; head of history 1989-92; deputy director 1992-2000,
director 21 st Century Trust 2000- *party* joined 1992 *special interests* international
relations, human rights, social policy *other mbrships* Fellow Goodenough College;
Amnesty International; Historical Association *recreations* theatre, music, trying to
find time to spend in Italy *publications Years of Renewal: European History 1470-
1600* (1988, 2nd ed. 1999); *The Tudor Years (* 1994, 2nd ed. 2003*); The
Communications Revolution (*ed. with Deniz Derman, 1995*); The Seven Ages of Life
(*Centre Forum, ed. 2002); introduction to *Florentine History* by Nicol ò Machiavelli
(Barnes & Noble, 2004); introduction to *The Book of the Courtier* by Baldesar

Castiglione (Barnes & Noble, 2005) *address* 56 Falcon Point, Hopton Street, London SE1 9JW *tel* 020 7261 0101 *e-mail* John.Lotherington@gmail.com

LOWE, Nicholas John (Nick) *b* Feb 27, *1954 m* Solange (née Terrière) *education* George Watson's School, Edinburgh; Univ of Poitiers, France (maîtrise ès lettres) *career* translator, interpreter, document editor, private tutor in English and French; school-governing body officer, London Borough of Brent 1984-86; policy analyst Westminster City Council 1986-94; public affairs manager London Insurance and Reinsurance Market Association 1995-98; director government affairs, International Underwriting Association of London 1999- ; *party* joined Sept 1999; chair Battersea and Tooting 2004, treasurer 2002-03 *special interests* Europe and foreign affairs, financial services, education, social services, Indian sub-continent: *other mbrships* former chair Central London Europe group European Movement; former council member London Civic Forum; former school governor *recreation* travel, novels, films, science fiction, history, classical music, swimming *address* 58 Garrick Close, Wandsworth, London SW18 1JJ *tel* 020 88701474 *e-mail* nichlowe@aol.com

LUDFORD, Baroness Sarah: Life Peer cr 1997, MEP (London) *b* Mar 14, 1951 *education* Portsmouth HS for Girls; LSE (BSc, MSc); Inns of Court School of Law *m* Steve Hitchins *career* barrister, called to the Bar, Gray's Inn 1979; official, Secretariat General and DG Competition EC 1979-85 (when Roy Jenkins was president); Euro and UK advisor Lloyds of London 1985-87; vice-president corporate affairs American Express Europe 1987-90; Euro consultant 1990-99; elected MEP 1999, re-elected 2004 *party* joined in early 1980s; mbr LB Islington 1990-99; Euro candidate Wight and Hampshire East 1984, London Central 1989, 1994, London list 1999 (elected), 2004 (re-elected); PPC Islington North 1992, Islington South and Finsbury 1997; mbr Federal Policy Cttee 1991- (vice-chair 1993-99); mbr DELGA; created life peer 1999; European Parliament: Liberal Democrat European Parliamentary Party spokeswoman on Justice and Home Affairs; deputy leader of LDEPP; vice-president Anti-Racism Inter-Gp; co-chair of European Muslim Forumn; mbr Cttee on Citizens' Freedoms and Rights, Justice and Home Affairs; sub-mbr Cttee on Economic and Monetary Affairs; mbr delegation for relations with SE Europe *other mbrships* Gray's Inn; Royal Institute of International Affairs (Chatham House); council mbr Liberty and Justice; patron of Fair Trials Abroad and Guantanamo Human Rights Commission *recreations* theatre, ballet *address* 36 St Peter's Street, London N1 8JT *tel* 020 7288 2526 *fax* 020 7288 2581 *e-mail* office@sarahludfordmep.org.uk *web* www.sarahludfordmep.org.uk

LYNNE, Liz MEP West Midlands *b* Jan 22, 1948 *education* Dorking County Grammar School *career* actress 1966-89; freelance speech and voice consultant 1989-92; MP 1992-97; MEP 1999- ; *party* PPC (Liberal Alliance) Harwich 1987; MP (Lib-Dem) Rochdale 1992-97, spokesperson on Health & Community Care 1992-1994, Social Security & Disability 1994-1997; MEP West Midlands 1999, re-elected 2004; member Cttee on Employment and Social Affairs; member Subcttee on Human Rights; member, delegation for relations with South Asia and South Asia Association for Regional Cooperation; Vice-President, All Party Disability Intergroup; Co-chair of the Parliamentary Intergroup on AGE; Co-Chair of MEPs Against Cancer (MAC); President of the Liberal Democrat Friends of Kashmir *special interests* employment and social affairs, Shadow Rapporteur Working Time Directive, human rights; Kashmir; Rapporteur for European Year of Disabled People

2003 and the EU Action Plan for Disabled People 2006-2007; Patron of Jennifer Trust for Spinal Muscular Atrophy; Patron, Blue Eyed Soul Dance Company; Patron, Friends of the Montgomery Canal; Patron, George Coller Memorial Fund: Vice President, the Droitwich Canal Trust; Patron, Tourism for all UK; Patron, Federation of European Motorcyclists'; Patron GUCH Patient Association (Grown up Congenital Heart); Patron, Worcestershire Lifestyles; Patron Shropshire and Wrekin ME support; Patron, Parkside Centre Trust; Association Founder and Chair for first seven years of the Indonesian Co-ordination for British Section of Amnesty International *recreations* motor-biking, tennis *address* constituency office 55 Ely Street, Stratford-upon-Avon CV37 6LN *tel* 01789 266354 *fax* 01789 268848 *e-mail* lizlynne@cix.co.uk or elynne@europarl.eu.int *web* www.lizlynne.libdems.org.uk

LYON, George MSP (Argyll and Bute) Chief Whip in Scottish Parliament *b* Jul 16, 1956 *education* Rothesay Academy 1972; Nuffield Farming Scholarship (New Zealand & Australia) 1986 *m* (sep) 3 *d career* farmer; resident, National Farmers' Union 1997 *party* mbr Argyll and Bute LP1997; elected Scottish Parliament 1999; Chief Whip, Parliament business manager 2003- ; former spkspn Industry, Enterprise (Industry Team Leader): spkspn on Agriculture, Home Affairs and Land Reform 2001-03; convener, Scottish Parliamentary Party 2001- ; spkspn on Enterprise, Life Long Learning1999-2001; co-convener Cross-Party Gp on Scottish economy; mbr, Audit Cttee 2003- ; substitute mbr Equal Opportunities Cttee *other interests* former mbr, Argyll & Isles Enterprise Company *recreations* skiing, football, reading, keeping fit *clubs* Farmers Club *address* Scottish Parliament, Edinburgh EH99 1SP *tel* 0131-348 5787; *constituency* First Floor, 7 Castle Street, Rothesay, Isle of Bute, PQ20 9HA *tel* 01700-500222 *e-mail* glyon1@supanet.com or george.lyon.msp@scottish.parliament.uk *web* ww.kirtel.demon.co.uk/argyll_libdems

M

McCARTIN, Eileen *b* Mar 6, 1952 Glasgow *m* Allan Heron *1 s* aged 15 *education* Diploma/Domestic Science (Nutrition) 1973; Cert. Secondary Educ.1974; HNC Business Studies 1978; post- grad in Social Work Management, 1994 *career* teacher; Family Aides co-ordinator; Glasgow Meals organiser; Strathclyde Regional Catering Advisor; Contracts Officer; self-employed Herb & Nutrition specialist *party* mbr Paisley and District LP, held every office except treasurer over last 20-odd years!; cllr 1988 - ; Leader, Scottish LD gp, Renfrewshire Council; PPC Paisley North (3 times), PPC Paisley South (3 times) and at 1997 by-election; PSPC Paisley South (twice); mbr Scottish Exec 1995- ; ASLDC WLD *recreations* wider family; singing; health and wellbeing; friends *special interests* abortion: I believe that abortion does great damage to women in terms of both physical and mental health and wellbeing, as well as the obvious damage done to the baby/foetus/conceptus; Fairtrade/ trade justice *style* Cllr *address* 13 Greenways Avenue, Paisley PA2 9NS *tel* 01505 814676 *e-mail* eileen.mccartin@ntlworld.com *web* www.heronnaturalhealth.co.uk

McDONALD, Ian Richard *b* Sept 2, 1958 *m* Heather (linguist: Hausa, French, some Japanese) 2 *d education* Sudbury Junior, Brent; Malden Parochial, Kingston upon Thames; Beverley Boys' School, Kingston upon Thames; part time Kingston College; Portsmouth Univ (applied physics) 1980; Westminster Univ (electronics, computer technology) 1988: London Institute of Education (secondary science PGCE) 1989; Open Univ (science: biology, chemistry, ecology, astrophysics, mathematical modelling) 1997; mbr Institute of Physics (MInstP); Chartered Physicist (CPhys); European Physical Society (EurPhys); mbr British Computer Society (MBCS); Chartered Information Systems Practitioner (CITP); mbr Institute of Electrical Engineers (MIEE); registered UK Engineering Council as incorporated engineer (IEng) *career* helped at weekends, holidays in parents' TV and retail business, designed UK military, civil air traffic control systems for clients in Africa, South America, UK, Middle East (work exhibited at Farnborough, Paris air shows) Radar Company 1980-86; designed airborne satellite telephone communications systems (work exhibited at Farnborough Air Show, BBC *Tomorrow's World*) blue chip communications company 1986-88; teaching (career break), head of environmental science Chessington Community College, head of physics, electronics Southborough School 1989-94; air traffic control systems for number of European Govts 1994-96; senior quality assurance manager, international company 1996-97; consultancy working for number of Blue Chip companies 1997- *party* joined 1991; having previously delivered *Focus*, Kingston upon Thames; mbr LP Exec, vice chair, ward election agent; mbr (Malden Manor ward) Kingston Council (from third place, took one of safest Tory seats in London) 1995, re-elected 1998, 2001, mbr environment, education, community services Cttees; standing deputy Heathrow Airport advisory Cttee; helped Liberal Party in Canadian general election 1997; deputy mayor Kingston upon Thames; Euro candidate London List 2004; representative ELDR Congress in Brussels 2004; mbr Aviation Policy Gp; mbr Air Transport Policy Working Gp; mbr PCA, ALDC, Association of Liberal Democrat Engineers and Scientists *special interests* community politics, environment, ecology, transport – especially air traffic; Europe *other mbrships* Association for Science Education; RSPB; Wildfowl and Wetlands Trust; Bat Conservation Trust; World Wide Fund for Nature; Friends of the Earth; Movement for Christian Democracy; past mbr Save British Science *recreations* helping arrange biennial family clan reunions in Ireland; learning languages (Greek, Hebrew, Gaelic); writing (book, educational software); ten pin bowling, judo, aikido, fencing, rowing, photography *publications* articles on engineering, teaching, alternative transport, regeneration *address* 83, Knightwood Crescent, New Malden, Surrey KT3 5JP *tel* 020 8949 1095 *e-mail* ianmcdonald@cix.co.uk or ian.mcdonald@libdems4london.org.uk

McGUINNESS, Justine *education* St Antony's-Leweston, Sherborne; Heythrop College, London Univ (BA, Philosophy and Theology) *career* Public Affairs consultant *party* mbr Federal Conference Cttee 2005-06; PCA Exec, Policy Officer 2005-06; mbr Tax Commission 2005-06; ELDR Council 2004-06; aide to Sir Menzies Campbell, 2006 Leadership campaign; PPC West Dorset 2005, Holborn & St Pancras 1997; mbr General Election planning cttee 1996-97; chair Women Liberal Democrats 1996-97; mbr LDiPR, Green Lib Dems *special interests* environment, corporate governance, rural affairs, economics, the Arts, political presentation, Australia, Africa *other mbrships* Institute of Directors, RSA, CPRE, Greenpeace and Friends of the Earth *recreations* murder mysteries, jam and chutney making, ballet, Art, travel *publications* various articles on environmental issues and Corporate Social Responsibility *address* c/o 3 Church Close, Bradford Peverell, Dorchester, Dorset DT2 9SA *e-mail* justine.mcguinness@googlemail.com

215

MACKIE of Benshie, Baron George Mackie: LLD 1982, Life Peer UK cr 1974, CBE 1971, DSO 1944, DFC 1944 *b* Jul 10, 1919 *education* Aberdeen GS; Aberdeen Univ *m* 1 Lindsay Lyall (died 1985) 3 *d* Lindsay (Mrs Rusbridger), Diana (Mrs Hope), Jeannie (Mrs Leigh) 1 *s* decd *m* 2 Jacqueline Rauche Lane 1988 *career* RAF Bomber Command WWII; farmer 1945-89; chairman Mackie Yule & Co, Caithness Glass Ltd 1966-85, Caithness Pottery Co 1975-84, Cotswold Wine Co. (UK) Ltd. 1983-85, Benshie Cattle Co Ltd, Land and Timber Services Ltd 1986- ; *party* PPC (Lib) Angus South 1959; Caithness & Sutherland 1964 (elected MP), 1966 (lost by 64 votes... to Bob Maclennan *qv*); Euro candidate Scotland NE 1979; chair Scottish Liberals 1965-70, 1986-88, president 1974-88 (became Lib Dems); cr Life Peer 1974; House of Lords spksn on devolution, agriculture, Scotland; mbr Parliamentary Assembly Council of Europe 1986-97, Western European Union 1986-97; president Scottish Liberal Party until 1988 (became SLD) *other interests* Rector Dundee Univ 1980-83, Hon LLD 1982 *recreations* walking the farm, classical music, reading *publications* Policy for Scottish Agriculture 1963 *clubs* Garrick, Farmers; RAF *style* Rt Hon Lord Mackie of Benshie, CBE, DSO, DFC *address* Benshire Cottage, Oathlow by Forfar, Angus DD8 3PQ *tel* 01307 850376

MACKINTOSH, Fred *b* Feb 21, 1970 London *m* 3 *ch education* Univ of Edinburgh (MA Geography; LLB Scots Law *career* advocate 2000- ; *party* mbr Edinburgh South, vice convenor 2001-04; GE agent Edinburgh South 1997; councillor, City of Edinburgh Council, Newington Ward; mbr Scottish Liberal Democrats Policy Cttee; cttee mbr, Association of Scottish Lib Dem Councillors 2000-04; vice convenor, Lothian Lib Dems 2000-02; vice convenor, Scottish Young Liberal Democrats 1990-92; PPC Livingston 1992, Midlothian 2005, Edinburgh South 2006- ; mbr ASLDC special interests transport, environment, school food, civil liberties, criminal law and parliamentary reform *LD quirks you'd like to tell us about?* Edinburgh South is the party's top target seat against Labour for the next general election *style* Councillor *address* c/o Edinburgh South Liberal Democrats, 4 Grange Road, Edinburgh EH9 1UH *tel* 0131 662 1513 home *e-mail* mail@fredmackintosh.com *web* www.fredmackintosh.com

MACLENNAN of Rogart, Baron Robert Adam Ross: Life Peer cr 2001, PC: Lords Spokesperson on Scotland *b* Glasgow Jun 26, 1936 *education* Glasgow Academy; Balliol College, Oxford (Law); Trinity College, Cambridge; Columbia Univ, New York *career* called to the Bar 1962; international lawyer; MP 1966-2001 *m* Helen 1 *s* 1 *d* 1 *ss party* Labour PPC Caithness and Sutherland 1966 (took seat from Liberal George Mackie *qv* by 64 votes; represented that and revised constituency Caithness, Sutherland and Easter Ross until 2001; parliamentary roles: PPS to Secy of State for Commonwealth Affairs 1967, opposition spksn Scottish Affairs, Defence 1970-74; Minister, Department of Prices and Consumer Protection (responsible for competition policy 1974: helped pilot Consumer Credit Act 1975); left Labour, founder mbr SDP, Mar 1981; elected Leader of SDP Aug 1987, successfully led negotiations to create Liberal Democrats, Mar 1988; co-author new party constitution; spokesman Home Affairs, National Heritage 1988-94; Constitutional Affairs, Culture 1994-2001; mbr Commons Public Accounts Cttee 1980-99; President of party 1994-98; co-chairman (with Robin Cook) Joint Consultative Cttee on constitutional reform 1997-2001; created life peer 2001; Lords spokesperson on Europe, party representative on European Convention *recreations* theatre, music, visual arts address House of Lord, London SW1A OPW *e-mail* bobmaclennan@cix.co.uk *web* www.scotlibdems.org.uk/lp/caitsuth/maclenmp.htm

McNALLY of BLACKPOOL, Baron Tom: Life Peer cr 1995: Leader of Liberal Democrats in the House of Lords *b* Feb 20, 1943 Thornton-Cleveleys *m* Juliet (nee Hutchinson) 2 *s* John and James 1 *d* Imogen *education* College of St. Joseph, Blackpool; Univ College London, BSc (Econ) in Economics and Social History, President of the Union, v-President NUS *career* Fabian Society Assistant General Secretary 1966-67; Labour Party researcher 1967-69; International Secy of Labour Party 1969-74; Political Adviser to Rt Hon James Callaghan MP at Foreign Office 1974-76, at 10 Downing Street 1976-79; Labour MP for Stockport South 1979-83; mbr Select Cttee on Industry and Trade; left Labour Party 1982 to join SDP; lost 1983 General Election as SDP candidate for Stockport; parliamentary adviser to GEC 1983-84; Director General of Retail Consortium 1985-87; Head of Public Affairs Hill and Knowlton 1987-93; Head of Public Affairs and then Vice Chairman WeberShandwick 1993-2004; *party* elected Leader of the Liberal Democrats in the House of Lords 2004 (Deputy Leader 2001-04); entered House of Lords as a Liberal Democrat peer 1995; mbr Federal Exec 1988-98, adviser to Rt. Hon. Paddy Ashdown 1988-98; Lords spokesman on Home Affairs, Broadcasting; president St. Albans LP 1991- ; president Eastern Region 2004- ; *special interests* Europe, trade, tourism *other mbrships* Fellow of Univ College London, Fellow of the Chartered Institute of Public Relations, Fellow of the Industry Parliament Trust; mbr of the Privy Council since 2005 *publications* pamphlets and articles; but no memoirs *recreations* watching sport; enjoying family *LD quirk* I love speaking at annual dinners – same jokes to a different audience *address* 30 Cunningham Avenue, St Albans, Herts AL1 1JL *tel* 01727 760689 home 020 7219 5443 Lords *e-mail* McNallyT@parliament.uk

MACPHERSON, Fraser *b* Feb 24, 1963 *education* Grove Academy Dundee; Univ of Dundee *career* development manager, Institute of Revenues, Rating & Valuation *party* mbr (Tay Bridges Ward) Dundee City Council 2001- ; education convener 2003-04; finance convener 2005- ; gp leader 2003- ; *special interests* local Govt; planning, education *other mbrships* Amnesty International, Liberal International, Association of Scottish Liberal Democrat Cllrs and Campaigners *address* 2a Argyle Street, Dundee DD4 7AL *tel* 01382 459378 home 01382 434985 business *fax* 01382 434120 *e-mail* fraser.macpherson@dundeecity.gov.uk

MADDICK, Henry *b* Jun 3, 1915 *m.* 1939 Winn Pollard (daughter of suffragette: splendid activist) widowed 2000 3 *s* 1 *d education* King Edward VIth Grammar School, Totnes 1923-31; UCSWE Exeter 1931-32); Keble College Oxford (MA Oxon) 1946-48 *career* bank clerk 1932-40; RAF 1940-46,commissioned 1941; Univ student 1946-48; lecturer, Wadham College Oxford 1948-50; lecturer Univ of Birmingham 1950; Founder Director, Institute Local Govt Studies (INLOGOV) 1964; 1968 - 1977 Professor Local Govt &Development Administration (first such Chair in Europe) 1968-77; Emeritus Professor 1977 *party* activist GE 1945; 1948 secy, North Oxford 1948; various offices Roseland Branch, Truro 1977-87; president , Truro LP 1983-86; president Devon & Cornwall Region 1985-86; treasurer, chairman Romsey and district branch, Romsey and Waterside LP 1987-96; president 1996- *special interests* local Govt structure, management; Third World local Govt and field administration; India *other mbrships* AIB, RAF Association *recreations* gardening; bowls; travel; theatre; reading **publications** *Democracy, Decentralisation and Development, Panchayati Raj-Indian Rural Local Govt*; plus numerous articles on British, foreign local Govt; contributions to international, UN seminars **address** Velwell, 18 The Harrage, Romsey, Hants SO51 8AE **tel** 01794 515884 **e-mail** henrymaddick@waitrose.com

MADDOCK, Baroness Diana: Life Peer cr 1997 *b* May 19, 1945 *m* Rt Hon Alan Beith MP *qv* 2 *d* **education** Brockenhurst Grammar School; Shenstone College, Worcestershire (teacher training); Portsmouth Polytechnic (post graduate) *career* teacher Southampton, Bournemouth, Stockholm; MP Christchurch 1993-97; mbr House of Lords 1997; previously Lords Spokesperson on Housing; former mbr Lords Select Cttee on European Union; joint chair All Party Parliamentary Univ Gp; mbr Cttee for Standards in Public Life; mbr Lords Select Cttee on Merits of Statutory Instruments *party* joined Liberal Party 1976; mbr Southampton City Council 1984-93, gp leader 1986-93; federal president 1998-2000 *special interests* housing; energy efficiency (successfully sponsored Home Energy Conservation Act as Private Mbrs Bill 1995), education, local govt, environment *other mbrships* president Micropower Council; president National Housing Forum; vice president National Housing Federation; National Liberal Club; National Trust; Electoral Reform Society *recreations* theatre, music, reading, travel *address* House of Lords, London SW1A 0PW *tel* 020 7219 1625 *e-mail* maddockd@parliament.uk

MAIN, James Russell BDS (Edin) DGDP RCS Eng *b* May 21, 1962 *education* King George V, Hong Kong; Morris Academy, Crieff; Edinburgh Univ (Bachelor of Dental Surgery: Royal Navy Scholarship; Diploma in General Dental Practice Royal College of Surgeons) *m* 1 *s* *career* Royal Navy (retired as surgeon lieutenant commander (D); honorary clinical tutor, Manchester Univ Dental School; general practice British West Indies, UK *party* joined 1988 in Edinburgh; former mbr Exec Chester, Cheadle, Isle of Wight; former mbr Exec EMLD and Western Regional Exec; former training officer EMLD; Chester City Council candidate 1992; PPC Bristol South 2001, and Bridgwater 2005 *special interests* foreign affairs, health, economy, ethnic issues *other mbrships* former mbr Chester & Ellesmere Port CHC; mbr board homeless charity, Taunton *publications* scientific papers; poetry *recreations* golf, sailing, Tai Chi, family *style* Dr James Main *address* Hollyspring, 14 Blackdown View, Curry Rivel, Langport, Somerset *tel* 0796 0011879 *e-mail* jrmain13@aol.com

MAKKI, Rabih *b* Jan 10, 1974 *m* Adele (nee Jones) 1 *s* Connor *education* Andrew Ewing School 1981-85; Cranford Community School 1985-92; Portsmouth Univ 1992-94 (HND Business & Finance); Wolverhampton Univ 1994-95 (BA Hons Business Enterprise) *career* senior sales Exec, Channel 4 Television 1995-present *party* joined Liberal Democrats 1991; mbr Thurrock LP Exec 2000-2003; Thurrock local election campaign co-coordinator 2001-2003; council candidate, Thurrock Stifford Ward 2001, 2002, Milton Keynes (Walton Park ward) 2006; mbr Milton Keynes LP Exec and Moving Forward Gp 2006- ; mbr Liberal Democrats in Business, ALDC and PCA *special interests* politics, electoral reform, Europe, transport, media, foreign affairs, business affairs *other mbrships* Election Reform Society; Britain in Europe; Republic; No2ID *recreations* tennis, gym, badminton, football, computing, music, reading, travel, TV *address* 34 Pascal Drive, Medbourne,

Milton Keynes MK5 6LS *tel* 01908 507 434 home 0207 306 8226 business *e-mail* r.makki@btinternet.com

MALCOLM, Gary *b* Nov 24, 1973 Wigan *single education* Sheffield Univ, BSc (Hons) Genetics; Lancaster Univ, Business Management *career* database administrator, London Business School 1999- ; market research exec, BMRB 1997-1999; public house manager, Bass 1996-1997 *party* PPC Ealing, Acton & Shepherds Bush 2005; Cllr Southfield ward, London Borough of Ealing 2002- ; Lib Dem Engineers & Scientists exec 2000-2005; Ealing, Acton & Shepherds Bush secy 2000; Ealing, Acton & Shepherds Bush mbrship secy 1999; Ealing, Acton & Shepherds Bush exec 1999- ; mbr Green Lib Dems, ALDC *other mbrships* Electoral Reform Society, AMICUS, Living Streets *special interests* transport, environment, consumer rights *LD quirk* probably only Lib Dem male PPC with long hair and less than 5ft 5in tall *recreations* cricket, touch rugby, football, card tricks, writing, pool *style* Cllr *address* 14a Twyford Crescent, Acton, London W3 9PP *tel* 020 7000 7386, 07813 205218 mobile *e-mail* gary.malcolm@ealing.gov.uk *website* www.ealinglibdems.org.uk

MAR AND KELLIE, 14 and 16 Earl of (Scotland 1565, 1619): James Thorne Erskine; DL (Clackmannanshire, 1991); also Lord Erskine (Scotland 1426), Baron Erskine of Dirletowne (as stated by *The Complete Peerage, Scotland 1604*), Viscount of Fentoun and Lord Dirletoun (Scotland 1916); Hereditary Keeper of Stirling Castle **cr Life Peer 2000: Baron Erskine of Alloa Tower** *b* Mar 10, 1949 *education* Eton, Moray House College of Education, Edinburgh (Dip Social Work, Dip Youth & Co Work); Inverness College (Certificate in Building) *m* Mary Irene 5 *sch* heir bro Hon Alexander David Erskine *career* estate manager; Pilot Officer RAuxAF Regt 1979-82, Flying Officer 1982-86 (Highland Squadron), mbr RNXS 1985-89; Page of Honour to HM The Queen 1962-63; community volunteer York 1967-68; community worker Craigmillar 1971-73; social worker: 1973-1982; supervisor Community by Offenders, Inverness 1983-87; mbr Visiting Cttee HM Young Offenders Institution, Glenochil; building technician 1989-91; project worker Central Intensive Probation Project Falkirk 1991-93; canoe and small boat-builder 1993-94; chair Strathclyde Tram Inquiry 1996; commissioner Burrell Collection (lending) Inquiry 1997; Liveryman Worshipful Co of Cordwainers *party* Scottish PPC Ochil 1999, mid-Scotland and Fife Regional List; took seat in House of Lords 1994 as Lib Dem peer; mbr Select Cttee on the Constitution 2001- , Religious Offences Select Cttee; assistant Whip; party spokesman on Scotland *recreations* open canoeing, Alloa Tower, cycling, gardening, railways *clubs* Farmers *style* The Earl of Mar and Kellie *address* House of Lords, London SW1A OPW

MARKS, Jonathan Clive QC *b* Oct 19, 1952 *m* Medina 3 *s* 3 *d education* Harrow School; Univ College, Oxford; Inns of Court School of Law *career* barrister, Inner Temple 1975; in practice general common, commercial law; visiting lecturer in Advocacy, Univ of Malaya, Kuala Lumpur 1985, 1989-91; Univ of Mauritius 1988; Sri Lanka Law College 1992; QC 1995 *party* founder mbr SDP 1981; deputy chair Kensington and Chelsea SDP 1981-83; European PPC Cornwall and Plymouth 1984; PPC Weston-Super-Mare 1983, Falmouth and Camborne 1987; mbr Lib Dem Cttee for England 1988-89; chair, Broadcasting Working Party 1989; chair Buckingham LP 2000-02; mbr Crime and Policing Working Party 2001-02, Children and Families Working Party, 2005-06, Royal Mail Working Party 2005-6; elected to Federal

Policy Cttee 2004 -; Interim Peers List; chair Lib Dem Lawyers Association 2001- ; moved conference policy motions on Legal Aid 1999, Human Rights 2003, a Right to Justice 2004 *special interests* human rights, home affairs *recreations* ski-ing, tennis, theatre, food, wine, travel *address* Tythrop Park, Kingsey, Bucks HP17 8LT *tel* 01844 291310 *fax* 01844 291102 *e-mail* jonathanmarksqc@btinternet.com *chambers* 4 Pump Court, London EC4Y 7AN *tel* 020 7842 5555 *fax* 0207 583 2036 *e-mail* jmarks@4pumpcourt.com

MARRITT, Francesca Jane *b* Mar 30, 1974 *partner* Stuart Marritt 1 *s* Luke 2 *d* Eleanor, Daisy *education* Blanchelande College, Guernsey 1985-92, MA French, Spanish, Jesus College, Cambridge 1993-97 *career* administrator, States of Guernsey, 1992-95; CUSU Welfare Officer 1995-96; admissions officer, Trinity Hall, Cambridge 1997; quality co-ordinator 1997-1998, project manager1998-2003, Cadcentre (now Aveva) Ltd; Liberal Democrats GBTF administrator 2003-06; acting Exec secy to chief Exec, October-Dec 2003; local development officer, Humberside Scout Council 2006- ; various professional qualifications including project management, facilitation, quality management systems development, internal auditing *party* joined 1998; campaign manager for Sal Brinton, SE Cambridgeshire 2001 (moved from third to second place); secy SE Cambridgeshire 2002, chair 2003; secy East of England Region 2003; English Council rep 2003; conference rep federal, regional conferences 2002- ; agent, Soham by election 2002 (moved from third to second place, losing by 15 votes); mbr Equal Opportunities Policy Audit Gp 2004- ; accredited party trainer *other mbrships* women's officer Jesus College, Cambridge 1994; CUSU Exec SWD Officer 1995; welfare officer (sabbatical) 1996; independent mbr NUS Cttees including Regional Exec 1995-96; National Women's Cttee 1996; SWD Exec 1996-97; secy to Board of MOSAIC (European Student Organisation) 1996-97; former chair, MOSAIC, NUS SWD conferences *special interests* equal opportunities, access work (within and outside politics); getting more women elected to Parliament; ensuring there are no barriers to anyone interested in a political career at any level; training (former NUS and workplace peer-gp trainer); quality, process management *recreations* spending time with family, Brownie Guider (since 1992), reading *address* 7Burgon Crescent, Winterton, N Lincs *tel* 01724 733594 *e-mail* fmarlow88@hotmail.com

MARSHALL, Paul *b* Aug 2, 1959 London *m* 2 *ch education* BA (Hons) History & Modern Languages, St John's College, Oxford University; MBA, INSEAD, Fontainebleau *career* Mercury Asset management plc, Director, Chief Investment Officer, Europe 1985-1996; Marshall Wace Asset Management Plc, Founder Partner and Chairman 1997- ; *party* research assistant to Rt Hon Charles Kennedy, MP 1985; Secy Putney SDP 1986; chairman, City Liberal Democrats 1993-99; chairman, Lib Dem Business Forum 1999- ; SDP/Liberal Alliance PPC for Fulham 1987; *other mbrships* chairman, Centreforum 2005- ; currently mbr Richmond Park LP *special interests* education (co-chairman ARK Education) *publications* editor, Market Failures Review 1998; co-editor, *The Orange Book* 2004; assistant editor, *The Social Democrat* 1986 *recreations* music, history, trees *e-mail* p.marshall@mwam.com

MARSOM, Victoria Fiona *b* Oct 16, 1973 *education* Teignmouth Community College 1985-92; Univ of Stirling 1992-1996; Univ of Illinois 1994-95 career taught English as a foreign language Japan, Australia, UK 1997-2000 *party* joined 1996; active in Teignbridge campaign 1997; agent for Oxford West & Abingdon LP 2000;

agent for Dr Evan Harris MP (3.9% swing Con to LD), sixteen candidates county council elections 2001; London Region Campaigns Officer 200; agent for Brent East Parliamentary By-Election (29% swing Lab to LD) 2003; agent London elections including mayor, London Assembly, Europe 2004; chair Agents & Organisers Association 2002- ; accredited party trainer *recreations* American politics, travel, spending time with friends, reading, trashy TV *address* 4 Cowley St, London SW1P 3NB *tel* 020 7227 1214 *e-mail* v.marsom@libdems.org.uk

MARTIN, Maureen BA MA *b* Saskatchewan, Canada Sept 17, 1945 *education* Univ of Saskatchewan (BA Economics & Political Science, 1966); Univ of Reading (MA 1968) *m* Stephen *qv* 2 *ss*1 *d career* programming, systems analysis, MIS, ICT training in local Govt, Plymouth Polytechnic, BBC Wood Norton, local colleges and independently *party* joined Liberals in Devon 1971; now Exec mbr Mid Worcestershire LP; agent 2001 general election s*pecial interests* education (governor, two local schools) *recreations* walking, swimming, travel, reading, theatre, music *address* Orchard House, Long Hyde Rd, South Littleton, Worcs WR11 8TH *tel* 01386 832806 *fax* 01386 832806 *e-mail* mmartin@lineone.net

MARTIN, Prof Stephen BSc, PhD, FIBiol, FI Env Sci, FIHort, FRSA *b* Feb 28, 1944 *education* High Pavement School, Nottingham; Nottingham Univ; Univ of Saskatchewan; Univ of Reading *m* Maureen *qv* 2 *ss* 1 *d career* principal lecturer, HoD Plymouth Polytechnic; HMI for Education; chief Exec, Countec Ltd; director of learning Forum for the Future; independent consultant *party* former chair Mid Worcestershire LP; Euro candidate 1999; PPC Tewkesbury 2001 *special interests* education policy, transport, health, environment, sustainable development (former trustee WWF; mbr of Toyne Cttee; council mbr Institution of Environmental Sciences; visiting professor, Open Univ *recreations* theatre, walking (mbr Ramblers, YHA), gardening, cycling *style* Dr Stephen Martin *address* Orchard House, Long Hyde Rd, South Littleton, Worcs. WR11 8TH *tel* 01386 832806 *fax* 01386 832806 *e-mail* esm@esmartin.demon.co.uk

MATHON, Dominic *b* Oct 7, 1973 *education* Univ College School; Christ Church, Oxford *career* Chartered Accountant 1997; corporate tax manager (PricewaterhouseCoopers, NatWest, Sema Plc, Atos, Schlumberger, Atos Origin) 1994- *party* joined 1991; agent, Islington Borough 1999-2001; Islington LP Exec 1999-2001, chair 2002-04; president 2005-06, London Region Exec 2006 *special interests* election campaigns, PR, EU affairs, devolution, Central/Eastern Europe, fiscal policy *other mbrships* Electoral Reform Society, European Movement, Charter 88, LDEG, Lib Dem History Gp *recreations* leaflet delivery; armchair sportsman, lapsed cellist *address* Tower Cottage, Rear of 12 Culvers Ave, Carshalton SM5 2BS *tel* 07949 086 044 *e-mail* dominicmathon@hotmail.com

MAYER, Andy *b* Nov 21, 1974 Birmingham *ptnr* Helen Jardine-Brown *ch* none *education* King Edward's, Birmingham, Brasenose College Oxford (BA Politics, Philosophy & Economics) *career* consultant, Accenture 1997-99; General Secy, Pro Euro Conservative Party 1999; New Media Strategist, Wheel 2000-01, Netpoll 2001-02; Global Corporate Intelligence Manager, NOP Research Group 2002-05; Global Future Trends Manager, BP International Ltd 2005 *party* mbr North Southwark & Bermondsey, London; participant in Tax Commission, Trade Union policy working gp, andBusiness Tax working gp; contributor, Meeting the Challenge; formerly

Director of Liberal Future, founder yes-campaign.com, Euro Information Network; candidate European Parliament 1999, Yorkshire & Humberside, Southwark Council, Faraday Ward 2005; mbr PCA, ALDC, Green Liberal Democrats, LDEG, Friends of LDYS *other mbrshps* Centre Forum, Fabian Society (associate), World Future Society special interests future of liberalism, tax, business, environment *publications* Mapping the Liberal Future, Reform Journal, Challenge, Liberator, Open Democracy *recreations* running, photography, poker *address* 37 Tyers Estate, Bermondsey Street, London, SE1 3JG *tel* 020 7407 2312, 079 7342 4274 mobile *e-mail* andymayer@f2s.com

MAXFIELD, Edward Robert *b* May 20, 1967 *m* Daniela *1 d* (Hannah) 1 *s* (William) both from first marriage *education* De Aston School, Market Rasen, Lincs, 1978-85; Univ of East Anglia 1985-88 (BA Hons, Economic and Social Studies); Birmingham Univ (MA in European Studies); currently studying part-time for doctorate at Sussex Univ *career* civil servant 1988-96; tax consultant: (Coopers & Lybrand, KPMG Polska (Poland), Price Waterhouse Coopers Romania) 1996-2000; campaign manager, North Norfolk Lib Dems 2000-01; training consultant, BPP International (Bucharest) 2001; East Midlands Campaigns Officer, Lib Dems 2002-03; Hants & Wight campaigns officer, Liberal Democrats Jan 2004- ; *party* joined Liberal Party 1983, aged 16; serial election agent; various local party offices held; mbr East Midlands regional Exec *special interests* campaigning, Eastern Europe, fading attachment to indirect tax policy *other mbrships* Chartered Tax Adviser *recreations* beating Tories, watching Norwich City *address* 34 Ellis Close, Old Coulsdon, Surrey CR5 1BQ *tel* 0208 407 3437 *e-mail* maxfield@cix.co.uk

EMERSON, Merlene Toh *b* Oct 11, 1960 Singapore *m* 3 *s education* Singapore Chinese Girls School, Kings College, Univ of London (LL.B.), Clare Hall, Univ of Cambridge, (LL.M.) *career* former Solicitor at firm in City of London and Partner at law firm in Singapore; C.E.D.R. accredited mediator; Director of international property and investment company *party* mbr Twickenham & Richmond (London); currently LD Council Gp Secy, Richmond Council; candidate in May 2006 local elections for Barnes ward; exec post on local Housing Association and Youth Group *other mbrships* Law Society (Eng & Wales), Chinese Liberal Democrats, Chinese in Britain Forum, Royal Commonwealth Club, UN Association, LDEG *special interests* diversity within the party, Europe, international development *recreations* yoga (B.W.Y. diploma), learning French, volunteer for Save the Children and C.A.L.M. *quirk* equality issues *style* Ms *address* 8 Lonsdale Road, Barnes, London SW13 9EB tel 07808480550 *e-mail* merle@markemerson.net

METHUEN, Baron: 7th Baron Methuen (Robert) *b* Jul 22, 1931 *education* Shrewsbury School; Trinity College, Cambridge (BA in engineering 1957) *m* 1958 (dis) 2 *d* m2 1994 *career* design engineer Westinghouse Brake and Signal Company 1957-67; computer systems engineer IBM UK Ltd.1968-75, Rolls Royce plc 1975-94; entered the House of Lords 1997, elected hereditary peer 1999 *party* active mbr of Lords' Cttees covering energy, industry, science & technology, micro-processing innovation, Regional Development Agencies and transport (including Channel Tunnel Rail Link, aircraft cabin environment); mbr Lords Cttees on office administration & works; offices, library and computers sub-Cttee *other interests* patron Lady Margaret Hungerford Charity *recreations* walking, horse trekking, industrial archaeology *address* House of Lords, London SW1A 0PW

MICHIE, Baroness Ray: Life Peer cr 2001 *b* Scotland Feb 1934, daughter of late Lord and Lady Bannerman of Kildonan *m* (to consultant physician) 3 *d education* Aberdeen High School for Girls; Lansdowne House School, Edinburgh; Edinburgh College of Speech Therapy career area speech therapist Argyll and Clyde Health Board; MP 1987-2001; mbr House of Lords 2001- *party* PPC 1997, 1983, 1987 (elected) re-elected 1992, 1997 (stood down 2001); mbr House of Commons Select Cttee on Scottish Affairs 1992-97; mbr Chairman's Panel 1997, joint vice-chair Parliamentary Gp on Whisky Industry; former vice-chair Scottish Liberal Party, chair Scottish Liberal Democrats 1991-93; spokesperson on Scottish Affairs (strong advocate of Home Rule for Scotland, promotion of Gaelic language); mbr of the House of Lords 2001, first peer to pledge oath of allegiance in Gaelic *other mbrships* An comunn Gaidhealach, NFU Scotland , Scottish Crofters Union former vice-president Royal College of Speech and Language therapists; honorary associate National Council of Women of Great Britain; president Clyde Fishermen's Association *recreations* golf, swimming, gardening, watching rugby (father played 37 consecutive games for Scotland) *address* House of Lords, London SW1A 0PW

MILLARD, Brian John *b* Nov, 17 1937 Cardiff *m* Sandra Rae nee Colebrook, Jun 11 June, 1966, 2 *s education* Lewis School, Pengam, S.Wales, Sheffield Univ (BSc (Hons) Chemistry, PhD) *career* research chemist, Fisons Pharmaceuticals Ltd 1962-63; post-doctoral research, Univ of Liverpool 1963-1966; lecturer, Liverpool College of Technology 1966-67; lecturer, School of Pharmacy, Univ of London 1967-1979; visiting scientist, FDA, Washington DC 1979-80; senior lecturer, Institute of Neurology, Univ of London 1980-81; MD, Qudos Publications Ltd 1985- ; *party* mbr Cheadle LP Cllr and Leader Stockport Metropolitan Borough Council 2005- ; *special interests* economics, environmental issues publications Quantitative Mass Spectrometry (Heyden 1979), Stocks and Shares Simplified (Heyden, 1981), Traded Options Simplified (Qudos, Wiley 1988), Profitable Charting Techniques (Qudos, Wiley 1989, Channel Analysis (Qudos, Wiley 1991), Channels and Cycles (Trader's Press, 2002) *recreations* watching football and rugby, fine wine and food, travel *style* Cllr *address* 16 Queensgate, Bramhall, Stockport, Cheshire SK7 1JT *tel* 0161 439 3926 home 0161 474 3302 work *fax* 0161 474 3308 *e-mail* cllr.brian.millard@stockport.gov.uk

MILLER, John Christopher Chippendale Deputy Director of Campaigns (South West) *b* July 20, 1948 *m* 1 Melissa Brooks (divorced 1977) *m* 2 Susan Taylor (divorced 1997) 2 d Madeleine, Charlotte (deceased) *m* 3 Pascale Jenkins 2005 *education* Emanuel School, London; Middlesex Univ (MA History of Design) *career* lecturing in design, marketing, media planning in FE college; publicity and public relations manager, later marketing director general and educational publishers, London, Devon; owner two successful bookshops in West Country 1979-89 Council group support officer ALDC 1997-2004; Deputy Director of Campaigns (South West)2004- ; *party* joined Liberals 1979; parish councillor 1981, chair of Parish 1982; mbr South Somerset DC 1991-2003, Deputy Leader in 1992, Leader of Council 1993-96, Chair Policy and Resources, Chair of Arts and Leisure 1993-1996; co-ordinated DC election in 1995 (Lib Dem majority increased from 41 to 46 out of 60), decentralised council services, budgets to four area Cttees; Deputy Leader 1999,

Exec Mbr for Arts and Leisure 1999-2003; Mbr Local Government Association Arts Policy Exec 2000-2003; Party Arts Policy working Groups; mbr Yeovil exec, secy, vice-chair Yeovil Constituency 91-96; mbr English Council 1995; Agent/organiser for Paddy Ashdown in Yeovil 1991-2; PPC Westbury 1997 (halved Tory majority to 6,000); ALDC Council Support Officer 1997 with responsibility for political and campaign advice to Lib Dem Council Groups nationally and as part of the ALDC training team at Federal and regional conferences; Deputy Director of Campaigns (South West) for region from Gloucester to Cornwall *special interests* arts in rural areas, ecological design and planning, Europe (lived in France for two years 1989-91) *other mbrships* former Governor Yeovil FE College and local secondary school; director South West Arts; Arts Council Regional Arts Board 1997-2002 *publications* A Councillor's Handbook Volumes 1, 2 (co-author); Thriving in the Balance-Making the most of NOC; Modernisation in Practice-Cabinets and Scrutiny; Liberal Democracy in Action; co-author Read All About it! - a Councillor's Guide to Media Relations; contributor Winning Elections, Grassroots Campaigner *recreations* reading, sketching, classic cars, jazz, Dutch barges in France *address* 9 Quaperlake Street, Bruton, Somerset BA10 0HF *tel/fax* 01749 812530 mobile 07768 452062 *e-mail* johnmiller@cix.co.uk

MILLER of Chilthorne Domer, Baroness (Sue): Lords Spokesperson on Environment, Food and Rural Affairs *b* Jan 1, 1954 *m* Humphrey Temperley 2 *ss* 2 *d* (one deceased) 1 *sd education* Sidcot School; Oxford Polytechnic *career* publishing, David & Charles, Weidenfeld & Nicolson, Penguin; book-selling PR consultancy *party* joined 1985; district Cllr South Somerset, area chair, Leader of Council 1991-98; Somerset County Cllr 1997- ; mbr FPC 2004; Lords spokesman Agriculture Rural Affairs 1998-2002, Environment, Food and Rural Affairs 2002- *special interests* environment, oceans, street children *other mbrships* Wildlife Trust, Baby Milk Action, Fawcett Society, WLD *recreations* walking, sailing gardening reading *e-mail* millers@parliament.uk

MOLLER, Knud Valdemar *b* May 27, 1942 *education* Birmingham Polytechnic (diploma, town planning) 1981; Univ of Keele (MA Geography) *career* senior planning officer, City of Stoke-on-Trent 1974-2002; principal analyst and information officer 2002- *party* mbr Radikale Venstre (Danish Social Liberal Party), Radikal Ungdom (youth section) 1969-74; joined Liberals in Stoke-on-Trent 1974-83, various offices including secy, treasurer; Newcastle-under-Lyme LP 1983-97, various offices including secy, treasurer and chair; Congleton LP 1997- , treasurer 2004- ; vice-chair Odd Rode-Smallwood branch; chair Odd Rode-Smallwood PC 2003-04 *other mbrships* Royal Statistical Society; secy Local Authorities Research and Intelligence Association *recreations* antiques, art, cooking, gardening, nature, music *address* 1 South Street, Mow Cop, Stoke-on-Trent ST7 4NR *tel* 01782 518074 home 01782 232347 business *e-mail* moller@knud2705.fsnet.co.uk

MOON, Christian *b* Oct 6, 1965 *education* Monmouth School 1977-84; Brasenose College, Oxford (BA Hons Modern History) 1984-87 *career* Liberal Democrat Deputy Head of Policy and Research 2006- ; Head of Policy Unit, Liberal Democrat HQ 1999-2006; deputy director Policy and Research 1998-99; parliamentary researcher to David Heath MP 1997-98; organiser, Graham Watson MEP 1995-97 *party* joined 1990; secy Monmouth LP 1994-95; local candidate, agent Monmouthshire 1995; candidate LB Wandsworth 2002; mbr London Region selection panel for 2004 European elections *special interests* environment, health, Europe *address* 130 Beechcroft Road, London SW17 7DA *tel* 020 7227 1386 *fax* 020 7799 2170 *e-mail* c.moon@libdems.org.uk

MOORE, Ann DL (East Sussex 1996) *m* Richard Moore 1955 *qv* 1 *s* Charles 2 *d* Charlotte, Rowan *party* Liberal, Liberal Democrat county cllr East Sussex 1973-77, 1981-97; gp leader 1974-77; deputy leader 1977-87; member, gp leader Rother DC 1977-87; chair Liberal Part Envireonment Panel 1977-83; chair Liberal Summer School cttee 1989-2001; agent for husband's GEs October 1974, 1979, Euro election 1979 *address* Goldsmiths, Whatlington, Battle TB33 0NX

MOORE, Michael MP (Berwickshire, Roxburgh & Selkirk maj: 5,901**) Shadow Foreign Secy; Deputy Leader, Scottish Liberal Democrats** *b* Jun 3, 1965 *education* Strathallan School, Perthshire; Jedburgh Grammar School; Edinburgh Univ (MA Hons Politics & Modern History 1987) *career/party* research assistant Archy Kirkwood MP 1987-88; Scottish Chartered Accountant, Coopers & Lybrand, Edinburgh 1988-97; elected MP Tweeddale, Ettrick & Lauderdale 1997, re-elected 2001; elected MP Berwickshire, Roxburgh & Selkirk 2005; Scottish Party Campaigns Chair 1998-2003; deputy leader, Scottish Liberal Democrats 2002- ; Parliamentary Transport Spokesperson 1999-2001, deputy Foreign Affairs Spokesperson 2001-03; Shadow Minister for Foreign Affairs Oct 2003-05; mbr Scottish Affairs Select Cttee 1997-99; vice-chair All Party Rail Gp; treasurer All Party Textiles Gp; vice-chair All Party Corporate Social Responsibility Gp; Council Mbr, Royal Institute of International Affairs 2004- ; Parliamentary Visiting Fellow, St. Antony's College, Oxford, 2003-04; former governor, vice-chair, Westminster Foundation for Democracy *other mbrships* Amnesty International *recreations* jazz, hill-walking, supporting local rugby teams *address* House of Commons, London, SW1A 0AA *tel* 020 7219 2236 *fax* 020 7219 0263 *constituency* 11 Island Street, Galashiels TD1 1NZ *tel* 01896 663650 *fax* 01896 663655

MOORE, Richard *b* 1931 *education* Cambridge Univ (president Univ Liberal Club 1954, president Cambridge Union 1955) *career* journalist: leader writer *News Chronicle* 1956-60; secy-general Liberal International 1961-64, 1975-78 (part-time); political officer Liberal Party Organisation 1965-66; secy Liberal peers 1966-67; political secy Jeremy Thorpe 19678-74; assistant to British Liberal MEPs 1974-79; political adviser Liberal Gp (ELDR) in European Parliament 1979-96 *party* joined Liberals 1951; National chair Union of Liberal Students (then UULS) 1954-55; PPC Tavistock 1955, 1959, Cambridgeshire 1961 (by-electon), 1964, North Antrim 1966, 1970 (against Rev Ian Paisley), North Norfolk 1974 (both elections), Rye 1979, Euro elections East Sussex 1979, Somerset and West Dorset 1984; chair Liberal European Gp (now LDEG) 1970-75; chair Liberal International British Gp 1997-2000; elected patron Liberal International at Dakaar Congress 2003; mbr Liberal Summer School Cttee (since 1959; attended every autumn conference since 1953, spoken at all except 2002; initiated (with French, German and Italian colleagues) Federation of Liberal Parties to contest Euro elections; mbr cttee to draft ELDR constitution, declaration of aims for founding Congress Stuttgart 1976 *address* Bankside, Battle, Sussex TN33 0JS *tel* 01424 774021

MUGHAL, Fiyaz: Chair Ethnic Minority Liberal Democrats *b* Sept 14, 1971 *education* Univ of North London (MBA Exec, MA Education); Univ College

London (BSc Hons); Latymer School, London; St Ignatius College, London *career* lecturer, Oxford College of Further Education 1999- ; social policy manager National Association of Citizens Advice Bureaux 1996-99; deputy manager Education Service, Haringey Council 1995-96 *party* mbr Oxford City Council 2002- ; chair Community Scrutiny Cttee 2002-03, lead mbr on Revenues and Benefits 2003- ; Local Govt Association Social Inclusion Exec mbr 2003- , mbr Community Cohesion Working Gp, Joint Negotiating Cttee for Youth Workers, Cttee on Prostitution; mbr Ethnic Minority Liberal Democrats, campaigns co-ordinator 2000-01, chair 2002- ; mbr Race Equality Advisory Gp 2001-03; chair Black Leadership Network, Oxford; chair Oxford Neve Shalom Wahat-Al-Salaam Middle East Peace Gp; prospective PPC, London Bethnal Green and Bow *other mbrships* governor Oxford Community School 2002- , Earlham Primary School 2003- *special interests* developing new, innovative social capital projects; strategic project based partnerships; new social mechanisms to enhance community cohesion; race, changes in migrant gps in 21st century UK; European Union and impact of asylum; European legislation and its impact on minority ethnic gps; minority faiths in multi-cultural Britain *address* 53 Russell Avenue, Wood Green, London N22 6QB *tel* 0793 960 9481 *e-mail* fiyaz@fiyaz.freeserve.co.uk

MULHOLLAND, Gregory Thomas (Greg) MP (Leeds NW maj:1,877) *b* Aug 31, 1970 *m* Raegan Hatton, Aug 13, 2004 1 *d* Isabel b 2005 *education* St Ambrose College, Hale Barns; York Univ (BA politics, MA public administration and public policy) *career* sales promotion, events in England, Scotland for several leading marketing agencies 1997-2002; Leeds City Councillor 2003-05; elected MP for Leeds NW May 2005 *party* joined 2000 (having been activist previously); mbr exec Edinburgh Central LP 2001; Moortown ward exec 2001-02; Leeds NW exec 2002, vice chair 2003; selected PPC Leeds NW Dec 2002; chair campaign, development team 2003- ; elected Leeds City Council (Headingley ward) 2003; mbr International Development working party 2002-04; elected MP Leeds NW 2005; mbr All Party Work and Pensions Cttee *special interests* development issues (campaigner and schools volunteer for CAFOD, TIDAL) *other mbrships* CAFOD, Trade Injustice Debt Action Leeds (TIDAL), Amnesty International, Long Distance Walkers Association (LDWA), CAMRA *recreations* hill-walking, long distance walking, skiing, rugby league, football (Middlesbrough fan) real ale and pubs, spending spare time with wife and daughter *address* 427 Otley Road, Leeds LS16 6AJ *tel* 0113 2266519 *e-mail* info@gregmulholland.org

MUNRO, John Farquhar MSP (Ross, Skye and Inverness West) Scottish Spkspn Highlands, Islands and Gaelic Issues *b* Aug 26, 1934 *education* Plockton High School; Merchant Marine College *m* 1 *s* 1 *d party* elected Scottish Parliament 1999; Scottish Spkspn on Gaelic Issues and Forestry 2001- 03; spkspn on Highlands and Islandsand Gaelic 1999- ; spkspn on Transport and Gaelic Nov 2000-1; former spkspn for Education, Heritage, Gaelic, Culture; mbr, Public Petitions Cttee; substitute mbr Local Govt and Transport Cttee; former gp leader, chair Highland Council; mbr Roads and Transport Cttee; former chair, Highland Council Rail Network Partnership *other interests* board mbr, Highland Opportunity Ltd, Skye and Lochalsh Enterprise; chair, Caledonian MacBrayne Shipping Service Advisory Cttee; v chair, Skye Mod Cttee; trustee, Skye Gaelic College *recreations* sailing, fishing *address* Scottish Parliament, Edinburgh EH99 1SP *tel* 0131 348 5790; 1A

Montague Row, Inverness, IV3 5DX 01436 714377 *e-mail*
john.munro.msp@scottish.parliament.uk

MUNT, Tessa J: Deputy Chair, PCA 2005- ; *b* Oct 16, 1959 Surrey *m* Martin 1 *sd*
Sarahjane 1 *d* Emma 1 *s* Harry *education* convent, girls' grammar school,
independent school, college *career* currently London law firm; previously sales,
marketing, personnel and training, Social Services manager, teacher, lecturer FE
college *party* PPC South Suffolk 2001, Ipswich by-election Nov 2001, Wells 2005;
mbr Federal Exec 2005 - ; party trainer; PCA Vice Chair 2002-05 *other mbrships*
vice-chair Mid Somerset CND; Greenpeace, Friends of the Earth, Environmental
Investigation Agency, Amnesty International; Eastern region advisory panel National
Lottery Charities Board 1994-99; Childline; Domestic Violence Fora; Suffolk branch
of Families Need Fathers *recreations* radio, listening to music, East African history;
reading *address* Yarrow Orchard, Yarrow Road, Mark, Somerset TA9 4LW *tel*
07714 599669 *e-mail* tessa@tessa4wells.com

MURPHY, Laura Jane *b* Feb 2, 1956 *m* Steve *education* Portsmouth Southern
Grammar School for Girls; various FE colleges, Open Univ; Brighton Univ (MBA)
2000; Sussex Downs College (teaching qualification, 7407 FE) 2003 *career* IBM,
Portsmouth; NRPB Oxfordshire; after family break re-entered employment as
volunteer advocate for various health, education and youth charities; child-protection
East Sussex Social Services 1993; project manager (programme for people with
disability) East Sussex Employment Services; project manager (training programme
for SMEs) Sussex Downs College; management training, consultancy; trustee
Hailsham CAB, vice-chair 2000-03; board mbr Freedom Leisure 2003- *party* joined
1994; mbr Hailsham town council 1995-99 (stood down), Wealden DC 1995, re-
elected 1999, 2003 , chair Economic Review Cttee; chair, Wealden LP 2000-03
special interests equal opportunities, disability rights, education, employment *other
mbrships* MCMI, Licentiate mbr CIPD *recreations* theatre, music, travel, keeps fit
(and sane) through body combat *address* 2 Old Orchard Place, Hailsham, E Sussex
BN27 3HY *e-mail* sja.murphy@virgin.net

MURRAY, David RV C.Eng MIEE DMS DipM MCIM *b* Mar 27, 1939
education Culford School, Bury St Edmunds (1949-57); RAF Ground Radar: 61
Signals Unit (1958-60); Cambridgeshire College of Arts & Technology (1965-72);
Wolverhampton Polytechnic (1987-89) *career* part-time lecturer Maths (Engineering
& Construction); worked in Stevenage (1974-76), EMI Medical on CT scanners
(1976-79); founder MD Meditech Engineering Ltd (1979-86); new product
development (1986); business advisory role/consultancy (1992-2002) *party* joined
Cambridge Liberal Party 1967; local council candidate, St Matthew's Ward 1967;
launched City Centre Circular 1968; candidate, Market Ward 1968, 69, 70 (elected
by 5 votes a month later; in same ward, Chris Bradford elected with over 300 votes);
press officer, secy, chair at various times; Eastern Region industrial relations
spokesman during Barbara Castle's In place of Strife and Tom Jackson's PO strike;
helped Stafford LP 1990-92; joined Wolverhampton LP 1993; candidate St Peters
Ward 1994, 1995; candidate Shropshire CC elections 1997, 2001; secy Wrekin &
Telford LP 1997-98; candidate Albrighton parish council by-election 1998, elected
1999, 2003; candidate Bridgnorth District Council 1999, elected 2003; president
Wrekin & Telford LibDems 2003- , chair 2004- ; candidate for Shropshire CC
elections 2005 *other interests* manufacturing, engineering in schools, planning,

housing *recreations* DIY, YHA, walking, travel, classical music *address* 74 Ashgrove, Albrighton, Wolverhampton WV7 3QX *e-mail* drvmurray@hotmail.com

MURRAY, James *b* Dec 13, 1950 *m* Sara (nee Rowan) 1988 2 *s* George, Richard *education* St Matthews Primary, Liverpool; St Bonaventures Grammar, Liverpool; De La Salle Sixth Form, Liverpool; Leeds Univ (BSc Pure Chemistry - terrible degree mark, but caroused a lot while drinking a lot of beer); Law Society Solicitors Qualifying Exams Part I in 1979, Part II 1980 (3 distinctions, second in country out of 5,000-plus candidates *and* without attending formal law course *and* while working full time as social worker *and* taking only 20 months from start to finish for both parts *and* still managing to carouse a lot *and* drink a lot of beer); Nottingham Law School (LLM Advanced Litigation)1999 *career* teacher, English as Foreign Language, Iran 1970; pharmaceutical salesman 1973, community worker 1974; generic social worker 1975; welfare rights officer 1979, Legal Articles 1980-82; 1983 bar steward Liberal Club1983; solicitor 1984- ; own firm, James Murray Solicitors1991, now senior of five partners, staff of sixty, biggest of type Merseyside *party* joined Liverpool Clubmoor Liberals 1982; Liverpool Crosby 1989; Exec mbr 1980s; PPC North Knowsley (2,500 votes) 1992, Liverpool Bootle (not much better but beat Tory into third place) 2001; PPC Liverpool Crosby *special interests* drug related crime, police misconduct *other mbrships* Crosby Speakers Club, Liberty, school governor *recreations* none: no time to spare *address* 9 Far Moss Road, Crosby Merseyside L23 8TG *tel* 0151 024 9020 home 0151 933 3333 business *fax* 0151 933 3343 *e-mail* jamesmurray@mersinet.co.uk

N

NAPIER, Sir Oliver John kt (1985) *b* Jul 11, 1935 *education* St Malachys College Belfast; Queen's Univ Belfast (LLB) *m* 1961, Kathleen Brigid 3 *s* James, John, Kevin 5 *d* Brigid, Veronica, Nuala, Emma, Mary-Jo *career* solicitor, mbr Board of Examiners Law Society of NI 1964-68; Minister of Law Reform NI Exec 1973-74 *party* Alliance Party of Northern Ireland: mbr Belfast City Council 1977-89; NI Assembly 1973-74, 1982-86; NI Constitutional Convention 1975-76, Leader Alliance Party 1973-84; chair Standing Advisory Commission on Human Rights 1982-92; elected to NI Forum 1996; mbr Alliance Team in inter-party peace talks 1996-98; negotiator *Good Friday Agreement recreations* gardening *clubs* Northern Law *style* Sir Oliver Napier *address* Glenlyon, Victoria Road, Holywood, Co Down, NI *tel* 012317 5986; Napier & Sons Solicitors, 1/9 Castle Arcade, High Street, Belfast *tel* 028 90244602

NATION, David John *b* Nov 5, 1944 *m* Mary (solicitor, former Lib Dem Cllr) 4 *d* (two from previous marriage) *education* Heles GS, Exeter; Bristol Univ *career* 20 years as qualified insurance technician, General Accident then Barclays Bank; after seven years as magistrate retrained as probation officer 1984; pioneered schemes bringing offenders face-to-face with victims; established one of country's most successful neighbourhood dispute-resolution services, Plymouth 1992-2002; full-time politics 2002- *party* joined Liberals 1974; held most LP positions including GE agent; Exeter city Cllr 1980-84; Mid Devon district Cllr 1995- ; deputy gp leader; mbr Crediton TC 1999- PPC North Swindon 2001; PPC Tiverton and Honiton 2003 *special interests* environment, housing, unemployed, young people *other mbrships* Dartmoor Preservation Association, European Movement, Action for South Africa *recreations* gardening, walking on Dartmoor, vintage cars, local and family history *publications* various in social work , criminal justice journals *address* 3 George Hill, Crediton, Devon, EX17 2DT *tel/fax* 01363 774441 *e-mail* nation@cix.co.uk

NEAL, Jon *b* Nov 12, 1975 *education* Kesgrave High School, Suffolk; Farlingaye Sixth Form, Woodbridge, Suffolk; Univ of Hull, Dept of Politics *career* marketing and PR, Senior Press Officer, international food and grocery think tank IGD 2005- ; PR manager, Business Link South Yorkshire 2002-05; communications officer, Diana Wallis MEP 1999-2002; research assistant (work placement) Paul Keetch MP 1997-98 *party* joined late 80s; twice PPC Haltemprice & Howden against David Davis; former Cllr, Howden, East Riding of Yorkshire Council (Unitary Authority); previously office-holder LDYS; accredited trainer *special interests* PR and communications, food, sport, heritage *other mbrships* The Ramblers Association; English Heritage, *Blue Peter* badge-holder *recreations* film, cinema, football (Spurs fan), reading (*Harry Potter, His Dark Materials, LOTR*) *publications* co-author *Mr Blair's Loyal Opposition? The Liberal Democrats in Parliament* published in *British Elections & Parties Review Vol 10*, 2000 *address* 60 Athelstan Walk South, Welwyn Garden City, Herts AL7 3SJ *tel* 01707 372878, 07958 703720 mobile *e-mail* jon_neal@yahoo.com

NEUBERGER, Rabbi Dame Julia Babbette Sarah: Life Peer cr 2004 *b* Feb 27, 1950 *m* Anthony John Neuberger 1 *s* Matthew 1 *d* Harriet *education* South Hampstead School for Girls; Newman College, Cambridge; Leo Baeck College, London *career* rabbi South London Liberal Synagogue 1977-89; visiting fellow King's Fund Institute 1989-91; visiting, Harkness Fellow, Harvard Medical School 1991-92; chair Camden, Islington Community Health Services NHS Trust 1982-97; chief Exec The King's Fund 1997- ; fellow King's Fund College 1992-97; chancellor Univ of Ulster 1994-2000; trustee Imperial War Museum 1999- ; mbr Human Fertilisation and Embryology Authority 1990-95; BMA Ethics Cttee 1992-94; General Medical Council 1993- ; Medical Research Council 1995-2000; Cttee on Standards in Public Life 2001- ; Civil Service Commissioner 2001- ; Chair of Commission on Future of Volunteering 2005- ; honorary doctorates universities of Liverpool, Humberside, Ulster, Stirling, Oxford Brookes, Teesside, Nottingham, Queen's Belfast and the Open Univ; honorary fellow Mansfield College, Oxford 1997; honorary FCGI 1998 *party* mbr SDP 100 1981; founder mbr SDP, founder mbr Liberal Democrats *special interests* community regeneration, health, religion, poverty *publications* *The Moral State we're in* 2005; *Rebuilding Trust in Healthcare* (foreword) 2003; *Hidden Assets: Values and Decision-making in the NHS* (ed with Bill New) 2002; *Dying Well: a guide to enabling a good death* (Hochland and Hochland) 1999; *On Being Jewish* (Heinemann) 1995, 1996; *Caring for Dying Patients of Different Faiths* (Lisa Sainsbury Foundation) 1986, (Mosby) 1994, (Radcliffe Medical) 2004; *The Things That Matter: An Anthology of Women's Spiritual Poetry* (Kyle Cathic) 1993; *Ethics and Healthcare: Research Ethics Cttees in the UK* (King's Fund Institute) 1992; *Whatever Happened to Women?* (Kyle Cathic) 1991; *A Necessary End* ed with John White (Macmillan) 1991; *Days of*

Decision series of four current affairs essays: edited with introductions (Macmillan) 1987; *The Story of Judaism* (for children: Dinosaur/Collins) 1987 *recreations* swimming, children *address* House of Lords, London SW 1A 0AA

NEWBY, Lord Dick: OBE, Life Peer cr 1997: Lords Spokesperson on the Treasury *b* Feb 14, 1953 *education* Rothwell GS; St Catherine's College, Oxford (MA) *m* 1978 Ailsa Ballantyne Thomson (vicar) 2 *s career* HM Customs and Excise administration trainee 1974, private secy to Permanent Secy 1977-79, principal, Planning Unit 1979-81; Secy SDP Parliamentary Cttee 1981 joined SDP HQ staff 1981; National Secy 1983-88; director, corporate affairs 1991; Rosehaugh plc; director Matrix Communications Consultancy 1992-9; Flagship Gp 1999-2001; chairman Live Consulting (an adviser on Corporate Social Responsibility) 2001- *party* became addicted to politics as teenager, active mbr Labour Party for ten years, at Univ and in several London Boroughs; during 1975 European referendum he was General Secy, Young European Left, the pro-European youth wing of the Labour Party; treasurer of newly-formed Liberal Democrats in England; press officer Paddy Ashdown 1992 GE; deputy campaign chair 1997 GE; Life Peer in 1997; Chief of Staff to Charles Kennedy MP 1999-2006; Treasury spokesman House of Lords; convenor Yorkshire Peers Gp; Advisory Board CentreForum *other mbrships* chair of sport at The Prince's Trust *recreations* family, football, cricket *clubs* MCC *address* 179 Fentiman Road, London SW8 1JY *tel* 020 7735 0855, 0780 887606 mobile *e-mail* newbyr@parliament.uk or dnewby@live-consulting.com

NEWMAN, David *b* Jun 10, 1969 2 *dog d* Masse, Libby *career* Royal Mail 1987-97; underwriter; programme manager; MD Zurich Financial Services 1997-2003; vice-president WNS Global Services, India 2003- *party* joined Liberals 1986; held various local party, constituency Exec positions; parish, borough Cllr 1991-99; PPC Surrey Heath 1997 *recreations* dog walking, socialising, Indian politics (even more frustrating than in UK!) *address* Christmas Pie Ramparts, 1003 Tower E, Daffodils Fort, Magarpatta City, Hadapsar, Pune, India 411 028 *tel* (cell) 0091 98233 97249 *e-mail* xmaspieuk@hotmail.com

NEWTON DUNN, Bill MEP East Midlands *b* Oct 3, 1941 *m* Anna 1 *s* 1 *d* *education* Marlborough College (scholar); Gonville & Caius College, Cambridge (MA Natural Sciences); INSEAD Business School, Fontainebleau, France (MBA) *career* Conservative MEP for Lincolnshire 1979-1994; MEP for East Midlands 1999-2004 (Conservative 1999-Nov 2000, Lib Dem Nov 2000) *party* joined 2000 when crossed the floor from the Tories; alternate mbr, Justice & Home Affairs Cttee; full mbr,Internal Market and Consumer Protection Cttee *special interests* Europe *publications* many political pamphlets including one in 1980s which coined the term 'democratic deficit'; *Big Wing* (biography of WW2 Air Chief Marshall Trafford Leigh-Mallory); *The Man Who Was John Bull* (biography of wonderful comic improviser Theodore Hook; and *The Devil Knew Not* (novel set in European Parliament) *address* 10 Church lane, Navenby, Lincoln LN5 0EG *tel* 01522-810812 *e-mail* wnewton@europarl.eu.int

NICHOLSON of Winterbourne, Baroness Emma: cr Life Peer 1997: MEP South East England *b* Oxford Oct 16,1941 *d* of Sir Godfrey Nicholson Bt. MP and The Lady Katharine Lindsay *m* Sir Michael Harris Caine (dcsd) 1 *ss* Richard 1 *sd* Amanda 1 foster son Amar Kanim *education* St. Mary's School, Wantage; Royal

Academy of Music; LRAM; ARCM *career* computer software developer; systems engineer; computer consultant; director of fundraising, Save the Children; consultant *inter alia* Dr Barnardo's, Westminster Children's Hospital, The Duke of Edinburgh's Award Scheme, Foster Parents Plan; chairman AMAR International Charitable Foundation; president Caine Prize for African Writing, Booker Prize for English fiction; Booker Prize for Russian fiction; founder, mbr and former trustee Parliamentary Appeal for Romanian Children Charitable Trust; honorary doctorate Univ of North London (now London Metropolitan Univ), Univ of Timisoara; Academy of Economic Studies, Bucharest *party* Conservative MP 1987-95, vice chairman Conservative Party 1983-87; joined Liberal Democrats Christmas Day 1995; Lib Dem MP 1995-97; created Life Peer 1997, mbr Lords Foreign Affairs Team 1997- ; elected MEP South East region of England, 1999 re-elected 2004;.vice-president Cttee on Foreign Affairs, Human Rights, Common Defence & Security Policy; *Rapporteur* for Iraq, *Rapporteur* for Romania; mbr, Cttee on Women's Rights and Equal Opportunities, Inter-parliamentary Delegation to Mashreq Countries and Gulf States, European Parliament Delegation to Euro-Mediterranean Forum, Stability Pact for South East Europe Parliamentary Gp; substitute mbr, Cttee on Agriculture and Rural Development, Joint Parliamentary Cttee for Romania, Parliamentary Cooperation Cttee for Kazakhstan, Kyrgyzstan, Uzbekistan, Tajikistan, Turkmenistan and Mongolia *special interests* foreign affairs; human rights; international development (WHO Envoy for health, peace and development); aid; defence *publications* co-editor *The Iraqi Marshlands* 2002; *Secret Society* 1996; *Why does the West Forget?* 1993 *clubs* Reform *address* European Parliament, ASP 10G209, Rue Wiertz, B-1047 Brussels Belgium *tel* +32 2 284 7625 *fax* +32 2 284 9625 *e-mail* enicholson@europarl.eu.int

NOBLET, Andrew *b* Nov 4, 1940 Preston *m* with children *career* retired teacher *party* Wiltshire rep on Western Region Exec; councillor; mbr North Wilts LP *address* 39 The Ridings, Kington St Michael, Chippenham, SN14 6JG *tel* 01249 750534 *e-mail* acgnoblet@beeb.net

NORTHOVER, Baroness Lindsay: Life Peer cr 2000: Lords spokesperson on International Development *b* Aug 21, 1954 Shoreham, Sussex *m* Prof John Northover, St Mark's Hospital and Imperial College, London 2 *s* Tom, Joe 1*d* Louisa *education* Brighton and Hove High School; St Anne's College, Oxford Univ (MA Hons); Bryn Mawr College/Univ of Pennsylvania (MA, PhD) *career* Fellow, Univ College London and St Mark's Hospital; Fellow, St Thomas's Hospital Medical School; lecturer, Univ College London and Wellcome Institute *party* mbr LBC Haringey LP; PPC Welwyn Hatfield 1983, 1987, Basildon 1997; chair, PCA 1987-91; chair Women Liberal Democrats, 1992-95; mbr various party cttees, 1987- ; Health Spokesperson, House of Lords, 2000-2002; Lead Spokesperson on International Development, House of Lords, 2002- ; mbr House of Lords Select Cttee on Stem Cell Research, 2001-2; mbr House of Lords Select Cttee on the European Union on Foreign Affairs, International Development and Defence 2003-2004; Vice-Chair All Party Parliamentary Gp on Debt, Aid and Trade; exec mbr All Party Parliamentary Gp on Africa; Secretary, All Party Parliamentary Gp on Overseas Development; Secretary, All Party Parliamentary Gp on Cuba; invited mbr, Cancer Research UK Parliamentary Champions Gp *publications* various academic *style* Baroness Northover *address* House of Lords, London SW1A 0PW *tel* 020 7219 8623 *e-mail* northoverl@parliament.uk

OPQ

OAKESHOTT of Seagrove Bay, Lord: Life Peer cr 2000: Lords spokesperson on Work and Pensions *b* 1947 *m* Pippa (inner City GP) 3 *ch* education Univ and Nuffield Colleges, Oxford *career* Overseas Development Institute/Nuffield Fellow Kenya Ministry of Economic Planning 1968-70; special adviser to Roy Jenkins (in opposition and at Home Office) 1972-76; investing in small companies and commercial property throughout the United Kingdom for pension funds, charities and investment trusts since 1976: Warburgs (four years), Courtaulds Pension Fund (five years); started own business 1986 *party* former Oxford City Councillor; PPC Horsham and Crawley, October 1974, Cambridge 1983; was with Roy Jenkins at Limehouse for formation of SDP; mbr National Steering Cttee, Economic Policy Cttee; mbr Lords Economic Affairs Select Cttee; one of two Liberal Democrat peers on Joint Cttee of Parliament on House of Lords Reform *special interests* economic and pensions policy, constitutional reform, housing *recreations* music, supporting Arsenal, elections *address* House of Lords, London SW1A 0PW *e-mail* oakeshottm@parliament.uk

OATEN, Mark MP (Winchester maj:7,476) *b* Mar 8, 1964 *m* Belinda Fordham 2 *d education* Hatfield Poly (BA Hons) 1986; Hertfordshire College of FE, Watford (Dip in Public Relations) *career* consultant, Shandwick Public Affairs 1990-92; consultant 1992-95, MD 1995-97, Westminster Public Relations; director Oasis Radio 1995-96 *party* joined SDP 1983; mbr (elected when just 22) Watford Borough Council 1986-94; PPC Watford 1992, Winchester 1997 (elected with majority of two, re-elected at by-election caused by protest of beaten Tory) re-elected 2001, 2005; PPS to Leader of Lib Dems 1999-2001; spokesman: on disabilities 1997-99; foreign affairs and defence 1999-2001; chair Parliamentary Party 2001-03; spokesperson Cabinet Office 2001-2003; Shadow Home Secy 2003-06; contested party leadership election 2006 *special interests* mbr Select Cttee on Public Administration 1999-2001, chair All-party POW Gp 1998-2000; secy All-Party EU Accession Gp 2000-05; co-chair All Party Adoption Gp 2000-05; treasurer All-Party Human Rights Gp 2000-05 *recreations* gardening, swimming and jogging, cinema, football *address* G/01, Norman Shaw North, House of Commons, London SW1A 0AA *tel* 020 72192703 *fax* 020 7219 2389 *e-mail* oatenm@parliament.uk

O'DONNELL, Hugh Bede Butler *b* May 1, 1952 1 *s* 1 *d education* St Ninian's High, Kirkintilloch; Falkirk College of FE (HND communication, media studies) 1994; Queen Margaret College, Edinburgh; Southern Connecticut State Univ, USA (BA Hons communication) 1997 *career* former community care professional, FE college lecturer *party* mbr Scottish Liberal Democrat Exec 2000- ; council candidate Cumbernauld & Kilsyth, North Lanarkshire Council 2003; former mbr, Recruitment and Mbrship Cttee; mbr, campaign team for Donald Gorrie MSP 1999; assistant agent, parliamentary by-election Hamilton South 1999; Scottish PPC, Cumbernauld & Kilsyth 1999, 2003, 2007; Central Scotland list 2003; Westminster PPC Falkirk West by-election 2000, 2001 GE; Scottish election addresses co-ordinator 2001;

vice-convener, Central Scotland Lib Dems, treasurer 2004; mbr, Scottish Policy Cttee; mbr, federal Broadcasting Policy Working Gp; occasional advisor on broadcasting issues to Ian Jenkins MSP; winner – best conference speech, Scottish Conference – Spring 2006 *special interests* disability rights; media structure, ownership, influence; Freedom of Information *other mbrships* UN/OSCE Electoral Returning Officer Kosovo 2001; regional organiser, Scotland in Europe campaign; board mbr: RECAP (community recycling company) *recreations* historical research, writing for local press, DIY *address* 280 Oak Road, Cumbernauld G67 3LG *tel* 0845 600 9580 *e-mail* Hugh.O'Donnell@scottish.parliament.uk

OLIVER, Rachel BA (Hons) *b* Oct 13, 1964 *m* Patrick Gilmour (solicitor) 2 *s* Henry, Tom 1 *d* Sophia *education* Cheltenham Ladies' College 1977-83; School of Oriental and African Studies, Univ of London (LLB course) 1984-86; Kings' College, London (BA Hons English Literature) 1987-90 *career* public relations officer Taunton Deane Borough Council 1991-93; communications, policy adviser to Nick Harvey MP 1993-95; press, parliamentary communications officer, Association of Personal Injury Lawyers 1995-97; head of campaigns, RNID 1997-99; head communications, public affairs Everychild 1999-2001; marketing, communications consultant 2001-03; Director of Communications, National Farmers Union 2003-*party* chair, Liberal Democrat Disability Policy Cttee 1999-2000; PPC Nottingham North 1997, Totnes 2001; mbr Mid Devon DC 1995-96, school governor *other mbrships* Harlequins FC, Royal British Legion, Amnesty International, Small Farms Association, GMB *recreations* rugby union, literature (British, French and Latin); current affairs, music (flute, piano) *publications* author TUC Legal Services Report 1997, 2001.*address* Bean Close, Hemyock, Devon EX15 3RJ *tel* 01823 680975 *e-mail* pagalso@aol.com

OPIK, Lembit MP (Montgomeryshire maj: 7,173**) Shadow Cabinet spokesperson for Wales and Northern Ireland; Leader of Welsh Party** *b* Mar 2, 1965 (parents Estonians who fled Stalin after World War II) *education* Royal Belfast Academical Institution; Bristol Univ (BA Hons, philosophy) *career* brand assistant, corporate training and organisation development manager, global human resources training manager Proctor and Gamble 1988-97 *party* joined 1990; mbr Newcastle City Council 1992-97; PPC Newcastle Central 1992, Montgomeryshire 1997 (elected MP), re-elected 2001; Euro candidate Northumbria 1994; parliamentary spokesman for Wales, Northern Ireland and Youth affairs; mbr Welsh Affairs team; Leader Welsh Party 2001- , spksn on employment and training; spksn on Northern Ireland 1997- ; mbr Federal Exec; federal vice president *special interests* Northern Ireland, Baltic states, aviation, rural affairs *recreations* motorcycles, paragliding (no more!) aeroplanes, windsurfing, astronomy *style* Lembit Opik MP *address* The House of Commons, London SW1A 0AA *tel* 020 7219 1144 *fax* 020 7219 2210 *e-mail* opikl@parliament.uk

ORD, David *b* Oct 26, 1961 Wallsend *partner* Karen 1 s Ethan 1 d Charlotte *education* Burnside High School; Luton College of Higher Education *career* Coates Computer Services: analyst programmer; Newcastle Hospitals Trust: software architect *party* mbr North Tyneside LP (mbrship secy 2006, previously secy), Northern region; councillor and deputy ldr NT Council Gp; PPC South Shields 1997; Newcastle East and Wallsend 2001, 2005; elected councillor into 'safe' Labour seat 1998, re-elected in 2002 and 2004 *special interests* expanding democratic involvement recreations music (bassist in Geek Theatre) *style* Councillor *address* 71 Laburnum Avenue, Wallsend NE28 8HG (work – IT Dept, Freeman Hospital, High Heaton, Newcastle upon Tyne NE7 7DN) *tel/fax* 0191 2636026 home 07968507767 mobile *e-mail* David.ord@northtyneside.gov.uk

OSBORNE, David *b* Feb 25, 1942 *m* 1 *d education* Queen Elizabeth GS, Mansfield 1953-60; City of Worcester Training College 1960-63; Birmingham Univ 1987 (BPhil Ed) *career* teaching, lecturing *party* joined 1992; past secy local party; PPC 1992, 1997, 2001; mbr Birmingham City Council 1996- ; chair Birmingham Licensing Cttee 2006- ; chair Birmingham Yardley District Cttee 2006- ; *special interests* community politics, education *address* 27 Elan Road, Northfield, Birmingham B31 5EP *tel* 0121 476 8918 home 0121 303 4204 business *fax* 0121 475 4425 *e-mail* cllrozzy@aol.com

PALMER, Monroe Edward *b* Nov 30, 1938 *m* Susette 2 *s* John, Andrew 1 *d* Fiona *education* Orange Hill Grammar School *career* Chartered Accountant *party* joined Liberal Party 1964; national party treasurer 1976-83; elected Cllr (Childs Hill ward) LB Barnet 1986, gp leader; PPC Hendon South 1979, 1983, 1987; Hastings & Rye 1992, 1997; chairman Liberal Democrat Friends of Israel; president Finchley & Golders Green LP *special interests* foreign affairs, particularly Middle East; local politics; treasury matters *other mbrships* NLC; trustee Cricklewood Millennium Green; director Barnet Homes; governor Wessex Gardens School *recreations* horse riding, reading, photography *address* 31 The Vale London NW11 8SE *tel* 0208455 5140 *fax* 020 87317670 *e-mail* cllr.m.palmer@barnet.gov.uk

PANNICK, David Phillip QC *b* Jul 3, 1956 *m* *1* Denise Sloam (died 1999) *2* Nathalie Trager-Lewis 2 *s* 2 *d education* Bancroft's School, Woodford Green, Essex; Hertford College, Oxford *career* barrister 1980, QC 1992 *party* joined Liberals 1974; chair, Working Gp on Censorship 2003; mbr Liberty Network *special interests* legal affairs *other mbrships* Fellow of All Souls College, Oxford *recreations* sport, cinema, theatre *publications Judges* (OUP, 1987), *Advocates* (OUP, 1992), *Human Rights Law and Practice* (with Lord Lester of Herne Hill QC Pub: Butterworths, 2nd edition, 2004), and fortnightly column on the law in *The Times address* Blackstone Chambers, Temple, London EC4Y 9BW *tel* 077 47 612 674 home 0207 583 1770 business *fax* 0207 822 7350 *e-mail* davidpannick@blackstonechambers.com

PARMINTER, Kate *b* Jun 24, 1964 *m* Neil Sherlock *qv* 2 *d* Rose, Grace Sherlock *education* Millais School; Collyer's Sixth Form College, Horsham; Lady Margaret Hall, Oxford (MA Theology) *career* chief Exec Campaign to Protect Rural England (CPRE) 1998-2004; head press, public affairs RSPCA 1990-98; Juliette Hellman Public Relations Consultants 1989-90; parliamentary researcher for Simon Hughes MP 1988-89; graduate marketing programme, Nestle 1986-88 *party* joined 1987; elected mbr Horsham DC 1987-95; mbr Liberal Democrat GE campaign team 1997; mbr Animal Welfare Policy Review Working Gp 1992; elected mbr South East Regional Exec 1990-9); mbr Lord Sharman's Foot & Mouth Inquiry 2001; mbr Meeting the Challenge Policy Gp 2005- ; *special interests* environment, animal welfare, rural policy *other mbrships* advisory board National Consumer Council; NLC; RSPCA; National Trust; CPRE; NCC Policy Commission on Public Services 2003-2004 *recreations* family life, walking *publications A Third Sector as well as a Third Way in 'The Progressive Century'* 2001; *Pressure Group Politics in Modern*

Britain, Social Market Foundation, 1996 *address* 12 Binscombe Lane, Godalming, Surrey, GU7 3PN *tel/fax* 01483 428184 *e-mail* neil-kate@kateneil.demon.co.uk

PARRY, Ian Huw *b* May 12, 1962 *m* Sue (nee George) 2 *s* Huw, Rhys 1 *d* Anna *education* various schools, Reading 1965-80; Univ College Cardiff 1982-85 (BSc Econ: Economics and Industrial relations) *career* 1985-92 trained , qualified, as Chartered Accountant, Arthur Andersen and Touche Ross; 1992-99 various positions as auditor, accountant; 1999- Assurance Consultant, HEFCE *party* joined Union of Liberal Students 1982; chair Welsh Liberal Youth Movement 1984-85; Exec officer (various posts) Bristol North West LP 1990-98; mbr Bristol West 1998- ; mbr Western Counties Exec 1993-2003, 2005- ; PPC Bristol North West 1997, Cynon Valley 2001 *special interests* governance and accountability arrangements, education, local politics *other mbrships* Fellow, Institute of Chartered Accountants (FCA); National Trust, CADW *recreations* family, friends, staying fit and healthy *address* 28 Briarwood, Westbury on Trym, Bristol, BS9 3SS *tel* 0117 962 3830 *e-mail* i.parry@hefce.ac.uk

PARSONS, Adam Charles *b* Jan 15, 1985 Cuckfield *education* Westwood High School; Kidderminster College; Worcester College of Technology; currently Univ of Kent *party* recruitment officer Wyre Forest 2004-2005; West Midlands regional exec mbr 2004-2005; West Midlands LDYS GEM 2003-2004, social and events secreatry (joint office) 2004-2005; mbr Canterbury LP; chair Univ of Kent at Canterbury Liberal Democrats; Youth and Student representative on Canterbury and Whitstable LD exec; mbr LDEA and LDPG (Liberal Democrat Peace Gp); mbr National Union of Journalists and CAMRA *special interests* education, peace and security, political history *recreations* running, snooker, darts *e-mail* kentuni@hotmail.co.uk *website* www.ukcld.org.uk

PARSONS, Alexandra *b* Nov 16, 1984 *education* Univ College London studying BA (Hons) English Literature 2004- ; Central Saint Martin's School of Art and Design: Foundation Art 2003-04; James Allen's Girls School 1996-2003 *career* currently student and Administrator, Treasurer's Unit, Liberal Democrat HQ 2005- ; Volunteer Adult Literacy Support Teacher, Mary Ward Centre, Holborn 2004-05; CV Writer, The CV Company 2004-05 *party* mbr Hackney LP *other mbrships* Tate, Victoria & Albert Museum, Royal Academy of Arts *special interests* higher education, party development, human rights *recreations* theatre, literature, dressmaking, rock climbing, Japanese food *address* 7 Beatty Road, Stoke Newington, London N16 8EA *tel* 020 7340 4994 business *e-mail* alex.parsons@libdems.org.uk, alexandraparsons@hotmail.com

PATRICK, Zoé Anne FRSA *b* May 22, 1952 *m* Glenn 2 *ch education* Bremond College Grammar School, Coventry; Birmingham College of Food & Domestic Arts (Diploma) *career* accounts clerk at Lea Francis Engineering Ltd., secy to works manager at K.C. Jeavons Ltd; dept secy at Lancaster University Department of Mathematics; assistant at Waitrose; broadcast monitor for Broadcast Monitoring Company, London; freelance reporter for Oxford & County Newspapers; admin assistant for Thames Business Advice Centre; Community Development Worker for Age Concern Oxfordshire and currently Team Manager *party* joined 1996; PPC Banbury 2005; cllr Oxfordshire County Council; exec mbr Wantage LP; secy and chair local branch of Wantage constituency; deputy ldr Vale Liberal Democrats, deputy ldr Oxfordshire County Council Liberal Democrats and gp press officer for gp; **mbr** ALDC, PCA *other mbrships* Fellow Royal Society of Arts *special interests* health, special educational needs, HR & management, environment, public transport *recreations* walking, swimming, horse riding, wildlife, film, theatre, reading and writing *publications* articles and stories for local press, many Focuses! *address* 16 Churchward Close, Grove, Wantage, Oxfordshire, OX12 0QZ *tel* 01235 768809 *e-mail* zoe@patrickx.freeserve.co.uk

PAXTON, Wesley *b* Jun 23, 1946 Riddings, Derbyshire *m* Linda (nee Clifton) Dec 7, 1968 1 *s* 1 *d education* Brunts Grammar, Mansfield 1957-59; Bilboro' Grammar Nottingham 1959-64; Warwick Univ 1965-68 BA (Econ) 2.2 Economics + Industrial Studies; Hull Univ 1973-74 PGCE *career* apprentice United Steel, Rotherham 1964-5; Method Study Analyst, British Steel, Rotherham 1968-9; Glass Industry Research Sheffield 1969-71; teaching 1971-95 including Rotherham College of Technology, Mexboro' College of FE, Bransholme High School, Hull College; freelance writer & researcher since Aug 1995; British Exec Service Overseas 1998; project in Latvia Sep 2001 *party* PPC Glanford & Scunthorpe 1992, Pontefract & Castleford 1997, 2001, 2005; mbr Haltemprice & Howden, pavement pounder with leaflets *special interests* compiling a study provisionally entitled "Re-building Britain's Railways", re-afforestation in W Africa to make poverty history & create a carbon sink, modern languages, gardening, models, photography, travel, carpentry *other mbrships* Salvation Army, education trade union *address* 5a Hawthorne Avenue, Willerby, Hull HU10 6JG *tel* 01482 651701 *e-mail* wesley@paxton5a.freeserve.co.uk

PAYNE, Geoffrey Donald Stephen *b* Dec 28, 1975 *education* Crabtree Junior Mixed Infants, Harpenden, Herts 1980-87; Sir John Lawes School, Harpenden, Herts 1987-94; St Edmund Hall, Oxford, 1994-97 BA (Hons) Modern History; City Univ, London 1998-99; Inns of Court School of Law 1999-2000 Bar vocational course *career* vice-president (finance), Oxford Univ Student Union 1997-8; Higher Education researcher, Dr Evan Harris MP; chambers of D. Anthony Evans QC, 9-12 Bell Yard, London, pupil barrister 2000-01; chambers of Rock Tansey QC, 25 Bedford Row, London: barrister specialising in criminal defence, defended in several large-scale fraud cases 2002- *party* joined 2000 via Oxford Univ Liberal Democrats; previously active in what became Hitchin & Harpenden LP; treasurer, Oxford Univ Liberal Democrats 1996; campaigned Oxford West and Abingdon 1997 General Election; student development officer, LDYS (ran NUS campaign) 1999-2000; chair LDYS 2000-2001; mbr English Council Exec 2000- ; PPC, Bromley and Chislehurst 2001; mbr Federal Policy Cttee 2001- ; Crime, Policing and Drugs Policy Working Gp 2002; Euthanasia Policy Working Gp 2003-4; proposed motions at Federal Conference on higher education, cannabis; mbr Federal Conference Cttee 2002- (trained to chair conference sessions) *special interests* higher education, home affairs, crime and criminal justice *other mbrships* LDYS, Liberal Democrat Lawyers, Young Fraud Lawyers Association, Criminal Bar Association *recreations* travelling, drinking in pubs *publications* various articles in Legal Democrat, Free Radical and Liberator *address* Chambers of Rock Tansey QC, 25 Bedford Row, London WC1R 4HD *tel* 020 7067 1500 work 07956 472 769 mobile *fax* 020 7067 1507 *e-mail* geoff@geoffpayne.org

PHILLIPS of Sudbury, Lord Andrew: Life Peer cr 1998 OBE (1996) *b* Mar 15, 1939 *education* Uppingham school, Rutland; Trinity Hall, Cambridge (BA Hons, economics and law) *m* Penelope 2 *d* Hon Caitlin, Hon Alice 1 *s* Hon Oliver *career* qualified as solicitor 1964: Bates, Wells and Braithwaite, Sudbury, Suffolk 1964-65; Pritchard Englefield, City of London 1965-69; Lawford & Co 1969; founded Bates, Wells and Braithwaite, London (1970); fdr Parlex Gp of lawyers 1971; founder chair, Legal Action Gp 1971-76, Citizenship Foundation 1989- (both charities); hon legal adviser Council for Charitable Support 1985- (president 2002-); board mbr International Centre for Not-for-Profit Law; regular visitor to East European countries advising on charity law, charity organisation issues; Scott Trustee (*The Guardian, Observer*); freelance journalist, broadcaster: legal eagle on BBC's Jimmy Young Show 1975-2001; presenter *London Programme* for LWT 1982-83, regular panellist, occasional presenter on current affairs programmes Anglia TV; occasional interviews/appearances *Today, Newsnight, Any Questions party* Labour PPC Harwich 1970; expelled as Lab candidate North Norfolk 1973; Liberal candidate Saffron Walden 1977 (by-election); Euro candidate NE Essex 1979; Alliance candidate Gainsborough 1983; created Life Peer 1998; whip, House of Lords 1998-2001; mbr parliamentary joint Cttee on Consolidation of Bills; mbr Administration and Works Cttee; mbr Exec Lib Dem Lawyers Association; retired from House of Lords 2006 *special interests* former council mbr Charter 88; president Sudbury Society; president Solicitor's Pro-Bono Gp; he initiated Lawyers in the Community Scheme 1987; first chair, now president Citizenship Foundation; trustee, patron charities including Public Interest Research Centre, Gainsborough House, Me-Too, Council for Charitable Support, the Giving Campaign, VIRSA Trust, National Centre for Volunteering *publications* *Charity Investment: Law and Practice* (with Fiona Middleton), *Charitable Status - a Practical Handbook* (fourth ed), *The Living Law, Equal Justice, Justice Beyond Reach* plus freelance articles on charity law; regular radio, TV appearances on legal issues *recreations* the arts, local history, architecture, golf, cricket, walking *address* House of Lords, London SW1A 0PW *tel* 020 7219 3000

PHILLIPS, David *b* Feb 17 1933 *m* Jun (active Liberal Democrat, qualified pharmacist) 3 *ch* 8 *gch education* trained as Industrial Chemist, then as pilot *career* Post Office Engineering Department; twelve years as RAF pilot, mainly in Coastal Command, retired with rank of Flight Lieutenant; started own company distributing electrical and electronic components *party* joined Liberal Party 1973; various posts at constituency, regional level; PPC South Worcestershire 1979, 1983 Ludlow 1987, 1992; Euro candidate Hereford and Worcester 1984; currently president West Midlands region, mbr English Council; policy assessor for candidate approval; Returning Officer for candidate selection *special interests* voting reform, Europe *other mbrships* Birmingham and Midland Society for Genealogy and Heraldry, British Nuclear Test Veterans Association, Electoral Reform Society, Royal British Legion *publications* *The Castle at Elmley recreations* history, family history, lecturing, painting, sailing and skiing *address* Waverley, Elmley Castle, Pershore, Worcs WR10 3HS *tel* 01386 710337 *e-mail* aberic@v21.me.uk

PIDGEON, Caroline Valerie *b* Sept 29, 1972 Eastleigh *education* Thornden School, Barton Peveril Sixth Form College, Hampshire; Univ College of Wales, Aberystwyth *career* political assistant, researcher 1994-99; communications manager, Croydon Health Authority 1999-2002, Guy's and St Thomas' Hospital NHS Trust 2002-06 *party* women's officer Student Liberal Democrats/LDYS 1992-94; honorary vice- president LDYS 1995-97; elected LB Southwark May 1998 (taking a previously safe Labour ward), regeneration, environment spokesperson 1998-2000; chief whip 2000-02; Exec mbr for Education 2002-06; Exec mbr for Children's Services and Education; deputy leader of LD Gp 2006- ; deputy leader 2002-04; PPC Dulwich and West Norwood 2001; GLA candidate Lambeth and Southwark 2002 *special interests* environment, local Govt, women, health *recreations* cinema, modern art, walking *address* 12 Vestry Mews, Camberwell, London SE5 8NS *tel/fax* 020 7701 4648 *e-mail* cpidgeon@cix.co.uk

PICKSTONE, Tim Chief Exec, Association of Liberal Democrat Councillors *b* Nov 11, 1968 Chorley *education* Bishop Rawstorne CoE High School, Runshaw Tertiary College, Manchester Metropolitan University (DipHE Health Studies) *career* Deputy Chief Exec, George House Trust 1991-2006; Chief Exec, ALDC 2006- ; *party* mbr Bury LP, cllr and gp leader Bury Council, PPC Ashton-under-Lyne 1997, Bury South 2001; mbr ALDC, DELGA *address* 49 Heaton Street, Prestwich, Manchester M25 1HS *tel* 0161 773 8266 *e-mail* timpickstone@bigfoot.com

PIERCY, Candy BSc Hons *b* Sept 9 1952 *m* Mike 1 *d* Miranda 1 *s* Aidan (both active Lib Dems) 2 golden retrievers *education* assorted RAF Schools; Upper Chine School for Girls, Isle of Wight; St Nicholas School for Girls, Fleet; Univ College London (BSc Hons in microbiology) *career* medical research before moving to Suffolk in 1976; number of part time jobs while children were young; director family-owned Oakfield Consulting Ltd; Federal Campaigns and Elections Officer Lib Dems 1990-97; director Midas Training Solutions 1998, trained, mainly democracy-building, in 25-plus countries: in UK, specialises in communication, leadership, management skills *party* president Agents and Organisers Association 2000, 2004; vice president LDYS; vice chair Gender Balance Task Force. mbr FE 2000- ; editor *Election Agents Manual* 1996, 2001; lead party trainer, founder mbr Training Task Gp; key mbr by-election team throughout the 1990s, responsible for Rochdale, Bath 1992 GE; target seats officer Wessex Gp of seats in run up to 1997 GE (won 6 out of 8); agent Winchester by-election 1997; campaign director for John Farquhar Munro MSP in Ross, Skye and Inverness West, 1999; campaign director for Highlands 2001 (including Charles Kennedy MP, John Thurso MP and Patsy Kenton) *special interests* training women, youth, agents; winning elections UK, elsewhere in the world *recreations* wild birds, wild orchids, beaches *address* Malmsmead, Kiln Lane, Lacey Green, Bucks HP27 0PU *tel* 01844 344021 *fax* 01844 274145 *e-mail* candypiercy@cix.co.uk

PINDAR, John *b* Apr 1, 1955 *educated* Univ of Manchester, Crewe and Alsager College (teacher training); Newcastle Univ; King's College, London; Temple Univ Philadelphia *career* teaching, girls' comprehensive school; various sixth form and tertiary teaching posts 1988-93; geography, politics lecture West Thames College, Isleworth 1993-2003 *party* joined Liberals 1973; Southampton: agent, organiser East Hants Liberals; mbr LB Lambeth Council (Thornton ward) 1994-98; PPC Southampton Itchen 1979, Streatham 1992; candidate London Euro list 1998, 2003; active in local elections, avid national by-election helper; mbr PCA Exec 1986-05; Exec LDEG; mbr International Relations Cttee *other interests* speaker, Electoral Reform Society; *Liberator* subscriber; campaigned for independent US presidential candidate John Anderson 1980 *special interests* environment; central, eastern, south-eastern Europe; EU enlargement, single currency; constitutional reform; crime prevention; keen supporter Bosnian Institute; Events Organiser, Croatian Students and Young Professional *recreations* walking in countryside; foreign travel, cinema, trying to get novel published, photography, psephology *address* 13 Rosethorn Close, London SW12 0JP *tel* 020 8671 5938 *e-mail* pindarj@hotmail.com

PINKERTON, Barbara Jeanne JP *b* Mar 19, 1946 Plymouth *d* of late Len Greenfield (Kingswood & Avon Cllr for 30 yrs.) and Betty Griffiths (nursing sister St. John's Ambulance) *m* John Mitchell Pinkerton Apr 1964 1 *d* Carol 1964 1s Neil 1969 *education* Bishop Road; Oldland Girls School; Soundwell Tech College; awarded Retail Trades Cert *career* sales asst, Jones Of Bristol 1960-62; clerk at Fry's Keynsham 1962-67; Central Kitchens Somerset CC Sch. Meals 1967-69; child minder 1969-72; newsagent proprietor 1972-92; ptnr family market garden business 1992- *party* joined Liberal Party 1966; local election agent 1983; 1984; 1985; 1989; 2000; PPC Kingswood 1992, 1997, Stafford 2001; Cllr Bristol City 1986-88; Keynsham Town 1999-2003; chair Kingswood LP 1988-90; 1991; 1994-97, president Kingswood 1997- ; secy Wansdyke 1997-2000; 2004- ; English Council mbr 1986- ; Western Counties Exec 1998- ; regional candidates chair 2001-04; accredited returning officer; mbr ALDC; PCA; WLD; led successful campaign for the retention of the A&E dept at Frenchay Hospital 1994 *other mbrships* Howard League for Penal Reform; British Hedgehog Preservation Society; Magistrates Association; magistrate (Bristol Bench) 1990- ; Valuation Tribunal mbr; school governor Speedwell School 1986-91, Sir Bernard Lovell 1990-93, Summerfield Special School 1991- ; Girl Guide Ambassador 2000- *recreations* gym; swimming; time with family *address* Broadleaze Nursery, 283, Bath Road, Keynsham BS31 1TN *tel/fax* 0117 9863185 home 0117 9863185 business *e-mail* jeannepinkerton@blueyonder.co.uk

PINKETT, Jenny BA *b* Apr 23, 1945 *education* Sedgehill School, London; Cartrefle College of Education; Open Univ (Cert Ed BA Ad Dip) *m* (and soon-to-be grandmother) *career* teaching since 1966, Special Education since 1969 children with specific literacy difficulties; currently special educational needs co-ordinator, child protection co-ordinator, *Looked After Children* co-ordinator in mainstream high school; ambition is to see truly inclusive system and equality of opportunity in education before she retires; spent year out as wire-buyer in fastenings industry *party* former chair Tamworth LP; former Regional Candidates chair; mbr West Midlands Regional Exec, English Council; PPC Tamworth 1997, 2001; regional conference chair *other mbrships* National Association for Special Educational Needs, Tamworth Crime Prevention Panel, Tamworth Heritage Trust *recreations* walking, cooking, painting, visiting markets; delving into junk shops, forged, cut and wire nails, anything old, recycling or finding a million and one uses for things that most people throw away *address* 6 Ludgate, The Leys Tamworth, Staffs B79 7EG *tel* 01827 61170 *e-mail* jenny@jpinkett.idps.co.uk

POLLARD, Anne Kathleen (Kathy) *b* Nov 15, 1951 *m* Derek 2 *d education* Llwyn-y-bryn High School, Swansea; Birmingham Univ (MSc Work Design and Ergonomics); Swansea Univ (BSc Hons Electrical and Electronic Engineering) *career* BT Research and Development, latterly in usability and *web* design 1973-79, 1988-2002 *party* joined 1983; currently mbr regional Exec, East of England Regional Assembly Exec, Europe and international affairs Panel; district Cllr 1987-95, Suffolk county Cllr 1993- , currently Exec mbr; PPC South Suffolk 1992, 1997;

successful agent, leaflet writer for local elections; mbr ALDC, WLD *special interests* Europe, transport, road safety, food safety, getting other Lib Dems elected *other mbrships* LDEG, Women Liberal Democrats, PCA, National Trust *recreations* gardening, reading, walking *publications* Focus newsletters *address* 19 The Street, Capel St Mary, Ipswich IP9 2EE *tel* 01473 311384/313037 mobile 07889 123702 *fax* 01473 *312175 e-mail* Kathy.pollard@btinternet.com

POLLING, Ruth *b* Sept 4, 1980 *partner* Chris Gurney *qv education* Cator Park School, Beckenham 1992-99; London School of Economics (BA Hons International History) *career* support officer for Liberal Democrat Gp, Islington Council 2000-5; currently clerical officer for the Family Planning Association *party* joined Bromley and Chiselhurst LP 1998; mbr Federal Conference Cttee 2001-, vice chair 2005-, Conference communications cttee; LDYS 1998-2004, including Chair Conference Cttee 2001-4, exec mbr 1999-2003, vice chair 1999-2000, London Region chair 1998-2000; mbr Bromley & Chiselhurst LP exec 1998-2003, candidate Plaistow and Sundridge ward 2002; (hopefully, depending on LP elections) candidate Bunhill ward (Islington) 2006 *special interests* youth involvement in politics, young citizenship, local Govt, housing, pornography, sexual health *recreations* eating, sleeping, watching TV, cuddling partner, delivery *address* 26 Rahere House, Central Street, Islington EC1V 8DE *e-mail* r.l.polling-alumni@lse.ac.uk

POPE, Geoff *b* Islington *party* joined London Assembly on 6 Jun 2005, replacing Lynne Featherstone MP *qv*, who stepped down on election to Parliament; GLA candidate 2000, 2004 elections gaining over 30% of vote in SW London; Mayor of Richmond upon Thames 1989-90; chair of Richmond Social Services 1998, where he maintained the best day services for Older People in London; chair of Addiction Support and Care Agency Kingston and Richmond; President of Twickenham Club for the Blind; Trustee of Richmond's Ethnic Minorities Advocacy Gp *career* management consultant (voluntary sector) in service development across London; previously at Kodak Research Division in Harrow, Development Manager at Glaxo SmithKline *special interests* public transport, recycling *recreations* lifelong Charlton Athletic supporter *e-mail* geoff.pope@london.gov.uk

PORTER, Richard Jonathan *b* Jul 21, 1974 *education* King's College London (medical ethics) 1998-99; Univ of Amsterdam (Dutch) 2002- *career* hospital liaison manager Medical Defence Union 1996-99; paramedic London Ambulance Service 1999- *party* joined 1998 Carshalton and Wallington; Focus delivered Wallington North ward; moved to Southwark 2000, deliverer, elected Cllr LB Southwark 2002- , Exec mbr community safety, social inclusion 2002-04, regeneration, economic development 2002- ; vice chair Southwark Borough Action Gp (local campaign strategy gp) 2002-2004 PPC Camberwell and Peckham (Apr 2004) *special interests* policing, community involvement, equalities, regeneration, London and European politics, foreign affairs *other mbrships* PCA, DELGA, Liberty and Stonewall *recreations* football, athletics, running *address* 3 Donato Drive, London SE15 6BF *tel* 020 7967 9797 home 020 7525 7162 business *e-mail* richarddjporter@btopenworld.com

POWELL, Michael John *b* Sept 21, 1959 Pontypridd, Rhondda Cynon Taff *education* Coedylan Comprehensive School; Univ of Glamorgan *career* self employed plumbing and heating engineer *party* mbr and vice chair Rhondda Cynon Taff LP; Welsh Assembly Candidate Pontypridd 2003; PPC Pontypridd 2005;

County Council Candidate 1999, 2004; mbr ALDC; former chair of Welsh Conference cttee, former mbr Policy Cttee *special interests* environment, education *recreations* golf, pub quizzes *address* 8 The Parade, Trallwn, Pontypridd, Rhondda Cynon Taff CF37 4PU *tel* 07779 337839 *e-mail* mike.powell@rctlibdems.org.uk *website* www. rctlibdems.org.uk

PRICE Gareth John Welsh Liberal Democrats Head of Media, and Head of Assembly Group Office *b* May 28, 1975 Pontypool *m* Sarah. *1 d* Sylvie, born Mar 31, 2006 *education* Univ of Warwick, BSc in Mathematics with intercalated year at Universite des Sciences et Technologie, Lille; Pontypool & Usk College (now Coleg Gwent), Abersychan Comprehensive *career* currently Head of Media for the Welsh Liberal Democrats, and Head of Assembly Group Office for the party's Welsh Assembly Mbrs; previously worked as a journalist in Wales, and as a press officer for the Welsh Assembly Government *party* LD accredited media trainer. *other mbrships* governor, Tremorfa Nursery School. *recreations* keen hockey player/coach/writer/umpire (in that order!) and secretary Cwmbran Hockey Club *address* 46 Burnaby Street, Cardiff, CF24 2JX *tel* 029 2031 3400 work *e-mail* gareth.price@welshlibdems.org.uk

PRICE, Peter Nicholas, Honorary MEP *b* 19 Feb 1942 *m* Joy Bhola 1988 1 *d* Myfanwy Angharad *education* Worcester Royal GS; Aberdare Boys' GS; University of Southampton (BA Law); College of Law, Guildford; King's College London (diploma EC Law) *career* freelance broadcaster 1962-67; solicitor in full-time practice 1966-79; MEP 1979-94; European Strategy Counsel 1994-; part-time chair of employment tribunal 2000- *party* Conservative PPC Aberdare 1964, 1966, Caerphilly 1970; mbr Conservative NEC 1969-72, 1978-79; vice-chair Conservative Political Centre 1978-79; hon sec Foreign Affairs Forum 1977-79; vice-chair Conservative Gp for Europe 1979-81; mbr Council European Movement 1971-81; Campaign Co-ordinator Mid and South Glamorgan counties Britain in Europe Referendum 1975; elected Conservative MEP Lancashire W 1979-84, London SE 1984-94, (chair, Budgetary Control Cttee 1989-92, vice chair, 1979-84, gp spokesman Legal Affairs Cttee 1984-87, Budgets Cttee 1986-89; mbr:- ACP/EEC Joint Assembly 1981-94, External Economic Relations Cttee 1992-94, mbr delegations for relations with Japan 1989-92, US Congress 1992-94; co chair Euro-Arab group 1984-94, AWEPA anti-apartheid group 1985-94); Honorary MEP 1994- ; co-leader of 'Conservatives say Yes' in Welsh devolution referendum 1997; joined Liberal Democrats 1997; mbr:-Federal Policy Cttee 1998- , ELDR Council 1999- , Federal Finance and Admin Cttee 2000-06, Meeting the Challenge Working Gp 2005- , PCA, Lib Dem Lawyers, LDEG, ALDC; Euro-candidate Wales 1999 *special interests* mbr FPA NEC 1973-77 (chair long-term planning group); Fellow, Industry and Parliament Trust 1981-82; UK vice-president European Year of Small and Med-sized Enterprises 1983; parliamentary consultant NALGO/UNISON 1989-94; mbr NHS Service Cttee 1995-97; non-exec director NHS Trust 1998-99; Standing Orders Commissioner preparing for National Assembly for Wales 1998-99; mbr Richard Commission on Powers and Electoral Arrangements of National Assembly (recommended STV) 2002-04; mbr Royal Institute of International Affairs (Chatham House) 1977- ; vice-pres Llangollen International Eisteddfod 1981- ; non-exec director Bureau Veritas Quality International Ltd 1991-2001; governor Thames Valley University 1996-2005; board mbr Wales in Europe 2002- ; non-exec director Welsh Ambulance Services NHS Trust 2005- ; *address* Peter Price Hon. MEP, 37

Heol St Denys, Lisvane, Cardiff CF14 0RU *tel* 029 2076 1792; and 60 Marlings Park Avenue, Chislehurst, Kent BR7 6RD *tel* 01689 820681 home 07985 205480 mobile *e-mail* peterprice@btinternet.com

PRINGLE, Mike MSP (Edinburgh South): **Deputy Justice Spokesperson in Scottish Parliament** *b* Christmas Day, 1945 *m* 2 *s education* Edinburgh Academy; Scottish Institute of Bankers (Intermediate & Final) *career* Royal Bank of Scotland 1966-72; own company: TMM Ltd 1974-89; MSP 2003- *party* joined SDP 1982; Edinburgh Cllr 1992-2003: city council 1992-94; Lothian Regional Cllr 1994-95; City of Edinburgh Cllr 1995-2003; PPC Edinburgh South 1997; mbr Scottish Party Exec 1995-2003; former Arts, Sport & Leisure Spokesperson; Health & Social Services (disability issues) spokesperson; Scottish PPC Edinburgh South, List candidate Lothian 1999; 2003 (elected); mbr Justice 2 Cttee 2003-05; Justice 1 Cttee 2005- ; substitute mbr Justice 1 Cttee; deputy Justice spokesperson *recreations* cinema, wine collecting, sports (especially rugby, football) *address* Scottish Parliament, Edinburgh, EH99 1SP *tel* 0131 348 5788 *constituency* 4 Grange Road, Edinburgh EH9 1UH *tel* 0131 662 1513 *e-mail* mike.pringle.msp@scottish.parliament.uk

PSALLIDAS, Stephen *b* Sept 24, 1970 Jarrow *ptnr education* BEng (Hons) Newcastle Univ 1990, PGCE Newcastle Univ 1991; MSc Environmental Management Sunderland Univ 2001 *career* sustainable transport charity 2005- ; *party* mbr Newcastle City LP in NE Region; elected councillor; PPC Newcastle Central 2001, South Shields 2005; mbr ALDC, Green Liberal Democrats *other mbrships* greenpeace *special interests* environment, transport, international development *recreations* cycling, photography, travel, languages *address* 10 Falmouth Road, Newcastle upon Tyne, NE6 5NS *e-mail* stephen@psallidas.net

PUGH, John MP (Southport maj 3,838) **Shadow Health spokesperson** *b* June 28, 1948 Liverpool *m* 4 *ch education* Durham Univ (Doctorate in Logic) *career* teacher, head of philosophy at school in Crosby *party* joined 1974; mbr (Birkdale) Sefton BC, leader of council 1992-97; PPC Southport 2001 (elected MP in succession to Ronnie Fearn), re-elected 2005; Shadow Ministerial spokesman, Education 2002-05; Shadow Transport spokesperson 2005-06; mbr Transport, Local Govt and Regions Select Cttee *recreations* computers; weight-lifting *address* House of Commons, London SW1A 0AA; constituency 35 Shakespeare Street, Southport PR8 5AB *tel* 01704 533555 *fax* 01704 884160 *e-mail* pughj@parliament.uk *web* www.johnpughmp.com

PURVIS, Jeremy MSP (Tweeddale, Ettrick & Lauderdale) Scottish Parliament Justice Spokesperson *b* Jan 15, 1974 *education* Berwick-upon-Tweed High School 1992; Brunel Univ (BSc Hons Politics, Modern History) 1996 *career* research assistant to Sir David Steel MP, House of Commons 1993; parliamentary assistant, Liberal International 1994; parliamentary assistant ELDR Gp, European Parliament 1995; personal assistant to Sir David Steel MP 1996-98; Edinburgh Parliament Affairs Company 1998-2001; director, strategic communications consultancy 2001- ; Mbr Scottish Parliament 2003- *party* elected Scottish Parliament: Tweeddale, Ettrick & Lauderdale 2003; Finance Spokesperson 2003-05; Justice Spokesperson 2005- ; mbr Justice 2 Cttee; substitute mbr Environment and Rural Development Cttee *publications Fiscal Federalism* 2004 *other mbrships* Scottish Council of European

Movement; Amnesty International *recreations* classic cars, reading *address* Scottish Parliament, Edinburgh EH99 1SP *tel* 0131-348 5801 *constituency* 11 Island Street, Galashiels TD1 1NZ *tel* 01896 663656 *e-mail* jeremy.purvis.msp@scottish. parliament.uk *web* www.jeremypurvis.org

QUINLAN, James Alex *b* Aug 8, 1951 *m* Eija-Riitta 1 *s education* West Hatch High School, Chigwell; Univ of London (BSc Hons geography, sociology) 1972; Univ of North London (postgraduate diploma, town and country planning) 1976; mbr Royal Town Planning Institute 1981 *career* town and country planning, local Govt 1971-88; consultancy 1988- ; currently MD James A Quinlan & Associates Ltd Planning & Environment Consultants *party* joined 1996; chair Cambridge South Rural branch 1999-2003; chair Cambridgeshire South LP 2002-03, 2006- ; mbr South Cambridgeshire District Council (elected 1996, re-elected 2000, seeking re-election 2004; PPC Cambridgeshire South 1997 (swing to LD 8.7%: Tory majority reduced from 19,600 to 8,700); currently looking for a more winnable seat; Exec mbr PCA 2005- ; *special interests* foreign affairs, environment and planning, culture *other mbrships* Eastern Orchestral Board; Cambridge Cottage Housing Society Ltd (chair 2001-2004); chair Thriplow Village Shop Association Ltd *recreations* flying (glider pilot), music (passive, active: plays trumpet); art, architecture of 14th-15th century Italy *address* Forge House, Thriplow, nr Royston, Herts SG8 7RA *tel* 01763 208226/01763 208314 home/business *fax* 01763208226 *e-mail* james.quinlan@ntlworld.com

R

RADCLIFFE, Nora MSP Gordon *b* Mar 4, 1946 *m* Dr M A Radcliffe 1 *s* 1 *d education* Bowmore, Peterculter Primary Schools; High School for Girls, Aberdeen; Aberdeen Univ *career* management, hotel & catering industry; travel agency; community liaison, primary care development NHS Grampian Health Board *party* joined 1962; various offices including chair West Aberdeenshire Young Liberals, branch secy, branch chair; chair Gordon LP; treasurer ALDC; mbr Gordon DC 1988-92; elected MSP Gordon 1999, re-elected 2003, currently convener Parliamentary Gp *special interests* environment, rural development *other mbrships* National Trust for Scotland, Historic Scotland, Saltire Society, National Women's Register, Aberdeenshire Environmental Forum *recreations* reading; visiting gardens, historic houses; walking; knitting, sewing; eating out *address* 67 High Street, Inverurie, Aberdeenshire AB51 3QJ (constituency office); The Scottish Parliament, Edinburgh EH99 1SP; 3 King Street, Inverurie, Aberdeenshire AB51 4SY home *tel* 01467 622575 home 01467 672220 (constituency) 0131 348 5803/4 (parliamentary office) *e-mail* nora.radcliffe.msp@scottish.parliament.uk

RADFORD, Simon Wyn *b* Mar 4, 1982 *education* Eton College; Peterhouse, Cambridge Univ (Law, Social and Political Sciences); Brown Univ, USA (Master in Public Affairs) *party* joined 1999; LDYS activist at Univ and nationally; chair, Cambridge Student Liberal Democrats; Exec mbr, vice-chair (communications) LDYS; PPC Enfield North 2005 *special interests* foreign affairs, international political economy, civil liberties *other mbrships* Oxfam, Amnesty *recreations* travelling (especially to Russia), films and theatre, following travails of Brentford FC *publications* editor *Free Radical* 2003-04, various articles in press *address* 17 Rosslyn Hill, Hampstead, London, NW3 5UJ *e-mail* radford_simon@hotmail.com

RAMM, Benjamin *b* June 12, 1982 *education* University College School; St. Catharine's College, Cambridge *career* (re-)founded *The Liberal* magazine, July 2004; Editor and Publisher, 2004- *party* joined April 2001; chair, Cambridge Student Liberal Democrats, 2003-2004; prospective PPC, November 2003-March 2006; co-founder, Liberal Democrat Jewish Forum, March 2006 *special interests* Latin American affairs, particularly indigenous issues; cultural policy; commodification and the public sphere; radical/liberal humanism *other mbrships* William Blake Society; Keats-Shelley Memorial Association *recreations* travel, poetry, football, cricket *publications* upcoming book on liberalism and the sacred; an aesthetic theory of liberalism; articles/editorials on freedom of expression, scientism and the imagination, etc. *address* 208-210a High Road, East Finchley, London N2 9AY *tel* 020 8444 5413 home 07812 650 399 mobile *e-mail* ben.ramm@talk21.com

RAMPTON, Carolyn Mary *b* Jun 2, 1943 *m* Richard 2 *s* 1 *d education* St Michaels, Burton Park, Lycee Francais de Londres, Kingston Univ (MA Hons business and public sector strategy) *career* manager, Richmond Citizens Advice Bureau 1980-1995; senior researcher, Liberal Democrats, House of Lords 1995-2005; Head of Office, Liberal Democrats, House of Lords 2006 - *party* joined Liberal party 1987; vice-chair of Richmond LP 1990-92; chair Barnes Ward 1988-1990, 1994-1996; computer officer, Barnes Ward 1994 - ; Office Manager, Jenny Tonge MP's election campaign 1997, 2001; Campaign Coordinator, Susan Kramer MP's election campaign 2005 *special interests* politics and political writing *recreations* Italy and France and their languages, Italian renaissance painting, romanesque architecture, Mozart and 6 (at present!) grandaughters *address* 88 Castelnau, London, SW13 9EU *e-mail* ramptonc@parliament.uk

RAMSBOTTOM, Marc Steve *b* Nov 27, 1963 1 *s* born 1990 *education* Morecambe High School; Manchester Polytechnic (BA History and Politics); Univ of Leicester (MA Employment Law and Industrial Relations) *career* General Manager, Manchester Metropolitan University; trusteeships: Students Union Superannuation Scheme 1992- , Robert Stanley Armitage Trust Fund 2004- ; Director of Community Security 2004- ; *party* PPC Altrincham and Sale West 1997, Oldham West and Royton 2001, Manchester Central 2005; elected mbr Manchester City Council 2000- ; *special interests* higher education, urban regeneration, planning, criminal justice, foreign affairs *recreations* swimming, walking, golf, weight training, and entertaining *address* 107 Victoria Mill. Lower Vickers Street, Manchester M40 7LJ *tel* 0161 202 6603 home 07976 352 513 mobile *e-mail* cllr.m.ramsbottom@manchester.gov.uk *web* www.marc.ramsbottom.org.uk

RANDERSON, Jennifer Elizabeth (Jenny) AM (Cardiff Central) Chair, Welsh Assembly Business Cttee *b* May 26, 1948 *m* Peter Randerson 1 *s* 1 *d education* Wimbledon High School. Bedford College, London Univ, Institute of Education London Univ (BA Hons History, PGCE *career* teacher, FE Lecturer Coleg Glan Hafren, Cardiff until winning Assembly election in 1999 *party* joined Liberals 1979; elected Cardiff Cllr 1983-2000, opposition leader 1995-99; mbr National Assembly for Wales 1999- , Minister for Culture, Sport and the Welsh Language in Partnership

Govt 2000-03, currently chair Assembly Business Cttee, party spokesperson Economic Development, Transport and Equal Opportunities; first chair Welsh Lib Dems 1988-90, currently chair Welsh Campaigns and Elections Cttee, mbr Welsh Exec, Welsh Policy Cttee; AM representative Federal Policy Cttee; PPC Cardiff Central 1992, 1997, Cardiff South 1987 *special interests* economic development, Europe, disability issues, education *other mbrships* ALDC, PCA, Women Liberal Democrats, Association for College Management, Friends of the Earth *recreations* travel, theatre, concerts, gardening *address* 99 Woodville Road, Cardiff CF24 4DY *tel* 029 2066 8558 *fax* 029 2089 8355 *e-mail* jenny@jennyranderson.com *web* www.jennyranderson.org

RAVAL, Dave *b* Feb 9,1970 *education* St Olave's Grammar School, Orpington; St. Johns College, Oxford (MEng Engineering, Economics and Management); Wolfson College, Cambridge (advanced course in design, manufacture and management) *career* business mentor, The Technology Partnership, Cambridge, specialises in helping start companies on the basis of new technologies, in the management of science and engineering in large organisations, and in Government science policy implementation; previously manufacturing engineer and manager *party* PPC Bexleyheath and Crayford 2005, Walthamstow LP Exec and borough-wide Campaigns Coordinator, mbr Green Lib Dems, ALDES, EMLD *special interests* environmental issues, new business development, science and engineering, fair international trade sport *other mbrships* former Chair of Trustees of a charity providing counselling for people subjected to discrimination at work *recreations* football referee (Level 4; semi-professional leagues) *address* 6 Alander Mews, Walthamstow, London E17 9SA *tel* 07788 780250 *e-mail* dave.raval@ttp.com

RAVENSCROFT, (Penelope) Lynne MSc *b* Apr 28, 1944, *m* Pelham Francis *qv* 1966, 2 *s* 2 *d education* Pates' Grammar School, Cheltenham; LSE (MSc criminal justice policy); currently doing PhD research on youth courts *career* 1976-2000 JP (Hampshire) 1978-98; chair PTA 1978-81; 1978-1998 governor Alton (6th Form) College 1978-98; management Cttee hostel for ex-offenders; council mbr then trustee Howard League for Penal Reform 1981- ; chair then president local NSPCC 1984- ; Hampshire Probation Cttee 1986-89; chair Hampshire Association for Care and Resettlement of Offenders 1988-91; Hampshire Magistrates' Courts Cttee 1989-95; ethical research Cttee NE Hants Health Authority 1989-95; council Magistrates Association 1994-98,; researched, led campaign on child prostitution 1997, chair youth courts Cttee 1998; Children's Society advisory council on child prostitution 1998-2000; magisterial Cttee Judicial Studies Board 1995-2000; criminal Cttee Justice 1997-2000; NACRO working party, criminal justice 1999-2000; East Hants Domestic Violence Forum 1998- ; editor Children Law UK Conference papers 1999- ; writer, broadcaster on criminal justice; mbr Immigration Appeals Tribunal 2003- *party* joined Liberals 1969, local activist NE Hants; PPC Chichester 2001; administrator WLD 1999-2000; treasurer Lib Dem Lawyers Association 2000-; mbr Crime and Policing policy gp 2001 *special interests* - women's, children's rights; criminal justice policy; European Union *other mbrships* Amnesty, Liberty, Justice *recreations* making things; theatre, music, enjoying rural France *address* 78a Cambridge St. Pimlico, London SW1V 4QQ *tel* 020 7931 7724; Oakwoods Farmhouse, Selborne, Alton Hampshire GU34 3BS *tel* 01420-472470

RAVENSCROFT, Pelham Francis BA (Cantab) *b* May 10, 1930 *m* Lynne *qv* 4 ch *career* chartered accountant (FCA) *party* active in East Hampshire since 1968 (constituency has changed several times); chair Euro constituency for Nancy Seear's campaign; district Cllr 1987-99: chair 1992-3; chair, environment and planning Cttee 1993-99 *other interests* chair, Kingsley Centre (training physically disabled for greater independence); finance director Empire Museum Ltd; vice chair Earthworks Trust Ltd.(sustainability centre at East Meon); accountant, The Trollope Society *clubs* NLC *address* Oakwoods Farmhouse, Selborne, Alton Hampshire GU34 3BS *tel* 01420-472470

RAYNER, Claire Berenice OBE (1996) *b* Jan 22 1931 education City of London School for Girls; Royal Northern School of Nursing (SRN; awarded Hospital Gold Medal for outstanding achievement); Guy's Hospital School of Midwifery *m* Desmond 1957 2 *s* Adam, Jay career sister, Paediatrics Dept, Whittington Hospital, London; writer, broadcaster, public speaker: advice columnists various magazines, newspapers *party* joined Lib Dems Oct 2001 (after fifty years as prominent Labour supporter); contributor to party political broadcast 2002 *other interests* president Patients Association; Hon Fellow, Univ of North London (1988); hon doctorate Oxford Brookes Univ (1999); Freeman, City of London (1981); mbr RSM *publications* more than ninety (some under pseudonyms Sheila Brandon, Ann Lynton) including *The Performers* (12 volumes: translated into several languages), *The Poppy Chronicles* (six volumes), *The George Barnabas novels* *style* Clare Rayner OBE

RAZZALL, Deirdre: Editor, *Liberal Democrat News* *b* Feb 2, 1949 1 *s* Rupert Martineau 1 *d* Zoe Martineau 1 *sd* Katie Razzall 1 *ss* James Razzall *education* Sherborne School for Girls; Institute Videmanette, Rougemont (Alliance Francaise Diploma) *party* elected Cllr Mortlake Ward, LB Richmond 1977-94, chair housing 1983-90, chair education 1990-94; London Regional Media Co-ordinator 1992-97; mbr education, housing policy Cttees; chaired Federal Conference plenary sessions *special interests* Richmond Music Trust (chair 1994-2000) *recreations* music, food, wine, gardening *address* 4 Cowley Street, London SW1 3NB *tel* 020 7227 1361 *e-mail* ldn@libdems.org.uk

RAZZALL, Lord Tim: Life Peer cr 1997: Edward Timothy Razzall CBE 1993: Lords Spokesperson on Trade and Industry *b* Jun 12, 1943 *education* St Paul's School; Worcester College, Oxford *career* solicitor Frere Cholmeley Bischoff 1968-95, partner 1973-95, chief Exec 1990-93 *party* joined Liberal Party 1963; vice chair Acton Liberal Association 1967-68, elected Cllr (Mortlake Ward) LB of Richmond May 1974-98 (stood down), deputy gp leader 1978-98, deputy leader of council 1983-98, chair Policy Resources 1983-97; treasurer Liberal Party 1987-88, treasurer Liberal Democrats 1988-2000; chair Campaigns and Communications Cttee 2000-06; mbr National Exec Liberal Party 1986-88; mbr Federal Exec 1988- ; president ALDC 1990-95; Lib Dem Peer 1997, House of Lords spokesman on Trade and Industry 1998- *special interests* trade, industry *address* House of Lords, London SW1 0PW *tel* 0207 247 2280 *fax* 0207 247 2375 *e-mail* tim@Argonaut-associates.net

REDESDALE, 6th Baron UK Rupert Bertram Mitford cr 1902; also Life Peer Lord Mitford of Redesdale cr 2000; House of Lords Spokesman on Energy *b* Jul

18, 1967 *m* Helen 1998 1 *s* Hon Bertram David 1 *d* Clementine Amelia *education* Milton Abbey; Highgate School; Newcastle Univ (BA Hons archaeology) *party* candidate LB Camden council 1998; president of Holborn and St Pancras LP; chair International Development Working Gp; left House of Lords in 1999 reform but returned as youngest-ever Life Peer in 2000; front bench spokesman on Northern Ireland 1999-2001, international development 1994-99, defence 2000-04; energy 2005- ; mbr Select Cttee on Science and Technology 1993-97; European Union Select Cttee *special interests* International Development, environment *other mbrships* council of Institute of Advanced Motorists; proprietor The Redesdale Arms, Northumbria *recreations* caving, climbing, skiing, archaeology *address* 116 St Georges Avenue N7 0AH *tel* 0207 609 2049

REID, Alan MP (Argyll & Bute maj:5,636) **Shadow Northern Ireland spokesperson** *b* Aug 7, 1954 *education* Ayr Academy; Strathclyde Univ (BSc Hons) *career* computer project manager at Glasgow Univ; MP 2001- *party* mbr Renfrew District Council 1988-96; PPC Paisley South 1990, 1992; Dumbarton 1997; Argyll and Bute 2001 elected, 2005 re-elected; vice-convener Scottish Liberal Democrats 1994-98; mbr Scottish Party Exec to 2003; Scottish election agent - Argyll & Bute 1999; junior Whip 2001-05; Common Fisheries Policy Reform Spokesperson 2001-05; mbr Broadcasting Select Cttees 2001-05; Shadow DTI spokesperson 2005-06 *other mbrships* Association of Univ Teachers (AUT) *recreations* chess, walking, reading *address* House of Commons, London, SW1A 0AA; 44 Hillfoot Street, Dunoon, Argyll PA23 7DT *tel* 01369 704840 *e-mail* reida@parliament.uk *web* www.kirtel.demon.co.uk/argyll_libdems

RENDEL, David *b* Apr 15, 1949 *m* Sue (GP) 3 *s education* Eton; Oxford Univ (BA physics, philosophy; rowing blue: mbr record-breaking Boat Race crew 1974) *career* VSO teacher Cameroon, Uganda (during gap year);.financial and computing manager, energy industry (Shell International, British Gas, Esso) *party* mbr Newbury DC 1987, re-elected 1991 (when Lib Dems took control with 24 of 37 seats); chair Finance and Property sub-Cttee, Recreational Cttee; stood down 1995; PPC Fulham 1979, 1983, Newbury 1987, 1992 (elected in historic by-election May 1993 MP for Newbury maj 22,055 with swing which surpassed historic Liberal victory Sutton and Cheam 1972), re-elected 1997, 2001; re-selected as PPC Newbury 2006; front bench spksmn Local Govt & Housing 1993-97; Social Security (lead largest rebellion of MPs of the Parliament, against Govt plans to scrap single parent benefits) 1997-1999; Spokesman on Higher, Further Education; 2001- ; mbr Public Accounts Cttee 1999- ; secy All Party Parliamentary Gp on Cycling; joint vice-chair All Party Parliamentary Gp on Racing and Bloodstock Industries; candidate for Party Leadership 1999 *recreations* walking, classical music, playing trumpet (badly) *address* House of Commons, London SW1 0AA *tel* 020 7219 3000; *constituency:* Kendrick House, Wharf Street, Newbury, Berkshire RG14 5AP *tel* 01635 581 048 *fax* 01635 581 049 *e-mail* newburyldp@cix.co.uk *web* www.davidrendel.libdems.org.uk

RENNARD, Lord Chris: MBE, Life Peer cr 1999: Chief Exec, Liberal Democrats *b* Jul 8, 1960 *m* Ann McTegart *education* Liverpool Bluecoat School; Univ of Liverpool *career* agent Liverpool Edge Hill & Mossley Hill Liberal Associations 1982-84; HQ area agent, Liberal Party organisation, East Midlands 1984-88; election co-ordinator, Social & Liberal Democrats 1988-89; Director of

Campaigns & Elections, Liberal Democrats 1989-2003; Chief Exec, Liberal Democrats 2003- ; *party* past secy, treasurer Church Ward Liberals, secy Liverpool Wavertree constituency, chair Liverpool Young Liberals, Liverpool Univ Liberal and Social Democratic Society, deputy chair Liverpool Liberal Party; agent Liverpool City Council elections 1979-84, mbr various Liberal/Alliance parliamentary by-election teams including Edge Hill, Birmingham Northfield, Penrith, Chesterfield, Enfield Southgate, West Derbyshire (agent), Newcastle under Lyme, Greenwich; overall responsibility for Liberal Democrat parliamentary by-elections including Eastbourne, Ribble Valley, Kincardine and Deeside, Newbury, Christchurch, Eastleigh, Littleborough & Saddleworth, Winchester, Romsey, Brent East, Birmingham Hodge Hill and Leicester South; directed General Election target seat campaigns 1992, 1997 and overall responsibility for General Elections in 2001 and 2005 *publications* various ALC/ALDC publications including *Winning Local Election*, *The Campaign Manual* (1st & 2nd editions) *address* 4 Cowley Street, London, SW1P 3NB *tel* 0207 227 1202 *e-mail* c.rennard@libdems.org.uk

RENNIE, Willie MP (Dunfermline and West Fife maj: 1,800) **Shadow Spokesperson on Defence** *b* Sept 27, 1967 *m* Janet (neé Macfarlane) Oct 31, 1992 2 *s education* Bell Baxter High School, Cupar; Paisley College of Technology (BSc Biology); Glasgow College (PgDip Industrial Administration) *career* constituency organiser, North Cornwall Liberal Democrats 1990-94; Campaigns Officer, Liberal Democrats 1994-97; Chief Exec, Scottish Liberal Democrats 1997-2001; Independent Communications Consultant 2001-03; Account Director, McEwan Purvis 2003-2006; *party* Agent to Paul Tyler 1992; agent to Diana Maddock 1993, Robin Teverson 1994; elected MP in 2005 by-election *other mbrships* NLC, Carnegie Harriers recreations running and coal carrying *e-mail* renniew@parliament.uk *web* www.dunfermlinelibdems.org

RICH, Ben *b* March, 29 1966 *m education* (Dulwich College; York Univ (BA Hons Politics, English) *career* president York Univ Students Union 1987-8, chair Student Liberal Democrats 1989-90; Northern Ireland researcher to Lord Holme 1990-91; PCA Campaigns Officer 1991-95; PR consultancy Luther Pendragon 1995- , partner 1999 *party* vice chair Federal Policy Cttee 1997-2001; vice chair Brent East LP 1990-92; press officer, Harrow LP 2004- ; chair Urban Policy Working Gp 2000, Medically-assisted Dying policy working gp 2004 *special interests* media relations, communications, presentation skills training, public speaking *other mbrships* board mbr Reprieve (charity providing legal support to those facing death penalty in US, Caribbean); communications adviser Liberal Judaism Movement *recreations* chess; bridge; playing cricket badly, watching cricket *publications* endless policy papers! *address* 69 Cecil Park, Pinner, Middlesex HA5 5HL *tel* 0208 869 9539

RICKARD, Rear-Admiral Hugh Wilson CBE BSc MIL *b* Sept 1, 1948 *m* Tricia 2 *s* James, Tom 1 *d* Katie *education* Surbiton County Grammar School; London Univ (BSc Hons) *career* Royal Navy (28 years): appointments included Defence and Naval Attaché to The Hague; Commodore (chief Exec) HMS Raleigh; Senior Directing Staff (Navy); Deputy Chief Exec, Royal College of Defence Studies; Chief Exec Liberal Democrats until Oct 2003; Chief Exec Royal Anniversary Trust – Queen's Awards for Higher and Further Education May 2004- *party* closet Liberal Democrat following Madrid Summit, came out on leaving RN; joined party after being appointed chief Exec; elected mbr Federal Exec 2003-05 *special interests* sailing, skiing, character-development of young people, disadvantaged gps through medium of sail-training; skipper London Sailing Project; education director, Claremont Fan Court Foundation *recreations* family, skiing, sailing, music, spiritual development clubs Navy, NLC *address* High Burrows, The Drive, Sutton, Surrey SM2 7DP *tel* 020 8661 6258 *fax* 020 8661 6258 *e-mail* hugh.rickard@btclick.com

RIJKE, Nicholas David *b* Jun 7, 1966 *education* Staffordshire Univ (BA Hons International Relations); Exeter Univ (MA Middle East Politics) *career* Kleinwort Benson Ltd, Devon Liberal Democrats, David Rendel MP, Local Government Association, Environment Agency *party* joined 1981; PPC St Albans 2001; Federal Policy Cttee 2004; treasurer Bath LP *special interests* foreign affairs, international security, education, environment *address* 39 Longfellow Avenue, Bath BA2 4SJ *tel* 01225 314074 *e-mail* nick.rijke@virgin.net

RILEY, Dr Alan *b* Aug 19, 1964 *education* solicitor's finals Europa Institute, Edinburgh Univ, PhD, LLM European law; Durham Univ BA law *career* currently, associate research fellow, Centre for European Policy Studies, Brussels; Reader in Private Law, City Law School, City Univ; formerly research fellow Nottingham Law School, journalist writing on European issues for Economist Intelligence Unit, editor European Union News; temporary lecturer in law Faculty of Law, Edinburgh University; solicitor EC law unit Theodore Goddard, London, Brussels *party* joined 1991; Euro candidate Greater Manchester East 1994; mbr Federal Policy Cttee on trade, industry; Vice-Chair East Midlands Liberal Democrats; past chair Nottingham City LP *special interests* EU law, human rights, competition law *other mbrships* Law Society of England and Wales; chair Competition Law Scholars Forum; walking in mountains, skiing *publications* various specialist publications on EU law; currently writing book on European human rights law for Oxford University Press *address* Flat 2, 19 Chapel Market, London N1 9EZ *tel* 020 7278 0220 home 020 7040 4142 office 07799 413792 mobile *e-mail* dr.alan.riley@btinternet.com; alan.riley.1@city.ac.uk

RIMMER, Martin Edward BEng, FInstSMM, BPREA *s* of George and Pat (nee Bowden) Rimmer *b* Oct 3, 1952 *m* Isobel McTaggart 2 *d* Josie, Ellie 1 *s* Thomas *education* Belmont Abbey School, Hereford, Liverpool Univ (Electrical Engineering) plus research programme with Westinghouse Inc, Pittsburgh, USA; BPREA Beaune, France in Vinification and Viticulture; *career* GEC Machines, Rugby 1970-74; Sperry Gyroscope (became BAe) Bracknell, 1975-77; Opperman Gears (Hawker Siddeley Company), Newbury 1977-82; Digital Equipment Co. Reading 1984-88; started second career 1988, started new businesses including Masterclass and Just Great Wine, currently MD *party* founder mbr, organiser SDP 1981, Cllr Royal Borough of Windsor and Maidenhead 1987-97, chair Leisure Services 1991-94; PPC Basingstoke 1997, Spelthorne 2001; co-author Lib Dem Disability Policy 1994, 1999; held many Exec officer positions within party since 1981 *special interests* disabled and disability rights (elected mbr Scope); Europe (mbr, guest speaker European Movement); Charter 88 *recreations* off-piste skiing, Liverpool FC, cooking, travel, breeding Bernese Mountain Dogs, Bengal Cat Club rescue *style* Mr Martin Rimmer *address* Morningside, Knowle Grove, Virginia Water, GU25 4JD *tel* 01344 430505 *fax* 01344 845524 *e-mail* martinr@masterclass.co.uk or martinr@justgreatwine.com

RIPPETH, Thomas Philip (Tom) *b* Jul 29, 1966 Hexham *ptnr* Linda Scott *education* Ryton Comprehensive School, Reading University (BSc joint Hons Phys & Met), University of Wales (MSc Physical Oceanography; PhD Physical Oceanography) *career* Research Fellow, University of Wales Bangor, Institute of Ocean Sciences Victoria, Vancouver Island *party* various roles inc. mbr of Welsh Exec 2000, 2002 and Federal Exec 2000; stood as a candidate for Gateshead MBC 1988, 1990, 1991; Ynys Mon WBC 1999; Flintshire 2004; Welsh Assembly: North Wales List 1999, Wrexham constituency 2003; Westminster Parliament: Wrexham 2005; mbr ALDC, LDEngineers & Scientists *other mbrships* American Geophysical Union; Fellow of the Royal Meteorological Society, AUT *special interests* environment, energy, social justice, human rights *publications* over 30 publications in International Peer Reviewed Science Journals (eg. Phil Trans Roy Soc., J Phys. Oceanogr., Geophys Res Letts) *recreations* music (play traditional jazz trombone and piano), hiking, cross country skiing, cycling, astronomy *LD quirk* formerly mbr of Micheal Meadowcrofts Granny Lee All Star Jazz Band *style* Dr *address* 12, Pilgrim's Close, Northop, Flints, CH7 6BF *tel* 01352 840 972 home 01248 382293 work 0772 0399 298 mobile 01352 840973 (fax) *e-mail* tom.rippeth@tiscali.co.uk

ROAF, Dermot James CBE, MA, PhD *b* Mar 25, 1937 *m* Caroline (nee Hughes) MA, PhD, Visiting Research Fellow, Oxford Brookes Univ 1*s* 2*d* 6*gch education* Winchester College; Christ Church, Oxford (BA Maths); Trinity College, Cambridge (PhD Physics) *career* Fellow in Mathematics, Exeter College, Oxford 1961-2004, with periods as Senior Tutor, Bursar etc; Lecturer in Theoretical Physics, Oxford Univ 1962-2004, Senior Proctor 1974-75; Visiting Lecturer Monash Univ Australia 1968-69; Arthur Andersen Travelling Fellow (studying Inflation Accounting in USA) 1975 *party* after eight unsuccessful campaigns (including PPC Oxford City 1979) elected Oxfordshire County Council 1981 (since re-elected six times); gp leader 1995-2000, 2004- ; deputy leader of council 2004-05; mbr Association of County Councils 1985-1994, gp leader 1990-04 (hence third class honour); mbr South East England Regional Assembly 1999-2001, Exec 2000-01; mbr Education Exec of Local Govt Association 2003-4; vice-chair Local Govt Employers 2005- ; *special interests* local govt finance *recreations* bell-ringing, tower-captain St Giles, Oxford 1982- *address* 27 St Margaret's Road, Oxford OX2 6RX *tel* 01865 559467 home 01865 815285 work *fax* 01865 316388 home 01865 815323 work *e-mail* dermot.roaf@oxfordshire.gov.uk

ROAF, Susan *b* Oct 28, 1952 Penang, Malaya *m* Michael Douglas Roaf 1978, divorced 1995, 2 *s education* Talbot Heath School, Bournemouth; Manchester University (BA Hons in Architecture 1975); Architectural Association (AA Diploma 1978); Oxford Polytechnic (PhD on the Windcatchers of Yazd 1989); Registered Architect 1978; Fellow of the Schumacher Society 2000; Liveryman of the Worshipful Company of Chartered Architects 2000; Freeman of the City of London 2001 *career* practising architect in a range of practices 1975-present: including Manchester City Council, WRM, APP Horsham, John Perryman Oxford and in private practice and consultancy; field work in architecture anthropology and archaeology in Iran and Iraq 1975-86; lecturer at Baghdad Univ 1981-84; lecturer Oxford Polytechnic 1989-93; Principal Lecturer Oxford Brookes University 1993-2000; Professor Oxford Brookes Univ 2000-06; Arizona State Univ Visiting Professor 2006- ; trustee, The Michael Ventris Award 1982- ; trustee, The Anthony Pott Memorial Fund Award 1984- ; trustee, The Rawson Trust 2003- ; trustee, The

City of Oxford Charity 2006- ; Co-founder and Director of TIA, the Teachers in Architecture 1994- ; *party* Liberal Democrat Oxford City Cllr 2002- ; *special interests* the impacts of climate change on the built environment and mitigation and adaptation policies, strategies and climate change action planning and implementation *publications* co-author of books on ice-houses, energy efficiency, ecohouse design, benchmarks for sustainable buildings, adapting buildings and cities for climate change and a carbon counting handbook for buildings and numerous academic and popular papers and articles *recreations* family, gardening, films, reading *address* 26 Blandford Avenue, Oxford OX2 8DY *tel* 01865 515001 *e-mail* s.roaf@btinternet.com

ROBERTS, Karen *b* Jun 20, 1961 Clydach Vale, Rhondda *m* 2*ch education* Cwmclydach Infant and Junior Schools; Tonypandy Grammar School; Univ of Wales, Univ College Cardiff *career* former lecturer in retail studies; sales negotiator; development worker for Clybiau Plant Cymru *party* currently Gp Administrator Welsh Liberal Democrat Assembly Gp; part-time Party administrator; leader Welsh Liberal Democrat Council Gp until 2004; mbr and chair Rhondda Cynon Taff; PPC Rhondda 2005; County Council candidate 2004; mbr ALDC; previously Plaid Cymru cllr and Cabinet mbr for Education Rhondda Cynon Taff CBC; joined Welsh Liberal Democrats in 2002 as cllr Rhondda Cynon Taff CBC *special interests* education *recreations* reading, pub quizzes, work with a range of voluntary organisations *address* Pwwl Yr Hebog, Wern Street, Clydach Vale, Rhondda Cynon Taff CF40 2DH *tel* 01443 433648 home, 02920 898741 business, 07990 573591 mobile *e-mail* karen.roberts@rctlibdems.org.uk *web* www.rctlibdems.org.uk

ROBERTS of Llandudno, Rev Lord John Roger Roberts: Life Peer cr 2004 *b* Oct 23, 1935 *education* John Bright Grammar School, Llandudno; Univ College of North Wales; Handsworth Methodist College, Birmingham *m* (widowed) 3 *ch career* Methodist minister 1957- , superintendent Methodist minister Llandudno 1984- *party* five times PPC Conwy; president Welsh Liberals, Welsh Liberal Democrats; former gp leader Aberconwy Borough Council; board mbr Centre Forum *other interests* chair Aberconwy Talking Newspaper for the Blind, trustee Fund for Human Need *address* House of Lords, London SW1A 0PW

ROBINSON, Stephen John *b* Oct 3, 1966 Essex *m* Angela Staddon 1*s* Charlie *education* Buckhurst Hill County HS; Univ of Central Lancashire (BA Hons law with politics) *career* self-employed legal, political research 1989-94; regional director, RIBA (Royal Institute of British Architects) East/London 1995- ; *party* mbr Essex CC 1993-2001 (deputy gp leader); Epping Forest DC 1990-98, (jt council leader 1994-96); PPC Epping Forest 1997, Chelmsford West 2001, Chelmsford West 2005; various local party posts; mbr PCA, ALDC, LDEG *other mbrships* European Movement; Electoral Reform Society *address* 14 Paradise Road, Writtle, Chelmsford, CM1 3HP *tel* 01245 423084 or 0701 0702 500 *fax* 0870 321 1964 *e-mail* mail@stephenrobinson.org.uk *web* www.stephenrobinson.org.uk

ROBSON, Brian *b* Jun 9, 1981 *education* Sandhill View School, Sunderland 1992-97; City of Sunderland College 1997-99; Leeds Univ (BA Hons politics, parliamentary studies) 1999-2003 *career* campaign co-ordinator Orpington Liberal Democrats (just 269 votes to win at next GE) 2003- ; organiser Westminster Day 2002 (first, only appearance of Tony Blair); various internships during sandwich year: Department of Work & Pensions, Liberal Democrat Policy Unit, office of Phil Willis MP, Richard Allan MP *party* joined in Leeds, Sept 2000 (no-one had ever asked before); campaign Cttee, Leeds NW 2000-01; general Exec mbr LDYS 2001-02, vice chair (campaigns) 2002-03, chair 2003-04; approved PPC, party trainer *special interests* Europe *recreations* music, real ale, travel, Sunderland AFC *address* 7 Station Road, Orpington, BR6 0RZ *tel* 07949 297 030 *e-mail* mail@brianrobson.net

ROBSON, Euan MSP (Roxburgh & Berwickshire) Scottish Deputy Minister for Education and Young People *b* Feb 17, 1954 *education* Newcastle Univ (BA Hons History 1975); Durham Univ (PCG Education, Teaching Certificate 1976); Strathclyde Univ (MSc Political Science 1984) *m* 2 *d career* Scottish Manager, Gas Consumer Council *party* PPC, Hexham 1983, 1987; mbr Northumberland County Council 1981-89; elected Scottish Parliament May 1999; Deputy Minister for Education & Young People 2003- ; Scottish Chief Whip; Business Manager; Deputy Minister for Parliament 2001-03 ; spokesperson on Justice 2000-2001; Justice & Home Affairs 1999-2000; former spokesperson Rural Affairs, Team Leader *other interests* vice chair, founding mbr, Consumer Safety International; chair VAT on Fuel - Scotland Says No 1995-96 *other mbrships* Institute of Consumer Affairs; secy Kelso Angling Association; River Tweed Commissioners *address* Scottish Parliament, Edinburgh EH99 1SP5 0131-348 5806; 42-44 Horsemarket, Kelso, Roxburghshire TD5 7AEE *tel* 01573-228635 *e-mail* Euan.Robson.msp@scottish.parliament.uk *web* www.euanrobson.co.uk

RODGERS of Quarry Bank, Baron William Thomas Rodgers: Life Peer UK 1992, PC 1975 *b* Liverpool Oct 28, 1928 *education* Quarry Bank HS, Liverpool, Magdalen College Oxford *m* 1955 3 *d career* MP (Lab 1962-81, SDP 1981-83; director general RIBA 1987-94; chair Advertising Standards Authority 1995-2000; Hon FRIBA, Hon FIStructE *party* active in politics since 1945 GE; Exec Chairman of the Campaign for Democratic Socialism, supporting the leadership of Hugh Gaitskell against left wing. helping to resist Labour's drift to unilateral nuclear disarmament; PPC (Lab) Bristol West 1957, Teeside Stockton 1962 (elected) until 1979. when constituency changed to Stockton North 1979-83; served in Lab Govts as parliamentary under-secy(to George Brown) DEA (1964-67, FO 1967-68, Minister of State, Board of Trade 1968-69, Treasury 1969-70, MoD 1974-76, Transport Secy (under James Callaghan) 1976-79; General Secy Fabian Society 1953-60 (remained mbr until 1981); leader UK Delegation to Council of Europe, WEU 1967-68, chair Expenditure Cttee Trade & Industry 1971-74; one of *Gang of Four* set up SDP 1981; chair "Yes to Unity" campaign which won the ballot amongst SDP mbrs; created Life Peer 1992; spokesman Home Affairs 1994-97; succeeded Roy Jenkins as Lib Dem Leader House of Lords 1997-2001 *publications Hugh Gaitskell* 1963, *The People into Parliament* 1966, T*he Politics of Change* 1982, *Govt and Industry* 1986, *Fourth Among Equals* 2004 *style* The Rt Hon Lord Rodgers of Quarry Bank PC *address* 43 North Road, London, N6 4BE

ROGERS, David Owen *b* May 5, 1952 *partner* Alison Clish-Green (in Devon) 1 *s* 3 *d education* Royal Grammar School, Guildford; College of Commerce, Kingston-upon-Hull *career* entertainment/music business; OPCS; househusband; continuous elected and appointed public service over 27 years: East Sussex County Council 1977- , opposition leader; Brighton borough council 1979-91; Newhaven Town

Council 1989- ; Lewes District Council 1991- , deputy leader; Sussex Police Authority (past chair); East Sussex, Brighton & Hove Health Authority 1995-98; South East England Development Agency 1998-2001; Local Govt Association; chair Community Wellbeing Board *party* joined Liberal Party 1960s; Liberal Democrats from formation; former chair Brighton Young Liberals; Brighton Pavilion Liberal Association; Lewes Constituency Liberal Democrats; General Election agent to David Bellotti, Norman Baker; mbr of ALC/ALDC since 1977 *special interests* local, regional Govt; public health; community-led regeneration *other mbrships* chair, Asham Literary Endowment Trust *address* 74 Fort Road, Newhaven, East Sussex, BN9 9EJ *tel/fax* 01273 512172 *e-mail* cllr.david.rogers@eastsussexcc.gov.uk

ROGERSON, Dan MP (Cornwall North maj:3,076) *m* Heidi 1 *s education* Bodmin College; Univ of Wales, Aberystwyth (politics) *career* researcher Bedford Borough Council Lib Dem Gp, then councillor (elected 1999); admissions officer De Montfort Univ; party organiser in Cornwall 2002-04 *party* cllr Bedford BC 1999-2002 (deputy gp leader); PPC Bedfordshire NE 2001, Cornwall North 2005 (elected); DEFRA spokesperson 2005-06; mbr DEFRA Select Cttee 2005- ; mbr Communities and Local Govt team 2006- ; *special interests* promoting Cornish language, devolution and a Cornish assembly; affordable housing and shared equity schemes *recreations* Terry Pratchett fantasy novels, blues music, political history, Celtic culture *address* Church Stile, Market Street, Launceston PL15 8AT *tel* 01566 777123 *fax* 01566 772122 *e-mail* contact@danrogerson.org

ROPER of Thorney Island, Baron: John Francis Hodgess Roper: Life Peer cr 2000 *b* Sept 10, 1935 *widower* 1 *d* Kate *education* William Hulme's Grammar School, Manchester; Reading School; Magdalen College, Oxford; Univ of Chicago *career* National Service Royal Navy 1954-56; lecturer Manchester Univ 1961-70; MP Farnworth 1970-1983, Labour and Coop 1970-1981, SDP 1981-83; editor, researcher Royal Institute of International Affairs, 1983-90; director Western European Union Institute of Security Studies, Paris 1990-95; professor College of Europe, Bruges, 1996-99; House of Lords 2000- , Liberal Democrat Chief Whip in House of Lords 2001-05 *party* Labour Party 1957, SDP 1981, Liberal Democrats 1987 *special interests* foreign, defence policy, European integration, parliamentary process *recreations* walking gently, reading, talking *address* 21 Gladstone Court, 97 Regency Street, London SW1P 4AL *tel* 020 7976 6220 home 020 7219 8663 **office** *fax* 020 7219 2377 *e-mail* roperj@parliament.uk

ROSENSTIEL, Colin Richard *b* Oct 17, 1949 *m* Cllr Joye Rosenstiel 1978 2 *d* Katharine 1986, Lucy 1992 *education* London, Colet Court and St Paul's, Hammersmith, 1957-67; Trinity College, Cambridge, 1968-72 BA (Cantab) *career* 25 years in Pye/Philips/Simoco, Cambridge 1973-98, first in sales support, from 1990, in IT 1998-2000, in software support for asset-management software company, Cambridge; since 2001, IT support consultant, Lib Dem HQ, Cowley Street *party* first activity 1966 General Election, joined Putney Young Liberals later that year; active as Cambridge student from 1968, conference representative since 1969; Cambridge city Cllr 1973-88, 1992- ; Liberal/Alliance gp leader 1976-86, deputy leader Lib Dem gp, City Council since 2000; editor City Centre Circular (published since 1969); for much of the last 30 years mbr English Council; ALC/ALDC Management Cttee (previously Standing Cttee) since 1970s *special* *interests* count STV elections for party since 1981, Cambridge students union (since 1971); transport policy, especially cycling, railways and residents' parking schemes *other mbrships* chair Electoral Reform Society 2003- ; council mbr 1990- ; director, Glisson Printers Ltd recreations cycling and other transport interests *publications* *How to Conduct an Election by the Single Transferable Vote*, third edition (Joint ed) Electoral Reform Society, 1997; *The Four Least Solutions in Distinct Positive Integers of the Diophantine Equations* $= x3 + y3 = z3 + w3 = u3 + v3 = m3 + n3$, by E Rosenstiel, JA Dardis and CR Rosenstiel, The Institute of Mathematics and its Applications Bulletin July, 1991, Volume 27 *address* 17 Grafton Street, Cambridge CB1 1DS *tel* 01223 368326 home 020 7222 7999.business *e-mail* rosenstiel@cix.co.uk

ROSS, Colin Andrew *b* Oct 29, 1975 *education* Lucas Vale Primary School, Deptford, London 1979-87; Addey and Stanhope Secondary School, New Cross, London 1987-92; Orpington College of FE 1992-94; Univ of Wolverhampton (BA Hons politics, law) 1994-97 *career* sabbatical communications officer LDYS 1997-98; local youth council development officer, British Youth Council 1998-99; overseas 1999-2000; constituency organiser, campaigns officer 2000-02; overseas 2002-03; parliamentary campaigns officer, Royal Society for the Protection of Birds 2003-04; assistant to Liberal Democrat gp, Walsall Metropolitan Borough Council 2004- *party* joined Spring 1992 (following school mock election; various offices including mbr English Council; training officer, West Midlands Region; Exec Agents and Organisers Association; party trainer; former ELDR Congress representative; secy Agents and Organisers Association; chair West Midlands LDYS; communications officer LDYS; Exec mbr, Lewisham LP, Wolverhampton LP *special interests* international affairs (especially development of emerging democracies Eastern Europe, Africa); international aid, European Union, environment, equality, access, party development *other mbrships* Electoral Reform Society *recreations* travelling, swimming, chess, backgammon, cinema publications various youth rights publications, British Youth Council; LDYS guides, pamphlets *address* 54 Clifford Street, Wolverhampton WV6 0AA *tel* 07989 488105 *e-mail* colin@colin-ross.org.uk

ROSSI, Marie-Louise Elizabeth MA (Oxon), MIEx, FRSA; Chair, The Peel Gp *b* Feb 18, 1956 *education* St Paul's Girls' School; St Anne's College, Oxford (*Literae Humaniores*) *career* Hogg Robinson plc 1979-87, specialising in export credits, political risks; Sedgwick plc 1987-90; Tillinghast-Towers Perrin, management consultants and actuaries 1990-93; chief exec, London International Insurance & Reinsurance Market Association 1993-98; chief exec, International Underwriting Association 1998-2005 (www.iua.co.uk), representing £11 billion-plus market to Govts worldwide; deputy chair, European Movement UK 2004- ; visiting lecturer, Cass Business School 2005- ; head of Insurance and Risk Management, The New Security Programme (Centre for Defence and International Security Studies, Henley); formerly mbr, Bank of England City Euro Gp; General Cttee of Lloyd's Register; mbr Learning & Skills Council (London Central) 2001-05; governing Council, Univ of Nottingham 2001-05 *party* joined Liberal Democrats 2001, having led negotiations for the merger with the Pro Euro Conservative Party; Treasurer/Secy, The Peel Gp 2002-; Exec LDEG 2003-05 ; Exec PCA 2003- ; founder chair PCA Foreign Affairs Forum 2003-05; PPC Cities of London & Westminster 2005; number seven Euro candidate, Yorkshire & Humber 2003 (dropping to reserve on enlargement 2004); council candidate, St James's Ward, City of Westminster 2002; previously elected as Conservative to Westminster City Council 1986-94 (Baker Street Ward), chair of Education and Leisure 1989-92, chair Arts; chair Investments; chair, Bow Gp 1988-89; chair Foreign Affairs Forum, Conservative Party 1993-96; vice-chair Conservative Gp for Europe; chair Organising Cttee, Pro Euro Conservative Party 1999-2001 *special interests* international trade; financial services regulation; education; environment *other mbrships* Athenaeum Club; Special Forces Club; vice-president Insurance Institute of London; affiliate, Institute of Actuaries; council mbr Federal Trust; governor, new City of London Academy; associate, Foreign Press Assocation *tel* 020 8529 7339 *e-mail* mlrossi@cix.co.uk

ROULSTON, Gemma Mary *b* Jul 1, 1965 *m* Chris 1 *s* James 1 *d* Claire *education* Teesside Polytechnic 1984-87; Kirby College of FE 1987-88; St Mary's Sixth Form College 1981-84; Teesside High School 1976-81 *career* mbrship assistant Lib Dems 2001- ; mother, carer 1991- ; pensions admin Jan-Sept 1991; Crown Financial Management; admin officer Inland Revenue 1988-1990 *party* joined 1992; mbrship secy Reigate LP 1994-2001; mbrship secy LD Disability Association 1999- , chair 2002-05, vice-chair 2006- ; former secy ECC *special interests* disability, education, environment, and justice and peace (Make Poverty History, Oxfam, Christian Aid, etc) *other mbrships* RNID, AFASIC recreations supporting Middlesbrough FC, wine, food, sport *address* 98 Colesmead Road, Redhill, Surrey RH 1 2EQ *tel* 01737 277607 home 020 7340 4954 business *e-mail* gemma.roulston@ntlworld.com or g.roulston@libdems.org.uk

ROWEN, Paul MP (Rochdale maj:442) *education* Bishop Henshaw Memorial HS; Nottingham Univ (chemistry and geology) *career* teacher, deputy head Yorkshire Martyrs Catholic College, Bradford *party* worked on Cyril Smith's campaign in 1972; elected Rochdale MBC 1983, chair of housing 1985-86, leader LD Gp 1990, leader of council 1992-96; mbr ALDC Standing Cttee 1996-99; PPC Rochdale 2001, 2005 (elected); Shadow Transport spokesperson 2005- ; *special interests* education, housing, youth services, international development *recreations* hill-walking, travel, reading *address* 246 Queensway, Rochdale OL11 2NH tel 01706 355176 fax 01706 660295 *e-mail* rowenp@parliament.uk *web* www.rochdalelibdems.org.uk

ROWLANDS, Anthony Francis, Exec Director: Centre Forum *b* Shanklin, Isle of Wight Aug 11, 1952 *m* Harriet 1 *s* 1 *d education* Ryde School, Ryde, Isle of Wight; The Queen's College, Oxford (degree in Modern History); Churchill College, Cambridge (PGCE); Univ of London MA (in Educational Administration) *career* teacher/head of department, number of secondary schools; Director, Centre for Reform 2000-05 *party* joined Liberal Party 1974; volunteer in office of the late Steven Ross MP, 1978; secy, St Albans Liberal Party 1981-3; Cllr St Albans City and District Council 1986-2003, 2006- ; Hertfordshire County Cllr 1993-97; PPC St Albans, 1997; PPC Isle of Wight 2005 *special interests* education, economic development, constitutional reform *other mbrships* St Albans Striders; Shanklin Cricket Club; Friends of Brading Roman Villa; MCC; National Liberal Club; Burnley Supporters Club *recreations* soccer (watching Burnley stave off relegation, again!); cricket; running marathons (15 to date) *address* 106 Beaumont Avenue, St Albans AL1 4TP *tel* 01727 839132 home 020 7340 1165 work *e-mail* anthonyrowlands@hotmail.com

ROWLEY, Alexandra Margaret Bsc MA MCLIP DMS *b* Apr 24,1946 Horncastle *m* David 1967 1 *s* 2 *d education* Horncastle Grammar School; Nottingham Univ (BSc Hons Zoology); Loughborough Univ (MA Librarianship); Gloucestershire (DMS) *career* asst librarian, Nottingham Public Libraries; Wilts County Library; Learning Centre Manager, Cheltenham & Gloucester College of HE; librarian, Worcestershire Acute Hospitals NHS Trust *party* joined 1989; chair, Mid-Worcs LP 1995-99; chair, Worcs & S.Warks Euro Constituency 1993-4; mbr Wychavon DC 1995- ; chair, Environment Cttee 1997-9; gp leader 1999- ; PPC Bromsgrove 2001, Mid-Worcs 2005 *special interests* environmental, rural issues, transport *other mbrships* chartered mbr, Institute of Library and Information Professionals; secy, WM Branch CILIP 2004- ; mbr WMRA Sustainability Review Gp 2004; chair, Droitwich Canals Trust 1998- ; Worcestershire Wildlife Trust *recreations* walking, gardening *address* Old Park, Plough Rd, Tibberton, Droitwich Spa, Worcs WR9 7NN *tel* 01905 345307 home 01905 760601 business 07899 053700 mobile *e-mail* mrowley@worcs.com

ROWLEY, Simon *b* Mar 9 1949 *m* Gill *education* Wellington College, Berkshire; Univ of York 1969-71 (BA Maths and Economics); also ran the student newspaper *career* systems analyst Rolls-Royce 1971-73; selling computer services for NatWest bank company 1974-81; set up, ran Apple/IBM PC dealership, West London 1981-93; IT consultant 1993-99; accounts/IT director, magazine publisher 1999-2002; freelance IT/business consultant 2003- *party* joined Union of Liberal Students, York 1970; helped revive West Hampstead ward 1974; candidate Ealing local borough election 1978; PPC for Ealing Acton 1979; GLC candidate Ealing Acton 1981; chair Ealing North 2000; chair Ealing Lib Dem Borough Gp 2001, secy 2003; London Region Exec 2004 *special interests* community politics, transport, sustainability *other mbrships* 2002 joint founder/Cttee mbr EPTUG (Ealing Passenger Transport Users Gp); 2001 chair Ealing LA21 Transport Gp *recreations* tennis, cycling, travel *address* 3 Gordon Road, Ealing, London W5 2AD *tel* 020 8998 7982 *e-mail* srowley@dircon.co.uk

RUMBLES, Mike MSP (West Aberdeenshire and Kincardine) Scottish Parliamentary Health Spokesperson *b* Jun 10, 1956 *education* St James School, Hepburn, County Durham; Durham Univ (BEd Educational Studies1979); Univ of Wales (MSc Economic Strategic Studies 1990); Royal Military Academy, Sandhurst 1979-80 *m* 2 *s career* Education and Training Services Branch, British Army (retired as major); business management team leader, Aberdeen College; Fellow, Institute of Personnel & Development *party* joined 1974; parliamentary agent Jarrow 1974; policy officer, West Aberdeenshire and Kincardine LP; former secy, Kincardine and Deeside LP; PPC Aberdeen North 1997; elected Scottish Parliament May 1999; spkspn Rural Affairs 1999-2000; Rural Development 2000-03; Health Spokesperson 2003- ; substitute mbr Communities Cttee 2003- ; former spkspn Transport and Environment (Energy); chair, Scottish European Election Cttee 2004 *recreations* family, hill-walking, tennis, chess *address* Scottish Parliament, Edinburgh EH99 1SP *constituency* 6 Dee Street, Banchory Aberdeenshire AB31 5ST *tel* 01330 820268 *fax* 01330 820106 *e-mail* mike.rumbles.msp@scottish.parliament.uk

RUNCIMAN, Carol Elizabeth *b* Mar 27, 1943 Walton-on-Thames *partner* Ian Cuthbertson *qv* 1 *d education* Sir William Perkins School, Surrey; Gipsy Hill College, London; Leeds Metropolitan Univ; Manchester Metropolitan Univ *career*

teacher London, Surrey, Leeds; adviser for under fives, Leeds Social Services Dept; FE lecturer (Early Years) Leeds; FE section head, then head of department, Scarborough; Early Years Development Manager, NYCC; external examiner, moderator, verifier 1978- ; JP 1978- , and deputy chair Leeds Family Panel; exec mbr Children's Services, City of York Council 2003- ; *party* involved since childhood; cllr City of York, Huntington and New Earswick Ward 1999- ; Secy Wortley Ward, Leeds 1968-78; Leeds West GE Campaign Team 1983; Leeds West Exec during merger; Ryedale Exec 1988;Vale of York LP, Chair 1995-99, Treasurer 1999-2002, presently Vice Chair; Haxby and Wigginton Branch, York, (previously Chair); Conference Chair, Yorkshire and the Humber (2000-3). Candidates Chair, Yorkshire & The Humber (2003-4), Agent (Ryedale 2005 GE), Assessor, Returning Officer, Accredited Party trainer; English Council Representative; mbr ALDC, LD Agents & Organisers Association, LDEA *special interests* education, post-16 provision and early years; Children's Services; training, management development, candidate development, equal opportunities *other mbrships*: Magistrates' Association, Association of External Verifiers *recreations*: reading, music (singing, performing, listening), theatre, walking *publications*: *Early Years* Heinemann 2002 (2nd edition 2006); *Care for Young Children in Four English Speaking Countries* Phi Delta Kappa Educational Foundation 2002 *style* Cllr Carol Runciman *address* Spurr House, Plainville Lane, Wigginton, York YO32 2RG *tel/fax* 01904 764356, 07944 259072 mobile *e-mail* cllr.crunciman@york.gov.uk

RUSSELL, Robert Edward (Bob) MP (Colchester maj: 6,277**) Shadow Defence Spokesperson** *b* Mar 31, 1946 Camberwell *education* Myland Primary Colchester; St Helena Secondary Modern; North Essex Technical College *m* Audrey 2 (twins) *s* 1 *d career* journalist; reporter *Essex County Standard, Colchester Gazette,* news editor *Braintree and Witham Times*; in Mar 1968 became country's youngest editor (aged 21) *Maldon and Burnham Standard*; subsequently four years in London as sub-editor *Evening News, Evening Standard*; press officer Post Office Telecommunications/British Telecom in Colchester 1973-85; publicity, information officer Univ of Essex at Colchester 1986-97; MP 1997- *party* elected Colchester BC 1971 (Labour until 1981, then SDP) longest serving mbr; Mayor 1986-87; leader of council 1987-91; PPC (Lab) Sudbury and Woodbridge 1974, Colchester (which then included more than 30 villages plus town) 1979; first former mayor to subsequently serve town as MP when elected 1997; a further claim to fame: he could be the fastest typing MP (75 wpm); mbr Home and Legal Affairs team 1997-99; sports spokesman 1999-2005; *other mbrships* Queen's Scout; Duke of Edinburgh Gold Award *publications* foreword *History of Colchester FC recreations* season ticket holder Colchester United Football (more than 49 years) *address* House of Commons, London SW1A 0AA *tel* 020 7219 5150; *constituency:* Magdalen Hall, Wimpole Road, Colchester CO1 2DE *tel* 01206 506600 *fax* 01206 606610 *e-mail* brooksse@parliament.uk *web* www.epolitix.com/bob+russell

RUSSELL-JOHNSTON, Baron Sir (David) Russell Russell-Johnston: Life Peer UK 1997, Kt 1958 (assumed by deed poll 1997 the surname Russell-Johnston in lieu of patronymic) *b* 1932 *education* Portree HS, Isle of Skye; Univ of Edinburgh (MA) *m* Joan Graham 1967 3 *s career* National Service, Intelligence Corps 1958; history teacher Liberton Secondary school Edinburgh 1961-63; research assistant Scottish Liberal Party 1963-64; MP 1964-97; MEP 1973-75 *party* revived Edinburgh Univ Liberal Club, president 1956.mbr Exec Scottish Liberal Party 1961-94 ; research assistant Scottish Lib Pty 1963-64; MP (Lib until 1988, later Lib Dem): Inverness 1964-83, Inverness, Nairn and Lochaber 1983-97; Lib spksn on Foreign and Commonwealth affrs 1970-75, 1979-85; Scotland 1970-73, 1975-83, 1985-87; Alliance spksn, Scotland, EU Community Affairs 1987; Lib Dem spksn Foreign and Commonwealth affrs 1988-89, Europe and East/West relations 1989-97; one of first UK Liberal mbrs of Euro parliament 1973-75 and 1976-79 (vice pres Political Cttee 1976-79), stood in first Euro direct election 1979, and 1984; president Scottish Lib Dems 1988-94 (chair 1970-74, Leader 1974-88); Deputy Leader Lib Dems 1989-92; WEU Assembly (rep to Council of Europe 1984-86, 1987, 1988- , leader Lib Gp 1994-, president sub-Cttee on Youth and Sport 1992-95, president Cttee on Culture & Education 1995- ; vice president ELDR 1990-92, President of Assembly 1999-2002; president Liberal International **other interests** mbr Royal Commission on Scottish Local Govt 1966-69, parliamentary spokesman for Scottish National Federation for Welfare of the Blind 1967-97; for 20 years, Parliamentary Representative for RNIB; vice chair Board of Governors , Westminster Foundation for Democracy 1992-97; winner of debating trophies: *The Scotsman* 1956, 1957, *The Observe*r Mace 1961 **publications** *Highland Development; To be a Liberal; Scottish Liberal Party Conference Speeches 1971-78, 1979-86, Humankind has no Nationality; Human Rights and Wrongs; Moral Politics* **recreations** reading, watching shinty (former player), modern trams and photography **clubs** Scottish Liberal **style** Lord Russell-Johnston **address** House of Lords, London SW1A 0PW

S

SAMPLE JP, Paul *b* Mar 22, 1961 *m* Catherine 1 *s* Robert 1 *d* Sophia **education** Bishop Wordsworth's School, Salisbury; City Univ, London (BSc Hons) **career** research assistant parliamentary Liberal Party 1983; research, information officer, Liberal Party Organisation 1984; editor *Liberal News, Liberal Democrats News* 1985-89; senior press officer Help the Aged 1989-91; head of PR Crime Concern 1991-93; head of communications The Leonard Cheshire Foundation 1993-95; director of communications Winged Fellowship Trust 1995-99; MD Paul Sample Corporate Communications Ltd 1999- *party* joined Salisbury Liberal Association 1977; delegate since Blackpool Special Assembly to discuss the Lib-Lab pact 1978; international vice chair Union of Liberal Students 1980; political vice chair ULS 1981; Lib/SDP Alliance candidate ILEA 1986; mbr Salisbury District Council 1990, re-elected 1991, 1995, 1999, 2003 (now longest continuously serving mbr); PPC Salisbury 1992; mbr Wiltshire County Council 1993-2005 (retired); mbr Wiltshire Police Authority (including Vice Chairman and Chairman of Complaints Cttee) 1993-2005; 737th Mayor of Salisbury (his mayoral appeal raised £66,500 to provide respite breaks for carers) 1997-1998; gp leader Wiltshire CC 2001-2003; gp leader Salisbury DC 2005- ; appointed by Lord Chancellor as a Justice of the Peace 2005 (South East Wiltshire Bench) **special interests** community safety **other mbrships** Chartered Institute of Public Relations; Magistrates Association; Salisbury Rugby Football Club **recreations** charity work, golf, horse racing, rugby, fishing; working hard for my community and constituents and having bloody good time as often as possible *publications* Oldest & The Best - The Official History of Wiltshire Constabulary 1839-2002 now in second edition *address* 24 Queens Road, Salisbury, Wiltshire SP1 3AJ *tel* 01722 744033 *fax* 01722 744031 *e-mail* paul@paulsample.co.uk

SANDBERG of Passfield in the County of Hampshire, Baron Sir Michael Graham Ruddock Sandberg: Life Peer cr 1997, kt 1986, CBE 1982, OBE 1977 *b* Surrey May 31, 1927 *education* St Edward's School, Oxford *m* 1954, Carmel Mary Roseleen, nee Donnelly 2 *s* 2 *d career* 6 Lancers (Indian Army), King's Dragoon Guards 1945 (served in Palestine, North Africa); Hong Kong and Shanghai Banking Corp; joined 1949, chair 1977-86; treasurer Univ of Hong Kong 1977-86; chair British Bank of the Middle East 1980-86; director International Totalizator Systems Inc, New World Development Ltd, Windsor Ind Corp; mbr Exec Council of Hong Kong 1978-86; chair Board of Stewards, Royal Hong Kong Jockey Club 1981-86 (Hon Steward 1986); president Surrey CCC 1987-88; JP Hong Kong 1972-86; Freeman, City of London, Liveryman Worshipful Co of Clockmakers; FCIB 1977 (vice-pres 1984-87), FRSA 1983; created life peer 1997, regular attendee at debates *special interests* foreign affairs, the arts, sport *publications* The Sandberg Watch Collection 1998 *recreations* racing, horology, cricket, bridge *clubs* Cavalry and Guards', White's, MCC, Surrey CCC, Portland, Hong Kong *style* The Lord Sandberg, CBE *address* Waterside Passfield, Liphook, Hants GU30 7RT *tel* 01428 751225; Suite 9, 100 Piccadilly, London W1V 9FN *tel* 020 7629 2204

SANDERS, Adrian Mark MP (Torbay maj 2,029) **Deputy Chief Whip** *b* Paignton Apr 25, 1959 *m* Alison 1991 *education* Torquay Boys' Grammar School *career* seven years insurance industry; eight years information, campaigns officer Association of Liberal Cllrs, ALDC 1986-89, parliamentary Whips' Office 1989-90, Paddy Ashdown's office (responsible for *Beyond Westminster* tour, in which Paddy was first party leader to leave Westminster to live and work in various different communities across Britain) ; four years European grant-funding, voluntary sector *party* joined Liberals 1979; active in Young Liberals, vice-president National League of Young Liberals 1985; elected (Blatchcombe ward) as youngest mbr Torbay Borough Council 1984-86; Euro candidate Devon & East Plymouth 1994; PPC Torbay 1992, 1997 (elected maj 12), re-elected 2001 (with more than 50% of vote), re-elected 2005; regional whip, Housing spokesperson 1997-2002; Local Govt and Housing 2002-06; Deputy Chief Whip in House of Commons 2006- ; chair Devon & Cornwall MPs 2001- ; chair All-party Gp on Diabetes 1998- ; v chair Housing & Homelessness 1997- ; Charities & the Voluntary Sector 1998- ; mbr gps on housing co-ops, building societies, football, beer, cider, tourism, town centre management, osteoporosis, CPA, USA, IPU *special interests* diabetes, tourism *other mbrships* British Diabetic Association *publications* Using Parliament for Local Campaign 1989; *Service with a Smile* 1991, *Service beyond a Smile* 1992 (both on customer strategies in local Govt) *recreations* soccer, music, film clubs, Paignton Club *address* House of Commons, London SW1A 0AA *tel* 02072196304 *fax* 0207219 3963; and 69 Belgrave Road, Torquay TQ2 5HZ *tel* 01803 200 036 *fax* 01803 200 031 *e-mail* asanders@cix.co.uk

SANDERS, Darren *b* Feb 11, 1971 *education* St John's College, Southsea; King's College, Cambridge (MA Cantab Social and Political Sciences); Journalism Training Centre, Surrey (NVQ in Magazine Journalism) *career* publications manager British

Lung Foundation until Dec 2003; communication manager (contact lenses) Eyecare Information Service 1997-98; press officer, British Safety Council, 1995-97; account Exec MMD 1994-95 *party* joined 1988 in Portsmouth; helped Portsmouth South 1988-92, various elections since; Exec mbr Portsmouth LP 1992-93; helped in Newbury 1994-95; by-elections Littleborough & Saddleworth, Christchurch, Romsey, Winchester, Kensington and Chelsea, Brent East; candidate Clapham Park MB Lambeth 1998 (failed), elected Clapham Common ward 2002 (first ever victory for Lib Dems); PPC Portsmouth North, 2001 (failed); Exec mbr Streatham LP 1998 - , chair 2003- *special interests* housing, regeneration, decentralisation *other mbrships* director, Clapham Park New Deal for Communities project 2000- *recreations* watching sport, especially Portsmouth FC and Hampshire CC; travelling; listening to music *address* 74 Cavendish Road, London SW12 0DG *tel* 020 8675 5328 *e-mail* darrensanders@lineone.net

SANDERSON, Arthur Norman MBE: Convener, Greater Glasgow Liberal Democrats *b* Sept 3, 1943 *m* Issy (née Halliday) Jul 30, 1966 1*s* 1*d* 2*gds* 1*gdd* *education* Glasgow Academy, Fettes College, Corpus Christi College Oxford (MA *Lit Hum* & PPE), Edinburgh Univ (Dip Ed), Henley Management College (Dip Mgt) *career* teacher (VSO) Ghana 1966-8; economics & careers master, Daniel Stewart's College, Edinburgh 1969-73; British Council career service 1974-97: Nigeria, Brazil, Far East & Pacific Dept London, Ghana, Director West of Scotland, Director E. Nigeria, Director S. India, and Director Baltic States; consultant in public relations to Crown Agents Customs reform project, Mozambique 1997-2001 *party* convener, Greater Glasgow Liberal Democrats 2003- ; chair, Scottish transport policy gp 2004- ; candidacies: Glasgow Maryhill (Scottish Parliament) 2003; Glasgow South (Westminster) 2005; Glasgow Cathcart (Scottish Parliament by-election) 2005 *public service* board mbr, Citizens' Theatre Glasgow; treasurer, Claremont Trust; selector, Voluntary Service Overseas; advice worker, The Well Asian Advice & Information Centre, Govanhill, Glasgow; mbr, Scottish Episcopal Church Cttee for Relations with Peoples of Other Faiths *other mbrships* Liberal International; European Movement; PROBUS *special interests* international development and international affairs; transport; the arts *recreations* hill-walking, classical music, choral singing, languages *publications* Customs Reform Project Mozambique, a model for partnership *address* 1 Waterside Drive, Newton Mearns, Glasgow G77 6TL

SAUL, Hannah Mary *b* Nov 16, 1978 *m* Dean 2001 *education* Todmorden High School; Hull Univ *career* Policy and Public Affairs Manager, Cancerbackup: Parliamentary and Campaigns Officer, Action for Blind People 2001- 2004; Communications Assistant, BP Chemicals Hull 2000-01; Research Assistant for two Labour MPs, reason joined Liberal Democrats! 1999-2000 *party* joined 2002; PPC Daventry 2005; chair Daventry LP; mbr Buckingham Town Council; mbr PCA, LDO, LDYS *special interests* health and disability issues especially cancer and visual impairment *recreations* reading, arguing, science fiction *address* 24 Ridgmont, Deanshanger, Milton Keynes MK19 6JH *tel* 01908 263 754 mobile 07971 875 151 *e-mail* hannah_saul@hotmail.com

SCHARDT, Charles William (Bill) *b* Apr 24, 1950 *single education* Northampton Grammar School; St Catharine's College, Cambridge (BA, Natural Sciences) *career* clinical biochemist, Newcastle upon Tyne 1971- *party* former chair of Tynemouth

Liberal Party; local govt candidate on numerous occasions; elected to Newcastle City Council in 1999; Chair of Scrutiny Management Cttee May 1995- ; PPC Jarrow 1995 *special interests* philosophy of liberalism, economics, civil liberties *recreations* history, motor cycles, skiing, walking, architecture, travel *address* 3 Maudlin Place, Newcastle upon Tyne NE5 3LE *tel* 0191 2421448 *e-mail* bill.schardt@blueyonder.co.uk

SCOTT, of Needham Market, Baroness (Ros) Life Peer created 2000: Lords Spokesperson on ODPM *b* Aug 10, 1957 Bath *m (dis)* 1 *d* Sally 1 *s* Jamie *education* Whitby Grammar School; Kent School, Hostert; Univ of East Anglia (BA Contemporary European Studies) *career* board mbr Audit Commission; non-Exec director Entrust, Lloyds Register, Anglia Television *party* mbr Mid-Suffolk District Council 1991-94; mbr Suffolk County Council 1993-05; deputy leader, leader of Council 1995-2000; transport spokesperson, Local Govt Association; mbr UK Delegation to European Union Cttee of the Regions; vice chair, chair Local Govt Association Transport Exec 1997- ; mbr, Commission for Integrated Transport; Euro candidate (number two on list) Eastern England 1999; created Life Peer 2000; Transport spokesperson 2000-04; elected mbr Federal Exec 2004-05 *special interests* transport *recreations* walking, choral singing *address* House of Lords, London SW1A 0PW *tel* 020 7219 8660 *e-mail* scottrc@parliament.uk

SCOTT, Tavish MSP (Shetland) Scottish Minister for Transport *b* May 6, 1966 *education* Anderson High School, Lerwick; Napier Univ, Edinburgh BA Hons (Business Studies) *m* 3 ch *career* farmer *party* parliamentary researcher to Jim Wallace MP 1989-91; Scottish Lib Dem press officer 1991-92; mbr Shetland Islands Council 1994-99, vice chair council Roads and Transport Cttee; elected Scottish Parliament 1999; spkspn Transport, the Environment, Europe 1999-2000; Deputy Minister for Parliament Oct 2000-Mar 2001; Liberal Democrat Business Manager Oct 2000-Mar 2001; spkspn on Enterprise and Lifelong Learning, Highlands and Islands Oct 2001-03; mbr Parliamentary Bureau; convener Scottish Liberal Democrats 2002-03; Deputy Minister for Finance, Public Services & Parliamentary Business May 2003-June 2005 *other interests* chairman and trustee, Lerwick Harbour Trust 1994-99 *address* Scottish Parliament, Edinburgh EH99 1SP *constituency* 171 Commercial Street, Lerwick, Shetland, ZE1 0HX *tel* 01595 690044 *fax* 01595 690055 *e-mail* tavish.scott.msp@scottish.parliament.uk

SEEFF, Geoffrey Michael *b* Aug 29, 1947 *m* Deanna 2 *d* Monique Alison; Nicole Suzannah *education* Beal Grammar School, Ilford; Birmingham Univ 1970-73 *career* Chartered Accountant; management consultant; articled clerk, Wallace Cash & Co; Consultant Coopers & Lybrand, London, Tehran 1973-77; director Stoy Hayward Consulting 1977-89; seconded Head of Grants Appraisal Unit Department of the Environment 1986-87; director Widnell Consulting and Financial; director Widnell 1990-2000; (following merger) director Currie & Brown Consulting 2000- *party* founder convener Redbridge SDP 1981; treasurer 1981-83; chair 1983-86; Exec mbr Wanstead and Woodford 1990- ; vice chair Chingford and Woodford Green 1998-2000; chair 2000-03; vice chair Campaigns 2004- ; PPC Chingford and Woodford Green 1997, Romford 2005; GLA candidate Redbridge and Havering 2000; local election candidate various Redbridge wards 1982, 1986, 1994, 1998, 2002, 2006; mbr Liberty Network, LD Business Forum *special interests* urban regeneration; corporate governance; electoral, constitutional reform *other mbrships*

Fellow, Institute of Chartered Accountants in England and Wales; ctte mbr Faculty of Finance and Management, Institute of Chartered Accountants; Fellow, Chartered Institute of Management Consultants; mbr Academy of Experts; chairman Barking and Dagenham bereavement counselling service *recreations* family music (plays violin, saxophone), swimming, keep fit *publications* various technical articles in relevant professional magazines including several on subject of corporate social responsibility *style* Dr *address* 32c Churchfields South Woodford London E18 2QZ *tel* 0208 505 5969 home 0207 834 8400 business *fax* 0207 828 2030 *e-mail* geoffseeff@cix.co.uk

SEEKINGS, Gordon Kenneth *b* Dec 28.1953 *m* Linda (nee Smith) *qv* 1976 1 *s* Jamie 1 *d* Vicki *education* partially-educated Spencer Park Comprehensive, Wandsworth; managed to avoid Univ: Sixties' school drop-out, proud layabout career telecommunications apprenticeship PO/BT 1971-75; various engineering, customer service roles 1975-84; BT Customer Service Manager 1985-87; BT Quality Manager 1987-90; Security Manager BT 1991-95; HoC office manager Liz Lynne 1995-96; various jobs 1996-99; mbrship officer Cowley Street 1999- *party* joined Liberals 1985; Cllr 1987- ; PPC Crawley Borough 1992; Gp leader Crawley BC 1994- ; South East England Regional Planning Cttee 2000-01 *special interests* planning *recreations* industrial archaeology, gardening, walking, music (heavy rock: Hawkwind, Black Sabbath), blood sports such as baiting Tories, Socialists *other mbrships* Bluebell Railway; MENSA *address* 12 Green Lane, Northgate, Crawley, RH10 8JP *tel* 01293 416767/516767 *e-mail* gordonseekings@cix.co.uk or Gordon.Seekings@crawley.gov.uk

SEEKINGS, Linda Ann *b* Aug 25, 1953 *m* Gordon Seekings *qv* 1976 1 *s* Jamie 1 *d* Vicki *education* Ashburton High School; Southwark College (National Nursery Examination Board) *career* trained as NNEB nursery nurse; time out for raising family; now NNEB neo-natal unit East Surrey Hospital *party* joined 1975; Cllr 1994- ; chair Crawley LibDems 1998-2001; PPC Crawley Borough 2001 *special interests* planning, the environment *recreations* music (Prodigy, David Gray, Stevie Wonder), football (Wolves), steam railways, crochet, embroidery, *South Park other mbrships* Crawley Museum, Bluebell Railway *address* 12 Green Lane, Northgate, Crawley, RH10 8JP *tel* 01293 416767/516767 *e-mail* Linda.Seekings@crawley.gov.uk or via gordonseekings@cix.co.uk

SEWARDS, Geoffrey Brian BA, MSc, C Math, FIMA *b* Feb 4, 1936 *m* Ernestine 2 *s* 1 *d* 7 *gch education* Emanuel School, Wandsworth; Clare College, Cambridge; Univ of Nottingham *career* technical officer, Hawker Syddeley Dynamics, Coventry 1958-61; principal lecturer in mathematics, Coventry Univ (formerly Lanchester Polytechnic) 1961-96; retired 1996 *party* joined 1964, active in Coventry since 1973; chair, Coventry SW Liberals 1975-78; chair Coventry Liberal Party 1978-88; secy Coventry Liberal Democrats 1988- ; PPC Coventry SW 1992; Coventry NE 1997, 2001; European PPC Coventry & North Warwickshire 1994 *special interests* economics, constitutional reform *other mbrships* secy Finham Residents Association 1977- ; chair governors Finham Primary School 1989-2002; chair Coventry Governors Organisation 1995- *recreations* music, history *address* 8 Grange Avenue, Finham, Coventry, CV3 6PP *tel* 024 7641 2747 *e-mail* sewards@which.net

SEWELL, Nicola *Emma b* Jul 16, 1981 *engaged* Dave Wood *qv education* Hautlieu School, Jersey; Univ of Plymouth (BSc Hons Psychology) *career* management, Plymouth NightLine 2001-03); Student Union education officer Univ of Plymouth 2003-04); mbr national Cttee NUS Students with Disabilities 2004-05); currently charities, mental health sector *party* joined 2001; mbr local, regional party Execs; candidate local elections (achieved 20% swing) Exec Plymouth Univ LDYS, Devon & Cornwall LDYS 2002-03); NUS officer, lead candidate, LDYS UK 2003-04 *special interests* mental health, hidden disabilities, prison and offender reform, sex offending, charity and community sector, student movement, education issues *address* Kalina, Rue de Samares, St Clement, Jersey, JE2 6LS *tel* 07779 080869 *e-mail* nickysewell@hotmail.com

SEYMOUR, Caroline Margaret *b* Aug 2 1946 *m* John Seymour 2 *s* 2 *d education* Abbey School, Reading; Univ of Newcastle on Tyne *career* teacher, lecturer in politics, business *party* joined 1973; mbr North Yorkshire CC 1989- , gp leader, previously joint leader of council 1996-97; chair Combined Fire Authority 1996-99, chair Scrutiny Cttee 1999-2000, currently vice chair; mbr Hambleton DC 1985- ; deputy chair LGA Public Protection Exec 1999- ; director LACORS 1996- *special interests* community politics; public protection, fire issues *recreations* gardening, travel, family *address* White House Farm Stokesley Middlesbrough North Yorks TS9 5LE *tel/fax* 01642 710382 *e-mail* cmseymour@cix.co.uk

SHARMAN of Red Lynch, Lord Colin Morven Sharman: OBE, Life Peer cr 1999: House of Lords spokesman on Trade and Industry *b* Feb 19, 1943 *education* Bishop Wordsworth school; FCA *m* Angela 1 *d* Sarah *career* Peat Marwick Mitchell (later KPMG) 1966; manager Frankfurt office 1970-72, The Hague 1972-81 (partner 1973, partner-in-chief 1975), London 1981-99; senior partner (national marketing, industry gps) 1987-90; senior management consultancy partner 1989-91; senior partner 1994-98; chairman KPMG International 1997-99; House of Lords 1999; chairman Le Gavroche Ltd; non-Exec director AEA Technology plc, chairman of Audit Cttee; non-Exec director of BG International plc, Phocis plc; chairman Advisory Board Good Corporation. *party* business liaison; HoL spokesman Trade and Industry 2001- *other interests* Companion, British Institute of Management; mbr Chancellor of Exchequer's City Advisory Panel; council mbr CBI; Association of Business Sponsorship of the Arts; Appeal Cttee, Golden Jubilee Appeal; National Association of Almshouses; chairman Ocean Youth Club; Liveryman Company of Gunmakers 1992; hon mbr Securities Institute; Advisory Board of George Washington Institute for Management *recreations* outdoor and field sports, shooting, sailing *address* Manor Farm, Teffont Magna, Salisbury SP3 5QY

SHARP of Guildford, Baroness Margaret: Life Peer cr 1998: Lords spokesperson on Higher and Further Education and Science Policy (with Baroness Walmsley) *b* Nov 21, 1938 *m* 2 *d education* Percy Road Primary, Hampton; Pates' GS for Girls, Cheltenham; Tonbridge GGS; Newnham College, Cambridge (BA first class Hons in Economics, MA Cantab) *career* assistant principal Board of Trade, Treasury 1960-63; assistant lecturer/part time lecturer economics LSE 1963-72; guest fellow Brookings Inst, Washington DC (part-time honorary position while husband was diplomat in Washington); economic adviser NEDC 1977-81; fellow, senior fellow Science Policy Research Unit, Univ of Sussex

1981-1999; associate director ESRC Centre for Science, Technology, Energy and Environment Policy, 1992-1997; visiting fellow Univ of Sussex; Hon FCGI 2004; Hon Doctorate of Laws, Univ of Sussex 2005; Hon Fellow Birkbeck College 2006 *party* mbr Lewisham Labour Party 1969-71; founder mbr SDP 1981, chair Lewisham West LP; PPC Guildford 1983 (won 33% of vote), 1987, 1992, 1997 (reduced Tory majority to 4,800); active mbr SDP *Yes-to-Unity* gp; founder mbr Lib Dems; chair Guildford LP 1988-90; mbr regional Exec 1988-91 1997-98; chair W Surrey Euro constituency 1989, 1994; mbr FPC 1992-2003; chair working gps on science and technology 1991-92; economic policy 1995-96 *other mbrships* former chair Inner London gp CASE; helped develop neighbourhood schools complex in Washington, DC; PTA chair, governor daughters' comprehensive, Sydenham1978-82; Exec Cttee mbr Save British Science 1989-97; mbr editorial board *Political Quarterly* 1985-89; governor Stoke Hill School, Guildford 1998-2002; mbr local council Guildford High School 1998- ; governor Weyfield School, Guildford, 2004 - ; trustee/director Age Concern Surrey 2001- ; chair Age Concern Surrey 2004- ; mbr APPG (all party parliamentary gps) on universities, children, families and parenting, adult and continuing education; mbr Lords select cttees – European Select Cttee – sub-cttee A (Economic and Monetary Affairs) 1999-2003, Science and Technology Cttee (chair Science and Heritage sub-cttee) 2004- ; *publications* number of books, articles about UK science and innovation policy, and impact of new technologies in Europe; author of 2003 Lib Dem policy paper on higher education *address* 96 London Road, Guildford GU1 1TH *tel* 01483 572669 home *fax* 01483 502262; (020 7219 3121 office); *e-mail* sharpm@parliament.uk

SHARPLEY, Jamie Andrew *b* Jun 27, 1947 *m* Rosie (nee Horgan) *education* Box Hill School; Univ of London *career* Health Service manager 1970-99; non-Exec director, range of organisations 2000- *party* joined 1975; mbr South East of England region Exec 2002– , English Council 2003- *other mbrships* National Liberal Club *recreations* politics, gardening, life *publications* Industrial Relations in Hospitals *address* 13 Alterton Close, Woking GU21 3DD *tel* 01483 770053

SHAW, Joanna Elizabeth *b* Jun 1, 1972 Roehampton *div* no children *education* Drayton Manor High School, Univ of Leeds, Univ of Westminster, Inns of Court School of Law *career* barrister 2000- ; *party* mbr Camberwell & Peckham (London), paper candidate Southwark election 2006, former mbr of LP exec, ward organiser for target wards; Borough Action Gp mbr for Southwark 2006- ; co-opted mbr London Campaigns Cttee; press/publicity officer LD Lawyers' Association 2005- , exec mbr 2003- ; mbr ALDC, PCA, WLD; International Law working gp 2005-6; seeking approval as PPC in 2006 *other mbrships* Liberty; Justice; Amnesty International *special interests* making the party (and democratic institutions generally) more representative of the UK; civil liberties; human rights; access to justice; social justice; death penalty issues *publications* article on ASBOs, contributions to *LibDem News* **LD quirks** reported on BBC website for speech at Sept 2005 conference as referring to Tony Blair and Charles Clarke as 'the hideous spectre of a pair of truncheon-wielding jackbooted nannies'; only own one yellow item of clothing *recreations* running, reading novels, music, knitting, lying on my new sofa listening to Algerian pop, talking to and seeing my oft-neglected friends and family, writing bad poetry, dreaming of travelling to India *style* Ms *address* 96 Astbury Road, Peckham, London SE15 2NW *tel* 07951 743079 *e-mail* joannashaw2001@hotmail.com

SHAW, John *b* Oct 20, 1963 *m* Erica *education* King Henry VIII School, Coventry; Bristol Grammar School; Bedford Modern School; Aberdeen Univ (MA Hons) 1986 *career* trainee KPMG Peat Marwick McLintock 1986-90; project worker, later manager, Hyde Housing Association 1991-2002; community fieldworker, more recently Regional Community Development Manager, Scope 2002- *party* joined Liberal Party 1982 *address* 101 Penrith Road, Basingstoke, Hampshire RG21 8UR *tel* 01256 461776 *e-mail* johnandericashaw@btinternet.com

SHERLOCK, Neil Roger *b* Aug 13, 1963 *m* Kate Parminter (Jul 1994) 2 *d* Rose, Grace *education* Esher County Grammar School 1974-79; Esher College 1979-81; Christ Church, Oxford 1981-84 MA (Philosophy, Politics and Economics), President, Oxford Union *career* partner, Public Affairs and Corporate Social Responsibility KPMG 1985- ; *party* joined Liberal Party 1981; PPC South West Surrey 1992, 1997; vice president, South West Surrey Liberal Democrats 1999- ; mbr Federal Conference Cttee 1994; Federal Finance and Administration Cttee 1996-98, 2004; speechwriter Rt Hon Paddy Ashdown MP 1988-99; mbr Rt Hon Charles Kennedy MP General Election speechwriting team 2001; mbr Sir Menzies Campbell leadership election campaign team and transition team *special interests* electoral reform, business issues *other mbrships* ALDC, Electoral Reform Society, Make Votes Count, European Movement, CPRE, National Trust, Farnham Liberal Club, National Liberal Club, Royal Commonwealth Society, Liberty Network, Working Families (trustee), CentreForum (management team), mbr Armed Forces Pay Review Body 1999- ; *publications* The Progressive Century - the future of the centre-left (edited with Neal Lawson, Palgrave 2001) *recreations* football, cricket, golf *address* 12 Binscombe Lane, Farncombe, Godalming, Surrey GU7 3PN *tel* 01483 428184 home 020 7311 885 business *fax* 01483 428184 *e-mail* Neil.Sherlock@kpmg.co.uk

SHERVEY, Christopher *b* Dec 29, 1948 *m* Fiona (nee Fjaelberg) 2 *s* 1 *d* *education* Bristol Univ (MbChB) *career* GP Tewkesbury 1979- ; *party* mbr and chair Tewkesbury LP, Gloucestershire rep Western Counties 2005- ; mbr Green Liberal Democrats, ALDC *other mbrships* BMA, Royal College of General Practitioners *special interests* environment, special needs education *recreations* photography, jazz, *address* High Gables, Aston-on-Carrant, Tewkesbury Glos GL20 8HL *tel* 01684 773269, 0788 182 2374 mobile *fax* 01684 274911 *e-mail* chris@shervey.demon.co.uk

SHORTEN, Jenny *b* Sept 15, 1954 *education* grammar schools Berkshire, London; secretarial college; Univ of Leeds (BA Hons Psychology) 1977 *career* personnel, training, marketing and sales, including exhibitions, events; own business, freelance work for wide range of companies UK, Europe, worldwide *party* joined SDP at foundation; trainer, facilitator specialising in training trainers, communication and interpersonal skills, team building, training for women in politics; range of campaign-related disciplines national, regional, local level; also trains, supports returning officers and selection cttee mbrs throughout UK; campaign trainer in threatened democracies including Bosnia, Philippines and Angola; agent, organiser, local party, regional party Execs; currently mbr English Candidates Cttee, English Council Exec, GBTF, Training Task Gp; chair Selection Rules Working Party (reviewing, revision of PPC selection rules for England) *recreations* cricket, amateur mycology, embroidery *address* 45 Sevenfields, Highworth, Swindon SN6 7NF *tel*

01793 764649 home 01793 766759 business 07802 482993 mobile *fax* 0870 1369977 *e-mail* jennyshorten@cix.co.uk

SHUBERT, Elliot *b* May 16, 1943 St Louis, Missouri, USA *m* Dr Eileen J Cox 2 *s* Andrew, Nathan 1 *d* Angela *education* PhD in Botany & Phycology, 1973, University of Connecticut, Storrs, Connecticut USA; BS in Biology & Microbiology, 1966, University of Missouri, Kansas City, Missouri USA *career* Research Associate, The Natural History Museum and Scientific Consultant; previously Professor of Biology, University of North Dakota USA *party* exec mbr Greenwich LP 2006; candidate for Eltham South election 2006; exec mbr PCA (mbrship secy and Business Liaison Officer); *other mbrships* London Chamber of Commerce; Lions Clubs International; Building Hope (UK reg charity); Liberty; Community Governor for Eltham Hill Technology College for Girls; British Phycological Society; Phycological Society of America; International Diatom Society; International Phycological Society; Systematics Association; Society for International Limnology *special interests* presenter on effective public speaking: PowerSpeak and speech writing, humanitarian activities (Lions Clubs International, Habitat for Humanity International and Building Hope) *publications* author of one book, three book chapters and 30 peer-reviewed scientific papers *recreations* art museums, exercise, photography, DIY *style* Prof Elliot Shubert *address* 11 Everest Road, Eltham, London SE9 6PX *tel* 020 8333 8885, 077 6461 1401 mobile *fax* 020 7942 5529 *e-mail* e.shubert@ntlworld.com

SHUTT of Greetland and Stainland, Baron David Trevor: Life Peer cr 2000, OBE 1993: Chief Whip in House of Lords *b* Mar 16, 1942 *education* Pudsey Grammar School; FCA1969 *m* Margaret Pemberton 1965 2 *s* 1 *d career* articled clerk Smithson, Blackburn & Co, Leeds 1964-66; taxation assistant Bousfield, Waite & Co 1966, partner 1970-94, consultant 1994-2001 *party* Liberal PPC Sowerby 1970, 1974 (both General Elections), 1979; Calder Valley (Alliance) 1983, 1987, Pudsey 1992; mbr (Liberal, Liberal Democrat) Calderdale MBC 1973-90, 1995-2003, Mayor of Calderdale 1982-83; created life peer 2000; Lords spokesman for the Liberal on International Development and Northern Ireland 2001- ; Chief Whip (House of Lords) 2005- *other interests* director Joseph Rowntree Reform Trust 1975, vice-chair 1987; trustee Joseph Rowntree Charitable Trust 1985; treasurer Institute for Citizenship 1995-2002; Paul Harris Fellow of the Rotary Club 1999, Freeman of Calderdale 2000, awarded the Citoyen d'Honneur, Commune de Riorges, in France *recreations* travel, transport, singing (mbr, treasurer Parliament Choir) *address* House of Lords London SW1A 0PW

SIMPSON, Andrew *b* May 26, 1965 Welwyn Garden City *div education* Manshead Upper School, Dunstable, Beds; Nene College (now University of Northampton), BA (Hons) Combined Studies – History, Economics and English – awarded by University of Leicester; Student Union President, Nene College SU 1987-88; Post Graduate Diploma in Marketing (Chartered Institute of Marketing) *career* Nationwide Building Society 1988-95; Marketing Manager Dial Direct Insurance 1995-2001; Marketing Manager/Product Controller,Argos Retail Group Financial Services 2001- ; *party* PPC Northampton North 2005 (re-selected 2006), Northampton South 2001; former local party Chair and Treasurer, currently Vice Chair of Northampton LP; East Midlands Regional Exec (training officer); mbr PCA, ALDC, DELGA *other mbrships* Chartered Institute of Marketing, Institute of

Direct Marketing *special interests* local government, civil liberties, transport and environment *publications* Focus leaflets!!! *recreations* keeping fit, British science fiction and holidaying *style* just Andrew will do ! *address* 13 Beaconsfield Terrace, Northampton, Northants NN1 3ES *tel* 01604 634539 or 01908 296621 *e-mail* asimpson@cix.co.uk *website* www.andrew-simpson.org.uk

SIMPSON, Mike *b* Jan 2, 1939 Redhill *m* 1962 3 *ch* (adult) 2 *gdch education* National Service, Royal Air Force, Junior Technician *career* actuarial student, party organiser, salesman, sales manager, IT manager, marketing manager, IT and finance industry related consultancy and training *party* Chair SE Region, ECE, EFAC, FE, FFAC 2006; councillor on Tandridge DC from 1990-2002, council leader from 1995-2000; PPC Mitcham & Morden, in 1974 (2nd); mbr ALDC; done most jobs at LP level, currently mbrship secy for East Surrey *special interests* electoral reform and other constitutional issues; fighting centralisation of decision making in politics and business; practical educational issues via school governorship *recreations* range of local voluntary activity outside politics; carer *LD quirks* I expect things to be done efficiently *style* none - just "Mike" please *address* 38a Searchwood Road, Warlingham, CR6 9BA *tel/fax* 0845 330 3960 home 07985 291424 mobile - but not usually switched on, only occasionally used *e-mail* mikeg.simpson@virgin.net

SINGH, (Cornelis) Harjinder *b* May 6, 1947 *m* Satnam Kaur Khalsa *education* Willem de Zwijger School, Roermond, Limburg; Grotius College, Heerlen, Limburg; Casimir College, Amstelveen, Noord Holland; Univ of Amsterdam (where did few studies but lots of student politics!) *career* 1962-95 various capacities, travel trade (student travel, 'bucket shops' and later running international coach services, based in Amsterdam); MD, Magic Bus Company, Dublin, for three years; general usefulness at the Harmandar Sahib (Golden Temple) in the Punjab 1996-2004; Chandigarh, helping edit English language journal on Sikhi; learned IT skills on Sikh webs *party* joined Liberal Democrats 2000; treasurer EMLD; chair Hounslow borough party; candidate Syon Ward (Hounslow), 2003 (200 votes short of being elected) *special interests* local politics, foreign affairs, public transport *other interests* active in Sikh community, local and national level; Slough CRE, mbr chaplain's team, Heathrow *recreations* music, reading, walking *publications* weekly column, under by-line The Man in Blue, *The Sikh Times*; articles in Journal of the Institute of Sikh Studies: see www.surbut-khalsa.com *address* 39 Ash Grove, Heston, Middlesex TW5 9DU *tel* 020 8577 3148 mobile 07931 531639 *e-mail* harjindersinghkhalsa@btinternet.com

SMITH, Christopher Waldo *b* Sept 21, 1930 *m* Eleanor Beatrice 1 *s* 2 *d education* Wyggestin Grammar School, Leicester; St Michael's School, Limpsfield Surrey; The Nautical College, Pangbourne; BA Hons, Open Univ *career* Royal Navy 1948-70; chief summer schools officer, Open Univ 1970-96; Univ administration in Macau, Singapore; freelance editing Singapore, London 1990-96 *party* joined early 1970s Mid-Bedfordshire; treasurer, chairman (and supporter of Alliance with SDP) *special interests* foreign affairs (plus moral support for Simon Hughes, since the days when, with daughters, canvassed so successfully at his by-election *other mbrships* National Liberal Club *recreations* concert and theatre-going; running round Regent's Park *address* 9 Clarence Gate Gardens, London, NW1 6AY *tel* 020 7724 2984 *e-mail* cwandebs@tiscali.co.uk

SMITH, Sir Cyril kt (1988), MBE (1966), DL (Greater Manchester) *b* Jun 28, 1928 *education* Rochdale GS for Boys *career* MP (Lib until 1988, Lib Dem 1988-92) Rochdale, Liberal Chief Whip 1975-76; mbr Rochdale BC 1952-66, alderman 1966-74, mayor Rochdale 1966-67, mbr Rochdale MDC 1974-75 *other mbrships* president Greater Manchester Scouts 1994-99; freeman Borough of Rochdale 1992; Hon DEd Metropolitan Univ Manchester 1976; Hon LLD Univ of Lancaster 1993 *recreations* listening to music, reading, TV *clubs* National Liberal (chair 1987-88) *style* Sir Cyril Smith MBE DL *address* 14 Emma Street, Rochdale, Lancs *tel* 01706 648840

SMITH, Gerard Christopher Mark (known as **Gez**), *b* Jul 30, 1979 Stourbridge *ptnr* Anna Willcox *education* Oldswinford Hospital, Stourbridge, Univ of Bristol and Rutgers Univ, NJ, USA, BSc (Hons) Politics and Philosophy, MSc International Relations, ACMRS (BPP), Assoc Mbr Market Research Society *career* research and consultation posts, Bristol City Council 2002-2004; Project Manager, National e-Democracy Project 2004-2005; Local Govt Consultant (e-Democracy) Delib Ltd *party* mbr Bristol West,Western Counties region; general exec mbr LDYS, 2003-2004; vice-chair Communications LDYS 2004-2005; LDYS chair 2005-2006; Deputy President, Liberal Democrats (Youth & Students) 2005-2006; mbr Wired Working Gp 2005-2006; council candidate Southmead, Bristol 2005, 2006 *special interests* drug law reform, youth offending, organic farming *recreations* fine food, fine cider and music *publications* articles in *I&DEA, The Independent, Financial Times, LGC address* 30 Cromwell Road, St Andrews, Bristol BS6 5HB *tel* 07745 750072 *email* gez@gezsmith.com *website* www.gezsmith.com

SMITH, Graeme Donald *b* Apr 17, 1978 Boston *education* Spalding Grammar School; Loughborough Univ BSc (Hons) Computing and Management; Keele Univ PGCE (ICT and Maths) *career* head of ICT, Rawlins Community College 2005- ; teacher of ICT, Babington Community Technology College 2004-5; teacher of ICT, Wellington School 2002-04 *party* PPC Loughborough 2005; vice chair, Loughborough LP; mbr ALDC *other mbrships* Campaign for Nuclear Disarmament; Association of Teachers and Lecturers, European Movement *special interests* fair trade, education (secondary and higher), European issues, international development *recreations* church (Emmanuel Church, Loughborough) football and cricket (season ticket holder Leicester City and Leicestershire CCC), FA registered referee, theatre, singing, reading *address* 15 Mill Lane, Loughborough, Leicestershire, LE11 1EL *tel* 01509 554963, 07940 528079 mobile *email* graeme.smith1978@ntlworld.com *web* www.loughborough.libdems.org.uk

SMITH, Iain William MSP (North East Fife) *b* May 1, 1960 Gateside, Fife *ptnr* Matthew Clark *education* Bell Baxter High School, Cupar; Newcastle upon Tyne Univ (BA Hons politics & economics) 1981 *career* administrative assistant Northumberland County Council 1981; advice worker 1982, centre manager Bonnethhill Advice Centre, Dundee 1983-85 *party* voluntary agent NE Fife Liberal Assoc 1985-87; constituency researcher to Menzies Campbell MP for NE Fife 1987-98; constituency organiser, NE Fife Liberal Democrats 1998-99; Fife Cllr 1982-99; Alliance gp secy 1982-86; gp and opposition leader Fife Council 1986-99; elected Scottish Parliament 1999, re-elected 2003, deputy business manager, whip 1999-2000; Convener, Scottish Parliament Procedures Cttee 2003- , Local Govt &

Transport Cttee 2003- ; European and External Relations Cttee, Education Cttee; mbr ASLDC Exec, mbr Convenors Gp *special interests* education, transport, culture *recreations* sport (football, cricket), cinema, travel, reading *address* constituency: 16 Millgate, Cupar, Fife KY15 5EG tel 01334 656361 fax 01334 654045; Scottish Parliament, Edinburgh EH99 1SP *tel* 0131 348 5817 *fax* 0131 348 5962 *e-mail* iain.smith.msp@scottish.parliament.uk *web* www.iainsmith.org and www.scottish.parliament.uk/msp/membersPages/iain_smith/index.htm

SMITH, Jen Helen *b* Nov 12, 1976 *education* The High School for Girls, Gloucester; Univ of Wales, Swansea (BA international relations, politics) *career* welfare, education officer, Swansea Univ Students Union 1997-98, president Students Union 1999-2000; PA to Lembit Opik MP 2000-01; Head of Office David Chidgey MP 2001-02); public relations officer Circle 33 Housing Gp 2002- *party* joined 2000, PPC Basingstoke 2005 *special interests* penal reform, higher education, housing, regeneration *recreations* theatre, travel, running *address* 4 Ferguson Close, Basingstoke RG21 3JA *tel* 07989 267809 *e-mail* jennifer@libdemjen.freeserve.co.uk

SMITH (nee Smart), **Kate** (originally Catharine) **Mary** *b* Jun 4, 1957 *m* Paul Smith Apr 9, 1983 2 *s education* Cheadle Hulme School; New Hall, Univ of Cambridge (MA Modern and Mediaeval Langs); Newcastle Polytechnic (Postgrad Cert in Bilingual Administration (French)) **career** sales administrator, BBC Enterprises News & Current Affairs, 1979-82; trainer and course director in EFL and other business communication skills eg presentations, negotiating, Canning Ltd, 1982-87; training consultant Huthwaite Ltd 1987-88; freelance training consultancy 1988-91; French lecturer, Derby Univ, 1991-92; Chair, Secretary, Fundraiser at different times Mid-Derbyshire National Childbirth Trust (NCT) 1990-2000; NCT national cttee mbr 1991-2000; mbr Southern Derbyshire Community Health Council, 1994-98; NCT Trustee 1998-99; Presidential Candidate NCT 2000; mbr and subsequently Lay Vice Chair, Southern Derbyshire NHS Maternity Services Liaison Cttee (MSLC), 1991- ; *party* mbr Amber Valley LP in East Midlands Region; mbrship secy AVLD 2001- ; Media Officer 2002- ; PPC Amber Valley 2001, 2005; mbr WLD, LDDA *other mbrships* Assn for Improvements in Maternity Services, Birthcentres e-gp *special interests* education, food allergies and intolerances, disabilities, languages in the curriculum, devolved maternity and other healthcare *recreations* whole family are choristers (CofE); classical music; cookery; Jane Austen; keeping fit by jogging round village three times in the morning *publications* *Mother Nature under Threat in Maternity Care*, 1999; *Mother Nurture in Recovery* 2000 (known as "Good Friday Report") both NCT; various short pieces on policy *address* 1 Hillcrest, Crich, DE4 5DH *tel* 01773 856090 (not late) *e-mail* katesmithlibdem@aol.com

SMITH, Margaret MSP (Edinburgh West) *b* Feb 18, 1961 *m* (div) *civil partnership* Suzanne Main Mar 31, 2006 1 *s* 3 *ss* 1 *d education* Broughton High School, Edinburgh; Edinburgh Univ (MA Arts 1983) *career* Scottish Officer, United Nations Association *party* mbr Scottish Party Exec; cllr Cramond Ward 1995-99; spkspsn on transportation City of Edinburgh Council 1995-99; elected Scottish Parliament 1999; convener Scottish Parliament Health and Community Care Cttee 1999-2003; spkspsn Transport and Local Govt Feb-Aug 2005; Chief Whip 2005- ; Audit Cttee Aug 2005- ; Waverley Bill Cttee mbr 2006-06; spkspsn Equal Opportunities 2000-01; Health and Community Care 2001-03; Deputy Convener,

Equal Opportunities Cttee 2003-04; mbr Justice 1 Cttee; Justice spokesperson 2003-05 *other interests* former representative Forth Road Bridge Joint Board *recreations* reading, golf *address* Scottish Parliament, Edinburgh, EH99 1SP *tel* 0131-348 5785; 3 Drumbrae Avenue, Edinburgh, EH12 8TE *tel* 0131 317 7292 *e-mail* margaret.smith.msp@scottish.parliament.uk *web* www.margaretsmithmsp.com/

SMITH, Martyn George *b* Feb16,1946 *m* Sadie Laureina Smith 1 stepson *education* Wyggeston Boys' School, Leicester; Jesus College, Cambridge *career* computer industry 1967-75; chief officer, West Birmingham Community Health Council 1975-2003 (on abolition) *party* joined Liberal Party, 1963; currently treasurer, West Bromwich LP (and predecessors since 1976); mbr Sandwell MBC (since 1980 breakthrough); delegate Federal, Regional conferences; general factotum; PPC West Bromwich East 2005, West Bromwich East 1997, 1992, 1987, 1983, 1979, Stoke North (Oct 1974), Stoke South (Feb 1974; parliamentary agent, Leek 1970, Newcastle-under-Lyme by-election 1969; mbr Newcastle-under-Lyme BC, 1972-74; Liberal Party NEC 1971-74; Liberal Party Council 1969-merger; treasurer, West Midlands Region; chair, Liberal Party Health Panel; general secy, ALTU *other mbrships* Amnesty Intl *recreations* correspondence chess *publications* various party publications; various publications, West Birmingham CHC *address* 19 Newton Road, Great Barr, Birmingham B43 6AA *tel* 0121 358 2484 *fax* 0121 358 1593 *e-mail* msmithm@cix.co.uk

SMITH, Sir Robert Hill (Bob) 3rd Bart (UK 1945) MP BSc (Aberdeenshire West and Kincardine maj:7,471) *b* Apr 21, 1958 *m* Fiona 3 *d* Helen, Kirsty, Elizabeth *education* Merchant Taylor School, Northwood; Univ of Aberdeen (BSc) *career* family estate manager *party* founder mbr SDP 1981, Lib Dems 1988; PPC Aberdeen North 1987, mbr Aberdeenshire Council (Upper Donside) 1995-97; vice-convenor Grampian Joint Police Board; Scottish education spokesman 1995-97; MP for Aberdeenshire W and Kincardine 1997- , spokesman on Transport and Maritime Affairs 1997-99; parliamentary spokesman on Scottish Police & Prisons 1997-99; Shadow Scottish spokesman 1999-2001; mbr Scottish Affairs Cttee 1999-2001; vice chair All-Party UK Offshore Oil and Gas Gp 1999- ; Deputy Chief Whip 2001-06; mbr Trade and Industry Cttee 2001-06; Procedure Cttee 2001- ; *special interests* Offshore Oil and Gas Industry, rural affairs, electoral reform *recreations* hill-walking, sailing *address* Constituency Office: 6 Dee Street, Banchory AB31 5ST *tel* 01330 820330 *fax* 01330 820338 Home: Crowmallie House, Pitcaple, Inverurie, Aberdeenshire AB51 5HR; House of Commons, London SW1A 0AA *tel* 020 7219 3000 *e-mail* bobsmith@cix.co.uk

SMITH, Roy Alfred *b* Nov 27, 1948 *m* Liz 2 *ss education* Maldon Grammar School, Essex; Univ of Salford, (BA Hons Politics, Contemporary History); Associate, Institute of Management Accountants; *career* various jobs in engineering; switched to accountancy 1975; NCH, the children's charity 1985-2003, finance manager North West 1996-2003; project manager Halton Disability Services 2003- *party* joined Liberals 1987; founder mbr Liberal Democrats; campaigned for SDP/Liberal Alliance 1987; elected parish Cllr 1999; Warrington (Unitary) Borough Cllr 2000; PPC Warrington North 2001; vice chair Warrington LP 2000-2002; treasurer 2003- *special interests* social services, health, environment, voluntary sector *other mbrships* signatory Charter 88; Friends of the Earth; National Trust; Royal Horticultural Society; RSPB; MCC *recreations* cricket, rugby union, hill-walking, gardening, classical music, -reading including Victorian, contemporary fiction, poetry, biography, history, politics, collecting novels of Georges Simenon, Indian cookery *address* 25 Winchester Avenue, Great Sankey, Warrington WA5 1XU *tel* 01925 654950 home 07745 104307 business *fax* 01925 444537 *e-mail* rsmith@warrington.gov.uk

SMITH of Clifton, Baron Sir Trevor Arthur Smith: Life Peer cr 1997, kt 1996: Lords Spokesperson on Northern Ireland *b* Jun 14, 1937 *m* Julia 2 *s* 1 *d education* Chiswick Polytechnic; LSE *career* Univ teacher Universities of Exeter, Hull, Queen Mary London (professor), California State (Los Angeles), Ulster (Vice Chancellor) *party* joined 1955; chair LSE Liberal Society 1956-57, Union of Liberal Students 1958-59, mbr LPO Exec 1958-59; PPC Lewisham West 1959; served on various policy Cttees; president Yorks & the Humber YLDS 2004-05; patron LULDs 2006- ; Lords Front-Bench Spokesperson on Northern Ireland 2000- ; mbr, British-Irish inter-parliamentary body *special interests* Northern Ireland, higher education, constitutional affairs, fat-cat pay, PFI/PPP, charitable foundations, health, transport (air traffic *other mbrships* director (former chair) Joseph Rowntree Reform Trust Ltd 1975- ; *recreations* watercolour painting *publications* *Town Cllrs, Town & County Hall, Anti-Politics, Direct Action & Representative Democracy, The Politics of the Corporate Economy, The Fixers* and numerous articles *address* House of Lords, London SW1A OPW *tel* 020 7219 3563 *fax* 01347 824109 *e-mail* smitht@parliament.uk

SMITHARD, Jane Caroline Grantham: Vice-President PCA *b* May 2 1 *s* Oliver *education* St Paul's Girls Junior School, London; St. Mary's Hall, Brighton; Kingston Polytechnic; Inns of Court School of Law; Kings College London: qualifications: BA Hons, Barrister, FCI Arb, postgraduate diploma in European Law, Higher Certificate Wine and Spirit Educational Trust, ABRSM Grade VII singing *career* Legal consultant to international software companies; company secretary to UK listed plc *party* founder mbr Lib Dems and SDP; directly-elected Mbr Federal Conference Cttee; mbr PCA Exec 1990- , chair 1991-94, vice president 1994- chair Editorial Board *The Parliamentary Campaigner* 1995- ; PPC Basildon 2001, City and Westminster South 1987,1992; candidate Westminster borough council elections 1982, 1986, 1990, 1994,1998, 2006; former mbr Federal Exec, English Council; mbr SDP pro-merger gp; former organiser Surbiton Liberals; mbr Women Liberal Democrats, Liberal Democrat European Gp, Lib Dem Lawyers *special interests* Europe, civil liberties, foreign affairs, information technology, economy and business *recreations* foreign travel, art, architecture and design, music, singing, keeping fit *address* 24 Sutherland Street, London SW1V 4LA *e-mail* jane.smithard@btinternet.com

SOADY, Rev Mark *b* 1960 *career* various party posts, ordained minister (Church of Wales) 1996; chaplain HM Forces 1997 *party* mbr Federal Exec, Federal Finance Cttee, Welsh Exec; 1986-87 agent to Roy Jenkins in Glasgow Hillhead 1983-87; 1988-93 Cowley Street staffer; chair Welsh CEC 2000-01; chair, Welsh GE Campaign 2001, national agent for Wales *address* Hebron, Clifton Road, Newport NP20 4EW *tel* 01633 267191 *fax* 01633 211342 mobile 07811 439445 *e-mail* marksoady@onetel.net.uk

SPENCELEY, Lorna *b* Jersey, Dec 13, 1958 *m* Nick 1979 1 *s* Tom 1 *d* Georgina *education* Hautlieu School, Jersey; Selwyn College, Cambridge *career* education officer, Afasic (special educational needs charity) 1993-95; self-employed 1995-99; deputy chief Exec Afasic 1999-2000; marketing manage, Hertford Regional College 2000-2002; training administrator Liberal Democrats 2002- *party* joined 1987; gp leader Harlow District Council 1991- ; PPC Harlow 1992, 1997, 2001; Euro candidate (fourth on list) East of England 1999; former mbr Federal Conference Cttee *special interests* local Govt *recreations* walking with wolves (through UK Wolf Conservation Trust), reading, music, health club, regular visits home to Jersey *address* 171 Spring Hills, Harlow, Essex CM20 1TD *tel* 01279 324676 home 07930 337596 mobile *fax* 0871 224 7525 *e-mail* lspenceley@cix.co.uk

SPURLING, David John *b* Jul 24, 1940 *m* Anthea (neé Doddrell) *education* Diploma in Government Administration 1966; Bristol Univ, Economics with Statistics 1970; Fellow Chartered Institute of Logistics and Transport; PGCE 1976; Fellow Royal Statistical Society *career* Senior Lecturer, City of Birmingham Polytechnic 1974-80; Head of Economics and Government, Gravesend Grammar School for Boys 1990 -19-94; founder of Learning Through Cooperation Ltd, (LTC) *party* Councillor Southend on Sea 1973-74, Swale BC 1994-2002; PPC Meriden 1979 *publications* Pitman: *Business Calculations, Discover Business and Commerce, Discover Book-keeping and Accounts*; Penguin: *Economics Passnotes* (O Level), *Economics Passnotes* (GCSE), *Economics Master Studies* (A Level); Shaw and Sons: *Professional Competence for Road Haulage Operators, Test Yourself on Road Haulage Operations* (CPC); LTC Publishers: titles on Business and Management, Sociology *special interest* transport *address* 13 Periwinkle Close, Sittingbourne, Kent ME10 2 JT *tel* 01795 477122 home 01795 477122 business and fax *e-mail* davidjohnspurling@yahoo.com *web* www.ltcregency.co.uk

STACY, Terry *b* Jan 23, 1972 ptnr Paul Symes 1 *s education* Morpeth Secondary School; Tower Hamlets College *career* housing, regeneration consultant; freelance regeneration consultant 2003- ; programme manager, Hackney Wick SRB programme, LB Hackney/Renaisi 2000-03, community development manager 1998-2000; community development manager, LB Hackney 1997-1999; head, tenant services Harding Housing Association 1995-97 *party* joined 1986; Cllr, LB Islington 2002- , Exec mbr performance 2003- ; assistant Exec mbr community safety 2002-03, chief whip 2002-03; Cllr, LB Tower Hamlets 1998-2002, opposition spokesperson, housing & performance 1998-2002; chair, Tower Hamlets Stock Transfer Commission 2002; vice chair, Tower Hamlets Liberal Democrats 1995-98, chair, candidates selection panel 2001-2002; Exec mbr London Liberal Democrats 1993-96, vice chair (policy) 1994-95 *special interests* housing, regeneration, public service performance *other mbrships* chair Victoria Park Homeownership 2000-2002; vice chair Old Ford Housing Association 1999- ; vice chair Strutton Housing Association 1999- ; Cttee mbr Heritage Lottery Fund 2002- *recreations* Jazz Fair, wine (the more the better!), good food *publications* articles in *Inside Housing, Housing Today, Regen & Renewal address* 12E Sotheby Road, London N5 2UR *tel* 020 7704 6826 home 020 7527 3090 business *fax* 020 7527 3077 *e-mail* terry.stacy@islington.gov.uk

STAINER, Prof Alan Ivor MSc, PhD, CEng, FInstE, FIMM, FMS, FRSA *b* Nov 18, 1935 *education* Univ of Stirling (MSc technological economics) 1972; Univ of

Loughborough (PhD thesis: *Productivity in the Longwall Mining of Hard Coal*) 1979 *m* Lorice 1964 1 *s* 1 *d career* emeritus professor of productivity and performance management, head International Centre for Business Performance and Corporate Responsibility, Middlesex Univ Business School; Fellow, World Academy of Productivity Science 1992; founder, director International Society for Productivity and Quality Research 1991; editor *International Journal of* Business *Performance Management* 1997; productivity consultant and advisor; winner R *m* Currie fellowship to investigate productivity and quality management in Japan 1992 *party* joined Liberals 1959; mbr exececutive Enfield Southgate LP; mbr Lib Dem Business Forum; mbr Centre Forum; mbr City Lib Dems *publications* articles, papers on productivity, quality, business performance and business ethics; Literati Club prize for Excellence Award for the most outstanding paper *Ethical Dimensions of Environmental Management* (published in *Euro* Business *Review*) 1998 *recreations* cricket, music, theatre, good food *clubs* NLC, City Univ Club, MCC, Middlesex CCC, Surrey CCC, The Cricketers Club of London *address* 67 Arnos Grove, Southgate, London N14 7AG *tel* 020 8886 7604

STANIER, Eleanor Mary *b* Sept 2 1942 *m* Tom Stanier 3 *s* 1 *d* 2 *gs education* Oxford High School for Girls 1947-61; history degree St. Hilda's College Oxford 1961-4; PGCE London Univ Institute of Education 1964-5 *career* teaching, local schools; Richmond Adult College; Godolphin and Latymer School 1978-1991; regional director, Cambridge Occupational Analysts.1992-96 *party* joined 1984; elected LB Richmond 1997, 1998 for Mortlake ward, lost 2002; elected 2003 Mortlake and Barnes Common ward; Mayor, LB Richmond 2001-02 *special interests* education, the arts *other mbrships* Rotary International, Barnes and Mortlake History Society, Mortlake with East Sheen Society; chair Thames Concerts Society *recreations* family, piano playing, choir, France, local history *publications* articles on careers topics in local and national press *address* 74 Palewell Park, East Sheen , SW!4 8JH *tel* 0208 392 9366 *fax* 0208 287 8200 *e-mail* cllr.estanier@Richmond.gov.uk

STEEL OF AIKWOOD, Baron Sir David Martin Scott Steel: Life Peer cr 1997, KBE 1990, PC 1977, DL (Ettrick, Lauderdale and Roxburghshire 1990) *b* Mar 31, 1938 .*m* Judy 2 *s* 1 *d education* Prince of Wales School, Nairobi; George Watson's College, Edinburgh; Univ of Edinburgh *career* MP for Scottish Borders from by-election Mar 1965 to retiring in 1997; MSP, Presiding Officer, Scottish Parliament 1999-2003; mbr House of Lords since 1997 *party* president Edinburgh Univ Liberals 1960-61; assistant secy Scottish Liberal Party 1962-64; Leader, Liberal Party 1976-88; co-founder, Liberal Democrats *special interests* Scottish constitution, Africa, Middle East *other mbrships* president Anti-Apartheid Movement 1966-70; president Liberal International 1992-94 *recreations* fishing, classic cars *publications* numerous including autobiography *Against Goliath address* House of Lords, London SW1A 0PW

STEPHEN, Nicol MSP, Deputy First Minister; Minister for Education and Lifelong Learning: Scottish Parliament *b* Mar 23, 1960 Aberdeen *m* Caris (nee Doig) 2 *d* 2 *s education* Robert Gordon's College, Aberdeen; Aberdeen Univ, LLB; Edinburgh Univ, DipLP *career* solicitor, senior corporate manager, project manager, company director *party* councillor, Grampian Regional Council 1982-91, MP for Kincardine and Deeside 1991-92, MSP for Aberdeen South 1999- , leader Scottish

Liberal Democrats 2005- ; *special interests* education, health, economy *other mbrships* Law Society for Scotland, Aberdeen Chamber of Commerce *recreation* golf *address* 173 Crown Street, Aberdeen AB11 6JA *tel* 01224 252728 *fax* 01224 290926 *e-mail* nicol.stephen.msp@scottish.parliament.uk *website* www.nicolstephen.org

STEVENS, John Christopher Courtney Vice Chair PCA *b* May 23, 1955 *education* Winchester; Magdalen College, Oxford (BA) *career* foreign exchange dealer Bayerische Hypotheken Wechelsbank, Munich 1976-77; financial correspondent *Il Messaggiero*, Rome 1978; foreign exchange dealer Banque Indosuez, Paris 1979-80; Morgan Grenfell, London 1980-84; director Morgan Grenfell International (and head, Euro Govt Bond Trading) 1985-89; adviser, foreign exchange, interest rates J Rothschild Investment Management 1989- ; MEP (Conservative) Thames Valley 1989-99 *party* joined Lib Dems, Dec 2001; Euro candidate (number three on London List) 2004; vice chair PCA 2003- *publications A Conservative European Monetary Union* (1990); *On Line in Time - the Case for a Smart Citizen's Card for Britain address* 40 Smith Square, London SW1P 3HL *tel* 020 7222 8804 business 020 7222 0770 *e-mail* john.stevens@europachannel.net or jccs@dialin.co.uk

STONE, Greg Martin *b* Aug 30, 1974, York *education* Fulford School, York; Univ of Newcastle *career* Head of Northern England for sustainable development/ regeneration consultancy; previously university manager, management consultant *party* joined 1991; former chair Newcastle city party; Northern regional exec, regional media co-ordinator; PPC Vale of York 2001, Newcastle Central 2005 (12% swing to reduce Lab majority to under 4,000); Euro candidate North East 2004; councillor, Newcastle City Council 1998- , full time cabinet member (regeneration & transport) 2004-6; *special interests* regional development, regeneration *recreations* reading, football (York City FC Supporters Trust, Friends of Bootham Crescent) *address* 9 Marie Curie Drive, Newcastle upon Tyne NE4 6SS *tel* 0191 273 7838 *e-mail* cllrgregstone@yahoo.com

STONE, Jamie MSP (Caithness, Sutherland and Easter Ross) Secy, Scottish Parliamentary Party *b* Jun 16, 1954 *education* Tain Royal Academy; Gordonstoun; St Andrews Univ (MA History and Geology) *m* 3 *ch career* served in 2/51 Highland Volunteers; worked in oil fabrication Oil Exploration; cheese manufacturing; freelance newspaper columnist, broadcaster; Director, Highland Festival *party* former chair Ross, Cromarty and Skye LP; mbr Scottish Constitutional Convention 1989-96; mbr Ross and Cromarty DC 1986-96; v chair, Caithness, Sutherland and Easter Ross LP 1997- ; mbr Highland Council 1995-99, fmr vice chair Finance Cttee; elected Scottish Parliament 1999; Equal Opportunities; Fisheries (Holyrood Progress Gp) 2001-03; Secy, Parliament Party 2002- ; mbr Enterprise & Culture Cttee; Enterprise, Lifelong Learning and Tourism spokesperson *other interests* mbr Scotland Forward *other mbrships* Highland Preservation Building Trust; Edinburgh Club; Armagh Club*recreations* gardening, railway trains *address* Scottish Parliament, Edinburgh EH99 1SP *tel* 0131 348 5790 *fax* 0131 348 5807 *constituency* 26 Tower Street, Tain, Ross-shire IV19 1DY *tel* 01862-892726 *fax* 01862-821500 *e-mail* jamie.stone.msp@scottish.parliament.uk

STONEHAM, Ben *b* Aug 24, 1948 *m* Anne 2 *s* 1 *d education* Christ's College, Cambridge; Warwick Univ Business School; London Business School *career* research officer Nuffield College Oxford 1971-74; graduate management trainee National Coal Board 1974-76; staff officer NCB chairman Lord Ezra 1976-78; Wages Policy Manager, NCB 1978-79; National Education Officer-National Union of Railwaymen 1979-82; Industrial Relations Exec-Portsmouth and Sunderland Newspapers (PSN) Plc 1982-88; Development Director, Plc Board Director-PSN Plc 1988-90; MD Portsmouth Publishing and Printing Ltd (principal subsidiary PSN Plc) 1990-99; gp production director News International Ltd 1999-2002; HR Director, News International 2002-2003; HQ Director, Liberal Democrats 2004- ; *party* SDP founder mbr 1981- ; chair Camden LP 1981-82; Alliance PPC Stevenage 1983 (within 1800 votes of winning), 1987; mbr SDP Economic Policy Cttee 1982-85; Federal Exec 1985-88; mbr negotiating Cttee to form Liberal Democrats 1987-88; Hertfordshire county Cllr 1985-89; mbr Winchester LP 1993- ; ward organiser, currently Federal Conference representative; acting Chief Exec, Liberal Democrats 1999-2000; mbr Federal Finance and Administration Cttee 2003-04; chair-Federal Party Pensions Policy Working gp 2003-04; HQ Director 2004 *special interests* pensions, employment and media policy *other mbrships* director Thurrock Urban Development Corporation; director Portsmouth Harbour Renaissance Ltd; chair Portsmouth Housing Association *recreations* family, gardening, Portsmouth FC season ticket holder, cinema *address* St Clair's Farmhouse, Wickham Road, Droxford, nr Southampton *tel* 01489 878767 home 0207 227 1368 business *fax* 020 7799 2170 *e-mail* ben_stoneham@hotmail.com

STOREY, Michael John: Leader Liverpool City Council *b* May 25, 1949 *m* Carole Storey 1 *d education* St Katharine's College, Liverpool; Liverpool Univ (post-grad) career teacher, head teacher of two schools 19 years *party* joined 1970; chair Liverpool Liberals; agent to David Alton; city Cllr, chair Education 1978-80, deputy leader of council 1980-82, leader LD gp 1994- , leader of council 1998- *special interests* education, regeneration, social enterprise *recreations* swimming, film and theatre-going, travelling *tel* 0151 225 2319 *e-mail* mike.storey@liverpool.gov.uk

STORR, Debra *b* Feb 8, 1960 *ptnr* no *ch* 1 cat *education* King Edward VI Camp Hill School for Girls, Birmingham; Loughborough Univ of Technology, BSc. Mathematical Engineering *career* business analyst/project manager *party* mbr and vice-chair Gordon LP; vice-chair NE Scotland Region; mbr Scottish Party Exec; vice-chair Scottish Conference Cttee; Scottish Party rep to Federal Conference Cttee; PPC Falkirk East 1992, Moray 1997; local govt candidate many times from 1986 onwards; elected councillor Belhelvie, Aberdeenshire 1999 and 2003; exec mbr LDO; mbr Scottish Green Liberal Democrats, Liberal Democrat Humanist and Secularist Society, Scottish Association of Liberal Democrat Campaigners and Candidates *other mbrships* Mountain Bothies Association; John Muir Trust; Humanist Society of Scotland; Voluntary Euthanasia Society of Scotland; Unison (Steward); North East Scotland Kayak Club *special interests* planning and environment recreations sea kayaking in fine weather, dressmaking, cooking, borrowing neighbour's dog *style* Cllr *address* Westmost Cottage, Balmedie House, Balmedie, Aberdeenshire AB23 8XU *tel* 01358 742048 home 07812 116664 mobile *e-mail* debra@debrastorr.org.uk *web* www.debrastorr.org.uk

STREETER, Patrick Thomas *b* Aug 1, 1946 *m* Judy (nee Turk) 1 *d* 2 *s education* Harrow School *career* Chartered Accountant; Underwriting Mbr of Lloyd's *party* Liberal candidate, Croydon NE 1973, 1979; Cllr LB of Tower Hamlets 1982-1990 and Leader of the Opposition 1984-5; Chair, Housing and Planning (Bethnal Green and Spitalfields) 1987-89; Common Cllr, City of London Corporation, Bishopsgate Ward, 2004-05; Chair, Brentwood and Ongar Liberal Democrats 2006; other mbrships trustee, The Spitalfields Trust; director, The Tower Hamlets Development Trust *publications* author of five books *recreations* sport, local history *address* Watermans End Cottage, Matching Green, Harlow, Essex CM17 0RQ *tel* 01279 731308 *e-mail*, sptstreeter@aol.com, *mobile* 07941 173037

STUDD, Robin *b* Apr 28, 1941 *m* 3 *d education* King Edward VI School, Stratford-upon-Avon; Univ of Leeds (BA, PhD); Univ of London, Institute of Historical Research, Research Fellow *career* temporary lecturer in Medieval History, Univ of Leeds, 1966-67; temporary lecturer, lecturer, senior lecturer in History, Keele Univ 1967- ; director, Centre for Local History, Keele Univ; Fellow, Royal Historical Society *party* joined SDP 1985; chair, Newcastle-under-Lyme LP 1996-2000; PPC, Newcastle-under-Lyme, 1997; mbr Keele Parish Council 1975-2003 (chair for 22 years); Cllr, Keele and Parksite Ward 1992-6; 1999-2002 (Boundary Commission review); Cllr, Keele Ward 2002- ; cabinet mbr without portfolio, Newcastle-under-Lyme Borough Council, 2001-2003, cabinet mbr, community safety 2003-04, Liberal Democrat Gp Leader, 2002-06 *special interests* planning; heritage matters; community politics *other mbrships*: Fellow Royal Historical Society (council mbr 1996-2000); Victoria County History Central Cttee mbr; chair Staffordshire VCH *recreations* gardening *publications* 30-plus in Medieval History, Local History *address* home 3 Keele Farmhouse, The Village, Keele, Newcastle, Staffs ST5 5AR work School of History, Keele Univ, Keele, Staffordshire ST5 5BG *tel* 01782 626372 home 01782 583194 work *e-mail* studd@supanet.com home; j.r.studd@keele.ac.uk work

STUNELL, Andrew MP (Hazel Grove maj: 7,748) **Shadow Secy to Dept of Communities and Local Govt** *b* Nov 24, 1942 *m* Gillian 5 *ch education* Manchester Univ, Liverpool Polytechnic *career* various architectural posts 1965-85; ALDC 1985-97, political secretary ALDC 89-96; MP for Hazel Grove 1997- ; *party* PPC Chester 1979, 1983, 1987; elected Chester City Council 1979-90, Cheshire County Council 1981-91, Liberal/Alliance gp leader; Alliance Gp leader Association of County Councils 1985-90; PPC Hazel Grove 1992, elected MP Hazel Grove 1997, re-elected 2001 and 2005, deputy chief whip 1997-2001, Chief Whip 2001-06, Parliamentary Spokesman on Energy 1997-2006; elected Stockport Metropolitan Borough Council 1994-2002 *special interests* Third World issues, European affairs *publications* diverse ALDC publications: *Energy Clean and Green in 2050* (1999); *Cleaning up the Mess* (2001) *address* Constituency Office, 68a Compstall Road, Romiley, Stockport SK6 4DE; House of Commons London SW1A 0AA *tel* 0161 430 6739 home 0161 406 7070 business *e-mail* stunella@parliament.uk

SUTTON, Tony Bernard *b* Jan 13, 1948 Horsham *m* Valerie (nee Payne) Jul 12, 1969 1 *d* Philippa b 1974 1 *s* Simonb 1975 1 *gs* Joshua b 2001 *education* Westlain Grammar School; Brighton and National College of Food Technology, Weybridge; BSc 2.2 Food Technology; F.I.F.S.T *career* Batchelors Foods Ltd 1971–1978; The Boots Company Plc 1978-2004; retired early from Boots and now run a private Food

Consultancy business *party* mbr since early 80s, stood as paper candidate 5 times in Nottingham City and County Council in 90s for Wollaton Ward; mbr Nottingham City LP exec; PPC Nottingham South 2005; elected Nottingham City Cllr for Wollaton East and Lenton Abbey in by-election, May 2005; spokes for Education and Children's Services *address* The Council House, Old Market Square, Nottingham NG12DT *tel* 0115 915 9198 *e-mail* tony.sutton@nottinghamcity.gov.uk or tavylon-lib@yahoo.co.uk

SWINSON, Jo MP (East Dunbartonshire maj: 4,061) *b* February 5, 1980 *ptnr* Duncan Hames *qv education* London School of Economics (BSc Management, 1st class Hons) 2000; Douglas Academy, Milngavie 1991-97 *career* MP for East Dunbartonshire 2005- ; development officer, UK Public Health Association 2005; marketing manager SpaceandPeople Ltd 2003-2005; marketing exec and manager, *Viking FM* East Yorkshire 2000-02 *party* joined 1997; office holder, LDYS 1998-2001; vice-chair, Haltemprice & Howden LP 2000-01, PPC Hull East 2001 (achieved a 6% swing against Deputy Prime Minister); elected mbr Federal Exec 2002; PSPC Strathkelvin & Bearsden 2003; vice chair Gender Balance Task Force 2003- ; elected MP for East Dunbartonshire 2005; Shadow Arts Minister 2005-06; Shadow Scottish Secretary 2006 - ; *special interests* corporate social responsibility, gender balance and equality issues, human rights, youth participation *other mbrships* Amnesty International, New Economics Foundation *recreations* hiking, keeping fit at gym, reading and salsa dancing *address* 4 Springfield House, Emerson Road, Bishopbriggs G64 1QE *tel* 0141 762 2209 *fax* 0141 762 5604 *e-mail* jo@joswinson.org.uk *website* www.joswinson.org.uk

SWORD, Trevor *b* Mar 21, 1957 (with congenital disability) *education* Victoria Physically Handicapped School, Birmingham; Bournville FE College; Birmingham Polytechnic (studied law) *career* specialist training officer (including HIV counselling), Sandwell Social Services *party* joined 1981; PPC Birmingham Northfield 2001 *special interests* constitutional law, civil rights, welfare provision *address* 16 Dingle Close, Bournville, Birmingham B30 1RB *tel* 0121 459 5859 *e-mail* trevor@tpsword.wordonline.co.uk

SYKES, Howard *b* Dec 15, 1963 *m* (to secondary schoolteacher) 2 *ch career* family bakery business, Shaw, Oldham; regional organiser pro-Sunday trading Gp; Chief Exec ALDC 1986-2006 *party* mbr Oldham BC 1987- ; PPC Oldham East and Saddleworth 2001 *address* 27a High Street, Shaw, Oldham OL2 8RF *tel* 01706 880058 *e-mail* howard.sykes@aldc.org

SYMONDS, Roger Alan *b* Sept 22, 1941 *ptnr* Nic Rattle 1 *s* Tom 1 *d* Erica *education* City of Bath Boys School; Culham College of Education; Canley College, Coventry (BEd Hons degree, validated 1978 by Warwick Univ, in History of Education, Physical Education; graduate IDeA Leadership Academy 2002-03 *career* administrator British Gas, PE teacher primary, secondary schools 1979-94; part- time tour guide Open Top Bus 1994-2002); researcher Don Foster MP 1996; barman Old Green Tree Bath 1997-2000; accredited IDeA Peer Review 2003 *party* joined 1988; federal, Western Counties voting representative 1999- ;mbr English Council 2000; chair Bath, Wansdyke's joint campaign team for Euro, Westminster, local elections; mbr Bath City Council, Bath and North East Somerset Council 1991- , deputy gp leader 1998 -2003, Exec mbr Economic Development and Environment (EDEN

Portfolio) 2002, council's representative Bath Tourism Plus Board, Local Agenda 21 Initiative, Kennet and Avon Canal Trust; Lib Dem mbr LGA Waste Exec 2001- ; presented paper to R99 International Congress, Geneva 1999; conference speaker, national, regional conferences on Zero Waste 2001- ; moved successful Zero Waste motion 2003 Brighton (Lib Dems only major political party to do so); 777th Mayor of Bath May 2004-05 *special interests* environment (Bath and North East Somerset first LA to adopt Zero Waste); community *other mbrships* former captain, vice president Avon Rugby Football Club; Bath Rugby Supporters Club; mbr, trustee (for six years) *envolve* (Bath's Environment Centre); Combe Down Stone Mines Community Association, Combe Down Heritage Gp *recreations* watching rugby (mainly Bath), boule, cycling south of Italy, real ale (particularly Bath Ales), eating 'real' food from Bath Farmers market, good restaurants, politics *publications* Going to Waste paper to R99 Congress, Geneva *address* 22 Combe Road Combe Down Bath BA2 5HX tel*ephone* 01225 832144 *e-mail* mail@rogersymonds.org.uk *web* www.rogersymonds.org.uk

T

TAVERNE of Pimlico, Baron Dick: Life Peer cr 1996, QC 1965 *b* Oct 18, 1928 *education* Charterhouse; Balliol College, Oxford (First in Greats); mbr Oxford Union tour of US 1951 *m* 1955, Janice 2 *d* Hon Suzanna, Hon Caroline *career* called to the Bar 1954; MP (Lab) Lincoln 1962-72: Parliamentary Secy Home Office 1966-68, Minister of State, Treasury 1968-69, Financial Secy 1969-70; chairman Public Expenditure (General) Sub-Cttee 1971-72; first director Institute for Fiscal Studies 1971 (chair 1979-83); chair Public Policy Centre 1984-87; board mbr Spierenburg Cttee to examine working of European Commission 1979; director PRIMA Europe 1987-98 (chair 1991-94, president 1994-98); director AXA Equity & Law Life Assurance Society plc 1972- (chair 1998-) ; BOC Gp plc 1975-95; chair OLIM Convertible Trust 1989-99; deputy chair Central European Growth Fund; Hon Fellow Mansfield College Oxford 1997 *party* resigned Labour Party 1972; re-elected Independent Social Democrat MP Lincoln 1973-74; mbr National Cttee SDP 1981-87; PPC Dulwich 1983; founder mbr Liberal Democrats' mbr Federal Policy Cttee 189-90; created life peer 1996, sits as Lib Dem in House of Lords *publications* The Future of the Left-Lincoln and After 1974 *recreations* sailing *style* The Rt Hon Lord Taverne, QC *address* 60 Cambridge Street, London SW1V 4QQ *tel* 020 7828 0166; House of Lords, London SW1A 0PW

TAYLOR, Gordon Ian *b* May 10, 1950 *m* 2 *s* 1 *d education* City of London Polytechnic, North London Polytechnic 1969-72; Fellow, Chartered Insurance Institute; Fellow, Institute of Financial Accountants *career* director AHJT Taylor (Insurances) Ltd 1978-91; MD Taylor Acland & Co.Ltd. 1991-99; Chartered Insurance Broker in practice with Lark Insurance Broking Gp 2000- *party* party's insurance broker 1976- *address* Lark Insurance Broking Gp, Ibex House, 42/47 Minories, London EC3N 1DY *tel* 07768 607015 *fax* 07768 609045 *e-mail* gordontaylor@beeb.net

TAYLOR, Matthew Owen John MP (Truro and St Austell maj:7,403) *b* Jan 3, 1963 London, son of Ken Taylor, television author *education* Truro, London; scholarship to Oxford Univ; president Students' Union 1985-86 *party* economic research assistant to Parliamentary Party; seconded to David Penhaligon, MP 1986; PPC Truro and St Austell 1987 (by-election caused by death of David Penhaligon: elected with record maj, at 24 youngest MP, which he remained for 10 years), re-elected 1992, 1997, 2001, 2005; Alliance youth spksn 1987; Liberal spksn for Energy 1987-88; Local Govt spksn (handling Poll Tax Bill, overseeing development of party's alternative 'Local Income Tax' policy) 1989; Trade and Industry portfolio 1989-90; Education Spksn (responsible for developing 'penny on income tax for education' policy) 1990-92; chair Communications Cttee, responsible for communications, party political broadcasts, media relations, federal conferences presentation, creation of Bird of Liberty logo; mbr General Election Planning Gp 1992; chair Campaigns and Communications with overall responsibility for strategy, implementation 1992-94 (gp developed 'target seats strategy' for 1997 General Election which saw party win record 46 seats); Environment spksn (ex officio Deputy Convenor Liberal Democrat Treasury and Economics Affairs Cttee) 1994; won *Green Ribbon Award* (sponsored by *BBC Wildlife Magazine*) as most effective environmental MP 1997 (judges said: "Matthew Taylor is persistent, organised and energetic in his championing of the environment"); front bench spksmn on the environment; campaign chairman for Charles Kennedy in leadership election 1999; Shadow Chancellor 2000-03; chair Parliamentary Party 2003-06; chaired (wrote) 2005 GE manifesto *special interests* education, the environment *recreations* watching films, listening to soul bands, driving restored 1967 MGB *address* House of Commons, London SW1A 0AA *tel* 020 7219 6686; *constituency:* 10 South Street , St Austell, Cornwall PL25 4BH *tel* 01726 63443 *fax* 01726 68457 *e-mail* taylorm@parliament.uk *web* www.matthewtaylor.info

TEALBY-WATSON, Elfreda Drusilla Sarah *b* Mar 6, 1965 *m* Gregor Watson 1 *d* Phoebe *education* Springwood High School Comprehensive, King's Lynn; Perse School, Cambridge 1984-87; Queens' College Cambridge (MA History) 1987-88; Keele Univ (MA American History and Institutions); Cambridge Regional College (Foundation diploma in Fine Art & Design) 1997-98 *career* trainee accountant Price Waterhouse 1988; admin with Cambridge University graduate board 1989-90; project manager Careers Research Advisory Council 1991-93; freelance project management especially in business-education links, community & voluntary sector 1998-99; career break following surgery and birth of daughter; fine-art diploma 2000-03; freelance public affairs and community project work; ceased paid work 2004-05 to fight seat; unpaid chair and director of Homestart Uttlesford (charity supporting families in crisis with children under five) *party* joined 1995; Saffron Walden fund-raiser General Election 1997; won Tory seat Uttlesford District Council by-election 2000, re-elected 2003; PPC Saffron Walden 2001, 2005; exec mbr LP *special interests* visual arts; community development; lobby and advocacy politics; international affairs *other memberships* PitPat (network for pituitary patients); Amnesty International; Stop Stansted Expansion *recreations* family, friends; painting; cooking and eating; walking in Scotland; village cricket; horseracing *publications* occasional articles and sub-editing; unpublished BA thesis: 1936 Royal Commission to Palestine and British Public Opinion; unpublished MA thesis: American Presidential Decision-Making: Truman and the Declaration of Israeli Independence 1948 *address* Punters, 2 Haggers Close, Great Chesterford,

Saffron Walden, Essex CB10 1QN *tel* 01799 530175 home 07801 059 115 business *e-mail* elfreda.tw@virgin.net

TEATHER, Sarah MA (Cantab) MP (Brent East maj:2,712) **Shadow Secy of State for Education** *b* Jun 1, 1974 *education* John Ferneley HS, Melton Mowbray; Leicester GS; St John's College, Cambridge; Univ College, London *career* MRC research student UCL 1996-97; medical editor, pharmaceutical marketing agency 1997-98; science policy officer Royal Society 1998-2001; science policy consultant Technopolis Ltd 2001-02; health and social policy analyst Macmillan Cancer Relief 2002-03; MP for Brent East, by-election Sept 2003 *party* joined 1993; secy, Hackney LP 2000-1; PPC Finchley and Golders Green 2001; mbr Federal Policy Cttee 2001-03, Federal Conference Cttee 2001-02, Liberal Democracy Policy Working Gp 2001; mbr Exec ALDES, WLD, SE Region 2001; proposed motion on local cinemas, Federal Conference 2001; Cllr LB Islington (Hillrise ward), vice chair sustainability scrutiny Cttee, deputy Exec mbr sustainability; mbr Exec London Region 2002; chair Health Policy working gp 2003; MP for Brent East: by-election Sept 2003, re-elected 2005; Health spokesperson 2003-04; London spokesperson 2004-05; Shadow Secy for Community and Local Govt 2005-06; Shadow Secy Education 2006- ; *special interests* science, health policy, learning Gujarati and Urdu *recreations* Parliament choir, catching up with friends *clubs* National Liberal *style* Sarah Teather MP *address* constituency office, 1 High Road, Willesden Green, London NW10 2TE *tel* 020 8459 0455 *e-mail* teathers@parliament.uk *web* www.sarahteather.org.uk

TEVERSON, Lord Robin: cr Life Peer 2006; *party* one of the first two Liberal Democrats elected to the European Parliament; served as Chief Whip of the European Liberal Democrats 1997-99; appointed to House of Lords 2006 *address* House of Lords, London SW1A 0PW

THOMAS, Baroness Celia: cr Life Peer 2005; MBE *b* Oct 14, 1945 *education* St Swithin's School, Winchester *career* Winchester Diocesan Board of Finance, Winchester Cathedral; The Pilgrims' school, Winchester and Christ Church Cathedral School, Oxford 1964-74; agent to John Matthew, PPC 1974 GE; worked for Rt Hon Jeremy Thorpe in Leader's Office 1975-76; after six months with a head-hunter, produced the biggest-ever central London version of Britten's children's opera *Noyes Fludde* (almost as hard work as being an election agent, she says); Liberal Whip's Assistant, then Head of Whips' Office, House of Lords 1977- *party* joined 1964, started Winchester Young Liberals (played skittles quite a lot); probably all happened after falling under Jo Grimond's magic spell when he spoke to thirty young stalwarts in school hall in 1960s; chair Liberal Summer School 2002- *recreations* used to belong to lots of choirs, butterfly conservation and plant life; theatre, books; gardening; now particularly interested in alternative medicine *address* House of Lords, London SW1A 0PW

THOMAS, Richard *b* Jun 20, 1974 Swansea *m* 2 *ch education* St Michael's School, Llanelli; Gorseinon College, Swansea; Newcastle Univ *career* environmental campaigner, currently parliamentary officer with Association for the Conservation of Energy *party* mbr Dulwich and West Norwood; Southwark cllr 1998- ; exec mbr for Environment and Transport 2002-2006; PPC Lewisham East 2005, Lewisham West 2001; mbr Green Lib Dems other mbrships Friends of the

Earth; London Cycling Campaign *address* 165 Dunstans Road, East Dulwich *tel* 07960 688851 *e-mail* richard@richardthomas.org.uk

THOMAS of Gresford, Baron Donald Martin Thomas: Life Peer cr 1996, OBE 1982, QC 1979 *b* Mar 13, 1937 Wrexham *m* Nan 3 *s* 1 *d education* Grove Park GS, Wrexham, Peterhouse College, Cambridge (MA, LLB) *career* admitted solicitor 1961, lecturer 1966-68; called to the Bar, Gray's Inn 1967, bencher 1989, head of chambers; junior counsel Wales and Chester Circuit 1968-79, Recorder of Crown Court 1976- , deputy High Court judge 1985- ; mbr Criminal Injuries Compensation Board 1985-93; chair Marcher Sound Ltd (local radio for N Wales, Chester) 1992-2000 (v chair 1985-92); advisor to East Asia Institute, Univ of Cambridge 1998; patron China Law Conferences 1998-2001 *party* PPC (Lib) West Flint 1964, 1968, 1970, Wrexham 1974, 1979, 1983, 1987; president Welsh Liberal Party 1978 (chair 1969-71), president Welsh Lib Dems 1993-97; created life peer 1996; Lords spokesman Welsh Affairs, Home Affairs; mbr Commission on Local Govt Electoral Arrangements in Wales *other mbrships* president Gresford Memorial Trust; Friends of Gresford Parish Church; Friends of Wrexham Maelor Hospital; vice-president Llangollen International Eisteddfod *recreations* rugby, football, rowing, fishing, music-making (president London Welsh Chorale, mbr Parliamentary Choir); theatre (Wrexham Little Theatre); conservation (the capercaillie bird in Scotland) *clubs* Reform, Western (Glasgow), Wrexham RFC *style* The Rt Hon Lord Thomas of Gresford, OBE, QC *address* Glasfryn, Gresford, Clwyd LL12 8RG *tel* 01978 852205 *fax* 01978 855078; Ground Floor, 1 Dr Johnson's Buildings, Temple, London EC4Y 7AX *tel* 0171 353 9328 *fax* 0171 353 4410 *e-mail* thomasm@parliament.uk

THOMAS of Walliswood, Baroness Susan Petronella Thomas: Life Peer cr 1994, OBE, DL: Lords Spokesperson on Women *b* Dec 20, 1935 3 *ch* 6 *grch education* Cranbourne Chase; Lady Margaret Hall, Oxford, (degree in history; further education as a diplomat's wife in USSR, Portugal, United States and Cuba) *party* joined Liberal Party 1973; treasurer, chair Richmond LA; mbr London Liberal Party Council, standing policy Cttee; supported merger, served on policy Cttee during Alliance; elected Surrey CC 1985, chair Highways and Transport Cttee; chair of council 1996-97; PPC (Alliance) Mole Valley 1983, 1987; Euro candidate West Surrey 1994; created life peer 1994; speaks on transport in Lords *other interests* non-exec director East Surrey Hospital and Community Healthcare NHS Trust 1993-97; mbr Surrey Area Probation Cttee *recreations* talking, gardening, family, ballet, reading *style* Baroness Thomas of Walliswood *address* The House of Lords, London SW1A 0PW *tel* 020 7219 3599 or 01306 885590

THOMSON of Monifieth in the District of the City of Dundee, Baron Sir George Morgan Thomas: Life Peer UK 1977, Kt 1981, PC 1966, DL 1992 *b* Jan 16, 1921 *education* Grove Academy, Dundee *m* Grace (Lib Dem parish Cllr 1990-2000) 2 *d* Caroline (senior BBC Exec), Ailsa (vicar, married to Lord Newby *qv*) *career* various editorial posts on *The Dandy* to chief sub-editor 1930s; RAF 1940-46; assistant editor, editor *Forward* 1946-53; MP (Lab) Dundee East 1952-72, Minister of State FO 1964 66, Chancellor of Duchy of Lancaster 1966-67, 1969-70, jt Minister of State State FO 1967, Secy of State for Commonwealth Affairs 1967-68; Minister without Portfolio 1968-69, EEC Commissioner 1973-77; chair; European Movement in Britain 1977-80, Advertising Standards Authority 1977-80; director ICI plc 1977-90, Woolwich Equitable Building Society 1979-91, Royal Bank of

Scotland Gp 1977-90, English National Opera 1987-93, Value and Income Trust 1986-2000; First Crown Estate Commissioner 1978-80; chair Independent Broadcasting Authority 1981-88, vice chair European Institute of Media 1989-94; president History of Advertising Trust 1985-99, Voice of Listener and Viewer 1990-; Chancellor Heriot Watt Univ 1977-91; mbr Nolan Cttee 1994-97 *party* Labour PPC Glasgow Hillhead 1950, Dundee East 1952 (elected); served as MP, minister, shadow minister for twenty years; joined Liberal Democrats 1989; Lords spokesman Foreign Affairs, Broadcasting 1990-98; chair Scottish Peers Association 1996-98 *other interests* chairman Suzy Lamplugh Trust for three years; deputy chairman Ditchley Foundation, FRSE, FRTS (vice-president seven years); Pilgrim Trustee (twenty years); trustee Thomson Foundation 1977- ; trustee Leeds Castle Foundation 1978- (chair 1994-2000) *honours* Hon LLD Dundee 1967, Hon DLitt Heriot-Watts 1973, Hon DSc Aston 1976, Hon DLitt New Univ of Ulster 1984, Hon DCL Kent 1989, FRSE 1985 *style* The Rt Hon Lord Thomson of Monifieth, KT, PC, DL, FRSE *address* House of Lords London SW1A 0PW

THOMSON, Roy Hendry KStJ DL (City of Aberdeen) *b* Aug 1932 *m* Nancy 3 *d* 7 *gdch education* Aberdeen Grammar School, Univ of Aberdeen (MA Hons Psychology) currently Univ of Aberdeen M.Litt. *career* Industrial Psychologist, Rowntree & Co, Chair & MD various businesses in motor and radio trade; mktg dir Aberdeen Intl Youth Festival *party* convenor Aberdeen South LibDems, Past Pres, Past Convenor, Scottish Lib Dems, Scot rep on Fed Exec, previously Agent Malcolm Bruce, Cllr Aberdeen City 14 years, Leader of City Council 18 months, ELDR Council 3 years *special interests* electoral reform, mountain rescue, Order of St John *recreations* skiing, hill walking *LD quirks* presently carrying out study of 2007 Scot Local Govt elections by STV *address* 19 Westhill Grange, Westhill Aberdeenshire AB32 6QJ *tel* 01224 743858 home 07802 694998 mobile *e-mail* royththomson@aol.com

THORKILDSEN, William (Bill) *b* Aug 4, 1965 Southampton *m* 2 *ch education* 5 O-levels *career* sales exec for international company *party* mbr of Newcastle LP; elected councillor; director for D2 Youth Zone special interests working with consultants, reading, cycling, walking, dealing with people, China *recreations* drinking, socialising, making the most out of life *LD quirks* beating Labour! *style* Cllr *address* 19 Fetcham Court, Kenton Bank Foot,Newcastle upon Tyne, Tyne & Wear NE3 2UL *tel* 0191 286 5667 home 07929 464133 mobile *e-mail* bill@thorkildsen.fsnet.co.uk or william.thorkildsen@newcastle.gov.uk

THORPE, Rt Hon (John) Jeremy PC (1967) FRSA *b* Apr 29, 1929 *s* of Capt John Henry Thorpe OBE, JP (d 1944) Conservative MP for Rusholme, and gs of Sir John Norton-Griffiths, MP for Wednesbury and Wandsworth *education* Rectory Pomfret; Eton; Trinity College Oxford (president Oxford Union 1951) *m* 1 1968 Caroline (d1970) 1 *s m* 2 Marion, Countess of Harewood *career* called to the Bar, Inner Temple 1954; MP (Lib) North Devon; chair Jeremy Thorpe Associates Ltd (development consultants) consultant Stramit Ltd; Exec chair UNA 1976-80; mbr Devon Sessions; hon fell Trinity College Oxford, Hon LLD Univ of Exeter *party* Leader of the Liberal Party 1967-76, Hon Treasurer 1965-67 *clubs* NLC style The Rt Hon Jeremy Thorpe *address* 2 Orme Square, London W2 4RS

THORPE, Susan *b* Susan Lawes Dec 29, 1945, New Malden, Surrey *m* Tony 1985
2 *ch* 6 *gdch education* Ursuline Convent Grammar School, Wimbledon; Slough
College of Higher Technology (DMS) *career* various jobs in PR, the wine trade and
finance/marketing 1964–81; self-employed small business management accountant
1981- ; *party* joined in 1981; mbr Salisbury LP, Western Counties; mbr Regional
Exec 2006 ; mbr English Council 2006; former chair of Salisbury LP, and exec mbr
1994–2004; mbr Kingston exec 1983–87; elected Salisbury District Councillor
1995–2003, deputy leader 1995–99, chair: Finance 1995; Budget, Performance and
Review 1996-99; Partnership 1999-2001; mbr ALDC, Agents Association *other*
mbrships Treasurer, Community First, Wiltshire; Chair of Governors, St Osmund's
Primary School, Salisbury *special interests* economic development, transport and
environment, education *recreations* swimming, walking, gardening, travel *address*
Sandon, Mill Lane, Salisbury, Wilts SP1 3LJ *tel* 01722 411102 home 07973 452487
mobile *fax* 01722 411102 *e-mail* sthorpe@onetel.com

THURSO, Viscount John Archibald MP (Caithness, Sutherland and Easter
Ross maj:8,168) *b* Sept 10, 1953 *m* Marion Ticknor Sage 2 *s* 1 *d education* Eton
College; Westminster Technical College *career* hotelier, trained with Savoy Gp; MD
Lancaster Hotel Paris 1972-85; founder, general manager Cliveden, operations
director Cliveden House Ltd 1985- 92; CEO Granfel Holdings PLC 1992-95; CEO
Fitness and Leisure Holdings Ltd 1995-2001; non-Exec director The Savoy Gp PLC
1992-97,. Walker Greenbank PLC 1998-2001 Mossiman's Ltd 1998-2002,
(Chairman 1999-2001); deputy chairman Millennium and Copthorne PLC 2002- ;
chairman International Wine & Spirit Competition Ltd 1999- ; chairman Scrabster
Harbour Trust 1997-2001; president Academy of Wine & Food Service 1998- ;
patron HCIMA 1998-2003 *party* Liberal Democrat peer 1995-99; Lords spokesman
on tourism 1996-99 tourism and food 1998-99; mbr FPC 1999-2001, 2002-03; MP
Caithness Sutherland & Easter Ross 2001- ; Shadow Cabinet Scotland 2001-06, and
Transport 2003-05; Shadow Secy for Scotland 2006- *special interests* tourism,
transport, Scottish affairs *recreations* country sports, food & wine *address* Thurso
East Mains, Thurso, Caithness KW14 8HW *tel* 01847 892600 home 0207 219 1752
business *e-mail* thursoj@parliament.uk

TOD, Martin Paul Niebuhr *b* Aug 22, 1964 *m* Michaela *education* Lancing
College; St John's College, Cambridge (BA Hons Economics) *career* marketing
consumer goods UK, Austria, Germany, Czech Republic, Procter & Gamble 1987-
2002; head brand and marketing communication, Vodafone Ltd 2002-2005;
marketing & strategy consultant, 2005- ; *party* joined Cambridge Univ Liberal Club
1983; deputy president Cambridge Univ Students Union 1984-85; ULS delegate
World Festival of Youth & Students, Moscow 1985; treasurer, CULC, Michaelmas
1985; president Cambridge Union Society, Lent 1986; chair Liberal Democrats
Online 1999-2002, mbrship secy 2003, 2006; mbrship secy Ealing Acton &
Shepherds Bush Liberal Democrats 2000, chair 2001; PPC Ealing Acton &
Shepherds Bush 2001, North West Hampshire 2005; mbrship secy Newbury Liberal
Democrats 2006; chair, Wired Working Group 2005- ; webmaster
www.campbellcampaign.org 2006 *other mbrships* NLC, ERS *recreations* film,
travel, reading, gadgets *address* 25 Donnington Square, Newbury RG14 1PJ *tel*
07887 986048 *fax* 0870 4581619 *e-mail* martin@martintod.org.uk *skype* mpntod

TOOK, Chris *b* May 13 1980 Bridgend, South Wales *m* no children yet *education* Archbishop McGrath Secondary School (South Wales), Northwest High School (Michigan, USA); Univ of Kent (Canterbury) *career* Sales Manager for an HR software company in Canterbury *party* mbr Ashford LP, South East region; cllr Canterbury City Council; PPC Ashford *special interests* nutrition, cartoons *recreations* marathon running *LD quirk* lapsed mbr of the American Guild of Cartoonists *address* 21 Durovernum Court, Old Dover Road, Canterbury, Kent CT1 3DA *tel* 01227 450489 home 01227 780440 business 0772566969 mobile *fax* 01227 780447 *e-mail* chris@ashfordlibdems.org.uk *website* www.ashfordlibdems.org.uk

TOOLE, Dr Steven *b* Ashington, Northumberland Aug 1, 1972 e*ducation* Archbishop Holgate's School, York; York Sixth Form College; Univ of Newcastle-upon-Tyne (BA Hons geography); Univ of Wales, Swansea (PhD geography: *The Political Ecology of Small-Scale Agriculture in Barbados*) *career* part-time tutor in geography, Univ of Wales, Swansea; research fellow, Transport and Sustainable Development, Univ of Westminster; research officer Parliamentary Advisory Council for Transport Safety *party* policy adviser on environment and transport 2000- ; PPC Erith and Thamesmead 2005 *address* LibDem Whips Office, House of Commons, London SW1A 0AA *e-mail* tooles@parliament.uk

TONGE, Baroness Dr Jenny: cr Life Peer 2005; MB BS MFFP FRIPM *b* Feb 19, 1941 West Midlands *m* Keith (consultant radiologist) 3 *ch* 4 *gch education* Dudley HS; Univ College, London; UCH *career* family planning, general practice; Head, Women's Services Ealing Health Authority 1983-89, Medical Officer London Youth Advisory Service 1989-92, Community Services Manager Southall 1992; MP 1997-2005; mbr of House of Lords *party* joined Liberals 1959 (at Univ); chair, Richmond and Barnes LA (then biggest in country); mbr LB Richmond council 1980-90, chair Social Services four years; PPC Richmond and Barnes 1992, Richmond Park 1997 elected, 2001 re-elected (did not seek re-election at 2005 General Election); Shadow International Development Secy 1997-2003; mbr International Development Select Cttee; vice chair All-Party gp on AIDS; joint chair Breast Cancer, joint vice-chair Doctor-assisted Dying, joint vice-chair Pro Choice secy Landmine Eradication, treasurer Overseas Development, vice chair Rwanda, Great Lakes, vice chair Prevention of Genocide *special interests* international development, third world issues, health, environment, Europe, constitutional reform *recreations* bird-watching *address* House of Lords, London SW1A 0PW *e-mail* tonge@cix.co.uk

TOPE of Sutton, Baron Graham Norman CBE, AM, Life Peer created 1994 *b* Nov 30, 1943 *m* 1972 to Margaret *d* of Frank East 2 *s* Hon Andrew, Hon David *education* Whitgift School *career* Unilever GP 1961-69, insurance manager Air Products Ltd 1970-72; deputy general secy Voluntary Action Camden 1975-90 *party* MP (Liberal) Sutton and Cheam 1972-74; chair South East England Young Liberal Federation 1969-71; vice chair National League of Young Liberals 1971-74, president 1973-75; mbr LB Sutton 1974- , leader 1986-99, lead Cllr for Economic Development, Community Safety, Libraries and Culture 1999- ; president London Liberal Democrats 1991-99; Association of London Govt: Lib Dem leader 1997-99; vice president Local Govt Association 1997- ; education spokesperson House of Lords 1994-2000; UK mbr EU Cttee of the Regions 1994- , leader ELDR gp 1998-2002, chair Constitutional Affairs Cttee 2002- ; Greater London Authority: mbr, gp leader London Assembly 2000- , mbr Metropolitan Police Authority 2000- , chair Finance Cttee 2000- ; mbr Mayor's Advisory Cabinet 2000-4; Commission for Racial Equality London Advisory Board 2004-special interests London, Europe, policing and community safety, libraries, heritage *recreations* politics, history, reading, walking, gardening *address* 88 The Gallop, Sutton, Surrey, SM2 5SA; and GLA, City Hall, Queens Walk, London SE1 2AA *tel* 020 8770 7269 or 020 7983 4413 *fax* 020 8642 8595 or 020 7983 4344 *e-mail* graham.tope@london.gov.uk

TREGONING, Nicholas John *b* Feb 2, 1952 *m* Jane 2 *s* 1 *d education* Stoneham GS, Reading; Reading College of Technology; Manchester Univ *career* research & welfare officer, administrative and welfare manager, Bradford Univ Union; union manager Swansea Univ, Students' Union; regional and constituency manager South Wales West for Peter Black AM; deputy cabinet member for Education City and County of Swansea; equalities champion CCS *party* joined 1970s; chair, Bingley Liberals; council candidate Bingley 1979, 1984, 1987; elected City & County of Swansea councillor 1999; campaigns officer Swansea & Gower LP, secy South Wales West regional exec; mbr Welsh Campaigns and Candidates Cttee; rep to Welsh, Federal, Conferences *special interests* development issues; community entrepreneurship; environment; education, especially higher education; general manager South Wales West Liberal Democrat Printing Society *other memberships* Agents' Association; ALDC; LDEG; RSPB; chair LASA Credit Union Board; CPAG; NEF *recreations* badminton, theatre, opera, travel, hill-walking *address* 20 Glan Dulais, Dunvant, Swansea *tel* 07973 672580.business *e-mail* nick_tregoning@yahoo.co.uk

TRELEAVEN, Mike BTech (Hons), MIChemECeng *b* Aug 7, 1946 *m* Elaine nee Jones 1 *s* Tim 1 *d* Kate *education* Welwyn Garden City Grammar School; Bradford Univ (First Class Hons Chemical Engineering) *career* ICI Plastics 1969-72; production manager, then production director P Leiner & Sons (travelled extensively in Asia, South America) 1972-79; hotelier 1979-83; various enterprises to keep body and soul together! 1983- *party* finally joined 2000; chair Totnes LP 2001-02, PPC Totnes 2005 – halved Tory majority to 1,945; mbr Green Lib Dems, LDEG, Regional Exec, English Council *special interests* education, small businesses, sport *recreations* golf, sailing, theatre, travel *address*. Staunton Lodge, Embankment Road, Kingsbridge, Devon TQ7 1JZ *tel* 01548 854542 home 07773 792752 mobile *e-mail* miketreleaven@msn.com

TRUESDALE, Peter Jonathan *b* Mar 11, 1958 Rochdale *single education* Sandown High School, Isle of Wight, Merton College, Oxford *career* worked in Esso in Human Resources and Public Affairs, now Corporate Responsibility Consultant *party* mbr Vauxhall LP; leader Lambeth Council 2002- ; PPC Upminster 20001, 2005; councillor Bishop's Ward 1994- ; *style* Cllr *address* 14 Heralds Place London SE11 4NP *e-mail* ptruesdale@truesdale.demon.co.uk

TUFFREY, Mike: Greater London Assembly Mbr *career* chartered accountant, management consultant helping large companies be more socially and environmentally responsible *party* elected GLC/ILEA representing Vauxhall 1985; elected LB Lambeth 1990-2002, gp leader 1994-2002, joint council leader when Lib Dems were largest party without overall control; joined London Assembly as replacement for resigning mbr (Louise Bloom) Feb 2002, elected Jun 2004; mbr

Budget Cttee; Libdem Spokesman on Environment Cttee; and Audit Panel; deputy group leader London Fire and Emergency Planning Authority *special interests* environment issues and causes; economic development; inner city regeneration; Young Londoners; business in partnerships for sustainability; community, civil liberties *other mbrships* various regeneration boards including Brixton Challenge, Business Link London, London Development Partnership *tel* 020 7983 4383 *e-mail* mike.tuffrey@london.gov.uk

TURNER, Martin Marshall *b* Apr 2, 1966 *m* Marjolein Prins *education* St Chad's Cathedral School, Lichfield; King Edwards School, Birmingham; Hertford College, Univ of Oxford (Scholarship *career* Operation Mobilisation Belgium 1988-96, Exec officer West Midlands Arts 1996-2000, European communications manager, Lucas Automotive 2000-01, communications manager Walsall Community Health Trust 2001-02, head of communications Walsall Teaching Primary Care Trust 2002- ; *party* joined 1999; European PPC West Midlands 2004; PPC Sutton Coldfield 2001, Halesowen and Rowley Regis 2005; chair Liberal Democrat Christian Forum 2001- ; vice-chair PCA 2005- ; West Midlands spokesman on Culture, Media and Sport 2000- ; mbr policy working gp on Broadcasting *special interests* asylum, people trafficking, health, the arts, sports, broadcasting and media, Benelux, religious affairs *other mbrships* Institute of Public Relations, British Fencing, trustee Stechford Baptist Church, governor Arthur Terry School, Sutton Coldfield *recreations* fencing (ranked 69th in UK for foil, 2005), music (guitarist with band Str&nded), chess *address* 138 Manor Road, Stechford, Birmingham B33 8EQ *tel* 07753 683 337 home 0121 244 2724 *fax* 0121 244 2723 *e-mail* martin.turner@unforgettable.com

TURNER Peter John Russell *b* Jun 22, 1946 Ilford *m* Janet, two grown up children *education* Clark's College; Ipswich Civic College (CQSW); Anglia Management Centre (DMS); NottinghamTrent Univ *career* office junior, lighterman, engineer, sales exec, social worker, social work director, director of fostering agency *party* PPC Braintree 2005; leader Braintree District Council gp, chair Black Notley Parish Council ; chair of Braintree LP *special interests* transport, planning, health and social care, protecting our environment recreations walking, gardening, bird watching, and fanatical about Monty Python *address* 10 Spring Gardens, Cock and Bell Lane, Long Melford, Sudbury, Suffolk CO10 9JW *tel* 01787 468536 home 07776 182 860 mobile *e-mail* peter.turner52@btinternet.com

TYLER, Lord Paul: cr Life Peer 2005; CBE *b* Oct 29, 1941 *m* Nicky 1 *d* Sophie 1 *s* Dominick *education* Exeter College, Oxford *career* architectural Assistant 1963; housing, planning policy adviser, then Director of Public Affairs RIBA 1966-73; MP 1974, regional organiser, national board mbr Shelter 1975-76; MD Cornwall Courier newspaper group 1976-81; director Good Relations Public Affairs Ltd 1982-87, MD Western Approaches Public Relations Ltd 1987-92, MP 1992- *party* joined Liberal Party 1960; president Oxford University Liberal Club 1962; county councillor 1964-70; PPC Totnes 1966, Bodmin 1970, 1974 (MP March-October), 1979; regional chair; chair Liberal Party National Exec 1983-86; election campaign adviser to David Steel, mbr Alliance election team 1983, 1987; Euro candidate Cornwall and Plymouth 1989; MP for North Cornwall 1992- 2005; Working Peer 2005; Deputy Lieutenant Cornwall 2006; spokesperson on Agriculture & Rural Affairs 1992-97; Chief Whip 1997-2001; Shadow Leader, House of Commons, spokesperson on Constitutional Affairs 2001- 2005 *special interests* Lords reform, parliamentary reform, pesticide control (founder, Organophosphate Group, vice-chair Pesticide and Organophosphate All Party Group); Gulf War Veterans (mbr, Royal British Legion Group) *other mbrships* YHA, Friends of the Earth, Amnesty International, British Resorts Association *recreations* walking, gardening, food, Cornish ancestry *publications* *Power to the Provinces* 1968; *A New Deal for Rural Britain* 1978; *Country Lives, Country Landscapes* 1996; *Britain's Democratic Deficit* 2003 *address* House of Lords, London, SW10 0PW *tel* 020 7219 6355 *fax* 020 7219 1360 *e-mail* tylerp@parliament.uk

TYZACK, Peter *b* Dec 7, 1946 1 *s* George 1 *d* Rowena *m* (2) Fiona 1 *ss* David *education* Bablake School, Shoreditch College *career* teaching London, Coventry, Bristol from 1974; currently self-employed property agent *party* joined Liberals mid 70s; candidate Bristol City, Ashley 1979; mbr PC 1988- ; candidate Avon CC 1993; mbr Northavon DC 1994-96; mbr South Gloucestershire UA (Pilning and Severn Beach) 1995- ; chair Severn Estuary Partnership; chair EU Les Estuaries Network; chair Bristol NW constituency party; PPC Bristol East 1997, Bristol NW 2001 *style* Cllr Peter Tyzack *address* Crossings House, Little Green Lane, Severn Beach, South Glos BS35 4PA *tel* 01454 632764 *fax* 01454 633721 *e-mail* peter.tyzack@southglos.gov.uk

UV

UNDERWOOD, Jonathan William Rowland *b* Aug 24 1970 *m* Alison 3 *d* *education* King's School Grantham; Keble College Oxford (Physics) Trinity College Cambridge (Maths); Imperial College, London (PhD Theoretical Physics) *career* research physicist, Melbourne Univ, Swansea Univ; derivatives trader NatWest 1995-99; proprietary trader Deutsche Bank 1999-2001; analyst Standard Chartered Bank (part-time) 2002- *party* joined SDP 1987, Lib Dem founder mbr; treasurer East Devon 2001-2003; PPC Exeter 2005 *special interests* science, economic policy, environment *recreations* garden, chess, astronomy, wine, travel *publications* various academic articles *address* Millmead, Axmouth, Devon EX12 4AE *tel* 01297 625985 *e-mail* jon@exeter.libdems.org

VALLANCE, Lord Sir Iain David Thomas Vallance: Life Peer cr 2004, Kt 1994 *b* 20 May 1943 *s* of late Edmund Thomas Vallance, Janet Wright Bell Ross Davidson *m* 1967 Elizabeth Mary McGonnigill 1 *s* 1 *d* *education* Edinburgh Academy; Dulwich College; Glasgow Academy; Brasenose College, Oxford (Hon Fellow 1997); London Graduate School of Business Studies (MSc) *career* joined Post Office 1966; director Central Finance 1976-78; Telecommunications Finance 1978-79; Materials Department 1979-81; corporate director British Telecommunications 1981-2001; board mbr for Organisation and Business Systems 1981-83; MD Local Communications Services Division 1983-85; Chief of Operations 1985-86; Chief Exec., 1986-95; Chairman 1987-2001 (part-time 1998-2001); President. Emeritus, 2001-02; director Mobil Corporation 1996-99; president CBI, 2000-02 (mbr, president's Cttee 1988-); director Royal Bank of Scotland 1993- , vice-chairman 1994- ; mbr President's Cttee, Advisory Council BITC 1988-2002;

European Foundation for Quality Management, 1988-96; chairman European Advisory Cttee, New York Stock Exchange 2000-02 (mbr 1995-); European Services Forum 2003- ; mbr International Advisory Board British-American Chamber of Commerce 1991- ; board Scottish Enterprise 1998-2001; supervisory board Siemens AG 2003- ; European Advisory Council, Rothschild Gp 2003- ; vice president Princess Royal Trust for Carers 1999- (chairman 1991-98); trustee Monteverdi Trust, 1993-2001; deputy chairman Financial Reporting Council 2001-02; patron, Loughborough Univ 1996- ; Freeman, City of London 1985; Liveryman, Wheelwrights' Co 1986- ; hon governor Glasgow Academy 1993- ; Fellow London Business School 1989; Hon DSc Ulster 1992, Napier 1994; City 1996; Hon DTech Loughborough 1992, Robert Gordon 1994; Hon DBA Kingston 1993; Hon DEng Heriot-Watt 1995 *recreations* hill-walking, music *address* c/o Royal Bank of Scotland Gp, 2 Waterhouse Square, 138-142 Holborn, London EC1N 2TH

VERNON-JACKSON, Gerald *b* Jan 10, 1962 *education* St Edward's School, Oxford; Univ of Liverpool (BA Hons); Southampton Univ (MSc); Southampton Univ (Dip SW) *career* social worker Hampshire CC, LB Greenwich, Department of Health 1985-91; Head of Office to David Rendel MP 1994-99; Deputy Director of Campaigns and Elections, Liberal Democrats 1999-2003; lead Liberal Democrat, Improvement and Development Agency 2003- ; mbr Leadership Centre for Local Government Steering Group 2003- ; *party* joined 1988; mbr Federal Exec 1993-96, 2003- ; mbr New Forest DC 1991-94, chair Public Relations; West Berkshire Cllr 1994-2003, deputy leader, chair Social Services, chair Environment; Mayor of Newbury 1998-89; mbr national Exec of LGA 2001- ; chair Lib Dem gp LGA 2001-05, deputy chair 2005- ; Leader Portsmouth City Council 2004- , mbr 2003- , Exec mbr Housing, Health and Social Services; mbr Campaigns and Communications Cttee 1999- ; agent Romsey by-election 2000 *special interests* Africa, social services, housing, elections *other mbrships* Amnesty International, Friends of the Earth, Portsmouth Society, trusteeships: New Theatre Royal Portsmouth and Portsmouth Historic Naval Base Property Trust 2005- ; *recreations* winning elections, travel, food, wine *address* 39 Lindley Avenue, Southsea, Hampshire PO4 9NT *tel* 07976 949272 *e-mail* geraldvj@gmail.com

VICKERS, Anthony James Muschamp (Tony) *b* New Delhi Oct 13 1946 *m* Martha (nee Winston) 1969 3 *s* Edward, Ben, David *education* Wellington College, Berks; Brighton College of Technology (BSc Hons Building Technology & Management CNAA) 1969 *career* new town, spec-housing site engineer, manager Merseyside and south west 1969-72; planning engineer for regional construction company 1972-75; commissioned into Royal Engineers 1976, served Germany, Northern Ireland; Military Survey Branch 1980; Ordnance Survey HQ (Development Branch) 1981-83; Australian Survey Regiment 1983-85, Newbury -87, MoD 1987-91, Hong Kong 1991-95, usually as internal consultant on defence geographic services; retired Lt Colonel; independent consultant 1995- ; part time Head of Policy, National Centre for Volunteering 1997-99, chief Exec Henry George Foundation 1998-2001; currently independent land-policy researcher, writer, occasional lecturer and postgraduate student at Kingston Univ School of Surveying *party* joined Liberal Party 1964; vice chair South Gloucestershire Liberal Association 1973-75 (inactive 1975-95); secy Newbury LP 1997-2002; mbr Green Liberal Democrats, founder, chair ALTER; mbr Newbury District Council 1995-97; PPC Devizes 1997, Hackney South & Shoreditch 2001; mbr West Berkshire Council 2003- *special interests* land, tax policy; sustainable economics with free/fair trade; governance, citizenship; transport; housing; planning *other mbrships* TCPA, HGF, ERS, Refugee Trust, Catholic Justice & Peace, RA, RICS, Association for Geographic Information (founder mbr), Society of Property Researchers, Land Value Taxation Campaign *recreations* walking, choral singing, cinema *publications* Shifting the Burden (Progressive Forum 1999); numerous articles on land value taxation; contributing author to *Critical Issues in Environmental Taxation: International and Comparative Perspectives, Vol I* (Richmond Law & Tax 2003), *Land Value Taxation in Britain: Experience & Opportunities* (Lincoln Institute of Land Policy, Cambridge, MA USA 2004); Working Papers for Lincoln Institute: *Preparing for Land Value Taxation in Britain* (2000); *Preparing to Pilot LVT in Britain* (2002); *Blueprint for Smart Tax in Britain* (2003); *The land value effect of the Jubilee Line Extension* (with *s* Mitchell 2004) *address* 62 Craven Road, Newbury, Berkshire RG14 5NJ *tel* 01635 230046 *e-mail* tonyvickers@cix.co.uk *web* www.landvaluescape.org

VINCENT, John William *b* Mar 13, 1960 *m* Sue *education* King Arthur's School, Wincanton, Somerset; Yeovil College; Lanchester Polytechnic, Coventry (BSc Hons); Gloucester College of Art & Technology (DMS); Mbr Institute of Electrical Engineers (MIEE), Chartered Engineer (CEng) *career* Plessey Marine, Templecombe 1976-83; British Aerospace, Bristol 1983-84; Smiths Industries, Cheltenham 1984-89; Westland Helicopters, Yeovil 1989-91, Principal Systems Engineer; Civil Aviation Authority, Gatwick 1991-2004, Head of Strategic Safety and Analysis; European Aviation Safety Agency, Koeln, Germany 2004-, Head of Safety Analysis and Research *party* activist, Cheltenham 1985-89; Reigate BC candidate 1992, 2000, 2002, 2003; Surrey county councillor (Reigate division) 1993-97; Reigate borough councillor 1998-00; PPC Epsom & Ewell 1997, 2001; Euro candidate South East region 2004; former mbr Federal Conference Cttee, Federal Policy Cttee, Policy Working Group chair; chair Reigate LP 2002-04 ; exec mbr PCA 2003-04 *special interests* agriculture, aerospace, defence, trade and industry, science, environment, transport *other mbrships* European Movement *recreations* walking, countryside, travel *address* An der Muenze 10, 50668, Koeln, Germany *tel* +49 221 01208944 home +49 221 89990 2012 office *e-mail* johnwvincent@hotmail.com *web* www.john-vincent.org.uk *and* www.johnvincent.eu

W

WALKER, David *b* July 30, 1969 *education* Bridgnorth Endowed School, Bridgnorth: 1980-87; De Havilland College, Herts: 1987-89 (Land Surveying, Cartography OND); Hatfield Polytechnic 1989-91 (Engineering Surveying HND) *career* surveying (evolving into IT specialist) 1991- ; Invar Mapping Surveys (3 years); Total Surveys Ltd (5 years), Laser Surveys Ltd (3 years); MEB (9 months); Invar Mapping Surveys (a further 5 years); webmaster for Laser Surveys Ltd and subsequently Invar Mapping Surveys; worked variety of projects including Warwick, Napier & Cambridge Universities, West Midlands Safari Park, Millennium Dome, West Coast Mainline, Wolverhampton Mander Shopping Centre refurbishment,

Birmingham Northern Relief Road *party* joined 1992, after watching GE party political broadcast; 'paperless' candidate Much Wenlock ward, Bridgnorth DC 1995 (missed by 38 votes); attended Bridgnorth AGM 1996, left as vice-chair; elected as mbr for Morfe Ward, Bridgnorth DC 1999-, vice-chair policy, resources 2001-03, chair IT 2000-2002, member e-champion 2002-03; Bridgnorth TC 1999- , chair planning 2000- ; branch chair 2000-02; mbr for Bridgnorth Rural, Shropshire County Council 2001-2005, cabinet member education, demography 2003-2005; webmaster Ludlow constituency website 2002- ; *special interests* planning, highways, IT, economic development *other memberships* technical member Royal Institute of Chartered Surveyors; associate member, Institution of Civil Engineering Surveyors *recreations* watching American football, cricket, rugby union; IT, web design *address* 113a Hook Farm Road, Bridgnorth, Shropshire WV16 4RB *tel* 01746 767132 *fax* 01746) 769240 *e-mail* general@cllrdavidwalker.org *web* www.cllrdavidwalker.org

WALKER, Niall Robert *b* Jul 5, 1959 Glasgow *single education* St Andrews Univ, MA; Strathclyde Univ, Diploma in Accountancy; Glasgow Univ, MBA *career* accountant in various companies from 1981 till 1990; began own business in 1990 party mbr Glasgow Kelvin LP, councillor, PPC West Dunbartonshire 2005 *special interests* climate change, air pollution, health, civil liberties *publications* many articles and letters in local and Scottish media recreations swimming, tennis, cycling, writing *e-mail* niallwalker@lycos.co.uk

WALLACE, Jim QC MSP (Orkney maj 1,755**)** *b* Aug 25, 1954 Annan *m* 2 *ch education* Annan Academy, Downing College Cambridge (MA Economics & Law); Edinburgh Univ (LLB Legal Studies 1977) *career* advocate, practising at the Scottish Bar; QC 1997 *party* joined Scottish Liberal Party 1972, after reading Russell Johnston's book To be a Liberal; chair Edinburgh Univ Liberal Club; Euro cand South of Scotland Euro 1979; PPC Dumfries 1979, Orkney and Shetland 1983 (elected, succeeding former party Leader Jo Grimond), first person since World War Two to successfully inherit Liberal-held seat at a General Election; re-elected 1983, 1987, 1992, 1997 (stepped down 2001); first Chief Whip of the new LibDem party 1988-92; Leader of the Scottish Liberal Democrats 1992-2005; elected to the Scottish Parliament 1999, appointed Deputy First Minister 1999 and Minister for Justice 1999-2003 in partnership Govt; re-elected 2003, re-appointed Deputy First Minister (stood down 2005) and appointed Minister for Enterprise and Lifelong Learning 2003-05 in partnership Govt; as youngest mbr of the parly party at the time, he introduced Youth Charter Bill on the first sitting of International Youth Year 1985 mbr Scottish Liberal Party Exec 1976-1985 *other mbrships* mbr Scottish Constitutional Convention, played a leading role in the successful 1997 referendum campaign; mbr Consultative Steering Gp charged with drawing up preliminary arrangements, draft standing orders for the Scottish Parliament. other interests elder Church of Scotland; mbr Scottish Constitutional Convention *recreations* golf, reading and travelling *address* The Scottish Parliament, Edinburgh EH99 *e-mail* Jim.Wallace.msp@scottish.parliament.uk

WALLACE, Jonathan *b* Nov 24, 1963 *partner* David Randall *education* Lobley Hill Primary School, Gateshead 1969-75; Whickham Comprehensive, Gateshead 1975-82; Newcastle Univ 1985-88 (PhD 1988-94) *career* self-employed retailer 1982-85; manager Marks and Spencer 1993-94; constituency organiser Conwy

Liberal Democrats 1994-97; constituency organiser Harrogate 1998; co-ordinator North East Constitutional Convention 1998-2000; LGA Lib Dem Group political assistant 2000-2002; Federal policy officer 2002- ; *party* joined SDP 1981; Gateshead LP exec 1981-2000, secy 1985-90, media officer 1988, deputy chair 1992-95, chair 1995-98; Gateshead councillor 1987- ; PPC Hexham 1992, Tyne Bridge 2001; deputy chair Northern Region 1988-1990 mbr Federal Conference Cttee 1988-2002 *special interests* local election campaigning (edited *Focus* leaflets since 1985, produced one of the first constituency tabloid newspapers in 1987, used target mail for nearly 20 years); developing use of email, audio and video newsletters for communication with members and constituents *other memberships* Worldwide Fund for Nature, CentreForum *recreations* photography, reading history, writing, foreign travel, fund management *publications* Devolution by Evolution Centre Forum, 2001 *address* 7 Laburnum Grove, Sunniside, Newcastle upon Tyne NE16 5LY *tel* 0191 4883190 (Gateshead) 020 86538309 (London) home, 020 72271394 business *e-mail* j.wallace@libdems.org.uk

WALLACE of Saltaire, Baron William John Lawrence: Life Peer cr 1995: Deputy Leader of Liberal Democrats in House of Lords: Lords Spokesperson on Foreign Office *b* Leicester Mar 12, 1941 *education* chorister Westminster Abbey Choir; St Edward's School, Oxford; King's College, Cambridge (BA History); Cornell Univ (PhD Govt); Nuffield College, Oxford (MA); L'Universite Libre de Bruxelles; hon doctorate ULB *m* Helen (former president Cambridge Univ Liberal Club) 1 *s* 1 *d career* academic, Govt, international relations; Director of Studies Royal Institute of International Affairs 1978-1990; Walter Hallstein Senior Research Fellow at St Anthony's College, Oxford 1990-95; Professor of International Relations LSE 1995; Legion d'Honneur 2005 *party* joined Labour, Conservative and Liberal clubs at Cambridge; joined Liberal Party 1960; vice-president 1961 (beating Michael Steed), president Cambridge Univ Liberal Club 1962; assistant press officer (responsible for Jo Grimond's press realeases) GE 1966; national Exec NLYL 1967-68; PPC Huddersfield West 1970, Manchester Moss Side, Feb, Oct 1974, Shipley 1983, 1987; speech-writer for David Steel; vice-chair Party Standing Policy Cttee 1977-87; co-wrote GE manifesto 1979, 1997; president Huddersfield LP 1995- ; created life peer 1995; mbr Lords Select Cttee on Euro Communities 1997-01; spokesman on Defence 1997-2001; spokesperson on Foreign Affairs 2001- ; chair sub-Cttee on Justice and Home Affairs 2000; President, Yorkshire Regional Party 2004- ; *publications* The Transformation of Western Europe 1990; The Foreign Policy Process of Britain 1976; Policy Making in the European Community (jointly with Helen Wallace and others) 5th edition 2005; Regional Integration: the West European Experience 1994; Why I Vote Liberal Democrat 1997 General Election *special interests* foreign policy, defence, Euro affairs, constitutional affairs *recreations* swimming, singing, walking, gardening *style* The Lord Wallace of Saltaire *address* The House of Lords, London SW1A 0PW

WALLER, Andrew Michael *b* Jul 29, 1969 *education* Linthorpe Junior; Hustler Comprehensive; Acklam Sixth Form College, Middlesbrough; Imperial College Univ of London (BSc Hons Physics) *career* research scientist, Nestle-Rowntree York 1990-93; InterCity East Coast, GNER Finance 1994- , passenger accountant 1997-2006 *party* joined SDP 1985; Cleveland area Exec 1986-88, National Exec YSD 1988-merger; YLD representative Kensington LP Exec 1988-90; secy York LP 1990, chairman 1992-95, 1997-99, 2001- ; PPC City of York 1997, 2001, 2005; mbr

(Westfield Ward), York City Council 1994-96, City of York Council 1999- , deputy leader of council, Exec mbr environment, sustainability 2003- *special interests* environment, tourism, confectionery, railways *other mbrships* Friends of the Earth; Leeman Road Millennium Green Trust; St Olave's Church, York *recreations* gardening *address* 104 Askham Lane, York YO24 3HP *tel* 01904 337757 *e-mail* cllr.awaller@york.gov.uk

WALLIS, Diana Paulette MEP Yorkshire and Humber; Leader of the UK Liberal Democrat Gp in the European Parliament *b* Jun 28, 1954 *m* Stewart Arnold *education* Francis Combe School, Watford; North London Poly (BA History Hons); Univ of Kent at Canterbury (MA in Local Govt) *career* qualified solicitor 1983 *party* joined SDP 1986, Euro candidate NE Essex 1989, PPC Braintree 1992, Haltemprice and Howden 1997; Euro candidate Humberside 1994; elected Humberside County Council Sept 1994, elected East Riding of Yorkshire Unitary Council 1995-99, deputy leader; Euro candidate South Yorkshire by-election 1998, elected MEP Yorkshire and Humber 1999, 2004; Leader UK Liberal Democrats in the European Parliament 2001-04, 2006- ; vice president EP Delegation for relations with Switzerland, Iceland and Norway 1999-2004, president 2004- ; ELDR co-ordinator on Legal Affairs and Internal Market Cttee 1999–2004; ALDE co-ordinator Legal Affair Cttee 2004- ; substitute mbr Internal Market Cttee 2004- ; full mbr Petitions Cttee 2004- ; *special interests* direct democracy, usc of referendums, endometriosis awareness *other mbrships* president, Institute of Translation and Interpreting; mbr Law Society's EU Cttee *recreations* history, gardening, running *publications* *Forgotten Enlargement, EU relations with Iceland Norway and Switzerland;* European Movement Policy paper *Relegated to the Second Division? Why Associate Mbrship of the EU would be bad for Britain* *address* PO Box 176, Brough, East Yorkshire HU15 1UX *tel/fax* 01482 666898 *e-mail* diana@dianawallismep.org.uk *website* www.dianawallis.org.uk

WALMSLEY, Baroness Joan BSc (Hons), PGCE, Life Peer cr 2000: Lords Spokesperson on Education and Children *b* Apr 12, 1943 1*d* 1s 3 *s/d* 4 *s/s* *education* Notre Dame HS, Liverpool, Univ of Liverpool, Manchester Metropolitan Univ *career* cytologist, Christie Hospital, Manchester 1966-67; teacher, Buxton College 1978-86; countryside warden, Wigan 1987-88; PR consultant, Hill & Knowlton, Manchester 1989-97; PR consultant Walmsley Jones Communications 1997-2002 *party* Education spokesman and Shadow Minister for Children in HoL 2006- ; mbr FCC 1997-2002; mbr FE 2003-05, PPC Morley & Leeds 1992, Congleton 1997; former chair, now president Congleton LP; chair Crime & Policing Policy (including drug abuse) WP; chair Early Years Policy WP *special interests* prison education, drugs policy (trustee of drug rehab charity Adapt), child protection (Trustee of Unicef UK, Parliamentary Ambassador for NSPCC), women's rights, science *recreations* music, theatre, laughter, good company, dancing *style* Baroness Walmsley *address* House of Lords, London SW1A 0PW *tel* 020 7219 6047 *fax* 020 7219 8602 *e-mail* walmsleyj@parliament.uk

WALSH, Dr James Michael Meade MBBS, MRCS, LRCP, DObst RCOG, MRCGP, FRSM, OStJ, RD *b* Nairobi, Kenya Jan 11, 1943 *m* (dis):3 *s* Simon, Justin, Christopher educated: Wimbledon College; London Univ (The Royal London Hospital) *career* medical officer Royal Navy 1964-73, Royal Naval Reserve 1973-93, Medical Director RNR 1990-93, Surgeon Captain RNR; GP Rustington &

Littlehampton 1973-2003; police forensic surgeon 1975-2000 *party* founder mbr Leatherhead Young Liberals 1960; mbr Arun District Council 1976- , chairman 2003-04, gp leader 1986-2003; mbr Littlehampton Town Council 1976- , Mayor 1989-90, gp leader 1976- ;mbr West Sussex District Council 1985- deputy leader 1993-97, gp leader 1997-2001, chairman Social Services 1993-97, chair Europe Cttee 1993-97; Assembly of European Regions delegate 1993-97; mbr ACC Social Services Cttee 1993-97; mbr Sussex Police Authority 1989- , vice-chair 1993-97, chairman 1995-97; ACC Police Cttee 1993-96; CoLPA 1996-97; LGA Economic Regeneration Cttee 1997-2001 LGN, CCN 2001- ; South East Regional Forum, Exec mbr 1997-2000; full mbr EU Cttee of the Regions 1998-2002, Lib Dem spokesperson on transport, telecommunications; founder chair EU Airport Regions Conference 1994-98; vice-chair Arc Manche 1995-97; mbr European Health Forum 1998- ; PPC Hove 1974, 1979;Arundel 1983, 1987, 1992; Bognor Regis & Littlehampton 1997; Worthing West 2001; Euro candidate West Sussex 1979, 1984,1 989; South Downs West 1994; SE Region 1999, 2004 (fifth on list) *special interests* Worthing DHA 1983-90; chair Littlehampton School governors (largest in West Sussex) 1985-99; founder director Arundel Festival Ltd 1978- , chairman 2002- ;West Sussex Local Medical Cttee 1985- , chairman 2001-04; founder chairman Littlehampton Town Twinning Cttee 1981- ; Commander St John Ambulance, Sussex 2001- *other mbrships*: BMA; Amnesty International; LD Friends of India; reader, special minister Arundel Cathedral *recreations* skiing; opera; travel; gardening; swimming *publications*: *Air Transport & the Environment* (ARC 1998); *Improving Quality of Healthcare* (European Health Forum 1999); *Opinion on Prevention of Pollution and Maritime Safety* (CoR 2002); *Opinion on Maximum Dimensions & Weights for lorries in EU* (CoR 2000) *address* The Laurels, Ash Lane, Rustington, West Sussex BN16 3BT *tel* 01903 773771 mobile 07973 217243 *e-mail* james.walsh@westsussex.gov.uk

WALSHE, Roger Francis Croker b Apr 5, 1935 London **m** Pamela (nee Headon) 1963 **s** Richard **d** Miranda *education* Whitgift School, JSSL Bodmin, London Univ (Russian Interpreter) *career* Scantlebury & Hemingway; United City Merchants 1959-69; Lupton Morton et al 1969-71; created own Import/Export business 1971 specialising in Central & Eastern Europe, of which still Principal *party* joined Liberal Party 1960, Chr Croydon South LA 1960-63; Chr Croydon Liberal Pty 1961-63; V-Chr SE Surrey Area Gp 1962-63; V-Chr Reigate LA 1964-65; Chr Sevenoaks LA 1974-77, 1984-88; Merger Coordinator & Interim Chairman Sevenoaks 1988; Sevenoaks LP Exec 1988- ; SE England Regional Exec 1988-1995, 2001- ; Conf Chr 1992-93; Policy Chr 1993-95; PPC Sevenoaks 1992, 1997; Sevenoaks District Cllr 1987- ; Council Leader 1995-99; gp ldr 1995- ; Chair Environment Select Cttee 2003- ; mbr ALDC, PCA, ALTER, Working Gp on Local Govt 1990-91 *other mbrships* NLC, European Movement, U3A, National Trust, Inst Sales & Marketing Management, Sevenoaks Shakespeare Soc *special interests* languages, music, theatre, environment *recreations* gardening, reading, piano *address* Wayfarings, 8 Crownfields, Sevenoaks, Kent TN13 1EF *tel* 01732 454769 *fax* 01732 463823 *e-mail* rogerwalshe@supanet.com

WALTER, David Charles b Feb 1, 1948 **m** Pamela Port 1970 1 **s** Peter (TV producer) 1 **d** Natalie (actress) *education* Charterhouse; Trinity College, Oxford (President, Oxford Union); Massachusetts Institute of Technology (J F Kennedy Scholar) *career* BBC producer 1971-79; political correspondent ITN 1980-86;

political correspondent *Channel Four News* 1986-88; presenter *Talking Politics, Europhile* and *Education Matters;* BBC Radio 4 during 1990s; Paris Correspondent BBC TV 1990-91; Director of Communications, Director of Party Broadcasting, Liberal Democrats 1998-2005; Director, First Take Productions Ltd 2005- ; *party* joined Liberal Party 1967; PPC Torridge and West Devon 2005 *other mbrships* European Movement *publications* The Strange Rebirth of Liberal England Politicos 2003; *The Oxford Union, Playground of Power* 1984; *James I and VI* 1975 *address* 37b Queens Road, Kingston upon Thames, Surrey KT2 7SL *tel* 07768 616568 *e-mail* davidwalter@cix.co.uk

WALTER, Paul Robert *b* Aug 5, 1959 *m* Janet 1 *s* (deceased) 1 *d education* West Buckland School, North Devon; Reading Univ; Slough College *career* presenter, assistant Radio 210 Berkshire 1978-84; operations manager IT, Thames Valley 1982-Present day *party* supporter of Liberal Party since wearing complete orange clothing to primary school aged 10 on General Election day 1970; mbr Liberal Party 1987, Liberal Democrats 1992; recruitment officer, chair, vice-president, president Newbury Liberal Democrats 1992-2000; recruitment officer Chilterns Region 1997-99; Newbury town Cllr 2000- *special interests* politics of USA, Fiji; community case work *other mbrships* Church of England; Meningitis Research Foundation; Friends of the Earth; CAMRA *recreations* gym , 60s/70s music, genealogy, cooking badly, talking with daughter, current affairs via the internet, real alc, real food *publications* more than a thousand letters to the press published since 1989 *address* 12 Stanley Road, Newbury, Berkshire RG14 7PB *tel* 01635 846867 *e-mail* pw@bitsmart.com *web* http://paulwalter.blogspot.com/

WALTON, Ian Alexander *b* Feb 17, 1970 Beverley, East Riding of Yorkshire *education* Longcroft School, Beverley 1981-84; Bridlington School 1984-86; Hessle HS 1986-88; Coleg Y Drindod, Caerfyrddin (BA Humanities: 19th & 20th Century Studies) 1988-92 *career* Assistant to Director, International Students Housing Society, Woolwich 1994-98; Business Manager *Liberal Democrat News* 1995-98; Marketing & Promotions Manager Lib Dems 1998-2000; Assistant Conference Organiser, Lib Dems 2000-02; Target Seat Development & Deputy Campaigns Officer; Alliance Party of NI 2002-03; IT Department HSBC Global Markets 2004-05; IT Department LloydsTSB 2005; Party Manager, Welsh Liberal Democrats 2006- *party* joined Young Liberals 1987; chair, Humberside RP 1993-94; vice-president LDYS 1996-98; mbr LB of Lewisham Council 1998-2002; president LDYS 2000-01 *special interests* history of First World War, Irish History 1916-24 *recreations* reading, watching sport, collecting biographies of Prime Ministers *address* 6 Cumnock Terrace, Cardiff CF24 2AF *tel* 07879 630595

WALTON, Neil Christopher *b* May 10, 1969 *education* Royal Latin School 1983-87; Open Univ (BSc); CCNA, CCNP 2001' re-certified CCNP 2004 *career* MoD (and EDS when they took over) 1987-97;.Cable and Wireless 1997-2000; C-Pro International 2001-04 *party* joined 1998 mbrship secy Banbury LP 2002- , treasurer 2004; candidate district, town councils 2002- *special interests* IT, asylum, animal welfare, economics *other mbrships* ALDES; Liberal Democrat Disability Association; Lib Dem Online; British Computer Society; WWF; PETA; RNLI; FoE *recreations* reading (sci-fi, fantasy books, comics); watching good sci-fi, fantasy TV *address* 16 Westholm Court, London Road, Bicester, Oxon OX26 6UZ *tel* 01869 320948 home 07944 108778 mobile *e-mail* ncwalton@tiscali.co.uk

WARNER, Liz: Regional Candidates chair, South Central *b* Jun 25, 1942 *m* Alan Warner 1*s* Edward *education* splintered education, due to father moving around a lot; attended four primary schools in North East; two secondary schools; business studies, Sheffield College of Technology; obtained a qualification in Industrial Psychology later in life but was unable to complete course because employer closed down *career* banking, insurance, personnel officer, sausage factory, Winchester; returned to insurance, dealt in stock and shares, until move to Devon 1977; adopted son 1979 (agreed not to work until he was 15); with husband recently set up consultancy business (a success so far); as carer for mother has little time for much else *party* joined in 1961; delivered *Focus*, canvassed; variously chair, secy, press officer Gloucester City LP; assistant to agent, Devon; secy NW Hants LP, gp secy, Test Valley; conference organiser, secy Hampshire and Isle of Wight; regional candidates chair, South Central; candidates' assessor nine years; returning officer eight years including several target seats and Europe SW England *special interests* organisation of Region and Federal Party; community politics *other mbrships* Church of England: role mbr, former churchwarden; currently assists in inspection of churches; Gold Mbr ALDC, mbr PCA, and Liberal Democrat Christian Forum *recreations* walking, avid reader, PC fanatic, enjoys company of her cats, mother's dog *address* Staddles, Wildhern, Andover, Hants SP11 0JE *tel* 01264 735303 *fax* 01264 735303 *e-mail* lizwarner2000@hotmail.com

WATES, Julian *b* Jul 26, 1938 *m* Jean Wates 1 *s* 1 *d education* state scholarship, Newcastle Royal Grammar School; Cambridge Univ *career* FE lecturer, manager 1964- 95; Liberal Democrat HQ staff *party* joined Liberal Party 1959; PPC St Albans 1964, Belper 1974; Luton borough Cllr 1996 *other mbrships* mbrship secy Liberal Democrat Education Association *recreations* gardening, nature *address* 38 Lothair Road, Stopsley, Luton LU2 7XB *tel* 01582 615067 *e-mail* j.wates@ntlworld.com

WATFORD, Elizabeth Joanne (Liz) *b* Aug 29, 1983 *education* Univ of Sheffield BA in International History, International Politics; Worcester Sixth Form College; Pershore High School *party* joined 2002; treasurer, LDYS Sheffield 2003-04; GEM West Midlands 2003-04; mbr Cardiff LP *special interests* politics and rock music *e-mail* lizwatford@tiscali.org.uk *web* http://www.prettyinscarlett.blogspot.com/

WATSON of Richmond, Lord Professor Alan John: Life peer cr 1999, CBE *b* Feb 3, 1941 *m* 1965 Karen 2 *s* Stephen, Martin *education* Kingswood School, Bath; Jesus College, Cambridge *career* research assistant, Cambridge Professor of Modern History 1962-64; general trainee BBC 1965-66; reporter BBC TV's *The Money Programme* 1966-68; chief public affairs commentator LWT 1969-70; BBC: reporter *Panorama* 1971-74, presenter *The Money Programme* 1974-75; Head of TV, Radio, Audio Visual Division EEC; editor EC Newsreel to Lome Convention countries 1975-79; director Charles Barker City Ltd 1980-85 (Chief Exec 1980-83); deputy chair Sterling PR 1985-86; chair City and Corporate Counsel Ltd 1987-94; chair Thread needle Publishing Gp 1987-94; mbr Exec Board UNICEF 1985-92; board Prince of Wales Trust Business Leaders Forum 1996- ; non-exec director Community & Charities Cttee, BT 1996- ; chair RTS 1992-94; chair Corporate Vision Ltd 1989-98, Burston-Marsteller Worldwide 1992- , Burston-Marsteller UK 1994- , Burston-Marsteller Europe 1996- ; chair CBI Media Interests Gp 1995-98;

chair CTN (Corporate Television Networks) *party* president Liberal Party 1984-85; created life peer 1999; Front Bench spokesman on European Enlargement ,EU-US Relations *other interests* international chairman English Speaking Union; president British-German Association 1992-95; president Heathrow Association for Control of Tic Noise 1992-95; former chair Royal Television Society; chair Westminster College, Oxford; trustee Great Britain Studies Centre, Humboldt Univ, Berlin 1998- ; visiting professor Leuven Univ, honorary professor Birmingham Univ; chairman Cambridge Univ's Chemistry Advisory Board; visiting fellow Oriel College, Oxford *publications* Europe at Risk; The Germans: who are they now?; Thatcher and Kohl: Old Rivalries Revisited *address* 3 Cholmondley Walk, Richmond-upon-Thames, Surrey TW9 1NS *web* www.LordAlanWatson.com

WATSON, (George) Erlend *b* Nov 6, 1963 *education* Dauntseys School, Univ College London (BA Hons Scandinavian Studies) *career* EFL teacher, London, Czechoslovakia *party* joined in Orkney 1984 (but wore home-made rosette to school polling day Oct 1974); UCL branch secy 1989-90; candidate Wandsworth BC 1994, Cunninghame South 1997, Lambeth 1998 (target ward); assistant Lib Dems Candidates Office (working with Sandra Dunk) 1995-2000; agent Maidenhead 1997; winning agent Mid-Dorset and North Poole 2001; organiser Teignbridge 2001-03, Watford 2003, Hertfordshire 2003- (of 51 Tory losses nationally, 11 were in Hertfordshire); St Albans 2004- ; honorary vice president LDYS 2002- ;.since 1997 encouraged dozens of party's youth wing to be PPCs; by-election junkie turned 'Riso King,' printed a million-plus leaflets at Brent East; did most of in-house printing at Leicester South; co-moderator of cix Lib Dem conferences on election law, boundary changes (created conference in belief that party ignores changes at its peril); urges activists to use EARS, Pagemaker and any other useful tool to win seats locally but still believe party will only win if elected representatives continue to practice community politics *special interests* constitutional reform; community politics *other mbrships* Norwegian Church, London; St Albans Liberal Club *recreations* philology (languages), Orkney history, Sci-Fi, travel *address* Liberal Democrats, 9 Hatfield Rd, St Albans, AL1 3RR *tel* 01727 85523 office 07932 456378 mobile *fax* 01727 860896 *e-mail* erlend@cix.co.uk or erlend_w@yahoo.no

WATSON, Graham Robert MEP South West Region, Leader of ALDE Gp in the European Parliament *b* Mar 23, 1956 *m* Dr Rita Giannini 2 *s* 1 *d education* City of Bath Boys School; Heriot Watt Univ (BA Hons interpreting and translation) *career* freelance interpreter 1979-80; administrator Paisley College of Technology (now Univ of Paisley) 1980-83; head private office, Rt Hon (now Lord) David Steel MP, Leader of the Liberal Party 1983-87; banker TSB Gp 1987-88; The Hong Kong and Shanghai Banking Corporation 1988-94; MEP Somerset and North Devon 1994-99 (first ever UK Liberal Democrat), South West Region 1999- ; chief whip ELDR gp 1994-96; leader Lib Dem gp, European Parliament 1999-2002; Leader European Liberal Democrat and Reform Gp, European Parliament 2002- ; Cttees: chair Citizens' Freedom and Rights, Justice and Home Affairs 1999-2002; mbr delegation for relations with Japan *party* international officer Scottish Young Liberals 1975-77, vice-chair 1977-79, vice-president 1977-79; secy general International Federation of Liberal and Radical Youth 1979-81, founder EU's Youth Forum 1979; chair Paisley Liberal Association 1981-83; Exec Cttee mbr Scottish Liberal Party 1981-83; PPCs by-elections Glasgow Central 1980 (YL candidate), Glasgow Queens Park 1982; local Govt candidate Strathclyde region 1982, LB Lambeth 1986; representative

ELDR, LI Exec Cttees 1983-87 *other mbrships* Royal Commonwealth Club *recreations* sailing, listening to jazz *publications* publisher YL magazines *Libra* and *Radix*; occasional contributor of articles to other Liberal and Lib Dem periodicals, national newspapers; editor *The Liberals in the North-South dialogue* (Friedrich Naumann Stiftung, Bonn 1980); *To the Power of Ten* (Centre Forum 2000); *2020 Vision: Liberalism and Globalisation* (Centre Forum, 2001); *Liberal Language* (Bagehot Publishing, 2003 *address* European Parliament, Brussels *fax* 00 322 284 9626 *e-mail* gwatson@europarl.eu.int *web* www.grahamwatsonmep.org

WATT, Lucy Elizabeth *b* Dec 16, 1977 *education* Univ of Southampton (BA Hons English 1999); Lambeth College, London (NCTJ Pre-Entry Journalism); Fearnhill School, St Christopher School, Letchworth *career* variously recruitment consultant (Tower Hamlets Action Team for Jobs, Employment Zone), business development manager (Corporate Centre), public affairs manager (Corporate Centre) Working Links (Employment) Ltd; briefly with Stonewall, *Pink Paper party* joined 2000; Cllr, LB of Islington 2000- , *special interests* employment; regeneration; lesbian, gay and bisexual issues; equal opportunities; youth issues; London; crime; safety issues *e-mail* lucywatt@o2.co.uk

WATTS, Keith *b* Oct 5 1942 *m* Jean (aka Roberts) 3 *s* 1 *d education* Hertford Grammar; Slough College *career* computer programmer ICT 1960-4, Eng Electric-Leo 1964, Calor Gas 1965-72; IT manager Thames Conservancy1972-9; project manager ICL Dataskil 1979-3; gp quality audits manager ICL 1983-5, director, quality software sciences 1985-90; technical manager Bureau Veritas1993-8, IT quality director Rolls-Royce plc 1998-2002; independent consultant, commercial mediator (trading as putITright) 1990-3, 2002- *party* joined Liberal Party 1967; agent Woodley Liberals 1969; Cllr, Wokingham RDC 1972, Wokingham DC 1973-6, Woodley TC 1973-91; chair, Berks Assoc of District Councils 1975-6; national chair, Assoc of Larger Local Councils 1988-9; PPC, Reading North Oct 1974, Reading South 1979; chair, Reading South LA 1975-7, president Wokingham LA 1984-8; founding treasurer, John Stuart Mill Institute 1991-3; chair, Abbey, Allestree & Darley Branch, Derby Lib Dems 2001-2; chair, Whitchurch Branch, NW Hampshire Liberal Democrats 2002- *special interests* real community politics (not the industrialised kind); European democracy; devolution in South East England *other mbrships* Fellow, British Computer Society; Mbr, Chartered Management Institute; ERS; Friend of John Stuart Mill Institute *recreations* walking, talking *address* Causeway House, 15 Newbury Street, Whitchurch, Hants, RG28 7DW *tel* 01256 896969 *e-mail* keith.watts@tiscali.co.uk

WEBB, Steve Professor MP (Northavon maj: 11,033) **Shadow Secy of State for Health** *b* Jul 18, 1965 Birmingham *m* 2 *ch education* Dartmouth HS, Birmingham; Hertford College, Oxford Univ (PPE 1st) *m* Helen (hospital chaplain) 1 *d* Charlotte 1 *s* Dominic *career* economist, Institute for Fiscal Studies (non-political research), specialist advisor to Social Security Select Cttee (then chaired by Frank Field), mbr IMF technical assistance mission to The Ukraine (advising on Welfare Reform); Professor of Social Policy, Bath Univ 1995-97; MP *party* PPC Northavon 1997 (elected maj: 2,137), re-elected 2001, 2005; Shadow Secy for Health 2006- , for Work and Pensions 2001-05; mbr Social Security and Welfare Team 1997- ; mbr Commission on Social Justice *publications For Richer, For Poorer: The Changing Distribution of Income in the UK 1961-91* (Institute for Fiscal Studies 1994);

contributed chapter 'Children, the family and the state' to the *Orange Book*; runs
www.libdemnhswatch.com *address* House of Commons, London SW1A 0AA
constituency Poole Court, Poole Court Drive, Yate BS37 5PP tel 01454 322 100 *fax*
01454 866 515 *e-mail* steve@stevewebb.org.uk *web* www.stevewebb.org.uk

WELCH, Anthony Cleland: OBE *b* Sep 15, 1945 *m* Pamela (neé Darnell) May 6,
1983 1*d* 1*s education* Prior Park College, Bath; St. John's College, Southsea, Army
Staff College (psc), Defence Staff College (hcsc), Univ of Portsmouth (MA,
European Studies) *career* Commercial Sales Mngr Rediffusion Television, Hong
Kong/Singapore 1961-67; Exec Manager, Hutchison Gp, Hong Kong 1967-68;
Brigadier, British Army 1969-1993; Chief of Staff/ SRSG, United Nations in former
Yugoslavia 1993-1994; Manager, Allmakes Ltd, Oxford 1994-1995; European
Union/ OSCE representative, Albania/Serbia 1995-1998; Conflict & Security
Adviser, DFID 1998-2000; UN Regional Administrator, Northern Kosovo 2000-
2001; Director, DynCorp International 2001-2005; National Security Co-ordinator,
Govt of Kosovo 2005- ; Trustee, Centre for South East European Studies,
Sofia (www.csees.net); Trustee, Vencorp, Geneva *party* PEPC South West Region
2004; Cllr. Havant Borough Council 2001- ; *special interests* international affairs,
post-conflict security, European security & defence policy *mbrships* Institute of
Directors; Army & Navy Club *recreations* jogging, flying, reading *publications*
Donini, A, Minear, L, Smillie, I, van Baartha, T and Welch, A.C. (2005) – *Mapping
the Security Environment. Understanding the Perceptions of Local Communities,
Peace Support Operations and Assistance Agencies* Medford, MA: Tufts Univ;
Welch, A (2005), *A successful Security Pact: European Union policy in South East
Europe.* In Brown D & Shepard, A (Eds), *The Security Dimensions of EU
Enlargement,* Manchester Univ Press, due publication: 2006 *address* White Lodge,
24 Bellair Road, Havant, Hants, PO9 2RG *tel* 023 92365078, 07768 715494 mobile
fax 023 92450488 *e-mail* acwelch@aol.com

WHEELER, Alison *b* Apr 13,1956 *education* Apsley Grammar School, Hemel
Hempstead; Imperial College; Open Univ (Cert Nat Sci); OUBS (MBA) *career* IT
with Spillers, Olivetti, Sperry Univac, freelance business consultant; global internet
program mgr, CHS Electronics; Head of Technology, Capital Radio; CTO Narrateo;
CTO NNWA; also sound engineer for radio and theatre; LD Mbr Services 2002-3;
currently chief exec Wikimedia UK *party* though a supporter for more than 20 years,
eventually joined Oct 2001 while watching conference on BBC Parliamentary
Channel; mbr Camden Borough LP Exec 2002-05; London Regional Exec 2003-05;
English Council 2003-05; DELGA chair DELGA 2004, exec 2003-04, vice-
president 2003-06; Exec, Lib Dems Online 2003-05; *special interests* life-long
learning, finance, transport, town planning *other mbrships* chair, Holly Lodge T&L
Association 2001-03; Exec Cttee OUSA (representing London Region) 2002-03;
Open Univ in London Cttee 2002-03; Open Univ Central Consultative Cttee 2002-03
recreations clubbing, friends, conferences, IT, good food in good company, *The
Archers address* 76 Holly Lodge Mansions, Highgate, London N6 6DS *tel* 020 7419
1017 mobile 077 1017 2564 *fax* 0870 133 6998 *e-mail* libdems@alisonwheeler.com
web www.alisonwheeler.org.uk

WHITE, Chris *b* Jun 8, 1959 Coventry *m* 2 *d education* Merchant Taylors' School,
Northwood, Herts; Corpus Christi College, Oxford (*Literae Humaniores*) *career*
trained with Arthur Young, qualified Chartered Accountant 1984; Ernst & Whinney

1987-88; accountancy lecturer with BPP plc 1984-87, ATC 1988-91; now freelance *party* mbr Hertfordshire CC (St Albans Central Division) 1993- ; chair St Albans Lib Dems 1990; trsr Chilterns Reg 1988-91; PPC Hertford and Stortford 1992, Hitchin and Harpenden 1997; PEPC Eastern Euro reg list 1999, 2004; gp leader Herts CC 1994-2003, 2005- ; deputy leader of Council 1997-99; mbr Herts Police Authority 1996-2003; ldr of Lib Dem Gp on East of England Regional Assembly 1998- ; chair of Campaigns Cttee, East of England Region: 2004-05; mbr Federal Exec 2004- ; chair LGA Mgmt Exec 2003-04; chair LGA Regeneration Board 2004- ; Audit Commissioner: 2005- ; mbr ALDC, PCA *special interests* developing regional govt *recreations* in the kitchen *style* Chris White *address* 17 Cunningham Avenue, St Albans AL1 1JJ *tel* 01727 845300 *e-mail* chriswhite@cix.co.uk

WIGLEY, Christopher John *b* Apr 10, 1963 *m* 2 *d education* Ryde High School, Isle of Wight 1976-81; Univ of Essex (BA Hons philosophy, literature upper second) 1981-84 *career* Treasury, Citicorp - Channel Islands 1986-87; portfolio manager Mitsui Bank, London 1987-96; chief investment manager Aioi Insurance Company of Europe Ltd, London 1996-2003- *party* joined 1995; mbr (Pantiles ward) Tunbridge Wells BC 1997-2000; chair Tunbridge Wells Lib Dem strategy gp 2000-2002; chair Tunbridge Wells LP 2002-04; mbr English Council 2003- ; mbr South East regional Exec 2004- *special interests* finance, environment, constitutional affairs, international development *other mbrships* Association for Investment Management and Research; UK Society of Investment Professionals; UK Social Investment Forum; Lib Dem Business Forum; Green Liberal Democrats; UNA, Amnesty International *recreations* travel, swimming, reading, movies address Cranbourne, 4 Broadwater Rise, Tunbridge Wells, Kent TN2 5UE *e-mail* chrisrtw@cix.co.uk

WILCOCK, Jeremy David *b* Dec 4, 1950 Taunton *m* Liz 2 *d* Annaliese, Madeleine *education* King's College, Taunton; London Univ (Queen Mary College BA (Hons), French and Spanish; Buckinghamshire College, Postgraduate Diploma in Export Marketing; INSEAD (Fontainebleau) Advanced Management Programme ABPI Prof Med Reps' Exam *career* Reckitt & Colman (now Reckitt Benckiser) 1974-2002; various senior posts in export sales, marketing, international development, business transformation and strategic planning before gleefully taking retirement in May 2002; now Business Development Manager – Corporate Programmes and visiting lecturer Hull Univ Business School, mainly on MBA programmes in Middle East, Far East; also supervise postgraduate research and undergrad tutorials; mbr of Hull Univ Business School Advisory Board *party* joined 1988; chair, Beverley & Holderness LP 1997-2003; chair, York Lib Dem Federation 2001-03; PPC Selby 2001, Vale of York 2005 (securing 23% increase in vote ("most significant result" – BBC) and coming within 300 votes of Labour; regional , federal conference rep *special interests* constitutional reform, Europe, foreign affairs (especially Middle East and Africa), rural affairs *other mbrships* chair, Beswick Parish Council; former chair of governors, Lockington CofE Primary school (resigned in protest at intolerable govt bureaucracy); vice-chair, Beverley Police Community Liaison Cttee; trustee, Nunburnholme Trust; mbr League Against Cruel Sports, CPRE, Da Engliscan Gesidas (Anglo-Saxon cultural society). MIEx (Grad), MCIM, AIL *recreations* walking two daft cocker spaniels; bringing up two beautiful daughters; reading political and historical subjects; foreign languages (studying Arabic and Turkish); travelling; collecting world coins; watching cricket and rugby; delivering

FOCUS *publications* large number of letters in local press *address* 8 Main Street, Kilnwick, Driffield YO25 9JD *tel/fax* 01377 270677 *e-mail* j.wilcock@hull.ac.uk

WILCOCK, Peter Anthony *b* Aug 20, 1953 Totnes **m** Shirley 1986 3 *d education* Magdalen College School, Oxford 1964-71 *career* Food Store Development 71-05; Market Research; Admin Officer Harlow Lib Dems *party* elected District Cllr, Newport Ward, Uttlesford DC 1995, Chair of Airport Working Party 1995-97; Vice Chair Staff Appeals panel 1995-99; elected Deputy Gp Leader 1998-2005; PPC Harwich 2001; Deputy Leader of Council 2003-05; Chair of Constitution Task Gp 2004-05; Chair of Stansted Airport Advisory panel 2003-06; Chair of Strategic development advisory gp 2005-06; Chairman of District Council 2005-06; narrowly failed to win Essex CC seat for Stansted division in 2001 and 2005 *other mbrships* Amnesty International, Liberal International, CPRE *special interests* Governor Henham & Ugley CP School 1994- ; theatre, dining out *address* 4 Pimblett Row, Henham, Bishops Stortford, Herts CM22 6BT *tel* 01279 850198 *fax* 01279 850163 *email* cllrwilcock@uttlesford.co.uk

WILDIN, Julia Alicia *b* Jun 16, 1958 *m* Roger Oliver Wildin 1 *s* Patrick *education* Henley College *career* secy Gallaher Ltd, London; area manager Southern Europe Gallaher International 1978-88; aromatherapist 1994–2000; Turning Point Malvern Druglink (drugs counselling service) 2002 *party* joined 1990, galvanized into action following move to Malvern in 2001; elected (Longdon ward) Malvern Hills District Council May 2003; chair Policy Development and Review Panel; Malvern Hills Conservator; member West Worcestershire strategic campaign team; Chair of Council 2006-07 *special interests* young people, education, environment *recreations* rugby, coastal walking, reading *address* The Jingle, Marlbank Road, Welland, Malvern WR13 6NE *tel* 01684 311322 *fax* 01684 899165 *e-mail* julia.wildin@btinternet.com

WILKINS, Penny *b* Apr 26, 1951 *m* Brian Stevens 1 *s* 1 *d education* St Albans Grammar School for Girls *career* local Govt officer until 1979 when ill-health forced resignation *party* joined Liberal Party 1980; chair SW Beds Liberals 1986-87; secy Hexham LP 1988-92; chair Wellingborough LP 1999-2002; regional candidates chair East Midland 2000- *special interests* campaigning, candidates *recreations* reading, music *address* 16 Fowey Close, Wellingborough NN8 *tel* 01933 674086 *fax* 01933 674081 *e-mail* penny@rock-design.demon.co.uk

WILLIAMS, Benjamin Paul: Secy to Parliamentary Party *b* Sept Day 23, 1972 *education* Univ of Hull (BA Special Politics); Coopers' Company and Coborn School, Upminster, Essex *career* researcher for Nick Harvey MP 1996; researcher for Paul Tyler MP, South West Team co-ordinator 1996-98; Secy to the Parliamentary Party 1998 *party* joined 1991; mbr (Nethermayne ward), Basildon DC 1996, re-elected 2000, 2002, 2003 *special interests* defence, foreign affairs, developing world, environment and conservation, computers *other mbrships* Greenpeace, National Trust, Dry Street Interdenominational Church *recreations* classical music, opera, theatre, singing, walking, reading, cooking, computer games *address* Liberal Democrat Whip's Office, House of Commons, London, SW1A 0AA *tel* 020 7219 5654 *fax* 020 7219 5894 *e-mail* williamsbp@parliament.uk

WILLIAMS, Caroline *b* Jun 9 1970 *m* 1 *s education* John Beddoes; Herefordshire College of Art; GLOSCAT; Staffordshire Univ *career* international sales account manager, land and airborne communications; sales co-ordinator private airline; extended baby break; law degree (LLB) *party* joined 1997; Exec mbr Leominster LP; PPC Leominster *special interests* human rights, international civil liberties *other mbrships* Students Union *recreations* walking family dogs, shooting, riding, fishing, family sports *address* Longwall, Westhope, Hereford HR4 8BT *tel* 01432 830114 home *fax*/business 01544 319005 *e-mail* ppc@leolibdems.org.uk

WILLIAMS, David John *b* Usk, Monmouth Jun 25 June, 1949 *education* King Henry VII Grammar School, Abergavenny; Hatfield Polytechnic, Hertfordshire (BSc. Applied Biology) *career* scientific translator, editorial consultant *party* joined German Liberal Party (FDP) 1979, chair Heidelberg local party, chair regional party; joined Lib Dems 1991; Euro candidate Sussex 1994; PPC Ashford 1997 *special interests* foreign affairs, economic development, agriculture, regional policy, institutional reform of EU; scientific witness at BSE Inquiry 1998 *other mbrships* Anglo-German Association *recreations* mountain climbing, travel, photography *address* Conamore, Warrage Road, Raglan NP15 2LD *tel* 07733162744 *fax* 01291690914 *e-mail* dj.williams@zmbh.uni-heidelberg.de

WILLIAMS, Sir David Reeve Kt (cr 1999) CBE (1990) *b* Jun 8, 1939 *m* Christine *education* Eltham College, 1949-58; St. Cuthbert's Society, Univ of Durham (BA Honours Politics and Economics) 1958-61 *career* systems engineer IBM 1961-70, computer consultant, Insurance Systems and Services 1970-78, David Williams and Associates 1978-91, Teleglobe Ltd.1991-95 *party* joined Liberal Party 1958; president Durham Colleges Liberal Club 1959-61, treasurer Union of Liberal Students 1960-61; Cllr (Ham and Petersham ward) Richmond upon Thames 1974- , leader of opposition 1978-83, leader of council 1983-2001; leader of Association of Metropolitan Authorities Lib Dem gp 1986-97; leader of Local Govt Association Lib Dem gp 1996-2001, gp chair 2005- ; directly elected to Federal Exec 2003- ; inventor of the Richmond Formula; political hero David Lloyd George *special interests* local democracy, winning elections, campaigning with community politics *other mbrships* Electoral Reform Society *recreations* books, jazz, politics *publications* The Richmond Judgement (Adrian Slade's election 1982 petition) *address* 8 Arlington Road, Petersham, Richmond, TW10 7BY *tel* 020 8940 9421 *e-mail* cllr.dwilliams@richmond.gov.uk

WILLIAMS, Geoffrey *b* Chelmsford Jan 26, 1947 *m education* King's College, London (BA Hons, MPhil) *career* lecturer in modern languages *party* mbr Basildon DC 1981, re-elected 1986- , gp leader; parliamentary agent Basildon 1987; PPC Basildon 1992, Billericay 1997, Rayleigh 2001; European candidate Essex South 1994, mbr Essex County Council 1993-97; chair Eastern Region 1994-97; candidates chair Eastern Region 2000- ; chair, secy, mbrship secy (in due order) Basildon and Thurrock LP *special interests* Europe, education, NHS *recreations* singing; gardening; being in Cornwall *other mbrships* National Liberal Club; St James's Club *address* Hillcroft, Dry Street, Basildon, Essex SS16 5LT *tel* 01268 415348 *fax* 01268 490359 *e-mail* geoffwilliams@cix.co.uk

WILLIAMS, Kirsty AM (Brecon and Radnorshire) *b* Mar 19, 1971 *m* Richard Rees 2 *d* Angharad, Lowri *education* St Michael's School, Llanelli; Univ of Manchester;

Univ of Missouri (American Studies BA Hons) *career* marketing, PR Exec; AM 1999- ; *party* joined 1985; vice chair Llanelli LP 1987-89, chair 1994-95; mbr Welsh Campaigns and Communications Cttee 1994-96; Welsh National Exec 1994; Welsh Policy Cttee 1995; Welsh GE team 1995-97; deputy president Welsh Liberal Democrats 1997-99; PPC Ogmore 1997; mbr National Assembly Advisory Gp; elected AM 1999, re-elected 2004; mbr National Assembly Economic Development and Transport Cttee, Business Cttee, Standards Cttee *special interests* health, agriculture *recreations* helping on family farm, horse riding, collecting antiques *address* 4 Watergate, Brecon, Powys LD3 9AN *tel* 01874 625739 *fax* 01874 625635 *e-mail* Kirsty.Williams@wales.gov.uk

WILLIAMS, Mark MP (Ceredigion maj:219) *m* 2 *d education* Richard Hale School, Hereford; Univ College of Wales, Aberystwyth (politics); Univ of Plymouth (PGCE) *career* teacher, deputy head Ysgol Llangors 2000 *party* research assistant Liberal/LibDem peers 1987-92; mbr Welsh Liberal Democrats Exec 1991-92; constituency assistant to Geraint Howells MP 1987-92; President Ceredigion Liberal Democrats 1998-2000; mbr Welsh Lib Dem campaign Cttee 2000; PPC Monmouth 1997, Ceredigion 2000 (by-election), 2001, 2005 (elected); mbr Welsh Select Cttee 2005- ; Shadow Education minister 2005-06; Shadow Welsh Affairs spokesperson 2006- ; *other mbrships* NASUWT, Countryside Alliance *special interests* education, rural affairs *recreations* walking, camping, reading biographies *address* 32 North Parade, Aberystwyth, Ceredigion SY23 2NF *tel* 01970 615880 *fax* 01970 627708 *e-mail* williamsmf@parliament.uk

WILLIAMS, Roger MP (Brecon and Radnorshire maj:3,905) **Shadow DEFRA Spokesperson (Rural Affairs)** *b* 1948 *m* 2 *ch education* Llanfilo County Primary School; Christ College, Brecon; Selwyn College, Cambridge (degree in agriculture) *career* farmer; chairman Mid-Wales Agri-Food Partnership; MP 2001- *party* MP Brecon and Radnorshire 2001- ; mbr Welsh Affairs Select Cttee, and Shadow spokesperson for Wales 2003- ; Shadow spokesperson DeFRA (Food and Rural Affairs) 2002-05; mbr DEFRA Select Cttee 2005- ; county cllr for 20 years; Welsh Assembly candidate Carmarthen West, South Pembroke 1999 *special interests* education, economic development *other mbrships* Farmers Union of Wales; Brecknock Access Gp (rights for disabled people); governor Llangorse CW School; Inspector of Schools; former chair Brecon Beacon National Park; vice-chairman Powys TEC; Development Board for Rural Wales (nine years); past-chair Brecon and Radnor NFU *recreations* walking, reading, cricket, rugby *address* House of Commons, London SW1A 0AA; 4 Watergate, Brecon LD3 9AN *tel* 01874 625739 *e-mail* williamsrmp@gmail.com *web* www.rogerwilliams.org.uk

WILLIAMS of Crosby, Baroness Shirley: Life Peer cr 1993 *b* Jul 27, 1930 *d* of Prof Sir George Catlin and writer, Vera Brittain (Mrs Catlin) *m* 1 Prof Bernard Williams (dis 1974) 1 *d m* 2 Prof Richard E Neustadt *education* Somerville College Oxford, Columbia Univ New York *career* journalist; general secy Fabian Society; MP (Labour) Hitchin 1964-79; professor of elective politics Kennedy School of Govt, Harvard Univ 1988-2000; visiting fellow Nuffield College Oxford 1966-74; assoc fellow Centre for European Studies; hon fellow Somerville College Oxford, Newnham College, Cambridge *party* PPC (Lab) Harwich 1954, 1955, Southampton Test 1959; Hitchin 1964 (elected) MP there until 1974, then Hertford and Stevenage 1974-79; Secy of State Prices and Consumer Protection 1974-76; Secy of State for

Education and Science and Paymaster Gen 1976-79; chair Fabian Soc 1980 (general secy 1960-64); mbr Lab NEC 1970-81; one of original Gang of Four who left Labour to co-found SDP 1981; president of the party 1982-88; PPC Crosby 1981 (by-election: converted Conservative majority of 19,272 to SDP 5,289); founder mbr Liberal Democrats; Life Peer 1993; Lords spokesperson on Foreign and Commonwealth Affairs 1998-2001; elected Leader in the Lords 2001-04 *other interests* president British-Russian Society, East-West Centre; mbr; Advisory Council to Secy-General UN Fourth World Women's Conference 1995, Comite des Sages European Commission 1995 *publications* Politics is for People (1981), A Job to Live (1985), God and Caesar (2004) *recreations* hill-walking, swimming, music *style* The Rt Hon Lady Williams of Crosby, PC address House of Lords, Westminster, London SW1A 0PW *tel* 020 7219 5850 *fax* 020 7219 1174

WILLIAMS, Stephen MP (Bristol West maj:5,128) *education* Mountain Ash Comprehensive; Bristol Univ (history) *career* tax consultant for international business advisory companies *party* cllr Avon County Council 1993-96; cllr Bristol City Council 1995-99, leader of LD Gp 1995-97; PPC Bristol West 1997, 2001, 2005 (elected); mbr Education and Public Accounts Select Cttees; Health spokesperson 2005-06; FE and HE spokesperson in Education team 2006- *other mbrships* Amnesty International, Bristol Civic Society, Chartered Institute of Taxation, Friends of the Earth, National Trust, WWF, Stonewall; director of Watershed Arts Centre *recreations* art galleries and historic sites, theatre and cinema, gym, swimming, playing pool *address* PO Box 2500, Bristol BS6 9AH *tel* 0117 942 3494 *e-mail* stephenwilliamsmp@parliament.uk *web* www.bristolwest-libdems.org.uk

WILLIAMS, Stephen Roy *b* Oct 11,1966 *education* Mountain Ash Comprehensive School, Glamorgan; Bristol Univ (BA History) 1988 *career* chartered tax adviser, worked mainly for international accounting firms (PWC, Grant Thornton), large companies (Kraft, Orange, Wincanton); also spells working as children's play-leader, a bookshop assistant *.party* joined SDP 1983; secy Cynon Valley SDP 1985-87; mbr Council for Social Democracy, SDP Welsh Exec 1986-88; chair Bristol Univ SDP 1986-87; Bristol West Lib Dems Exec 1988– ; mbr Avon CC (Bristol Cabot ward) 1993-96, deputy leader, chair Lib Dem Grp 1993-95; mbr Bristol City Council (Cabot ward) 1995-99, gp leader 1995-97; PPC Bristol South 1997, Bristol West 2001, reselected PPC Bristol West 2002 *special interests* arts, civil rights, constitutional reform, Europe, preventative health care, taxation *other mbrships* ALDC, Amnesty, Cadw, National Trust, Stonewall, WWF; board mbr Watershed Media Centre *recreations*: cinema, eating out, gym, visiting places of historic interest, genealogy, psephology *address* Flat 6, 14 Portland Street, Kingsdown, Bristol, BS2 8HL *tel* 0117 9441714 *e-mail* stevewilliams@cix.co.uk

WILLIS, Phil MP (Harrogate and Knaresborough maj: 10,429) **Chair, House of Commons Science and Technology Cttee** *b* Nov 30, 1941 *m* Heather 1 *s* Michael 1 *d* Rachel *education* Burnley Grammar School 1953-60; City of Leeds and Carnegie College 1960-63; Birmingham Univ 1976-78 *career* teacher 1963-72; deputy head-teacher West Leeds Boys High School 1973-77; head-teacher Ormesby School, Cleveland 1978-82; head-teacher John Smeaton Community High School, Leeds 1983-97; MP 1997-*party* joined 1985; mbr Harrogate Borough Council 1988-99, council leader 1990-97; mbr North Yorkshire County Council 1993-97, deputy gp leader; PPC Harrogate and Knaresborough 1997: elected MP, re-elected 2001 and 2005; parliamentary spokesperson FE, HE, adult education 1997-2001; Shadow Secy for Education and Skills 2001-05; chair, House of Commons Science and Technology Select Cttee *special interests* special education needs, inclusion education *other mbrships* chair All Party Gp: Mobile Telecommunications; treasurer: All Party Gp: Medical Research; vice chair, All Party Gp: Adult Education and Further Education *recreations* season-ticket holder Leeds United FC *address* Ashdown House, 75 Station Parade, Harrogate HG1 1ST *tel* 01423 528888 home 0207820039 business *fax* 02072190971 *e-mail* willisp@parliament.uk

WILLOTT, Jenny MP (Cardiff Central maj 5,593**)** *b* May 29, 1974 *education* Wimbledon High School 1979-90; Uppingham School 1990-92; Durham Univ BA in Classics 1993-96; London School of Economics MSc (Econ) in Development Studies 1996-97 *career* voluntary sector and politics: Area Manager, Victim Support South Wales October 2003-05; Head of Advocacy at UNICEF UK 2001-03; Derwen Project Administrator Barnardo's, Cardiff 2001; Oxfam 1996; Adithi (charity working with women and children) in Bihar, Northern India 1995; in politics: head of office for Lembit Opik MP 1997-2000; worked for number of Welsh Liberal Democrat Assembly Mbrs 2000 *party* joined in 1994 but was active for many years before that; she was a child deliverer: "I hold my mother entirely responsible for the position in which I now find myself!" she says; LDYS in 1997; Cllr, LB of Merton 1998-2000 (resigned to move to Wales, on selection as PPC Cardiff Central; in 2001 reduced Labour majority from nearly 8000 to just 659; reselected at end 2001; elected May 2005 with majority of 5,593; deputy whip in Parliamentary Party 2006-; mbr of two select cttees (Public Administration, and Work and Pensions) 2005-; spokesperson for Youth Affairs 2006-; mbr of Parliamentary delegation to Council of Europe and Western European Union 2005-06; mbr PCA Exec 2003-05; mbr Welsh Campaigns and Election Cttee 2003-04; chair policy working gp on International Development 2003-04 *special interests* international development, foreign affairs, crime, work and pensions *recreations* travel around the world, music, reading, delivering leaflets! *address* 99 Woodville Road, Cardiff CF24 4DY *tel* 02920 668558 *e-mail* jenny@jennywillott.com; House of Commons, London SW1A 0AA *tel* 0207 219 8418

WILLOUGHBY, Laura Exec Mbr for Communities, LB of Islington *b* May 27, 1974 *education* Holyrood Community School, Chard, Somerset; Loughborough Univ, BSc Communication and Media *career* full-time Exec mbr Islington Council 2002-; senior peer at the Improvement and Development Agency 2006-; public affairs officer, YMCA England 2000-02; press officer, Stonewall Lobby Gp 1999-2000; public affairs officer, Institution of Mechanical Engineers 1998-99; public affairs officer, London Youth Matters 1997-98; researcher, Kingston-upon-Thames Lib Dem Gp 1996-97; Don Foster MP (Summer 1996); manager, Somerset College of Art and Technology Student's Union 1994-95 *party* joined 1994; PPC Islington North 2001, 2005; chair policy working gp on Sport (2003-); mbr Federal Exec (2000-02); ALDC Management Cttee 2005-; *public service* Association of London Government; LD lead mbr on the 2012 Olympic bid 2004-; Culture and Libraries Board; Joseph Rowntree Foundation – supporting backbench councillors 2004-; Cripplegate Foundation; Finsbury Park Partnership vice-chair 2000-; Finfuture 2004-; Lee Valley Regional Park Authority 2005-; *special interests* equalities and community cohesion, community engagement, regeneration, young people, young offenders *recreations* jazz, cinema, performing stand-up comedy, BSAC qualified ocean diver, good food and travel *address* 114D Blackstock Road, London N4 2DR; Islington Town Hall, Upper Street, London, N1 2UD *tel* 07968 708703 *e-mail* info@laurawilloughby.org.uk *web* www.laurawilloughby.org.uk and www.islington-libdems.org.uk

WILSON, Elisabeth Mary 1 *s* Daniel John Francis 1 *d* Rebecca Elisabeth *education* George Watson's Ladies College, Edinburgh; The Mount School, York; Univ of East Anglia (BA); Univ of Manchester (postgraduate diploma); Huddersfield Univ (MBA); Liverpool John Moores Univ (PhD) *career* social worker, manager; transferred to higher education; currently teaching management to students from lower income countries *party* joined 1972; currently mbr Yorkshire and Humber regional Exec; PPC Colne Valley *special interests* international development, environment, human resource development, higher education *other mbrships* chartered mbr, Chartered Institute for Personnel and Development; Development Studies Association *recreations* yoga, walking *publications* *Organizational Behaviour Re-assessed: The Impact of Gender, Sage 2000* *address* Pennine Acre, Pike Law Road, Golcar, Huddersfield HD7 4NL *tel* 01484 654930 mobile 07989 654018 *e-mail* elisabethwilsoncolnevalley@yahoo.com

WILSON, Willie *b* Nov 22, 1947 Dundee *m* 2 *ch education* MA Univ of Dundee 1970; postgraduate qualification in Health Care Management 1973 *career* previously senior manager in Health Service on Tayside; retired from full-time work in 2004 *party* joined in 1966; mbr and vice-convenor Perth LP; candidate and councillor for 30+ years; vice-convenor regional party; convenor Scottish Association of Liberal Democrat Councillors; mbr ALDC Management Cttee; mbr ASLDC *address* 3 Fairhill Avenue, Perth PH1 1RP *tel* 01738 626270 home *e-mail* wowilson@pkc.gov.uk

WISEMAN, Andrew LLB Hons *b* Nov 25, 1962 *career* solicitor specialising in environmental law; chairman UK Environmental Law Association 2003- ; partner, Head of Environmental Law, City law firm, listed in various legal directories as one of the countries leading solicitors specialising in environmental law; editor, editorial board mbr various environmental law publications *party* joined Liberal Party 1979; mbr LB Harrow 1986-97, former chair Policy & Strategy, gp leader (minority control); PPC Edmonton 1997, Lewisham Deptford 2001; chair Green Liberal Democrats 1993-96, chair ALDC 2001- ; mbr English Council 1998- ; vice chair Federal Conference Cttee 2003- ; former deputy chair LGA Waste & Environmental Cttee, deputy chair LGA Environment & Regeneration Board. *other mbrships* Chartered Inspire of Wastes Management, Fellow Royal Society of Arts, UK Environmental Law Association *address* 113 Radford Road London SE13 6SA *tel* 020 318 5164 *fax* 020 8473 8688 *e-mail* awiseman@cix.co.uk

WITHERICK, Allan Siao Ming *b* Aug 18, 1978 Luton *single education* Univ College London, Univ of London (BSc Hons) Physical Sciences 1996-2000; Manshead Upper School, Beds 1991-96 *career* Corporate Policy Support Officer, South Beds DC 2003- ; St Albans LD Agent and Organiser 2002-03; Community Safety Co-ordinator, St Albans DC 2001-02; Communications Assistant, Hertfordshire Police Authority 2000-01; Grocery Assistant, Sainsburys (Dunstable) 1995-2002 *party* mbr St Albans LP; Cllr St Albans North 2005- ; Hertfordshire

Police Authority Mbr 2005- ; EERA gp mr 2005- ; previously on International Relations Cttee and ELDR; candidate for South Beds DC 2003 (missed by 76), St Albans DC 2004, (missed by 34), Herts CC 2005 (won by 10!); mbr LDYS (International Cttee), ALDTU (exec), LI-BG, LDEG *other mbrships* UNISON - Eastern Regional Exec 2003- ; Fellow of the Royal Society of Arts; JEF-Bosnia and Herzegovina; Movimento Liberal Social Portugal; Honorary Life Mbr UCL Union; UCL College Dining Club; LYMEC-IMS *recreations* International Liberal Espionage and other related work on behalf of several organisations *publications* Editor/articles in LIBEL, The New Federalist, and various other magazines *address* c/o SALD, 9 Hatfield Road, St Albans, AL1 3RR or 1 Beacon Avenue, Dunstable, Bedfordshire, LU6 2AD *tel* +447957 464569 mobile +441727730838 business *e-mail* a@witherick.org *web* www.witherick.org.uk

WOOD, Antony Stuart *b* Sept 2, 1941 *m* Ursula 1 *s* 2 *d education* Aldenham School, Elstree, Herts; Leicester Univ (MSc Training) *career* Army Commission 1959-69; manufacturing (sales, personnel) Smith Kline Beecham, Metal Box 1969-1982; director, Understanding Industry Trust (for 3i) 1982-93; training consultant World Challenge Ltd 1994-2004 Praxis Training & Development 2004-*party* founder mbr SDP 1981; joined Liberal Democrats 1997; vice chair Windsor Local Party 2002, fund raising officer 2002; PPC for Windsor 2003 *special interests* education; Europe; defence, leadership and teamwork, public speaking , fund-raising *other mbrships* Fellow Royal Society of Arts (FRSA); SUSTRANS; council mbr Engineering Trust *recreations* theatre, film, reading, golf, running *publications* *Understanding Industry Today* (Editor) *address* 53 Clarence Road, Windsor SL$ 5AX *tel* 01753 771944 *fax* 01753 621571 *e-mail* antony@antony53.demon.co.uk

WOOD, Dave *b* Jun 24, 1981 *engaged* Nicky Sewell *qv education* Commonwealth School, Swindon; National Extension College, Cambridge; Univ of Plymouth with BSc Hons politics *career* co-ordinator, Plymouth Nightline 2001-03, Student Union president Univ of Plymouth 2002-03); public relations officer national Nightline 2003-05; currently developing own small business *party* joined 2001; served on local, regional party Execs; agent local elections (facilitating a 20% swing); chair Plymouth Univ LDYS 2001-03; chair Devon & Cornwall LDYS 2002-03); vice chair (mbrship development) LDYS UK 200304; NUS campaign agent 2003-04 *special interests* charity, community sector; student movement, education issues; Channel Isles (Jersey) politics *address* 4 Winifred Street, Swindon SN3 1RS *tel* 07973 146735 home 01793 343640 *e-mail* publicrelations@nightline.ac.uk

WOODCOCK, Geoffrey Laurence BA, MA, PhD, FRSA *b* Apr 1, 1936 *m* 1 *s* 1 *d career* research, lecturer, associate director Extension Studies, Univ of Liverpool 1970- ; lecturer in politics, senior fellow; mbr study team Mersey Estuary Management Plan (Univ of Liverpool) 1992-95 *party* mbr St Helens and Huyton Liberals 1970s; PPC Crosby 1974; mbr Liverpool Mossley Hill 1980s' secy, treasurer Liverpool Riverside 1995-2003, chair 2003- *special interests* the media, environmental politics recreations music, rugby *publications* *Planning, Politics and Communications* 1986 co-author *Democracy in Europe* (Parliamentary Affairs 64, 2) 1994; co-author *Environmentalism and UK Parties* (ibid 48, 3) 1995; co-author *A Sound Education?* 1996 *address* 42 North Studley Road, Aigburth, Liverpool L17 0BG *tel* 0151 727 8243 *e-mail* geoffwoodcock@onetel.net.uk

WOODS, Carol Ann *b* Dec 5, 1954 *m* (dis) *education* Durham Girls Grammar School 1966-73; Univ of Hull (Zoology 2i) 1973-76; Institute of Marketing, (Diploma in Marketing) 1986 *career* self-employed, owner and manager holiday cottage business 2003- ; career in sales and marketing management *party* local council candidate 1999; mbr (Shadforth & Sherburn) Durham City Council 2003- , cabinet mbr Finance 2003-06; cabinet mbr for Environment and Leisure 2006- ; mbr Sherburn Parish Council 2003- ; chair City of Durham Lib Dems 2001-02, secy 1999-2000; PPC City of Durham 2001, 2005 *special interests* public finance, NHS, getting fair deal for North East *other mbrships* SCR St Mary's College, Durham; Durham Forum for Health *recreations* reading, swimming, walking my dogs *address* Weardale House, 58 Front Street, Sherburn Village, Durham DH6 1HB *tel* 0191 372 1810 *e-mail* cwoods8652@aol.com

WOODTHORPE BROWNE, Robert: Vice President PCA; Chair International Relations Cttee; Deputy Federal Treasurer *b* May 26, 1943 *m* Barbara geb. Zwiauer May 28, 1966 1 *s* Robert Alexander 1975 *education* St Ignatius' College, Stamford Hill, Univ de Poitiers, Univ de Barcelona, Birkbeck College, London Univ (BA Hons Spanish) *career* reinsurance broker, consultant and underwriter 1961- ; president PLAIRE SA, Paris, GPH International, Warsaw; MD Robert Browne & Partners Ltd *party* chair, Liberal International (British Gp) 2001-04, vice-chair 2005 - ; v-pres Liberal International 2002-04; chair International Relations Cttee 2006- ; mbr ELDR Delegation; v-president, former chair PCA; Deputy Federal Treasurer; PPC Harlow 1979, Kensington and Chelsea 1997 and 1999 (by-election), Mid Worcestershire 2001, Sedgefield 2005; Euro candidate Central London 1979, East of England List 1999; Parish Councillor, Pebworth and District 2003- ; *other mbrships* Worshipful Company of World Traders; Lime Street Ward Club – Upper Warden 2006; Royal Geographical Society; Royal Forestry Society; English Ceramic Circle, Hon Sec British German Association 2004- ; English Speaking Union; Cotswold Line Promotion Gp *recreations* forestry, flying (PPL), travel, 18th C English ceramics (Lowestoft Factory); fine wines *address* 136 Coleherne Court, London SW5 0DY *tel* 020 7373 7570 mobile 0770 605978 *e-mail* robertbrowne@cix.co.uk

WRIGGLESWORTH, Sir Ian William kt (1991) *s* of Edward Wrigglesworth, of Stockton on Tees *b* Dec 8, 1939 Stockton-on-Tees *m* Patricia Susan, da of Hugh L Truscott 2 *s* 1 *d education* Stockton GS, Stockton; Billingham Tech College; College of St Mark and St John, Chelsea *career* various roles within students' unions 1964-68; PA to Sir Ronald Gould, General Secy NUT 1966-68; head Co-op Party Research Dept 1968-70; press and public affairs manager National Girobank 1970-74; MP (Lab and Co-op 1974-81; PPS to Roy Jenkins MP when Home Secy 1974-79; non-exec director: BAPAS Consultants Ltd 1975-76, Galleon World Travel Ltd 1976-81, Smiths Industries plc 1975-2000, Crabtree plc 1994-96; vice-chairman Anglo-Hong Kong Parly Gp 1976-87; Labour Shadow Minister Civil Service 1979-81; consultant to First Division Assoc (staff assoc of senior Civil Service) 1984-87, Barclays Bank plc 1985-87; deputy chairman John Livingston & Sons Ltd 1987-95 (non-exec 1995-99); p/t director CIT Research Ltd 1987-2003; director Fairfield Industries Ltd 1988-95 (non-exec 1996-99); chairman Northern Region CBI 1992-94; mbr: CBI National Council 1992-2002, advisory board North of England Ventures 1992-97, and deputy chairman Board of Governors Univ of Teesside 1993-99, board of Northern Development Company 1993-95, council of the Foundation for Manufacturing and Industry 1993-95, CBI Management Cttee 1996-2004; exec-chairman UK Land Estates (founded with Chris Whitfield) 1995- ; founder and chairman Northern Business Forum 1996-98; chairman Prima Europe Ltd 1996-98, sold to Omnicom and merged with GPC of which chairman 1998-2000, NewcastleGateshead Initiative 1999-2004; non-exec chairman Corporate Citizenship Co 1998-2005, Port of Tyne 2003-05 (chairman 2005- ;), Tyne Tees Television 2002-05; Liveryman of the Founders Company; Freeman of City of London; Deputy Lieutenant, Tyne & Wear 2005- ; chairman Baltic Centre for Contemporary Art, Gateshead 2005- ; *party* left Labour to co-found SDP 1981; MP 1981-87 (Thornaby, Teesside Feb 1974-83, Stockton South 1983-87); SDP Trade & Industry spkspn 1981-83; Alliance Trade & Industry spkspn 1984-87; SDP mbr 1981-87; first President of Liberal Democrats 1988-90; chairman, now President, Liberal Democrat Business Forum 1991- ; chairman Liberal Democrat Trustees 2002- ; *recreations* books, music, running, windsurfing, skiing *clubs* Reform, NLC, Groucho *style* Sir Ian Wrigglesworth *address* UK Land Estates, Picture House, Queens Park, Queensway, Team Valley, Tyne and Wear NE11 0NX *tel* 0191 440 8880, 07860 391494 mobile *fax* 0191 440 8881 *e-mail* ian@uk-land-estates.co.uk

WRIGHT, Simon James *b* Sept 15,1979 *education* King's College London, Imperial College of Science, Technology and Medicine; Dereham Sixth Form Centre, Dereham Neatherd High School *career* constituency organiser, North Norfolk Liberal Democrats, Norman Lamb MP 2003 - ; teacher of mathematics, Alderman Peel High School, Wells-next-the-sea, Norfolk *party* joined 2001; mbr Federal Exec 2006- ; mbr North Norfolk DC 2003- ; East of England Regional Assembly Europe Panel 2003- ; vice chair (campaigns) LDYS 2003-04; vice chair (communications) Jan to Jul 2003; elected mbr ELDR Council 2004 *special interests* Europe, local govt, elections *recreations* films, music production and technology, cooking *address* 10 Ellcar Rise, Norwich NR4 6HR *tel* 01692 403752 *e-mail* simon@simonwright.org.uk *web* www.simonwright.org.uk

XYZ

YOUNGER-ROSS, Richard MP (Teignbridge maj: 6,215) *b* Jan 29, 1953 *education* Walton-on-Thames Secondary Modern; Ewell Technical College; Oxford Polytechnic *m* Susan 1982 *career* architectural consultant; helped run father's insurance brokerage, family store in Shepperton Film Studios; political researcher House of Commons; worked in Iraq 1982 *party* impressed at age nine by Jo Grimond and has since been "marching towards the sound of gunfire"; joined Liberals 1970 (when 17); mbr Liberal Party Council 1979-82; v chair National Young Liberals; PPC Chislehurst 1987, Teignbridge 1992, 1997, 2001 (elected), 2005 (elected); mbr European, and Foreign Affairs Select Cttees 2005- ; *other mbrships* Howard League, British Kurdish Friendship Society, Anti Slavery International; co-ordinator Christian Housing Coalition, Teignbridge 1995; active Christian, mbr Our Lady and St Patrick's Church, Teignmouth *recreations* cooking, music (folk & blues), gardening, rowing (completed 22-mile Great River Race on Thames) collects old cook-books *address* House of Commons, London SW1A 0AA *constituency* 24/26 Queen Street Newton Abbot, Devon TQ12 2ET *tel* 01626 202626 *e-mail* yrossr@parliament.uk *web* www.teignbridgelibdems.com

YUILL, Ian *b* Feb 12, 1965 *m* Karen Freel *qv* 1 *d education* Robert Gordon's College; Robert Gordon's Institute of Technology *career* marketing manager Cornerstone 2002- ; Cllr Aberdeen City 1996-*party* joined Scottish Liberal Party 1983; founder Liberal Democrats (mbr 007); numerous offices include vice-convener 1996-98, convener Scottish Liberal Democrats, Federal vice president 1998-02; secy ASLDC 1995-97, convener 1997-04; mbr Scottish party Exec 1994- ; mbr Scottish Conference Cttee *special interests* the environment, community politics *other mbrships* National Trust for Scotland, RSPB, Friends of the Earth, Friend of Aberdeen International Youth Festival *recreations* gardening, reading *address* 57 Countesswells Crescent, Aberdeen AB15 8LN *tel* 01224 310746 home 01224 522220 business *fax* 01224 310746 *e-mail* iyuill@aberdeencity.gov.uk

The Liberal Democrats exist to build and safeguard
a fair, free and open society in which we seek to
balance the fundamental values of liberty, equality
and community and in which no one will be enslaved
by poverty, ignorance or conformity
Preamble to Federal Constitution

Liberal Democrat Parliamentary Candidates Association

The PCA exists to support all Liberal Democrat
parliamentary candidates and
aspiring candidates for Westminster,
the European and Scottish Parliaments, and
the Welsh and Greater London Assemblies.

It provides regular training, political briefings and
campaign support to its members,
and publishes *The Parliamentary Campaigner*,
The Candidate and *Who's Who in the Liberal Democrats*.

For further information, contact PCA Chair Gary Lawson
on 07941 553859 or by e-mail: gary@lawsononline.org

To join, contact PCA Membership Secretary Elliot Shubert
on 07764 611401 or by e-mail: membership@libdempca.org.uk

Membership is open to all candidates and aspiring candidates,
and costs £30 if paid by cheque,
or £25 if paid by direct debit.

Whilst every effort has been made to verify all the information
contained herein, please advise any omissions or errors to the Editor,
Linda Forbes
linda@lindaforbes.co.uk
for inclusion in the 6th edition

NOTES

NOTES